Personal History

Katharine Graham

PERSONAL HISTORY

ALFRED A. KNOPF   *New York*   1997

http://www.randomhouse.com/

Grateful acknowledgment is made to the following for
permission to use previously published and
unpublished material:

Alfred A. Knopf, Inc., and S. Fischer Verlag: Excerpt from *Letters of
Thomas Mann, 1889–1955,* selected and translated by Richard and
Clara Winston, copyright © 1970 by Alfred A. Knopf, Inc.
Rights in the United Kingdom from *Thomas Mann / Agnes E.
Meyer Briefwechsel 1937–1955,* edited by Vaget, copyright © 1992
by S. Fischer Verlag GmbH, Frankfurt am Main, administered by
S. Fischer Verlag GmbH. Reprinted by permission of Alfred A.
Knopf, Inc., and S. Fischer Verlag GmbH.

Yale University: Excerpt from Walter Lippmann letter. Walter
Lippmann Papers, Manuscripts and Archives, Yale University
Library. Reprinted by permission.

Library of Congress Cataloging-in-Publication Data
Graham, Katharine, [date]
Personal history / Katharine Graham. — 1st ed.
p.   cm.
ISBN 0-394-58585-2 (alk. paper)
1. Graham, Katharine, [date]. 2. Newspaper publishing—
Washington (D.C.)—History—20th century. 3. Publishers
and publishing—United States—Biography.
4. Washington post. I. Title.
Z473.G7A3   1997
070.5'092—dc21   96-49638
[B]   CIP

Manufactured in the United States of America

First Edition

*I would like to dedicate this book to
the most important people in it:*

my parents, Eugene and Agnes Meyer,

my husband, Philip L. Graham,

*my children, Elizabeth (Lally) Weymouth,
and Donald, William, and Stephen Graham*

— *Acknowledgments* —

F ROM THE START, I very much wanted to write this book myself, although I realized I wasn't a real professional. I well remember the columnist Walter Lippmann once telling me how
hard it was, even for him who wrote all the time, to get back into writing
after a hiatus of only a few weeks. That thought kept recurring when I
considered whether or not to write on my own rather than with a co-
author. But because I wanted this to be a personal story, I knew I had to
tell it myself. If I've succeeded at all, it is due to two people: my researcher,
Evelyn Small, and my editor, Robert Gottlieb.

Ev came from The Washington Post Company, where she was in corporate communications, producing an internal newsletter and doing research for speeches, including mine. She worked for several years at
organizing my papers in such a way that we could together take a look
back. As time passed, her role grew in importance. She knew as much
about my life as I did. She took the words I wrote and shaped them, reminding me of important details, tactfully eliminating others, adding
things from the research that I'd overlooked. This book could not have
happened without Ev. For four years, she was ably assisted by Todd
Mendeloff.

Only a small percentage of the stories Ev unearthed and brought to
light again could find their way into the book itself, which was also true for
the more than 250 interviews we conducted with people ranging from
childhood classmates and lifelong friends to many of those who were involved with the Pentagon Papers, Watergate, or The Washington Post
Company. But they all added to my perspective.

Bob Gottlieb, whom I first talked with about a book in 1978, became
my editor when he returned to Knopf from *The New Yorker.* He has mas-
terfully edited my copy with meticulous care and a ruthless eye for repetition, tediousness, and sequence. Quite often I found "we don't need this"
written in the margins. Even when he axed a story I might have particu-

larly liked—always in the interest of space, according to Bob—there were few squeals of protest from me. I may have grieved for the fallen pages, but he, Ev, and I always had the same goal in mind. And on those occasions when I thought something essential lay on the floor, Bob generously acceded to my pleading.

My friend Meg Greenfield, editorial page editor of the *Post*, and *Newsweek* columnist, whose editing skills and advice have been sought out by me and on whom I have relied for much of my professional life, also read and commented on the manuscript. Meg's mind and mine work in similar ways, as do our judgments about people and situations, about what is funny and what is intolerable. Our friendship has endured and grown almost from the moment of her arrival at the *Post*.

Five other important people also read and commented on the manuscript and were exceedingly helpful: my daughter, Lally, my sons, Don, Bill, and Steve, and my friend Warren Buffett.

This project has renewed my appreciation for the value of archival material. I have spent innumerable hours poring over old letters and memos from and between my parents, my husband, and myself, as well as communications involving *Post* and *Newsweek* executives and editors. I am thankful that we all wrote letters in those days. For saving much of this material and organizing it originally, I must acknowledge the late, and incomparable, Charlie Paradise, secretary and assistant to my father, to Phil, and then to me for some years. Charlie used to answer the phone by singing out "Paradise." My thanks go also to all of those from whose letters I quote.

I am indebted to Chalmers Roberts, whose living history of the *Post*— *The Washington Post: The First 100 Years* (Houghton Mifflin Co., 1977)— has been a constant source of information, and to Merlo Pusey, for his biography of my father, *Eugene Meyer* (Alfred A. Knopf, 1974). Both books informed our research and my thinking.

In my office, I am grateful to Liz Hylton for her devoted and patient work over thirty-three years, including help on the book. She has not only run my office, keeping all my papers and my business and social calendars, but she has managed my houses as well. In many ways she has been my alter ego. For the last two years I have also been greatly helped by my assistant, Barry Tonoff.

I have worked closely for fifteen years with Guyon (Chip) Knight, vice-president for corporate communications at The Washington Post Company, whose extraordinary talents have crafted all my public utterances.

In addition, I want to thank the people in the *Post*'s News Research Center, on whom we relied time and again, for their ever-ready and always accurate information.

I also want to thank the many people at Knopf who have helped me with this book: Sonny Mehta, Jane Friedman, Bill Loverd, and Paul Bogaards for their interest and support; Carol Carson, Virginia Tan, Cassandra Pappas, and Tracy Cabanis for their talented design and production; and Kathy Hourigan, Leyla Aker, Karen Mugler, Amy Scheibe, and Ken Schneider for their editorial assistance.

Of course I am responsible for the final contents of the book. I have tried to be frank and honest while honoring privacy, particularly that of my children, who are, naturally, more important to me than I can describe here and have achieved so much in their own lives. They, too, were deeply and permanently affected by all that happened.

My two surviving sisters, Elizabeth Lorentz and Ruth Epstein, have also been involved, helpful, and interested, sharing with me their own memories and judgments. My late brother, Bill (Eugene Meyer III), was always supportive during his lifetime, and I am eternally grateful for that, although he died before I began the book.

With all of my trepidations about writing, and with all of the complications inherent in looking back over a long and full life, writing this book has been a rigorous and absorbing exercise, one that I've enjoyed immensely. Throughout the book I hope I've given credit where credit is due and haven't neglected those to whom I owe so much. Necessarily many names have been left out, but they are in my head and in my heart.

Personal History

— *Chapter One* —

MY PARENTS' paths first crossed in a museum on 23rd Street in New York. It was Lincoln's Birthday, 1908. Eugene Meyer, who was thirty-two years old, had been in business for himself for only a few years, but had already made several million dollars. Agnes Ernst, just twenty-one and a recent graduate of Barnard, was strikingly beautiful. She was earning her own living and helping to support her family as well by her free-lance work for a newspaper, the old *New York Sun*. She was also interested in the art world, which was what brought her to the exhibit of Japanese prints. Both her interests and her work were unusual for a woman in those days.

On his way down to Wall Street, my father, who was driving a Stanley Steamer, one of the earliest automobiles, noticed an acquaintance whom he didn't especially like. But Edgar Kohler looked frail and dejected and my father felt sorry for him, so he offered him a ride, mentioning that he was going to stop off at a Japanese-print exhibit. Kohler decided to accompany him.

Going into the gallery, they met two friends coming out, who assessed the exhibition this way: "There's a girl walking around who's better-looking than anything on the walls." Once inside, Kohler and my father immediately spotted her—a tall young woman with fair hair and blue eyes, clearly strong, dynamic, and self-assured. My mother always remembered what she was wearing that day, because she felt that her "costume," as she called it, had played a part in her destiny. She must have been quite a sight in her gray tweed suit and small squirrel cap adorned with an eagle feather. My father, on seeing her, said to Kohler, "That's the girl I'm going to marry."

"Are you serious?" Kohler asked, to which my father responded, "I was never more serious in my whole life." Kohler, supposing that they'd never run into her again, suggested that my father speak to her. "No. That would offend her and spoil everything," my father replied. The two men

then agreed that whoever subsequently might meet her first would introduce her to the other.

Just a week later, Kohler called my father and said, "Guess what happened?" "You met the girl," was the ready answer. "Damn you, I did,"
Kohler responded. He had been to a party at the home of one of Agnes's
Barnard classmates, where they were giving an amateur performance
of *The Merry Widow* in which my mother was playing Count Danilo.
When she appeared after the performance out of costume, Kohler realized
that she was the girl from the art show. He introduced himself, told her
about the pact with my father, and arranged a lunch for the three of them.

My father's friend had fulfilled his pledge by introducing Eugene and
Agnes to each other. On Lincoln's Birthday in 1910, two years to the day
after Eugene had first seen Agnes in the gallery, they were married. When
I look back over my long life, if there is one thing that leaps out at me it is
the role of luck and chance in our lives. From this particular string of accidental happenings all the rest followed.

MY FATHER came from a distinguished Jewish family with roots going
back many generations in Alsace-Lorraine, France. It was a family that
numbered many rabbis and civic leaders. Jacob Meyer, my great-great-
grandfather, who was awarded the Legion of Honor, had actually been
a member of the Sanhedrin, the college of Jewish notables called by
Napoleon I in connection with recognizing the rights of Jews as citizens.

My paternal grandfather, named Marc Eugene Meyer, but always
called Eugene, was born in 1842 in Strasbourg, the youngest of four children by his father's second wife. When his father died, his mother was left
penniless, and Eugene could stay in school only until the age of fourteen;
then, as his siblings had already done, he went to work to help support the
family. He first worked for two Blum brothers who owned one store in Al-
sace and another—improbably—in Donaldsonville, Mississippi, and when
one of young Eugene's bosses said he was going to America, my grandfather decided to go with him. In Paris, on the way, he was introduced by
Blum to Alexandre Lazard of the firm of Lazard Frères, who gave him an
introduction to their San Francisco partner. Eugene traveled to New York
on the fastest boat going, a side-wheeler, for a third-class fare of $110,
leaving Europe in September 1859. From New York he took a steamship
to Panama, crossed the Isthmus by rail, and then caught another steamer
to San Francisco, at that time a city of fifty thousand or so people. He
spent two years there, learning English and saving a little money from his
job at an auction house, until in 1861 he moved to Los Angeles, where a
cousin of the Lazards' was said to need a clerk for his store. As described
by Eugene himself, the town was made up of only three or four thousand

inhabitants, mostly foreigners. There were four brick houses—the rest were adobe with roofs that cracked. There were no paved streets or sewers. The water for both drinking and irrigation came from ditches. My grandfather stayed in Los Angeles for the next twenty-two years.

He started as clerk and bookkeeper, living in the general store's back room. Sometimes he slept on the counter with his gun, to protect the merchandise. As his reputation for reliability and sobriety spread, some of his new friends began leaving money with him, for there were no banks. Within three years, he became a general partner in the store, which came to be known as "The City of Paris." Within ten years, he and his brother Constant had taken it over. He also started lending money, became director of a bank and organizer of the Los Angeles Social Club, and helped maintain law and order as a member of the Vigilance Committee. He was an incorporator of the city water system, involved in real estate and mining investments, and doubled as the French consular agent. In 1867, he married the sixteen-year-old Harriet Newmark, whose father, a rabbi, performed the ceremony, following which a sumptuous dinner was served at the couple's new home—complete with ice cream, something new to Los Angeles.

My father, named Eugene Isaac Meyer after his father and grandfather, was born in 1875, the first boy in the family after three girls, Rosalie, Elise, and Florence. Four more children followed: two daughters, Ruth and Aline; and two sons, Walter and the youngest child, Edgar. Harriet, not as strong as her husband, became a more or less permanent invalid—whether from having eight children by the age of thirty-two under pioneering medical conditions or because there was some depression involved, or both. As a result, my father's mother-figure in his youth was his sister Rosalie, six years older than he, who left school to help raise her siblings.

These early circumstances help me understand my father's personality. His father was very strict and not particularly loving, as far as I can tell, and the only real mother-figure was a near-contemporary, sweet and sensitive but overwhelmed by being thrust into a position of authority well before she was ready for it. There couldn't have been much parental love for all those children, with the father ambitious and driven and no real mother. My father himself was never very good at personal relations of the intimate kind; the feelings were there, but they went unexpressed.

Early in 1884, my father moved with his family back to San Francisco, a city by then of 225,000 with much better educational and medical facilities than Los Angeles could offer the large Meyer family. It was also safer. I remember my father saying of his early days in Los Angeles that everyone carried a Derringer and almost every night someone was shot. But though my grandfather may have been pleased with the move, my father, a young boy of eight, immediately became embattled. He was a loner and a fighter, forced by his family to wear clothes—including a white starched Eton collar—that made him look "different." Older boys at school would put the younger ones in a circle, pitting them against each other. The fights would stop only when someone had a nosebleed, and this was usually my poor father. Nonetheless, he was forced to learn to fight to defend himself, all the while receiving severe reprimands from his father for his rough behavior. These encounters toughened him to the point where, when the family moved to Alameda, to improve his mother's health by removing her from San Francisco's fog, young Eugene outfought the local bully, who had previously ruled the playground. This victory had the dubious effect of making him the top troublemaker, both at school and at home. He led the younger children in rebellion against the housekeeper, generally made mischief, and teased the girls, especially harassing poor Rosalie.

Alameda had done my grandmother no good, and it proved too remote to be practical for my grandfather, so after a short time the family moved back to San Francisco. It was the third change of school for my father. After getting hit in the eye by a baseball, he was forbidden to play, on the grounds that it would worry his mother. Football and sailing on a nearby lake had also been forbidden. He was, however, allowed to take fencing lessons, and boxing lessons from Gentleman Jim Corbett, later heavyweight champion of the world, but these too were stopped when a picture appeared in the paper of the lesson with Corbett, who was seeking publicity. He went on having a difficult time in school, and endured being called a sheeny, along with others who were called wops, micks, and chinks.

The family belonged to a Reformed Jewish congregation, and Eugene was instructed in Jewish history, Hebrew, and the meaning of religion, but when it came time for his bar mitzvah, he declined. Asked to declare "perfect faith," he said, "I believe some of these things, but I don't believe them all with *perfect* faith." He was never overtly religious, yet was later involved in Jewish charities, causes, and international issues. He was not a Zionist, however, believing strongly that he was an American citizen first and foremost.

School didn't interest him, but he read a lot. When he came out third in his grammar-school class, his father reproached him with not being first, largely because he knew the boy wasn't working, but eventually Eugene developed a true passion for learning, enhanced when his father included him more and more in his business meetings and discussions of politics and high finance.

Like my father, Rosalie became a strong and dominating person. She married Sigmund Stern, and her next-younger sister, Elise, married Sigmund's brother, Abraham. The Sterns were nephews of Levi Strauss, who had gone to San Francisco at the height of the Gold Rush with heavy denim material for tents to sell to the miners. Either it didn't sell as tent material or it made better pants, sealed with rivets, but Levi Strauss made his fortune through those pants, and "Levi's" eventually became known throughout the world. Because Strauss was a bachelor, the Sterns, who managed his business, inherited the company, which was handed down through Sigmund and Aunt Ro to their daughter, Elise, and her husband, Walter Haas, and eventually to their children and grandchildren.

My grandfather was offered a partnership in Lazard Frères, and although the family hated leaving San Francisco—which was now the home of the oldest two daughters, who after marrying had built two large houses next door to each other—he saw the offer as a fine opportunity. They made the move to New York in 1893. At that time my father was seventeen and had completed his first year of college at the University of California at Berkeley. For the first time he saw the vastness of this country and the awesome size of New York, then a city of three and a half million, with its great luxuries and contrasting slums.

He went to work as a messenger at Lazard with the full expectation that someday he would succeed to his father's position there. With just three weeks' notice and only an average recommendation from Berkeley, he crammed for the Yale entrance examination and was accepted, settling down to an excessively grueling schedule. He knew very few people—he was a lonely Jewish boy from the West—so he studied all the time and took extra credits, with an occasional break for a workout in the gym, no doubt both to compensate for the lack of social life and because he was driven to excel. He emerged as a Phi Beta Kappa, and, with his extra credits, skipped his junior year and graduated in two years—nineteenth in a class of 250. He was not yet twenty.

After a brief stint back at Lazard, he went abroad for a year and a half to be apprenticed in banks in Germany, England, and France. He arrived first in Paris, where he worked without pay but was rewarded with a beautiful pearl stickpin, which he wore always, at least in my early childhood memories. He also started investing in the market with $600 his father had given him for not smoking until he was twenty-one. (Years later, my father offered all of us children the same deal, but I believe no one took him up on it, or possibly none of us made it to twenty-one without experimenting with smoking. No doubt the $1,000 he offered us meant a great deal less to us than the $600 did to him.)

My father's first exercise in adult independence occurred on his return from Europe. His father had groomed him, and certainly expected him, to enter the firm of Lazard. What he found when he returned there was that nothing had changed: his year and a half of learning banking counted for nothing. He was started at $12 a week and increased only incrementally. In addition, he was working for his brother-in-law George Blumenthal— a difficult man, with a big ego and a quick temper, whom he never really liked. Already an extraordinary foreign-exchange banker, Blumenthal later became even more successful as head of Lazard in the United States. He had married my father's much-loved sister Florence, or Florie, as the family called her.

When I first became aware of the Blumenthals, they lived winters in New York and summers in France or on yachts in the Mediterranean. Their enormous and elaborate house in New York occupied half a city block and had an indoor tiled swimming pool. Florie brought home immense quantities of French clothes every year, so many that once, when her trunks were brought down from the attic for packing to leave for Paris, one was discovered full of clothes that had never been unpacked from the previous trip. My father once jokingly moaned to George about my mother's extravagant taste in clothes, exaggeratedly claiming she hardly ever wore the same dress twice. George turned to him and said in all sincerity, "Eugene, you don't expect your wife to wear the same dress twice, do you?"

Florie had a perfect figure—one Christmas, instead of cards, they sent out plaster casts of her very delicate foot and ankle. She had only one child, whom George didn't allow her to nurse lest it spoil her beautiful figure, and she never got over this son's early death.

In any event, whether it was because of my father's feelings about George Blumenthal or because of his instinct to go it alone, he began to veer from the path his father had laid out for him. After a variety of adventures and false starts in other fields—he had tried learning law at night, but it bored him—he came upon a book, *The Map of Life*, by William Edward Hartpole Lecky, that suggested "that a man's life should be planned as a single whole in which each stage would be a prologue to the stage that followed," and he outlined such a plan for himself. The first twenty years were over—they were generally called "school." Twenty to forty would be given to growth and experimentation, during which he would earn a "competence," marry, and start a family. Forty to sixty would be a time for implementing all that he had learned and done prior to this, which, "if feasible," my father wrote, "should be devoted to public service." He would retire at sixty to grow old gracefully and help young people.

As he looked around at Lazard and even at his father, he was more than ever convinced of the rightness of his plan for life. The Lazard bureaucracy was hopeless, with older men making all the decisions and little opportunity for a bright young man to make a significant contribution.

The Paris partners controlled the company. He was taking out many young ladies, and there was one in whom he was really interested, Irene Untermeyer, the daughter of the lawyer Samuel Untermeyer. I think this was his only genuine romance before he met my mother. At Lazard, however, he was even now making only $200 a month, and realized—as did Irene's parents, I'm sure—that he couldn't support a wife on that.

By this time, the cigarette money had been well invested, and he had $5,000 saved. He parlayed this into $50,000 by investing in railroad stocks and then faced his father with his determination to leave Lazard and start out for himself. It was an emotional moment. His father viewed this decision as the rejection of his lifetime of toil in his son's behalf. When the younger man went further and told his father that he was going to buy a seat on the stock exchange, his father said he wouldn't help him, but my father announced that he had accumulated the $50,000 then necessary and could do it without any help. My grandfather said, "Eugene, you've been gambling," which is how he viewed playing the market.

My father's first move on his own, quite soon after leaving Lazard, turned out to be trouble: he unknowingly affiliated with a bucket shop—a kind of fraudulent brokerage house. When he discovered the nature of his associates, he left immediately. It was a blow, but now his father stood behind him, stating that he wanted his son to invest his own funds and expected others in the family to do the same. Even Blumenthal did.

After this rocky start, my father withdrew to Palm Beach to think things over, and there he drew up a "Plan for Developing a Business." This memo outlined a very simple but high-minded strategy of associating with the best people, acquiring known securities, staying with them, and being constructive, not destructive. Such thinking led him to start his own firm, Eugene Meyer and Company, which opened in 1904, and gradually, he began to make his mark on Wall Street and to do well for himself and his associates. By 1906, he had made several million dollars. At the time he started the firm, it must have been very difficult competing with the larger and better-known houses. In time, however, he came to know the heads of these firms. I always heard him say he had the greatest admiration for E. H. Harriman, father of Averell, and a very dominant figure. I think he felt very small and insecure next to Harriman, Morgan, and the other then-reigning titans, and he was gratified when they started to notice what he was doing. He quoted one of them as saying, "Watch that fellow Meyer. He'll have all the money."

His philosophy of investment involved careful research into companies—the first in-depth economic analysis of its kind. This was typical of his lifelong impulse to get at the facts before making judgments. Eugene Meyer and Company, in fact, had the first research department of any

Wall Street house. As time passed, my father became more and more adept at analyzing economic trends. He foresaw panics and violent swings in the market and got out when he reasoned that things were going to go to pieces. Although he made a large fortune, he was also willing to take great risks, and twice he was wiped out, at least by Wall Street standards.

He was very devoted to his family, then and always, and his great wealth allowed him to improve the situation of his parents. The entire Meyer family remained a close but combative one. My father stayed especially close to his sister Ro. In 1906, when the terrible earthquake and fire hit San Francisco, cutting the city off from telephone communication with the outside world, he decided to go out there immediately to see what he could do to help. He boarded a train in New York with a money belt containing $30,000, a small suitcase, and a pistol.

Rosalie, Elise, and their families were safe. They and their combined households, numbering twenty-eight, had taken shelter at Ro's for two days. As the fire approached, they had moved first to the Presidio, then to Golden Gate Park, then to a summer cottage at Fair Oaks that one of them had rented. There my father found them. Ro looked up as he approached and said, "Eugene, I knew you'd come."

Quite early on, my father became a collector, with a particular interest in Dürer and Whistler etchings, first editions of American manuscripts, and Lincoln letters. He met the sculptor Gutzon Borglum, who was working on a head of Lincoln, and volunteered to buy it and give it to the nation. President Theodore Roosevelt agreed to Borglum's request to show the bust at the White House before it was placed in the Capitol. My father thus went to Washington for the first time in his life, and met Roosevelt. With great foresight, he wrote to his sister Rosalie that Roosevelt should have worked out a "monetary mechanism that can prevent the kind of panics we have lately experienced. I should like myself to come to grips with these problems. But I have no doubt that they will still be with us by the time I am in a position to leave business behind me and follow through on my long-standing plan for some sort of direct participation in the management of government affairs."

This was the man who entered the art gallery on that February day in 1908—a successful businessman, a person interested in the art world, a collector of manuscripts, and a man who was already thinking about public economic issues. Although he was wealthy, he was aware of the problems of poverty. He had high values and aspirations, but he was something of a loner, driven, a workaholic. He was very family-oriented, despite complicated relationships with his father and his brother-in-law George Blumenthal. He also was fundamentally shy, but at the same time he had a fierce temper. No doubt he must have been bruised by discrimination in college, on Wall Street, and socially, but withal he was strong, brilliant, able, witty, and self-confident.

THE YOUNG WOMAN Eugene Meyer had seen walking through the gallery had a thirst for the avant-garde of the art world and thought of herself as somewhat bohemian. She, too, was full of determination and self-confidence, but she was, in addition, completely self-absorbed. Born in 1887, in New York City, my mother had roots that were in some ways quite similar to my father's and in others quite opposite. Their differences made for a complicated relationship.

On her father's side, my mother came from a long line of Lutheran ministers in Hanover, in North Germany, whose number included, at least in more recent times, not a few black sheep. The Ernst family was handsome, gifted, driven, and, unfortunately, riddled with a tendency toward alcohol addiction. My great-grandfather Karl Ernst was clergyman to the last king of Hanover, but when Hanover was conquered by the Prussians in 1866, he sent his seven sons out of Germany to keep them out of the army. All but one came to America, which is how my maternal grandfather got to New York, where he became a lawyer, and later persuaded Lucy Schmidt, my grandmother, here on a visit, to stay and marry him. She, too, hailed from North Germany, her family, mostly seafaring men and merchants, having lived in a small village near Bremen for more than three centuries.

My mother grew up in a then-small country community, Pelham Heights, just outside New York City, where the young family moved when she was three. Describing the atmosphere in which she was reared as puritanical, austere, and familial, she wrote:

> It was a curious obsession of our Lutheran parents that the more we disliked doing something the better it was for our soul's salvation. . . . We ate what was set before us without complaint even if it nauseated us. As I hated sewing lessons I was incarcerated for an hour every Saturday morning to stitch a hem. . . . But the real torment of our lives, considered vital to the formation of a sturdy character, was the cold bath into which we plunged every morning, winter or summer.

So conditioned was she to the virtues of this ritual bath that she continued it until after she was married.

Only when she was six or seven did her father, Frederick, become an important figure in my mother's life. When she first became aware of him, "he was a hard-working lawyer who supported his family in modest but comfortable circumstances." Money was never mentioned in her family, a tradition she carried on into ours. More and more, her father became a dominant influence in her life, and she developed what she herself referred to as an "extraordinary Oedipus complex." Her early childhood was infinitely brightened by this "luminous personality," as she referred to him. My grandfather would take her for walks to see the sunrise, talking to her about music, poetry, and art. He spoke of the joys of Wagner's "Ring" and sang Mozart arias around the house, particularly one from *Don Giovanni*, which I well remember, since, in her excitement, she hummed it out loud when we went to see the opera together much later in her life. She was certainly infatuated with her father, and he with her. Unfortunately, as time went on he philandered, tippled, and ceased paying the family bills, and she felt betrayed by him. The man she had loved as a child was replaced by what she called a "somber figure that haunted my adolescence like a nightmare."

In addition to their schoolwork, my mother and her three older brothers were tutored at home in German and math. When Bill and she—both in the same class—were ready for high school, and Fred for college, the family moved to New York to benefit from its excellent free public education. She had to adapt to new ways, to cease battling with boys, to go to an all-girls school. She thrived, however, in the stimulating learning atmosphere of Morris High School, where she studied Latin, Greek, ancient history, math, French, and American and English literature.

During her high-school years, her relationship with her father continued to deteriorate, as he got further involved with women, drank more, and increasingly neglected his work and his family. He no longer earned a living but instead wrote what his daughter frankly called "incredibly amateurish" books and dramas. The family bills went unpaid and Agnes's mother grew more and more anxious. This undoubtedly was the dominant emotional shock of my mother's life. It turned everything upside down, and her adoration of her father turned to shame and even to hatred. Worst of all, having taught her to love learning, he no longer cared if she went to school; he would have preferred her going to work to help pay the bills. So long-lasting and painful were these emotions about her father that, although she spoke often with us about him, she hardly ever mentioned this dark side, and then only by allusion. I eventually came to realize that her very ambivalent attitude toward men clearly sprang from this experience. She was both attracted and repelled by the whole idea of sexual relations. However, she did keep his picture on her desk always, a handsome man.

The estrangement from her father had the salutary effect of making her realize she had to work even harder to win scholarships to college and earn the money to pay her own expenses. Hard work also helped counter-act her fears that in many ways she was much like her father and had within herself some of his weaknesses.

She won a scholarship and entered Barnard in 1903, focusing initially on math and physics but later turning to philosophy and literature. She was very independent and irreverent, and as a result was labeled "too irre-sponsible" to deserve further scholarships, at which point she determined to earn the daunting sum of $150 that was necessary for her to re-enter Barnard for her second year. She worked at least twelve hours every day. In the mornings and early afternoons, she was the principal of a Baptist summer school. From 6 to 10 p.m., she had charge of the Hudson Guild lending library. She was still short $50 when the superintendent of her school announced that two male principals had been driven to leave their schools in Hell's Kitchen, the toughest section of the city, and called for volunteers at double pay; she volunteered and got the job. On her first day, she walked into a scene of turmoil, which she turned around by ejecting from the classroom a fourteen-year-old who turned out to be a gang leader and whose gang (half the boys in her class) followed him out. Quickly reading the situation, she parlayed with the ousted gang leader as well as with his chief rival, got the two leaders on her side, enlisted their help in keeping order, and thus came out on top of a difficult situation. She was only seventeen.

When she returned to college, Agnes was informed that the faculty had decided to give her the scholarship after all. It was manna from heaven. She didn't have to earn extra money by tutoring, and she could help her mother pay the household bills, to which her father was now in-different. She sailed through college thereafter, generally popular and beloved by various males. Alas, as she said, this gift "made me conceited and self-centered to an unbelievable degree. . . . For several years to come I was in love chiefly with myself, an ecstasy that cost me and others much pain before life cured me of this intoxication." Not to put too fine a point on it, life had hardly cured her of her self-absorption.

Agnes was forced to return for her senior year with only two hours of formal study to complete, but this turned out to be a blessing in disguise, because it was in her final year that she developed the first of a series of in-tellectual, yet highly emotional, crushes on men of distinction—most of them in arts or letters. She was often consumed by these strangely pas-sionate friendships with well-known men. My father was once heard to mutter, "There's always a stranger in the house."

The first of these crushes was on John Dewey. As president of the col-lege's Philosophical Society, she had invited Dewey to speak and then got to know him better through his daughter Evelyn, a classmate, who would take her home to family meals. And she read everything he'd written. She believed that his teaching to live life on a high plane made her come to terms with "the many frustrations, hardships and disappointments of my college years. . . . I believe I would never have married the man I did—the greatest good that ever befell me—if Dewey had not counteracted my *Sturm und Drang* with his inspired common sense."

As she wrote later, when she told her family that she intended to do newspaper reporting, "My mother wept and my father said solemnly: 'I would rather see you dead.' " In those days educated women worked either at teaching or at clerical work, and there were only a half-dozen women in journalism, most of them sob sisters, so it was quite a remarkable feat when my mother first started working on a free-lance basis for the *New York Sun*. She did "piece work," which put a terrible strain on her to get or think up enough stories to support her family. Her income ranged from a high of $40 a week to a low of $5 or $10, but she persisted and soon became known as the "*Sun* girl."

The quest for copy led her one day to a new modern-art gallery at 291 Fifth Avenue. There, for the first time, photographs were presented as art, and she thought that the very avant-garde group of Photo-Secessionists working there, led by Alfred Stieglitz and Edward Steichen, and including the painters Georgia O'Keeffe, John Marin, and Marius de Zayas, made a real story. She became so excited about the ideas and people she found there—they were ever after to be known as "291"—that, ignoring the rest of her duties, she sat down and talked for six hours straight. Though my mother had no sympathy with political radicals, she related totally to the artistic rebellion led by the group at 291. She made great friends there, especially with Steichen, and with Marion Beckett and Katharine Rhoades (they were known as the Three Graces), after whom I was named.

From then on, she had quite a flourishing artistic and social life. Despite my father's interest in her at that time, he seems to have been only one of several beaux, and not taken very seriously except, possibly, for his affluence and what it could bring her. One important thing it brought her was a companion for her long-planned and yearned-for European sojourn. She had borrowed $500, which she thought could last her six months, but two days before she was to leave she confided to her wealthy new suitor that her friend Evangeline Cole—or Nancy, as she was known—found that she couldn't afford to go with her. My father, wanting her to have company and a chaperone, loaned Nancy the money to go too. The two girls set off for France on August 4, 1908.

Agnes Ernst's determination to go to Europe, undeterred by her pursuit by Eugene Meyer and at least two other young men, took her away from her family problems—leaving it up to her father to support his family while she was gone—and exposed her to a whole new world. In Europe, she plunged into a rich life of museums, theater, ballet, music, and opera, often standing in line for hours for tickets. The two girls, Agnes and Nan, found a four-room apartment in Paris for $36 a month, including food and laundry and all minor expenses. This apartment quickly became a gathering place for students of all nationalities. The half-day-a-week cleaning lady earned thirty cents, including a five-cent tip.

Her only real entrée to the artistic and literary world was Steichen, who was in France with his family, but he proved to be enough. Through him, she met and became friends with many of the artists and intellectuals in France at the time. It was here that she deepened her friendship with Steichen, who remained close to her and to all of us for life. She met Leo Stein and his sister Gertrude—Leo, she admired and even adored; Gertrude, she dismissed as a "humbug." She came to know contemporary French musicians, led by Darius Milhaud and Erik Satie. She dismissed Picasso as superficially clever. The only woman in Paris who impressed her was Madame Curie, whom she met twice a week when they appeared at the same place for fencing lessons. Here was a woman to emulate, my mother thought—the first woman to so inspire her.

Two of the more important relationships she began while in Paris were with Brancusi, who also became a lifelong friend of hers and our family's, and with Rodin. It was my father, passing through Paris, who introduced her to Rodin. Rodin was famous for his amorous advances to young women, and she felt threatened one day when he locked the door of the studio, turned off the telephone, and started to embrace her. She pleaded with him that she loved him for his great art and his teaching, which she didn't want to lose, and, amazingly, he accepted this. He still couldn't understand why she was unwilling to pose nude on horseback, javelin in hand, for a statue of Boadicea, but he nonetheless took her under his wing.

My mother fell in love with Paris. She lived it up in the Latin Quarter, attended high mass at Notre Dame and Chartres, studied voice and singing, took French lessons, attended endless lectures, and generally delighted in her youth, her encounters, her gay life. A diary she kept in Paris displays her high values, a good deal of learning, and a great passion for all that was going on in the world of art and ideas.

When my father appears in the diary, he is described by her, with some condescension and little apparent interest, as her rich Jewish beau. Judging also from the many letters she wrote from Europe, he was regarded as the giver of loans to her friend Nancy and other friends and the provider of lavish meals that the Left Bank student group all enjoyed enormously. On his few visits to her in Paris, my father was principally greeted with joy for taking everyone out to dine at the Tour d'Argent.

Far from taking him seriously as a suitor, my mother—for the entire time she'd been in Europe—had been writing to Otto Merkel, a German-

American friend of the family, living in New York, to whom she seemed to consider herself engaged. The whole correspondence with Merkel was saved—he must have returned her letters. He is obviously withdrawing—disappointing her by not coming to visit after saying that he's coming—but she seems not to notice and keeps on writing passionately and in detail about her life and their future together. At one point she says she bought a beautiful first edition for "our library" instead of a fur coat she had saved up for. Anyone reading these letters can tell that he's lost interest, but, not untypically, she doesn't understand that his continuing nonappearance and his increasingly infrequent and colder responses are sending a message.

Nancy left for home in February 1909, and my mother moved into a room in a sixth-floor flat with neither bathroom nor heat. She earned enough to stay in Europe by sending stories to the *Sun* and a few magazines, including *St. Nicholas*, for which she also took some photographs. That spring she went to London for Easter vacation and, quite by accident, stumbled upon a small room of Chinese paintings. There she suddenly and inexplicably "fell in love at first sight completely, hopelessly, and forever with Chinese art." She vowed to explore this "attitude toward life" to "its uttermost depths," which she did over the next several years.

After a stimulating swing through Germany, Austria, and Italy, she finally returned home to discouraging problems. She was torn between devotion to her artist and bohemian friends and my father's renewed attentions. And she must have discovered the awful truth that the beloved Merkel was no longer interested in her. In any case, she grew more interested in my father. At a lunch at the Waldorf-Astoria she told him that she felt the need to go back to Europe to think things over. Having decided that problems in the Taft administration would lead to a recession, he had converted his assets to cash to wait out the inevitable effect on Wall Street, so he responded, "I have decided to get away for a bit myself," and told her of his plans to take time off for a trip around the world.

"Why, how long are you going to be away?" she asked in hurt surprise.

"Oh, at least six months," he replied.

When she suddenly realized that he might not be there waiting for her forever, she quickly responded, "I'm going with you."

"I know," he replied. "I have your tickets."

Three weeks later, they were married at her home in a very simple Lutheran ceremony with only the two families present. Even the accounts in the New York papers mentioned that their friends were surprised. He was thirty-four, she only twenty-three. What were her motives? And, indeed, what were his? Did she marry him to escape the problems of her family, for security, for money? Certainly she conceded that his money was not irrelevant to her decision. In her autobiography, she admitted:

. . . it would have been impossible for me to marry anyone who was not well-to-do. For the only dowry I had to bring a husband were my father's debts and my own. The fact that I could confess to Eugene the perpetual nightmare of my relationship to my father was a release from deep inner tensions. It gave me the sharpest realization that I was no longer alone in the world and the added blessing that henceforth I would be free of a crushing burden of debt. Let no one undervalue the importance of economic independence.

Hers was secured, to be sure: my father not only paid off her father's debts even before they left on their honeymoon, but also generously supported Frederick Ernst until his death, in 1913. And her mother was secure.

And yet Mother certainly loved my father in her own peculiar way all her life. She looked up to him, admired his brains, strength, and qualities of leadership. Perhaps one passage in her European diary provides some insight into why she married him, as well as some insight into her own consuming sense of self:

I wrote E.M. Jr. a birthday letter yesterday—one of the greatest things I have ever written. If I had any doubts of the value of his personality, they would be swept aside by this one fact, that he demands greatness of me. With all people that is the test of tests for me.

For his part, he was ready to be married and have a family. Her pictures show her as marvelously good-looking, and she was obviously a highly sought-after, intelligent young woman. From the first sighting in the museum, he must have been dazzled, determined, and patient.

Did the fact that he was Jewish trouble her? I think it must have. She refers to it in her early letters home from Paris. Despite her strong Lutheran background, my mother was not particularly religious either, but clearly she shared the latent anti-Semitism of the period, at least to some extent. My guess is that from her point of view his being Jewish was outweighed by his other strengths and appeal. I think she also was so young and unrealistic, and had had so much go her way despite her family problems, that she thought his being Jewish wouldn't affect *her*. I can only surmise that her ego and self-assurance were such that when she married my father she thought he might come to be considered as not Jewish rather than she as Jewish. She was deeply hurt, however, after her marriage by suddenly being touched by social discrimination in New York.

Her decision to marry Eugene Meyer sprang, no doubt, from a mix of reasons. In any case, she certainly startled everyone by this marriage, and there were those who thought it wouldn't last. But of one thing I am sure:

despite moments of great stress and difficulty in my parents' marriage, they never looked back.

AFTER TWO WEEKS at my father's farm in Mount Kisco, New York, which he had bought some years earlier, the newlyweds set out in a private railroad car, the *Constitution*, for their honeymoon trip around the world, he with a valet and she with a maid. They made their way across America, stopping at one point in Montana to see my father's copper-mining friend, "Big Bill" Thompson. My mother was wearing her wedding present, a string of perfectly matched pearls. Though they were not especially big, this was in the days before cultured pearls, and these were quite rare; she wore them all her life. As they were leaving, according to family lore, Mrs. Thompson turned to her husband and said, "Bill, do you see those pearls?" When he said yes, she queried, "Well, what are you going to do about it?"

By the time the newlyweds reached San Francisco, where they were to visit with the California members of the Meyer family for a week before going on, my mother's maid hadn't worked out. Rosalie found a trained nurse who wanted to travel and was willing to do what was necessary, although she knew nothing about what was expected or needed. So the unsatisfactory maid was replaced by a lady named Margaret Ellen Powell, a practical nurse and a Christian Scientist and the salt of the earth. It was the luckiest thing that ever happened for all of us Meyer children, since Powelly, as we all came to call her, stayed to bring us up.

When my parents returned from their honeymoon and settled back into New York, my mother was pregnant. My father went back to Wall Street, and she had to begin making the necessary adjustments to being a married woman. Overnight she found herself living a wealthy life and running households. She once told me of thinking, as she rode in a chauffeur-driven car, "Can this really be me?" As she herself acknowledged, she had a difficult time, especially in the first years, long before I was born, the fourth child of five. She had rarely thought about what marriage entailed in the way of relationships to spouse and children. I'm not sure she was ever really able to.

She seemed to regard her marriage as a contract she would always keep, and in her way she did. Her duty, as she saw it, lay in having and rearing children, running the houses, and being there when needed to fulfill her obligations as a hostess. After that, like so many of today's women but way ahead of her time, she was determined to maintain her own identity and intellectual life. In her own world, she went her own way. Later, in a memoir, she explained how she felt at the time:

I ... rebelled inwardly and outwardly against the suddenly imposed responsibilities of marriage. During the first few years . . . I
behaved as if the whole world were in a conspiracy to flatten out
my personality and cast me into a universal mold called "woman."
So many of my married college friends had renounced their intellectual interests and lost themselves in a routine of diapers, dinners, and smug contentment with life, that I was determined this
should not happen to me. I wanted a big family but I also wanted
to continue my life as an individual.

I believe she was often desperately unhappy in her marriage, especially at first. She went to a psychiatrist, on whom she leaned heavily. She
tried to escape any problems with her marriage and motherhood by studying Chinese art and language and by maintaining her connections to
"291" and developing an interest in collecting modern art. She had already met a man who was to be one of the great influences in her life, the
industrialist and pioneer collector Charles Lang Freer. They met at an exhibit of Chinese art, and he, having heard of her interest, invited her to
Detroit to see his collection. She responded, "Next week I am going to
have a baby, but I'll come as soon after that as I can." My father went along
as chaperone and he, too, became a friend of Freer's.

From January 1913 until his death, my mother studied under and collected with Freer. Often they would divide up the shipments from his
personal representatives in China. She had already studied the Chinese
language at Columbia from 1911 to 1913, and for the next five years, with
the aid of a Chinese scholar whom she often had in residence at Mount
Kisco, she amassed research materials for an analysis of the contributions
of Confucianism, Taoism, and Buddhism to the development of the T'ang
and Sung dynasties. This resulted in the publication, in 1923, of her book
Chinese Painting as Reflected in the Thought and Art of Li Lung-Mien. Unfortunately, Freer, to whom it was dedicated, had died in 1919. She visited
him constantly throughout his long, agonizing illness. At his death, Freer
designated five trustees for his gallery in Washington, of whom my parents were two.

As another outlet for her mind, she enrolled in postgraduate study in
biology, economics, and history at Columbia University, where she met
and became involved with the historians Charles and Mary Beard. When
the Beards, John Dewey, and others founded the free and liberal New
School for Social Research, she helped modestly to fund it and also helped
in psychology classes when it opened in 1919.

At the same time, she grew even more involved with "291" and with
Steichen in promoting modern art, especially that of John Marin, who

sent over his watercolors from Paris. She was instrumental in founding the periodical named for the gallery, "*291*," and became an editor of this first avant-garde journal in America. My mother was already caught up in these activities by the time the first baby, my oldest sister, Florence, was born. She later told stories of deciding to nurse the baby but forgetting to come home from her "extramural activities" and racing home to find a screaming baby being pacified by poor Powelly.

During these first years of my mother's struggles with marriage, my father had some business setbacks. He had entered the budding automobile business in a big way, investing heavily in a company called the United States Motor Company, which produced the Maxwell. This company had run into trouble, and my father had helped reorganize it into the Maxwell Motor Company, which was still in trouble. His heavy investments in copper had not begun to pay off, and, for the first time, he felt financially squeezed. My parents had moved into a large, elegant house at 70th Street and Park Avenue. In an effort to retrench, they sold the house and moved into an entire floor at the St. Regis Hotel—not exactly poverty row, but enough to set off rumors that Wall Street's boy wonder had gotten into trouble.

He eventually emerged from the tumultuous experience with Maxwell with a substantial profit and went on believing in the automobile business. A little later he made a brilliantly successful investment in the Fisher Body Company, run by seven able brothers. When Fisher sold to General Motors, however, he chose cash rather than stock, passing up the chance to become one of G.M.'s largest stockholders.

Around the same time, my father made another—less important—mistake. With his friend Bernard Baruch he invested in a gold mine, Alaska Juneau. The value of the mine went up and down, but at some point water, not gold, was found in it. For some reason, my father had invested in the mine for all of us children and told us about it. The price of Alaska Juneau was the subject of dinner-table merriment for many years, along with discussion of whether each child had profited or not. Eventually, it dropped farther and farther and finally disappeared altogether. Phil and I later named our golden retriever Juneau in honor of the mine—a much better investment.

My father's investments in copper, cars, and, later, chemicals were all indicative of his desire not only to make money but to participate in creating new frontiers. He very much admired E. H. Harriman for creating a railroad when railroads were new. That was the kind of thing he aspired to do, being in on the birth of an industry. He once asked James Russell Wiggins, when Russ was editor of the *Post*, what he would do if he could do exactly what he wanted. Russ replied that he supposed he'd write history, to which my father responded, "I wouldn't. I'd sooner make it."

In addition to his business problems, the first years following his marriage brought a number of personal troubles and tragedies. The worst was the loss of the youngest Meyer, Edgar, his partner and much-loved sibling, who went down on the *Titanic* after putting his wife and baby daughter in the last lifeboat. He was only twenty-eight. My father had been his much older brother—almost a father figure, and certainly a mentor—and he was painfully bereft. He was not close to many people; Edgar had been one of the very few.

He had my mother, of course, who always stood behind him staunchly when he needed it, but who seemed increasingly to resent running the big houses, who disliked social obligations, and who was shocked and discouraged by the pains of childbirth. She asked her obstetrician during Florence's birth why anyone had a second baby. As she herself wrote, "I became a conscientious but scarcely a loving mother."

By 1914, she had had my second sister, Elizabeth—or Bis, as she was always known—and was chafing so over what she felt as the "crushing" of her personality that my father encouraged her to go abroad. They initially thought of going together, but the gathering war clouds concerned him and he decided to stay home to look after his, by now, very large business. In addition, given her frustrations in acclimating to marriage and a family, they both saw the need for some distance between them, so they agreed that she would take the trip to Europe alone and they would correspond often. Indeed, all her life my mother found it easier to communicate from a distance, and she conversed with us children at least as much through letters as she did in person. I took this form of communication for granted.

For some reason, when she was in her old age and during my middle years, she suddenly gave me the letters that she and my father had exchanged while she was abroad in 1914. I'm not sure why. The strains between them were ill-concealed in these letters, which freely expressed their differences, his fairly unreasonable anger and jealousy, and her conflicting emotions.

Her first letters to him were written in May 1914, while she was still on the German steamship the *Vaterland*, headed for Bremen. Her very first letter asked why he had left the boat so long before it sailed. She was quite crushed, and ended the letter with "Kiss my babies. I have left my heart with you and them." She seems to have quickly got over any sadness at leaving them, however, since the next letter was full of details about her active social life on board—she had been taken up by the very distinguished Mrs. Stotesbury of Philadelphia. She alternated these social details with more intimate comments. At one point she asks,

Are you thinking of me lovingly in spite of the fact that I have temporarily deserted you? This is a revolutionary age even for the marital relationship and I hope that you will not cease having confidence in me and loving me when I have a period of thinking things out. It only means that my feelings for you will be clearer and therefore finer.

Much of the European trip was a reconstruction of the artistic life she had created as a student there. She looked at and bought books and art in Berlin, Vienna, and Paris. She went with de Zayas to see what she called the "ultra-moderns." She "expected to be horrified"—particularly by Picasso's work, since she had heard he used "pieces of wallpaper, newspaper and other actual things with which to construct his pictures"—but she found his work "large as life and fascinating" and bought a small still life of "a pipe, a glass, a bottle and some grapes," the grapes having been set in sawdust. She called it a "real work of art," and paid $140 for it.

Fairly early on, she committed an almost fatal error from the point of view of her relationship with my father. She went for tea to the apartment of an old friend, Alfred von Heymel, whom she had met in Berlin through her onetime beau Otto Merkel the summer of her student year.

Instead of making things better, as she thought her writing from this distance would, her letter about this unchaperoned visit prompted a wonderfully old-fashioned row. She had told my father quite casually about going to von Heymel's apartment alone, but added that he should not be shocked, since the place was "full of domestics." There followed from my father—all carefully preserved—two letters of uncontrolled and repetitive rage at her having "gone alone to a man's apartment."

She cabled and wrote back that there was a misunderstanding and tried to give her side of the incident, but it was no use. The details didn't matter to him; what did matter was that he had to have confidence in her. He enumerated other occasions when he felt she hadn't used good sense. He felt that the liberty he wanted her always to feel was hers was being abused, and that if she really cared she would understand the serious consequences of her thoughtlessness. Incredibly, after saying all this, he said he hoped "nothing in this sounds like lecturing and preaching," signing the letter "with fondest love."

Despite the misunderstandings on both sides about this ill-fated von Heymel visit, she carried on with her trip and her letters. She wrote my father that she recognized that her whole existence had been devoted to life, whereas his had been devoted to work. She also said she hadn't been giving to him, which she concluded was not entirely her fault: "We have often scarcely seen each other. We have lived in the market place instead of building up a shrine of our own." She thought even their town house reflected this distance between them: "We have no room where one feels you and I actually live." She admitted to him that in the last year she had been terribly restless and dissatisfied and could feel his uneasiness: "I do not blame you. Only a blind man could have failed to be uneasy about the woman who left you but I do not think you will be uneasy about the woman who returns."

Indeed, in the letters she wrote during this interlude she tried to be supportive of him and analytical about herself, but to little avail. He wrote a final letter complaining that she hadn't written as often as she had promised, that she was always in a hurry, and that she would be coming home tired instead of rested. This letter ended with:

> You say "Be happy and know that I shall work for you always in any and every way." This is a smart expression and I am sure you would do so—if you happened to think of it. Thinking after all is what counts.

Her last full week of what turned out to be more than two months in Europe she spent with the Steichens in their simple house in Voulangis, where he was growing and breeding delphiniums, a lifelong passion. With little to do, she wrote my father that she had grown "uneasy about you, the kids, the cook, the strawberries that weren't being preserved. . . ."

She sailed for home on a Dutch steamer on July 31, as promised, and luckily, too, since it was one of the last boats to leave Europe before World War I erupted two weeks later. Steichen's house was near to what became the front as the Germans threatened to break through at the first Battle of the Marne. Ignorant of his extreme danger, Steichen cabled my father asking what he ought to do. "Suggest immediate orderly retreat," was my father's firm reply. The Steichens were just able to leave for America and took refuge at Mount Kisco with my parents.

On her way home, my mother had a nightmare in which she saw herself as her father, irresponsible and self-absorbed to the extent of ruining his family's life and hers. She made up her mind not to be like that. And, in fact, the time away, despite the stormy exchanges, seems to have helped. She returned with a new commitment to this difficult relationship, determined to make it work. In a letter she had mentioned resting up before enduring more of "the baby business." I suppose her assumption was that she would have one every two years—and, indeed, she had my brother Bill a year later. And two years after that, on June 16, 1917, I was born.

— *Chapter Two* —

IN LINE WITH my father's "map of life," the time was right for him to turn his attention to public service. In the immediate years before my birth, he had begun to play a semipublic role in New York. In 1913, he had been elected to the board of governors of the New York Stock Exchange and had worked hard to effect the kinds of changes and reforms he had been espousing in financial circles. He was active in helping manage the various panics that hit the stock exchange as the threat of war in Europe loomed larger, and then later, as the likelihood grew of America's involvement in the war.

By the fall of 1914, for example, the war in Europe threatened the textile industry, largely because the German dye cartel at that time supplied at least 90 percent of our dyes. My father loaned Dr. William Gerard Beckers, a German-trained chemist, the money for plant facilities and a much-needed laboratory to continue his experimentation with manufacturing dyes. In 1916, Beckers's company merged with two other corporations to create the National Aniline and Chemical Company, and a few years after the war, my father negotiated a merger of National Aniline with four older companies. The integrated company thus created, the Allied Chemical and Dye Corporation, never missed a dividend throughout the Depression. By 1931, his holdings were worth $43 million, and the dividends were later to help cover losses suffered by *The Washington Post*.

Despite several financial setbacks, and even before the huge success of Allied Chemical, my father's wealth was considerable. By 1915, his fortune was estimated at around $40–60 million. But making money, satisfactory as it was, was never his primary objective. As he did throughout his life, he looked for ways to make his money work for the public good. He had become engaged in many welfare organizations. He was also president of Mount Sinai Hospital, and his interest in mental health was already evident in his support for building clinics. He had set up a fund at his alma mater, Yale, to train young men for public service. At the same time, he was beginning to hanker for some opportunity to serve the government himself. Being Republican, and having contributed to Republican campaigns and causes, he could see no immediate opportunities, since President Wilson was in office. He got involved in Charles Evans Hughes's campaign against Wilson in 1916, which, of course, was narrowly unsuccessful.

Shortly after the election, my father, even more eager to work for the government since he was certain America would be pulled into the war, offered his services to his friends Justice Louis Brandeis and Bernard Baruch, and even to Wilson himself. With no specific assignment, he went to Washington as a dollar-a-year man, and, after a few false starts, he eventually got various appointments and high-level government assignments under seven presidents, beginning with service on the Raw Materials Committee and the General Munitions Board, both eventually leading to the War Industries Board.

My father left New York for Washington early in 1917. My mother stayed in Mount Kisco that summer, following my birth in June. In October she joined him in Washington in a large rented house on K Street. For several vague reasons—Washington was crowded, there was a pneumonia epidemic at one point, they viewed their stay as temporary—they left us children in New York for the next four years, three of which they spent mostly in Washington with occasional visits back and forth. It's odd that they claimed not to have known how long they would be staying, since as soon as he got to Washington my father resigned as a governor of the stock exchange, gave up directorships in several companies, and sold all stocks that might involve him in a conflict of interest. In fact, in August 1917 he decided to dissolve his investment banking firm completely, since he knew even then that he would get deeply involved with the United States Treasury. He left only a small office for his personal business and several people who worked for him buying and selling stocks and paying taxes.

In 1917, we were occupying the entire top floor and half of the floor below at 820 Fifth Avenue, which is where I was born. We—"the babes," as Mother often referred to us in her diary—lived with Powelly in this Fifth Avenue apartment. A governess, Anna Otth, had been added after Bill was born. I can't remember the years in New York, and since I was a baby, those very early years of separation and substitute parenting had the least effect on me of any of the children. Only psychiatrists can guess about their effect on my older siblings. Much later, my brother, when he was in the process of being analyzed to become a psychoanalyst himself, got very angry thinking about the separation and testily asked my mother how she could have left her children in New York for those early years. She said, "Well, you were all in school." But the older children were two, four, and six, and I was a few months old, when our parents first left for Washington.

WHEN SHE WENT to Washington, my mother's life changed drastically—and for the better. She was part of a team for the first time, going into a strange city in which she and my father were both new. There seems to have been less anti-Semitic prejudice in Washington than in New York. And in Washington, unlike the many women who to this day find the city distasteful because they are regarded as appendages of their husbands, my mother found a wide canvas on which to paint.

She continued to maintain her old interests, particularly in Chinese art, even admitting in her autobiography that "I was so engrossed in translating Chinese texts and in writing a book on the philosophy of Chinese art that it never occurred to me to make any active contribution toward the war effort. In plain truth I sat out the First World War." At the same time, however, she threw herself into Washington's social life in a determined way, partly because she enjoyed it but also because she saw immersion in social life as the way she could help further my father's interests.

Mother began another diary at the time they moved to Washington, which makes it clear how devoted she was to him. She often worried that his talents weren't sufficiently recognized, and she constantly noted the progress of his career and her faith in his abilities: "He is so big that I want him to be of more help in this terrible situation of chaos produced by incompetence and politics mixed."

Although she never quite said so, and often claimed the contrary, she clearly thrived on the range of new and varied people she met. My parents, separately and together, attended dinners, lunches, and teas almost nonstop—including the famous Ned and Evalyn McLean Sunday lunches for eighty or a hundred people entertained by a full orchestra, held at Friendship, the McLeans' "country" place on Wisconsin Avenue in Washington, where McLean Gardens is located today. The names she mentioned in her diary escalate in both prominence and interest as the months mount, starting with Cissy Patterson, then known as Countess Gizycki. She fascinated my mother, who wrote of her: "Pugnose, red hair, a ready wit and charm, what more can a woman have? As she is extremely feline I shall see to it that I do not get scratched but with that in mind I intend to see what there is in it."

As she had done in Paris, my mother rapidly got to know extraordinary people: Baruch, Brandeis, Frankfurter, who took her to see Oliver Wendell Holmes, Jr., Elihu Root, and Charles Evans Hughes. She met and, as she said, tried to impress H. G. Wells. She began a flirtation with Shrinivasi Sastri, a delegate from India to the nine-power peace conference that took place in Washington in 1922. She is very self-analytical in the diary, and mentions feeling not always mentally at her best, "but when I like people I have a silly wish to glitter that no one really could satisfy."

She also got to know Alice Roosevelt Longworth and her husband, Nick. She was always ambivalent about Mrs. Longworth, and Mrs. L., as we all always called her later on, returned the feeling. My father and Mrs. L. became good friends and, later, bridge-playing companions, but my mother kept her distance. "What a brilliant but sterile mind!" she wrote after one meeting with her. "It is exactly like her father's and helps me to understand T.R. perfectly.... The thought of her undoubtedly makes my winter look more interesting." After one party that they both attended early in 1920, my mother described Alice as having been in a "very carnal sort of mood. She ate three chops, told shady stories and finally sang in a deep bass voice: 'Nobody cultivates me, I'm wild, I'm wild.'" Mother kept halfway admiring her, though, while also constantly criticizing her. "There is something depressing about her very keenness," she wrote.

Despite her seemingly happy immersion in the social whirl, her diary is peppered with critical comments, both about the city and its people: "Washington is not in the least intellectual. Of that there is no doubt whatever"; "Roosevelt [Franklin—then Assistant Secretary of the Navy] is very pleasant but his wife [Eleanor] like all officials' wives is terribly aware of her position"; "I came home very blue as the dinner party as a form of human intercourse seems to me very poor indeed."

She may have scorned dinner parties, but she took great delight in the "breadth and depth" of her life. At one point she exclaimed, "At last je m'en fiche de Mt. Kisco. I really believe that complex is eliminated"—the only reference to the fact that the social snobbery there had hurt her.

What the diary also indicates is that motherhood was not exactly Mother's first priority. She rarely mentioned any one of us children individually. I appear in the diary for the first time by name (or by initial, I should say) in February 1920, two and a half years after my birth: "The babes (Bill and K) take some of my time this week. At breakfast yesterday Euge said: 'K will be a big woman.' Bill (4½): 'She isn't going to be a woman, she's going to be a lady.' K: 'No I'm not, I'm going to be a woman.'"

There are sporadic mentions in the diary of visits to Washington by the children, or of parental visits to New York. These references focused on how much we were learning, and our development under the care of Powelly and Mrs. Satis N. Coleman, a teacher who later became well known for her program for the early musical training of children—she believed that music education should make a contribution to character building, home life, and society. My sisters played the violin, which she helped them learn by first teaching them to make violinlike instruments out of cigar boxes, and I did things like tap on glasses filled with varying amounts of water. In December of 1918, my mother noted, "The children delighted me with their progress and their happiness under Mrs. Coleman's influence." When Mother visited New York, she would often have a few people in, and we—especially Flo and Bis—would dance or perform for them in some way. Mother seemed to view this kind of thing as the essence of a happy childhood, making passing comments about everybody being pleased with the children and "their unconscious joy," or that everyone was "enchanted with the accomplishment, the promise and all pervading atmosphere of childish happiness." These remarks typify her talent for seeing things as she wanted them to be.

In the absence of a mother's day-to-day affection, we grew devoted to Powelly. She supplied the hugs, the comforting, the feeling of human contact, even the love that my mother did not. She was kind and wise and, above all, warm. Powelly was always there, sensibly solving our problems and salving our hurts, even if her methods were somewhat unusual.

My mother didn't much believe in doctors—I hardly ever saw one through most of my youth—and Powelly was a devout Christian Scientist, so illness wasn't acknowledged by her. If we said we had a tummy ache or a cold, she would say, "Just know it's going to be all right"—and off we'd go with any disease or even a fever. I did stay home from school briefly with the mumps and was permitted to lie down on the couch for half a day. Another medical problem was a sprained finger the size of a good cigar from a basketball bouncing off the end of it. My mother sent for her masseuse. The lovely Swedish lady took one look and suggested a doctor, who put it in a splint. My freshman year in high school, I had a loud, racking cough the entire winter. This was overlooked at home but much discussed in a deafened school as I barked my way through the year. Finally, toward spring, my mother decided that a weekend away in Atlantic City would be beneficial, so she dispatched me with the governess, Mademoiselle Otth, to a hotel on the boardwalk for a cure. A cold rain fell the entire time, and we ran out of money. Only thirty years later, when I was diagnosed with tuberculosis, was it observed by the doctors that the scars on my lungs indicated I had had a previous attack. Whatever it was, I got over it.

Luckily, I have always had rugged good health and a really strong constitution. The happy result of having Powelly's philosophy embedded in me was that, if I did get anything, I, too, tended to disregard it, and have always been able to keep going through minor afflictions. Year after year went by with perfect attendance at school, and no doubt many germs spread generously around.

When you outgrew Powelly, there was Mademoiselle Otth, who was somewhat disorganized but did her best and meant well. She was sweet but unable to ride herd on us as we grew older. Another much-loved influence on our early years was the family chauffeur, Al Phillips, known as Phil. He was our friend, colleague, supervisor, and protector.

After the first year in Washington, my mother went with us to Mount Kisco for the summer; then she returned to Washington to live in Mrs. George Vanderbilt's house, "a much more charming milieu than that of last year." She again decided to leave the children in New York, fearing the Washington winters. She wrote her justification in the diary: "The influenza has been raging all over the country with very high mortality, but here in W. [Washington] the conditions were disgraceful. People died right and left from pure neglect, and bodies were lying about everywhere because there were no undertakers and no grave-diggers to dispose of them."

She returned to a new round of people and dinners. And she helped start a ladies' lunch club and wrote of the first meeting in 1920: "We discussed 'What is the most outstanding figure developed by the war?' Mrs. Hard supported Lenin and Mrs. Harriman, Hoover. The feelings flew on occasion. . . . We decided to discuss at the next meeting 'Decided that the Russian blockade should be lifted.' It was great fun on the whole and among the women are the most intelligent in Washington." Alice Longworth was pointedly omitted from the invitees.

Making himself helpful in Washington, my father had moved through the War Industries Board and the War Savings Committee, and in January 1919 he had been made chairman of the War Finance Corporation. When its work came to a halt for a while in May 1920, my parents briefly moved back to New York one last time, but Washington, with its allure of politics, had captivated them both. They were drawn to its openness and what she called "the tenseness of interest that the life here has for us." In New York he toyed with buying the Missouri Pacific Railroad, or joining Adolph Ochs, who invited him to come on *The New York Times* on the business side, but that side alone didn't interest him.

When the Republicans were elected in 1920, there was talk of my father's returning to Washington. After a congressional struggle precipitated by the opposition of much of Wall Street, which viewed it as too much government interference, the War Finance Corporation was revived and my father was appointed to it by President Harding and was elected its managing director in March of 1921. This new appointment finally made my parents realize they would be in Washington for some years, so, when they returned to Washington that fall, we were at last brought down to live with them.

My mother threw herself into the social and political scene with renewed vigor, having found that she had to re-establish their position after their absence and, of course, a changed administration. For instance, she made three hundred social calls in a relatively short period of time, which meant leaving calling cards with one corner turned down, signifying that she had personally left them. She despised doing this, saying she did it "not only because of Eugene's much wider associations, but because I have to put us back on the social map. . . . This game takes more persistence and courage than anyone will admit." She confided to her diary that "I cannot hide the fact that my sympathies are deeper, my interests more serious than those of most of these women." In fact, that was true; they were.

As for me, when I reached the age of four, Washington became my home and remained so forever. At first, we moved into a large, dark, red-brick house on Connecticut Avenue, described by my mother in her diary as a "big, old-fashioned barn." She added: "The children are happy in their semi-country life, and we are all glad to be living together again." My earliest memories are of this house, where I was quite content. The house was a sprawling Victorian mansion with a stained-glass bay window in the dining room. It was rented from the Woodwards of the Woodward and Lothrop department-store family, the Lothrops having built an equally large stone house a block away. The land around the house extended the length of the block, and the yard became a playground for the whole neighborhood.

One of the earliest transactions I had with my father about the future took place in this Connecticut Avenue house when I was about eight. He kept asking if, when I grew up, I would be his secretary. I had no idea what a secretary was or did, but the whole idea struck me as distasteful. At the time, my father himself seemed to me a rather remote and strange male figure whom I liked from a distance but thought very different. My answer was a constant and firm no. Although I had an awareness that this was a tease, I knew it was something I didn't want to do. However, I had a bank in which you inserted nickels, dimes, and quarters, and when it reached the vast sum of $5.00 it would spring open. I had been collecting coins for months on my tiny allowance, and finally I needed only one nickel to have all this vast wealth at my command. When I asked my father if he would give me a nickel, he said, "Well, *now* will you be my secretary?" I agreed. I sold out for a nickel. My father would occasionally refer to this future, making me slightly puzzled and anxious, but I never thought of reneging on the bargain and was always referred to as his future secretary.

IN LARGE FAMILIES, it seems it is hardest to be either the first or the last child. That was certainly true in ours. Florence, the first—conceived on the honeymoon trip and born in 1911—was the only Meyer girl who was beautiful in the classical sense. Flo was both smart and vulnerable. Her tastes were artistic and literary: she could often be found reclining with a book in her hand. According to my mother's ideal, Meyer girls were supposed to be competitive and athletic. Flo was neither. She always wore a large picture hat on the tennis court to indicate that she wasn't seriously trying. Instead of sports, she immersed herself first in music, later—much too late, as it turned out—in dance, making her professional debut in Max Reinhardt's *The Eternal Road* in 1935. Despite my parents' interest in and support of her dancing, Flo never received from them the emotional support she needed while growing up. She had an especially difficult time with my mother, no doubt because of Mother's inexperience with motherhood and her lack of interest in it. An attempt to elope at sixteen was foiled by the chauffeur, Phil. Throughout my childhood, Flo was a distant though appealing figure to me. For Flo, I didn't exist until we were both grown up.

Whereas Flo may have bent, however unwillingly, to my parents' wishes, Bis—born two years after her— lived in a state of constant rebellion. "My whole life was malefaction," Bis later told me. "I was against adults." She resented the power our parents had over her and met power with power in whatever way she could—and she found a number of ways. As she said many years later, "I led an illicit life to a rather large degree."

Bis had an expression—"you haven't lived until . . ."—that both got her into trouble and led her into great adventures. Her life-sustaining escapades included attending a burlesque show and a wrestling match. When she was very young, Bis decided she would not have lived until she had hocked something, so she pilfered a necklace from my mother's room and asked Al Phillips to drive her and a friend across the Potomac River to Rosslyn, Virginia, which was then a dusty semicountry crossroads with a strip of pawn shops. "My good man, what will you give me for these jewels?" Bis demanded authoritatively of the bemused pawnbroker. "Little girl," he replied, "I suggest you return that necklace to your mother." When Bis and her friend turned around, they found Phil doubled over with laughter at the door.

Bis was popular with boys. She entered Vassar at sixteen and later went on to study in Munich and at Barnard. She often brought glamorous figures home for house parties, where my pedestrian young male friends paled in their shadow.

In 1915, along came Eugene Meyer III. Any boy with that name was going to have a hard time, and Bill, as he was always known, did, especially as he got older. Being the only boy of five children would be difficult in any family, but it was particularly so in ours, both because of my father's unapproachability and prominence and because of my mother's awkwardness with men. But my mother was elated at his birth. She had wanted nothing but sons and she felt, as she admitted, "a ridiculous sense of achievement."

Even as a young child, Bis found, or recruited, a companion rebel in Bill. The two of them formed a team; like Bis, Bill assumed a defiant stance toward the grown-up world. We were all away once on a yacht trip and Bill had stayed home, learned to fly, and gained his pilot's license. He told my mother he had something to show her. She held her breath, fearing it was a marriage license, in comparison with which a pilot's license seemed benign. He then "showed her" by buzzing our house in Mount Kisco, dipping his wings in acknowledgment.

From as early as I can remember, I adored my older siblings, but particularly Bis and Bill. I was desperately eager to be part of their adventurous life and terribly envious of Bis's nonconformist image. I really even wanted to *be* her. I envied her self-assurance, her independence, her daring, her willingness to cut up and row with the family. I would have liked to be a dashing law-breaker, but I didn't have the proper instincts or the courage, and I was always scorned for passively going along. Where Bis was a rebel, I followed the rules. I was Goody Two-Shoes, begging to be taken along with Bis and Bill wherever they went. Naturally, they considered me a pain.

Worse, when I was very young I was the world's most ignoble tattletale—without even realizing what I was doing. I didn't tell on the older ones to be mean, get even, or ingratiate myself with my parents. I simply had no idea that I had transgressed. I shared their lives so little that I didn't understand that their activities were meant to be secret, and was merely reporting. After one episode when I was about four, Bis, Bill, and Flo took me into a bathroom at Mount Kisco and carefully taped my mouth shut. As Bis remembers, "The big tears on those very fat cheeks almost undid me. It was so sad, but the cause was just."

As the fourth of five children, I was oddly shielded from the rigors of living with parents who demanded perfection and from some of the eccentricities of our curious upbringing. More so than the older children, I was supervised by our parents from afar. This was in certain ways lucky, because, growing up somewhat alone, I didn't experience the rules and heavy hand to which the older children were subjected.

By the time I was growing up, the battles between the children and the parents had already taken place. Not only were our parents busier and more preoccupied than ever, but my impulse was always to please. Only later did I observe that this curious passivity left me freer than both my older sisters and brother: their rebellion somehow left them more enslaved and affected by the family's myths and wishes. Somehow, in their defiance, my siblings were more captives of the negative part of our upbringing. So my position in the family turned out to be a lucky one; I bore neither the brunt of my mother's newness to parenthood nor the force of her middle-aged traumas, as my younger sister, Ruth, did. I was somehow protected. Luck helped me be a survivor and gave me strength, but at the time what I really wanted was a place in the remote and exciting world of my older sisters and brother. As Bis succinctly put it later, I was "safe but gypped."

My difficulties were much more tied to a lack of guiding personal relationships, for I had more or less to bring myself up emotionally and figure out how to deal with whatever situations confronted me. At the same time that I was surrounded by extreme luxury, I led a life structured and in many ways spartan, circumscribed by school and lessons, travel and study. The only person who was physically affectionate with me was Powelly, whom I emotionally outgrew when I was about seven. From then on I was on my own.

The youngest of us, Ruth, was born in Mount Kisco in July 1921. I was led in to see the new baby lying on the bed in the guest room. I hadn't the remotest idea how the baby arrived or whence it came and don't remember being curious. I was just in awe of her, with her tiny curled-up fingers.

Ruth's birth, the last in our family, sealed my separation from the older three, who viewed Ruth and me as a pair of infants. Ruthie was an enchanting child and I was jealous that she was blonde, blue-eyed, and beautiful, whereas I was dark and pudgy. I once tested family members by suggesting that if a fire broke out we'd all meet in Ruthie's room because we'd rush to save her first. No one contradicted this thesis or got the point of my test.

Ruthie and I were set apart as a duo in other ways. We both remained under Powelly's care as the older ones outgrew her, even sharing a room until I was twelve. When guests were present at dinner, which was nearly every night, Ruthie and I had to eat alone at an earlier hour. Every summer until I was nine and allowed to join the older contingent, my parents took the three of them on a trip to Europe or, in alternate years, on a camping trip out west. While the others were off enjoying exciting adventures, Ruthie and I were left in Mount Kisco with our governess.

As the fifth and last child, Ruthie received even less in the way of parental attention and interest, and more in the way of being attended to only by a governess or nurse. Naturally, because we were always considered a separate unit and I was four years older, I became a sort of parent to her, or at least an important mentor. She grew increasingly shy, gentle, and unassertive. For the most part, she lived in a world of her own, eventually becoming a gifted, devoted horsewoman. Her attention was focused on a Springer spaniel named Cricket and the governess, Mademoiselle Otth, whom she loved very much. When Ruth was fifteen, the dog died and the governess was sent away at about the same time. Needless to say, Ruth's heart was broken. When Mademoiselle left, Ruth wrote me:

I miss her so very, very much. If somebody that I didn't know very well asked me which I loved better, Mother or Mlle, I would probably say I loved Mother better, but I'll tell you and nobody else that I love Mlle better. You see, I can really discuss and talk things over with her. I guess I could do it with Mother, too, but boy oh boy, I would feel so small afterwards.

I understood only too well how she felt. My mother later wrote up these events in a story that she tried to sell to one of the women's magazines. I was indignant that she was using her daughter's grief and wounds in this way, but she calmly replied that she'd shown it to Ruthie and that Ruthie had liked it. I didn't believe it at the time, but she proved to be right. When Ruthie and I were going over my mother's papers after her death, the story reappeared. I stupidly tore it up, my anger returning at the sight of it. Years later Ruthie told me she had resented my tearing it up and thought I was jealous because it was about her, not me. The complexity of family relations is too deep to comprehend. This incident certainly testifies against moral certitude—mine.

MY LIFE AS a child was centered in the house in Washington and in our summer home in Mount Kisco. At that time it was an eight-hour train trip from Washington through New York and on into the country, but we made the trip regularly, those treks engineered by Mother, traveling with five children, several canaries, and all the baggage. The horses went separately.

The ambience of the huge country house was wonderful, making up in gaiety what it may have lacked in warmth. As a bachelor, my father had bought an old farm and had added to it over the years until his property reached seven hundred acres at its peak, which was most of my childhood. Originally, there was a beautiful old farmhouse, which he had used and where the family lived in summers in the early years of my parents' marriage, before they decided to build a larger home.

Designed in 1915 by Charles Platt, the architect my mother's friend Freer had selected to build his Oriental-art gallery in Washington, the new stone house was built to be lived in year-round, so that my father could commute to Wall Street by car or the excellent commuter train. Since my parents moved to Washington in 1917, we used it only from early summer until early fall.

The new house—surrounded by enormous trees, all transplanted—stood on top of a previously barren hill overlooking the old farmhouse. In the other direction, the house overlooked Byram Lake, a New York City water supply, but also our boating-and-fishing hole in a once-a-summer event. We always referred to this neoclassical country house as "the farm," because my parents thought of it as that and because it was a regular working farm. There were pigs and chickens, as well as Jersey milk cows, from which we got unpasteurized milk, buttermilk, and rich cream. There was a large and bountiful orchard and a garden at the foot of the hill, from which we ate fresh vegetables and enjoyed magnificent bouquets of flowers all over the house, refreshed and replaced every day. Flowers were even sent to Washington for our successive houses there, and in winters, many of the farm's products were delivered by truck to our Washington house. The care of the gardens, at least in summer, took a dozen men. Another dozen ran the farm. They all lived at the old farmhouse in a bachelor establishment.

The house itself was large but simple in lines. Though it was very grand in concept, it managed to retain a feeling of informality. Made of rough-hewn pinkish-gray granite blasted out of huge rocks from a quarry on the place and chipped and carved into immense brick-shaped slabs by stonemasons, it took two years to build. Samuel Gompers, head of the American Federation of Labor, had to be summoned to settle a jurisdictional dispute between two unions involved in the construction—stonecutters and bricklayers, I believe.

The rooms were all big. Most of the bedrooms had screened sleeping porches attached. There was an indoor swimming pool and a bowling alley, as well as a tennis court. There was a beautiful formal garden next to the house at one end, which was completed by a separate large, classical orangery. Two massive Italian birdbaths were situated on either side of a pond containing large lotuses at both ends and water lilies in the middle.

Most surprising was a big organ with pipes that wove through the house on every floor. My father loved to blast us out of bed on Sunday mornings by playing "Nearer My God to Thee" at its loudest, saying, "Everybody up!" We also had a grand piano, and both the organ and piano had mechanical attachments for playing rolls of music. We had scores of piano rolls, including many by Paderewski, a great friend of my mother's. One of my principal childhood memories is hearing one of the Liszt Hungarian Rhapsodies waft throughout the house.

My mother prided herself on not having had a decorator. She and Platt together had chosen the furniture, with curious and not very practical results. Since both of them were tall, they had naturally chosen chairs for the living rooms that were quite large. In several, my father's feet barely touched the ground, since he was a few inches shorter than she. None of the rooms had proper reading lights near the beds, or desks with appropriate chairs and lights. My father complained loudly that he didn't have a reading light in his bedroom—I think he finally managed to secure one by buying it himself. My mother's bedroom was the only room in the house that was both beautiful and livable, in the sense that it had proper lights and comfortable chairs.

No room on the ground floor had enough chairs for a cozy group to sit and talk, except for an outdoor porch off my father's study. We just about lived on this porch, which was open but roofed. It was in my father's study that we always gathered after dinner. There, too, there were only two large chairs, placed on either side of the fireplace. My father's desk and chair and a sofa were way off in opposite corners, so the conversation group had to be created anew each evening by bringing extra chairs in and pulling them close to the fireplace.

Not only did my mother never have a decorator, but she never changed anything once it was in place, except as we children grew up and altered our room arrangements. At first, I lived with Ruthie and a nurse, later a governess, in a room with a porch off it, on which we slept, and a playroom next door. Flo and Bis and their governess lived in a similar arrangement. My parents had a suite at the end of the hall. Bill and his tutor lived up on the third floor.

The whole house was lined with large Chinese paintings. In the biggest living room was a table on which sat many of my mother's beautiful bronzes, vases, and other objects. In her study stood two Brancusis—*Danaïde* on the mantel and *The Blonde Negress* at the door. In the library there was the large white marble *Bird in Space*, on a wooden base that Brancusi had carved in our garden on his first visit to the United States, when he had stayed with us at Mount Kisco. I remember sitting around watching while Brancusi hacked away and chatted with us simultaneously.

As Ruthie and I got older, meals were mostly taken together, the whole family gathered, especially on weekends, when my father arrived from Washington. We had two dining rooms. If there were a lot of us, we used the larger, more formal, marble-floored inside dining room, which was rare and special. When it was just the family and a few friends we would eat in what we called the "outside" dining room, which could still seat about twenty. It had a green Venetian dining-room set and was enclosed by large glass windows that provided views of the terrace and woods beyond the house. The only decoration in this room was a sculpture by Brancusi, his rendition of my mother. Needless to say, this was a very abstract black marble, which he called *La Reine pas Dédaigneuse*, or *The Not-Disdainful Queen*. Many people laughed at it, describing it, among other ways, as a horse's swollen knee. Only once was it shown in a Brancusi show, at which my sister Bis heard someone remark, "What the hell is that thing?" She turned to the poor baffled stranger and said, "Sir, that is my mother!" I've always found it extraordinarily beautiful.

In my early childhood, there was a household staff of roughly ten to twelve servants. Most of them stayed a long time and became acquaintances, confidants, and sometimes friends. There were two bells in each of the bedrooms by which you could summon a maid or the butler. I never did, but I think my older sisters did, and my parents certainly did. In addition, there were the chauffeur, Phil, and the groom and his assistant, who cared for as many as eight or nine horses.

All this was supervised first by a farm superintendent named John Cummins, and after him by the head gardener, a Scottish gentleman named Charles Ruthven, who lived in a nice white farmhouse on the place. His daughter, Jean, and her younger brother, George, were my playmates when we were in Mount Kisco. The groom and his wife lived in another cottage, and Al Phillips and his wife lived in an apartment over the garage. Their son, Tom, was another of Ruthie's and my playmates. We all had a happy time together, picking fruit in the orchards and riding on the hay wagons in the afternoons, after mornings spent on lessons.

All my life I had ambivalent emotions about Mount Kisco. On one level I deeply loved it and had happy times there when I was young, largely because there were children on the farm. As I grew older—say, from twelve to eighteen—I went on thinking of the farm as wonderful because as a younger child I had thought it was, but in reality, throughout my later childhood I had no friends in the neighborhood and felt completely alone there.

It was not until I was much older that I realized we were almost totally isolated. Though we had many visitors for weekends or longer, there was little or no local social life. Only later did I learn that my parents had suffered from local anti-Semitism. They had, I believe, been warned when they first started to build the large stone house that they would be snubbed socially. And, in fact, they were never invited to their neighbors' houses and were excluded from the country club until it went broke, at which time they were asked to join (and, I think, may have, just to help). But I never went there or even saw it.

Until the end of my mother's life, after countless return visits either with my children, who adored the farm, or later to visit one or both parents, I looked forward to being there, only to have painful realities return five minutes after entering its beautiful large front hall. The older I got, the more I disliked the loneliness of the farm, but in my childhood days, it was, as I wrote my father when I was ten, "a great old Place."

DURING THE YEAR I was in the fifth grade, we moved out of the Woodward house, which had been sold, and into a red-brick house on Massachusetts Avenue, a couple of blocks from Dupont Circle. My commute to school was a little longer. I used to walk up the avenue every morning, about eight blocks uphill, carrying my roller skates. Coming back was easy—I simply whizzed home downhill, carrying my book bag in one hand and reserving the other to grab the lamppost at each corner in order not to go flying into the street.

After a two-year interim on Massachusetts Avenue, we moved to a large house owned by Henry White, an ex-ambassador to France, at 1624 Crescent Place, just off 16th Street. I was then in the seventh grade, and this was the real house in which I grew up, my home in Washington, and where my mother lived for the rest of her life.

The house on Crescent Place, which my father rented for several years before eventually buying it in 1934, was designed in 1912 by the well-known architect John Russell Pope and initially had forty rooms. It was a very grand and rather formal house. The only somewhat cozy room on the main floor was the library, in which we spent most of our time. My sister Ruth and I again shared a large room, but as the older girls left for college, the house was done over and I was allowed to choose my own room and decorate it. I said I would like it to be modern. A special modern designer created a plaster fireplace, painted white, with no mantel, and the room had quite beautiful made-to-order modern furniture. It was a strange contrast to, and an odd oasis in, a period house full of Chippendale furniture as well as paintings and sculpture—Cézannes, a Manet, a Renoir, two Brancusis, a Rodin, and, in the upstairs hall, the Woolworth watercolor series by Marin. In the front hall there was a beautiful Chinese screen, a bronze Buddha, and a gilt mirror, which later went to the White House to join its twin, already there.

Although I didn't realize it at the time, the atmosphere of the Crescent Place house intimidated some of my friends. One of them remembers lunching in the vast dining room, just the two of us and my governess, attended by the butler and a maid. When my mother was there, she was served first and ate at once and so quickly that she would finish before the last person had been served. We called that unfortunate seat "Starvation Corner" and tried not to sit there. We learned to keep a hand on our plates; otherwise they would be removed before our forks returned from our mouths. To this day, I eat much too fast. It's odd how long childhood habits stay with us.

When I was in high school, one friend, Mary Gentry, came home with me for the weekend and remembers coming down to breakfast alone. She was seated in the huge dining room when the butler approached and asked what she would like. She was so terrified that all she could think of was Grapenuts. The Grapenuts were brought and set before her by the butler, who stationed himself behind her chair. Mary remembers her horror as the sound of each bite echoed from every corner. She says she just stopped coming down to breakfast, even though she spent several weekends with me when her father and mother were away.

Wherever we were living, in Washington or at the farm, we were invariably busy. We always existed on a strict regimen of lessons and a multiplicity of planned activities after school and during the summer, too. We spent a lot of time riding, especially on the miles of trails surrounding the farm, or in Rock Creek Park in Washington. When I was nine, the *Washington Evening Star* carried a photo of me on Pete, my small horse, giving me credit for being an "accomplished equestrienne." I actually wasn't very good at riding and didn't like it much, either. Nonetheless, riding was part of our routine, and I had to do it.

There were music lessons, carrying on the traditions of Mrs. Coleman. There were even posture lessons, for I was thought to stoop too much—and still do, despite the lessons. We also all received instruction in the Dalcroze method, a kind of dance that gave you a sense of rhythm. One thing I remember is using my arms to a one-two-three beat as my feet were marching to a one-two beat. It wasn't easy.

There were also French lessons, with a woman who lived with us for years at a time to teach us. She was not a relative, but her last name was the same as ours, Mademoiselle Gabrielle Meyer. On weekends we would be called on to give recitations in French. To this day, nearly seventy years later, I can still recite bits of La Fontaine's *Fables* and certain speeches from *Cyrano de Bergerac*, which I adored. For some reason, Mademoiselle Meyer departed for France when I was nine. Even though I went on with French through high school and my French today is fairly fluent, it remains nine-year-old French.

Sports were a major part of our program. In summers, there were tutors for my brother, one of whom organized the making and flying of kites. Bill even had a wrestling teacher, and my sister Bis occasionally inserted herself into his lessons. As we grew older, there was tennis all the time. For a few years in the very early 1930s, a tennis professional lived with us in the summer and worked as a coach, mostly for Bis. I had one short lesson a day.

My mother was more actively involved with us on the every-other-summer camping trips we took, although at least one of the governesses usually came along. My father never took to camping the way my mother did; he didn't like the cold and was uncomfortable in it. He would ride for about ten minutes into the wilderness, then turn to the guide and demand, "Is there a phone anywhere around here?" (Of course, now there would be.) One night, on a later trip, the full moon lit up the sky so brilliantly I heard him call out, "Someone turn out the moon."

My mother's diary about Bill's first camping trip contains some of the few negative notes she ever wrote about the children. This time, they—I was still too young to go—were described as quarrelsome and "need much careful handling. I had not realized that they have been getting rather selfish and spoiled." She was distressed at the difficulties of three as opposed to two children, comparing them to a basket of eels.

Mother saw these trips as bringing us closer to the realities of life and making us more independent. She once said that this was a way to show us life outside large houses. I suppose it did, but the lesson had its limits. There were five ranch hands on the trip to California, eleven saddle horses, and seventeen packhorses—not exactly roughing it.

I was taken on the last of these camping trips, one to the Canadian Rockies in August of 1926. We rode through the mountains on Western saddles and camped at night, with occasional fishing excursions. Again, there were a lot of packhorses carrying our gear and cowboys to put up the tents. We children and our guides caught fish, and my father caught colds. Mother kept a brief diary of this expedition, too, and the following excerpt represents an aspect of her philosophy that she imposed on us:

> The fatigue of the climb was great but it is interesting to learn once more how much further one can go on one's second wind. I think that is an important lesson for everyone to learn for it should also be applied to one's mental efforts. Most people go through life without ever discovering the existence of that whole field of endeavor which we describe as second wind. Whether mentally or physically occupied most people give up at the first appearance of exhaustion. Thus they never learn the glory and the exhilaration of genuine effort. . . .

Mountain climbing was one of Mother's favorite occupations, but she never succeeded in inculcating this passion in any of us.

Some years we would make trips to Europe, my first when I was eleven. One of the few diaries I ever started and kept was from this trip to Europe in the summer of 1928. We went from France to Germany, Austria, Switzerland, Italy, and back to France. My diary reflects all the interests of an eleven-year-old: noting that our cabin on the old British liner the *Berengaria* was the "Prince of Whales suite," giving the number of steps between floors on the Eiffel Tower, and retelling the story of the opening of Napoleon's casket when it was moved to Les Invalides. I remember being reinforced in my idea of being separate from the older children by having to stay with Ruthie in Switzerland in our hotel while my mother climbed to the top of the mountain with Flo and Bis, as well as staying on in Switzerland when the older children and my parents went to Italy. Ruth and I were deemed not old enough to appreciate museums; instead, we were parked in a resort hotel with the governess, where we took part in diversions created by the hotel to occupy their little guests. One old photo shows a fancy-dress party, which I actually remember enjoying; I went as a goosegirl with Ruthie as my goose.

Despite swimming in the Marne and visits to Notre Dame and Versailles, my only really vivid memory of this entire trip is of the suffocating, swirling cigar smoke in the car with all the windows closed as I rode with my father. He smoked only cigars, long rich expensive cigars made of Cuban tobacco, and had one lit pretty constantly. It was almost unendurable in small spaces, usually cars or trains with closed windows, but I gradually got used to it or at least came to terms with it. He had a private keg at Dunhills, where they kept his special brand of tobacco. He also had his own brand of extremely strong bourbon, with his name on it. I still have the top of one of the barrels.

Three years after this first trip to Europe, we returned, this time spending a lot of time in Germany. Most memorable for me was a visit to Einstein at his home, which I described in a letter to my father, who had remained at home at work:

> I suppose Mother has told you that we met Einstein. He was simply grand! His hair is positively a nest and he had on a bright blue sort of "over all" suit, and a pipe in hand. His wife won't let him smoke cigars. . . . Their house is very plain but awfully pretty— near a lake. He sails a boat alone. It's built with a very flat bottom so it won't tip over when he gets absent minded. When people see his boat running around in circles they know that a new theory is being formed.

In 1929, my father bought a ranch in Kelly, Wyoming, in the Teton Valley. The ranch, Red Rock, was beautiful, and in those days very remote, reached only after a two-hundred-mile drive from Rock Springs, the last thirty miles over winding mountain roads. Red Rock Ranch's seven hundred acres lay right at the foot of the beautiful Tetons, a dramatic red clay range. Dad took Flo, Bill, and me there in September of the year he bought it, when I was twelve, and we spent time riding, fishing, hiking, and target shooting. Because we were teenagers or soon to be and preoccupied with our various activities, we were somewhat unenthusiastic about going, although we loved it once we arrived. It makes me sad that my father sold the ranch after some years because he couldn't get us interested in it.

All of these trips and lessons did a great deal for our informal education. Our more formal education developed in some ways as oddly as did our informal one. The older children had started at the progressive Lincoln School in New York. When we moved to Washington, they went to the Friends School. I began my education in a Montessori school, another progressive school, where we were encouraged to pursue our own interests at our own pace—in other words, to do the things we liked most to do whenever we wanted to. I started by learning to tie shoelaces and progressed to reading a lot, which I enjoyed, and avoiding math, which I didn't. As a result of a rhythmic-dance class, using fancy tie-dyed scarves, I became adept at standing on my head and turning cartwheels. I spent the years from kindergarten through the equivalent of the third grade there and left happily proficient in acrobatics and sadly delinquent in arithmetic.

At the age of eight, I entered the fourth grade at Potomac School, only two blocks from our house. Potomac was a private conventional grammar school, and so I went from a free-form, permissive society to a completely structured school where the desks were in rows, the school day was programmed, there was homework, and—worst of all—they were starting fractions, which looked like a foreign language to me.

Entering Potomac as a new girl was difficult. I think of my life in my early years there as being solitary. I felt awkward, out of place, and different, especially in the ribbed socks that no one else wore. It was the last class in which there were both girls and boys; from fifth through eighth grades, beyond which Potomac didn't go, there were only girls, as was the case at Madeira, where I went to high school, and for my first two years of college, at Vassar.

Potomac School proved to be my first big adjustment—one that helped me with a basic lesson of growing up: learning to get along in whatever world one is deposited. I had to observe what was done, to imitate. I had to cope with my loneliness, my differences, and become some other person. I was more or less alone until my second year there, or fifth grade, when I figured out how to start making friends by inviting people over to the house. Rose Hyde became my best friend, despite the way I extended my initial invitation to her: "Rose, I've called everyone else and nobody can come over. Can you?" She could, and it was the beginning of a long friendship.

By the seventh and eighth grades, I had made some other friends: Julia Grant and Madeline Lang—both daughters of army officers, and Julia the granddaughter of President Grant. When we studied the Civil War in sixth grade, the students brought in pictures of their relatives who had fought in the war. Rose brought one of her great-grandfather, who was a clergyman in the Confederate Army. Julia came with the famous photograph of General Grant leaning against a tree. "Guess why he's leaning up against that tree," Rose cracked. "Because he's too drunk to stand up." Julia socked her, knocking her down in the playground. Rose's mother had to write a note of apology to Mrs. Grant, and peace was restored.

Julia and Madeline visited me at the farm in Mount Kisco when I was twelve or thirteen—my first houseguests, an exciting event. I didn't exactly know what to do to entertain them, so I kept asking my mother, "What shall we do?" I remember being solidly scolded for asking such a stupid question when we were surrounded by swimming pools and tennis courts and bowling alleys. Mother's point of view was understandable, given the environment of luxury, but I felt ill-at-ease entertaining and unable to cope.

My early dancing and acrobatics helped me athletically. By the fifth grade, I was fairly coordinated and had become proficient at team sports. Potomac was divided into two groups, the Reds and the Blues, which competed fiercely in games, races, volleyball, and other sports. I was on the Red team and was inclined to be bossy, a trait of which I was quite unaware until Miss Preisha—the gym teacher, on whom I had a crush—pulled me aside one day and told me she thought I might be elected captain of the Reds if I didn't tell people what to do so much. Suddenly I could hear myself egging people on or giving orders. I took her advice and, miracle of miracles, it worked! I became captain. This small triumph gave me great secret satisfaction. I had had my first social success, a sign that something was working.

When I got to the eighth grade, I was sent to Miss Minnie Hawkes's dancing school. My shyness made the class an ordeal to begin with, but adding to my torture was my height. I had grown tall—one of the tallest in the class—and had feet that were pretty big, too. During this time, my mother had a sudden fit of economy—or it may have been a genuine inability to shop—so I went off to dancing school in two hand-me-down dresses of Bis's. I still remember that one was pale-peach velvet and the other was red silk. Since the back of the latter was thought to be too low, it was filled in with other material in a not inconspicuous patching job. To complete the ensemble, my governess bought me gold kid shoes. The other little girls had flat pumps and puff sleeves. My shoes were high heels—that's all the store had in my size—adding at least two inches to my height. This odd apparition, of course, towered over the little boys, with the expectable disastrous results.

At about this period, we girls were all sending away for samples of soap and shampoo and trading them in the playground. Like my friends, I also collected photographs of favorite movie stars, Greta Garbo and Marlene Dietrich, whose movies I saw on weekends. I memorized—in German—"Falling in Love Again," a song from *The Blue Angel*. And we voraciously read movie magazines.

Also like most young people, I had fantasies, but I recognized them even then as being just that. One was that it would be great to be a model. I once expressed this notion to my high-school friend Nancy White, who returned me to reality by asking, "What of? Houses?" The other fantasy I suppose I shared with many children was that of being "famous"—maybe not a movie star (although I had wispy visions of entering a room like Dietrich)—but in some way being successful and having people know who I was. The strange thing is that after Watergate to some small extent the fantasy came true. I always found this hard to believe—both pleasurable and a little embarrassing—but the shadow of my mother's enormous ego lent the whole thing a healthy reality check.

For high school, I attended Madeira, which, when I was a freshman, was located in Washington, near Dupont Circle. My father greatly admired Madeira's founder, Lucy Madeira Wing, and was involved in helping her finance the school and move it to a beautiful new site in Virginia in my second year, when I became a five-day boarder, returning home on weekends. (Much later, my parents donated to the school the 178 acres they owned adjoining its original land.)

The Meyer girls were all automatically sent to Madeira. Miss Madeira had some advanced ideas and attempted to broaden our horizons. She believed, for instance, that God was a woman. Under the guise of Bible class, she attempted to enlighten us about poverty. She used her bully pulpit to try to mold us into some species of "Shavian Fabian," as Rose Hyde called it. The school itself evidenced a very egalitarian spirit. Our uniforms helped obscure our differing financial backgrounds, and we generally didn't know or care about anyone's social standing. But, not surprisingly, we were rather narrowly cast. The Depression raged all around us at Madeira, but rarely hit home hard. A "Poverty Party" was held, with the proceeds donated to the Social Welfare Fund.

Miss Madeira ran a tight ship in a strict age. Her motto, which she often included in her talks to the school assemblies, was full of puritan drive: "Function in disaster. Finish in style." Boarders were allowed to go into town to shop at one department store, though a chaperone had to stand guard in the shoe department because a man held your foot. One of my friends, Jean Rawlings, was invited to have lunch with her roommate and her roommate's father. "Impossible," said the housemother, "you can't go out with your roommate's father." Apparently, several years before, a girl had run away with another student's father.

Despite my penchant for law-abiding ways, I participated in one illegal activity. I joined a secret society, Vestes ad Mortuum, or Virgins Unto Death—an odd goal, I must say. In the middle of the night, we virgins arose, donned heavy rain-capes that Miss Madeira had procured from a French monastery, hiked a mile into the woods, and buried a pair of galoshes—the significance of which is unfortunately lost on me now. Vestes ad Mortuum flourished for several years after I graduated, until one envious girl who had not been tapped for membership squealed to Miss Madeira.

Dances were held at school about twice a year. Of course, no boys were allowed, so all the girls put on their evening dresses and corsages and danced with each other. The taller girls, who led, as I did, often found it difficult adjusting to male dancing partners in later life.

Social progress came slowly. I didn't get around to boys for years. One New Year's Eve during high school, when I was about sixteen, I went with my family to one of the famous dances given by Evalyn Walsh McLean. My brother was nice enough to cut in on me. Since I knew virtually no one, we danced on and on together. The lights finally went out, an electric sign lit up saying "Happy New Year," "Auld Lang Syne" was sung, and my brother looked at me and said, "This is the last New Year's Eve I'm ever going to spend with you."

When I was about seventeen, I made a determined effort to learn how to appeal to the boys in the stag line at parties and dances. I noticed that if you laughed uproariously at the silliest joke and acted lively, as though you were having a wonderful time, the boys thought you were attractive and appealing. I applied this knowledge shamelessly. I faked it, but achieved a passing measure of popularity. So I gradually made my way through parties in Washington, at which I managed not to get "stuck" with one boy, which was the nightmare. I knew one or two of my brother's friends from his Washington school days, and there were boys who occasionally took me to the parties and sometimes to movies. While at Vassar, I was invited to a few weekends at male colleges. But not until I got to the University of Chicago, years later, did I finally find real male friends and occasionally beaux, many of whom I frightened away through diffidence and not knowing how to cope.

I worked hard to be like everyone else at Madeira. I played on the varsity team in basketball, hockey, and track. I sang in the glee club. I was made to take piano lessons and practiced the same Beethoven sonata, the second movement of the *Appassionata*, every day for about a year. My schoolmates came to dread the never-changing clanging that emanated from my practice room, but I did learn something about musical structure in the process. I also appeared in a one-act melodrama produced by the Dramatic Association. My role was that of a handsome duke who was the cause of numerous deaths.

I was interested in journalism and joined the staff of the school magazine, appropriately called *Tatler*. Although we aimed to be "influential and stirring," our editorials focused as much on the weather as on social issues. Many advertisements appeared as well, including one with a headline that read: "Give those developing curves a good home in a Redfence corselette."

At Madeira, as an upperclassman, I also had my first certified success of a worldly kind. To my stunned amazement, I was elected president of the senior class. I had no idea of anything approximating general liking and/or approval of me by others. It gave me inordinate pleasure, but it gave my father even more.

At school we were much more concerned with sports, friends, and vacations than with the real world. In fact, my interest in politics was nil through most of my early school years. I remember one debate during the presidential campaign of 1932, in which, following the Republican pattern of my parents, I spoke for Hoover. I couldn't have known what I was talking about; I only knew that my father worked in the Hoover administration, and I believed in my father. My classmate Robin Kemper, daughter of James Kemper, a prominent Chicago Democrat, spoke for Roosevelt. It seemed almost automatic that we should all espouse our parents' views.

Despite my successes in high school, I left Madeira with scant training for the life I was later to lead. I still felt fairly different and shy and believed I had only a few friends. Apparently my classmates didn't see me the way I saw myself. My senior yearbook entry describes a girl known for her laugh and her manly stride. My class prophecy read: "Kay's a Big Shot in the newspaper racket." But I envisaged no such future for myself or, in fact, any specific future at all. Rather than creating my own way, what I was trying to do all the time was figure out how to adjust to whatever life I found. I would have preferred to be trailblazing, and of course adventurous and daring like Bis, but the poem chosen to accompany my class picture at Madeira reveals a different kind of person: "Those about her from her shall read the perfect ways of honor." In other words, Goody Two-Shoes.

IN 1921, my mother had met William L. Ward, one of the last of the great old-time enlightened political bosses. He pretty much ran Westchester County, where Mount Kisco was located, and he lured her into more active involvement in the county's Republican politics. Bill Ward became her mentor, her supporter, her leader, and her close friend, and persuaded her that she should get more involved in civic affairs. Her passionate acceptance of this idea and espousal of public service, added to that of my father, meant that we grew up with the belief that no matter what you did professionally, you automatically had to think about public issues and give back, either in interest in your community or in public service—you had to care.

Soon Ward had created a county Recreation Commission, consisting of five women, with my mother as chairman. Under her leadership, the commission started summer camps for underprivileged children. She helped found choral groups all over the county, and she organized a big annual music festival for adults and children, which at first took place under a huge tent. Then, largely at Mother's instigation, Bill Ward built a County Center, which opened in May of 1930, a large, all-purpose auditorium in White Plains that is still in use. The center housed everything from plays and concerts to poultry and other animal shows. Over the years my mother presided at various events held there, including a performance by the Metropolitan Opera that coincided with the annual poultry show in the basement. To ensure that the roosters wouldn't be crowing at the same time as the divas, she rigged up a system whereby cardboard was put in their cages so they couldn't raise their heads to crow.

Mother also went to work in Republican politics, and with such vigor that by 1924 she became a delegate to the Republican Convention. Later, as she became even more involved, she traveled in support of her candidates and causes. We composed a poem during the 1924 campaign year: "Coolidge and Dawes, Coolidge and Dawes. When Mother's away, they're the cause." When she was invited to state office and urged by women to run for Congress, she refused, on the grounds that "my husband and my family must come first." I went with her to Franklin Roosevelt's first inaugural in 1933 and watched Roosevelt come out in front of the Capitol and make his famous address. I distinctly recall Mother looking at the pathetic departing figure of Hoover contrasted with the triumphant Roosevelt, who appeared beaming on the platform just as a rain shower ended, the clouds parted, and a strong ray of sunshine illuminated his handsome, glowing face. She turned and said to me with remarkably little foresight, "Just wait. We'll be back in four years." Mother was an especially emotional Roosevelt-hater.

My father was also involved in Republican politics, though in a less active way. He, in fact, worked for both parties on nonpartisan things, from the War Industries Board to the Farm Loan Board to the Federal Reserve Board. By the mid-1920s, he had helped revive American agriculture through his work on the War Finance Corporation, which had special authorization to make loans for the benefit of farmers and livestock growers. He liquidated the corporation early in 1925 in an achievement that was widely recognized as remarkable. As Merlo Pusey described it in his biography of my father:

> Meyer had handed the Treasury a check for $499 million. It was ultimately sent to the National Archives in the belief that it was the largest check ever drawn in the history of the world. . . . [The WFC] had lent $700 million—$300 for war purposes, $100 to finance postwar exports, $300 million to aid farmers—without loss and with enough return to pay interest on the bonds it had issued and the funds obtained from the Treasury. . . . [M]any were saying he had saved American agriculture from disaster.

During my childhood, when my father was busy with his series of government jobs, my parents were mostly absent. When they were home, there were formal moments when we would see them. My mother always had her breakfast in bed, and my father usually had his in her bedroom, on a small table beside her. We went upstairs to see them for a little while before we went our separate ways. Mother sometimes took one of us for a drive in the park in the afternoon or had us in for a talk in her bedroom, but these occasions were few and far between, and more often than not the exchanges were one-way. Nonetheless, I loved these times and once commented that since she was so busy, perhaps we should make appointments to meet—a story she used to repeat as quaint.

My parents went out to dinner most evenings, or entertained elaborately at home. Sometimes I visited with Mother as she dressed, or when she was being massaged or manicured. My mother impressed me as being incredibly glamorous, regal, and beautiful, and I was secretly proud when she appeared at school functions elegantly dressed. But though I was deeply fond of her when I was very young, I was awed by and terrified of her at the same time. With the rarest exceptions, I was much too scared ever to consider disobeying. On the few occasions I did, the results made a lasting impression. On my first trip to Europe, when I was eleven, Mother told Bill and me to go to the ship's barber to get our hair cut. We had another plan. Bill told me to tell her there was a line waiting and that we would go later, and I mindlessly carried out his order, something I tended to do too much throughout my life. Mother somehow found out there wasn't any line at the barber's and severely reprimanded me for lying, which I wasn't even aware I was doing, and put me alone in my cabin. I was crushed, but the episode made an indelible impression on me about the importance of telling the truth.

A few years later, as a freshman in high school, I transgressed again on the coiffeur front—I cut my long curly black hair against my mother's will. I awaited her reaction with fear and trepidation and was puzzled and a bit humiliated when she failed to notice the change until at last I called her attention to it. She then shrugged it off, leaving me confused. It had taken such courage to do.

Children watch and listen to their parents, sometimes critically but sometimes unquestioningly. Each of my parents influenced us in large ways and small. Certain of their habits rubbed off and left their mark. One very peculiar habit I picked up unconsciously from my mother was a tendency to be suspicious and tight and ungenerous about small things. Though she was very lavish in some ways, she would complain about small bills she received, certain that people were cheating her. She would buy a fur and say, "You have to be careful, because you can choose one and they'll substitute another." She said, "If you have your pearl necklace restrung you have to sit and watch to be sure you get your own pearls back." She was mean about raises for people in the house. She literally hated to give things away, even praise or encouragement. I, too, developed an inability to spend money, along with a dark suspicion that people were taking advantage of me and an inability to enjoy giving.

Many of these habits were overcome when I married Phil Graham, who was exceedingly generous and imaginatively giving. Some habits I have never overcome are odd ones I inherited from my father. Despite the vast scale on which we lived, my father had peculiar fixations on certain small expenses. He preached tiny economies with zeal—using things up completely, never wasting, never phoning if you could wire, or better still, write. The compulsion I am still left with is turning out every light before I go to bed at night. To this day, alone in a house I am totally unable to leave a light on—I will go up and down halls and staircases if I know a light is on. I tell myself to stop, that it doesn't matter, yet then I go and turn it off.

Some lessons were impressed on me by reverse example. When I was young I perceived grown-ups behaving quite oddly at times. I remember being shocked or dismayed by things I observed and making silent vows not to behave as they did when I grew up. For instance, my mother, when confronted with a line waiting at the movies, would go up to the box office and say, "I am Mrs. Eugene Meyer of *The Washington Post*," and demand to be taken in and seated. At that time, she did indeed get in. I cringed with embarrassment and hoped the ground would swallow me up. It had such a lasting effect on me that I have never been able to deal with headwaiters in restaurants who put you "in Siberia" rather than the better part of the restaurant. I just go meekly to Siberia.

As the years went on, my mother seemed to have a more and more difficult time emotionally. She became increasingly engrossed in her friendships with the series of men in her life, only one of which, I believe, may have been a true affair—the one with Bill Ward. She was constantly beset with colds, pneumonia, or various other illnesses, and she reacted to each one with the greatest amount of care, self-pity, and drama, demanding and receiving constant visits, with all of us dancing attendance. In retrospect, I wonder if depression contributed to this intense concentration on her health.

She also started to drink more heavily, sometimes starting as early as ten in the morning, at least during one period in her life. This was a problem that greatly worried my father and was an escalating burden to him and to all of us. Even her drinking was done in a somewhat eccentric way. There was an old-fashioned locked whiskey-and-wine closet in the basement to which only my father had the key, so he would have to make repeated trips to the cellar and therefore knew exactly how much she was drinking. Of course, admonishments on this score never had an effect. The surprising thing is that she never bought whiskey herself or asked him for her own key.

My mother's effect on us was often contradictory. We received every encouragement for what we accomplished, yet her ego was such that she trampled on our incipient interests or enthusiasms. If I said I loved *The Three Musketeers*, she responded by saying I couldn't really appreciate it unless I had read it in French, as she had. Mother herself read constantly until the week she died—philosophy, history, biography, and all the English, American, French, German, and Russian classics. She had only scorn for people who read light novels, let alone trash or time-wasters.

The summer between fourth and fifth grades I spent almost entirely by myself reading in a room on the third floor of Mount Kisco, where I went through all of Dumas, eight volumes of Louisa May Alcott (starting with *Little Women*), *Treasure Island*, and a stirring adventure series by a man named Knipe. I counted up at the end, found that I had read around one hundred books, and wrote my parents that I was "positively floating in books." I couldn't have been happier. Unfortunately, this early passion for reading somehow diminished after the fifth grade, until I read only sporadically. A little later on I was concentrating on movie magazines, *Redbook*, and *Cosmopolitan*. Later still, I resumed reading, particularly loving Dickens's *Great Expectations* and Dostoyevsky's *Crime and Punishment*.

Mother set impossibly high standards for us, creating tremendous pressures and undermining our ability to accomplish whatever modest aims we may have set for ourselves. Fundamentally, I think we all felt we somehow hadn't lived up to what she expected or wanted of us, and the insecurities and lack of self-confidence she bred were long-lasting. But despite whatever personal doubts about us she may have had, the picture of her family she presented to the world was unblemished. She created and then perpetuated the myth of her children's perfection. From her point of view, we were all happy, bilingual overachievers. Indeed, on some levels she was proud of us. She used to compare us to the characters in a then-popular novel called *The Constant Nymph*, about an eccentric, boisterous, and madly funny family known as the Sanger Circus. Other myths she propagated about us were that Meyer girls were brighter, more attractive, funnier, smarter, more successful, this or that—in short, better than anyone else. Most important, she felt we *should* be different, more intellectual, eccentric even.

In addition, there were expectations of us for social success, also difficult to define and deal with. Popularity at school or parties was thought to be a necessity for Meyer girls. I always said I had a wonderful time at a party whether I did or not, and quite often I didn't. If one of my parents came to school or college, I thought I had to assemble a group of

friends so that I could at least give the appearance of being in an acceptable swim.

When we were very young, the McLeans, who then owned *The Washington Post*, gave children's parties at which expensive favors—even
watches—were given to their guests. Mother told me in what poor taste
this was, and that she wouldn't let my sisters go. A friend of hers suggested
that perhaps it was important to be seen there, to which my mother responded, "I want my children to be the ones to want to be with."

Her predisposition to think this way also meant that she condescended to the average, to the pedestrian, to the everyday. This negative
view of the commonplace became very much a part of me and my confusion. I knew that I wasn't any of the things that were held out as desirable.
I also knew that I wanted to fit into the world—to be liked by people
around me. Yet I adopted a lot of the family's philosophy, as did my older
sisters and brother. I remember in college saying to my friend Mary Gentry as we crossed the Vassar campus, "Do you like the girls here?" "Yes,"
she said, bringing me up short to the possibility that my criteria were suspect. I thought I should be condescending toward nice, normal people and
only like the brilliant eccentrics. It took me a long time to stop thinking
that I had to be different and that there was something wrong with being
normal or average, and to get to the point of enjoying a variety of people
for what they were.

I can't say I think Mother genuinely loved us. Toward the end of her
life, I was a success in her eyes, and perhaps that is what she loved. Yet,
with all her complexity, I felt closer throughout my early childhood to my
mother than to the very distant and rather difficult figure of my father. I
liked him, but always from a distance. Actually, he delighted in children
and was rather jolly with us, but a little awkward. At most, he would take
one of us as a small child onto his lap and dangle a watch at our ear. When
Ruth and I were very young, he would come into our bedroom before
breakfast for a short period of roughhouse play.

But though he lacked the gift of intimacy, in many ways his supportive love still came through to me. He somehow conveyed his belief in me
without ever articulating it, and that was the single most sustaining thing
in my life. That was what saved me. I realized this only in retrospect, however, since our relationship took time to grow.

SENSITIVE SUBJECTS were rarely mentioned at our house, but three
were particularly taboo—money, my father's being Jewish, and sex. None
of the three was ever articulated by any of us in the family; in fact, *nothing*
difficult or personal was discussed among us. There was such an aversion
to talking about money or our wealth that, ironically, there was, in some

odd ways, a fairly spartan quality to our lives. We were not showered with conspicuous possessions, elaborate toys, or clothes. At one point, when Florence was eleven, my mother wrote in her diary that she had gotten Flo very modest presents for her birthday—"books, pralines and other simple things." Though Mother felt that she had been a bit mean, she also felt that "it is the best way to continue their chance for happiness to restrain the desire for possessions."

I had less than most of the girls in my class—certainly fewer clothes. My spare wardrobe in grammar school consisted of one or two jumpers and blouses for school, and one best dress. We were also treated strictly in the matter of allowance. I still remember a telegram Bis sent my father from Vassar: "Allowance early or bust." He wired back, "Bust." The only discussions I do remember relating to wealth had to do with being told that you couldn't just be a rich kid, that you had to do something, to be engaged in useful, productive work; you couldn't and shouldn't do *nothing*. Working was always a part of my life. I remember one Christmas vacation, when I was probably about fifteen, spent at the Federal Reserve Board learning to draw graphs.

My mother's ambivalence about money and what it brought to her no doubt contributed to her own unwillingness to talk about it. Once, in 1922, after a visit to a Utah copper mine that had yielded my father great financial gains, she wrote in her diary: "[The mine] was an interesting sight but the village that led up to it appalled me. . . . This is where [the money] comes from and I spend it on Chinese art but it was a shock to think that we live on money that is produced under such conditions."

Remarkably, the fact that we were half Jewish was never mentioned any more than money was discussed. I was totally—incredibly—unaware of anti-Semitism, let alone of my father's being Jewish. I don't think this was deliberate; I am sure my parents were not denying or hiding my father's Jewishness from us, nor were they ashamed of it. But there was enough sensitivity so that it was never explained or taken pride in. Indeed, we had a pew in St. John's Episcopal Church—the president's church, on Lafayette Square—but mainly because the rector was a friend of the family. When I was about ten, all of us Meyer children were baptized at home to satisfy my devout Lutheran maternal grandmother, who thought that without such a precaution we were all headed for hell. But for the most part, religion was not part of our lives.

One of the few memories I have of any reference to my being Jewish is of an incident that took place when I was ten or eleven. At school we were casting for reading aloud *The Merchant of Venice*, and one classmate suggested I should be Shylock because I was Jewish. In the same way I had once innocently asked my mother whether we were millionaires—after someone at school accused my father of being one—I asked if I was Jewish and what that meant. She must have avoided the subject, because I don't remember the answer. This confusion about religion was not limited to me: my sister Bis recalls that at lunch in our apartment in New York once, with guests present, she blurted out, "Say, who is this guy Jesus everyone is talking about?"

My identity as Jewish did not become an issue until I reached college and a discussion arose with a girl from Chicago who was leaving Vassar. She had been asked if she would see another acquaintance, a Jewish girl, also from Chicago. "Oh, no," she replied, "you can't have a Jew in your house in Chicago." My best friend, Connie Dimock, later told me how horrified she was to have this said in front of me. Only then did I "get it"—and this was 1935, with Hitler already a factor in the world.

About the third thing that was never discussed in our family, sex, I knew nothing for a surprisingly long time. I had no idea what sex was or how babies were conceived. In fact, it was as if our rigorous schedules and exercise and athletic program were constructed to keep us from thinking too much about it. I once asked my mother what really happened during sex, telling her I'd read about the sperm and the ova but wondered how it all worked. She responded, "Haven't you seen dogs in the street?" Although unfortunately I hadn't, I naturally said, "Of course," and that was the end of the conversation. Mother finally brought herself to speak to me about having periods, or "becoming a woman." "Don't worry about it, Mother," I replied, "it happened months ago."

Because these matters were never discussed, I was almost totally unaware of all of them—money, religion, and sex. It's peculiar: I realized, of course, that the houses were big and that we had a lot of servants, but I didn't know we were rich any more than I knew we were Jewish. In some ways it was quite bizarre; in others, quite healthy. Equally odd was how little we were taught about the practical aspects of life. I didn't know how to manage the simplest tasks. I didn't know how to dress, sew, cook, shop, and, rather more important, relate to people of any kind, let alone young men. My governess and I did some minor shopping, but as I grew up I mostly inherited party dresses from my sisters, until, when I was eighteen, Mother took me to Bergdorf Goodman for French clothes of staggering beauty and sophistication, which were well beyond my years and whose quality was wasted on young people who dressed appropriately. There was nothing in between for everyday.

I was always well fed and cared for, of course. In fact, my mother was constantly reminding us of how lucky we were, how much we owed our parents, how far-seeing and wonderful my father was to have taken care of us all. And we were indeed lucky. We had vast privileges. We had parents with solid values. Our interests were aroused in art and politics and books. But to all of this I brought my own feelings of inability and inferiority—

not only to my mother, but to my older sisters and brother. I was, I thought, realistic about my own assets and abilities as I grew older. I was not very pretty. I grew tall early, and therefore seemed ungainly to myself. I didn't think I could excel, and was sure I'd never attract a man whom I would like and who would not be viewed with condescension by my parents and siblings.

In all the turmoil of the family and our strange isolation both from our parents and from the outside world, we children were left to bring ourselves up emotionally and intellectually. We were leading lives fraught with ambivalence. It was hard to have an identity. An early example of this came one day when the telephone rang in the playroom and there was no grown-up present. Bis very fearfully picked up the phone and said hello. A male voice impatiently asked, "Who is this? Who is this?," to which Bis replied, "This is the little girl that Mademoiselle takes care of." That was the only way she could think of to describe herself to a strange grown-up.

So the question of who we really were and what our aspirations were, intellectual or social, was always disquieting. The more subtle inheritance of my strange childhood was the feeling, which we all shared to some extent, of believing we were never quite going about things correctly. Had I said the right thing? Had I worn the right clothes? Was I attractive? These questions were unsettling and self-absorbing, even overwhelming at times, and remained so throughout much of my adult life, until, at last, I grew impatient with dwelling on the past.

— *Chapter Three* —

I N J U N E O F 1 9 3 3, my father bought *The Washington Post*. None
of us could have known then what a transforming event this would
be in all our lives. The paper had fallen on hard times, brought on in
large part by the aimless ways of its owner, Edward Beale McLean, a dap-
per playboy whom Alice Longworth later described as a "pathetic man
with no chin and no character." Ned, as he was known, had been a poker
and golf companion of President Harding, though their relationship
ended badly for Ned when he—along with the paper—was linked to the
Teapot Dome scandal.

From the time he inherited the *Post* in 1916 until he lost it a decade
and a half later, Ned had paid scant attention to either its news or its business side. He brought his mistress to editorial meetings, or so it was alleged by his wife, Evalyn, in divorce proceedings. In fact, concerning his
news sense, Evalyn memorably said, "He would not have recognized a
piece of news—not even if the man who bit the dog likewise bit Ned
McLean." Evalyn, for her part, operated on a grand scale. The wealthy
daughter of a mining tycoon, she lived in huge houses, gave lavish parties,
and owned—and wore—the famous Hope diamond, which was reputed to
bring bad luck to its owners, and seems to have done so for her. She had
every intention of saving the *Post* for her sons and so had turned down several offers to buy it—or urged her husband to do so—including at least
one from my father.

In fact, my father had several times before expressed interest in the
Post and other papers. As early as 1925, when he realized that Hearst had
two papers in Washington, both losers, he thought Hearst might be willing to sell one, and tried to acquire the morning *Washington Herald*.

Four years later, in 1929, he tried to buy the *Post* for $5 million, cer-
tain that this price was so high that the American Security Trust Company, which controlled the paper then, couldn't possibly afford to turn
him down. But it did. Other offers for the *Post*, including two in 1931,

each for $3 million, were also rejected. This was because Evalyn McLean held on—despite divorce proceedings and court fights. So the profitable paper Ned had inherited from his father continued its downhill slide. Poorly managed, with at least a half-million dollars in debts, it was forced into receivership in March 1932, unable even to pay its newsprint bills, and was to be sold at public auction.

Meanwhile, in September 1930, my father had been appointed by Hoover to be governor of the Federal Reserve Board. What he undertook in this job was nothing less than an attempt to turn around the Depression. He guided the banking and monetary policies of the United States domestically and abroad. He conceptualized the Reconstruction Finance Corporation, writing the legislation to set it up, shepherding the bill through the Congress, and serving as chairman of the new credit agency—his name was specifically written into the legislation as chairman so that the bill would be sure to pass—as well as keeping his responsibilities as governor of the Federal Reserve. But the strain of running one institution in the morning and another in the afternoon—and both during the worst of the Depression—was too great, and he nearly broke under the pressure. My mother went to see President Hoover to say that these intolerable professional burdens could not continue and that the president would have to relieve my father of some of his duties before he had a complete breakdown. In her diary she gave a graphic description of her visit to the president:

> Yesterday was . . . Eugene's low water mark in physical fatigue. He was so much harassed by White House pounding . . . that I made a secret appointment with Hoover, and frightened him thoroughly by telling him E. would break physically unless he H. helped protect him from Senatorial greed. The plan worked and I am sure H. will move carefully from now on in his whole attitude toward E. Without accusing H. of anything I forced him at least temporarily into the position of ally—which he never can be permanently because of his unfortunate disposition which sacrifices everybody and everything to what momentarily seems advantageous to his own position and objectives. . . . During my conversation with the Pres. I was surprised after hearing only E's version of their ever stormy relationship to have him begin by saying emphatically "Eugene Meyer is the most valuable man I've got." My chief occupation is to keep E. well.

In the end, what helped relieve the pressure a little was congressional passage of the Emergency Relief and Construction Act of 1932, which separated the two jobs of the Federal Reserve and the RFC, and allowed my father to give up the latter.

The election of Franklin Roosevelt in the fall of 1932, of course, created a different problem for my father, a Hoover appointee. He felt that what he had attempted was for the public good, so he saw no point in resigning—even though Hoover wanted him to. My mother's interpretation of Hoover's repeatedly urging my father to resign before Roosevelt's inauguration was typically to the point:

> Perhaps like an Oriental widow he is expected to hurl himself upon his Master's funeral pyre. I think H [Hoover] would like to go down to his political grave with all his retainers, household and even the pet dogs buried with him like the Iranian or Scythian chiefs.

My father may have felt similarly, but he had no intention of making his job as governor of the Federal Reserve look like a political position, which he felt it was not meant to be nor should be. On the other hand, he didn't see any sense in remaining in the government, since he felt he was tilting at windmills. When Roosevelt asked him to stay as head of the Federal Reserve, he agreed to do so, but in late March, he sent FDR his letter of resignation. In his eyes, Roosevelt's sins were many, but a few stood out: his experimentation with the dollar, his disregard for the gold standard, and his general lack of sophistication about economic and financial policies—a lack shared, I must say, by every other president.

So the bankruptcy of the *Post* came at a propitious time for my father—just as he was leaving the government. He and my mother had clearly discussed the possibility of buying the paper, since she wrote in her diary on May 7, nearly a month before the purchase and the day before my father's resignation from the Federal Reserve Board was accepted by FDR:

> . . . he [Eugene] has suddenly decided to buy T.P. If he succeeds it will be a sensation and we shall have a reputation for Machiavellian behavior. I was reluctant at first because it means more hard work at once but after all these are not times in which to loiter. Also it means a heavy expenditure but what after all is money for if not to be used. . . .

Yet, sometime after this diary entry, my father had still not decided to make the purchase. Instead, the first thing he did was retire to Mount Kisco. The story goes that, after his second week of retirement, he came down the stairs trailing his finger on the banister and claiming to find dust. He murmured something about the house's not being properly run, to which my mother responded, "Eugene, it's time you bought the *Post*."

He himself explained what happened to a group from the American Society of Newspaper Editors in 1934:

> Like the Oriental philosophers of olden days, I was determined to leave a chaotic world in order to enjoy the peace and seclusion of an agricultural existence. This benign mood lasted just two weeks when I decided, and I am afraid my family also decided, that the contemplative life was not for me.

Ironically, he was prompted to reconsider the *Post* by a visit to Mount Kisco from Cissy Patterson—Eleanor Medill Patterson—who had been a longtime friend of both my parents. Cissy was the sister of Joe Patterson, founder of the *New York Daily News*—at that time the great tabloid—and the cousin of Colonel Robert McCormick, owner and publisher of the *Chicago Tribune*.

The McCormick women were strong and intelligent, and Cissy was all of that. She was what the French call a *"jolie laide"*—a woman who is feature for feature ugly but succeeds in being beautiful. She lived in a mansion on Dupont Circle, now the Washington Club, became the editor of Hearst's morning *Herald*, and later was also editor and publisher of the afternoon *Washington Times*, leasing the papers from Hearst until she finally bought them and combined them into one all-day paper. At this point, in 1933, she knew one important thing: that her future depended on who owned *The Washington Post*.

Aware of my father's previous attempts to buy Washington newspapers, she came to ask if he meant to buy the *Post* now, and her question actually re-aroused his interest. This time it held, and he came down to Washington to pursue the paper. Since it was known that he had at one time been willing to pay $5 million for it, he didn't want to escalate the bidding at the auction by revealing his identity. Consequently, he had a lawyer, George E. Hamilton, Jr., do the bidding for him, and instructed Hamilton to raise anybody's bid by $50,000 or even $100,000 immediately, as though he were going to go on forever, then to jump in increments of $25,000 once the bidding reached $800,000. He also gave Hamilton an outside parameter of $1.5 to $1.7 million, and sent him off to the auction on his behalf. He himself remained out of sight at Crescent Place, which was essentially closed up for the summer, hiding with his friend and lifelong assistant, Floyd Harrison.

The auction was held on the steps of the *Post*'s gray gingerbread building at E Street on Pennsylvania Avenue on June 1, 1933, just a few weeks after my father had ostensibly retired. Gathered there on the steps of the building that day, among others, were Ned McLean's estranged wife, Evalyn, dressed in black and wearing the Hope diamond; her two sons; her friend Alice Longworth; David Bruce, then Andrew Mellon's son-in-law; the *Washington Star*'s president, Victor Kauffmann, and its business manager, Fleming Newbold; and representatives for the McLeans, Hearst, and other bidders. All that was being sold at auction was what was left of the fifth of five newspapers in town: a circulation reduced to fifty thousand, the quaint, run-down old building, and an AP franchise—in short, a decrepit paper with debts of $600,000.

Mrs. McLean's attorney and Hearst's lawyers, urged on by Cissy, were the only bidders who stayed with Hamilton's bids initially, but Mrs. McLean dropped out of the bidding at $600,000. Hearst's people kept pace with Hamilton's bids until the price reached $800,000. Hamilton, as instructed, went to $825,000. Hearst must have instructed his bidders to stop at $800,000, because they then dropped out. Cissy Patterson begged the auctioneer to delay the award so that she could telephone Hearst for his authority to go higher. She received three delays, but then Hamilton threatened to withdraw his bid. Hearst, who was no doubt cash-poor in 1933, finally refused to go on. The gavel came down to Hamilton, acting on behalf of an anonymous bidder. My father had bought *The Washington Post*—for which he had five years earlier offered $5 million—for $825,000.

WHAT IS MOST amazing to me about the purchase of the *Post*—especially given its importance to my future life and that of my family—is that I knew nothing about it. No one in my family had mentioned it to me either before or even immediately after, nor were they aware they hadn't told me about it.

At the time of the auction, I had just finished my junior year at Madeira and was still there, preparing to take college boards. Nancy White roomed next door to me. She was the daughter of Tom White, the general manager of all of Hearst's enterprises—his right-hand man, in effect—and also a close friend (some said lover) of Cissy Patterson. Nancy and I, naturally curious because of her father's interests in journalism and my father's years of public service, discussed the auction and speculated on the anonymous purchaser of the paper. When I finished my college boards, I went home to Mount Kisco, where the family had already settled for the summer. As we were sitting on the porch, my mother mentioned something to my father about "when you take over the *Post*," and so remote in my mind was the possibility that he might have been the anonymous buyer that I asked in all innocence what she was talking about. "Oh, darling," she said, "didn't anyone tell you? Dad has bought the *Post*." "No," I said, "as a matter of fact, no one did."

Shortly after I discovered the secret purchase, it was announced publicly. The delay between the purchase date and the date of revelation of its new owner was necessary so that the courts could approve the sale. My father had agreed to a ten-day delay by the court, at the end of which Charles Evans Hughes, then a lawyer for Evalyn McLean, sought to re-open the bidding. When the receiver reported that the anonymous bidder was ready to pay cash, the court finalized the sale to my father, which was announced in a box on the front page of the *Post* on June 13, 1933.

The first time I was ever in *The Washington Post*'s building was a day or two after that, when my brother Bill and I traveled from Mount Kisco to Washington with my father and were taken on a tour through the build-ing at night by what must have been some very nervous individuals. There was a skeleton staff that had remained through the difficult last days of the McLean era—a few fine people who had kept the paper going and some others who had nowhere else to go.

Much of the reaction—at least what appeared in print—to the an-nouncement of the new owner was favorable. Privately, however, there were doubts, which lingered on for years, both about the possibility of the *Post*'s being a nonpartisan paper and about whether the number-five paper in town, run by an inexperienced publisher, would ever make it. On the latter point, Gardner Cowles, one of the most able independent publish-ers in the country, warned my father that Washington was an afternoon-newspaper town, with the government workers getting to their jobs early and home by four-thirty. He said no morning paper, especially the *Post*, would ever amount to anything. The *Star* had the town by the throat. To Cowles, my father rather piously responded: "The Capital of this great nation deserves a good paper. I believe in the American people. They can be relied on to do the right thing when they know the facts. I am going to give them the unbiased truth. When an idea is right, nothing can stop it."

As to whether the paper would or could be nonpartisan with a Repub-lican owner like Eugene Meyer, my father emphasized from the start that the *Post* would be independent. Even in the announcement about his own-ership, there were several key statements that proved to be the underpin-nings of Eugene Meyer's *Post*. It was his aim to improve the paper, and he would do so by making it an independent voice. He explained that, in pur-chasing the *Post*, he had acted in his own behalf and without persuasion from "any person, group or organization." Although many people did not quite believe this at the time, it was true, and he was trying to assure the public that the *Post* would not be a toy: it would not be the voice of the Re-publican Party, and it would not be used to fight Franklin Roosevelt (al-though it later did, to some extent).

From the beginning, my father was excited. The challenge seemed to have rejuvenated him. Morale at the paper improved immediately after he reversed the 10-percent pay cut that had been imposed by the receivers and told the employees they could all keep their jobs if they just "made good." Then he looked around and very quickly began to face the stark reality of the wreck he had acquired—a paper with a reduced number of pages that had lost most of its good people, a paper with drastically diminished circulation and advertising, and one that had been operating without knowing whether the presses would run the next day. On the very day he was announced as the owner, the paper was only eighteen pages, with a total of nineteen columns of display ads and less than two pages of classified ads. As my father said, it was a paper that was "mentally, morally, physically and in every other way bankrupt."

At the outset, in attempting to reorganize the paper, he had rather naïvely felt that since he had been a success at business and government he could apply what he had learned to the realm of journalism. Though he didn't understand newspapers, he thought he could turn this one around simply by investing heavily and running it better. Instead, there followed years of struggle and discouragement and investment with only minimal success. He learned some expensive lessons. The going-in price was just the beginning of the financial drain and mental strain that went on for most of the next twenty years, and there were many moments during these years of uphill battle when he had his doubts about whether he could ever succeed. He would moan to us and even talk about selling it, although never, I think, seriously.

One of those moments and one of his roughest experiences came almost at once. His erstwhile friend Cissy Patterson, having been disappointed at losing her golden opportunity, now taught him a lesson in cutthroat competition which led to a spectacular brawl between the two of them. Cissy swiped the *Post*'s comics by getting her cousin Bertie McCormick to switch them to her. McCormick not only ran the *Chicago Tribune* but owned one of the most powerful syndicates that sold features to newspapers nationwide, and Cissy herself was a shareholder in his *Tribune*. She had the syndicate inform my father that the sale of the *Post* voided the contract for four of the most popular comics—"Andy Gump," "Dick Tracy," "Gasoline Alley," and "Winnie Winkle." The comics would go to the *Herald*, and Cissy proudly advertised the shift.

My father had never read comics and asked the *Post*'s business manager, A. D. Marks, whether they were important. Marks was deeply shocked at this amateur's lack of understanding about what attracted circulation. Comics were all-important to circulation—then even more than now—and indeed were the best and most important asset the paper had, he assured the new owner, who promptly sued Cissy.

Cissy then phoned him, saying that her brother, Joe Patterson, had created these comics, and that her relationship to McCormick and Patterson somehow gave her the right to them. When my father pointed out that he now owned the rights in Washington, she responded, "This means a fight."

And it did. For two years the legal battle of the funny pages was waged, ending the long, close friendship between Cissy and my parents. My father first won a temporary restraining order in New York that prohibited the *Herald* from publishing the comics, but this order was later dissolved, and for a while both papers were printing them. Then she won and the *Post* filed against the syndicate that distributed the comics, winning the case against the *Chicago Tribune* in New York in July of 1934, when a judge ruled that the *Post* was the legal owner of the rights. The case against the *Herald* was heard in Washington, where the U.S. Court of Appeals for the District of Columbia came to the same conclusion in March 1935. Cissy took the case to the Supreme Court, which refused to hear it. On April 10, 1935, victory was his.

When the final decree came down forbidding Cissy to print the comics in the *Herald*, she asked my father's permission to print the ones scheduled for the following Sunday, since the color comics were printed in advance and she already had them. So intense had the bitterness grown that my father gave his approval on the condition that she give the *Post* credit and note that henceforth the comics would appear only in the *Post*. Not only did Cissy refuse, naturally, but not long after, in retaliation, she sent my father an ornately wrapped florist's box inside which orchids surrounded a smaller package that contained a piece of raw meat; Cissy had written a card to drive home the point about the pound of flesh—"So as not to disappoint you." This unpleasantly loaded reference to Shylock shows how brutal the fight had become. From then on, she kept goading him and the *Post* in every possible way. If the *Post* made a mistake, she exploited it. Finally, my father called her and said, "Cissy, if you don't stop lying about me, I'm going to start telling the truth about you."

Twenty-two months after the end of the lawsuit, she got the comics anyway, when the contract for the *Post* finally expired. She and my father didn't speak again for years, except once when they were both asked to dinner by Mrs. Sumner Welles, the wife of the undersecretary of state, a lady unconscious of strains in relationships. My friend Luvie Pearson, who was there, later told me that they sat down together and talked most of the night.

All the while the intense fight over the comics was going on, my father was hard at work trying to improve the paper and to make it financially solvent. He soon realized that the newspaper business was like no other business he knew—you couldn't use ordinary techniques for improving a business and then look for results. He had very little idea of what could be done to make the paper a financial success, particularly since there were so many papers in Washington.

What he did have was a well-developed philosophy, which he spelled out in an early editorial, in 1934, and in several speeches over the next few years. He felt a newspaper was a public trust, meant to serve the public in a democracy. My father wanted a paper that would advance beyond what it had achieved even in its heyday and "take a leadership which could be achieved only by exceptional quality." In one address, on March 5, 1935, he spoke about the principles that he insisted on from the beginning, outlining them as follows:

1. That the first mission of a newspaper is to tell the truth as nearly as the truth may be ascertained;
2. That the newspaper shall tell ALL the truth so far as it can learn it, concerning the important affairs of America and the world;
3. That as a disseminator of news, the paper shall observe the decencies that are obligatory upon a private gentleman;
4. That what it prints shall be fit reading for the young as well as for the old;
5. That the newspaper's duty is to its readers and to the public at large, and not to the private interests of its owner;
6. That in the pursuit of truth, the newspaper shall be prepared to make sacrifice of its material fortunes, if such course be necessary for the public good;
7. That the newspaper shall not be the ally of any special interest, but shall be fair and free and wholesome in its outlook on public affairs and public men.

These principles were the heart and soul of his convictions, but how to translate them into action was the challenge. The first thing he worked on was the people needed to undertake the daunting task of turning the paper around. To begin with, he didn't know who the good people were, or how to find them. When he did find good people—some newsmen he'd heard about or others he had scouted out—it was almost impossible to persuade them to come to work for what looked like a failing newspaper. In addition, the professionals continued to be unsure about my father's motives. His statements to the contrary, many went on believing that he was there to run a Republican paper, or at least use the *Post* to set right the Roosevelt administration. My father always claimed that the competing papers in Washington kept circulating rumors that added to the uncertainty and difficulty of acquiring a first-class staff.

The search was on for staff people for the editorial-and-news side of the paper as well as for the business side. People of uneven quality were hired; others were brought in for advice or appraisal. Management problems at the *Post* vexed him from the beginning. As general manager to oversee everything except the editorial page, he hired Eugene MacLean, from the *San Francisco News*, who lasted about two years. He recognized that although MacLean was a superior reporter, he did nothing to build up good people in the organization. He saw him as lazy, a drunkard, and a womanizer. I myself was quite surprised during one of MacLean's visits to Mount Kisco when, during the course of an earnest conversation about newspapers, he suddenly grabbed me—a seventeen-year-old—and kissed me. I told nobody about this.

My father knew nothing about advertising, but after one false start he hired a first-class business executive, Don Bernard, whom he had found at the *Knoxville Banner* and who eventually helped him bring order to the chaotic business side. Editorially, too, the dark preceded the dawn, for my father soon found Alexander F. Jones—Casey, as he was known—who appeared on the scene in November 1935 as the *Post*'s new managing editor. Casey was just what the *Post* needed. He came from the blood-and-guts school of journalism, and was a fine, solid, slam-bang, hard-news, straight-ahead editor, perfect for a transition period. He brought substantial professionalism and journalistic standards to the job, as well as technical knowledge and expertise in newspaper management and production. Together, Casey Jones and my father went on a hiring spree, in some cases paying high salaries out of line with the times, and brought on many people who became important to the future of the paper. Recognizing the significance of a paper in the nation's capital, they began to assemble a separate staff of national-news writers to give full coverage to government news, particularly the affairs of the federal government. From the beginning, my father also had seen the importance of the local aspect of the paper, particularly in light of the strange way in which the city was governed.

In sports, my father had the benefit of a holdover from the old McLean regime, Shirley Povich, a brilliant sportswriter and editor hired in 1921 by Ned McLean, for whom he had once caddied in Maine. After a sensational career of more than seventy years, Povich still goes into the office frequently, and occasionally writes for the paper. Povich later told the story of another area—like the comics—about which my father was an innocent. In 1934, when the Senators, the local baseball team, were finishing a disastrous seventh in the American League, my father, thinking the team was supposed to win the pennant every year, as they had in 1933, asked him what was wrong with the ball club. "Pitching, no pitching, Mr. Meyer," Povich told him. "Tell me, maybe it would be good for *The Washington Post*, how much does it cost to buy a pitcher?" my father innocently inquired. He had already grown to realize the importance of sports to newspaper readership.

In those days, the people in Washington often found out what was happening at the ballpark by watching the big scoreboard in front of the *Post*'s E Street building, where the scores were posted in chalk. Occasionally my father himself carried the scores from the telegraph man to the man at the scoreboard. Once, when Goose Goslin hit a home run to win a big game, he asked that the scores not be posted until he could get there and see the pleasure of the large crowds that always gathered to watch.

Understanding the limits of syndicated material and the extent to which it caused newspapers to lose their individual character, my father was determined that the *Post* attempt to be as original as it could. One area he focused on was the women's pages, building them up under a highly intelligent editor, Malvina Lindsay, who also wrote a column, "The Gentler Sex." He thought the *Post*'s material for women was dreary, and began to create a staff of writers, as he said, "who would write for Washington women, among Washington women, and about the interests of Washington women." Even within a year of his purchase of the paper, he considered this revitalization of the women's pages to be one of the *Post*'s most successful accomplishments.

Unusually for the times, he hired women for those pages and gave them prominent roles on the paper. His interest in psychiatry and mental health led him to look for a psychiatrist to write an advice column for people with problems. When he couldn't lure a psychiatrist to the task, he selected Elizabeth Young, a staff reporter on the women's pages, to write it, and had her work overseen by a psychiatrist for the first few months. Young, who wrote under the name Mary Haworth, was so capable that her column became one of the most popular features on the paper, receiving more than twenty thousand letters a year seeking advice. It's hard to convey how groundbreaking and successful this column was, but it was eventually syndicated and read by twenty million people.

Another successful initiative of his was introducing the publication of reader opinion polls. Dr. George Gallup was just starting his American Institute of Public Opinion, and his polls weren't taken very seriously. Ever the logical thinker, and having always put a premium on the importance of research, my father signed the first contract with Gallup and ran his polls on the front page.

Most important, what he worked on from the very start of his ownership was developing the editorial page. He believed that the editorial page as a force in American life had dwindled in power and prestige and felt that a rejuvenated page on the *Post* would make the paper—that a good editorial page was more important in the nation's capital than anywhere else in the country. He tried always to instill in the editors the importance of avoiding emotional, vindictive, or partisan voices. And he vowed never to subscribe blindly to a government policy simply because it was a government policy, not to submit to domination by officialdom, and to avoid the "subtle influence of mob psychology." He had his own philosophy in place, but the challenge was to find a really distinguished editorial-page editor, one who shared his ideals and his aspirations.

After making several efforts to hire high-profile writers from other papers, he began to look for a "vigorous, unlabeled young man" and settled on Felix Morley, who arrived at the *Post* in December 1933. Morley had been a Rhodes Scholar and a research fellow at the London School of Economics. He had also been an editorial writer and a foreign correspondent for the *Baltimore Sun* and was the author of a book on the League of Nations. The brother of novelist Christopher Morley, Felix was very bright, literate, and a Quaker. Again, my father started a tradition—carried on to this day by the publisher of the *Post*—by making an arrangement with Morley that he would never be asked to write something with which he disagreed. The two men agreed that in case of a showdown the publisher reserved the right to have his view prevail, and their relationship evolved into a collegial one and remained so until their strong disagreements prior to America's entry into World War II, when Morley's pacifist views made him more of an isolationist.

The important thing was the establishment of an independent voice on the paper, which was its first distinguishing characteristic. Morley quickly began to make his mark on the page and on the paper. A *Fortune* article from 1944 that took a retrospective look at the *Post* said that "with his arrival the *Post*'s editorial page at once began to acquire insight, vigor, and prestige." Morley himself started another tradition that has prevailed—that of editorialists doing some of their own reporting, as well as talking to the reporters who were working on stories and to outside sources, carefully researching both sides of an issue before forming an opinion.

As he and Casey had done for news, my father and Morley began to build an outstanding editorial staff. They hired a brilliant economic and financial writer, Anna Youngman, who had been a professor at Wellesley and was on the research staff at the Federal Reserve Bank in New York. She wore her gray hair clipped short like a man's and was a bundle of hardheaded, honest rectitude. Morley held on to an invaluable asset from the McLean regime in Merlo J. Pusey, who had arrived in 1928 and remained for thirty-eight years. Until he retired, he was a sage, somewhat conservative, and steadying influence on the paper, in the process winning the 1936 Pulitzer Prize—the *Post*'s first—for editorial writing. (Eventually he was to write my father's biography.)

Even my mother tried her hand at editorials. She sent one to Morley in October 1935, saying, "If my first efforts are too inexperienced, pray put them aside until I can write things in such shape that you can use them without too many changes. The medium is new to me and makes me rather self-conscious"—not self-conscious enough not to attempt them, however. She also wrote provocative letters to the editor, one of which concluded, "Yours for more and better rows in the letter column," and was signed "Jonathan Swift."

Post editorials began having an effect on Congress and the government, and although the paper often quarreled with the administration, it backed the government, my father claimed, on as many measures as it opposed it. The *Post* engaged in campaigns on various fronts, fighting against what my father saw as the inflationary policies of FDR, the NRA, Rexford Tugwell, and Henry Wallace, and fighting for SEC rules that would protect investors against fraud, cleaning up Washington's hidden slums, and coming out strongly for Roosevelt's "quarantine" speech in 1937.

Despite my father's desire that the *Post* be independent and objective, someone remarked that the front page at first read like a Federal Reserve Board Bulletin. It seems that many of the editors and reporters were aiming to please by giving him what they thought he wanted. Indeed, in the very earliest period of my father's publishership, the staff persisted in focusing on stories about finance, banking, and taxation. They soon discovered he was quite serious about the independence of the paper and the autonomy of its reporters and editors within the limits of his principles. He worked out a system that endured, one of delegating autonomy to his managers on both sides—editorial and business—provided they performed according to his standards and ambitions. Since three of the last five *Post* publishers—my father, Phil Graham, and myself—came to work inexperienced in different ways, this was the only practical way to run things anyway. But I still believe it's the best way for newspapers to be run editorially.

In 1935 alone, my father lost more than $1.3 million. From that year on, he made the *Post* a partnership with my mother, with any profits and losses to be divided between the two partners, my father bearing 93 percent and my mother 7 percent. Despite the losses—which were now partially tax-deductible—real progress had been made, but the progress was more in news than in advertising and circulation.

His quest for integrity clearly extended to the business side. He wanted to be sure the advertising-sales people would study the needs of advertisers and honestly try to fulfill them. The story of the *Post*'s editorial transformation had to be sold to retail advertisers, and my father was deeply involved in that sales effort. But real circulation success continued to elude him until over a decade later, after the war.

By 1935, my father had begun to understand what the newspaper business was all about. Gradually an organization was put in place that worked well for its time. He installed a better typeface and improved graphics to make a more readable paper. He enlarged the E Street building by adding a wing and renting space in the Munsey Building next door. He even reported some stories himself, or at least passed on stories to his reporters. (It was he who provided the *Post* with its scoop that King Edward VIII planned to marry the divorced American Wallis Simpson.) He took great pride in delivering any tip that turned into a big story—as did I many years later.

Little by little, despite the fact that within the walls of the *Post*'s building during the first few years there seemed to be nothing but trouble, uphill struggle, a revolving door of people coming and going—some failing and some leaving for better jobs—and money hemorrhaging, the paper was making progress, so much so that Senator Arthur H. Vandenberg credited the *Post* "with the most amazing improvement in the past 12 months of any newspaper ever to come to my attention." Prospective buyers turned up from time to time, from Andrew Mellon to Walter Winchell, all of whom my father flatly rejected, while on the other hand his own attempt to buy the *Washington Herald* from Hearst in 1936 was foiled when Cissy Patterson heard of the negotiations and phoned Hearst, weeping until he submitted. Nothing was going to come easily.

FROM MY FIRST visit to the paper in June of 1933, *The Washington Post* was constantly part of my life. My family owned it, cared deeply about it, and was immersed in the minutiae of its daily travails. My father, the paper's owner and publisher and president of the new Washington Post Company, became its best salesman, never missing an opportunity to sell an ad, offering subscriptions to cab drivers, calling the news desk frequently to ask "What's new?," stopping by nightly, often in his tuxedo after a late dinner, to check on things.

My mother's level of enthusiasm and involvement was no less than his. Her bylines appeared frequently in the paper, particularly in the early years, and the extent of her caring was evident in a memo she sent my father complaining about the lack of *Post* boxes compared with the number for all the other Washington papers she had observed on one of her forays into the countryside. She stopped to interview people along the way to find out what the problem was and reported that "The Washington Post has lost a vast amount of subscriptions because for a long time it had an unreliable carrier boy. The impression of the people living there is that this circulation could easily be regained by a little special attention and a good carrier boy."

I worked for the *Post* as early as the summer of 1934—between high school and college. I was mainly a copy girl or messenger in the women's department, but I became friends with those two fine newswomen, Malvina Lindsay and Mary Haworth. From then on, I had occasional summer jobs at the *Post*.

When I went to college a year after the purchase, my parents and I corresponded constantly about what was happening. I read the *Post* daily, commented, encouraged, and even criticized, while my parents, particularly my father, told me in great detail about what was going on. I found myself deeply involved with the struggle to improve the paper. Somewhat to my surprise, given that I thought of myself during this period as unsophisticated, unworldly, and fairly unopinionated, I seem to have been full of independent appraisals of the paper and what it was printing. For instance, at the age of seventeen I wrote my parents:

> Have been reading the Post faithfully. I think it really is getting very good. The "human interest" that was jammed down its throat at first and looked so awkward, seems to be getting underneath the news now. I find myself unconsciously picking it up before my New York paper. . . . I think you slipped up once when you put the over pathetic community chest advertisement depicting the children on the streets opposite the page showing society at a dance. It might have made people give or it might have been unintentional but the effect was rather startling—especially I should think to the unemployed. However, that is a minor detail. I should think you would be encouraged as a whole.

Much later, the depth of my caring was pointed out to me by Phil's psychiatrist, who told me that Phil and I both had a problem: we cared too much about the *Post*. I told him, in one of the great understatements of my life, that I feared there was little he could do about that.

— *Chapter Four* —

I N T H E F A L L of 1934, I left for Vassar, which I had chosen by a process of non-thought; that is, next to no thinking went into my decision to go there. It simply was the "in" place at the time. Most Madeira seniors went there, as had Bis, whom I always wished to emulate. At the time I arrived on campus for my freshman year, Bis and Bill were in London living together in a small flat. Bill was taking his junior year abroad at the London School of Economics, where my parents had sent him out of discouragement with his Yale career. He had been on the diving team and was an accomplished athlete; however, he was on probation academically. In London he was to study with my father's friend Harold Laski, that brilliant, erratic, left-wing professor and intellectual.

Bis had spent her junior year abroad in Munich, where she had cut her usual glamorous swath, studied some, gone on with her violin, and enjoyed life with at least one or two heavy beaux in different countries. Instead of returning to Vassar, she had gone to work for Alexander Korda, the British movie producer, working with her friend the playwright Sam Behrman on *The Scarlet Pimpernel*.

Flo was dancing—with a Greek partner at least a foot shorter than she. One of her first appearances occurred at a party given by my mother at Crescent Place. Mother wrote me a characteristic letter in May of 1935, describing the event:

> Wish you had been here for my big dinner. Mme. Peter [wife of the Swiss ambassador] said it was the best party she had seen at Washington. Flo danced on a platform on the terrace because we recognized at last moment that drawing room was much too small. As it was drizzling we had to toss huge awning over everything. Jules [the butler] went to hospital the day before with kidney stones and Robert [the other butler] had just had his appendix

out. But I just ignored difficulties and we came through with the Meyer social colors flying higher than ever.

While my older sisters and brother were thus venturing into the real world, I was so unworldly that it was difficult for me to function. My new circle of friends and range of activities all looked appropriate and right, but I found them confusing and felt lost. I had a particularly hard time concentrating on my work and reading. My mind constantly wandered to where I was going and what I was doing—to the problem of how not to be lonely. In addition, I was coping with difficulties stemming from my protected and waited-on background, which I had always taken for granted. Not being very conscious of fashion, I had only the few elegant made-to-order dresses chosen by my mother and nothing for everyday. Before college began, I had set forth to buy clothes with no idea where to go or what I would need, and I somehow outfitted myself with skirts and sweaters. But I wore one yellow cardigan through the first weeks of school until Thanksgiving, when someone finally suggested it should be washed. I had noticed girls' sweaters stretched out on towels but had no idea either that I should be following their example or even *how* to. At home, someone had always removed dirty and discarded clothes, which later reappeared in my drawers. I resolved that problem by sending the yellow sweater out to a cleaner, and never did learn how to wash one.

This ignorance of practical matters applied to every aspect of daily life, whether it was cooking or cleaning or decorating or buying my clothes or knowing how much I could spend or how much others spent. I had to learn from life, from bumping up against reality or from my friends. Even so, I muddled through and learned a great deal my freshman year. In particular, I became aware of the issues surrounding the Roosevelt administration. The New Deal became a reality for the first time, and I began to be interested in it in a less-than-abstract way. The atmosphere at home was so anti-Roosevelt—Dad in a rational, measured way, Mother more emotionally—that I had never really heard a pro–New Deal position. Between the professors, the radical girls on the Vassar newspaper, which I went out for, and a new good friend, Connie Dimock, who gradually turned extremely left-wing, I became converted to the goals of the New Deal. In fact, the three middle Meyer children all became New Dealers, our views resulting in wild and vociferous political arguments with both parents, but mostly my mother.

Perhaps because of my conservative temperament, I slowly developed ideas that have remained fairly consistent throughout my life, with variations now and then. I believed—and believe—that capitalism works best for a freedom-loving society, that it brings more prosperity to more people than any other social-economic system, but that somehow we have to take care of people. These ideas converted me into an ardent Roosevelt advocate at that time and for all three of his re-election campaigns.

I was taking freshman German and became a great devotee of Thomas Mann, particularly of his novella *Tonio Kröger*. In it Mann talks about the ambivalence and conflict within Tonio caused by the natural rift between his Prussian father and his warm-blooded, emotional South German mother. The splintering caused by the pulls of these two opposites makes him feel different from others, and he longs to be like everyone else. That may or may not be an accurate reading of this lovely story, but that's how it struck me. I was so carried away and personally involved with the theme that I picked up an English translation and galloped through it, unwilling and unable to struggle with my beginning German.

So I *was* learning. But my work was spotty and disorganized. I had come to college unprepared, lacking the kind of self-discipline needed to read with concentration and the skills necessary to assemble research, give it thought, and write an essay. A history paper I had been assigned to write by an unsympathetic and tough professor, Lucy Textor, is a case in point. I wrote my parents about our conflict:

> Am still disagreeing violently with my History teacher. Right now perhaps my ideas are too general but I think hers are too specific, i.e., she has taught history ten years too long. We have a long topic to write just now on anything we wish to. I chose the position of women in the Middle Ages tracing the similar customs by races from the Saxons in Germany to England and bringing out the differences in Italy, France, Germany, and England. As they had just begun to obtain rights it seemed interesting to me to do this for this period, and perhaps again at later periods when we study them. I realize what a tremendous job this is but she wanted me to take *one* woman and do her. If I took one woman she would have to be famous therefore she would be an exception which is not what I am after. I am going to try my topic despite what she said. Even if it doesn't make a good one I will get what I want out of it. All of this will probably result in a bad mark because we dislike each other—I do my history my own way and enjoy it.

The innocence—and arrogance—of youth are evident here, as well as a budding interest in the position of women. The hated Miss Textor and I came to grief over the ill-prepared paper. She suspected, I suppose, what was really the case, which was that I had done only a half-baked job, and said, "So, Miss Meyer, read us your paper." When I finished reading it she said, "That's a good introduction. Then what?" Well, it was the end of what I had done. She gave me a D, which resulted in my being put on probation, an embarrassing failure that I resented even while I recognized it as at least partly deserved.

Instead of being outraged at me, my mother was outraged at the college. She wrote from Miami Beach that she had

> ... raised an awful row with McCracken [then president of Vassar] because they sent me notice you were on history pro. Dr. McCracken assured me this mark would not stand against you and you may be sure it won't. In the meantime please work as never before and don't say a word about my fusillade against this female. I sent my letter to Dean Thompson. ... I am furious that they dared send me a report of your being on history pro, and shall shatter the quiet of Vassar if they don't change things PDQ.

I was embarrassed though somewhat relieved when I got her letter, but mostly I was worried that her scathing tirades to the dean and the president would create pressure on me to follow up with the goods and write a first-rate paper. In the end, I worked off the probation and passed the course.

Midway through my freshman year, I began to feel better about my schoolwork and also to feel that college was growing more interesting and alive. But I had some difficulty with the fact that my mother, it seemed, could outdo my every achievement. Throughout my years of college, it always turned out that she had read all the books assigned to me—read them, assimilated them, critiqued them, dismissed them, even committed them to memory. In a letter to my father in the spring of my freshman year, I wrote that I was reading Tolstoy on the "function of art" and found "that he agrees with Mother in most of his ideas." How odd that I should have put it this way and not the other way around.

What assuaged my spirits was that by this time Connie and I had become seriously interested in politics. We were opposed to a bill in the New York State Senate providing that every member of state-supported institutions (meaning colleges, too, because they were tax-exempt) swear allegiance to the Constitution. Hearst was a big proponent of this measure and was backed by the American Legion. I wrote my father: "I hear, Dad, that you disagree with me on this subject. This is not a bit of college communism however. ... I think it is absurd. You can't brush out communism by refusing to recognize it."

I was appointed treasurer of the college political club, and was about to refuse, fearing it was the road to becoming "president of the Oshkosh Women's Club," but then, as I wrote my parents:

On the other hand, my friends are good looking, amusing, and nice and I thought it would be amusing to see something of the girls that think of nothing but "p.p.," present problems, and how to convert America to communism. Most of them are madly radical but some are extremely intelligent about it. My little conservative voice will scarcely be heard above the uproar but it will be fun baiting the bears.

That summer I was planning to visit my Madeira friend Jean Rawlings in San Francisco. I still have her letter of invitation, telling me about the wonderful things we would do—trips to the mountains with boys who were friends of hers, a rodeo, all enticing. However, my dream of going was suddenly blighted one night when my parents reminded me that there was a serious polio epidemic out west and insisted that I could not go. I remember weeping and telling them that the idea of another summer alone at Mount Kisco was almost unendurable.

My parents came up with a solution—a job on one of the chain of suburban Westchester newspapers owned by Noel Macy, later bought by Gannett, and I eagerly grabbed at the idea and went to work on the *Mount Vernon Argus*. Each day I commuted in a Chevrolet convertible, my first car. It was a nonpaying job, but I enjoyed it and enjoyed my associates. I did the menial tasks of telephoning and taking messages, and even wrote a few elementary stories or announcements—including one on women doctors, which was printed with my byline and which I sent off to my father, who wrote back in an encouraging way: "I think it is very well written. It looks quite professional, in fact, to me." I liked the job because it kept me busy, gave me some time away from the farm, and also gave me a structured life and an idea of what working was like.

I was startled to find that the Newspaper Guild had formally protested my working at the *Argus* for nothing, though individual guild members were personally conciliatory. I had a message from the union head saying:

> I wish to explain that we feel no animosity towards you. Those who know you appreciate your efforts to succeed in the field you have chosen. Our action is and will continue to be a protest against any publisher who hires an employee without paying him. . . . We hope that you can see our point.

At the same time, I had a message from a friend of my mother's saying that she had "heard about the Guild's teapot furor over you. It was all that damned little Communist Dotty Loeb, president and agitator-in-chief, who was at the bottom of it, though . . . some women from Pelham, space writers, had whined a little. . . . [T]he Guild seeks to make mountains of any molehill they can find." It was my introduction to union politics.

MY FATHER and I were growing closer during my college years, while my mother and I were growing apart. He was so shy and inarticulate in expressing emotion that I was always surprised to find him making the attempt. In the fall of 1935, when I was leaving for my second year at Vassar, he wrote me: "I hate to think that soon you'll be off to college and I to Washington and then only to meet at holidays for another year." And again, when I went to Europe the following summer, he wrote me that he was leaving for the "lonely farm, with Kate no longer there to cheer me up." My father and, later, Phil Graham were among the very few people who ever called me Kate.

I was eighteen that second year of college. The conflict that had begun the year before between the social life and the intellectual and political life continued to grow. "Coming-out" parties were very much in vogue, the accepted thing in Washington, and a few people still spent the whole year going to parties in different cities where they had family or ties. My own debut was limited to a tea dance at Thanksgiving and a dance on December 26, done quite splendidly, with the house decorated in a Greek theme and my dress Greek in effect, and gold, not the traditional white.

I had learned enough to help with the invitation list and arrangements. My mother had suggested asking young Joseph Alsop, the brilliant, young reporter for the *Herald-Tribune*, whom she had recently met. When we were seating the dinner, I put him next to me, intrigued by her description. She had omitted one salient fact, however—Joe, who was fairly short, then weighed about 250 pounds. In addition, he was extremely sophisticated. I was appalled by his appearance and unable to cope with his mature mind and presence, though I got through dinner as best I could. Later, we became lifelong, devoted friends, but this was an odd and inauspicious beginning.

Accentuating my ambivalence about the two worlds in which I felt myself to be moving, on the day after my big party Connie and I left by train for Columbus, Ohio, to attend the meeting that established the American Student Union. We had been asked to cover it for the Vassar *Miscellany News*, on which we both now worked. The union was a combination of communist and socialist student groups, the liberals and the radicals willing to get along with each other and to combine with unaffiliated students for antifascist purposes. It was a kind of mirror image of what was happening in the older political world, where the same groups had formed the Popular Front to try to fight the rise of Hitler.

We found friends from Dartmouth of more or less similar views and had a good time with Budd Schulberg, later author and movie producer; Eddie Ryan, later on the *Post*; and Bill Leonard, later head of news for CBS. After going out together for a drink one evening, we returned to the meeting to find that I, who had come as an observer and a reporter, had been put on the National Executive Committee. This was part of a transparent ploy of the left-wing factions to be sure they had enough visible unattached liberals to be convincing. My first instinct was to remove my name quickly, but a second, which I followed, was to go along with the idea. I was entirely realistic about the reasons for my selection and knew that I was being used. At the same time, I found that this was an interesting and unfamiliar scene and thought I'd take a look and learn what it was all about.

When I told my father about being on the committee, he wrote me at length, arguing against journalists joining organizations and suggesting that "the fewer labels you wear the better." In responding to his counsel, I quietly but firmly told him I appreciated the thought he had obviously given to all sides of the question and agreed with most of his points, particularly that there are certain dangers inherent in so-called mass thinking. I also agreed that labels were undesirable, but I explained that it would be difficult for all concerned if I were to resign at that time. My father wrote back at once, thanking me for my letter and concluding with what is one of the simplest and best precepts for parents to live by that I have ever read. It meant a lot to me then, as it does even today: "What parents may sometimes do in a helpful way is to point out certain principles of action. I do not think I would be helpful in advising you too strongly. I do not even feel the need of doing that because I have so much confidence in your having really good judgment. I believe that what I can do for you once in a while is to point out certain principles that have developed in my mind as sound and practical, leaving it for you yourself to apply them if your own mind grasps and approves the principles."

This issue, which might have become a separating bone of contention between us, is a good example of how my relationship with my father worked, and the caring and concern that were evident on both our parts. He was probably gently trying to persuade me not to join a group that included communists. But he didn't persist.

My mother, on the other hand, did take stands and, indeed, political jobs. In the spring of 1936, she was running Alf Landon's radio campaign, although Dad had apparently tried to talk her out of it. As usual, she sprang into action with total enthusiasm. She wrote me that spring with her characteristic excitement about her current project: "Landon is a home run. Much more important than the writer chaps have pictured him. I have to do a job." Later, still besotted with her own contribution to his image, she wrote: "I am doing a red-hot talk on Landon the man on a national hook-up. Such fun. Landon's acceptance speech was good but I can always put him over better than he can (!) because he hasn't the habit of putting himself into speeches. I can't help wondering sometimes what he thinks of himself when I get through with him." She had blinders on to such an extent that, when election eve came around, she was still thinking Landon might defeat FDR.

At about the same time that she was becoming deeply involved with the Republican campaign, she spoke at a Town Hall program, a very prominent radio discussion group, with Mrs. Roosevelt presiding. As always, she wrote me in advance to make sure I would tune in and added as an incentive that she would "defend your students' union and jibe at teacher and pupil oaths." I was pleased that she might mention the ASU in her speech, but not a little worried about what she might go on to say. In fact, she got in a row about the New Deal with Mrs. Roosevelt. Her next letter to me expressed hurt feelings at my silence: "I judge from your silence that you did not care for my speech very much, but as far as the world is concerned I am a hero. Before I left the hall I began getting telegrams and when we got back to the hotel there were numerous long distance telephone calls, one from Bis very enthusiastic. The fan mail is coming in hot and heavy, and all of it approving and even enthusiastic. The animosity which the letters breathe for the Roosevelts is unbelievable. I enclose a typical one for your amusement." This was yet another of my one-way conversations with my mother that consisted entirely of her telling me of the overwhelming reception of her latest speeches—mass ovations, and demands for thousands of copies. This kind of self-delusion and overwhelming need for adulation made any exchange with her increasingly difficult for me and, I think, for all of us.

In the spring of 1936, I got involved in organizing a nationwide peace strike. As if on cue, something else happened that underlined the schisms in my thinking. Connie and I were invited by the seniors at Vassar to be among the few girls picked for the Daisy Chain—allegedly for pulchritude and other sterling qualities, but in reality because they liked you. We were somewhat embarrassed, since the Daisy Chain was an old-fashioned ritual, but secretly we were pleased and soothed our self-conscious selves by composing a poem of acceptance that was titled "To the Upper Class from Two in Chains." Only the second verse of this epic survives, and reads:

> We thank the class of 36
> They've put us in a "pretty" fix.
> Between class struggles we must choose
> The proletariat or youse
> But we'll not be the C.P.'s bane.
> We'll organize the Daisy Chain.

My mother, on receiving a copy of this poem, responded enthusiasti-cally about the verse—not the tapping—and philosophized, "In this demo-cratic country nothing makes so much impression as being elected to something; popularity counts, alas, for a darn sight more than merit. Look at Franklyn [meaning, of course, FDR]. The best we can hope is that pop-ularity without merit eventually becomes cloying."

Connie and I had discussed making a trip to the Soviet Union that summer following our sophomore year, the summer of 1936. Although my mother's first reaction had been positive, my father vetoed the idea with vehemence. I pleaded for Russia, arguing politely that we could book an exciting and cheap tour conducted by Intourist, which I called the reli-able and official Russian travel bureau. I added fuel to my argument, I thought, by saying that we would shorten our planned stay in the Soviet Union to two weeks. We would go in the early part of the summer, when Connie's family would still be in Western Europe and therefore close enough to help us if there were a problem, and I would be back to spend September on the *Post* with my father.

Dad did not agree with my logic. He telegraphed his okay to Western Europe only and followed up with a letter explaining his reasons:

> These are very troublous times, more so than I can expect you to realize. You know, I am sure, that I do not say no to you lightly— You are one kid that is generally so reasonable in everything that I am anxious always to say yes—to you. I can't see you going so far to the Eastern part of Europe—under present conditions—unless I was free to devote myself *solely* to the job of getting you out in case of trouble. I am not in that position now. Much love. Maybe you and I will go there together someday.

When Connie and I left for Europe at the end of June, we made quite a traveling troupe, given Connie's parents, her four sisters, and a nurse or maid. Her father was constantly calling to the French porters, "*Neuf per-sonnes et vingt-neuf pièces de baggages*" (nine people and twenty-nine pieces of luggage).

We went first to London, and although I recognized the seriousness of the political situation, I found it quite a gay place, with everyone excited about the king's garden parties. In Paris, Léon Blum, the socialist, was the head of a Popular Front government, and politics made themselves felt everywhere, exacerbated for us, no doubt, by our having arrived in the city on the day before Bastille Day. In addition to the usual military parade, there was a Popular Front demonstration, which gave me the most im-pressive feeling of communal strength I had ever had. There were two separate marching lines that eventually met and came together, singing, into the Place de la Bastille. The spirit with which the crowds poured in, about 750,000 strong, made it easy to visualize previous scenes at the same location.

Connie and I joined the march, attaching ourselves to the *boulangers*—a group of bakers—and walking with them for a couple of hours. As if to make an even greater point of our being pulled in opposite directions at once, we broke off from the Popular Front parade to have lunch with my aunt Elise, who had left San Francisco after her husband died and taken up residence in a beautifully decorated house in Paris, where she became a successful and prominent social figure. After some time, Elise married the Brazilian ambassador to France, Luiz de Souza-Dantas, who by length of service had become dean of the diplomatic corps, a position of some eminence. Our morning's march was in marked contrast to Elise's usual activities, and it amused her greatly that Connie and I had joined her lunch straight from the parade. She kept telling us throughout the meal to "tell Princess So-and-So and Sir So-and-So what you did this morning!"

So we led a highly varied life on our trip. In Paris I took Connie to have dinner with Brancusi one night. I was so eager to see him that I rang the bell madly and burst into the studio when the door opened, only to be confronted by a strange face. Full of the exuberance of youth, I exclaimed, "My goodness, where's Brancusi and who are you?" He turned out to be Pierre Matisse, Henri's son, and he stayed to dinner. The four of us ate in Brancusi's totally white studio, sitting on blocks of marble around another huge chunk of marble, which served as the table. When it was time to eat, Brancusi produced large sheets of a kind of shiny white paper, and put them around like placemats. My memory is that everything we ate was white, too, although I'm sure that wasn't the case.

We returned to England for a student meeting at Oxford and lunch with Harold Laski, and then were off to Salzburg, where Mother had treated us to the Hotel Bristol and tickets to the music festival there. Because I had heeded my father's instructions to stay well on the Western side of Europe, Connie and I now parted company as she headed for the Soviet Union. But though I was sad to see her leave without me for the great adventure, I don't remember any feeling of resentment at having been forbidden to go with her. I had accepted my father's verdict.

— *Chapter Five* —

Ｏ N A T R A I N T R I P to Mount Kisco with my father later that summer, I broached the idea of my studying at the London School of Economics (as my brother, Bill, had) the following year. It was met with an immediate "no." He believed that Bill had been too young intellectually, too immature, to put European social problems in context, and he thought I was, too. But he said that he understood *why* I wanted to leave Vassar and that it was all right with him if I went anywhere else in this country. I was so taken aback that I could hardly think of an alternative to London. But I thought I had to respond instantly rather than do the natural thing, which was to think it over, so I made an instantaneous decision. I hit on the University of Chicago not out of a sudden impulse toward serious study but simply because there flashed into my mind a picture I had seen while flipping through the pages of *Redbook* magazine of Robert Maynard Hutchins, the university's young, handsome, dynamic president. The cutlines under his picture said that he was revolutionizing the learning process and shaking things up with new and interesting ideas about college education, and that the university was in an intellectual ferment—or something of the sort. I hadn't focused on it as I flipped the page, but now I added things up quickly: it was in the Midwest (I had never lived off the Eastern seaboard); it was coeducational; and it was in a city. "Okay," I said, "I'll go to Chicago."

And, in fact, with no more thought than that, off I went, arriving in Chicago less than a month after our conversation on the train. I hadn't foreseen the magnitude of the decision I'd made and didn't realize what I was in for until I was already in the thick of it. My father had come with me to Chicago to enter me in the university and find me a place to live, but once he left I was completely on my own in a strange environment and a sea of thousands of students, with only one or two casual acquaintances. Maybe it was lucky that I hadn't had the time or the sense to envision being so alone; I might well have pulled back. Probably I reassured myself with the thought that I was planning to stay only one year and could always return to Vassar—indeed, I kept that safety net by telling the college I would be back. But little by little life sorted itself out, and the university was good for me. Eventually I found my way, growing to love the place and staying on to graduate.

I lived on the edge of the campus at International House, which was filled with foreign students, graduate students, and some transfer students like me. We all ate in the cafeteria, sitting at round tables that afforded opportunities for making friends and acquaintances of every kind. Before too long I met and became roommates with Tayloe Hannaford, a like-minded girl from Winnetka who had transferred from Sarah Lawrence, and gradually we assembled a nucleus of friends. We both were entranced with a graduate student, Sidney Hyman, who was much around the house. Early on, Sidney and I fell into conversation about our shared enthusiasm for Thomas Mann, and we talked for hours, cementing a friendship that moved with me through the years. "Fun" for our group was talk, exchange of ideas, laughter, close-harmony singing, and hours at the college beer parlor, Hanley's, which had a long bar, in front of which was a row of small square tables with red-and-white-checked tablecloths where you could sit with your friends and nurse a beer or two all night.

After a few months, I was approached by members of two different clubs, Mortar Board and Quadrangle, similar to sororities, suggesting that I join. I went to a meeting of one where lots of young women were sitting around, many of them playing bridge. It wasn't the kind of atmosphere I was used to, even at Vassar. Shortly afterwards, a friend of mine who was a member of Mortar Board asked if I was really interested in joining and said that if I was she would go to bat for me: she was willing to take on a fight about my being Jewish, but not if there was nothing to be served by fighting. Having had no idea that my being considered Jewish was an issue, I was startled, and assured her that I wasn't really interested. Later, a friend told me that the Quadrangle had actually disbanded over the question of admitting me to membership. This was one of the very few instances in which anti-Semitism touched me directly in those early years, and I was more surprised than distressed by it.

Chicago then was a center of intellectual turmoil. The university was a distinctly urban school, with mostly nonaffluent students, some excellent faculty, and high intellectual standards. Because Hutchins had become enthralled by the theory that education consisted in reading the great books of the Western world and absorbing their ideas, the academic program was very different from that at most colleges. Hutchins had been influenced by Mortimer Adler, who was the leading exponent of these ideas, and by St. Johns College, where they had previously been tried out. Hutchins had also abolished football and other athletics. The whole thing was slightly flaky but stimulating—a universe of its own, and, important for me, a far cry from Vassar.

I had decided on American history as my major, so I enrolled in survey courses in economics and in history and, despite some trepidation, the course in the great books taught jointly by Hutchins and Adler. It started with Plato and Aristotle, worked up through St. Thomas Aquinas and other philosophers, and ended with Freud and Marx and Engels. This class—which was supposed to teach you "how to read a book," as Adler later titled one of his own books—met once a week for two solid, sometimes torturing hours. About thirty of us sat around an oblong table, and Hutchins or Adler or both would use the Socratic method in discussing what we had read and testing us. For the whole two hours, the two men hammered away, bullying us unmercifully—"Well, Miss Meyer, tell us in your own words what Aristotle thinks about this." "What do you think about what he says?" "Do you really think that good behavior follows from good values?" "What are good habits?" "What are good values?" "If that's what you think, what if such-and-such happened?"

The methods they used often taught you most about bullying *back*, about standing up to Hutchins and Adler, about challenging them and fundamentally pleasing them by doing it with gusto and verve, so that they were amused. If you learned to cope with their methods, you could stay afloat. When I didn't do well, the most awful depression set in, because so much depended on that performance. When I did do well, my elation carried over to everything else I was doing at the university.

Despite its intimidations, the course was good for me, and I actually got an A in it at the end of the first year. My father, who strongly believed in Chicago's educational theories, was thrilled at my grade and sent me a check for $100, which I said I would spend on books by Plato and Aristotle to commemorate the event. I suggested he may have overreacted, because "marks don't mean much out here and Adler usually deals them out pretty irrationally. Though he teaches logic, he knows better than to base his conduct upon it." For all I knew, I added, "the marks may have been the result of the rides home in the car when, as I told you, we got on very well."

I was still finding it difficult to learn the right balance between social and academic activities. Mrs. Kellogg Fairbank, a friend of my mother's, who once described herself to me as "that person in Chicago who voted for Landon," was my one link, except for Tayloe, to the social scene beyond the university. She lived in a large, stylish lakefront apartment and occasionally included me in her lunch or dinner parties and invited me to her weekend house. After these events I always made what I thought was the polite card gesture, often worrying about whether I was supposed to leave one card or two and whether I had to turn the corner down. Even as a college junior, and while the outside world was changing so dramatically, I was concerned to make sure I was adhering to the proper ways, doing the correct thing, making the appropriate gesture.

Through an old beau of my sister Flo's, I met a classicist émigré professor, Giuseppe Antonio Borgese, whose book *Goliath* I had read and respected. I found him to be a bit of a madman, but very entertaining and very bright. Soon afterwards, I was excited and flattered to be invited to dinner by Borgese. We ate in downtown Chicago—a great treat, since we students lived almost exclusively in South Chicago, the area around the university. On the way back from dinner he quizzed me about how many of my classmates I thought were still virgins, a question entirely beyond my ability to answer or even guess at. There were other leading questions, followed by an invitation to inspect his apartment. I was still so young and unsuspecting that poor Borgese obviously took my acceptance as an agreement to amorous advances, but, being so naïve about sexual relations, I was surprised when the distinguished professor made a pass at me. When I resisted, he pursued me, and I found myself racing around his desk, the professor in pursuit. Finally, I insisted on leaving, and he drove me home. Surprisingly, he called and asked me out again. I was in such a panic about offending the great man that I went to the university's infirmary and insisted I had appendicitis. When the doctors assured me I was in fine health, I had to tell the professor I was unable to go out with him—a monstrously difficult thing for me to do. It almost killed me with mortification.

My political outlook developed further as a committed liberal—primarily passionately antifascist and sympathetic toward the labor movement. Yet, though I was engaging in liberal thinking and activities, I remained basically conservative. I had never encountered real communists until I reached Chicago. The American Student Union there was very different from the one I'd left behind at Vassar, which had been run by girls who were relatively new to politics and whose passions—the political ones, at least—weren't all that deep. I was greeted effusively by the Chicago branch of the union, which was mostly composed of communists and socialists of a rather boring mind-set. An exception was a young British graduate student, Norman O. Brown, a Commonwealth Fellow, who took me to a few meetings and to dinner. He kept suggesting that I join the Young Communists, since they and the parent party were the most effective antifascist forces in the world. At that time, with the rise of Hitler and Mussolini, and Franco fighting against the forces of Spanish democracy, this argument could be made with some force. The ghastly crimes of Stalin had not yet been revealed, and when the famous trials started, they were, at least initially, viewed ambivalently by even the liberals among us.

I remained unpersuaded, and wondered whether Brown might be a communist himself, assigned to convert me. In response to his proselytizing, I eventually wrote him a letter—which I later found in one of my textbooks and probably never sent—in which I said that, although my parents were doing certain things with which I disagreed, I loved them, was grateful for the circumstances into which I was born, appreciated what I had, and had no desire to revolt against any of it. I didn't want to help overthrow a system that I knew I belonged to, although I certainly understood that there were problems that should be addressed.

I'm not sure why when many of my friends had joined the party I had the resolve to reject it. Perhaps there was a balancing weakness at work, one that had long been a part of me—that inherent desire to conform, to please, to abide by laws; to be a good girl, if you will. Anyway, very luckily for *The Washington Post* during the McCarthy era, when we were constantly being attacked as "reds" by various constituencies, I never had been a member.

In the spring of my first year at Chicago, I took a course on labor relations from Paul Douglas, later a United States senator, and grew interested in labor problems. This was a time of broad-scale industrial organization that was being resisted by the steel, coal, and automobile companies in extremely forceful, even violent ways. My sympathies lay with the right to organize, and they haven't changed in that respect, although I have grown to regard some union leadership and tactics with a degree of skepticism. But at this time the great mass of workers in the industrial area had no way of dealing jointly with employers.

I became friends with Ralph Beck, a young man who was stringing for the *Chicago Daily News* and covering the Chicago steel strike. The Republic Steel plant in South Chicago, not too far from the university, was being struck, and Ralph called to tell me that there was going to be a confrontation of some sort between the strikers and the company and invited me to go with him to observe it. I agreed with enthusiasm. The picketers were facing armed Chicago police. I was not in danger, being at some distance, but I was scared. Ralph had left me behind for safety and had gone nearer. The steelworkers advanced and the guards or the police suddenly fired on them, killing seven and wounding others. Pandemonium and fear of arrest spread, even to where I was standing, and we all piled into any available vehicles and fled this horrifying scene.

After recovering from this traumatic event, we returned once or twice to the struck plant, and it occurred to us to wonder what was going on inside. Ralph suggested we try to find out. I asked for permission, mentioning *The Washington Post* as well as the *Daily News*, and learned a never-to-be-forgotten lesson about the power of a Washington newspaper, even though the *Post* was a minor one at that time. We were invited in and

Two early Edward Steichen portraits of my mother,
one showing the famous hat with the eagle feather

My father and his parents

My parents on their honeymoon, in Japan (top),
and out West (above and right)

Our houses in Washington, D.C. (top), and in Mount Kisco

Bis and Billy clambering over the Buddha in
the front hall of our New York apartment

Me sailing

With my father

One of Steichen's photographs of the family

Graduation from Madeira; I'm the first girl on the left.

Family dinner

Bill

Ruth

Bis

Flo

7

My coming-out dress

toured the plant with its officials, somewhat to my embarrassment and surprise—a college junior and her stringer friend.

I wrote Casey Jones, explaining and apologizing for using the paper's name to gain entry. He answered that he had gotten a bang out of our experience and thought the picture we'd received of the way a big strike works was equivalent to a year's work in any economics course, and graciously sent a letter of introduction for future use.

Many years later, I was to get a more graphic—and personal—lesson about labor relations.

My FATHER and I kept up a constant conversation through the mail in which the *Post* often figured. Although it was improving editorially and even attracting more ads, Dad was being worn down by the seemingly impossible task of getting it out of the red. Costs were rising. The *Herald* had the blue-collar readership locked up, in part because of its famous third page—the sex-and-crime page. The *Times* was the afternoon version of the *Herald*. Scripps Howard had a solid, jazzy, tabloid niche—newsstands and lunch sales—and the *Evening Star* seemed to own the market and the town. It was the respectable establishment paper, overflowing with ads.

Dad wrote me in the spring of 1938, almost five years into the struggle to make the *Post* succeed, that he had had one of those lucky breaks that sometimes occur. He was offered the *Herald-Tribune* service, which meant columns by Walter Lippmann, Dorothy Thompson, and Mark Sullivan, some desirable comics and Sunday features, daily crossword puzzles and bridge articles, and book reviews—a rich trove, which he grabbed. The *Star* had had the *Tribune* service, and through a difference of opinion over cost it landed in our lap. The *Post* also got some routine coverage from the *Herald-Tribune*'s Washington bureau, which relieved our small national staff. In addition, we got foreign news from their correspondents abroad, which we could not afford at that time.

My father wrote:

> Yesterday, Mr. Newbold of the Star, visited me and told me it was very disturbing to them and they would like to divide the service with us, but as they did not offer to divide it with us when they had it themselves, I don't know why we should divide it with them when we have it, do you?

He described a lunch at the French Embassy with Arthur Krock of *The New York Times*; Fred Essary of the *Baltimore Sun*; Felix Morley, then the *Post*'s editorial-page editor; Sir Wilmott Lewis of the London *Times*; and "myself from the Wash Post." He added charmingly, "Such things make me feel like a regular newspaper guy. . . . Circulation 108,500 and going up—110,000 by sooner than you think." Then he added movingly, especially in view of how small the *Post* was at the time and how difficult the struggle:

> P.S. If you don't soon get down here on the Post there won't be anything left to do but the routine jobs of trying to hold our position. You ought to be in on the job of putting it to the top. It is much better sport fighting to get there than trying to stay there after you have gotten there. When we get there I will go out looking for some trouble somewhere, and let you, Mother, Casey Jones and Felix Morley keep the machine running.

What did he mean and what did I think? Looking back, I can only assume that I wanted to be a journalist and that he had a newspaper. I'm sure that he wasn't writing to my sisters or even my brother in this way. I am equally sure that neither one of us saw me as a manager. It interests me how he—and I—assumed at the time that I would be a journalist.

One contribution I did make to the *Post* was in the all-important area of the comics. I told my father about the comic strip "Terry and the Pirates," which was the talk of Chicago, and was then relatively new. He found it available and picked it up with great success. I felt pleased to have helped.

Right after Roosevelt's overwhelming victory in 1936, someone wrote the *Post* a letter suggesting welcoming the victorious president back to town. Next day the paper published a front-page box headed "Let's give the President a real welcome." The response was remarkable: two hundred thousand gathered at Union Station at eight o'clock in the morning to hail "The Champ," who rewarded Dad with a special wave to his second-floor window on Pennsylvania Avenue.

I wrote a rather sour letter to my father about this event, saying that I thought it was corny and trying to have it both ways, and that, for me, this was one of the *Post*'s lower moments—to which he responded instantly and aggressively. He thought it was a great idea and reported that other papers had participated, too. He further defended himself by saying the Associated Press had carried the story and even *Time* had mentioned it. He added:

> I am afraid that your Chicago atmosphere and remoteness prevents your exercising the good, keen journalistic understanding on this matter which I know you would have been capable of had you been here on the spot.

This was as overt a difference as we ever had. Even when he was criticizing my judgment, he was always kind and supportive. It says a lot for my father's equanimity that he was unbothered by this kind of exchange; in fact, he relished differences of opinion and sharp exchanges as signs that people had minds of their own. For example, he had started small trust funds for all of us at birth. He did this because he felt his own father had used money to control his children, and he didn't want to do the same thing; he wanted us to be independent of his will.

What I didn't grasp at the time was my father's real bias in my favor, the depth of his caring. My mother's hints that he had a crush on me and the stories she relayed of his hoarding my letters didn't sink in. In retrospect, I can see this intense affection we had for each other and what an enormous influence he had on my life, my plans, and my thinking. I'm not sure why I wasn't aware of it at the time, but it's clear to me now that he believed in me, which became a very powerful emotional asset as I grew older and gave me a measure of security which I greatly needed.

Relations with my mother were different. She was becoming more and more difficult and self-centered. It was hopeless to ask her a personal question or for advice: she had constructed an image of what we were all like and what our lives were like, and she never really looked to see if the reality fit her image.

After the 1936 election, Mother returned to Washington a little sadder—not too much so—and a good deal wiser. My father, not really one to say "I told you so," did take some consolation from having advised her to stay out of the job she had gotten herself into with Landon. My one meeting with her candidate was a perfect example of the contrast between the two worlds in which I was moving—that of my Republican parents, and my more liberal university environment. Just a few weeks after the election, I was taking the overnight train home for the Thanksgiving holiday. Sidney Hyman and some other friends came down to the station to see me off and, as a goodbye bouquet, presented me with a real hammer and sickle tied up with a red bow. There was nothing to do with this awkward joke but take it with me. I arrived home next morning still carrying the unwieldy implements and walked into the Washington house, where the door was opened by the butler and I found my parents in the library conferring with the defeated candidate—Alf Landon himself. I hastily disposed of the hammer and sickle before joining them.

It was during the 1930s that my mother started seriously on her career of speechmaking on a variety of issues, particularly welfare and education. Her letters to me were fuller than ever of accounts of speeches, of audience sizes, and of the enthusiastic reaction she always received and the many demands for copies. She had enormous and wide-ranging intellectual interests and wrote on many subjects; in fact, at this point her life centered on her writing. For a couple of years, she often went alone to the "Cabin"—as we called the lovely smallish modern house my parents had built overlooking the Potomac River in Virginia, about half an hour from town—to work on her book on Tolstoy, Dostoyevsky, and Mann.

It was during this time that she began another of her passionate friendships with men—one that consumed her and threatened her equanimity even as it sustained and enriched her. This one was with Thomas Mann, and even before she met the man himself she had fallen for him through his writings. Having earlier discovered his novels for myself, I had become an enthusiast, but my mother went further. In April of 1937, she finally saw Mann in person when she went to New York to hear him lecture on Wagner at the New School and was completely bowled over by the experience, calling him an "absorbing if unrequited passion," admiring him as both a writer and a human being. A second lecture, on Freud, only increased her first impression that here was one of the few authentically great men of the day. She was delighted to find that "such a great soul exists in our poor age," and immediately decided to interview him for the *Post*. She who was cynical about conspicuous members of society (or so she claimed), she who described herself as someone "who would rather meet an honest shoemaker than the average artist," was so overcome with emotion when she arrived for the interview (to be held in German, of course) that she "scarcely felt equal to the task." When she actually met him, her excitement was unbounded and contagious. In a letter to me she described the experience in great detail—and revealingly:

> His wife, a brilliant-eyed charming, rather elderly woman received me and my confusion increased when I realized I would have to interview him in front of her. Three men had to be put out before I was admitted and I could see other people waiting impatiently for me to get out. That isn't exactly conducive to a helpful atmosphere and together with my attack of hero-worship wellnigh made me speechless when the great man came forward to greet me. It took all the training in self-control that I have ever had to proceed but I had planned an intelligent question which I now heard myself reciting like a school-girl. A flash of recognition of my question's validity was visible and then I could almost see him reach up to a certain definite compartment of his mind where just the right answer was stored. For fifteen minutes he talked like a machine gun in the most fluent, subtle German with long perfect sentences and paragraphs just as precise and complicated as his written style. I never once looked up at him because I had to write like mad to get some of his vocabulary and a few of his ideas.

When he had finished, his wife indicated that my time was up, we exchanged a few more remarks revealing on my part a well-nigh subnormal intelligence and after a short exchange of courtesies with his wife, I took my broken heart and my wounded vanity into the street.

When my mother returned to Washington from the meeting, she was still so uplifted by Mann's words, the power of his personality, and her belief in his importance to liberal thought throughout the world that she wrote him her version of a fan letter. The next day, exhausted, as she said, "by the storm of my emotions," she set to work on the interview, which duly appeared in the *Post*. This experience with Mann—or, more important, the strength of her feelings for him—compelled her to advise me: "Be a newspaperwoman, Kay, if only for the excuse it gives you to seek out at once the object of any sudden passion."

Mother's physical problems were always dramatized, as were her emotional ones. As her attachment to Mann grew, so too did her emotional instability. The first overt evidence of a serious problem occurred the summer of 1937 at our ranch in Wyoming. My parents had picked me up that summer after I finished my courses in Chicago and took Ruthie and me to the ranch to spend some time there relaxing. It was a traumatic stay. Mother was going through a king-sized change of life, and, I suppose, depression exacerbated her already highly excitable state. She had started to drink noticeably by then.

One day, when we were all out for a ride in the beautiful valley, her horse ran away with her. Ruthie—an excellent rider, far better than I—was nearest to her and took out after her, as did the cowboys. Her horse was caught and somehow stopped, but something had snapped. It was an emotional explosion. She went completely to pieces, fought with my father, and generally retreated from him into her own cabin, where she started to drink seriously. We were all deeply disturbed.

My father could do nothing with her, and it fell to me to try to help her, to find out what was the matter and try to calm her down. The day after the runaway-horse scare, she climbed up a nearby mountain. I went after her, really worried about what she might do—she was so distraught—and finally caught up with her near the top, where we sat down and talked. Some of the time I talked while she wept. She had got so fervently involved with Mann and his writing that he seemed bound up in all her thoughts and feelings. When she talked, she concentrated on how wonderful he was, how much he meant to her, how brave and perceptive he was, how she understood him and could help him, what a terrible world it was in which he was an exile from his country and in which even people here in the United States didn't understand or appreciate him. Luckily, I could sympathize, so I was able to discuss—there, in the most incredible of settings—his writings and greatness with her, and eventually to calm her down enough to get her off the mountain. But for the rest of our stay on the ranch she remained more or less secluded, in bed or drinking but not communicating, especially not with my father.

From then on, I increasingly began to act as an adult, to help with Ruthie—still in high school at Madeira—and quite often with my mother. On a personal level, you had to sustain her, and very little came back in exchange. This was especially hard on Ruthie, who, being at home, was required to fit in with whatever Mother needed or wanted to do. Without realizing it, Mother was using Ruthie for company.

I found I actually enjoyed the responsibility and being of help. And during this time my father and I grew even closer. The fact that I shared his interest in journalism and public issues no doubt increased our closeness, but so did my helping with my mother's distress.

BY THE END of my first year at Chicago, I had decided I wouldn't return to Vassar but would stay on. I had found an intellectually stimulating academic environment, had developed wonderful friendships, had grown up significantly and enjoyed myself very much indeed. But I went on experiencing the usual angst about "who I was" and how to survive the great strength and influence of the family. I had occasional romantic flirtations—sometimes on my part, sometimes on a young man's, but rarely both at once. One of these attachments was a strange emotional relationship with a political scientist, Hal Winkler, who was much shorter than I but very intense and passionate. I was always attracted physically to brilliance, and he was brilliant—or so it seemed to me—but I was still shy and virginal and didn't know how to cope with sexual advances. I apparently went on looking a great deal more directed and together than I felt.

One of the most significant things to occur in the fall of my senior year was a visit from my sister Bis, who was then working in California. I was always excited at the prospect of seeing Bis, who had been in Europe, New York, and Hollywood while I was in Washington, Vassar, and Chicago. Her friends remained glamorous and even famous. In Europe, she had somehow grown friendly with Queen Marie of Romania and her daughter, Princess Illeana. In New York, she had been friendly with and even courted by the playwright Sam Behrman, and she saw a good deal of George Gershwin, Oscar Levant, and Harpo Marx, visited the famous Herbert Swope and his wife, and knew Alexander Woollcott, Dorothy Parker, and others of the Algonquin set. She had a serious romance with a movie producer whom she wanted to marry—an idea nixed by my mother, who thought it unsuitable. Mother once told me proudly how she had stopped Bis from going to Hollywood and marrying this young man. She said she went up to our family's New York apartment, where Bis was living, and argued with her for a week. Bis remained adamant until my mother said, "Bis, if you do this, it will kill your father." And that, said my mother with satisfaction, stopped her.

The visit Bis and I had in Chicago was extraordinary. We spoke at length about the complexity of being a member of this overwhelming Meyer family, of what it meant positively and negatively, and of what we both wanted to do with our lives. On the train, even as it was pulling out of the station, Bis began a long letter to me, so full of her essence and so full of insight into the family that I've kept it always. She wrote on November 20, 1937:

> I wish I had had time to talk about your own problems which in the light of my experiences seem very difficult and complicated. One of the hardest problems for all of us is the one which I believe is at the root of Flo's doings, and which I see little or no hope of her even realizing, let alone solving. That is the difficulty arising from the fact that from earliest childhood, we have all, through what is said and what is unsaid in the family circle, had the feeling that we were born to do big things! It was just a question of choosing the line best suited to us—hardly even the line we were best suited to! There was no question but that whatever it was we had to be best at it. Mother even used to say that, remember? "I don't care what any of you kids do—even if one of you should want to be an actress—just so you're the hell of a good actress!"
>
> We have all felt a compulsion to be terrific! And that is a dangerous thing.
>
> It is awfully hard for us really to give our best to something low, small, unimportant. We have lived so long at the top in every respect that it is hard to make ourselves really at home, with roots, at the bottom of the mountain. And that is the only way we will ever grow, if any of us do, to be able to climb under our own power.

It took me almost a month to reply, but when I did, it was a summation of what I was thinking about work, the family, the *Post*, and in particular my father. Bis kept my letter and returned it to me decades later:

> On the subject of Meyerdom, I have plenty to say, even though I don't pretend to understand it completely, either its causes or its effects. It can be compared, obviously enough, with an octopus whose tentacles stretch far and wide, and what is worst of all,

deep. In other words if you try to run from it you are apt to find it within. More concretely, this is the way it is working itself out for me at this point.

To begin somewhere in a circular situation, I think I want to go into the newspaper business. This is because I have certain political views which may or may not change combined with the fact that I like to write. . . .

Putting aside an unanswerable question at this time, my ability to be a good reporter, which is a gift given by God to a very few, I mean GOOD reporter, the fact remains that what I am most interested in doing is labor reporting, possibly working up to political reporting later.

As you can see, that is no help to Dad. He wants and needs someone who is willing to go through the whole mill, from reporting, to circulation management and problems, to editorial writing, and eventually to be his assistant. This presents the payoff in problems. One, I detest beyond description advertising and circulation and that is what a newspaper executive spends most of his time worrying about. Two, there is a question of point of view which would or might complicate things if I were to work under Dad. And three I doubt my ability to carry a load like the Washington Post, and four I know Dad needs a different kind of person, much more of an automaton under him, and five I damn well think it would be a first class dog's life. . . .

Discarding, finally, for a moment, the idea of ever having anything to do with the W. Post, there are more theoretical results to be questioned and tested. As I said long long ago at the beginning of this letter, Meyer tentacles clutch deep. From Dad's point of view, I think it would mean something; I may be flattering myself, but I think it would mean several things, such as companionship, a living connection with the next generation, and the knowledge that all that he was slaving to build was not going to stop with him.

From my point of view, it would be giving up a position that it is fair to say thousands would fight for, that is an influential position, in an influential paper in the capital of the world's most important country. Right now anyway. Besides that it would mean losing valuable help, company, and advice, which has already influenced me a great deal and which I respect highly. . . .

If I find for some reason that I am not fitted to do newspaper work, and this may happen as among other things, I function a little on the slow side, which is not good, I shall get out and consider it no disgrace. I don't think this is part of the success idea, because by fitted, I mean simply a competent, not scintillating job. Though that is made difficult by our heritage, I should think it could be worked out practically, though I can't tell from my present ivory tower window.

And someday I think I shall marry A MAN. That is because by nature I do not like to live alone. I like to live with somebody and if you live with someone it is nice to be married. So maybe I shall devote myself, as Flo always used to prophesy with hoots of mirth, to having sixteen small ones and bringing them up to be unsuccessful and rather animal in their desires, with as little as possible of that specialized human quality called the Rational. . . .

This letter seems to me to summarize who I was and what I was thinking after four years of college better than I can do it nearly sixty years later. I am puzzled that I had such reservations about working for my father, in view of the continuing conversations he and I were having about my education and career in journalism and the progress of the *Post*. I suppose the answer has to be that I was ambivalent, and maybe so was he, since he and I later both enthusiastically endorsed my husband's going on the *Post* and my going off to lead the life of wife, mother, and good works.

MY STAY at the University of Chicago—this "noble institution," as I referred to it to my parents—ended in early June of 1938. My marks throughout my tenure at Chicago were not as good—or as bad, in some cases—as they might have been. I didn't think it mattered, particularly since I felt I had learned a lot during my two years there. There seems to have been no discussion about my parents' coming to whatever graduation formalities there were. I don't believe I thought of graduation as a momentous event, but the fact that my parents didn't come has been built into a trauma in various accounts, in one of which I am portrayed as weeping. I can't, in fact, remember why they didn't come, and to tell the truth, I can't remember attending the graduations of my own children. Perhaps I inherited delinquency in this respect, or perhaps the sixties generation turned their backs on this kind of event.

We graduated in the beautiful Rockefeller-built chapel, the ceremony presided over by President Hutchins. And then, after partying with my friends, and with my formal education behind me, I left Chicago for Mount Kisco and a fairly uncertain future.

— *Chapter Six* —

W HILE I WAS home after graduating, my father suggested that I accompany him to California, land of his youth. I scarcely knew the California branch of my family, but I quickly fell in love with them, and with San Francisco as well—its beauty and its people, the civic feeling, the friendliness, the informality. Very soon I came to think that it would be wonderful to work in such a congenial atmosphere and beautiful environment, so I resolved to try to stay. I told my father that if he would help me find a job there, I would swallow my pride and give up a job I had earlier got for myself in Chicago.

There were four newspapers in San Francisco at that time. In the morning, the *Chronicle* was the predominant and most respected voice. The competition was Hearst's *Examiner*, the best and strongest Hearst paper of a then still-vibrant empire. The two afternoon papers exemplified typical old-fashioned razzle-dazzle street-sales journalism, bursting with huge headlines, late-breaking stories, and much more sex and crime than the morning papers. My father called his friend George "Deke" Parker of Scripps Howard, and it was on their paper, the *San Francisco News*, that he found me a two-month job. Our competitor in the afternoon was another Hearst paper, the *Call-Bulletin*.

I am surprised that my father didn't turn to his friends on the *Chronicle*, the better-known and more traditional paper, but the *News* turned out to be a great blessing for me, because it was a typically informal, understaffed, rowdy, scrappy, amusing afternoon tabloid—ideal for a beginner breaking in, since it afforded me opportunities I couldn't have had in a more structured, orderly atmosphere. But things didn't start out all that happily. I went to the city room knowing no one, and—worse—not knowing the elements of the job. I hadn't done much typing and certainly not much reporting. I didn't know the city or how to get around in it. Everything seemed so suddenly overwhelming. I sat down at my desk and was gripped by fear of failure, lost and defeated before I'd begun.

My father had stayed over a few days, and I went to his room one night and in tears told him that I was afraid I'd bitten off more than I could chew, that I felt unable to do the job and would be of little use to the paper, certainly not worth the $21 a week I was being paid, and that I wanted to go home with him. Dad said simply that everyone had to learn, that maybe I should take some more time before deciding to give up the job, and that if I wasn't worth the whole $21 a week now I'd be worth much more than that later, since I would gradually learn the things I was so discouraged about now. What persuaded me I'm not sure, but I agreed to stay, knowing I could always give up later.

Just one short month after my tearful desire to run away, my new life had become lots of fun. By mid-August, I was beginning to feel that there were more ups than downs. A touch of ambition was taking hold, and I could see further ahead than the next paragraph. I realized that not just the *News* but San Francisco itself was a good place for me to be starting work, since no one knew I was connected with newspaper big shots, and if some people did, they didn't care. Most people, in fact, had never heard of *The Washington Post*, and some, I suspected, hadn't heard of Washington.

On the job I was learning to write, or rewrite, from phoned-in news. It was still taking me too long to write, but my stories were appearing with fewer alterations by the editors on the callous city desk. I was also doing elementary jobs, like tracking down people for pictures. I even covered a bartenders' union convention. My first serious assignment was cooked up by some editor. The Women's Christian Temperance Union was meeting in town, and he suggested I lure some of the delegates to a bar with the simple proposition that they view the scene of the crimes they were railing against, and do a story on the visit. I duly got the deed done and written up.

After I had been on the job only a short time, my neighbor in the city room, Bob Elliott, the *News*'s experienced, professional labor reporter, leaned over and said that he had heard labor reporting interested me and asked if I would like to be his "legman," as it was then called, on two big issues he was covering—the growing confrontation on the waterfront involving a possible lockout of the Warehousemen's Union and a threatened retail-store clerks' strike against the city's department stores. I responded with a vigorous and enthusiastic assent, and thus began a long story that absorbed me for many weeks in the San Francisco waterfront and with many of the major figures involved in it.

At the time I began working on the lockout, the longshoremen and warehousemen—those who loaded and unloaded the ships and those who stored the goods from the port in the warehouses and removed them later—were organized into one big union, the International Longshoremen and Warehousemen's Union (ILWU). The distributors from all the industries, tired of being knocked over one by one and whipsawed against each other by this increasingly powerful union, got together and decided to exert their united front by locking out the ILWU so they could negotiate a master contract for the whole waterfront.

When a strike occurred at the Woolworth warehouse, the Distributors Association brought in a boxcar loaded by nonunion people and ordered it unloaded. The "hot car," as it came to be dubbed—meaning a railroad freight car loaded by strikebreakers—was sent up and down the waterfront, stopping at each warehouse, where the employees were asked to unload it. When the union members refused, they would either go out on strike or be "locked out" of work as a result.

One of my jobs as a reporter on this story was to follow the hot car on its journey along the waterfront, observe each warehouse on which it called and the ensuing work stoppage, and report back to Elliott. So my beat became the waterfront, and my ports of call were the ILWU, the Distributors Association, and the Pacific Coast Labor Bureau, another strong force in the picture. The bureau was a group of radical economists and professional negotiators for the unions, headed by Henry Melnikow. One of its ablest and toughest but most charming members was Sam Kagel, a highly successful negotiator for the ILWU, who had no love for newspaper people. Luckily for me, however, of all the papers covering the waterfront he disliked the *News* least, thinking it was the fairest of all the overtly antiunion press.

The ILWU was headed by Harry Bridges, the radical Australian immigrant who had led the violent longshoremen's strike in 1934. The warehousemen were headed by another very strong leader, Eugene Patton, one of a huge and authentic waterfront family, all of whom had grown up there and earned their living on the ships or around the harbor. Patton, or Pat, as he was known everywhere, was a wonderfully romantic figure. Smart, funny, and intuitive, though uneducated in any formal sense, he was a brave leader, and a charismatic one.

Each of these players said that I could make myself at home in his office and that if there were developments he would inform me. They all got together at the end of the day to trade information and unwind, usually at a bar at the foot of Sacramento Street, and I began going along. With Kagel, Patton, and occasionally Harry Bridges, I spent many hours up and down the waterfront in one of the twenty or more small, dark bars within a three-block area. We used to get boilermakers—a glass of beer and a shot of whiskey—at twenty-five cents each. If you bought two, you got the third one free—pretty heady stuff for a twenty-one-year-old.

We all became great friends. In fact—in a most unprofessional manner, I realize now—Pat and I became more than friends; he was an early romance of mine. We really liked each other—he was not only highly intelligent but very good-looking. Some weeks after we met, I realized that he was married. I also realized that he had a serious drinking problem. His courage and extraordinary leadership abilities revealed themselves during World War II, when, in the Battle of the Bulge, he was promoted from a private to an officer after all his officers had been killed and he took charge. Unfortunately, after the war he went on with his hard living and drinking, and eventually committed suicide by leaping off the Golden Gate Bridge.

I had carefully guarded my identity and was merely viewed by the labor leaders as the reporter from the *News* until my allotted time at the paper was about to expire. Patton had made some reference to future plans, and I said I wasn't sure I'd be there. "Why," he said, "are they going to fire you?" Not exactly, I responded, and then told them I had been hired only for two months at the request of my father, who was an Eastern publisher. They wanted to know who he was, of course, and what the paper was. When I told them, they were momentarily surprised and puzzled but accepted it, and we went on as usual.

It was lucky that they knew of my connection to the *Post*, because later Melnikow, a somewhat humorless and paranoid figure, said to them, "Be careful, we have a spy in our midst." Somehow he had found out that I was the daughter of a capitalist and therefore suspected I was a capitalist spy. Since I had already confessed, my pals were able to laugh and say, "Yes, it's all right, we know who she is."

There was no secret on the paper about my new friends, although the extent of our nightly forays was probably not known. I tried to be aboveboard. I told the paper and my family and felt I maintained objectivity in my reporting. Such behavior wouldn't be tolerated now: I shouldn't have been getting too close personally to one side of a dispute, no matter how useful my new friendships proved to the paper.

Things on the waterfront eventually came to an impasse and went into mediation, at which point the coverage scene changed to long waits outside the mediation-room door, with half a dozen of us sitting around for hours whenever we thought there might be a break. One day the principals were getting seated while the reporters were still inside the room. The night before had been the opening of the Opera, one of the biggest social events of the year in San Francisco, for which everyone dressed absurdly elaborately. I had been invited by my aunt and had sent east for my best dress from the previous year—it was long black velvet with leopard-skin shoulder straps forming a V in front and a lower one in the back. A photograph showing a large expanse of my back had appeared amidst the massive coverage of this event. Suddenly, to my consternation, Sam Kagel looked up and said to Bridges across the table, "Well, Harry, black velvet and leopard skin, what do you think of that?" Amidst peals of laughter from the table, I vanished.

After the lockout was over, I was assigned almost full-time to an even more important dispute from the point of view of the newspapers, the retail-store clerks' strike, which, like all San Francisco labor disputes, was long and violent and damaging to the economic prosperity of the community. By the time my two months on the paper were up, I was in the throes of all the excitement and wanted very much to stay on, but this was complicated by economic belt-tightening on all the papers due to linage losses caused by the retail-store strike. I wrote a troubled letter to my father asking for his advice on what to do next. He responded quickly by calling my boss, thanking him for the past weeks, and making it easy for him to close the incident. Happily, my boss said he wanted me to stay, that I was doing fine work, that they would be delighted to keep me permanently, and that my father had a right to feel proud of me. Dad said that from that point on I was there on my own, and I decided to stay until I thought the point of diminishing returns had been reached.

My social life in San Francisco was a curious but happy mix of my friends from work and the waterfront and the people I met through the family and a few old connections, each set of friends perfectly aware of the other. Through Aunt Ro, who with her wide range of artistic and civic interests had become a leader of the San Francisco community, I met Maurice Sterne, a fine artist, and his wife, Vera, and through them the Mexican artist Covarrubias, who was in San Francisco to do his murals for the upcoming Exposition. I went to the theater to see Gertrude Lawrence in *Susan and God* and then met her at a party given in her honor by Albert Bender, an elderly art-collector and bachelor friend of my aunt's, who became a friend of mine as well. It was Albert who gave Ansel Adams his first camera and Adams, the great photographer of Western scenery, and his wife, Virginia, were two other good friends out there. With Bill Hewitt, who ended up as the CEO of the John Deere Company, I went to Yosemite Valley to spend New Year's Eve with the Adamses, who were running a photography store there. The Adamses had only their guest bedroom, where I slept. Bill, amazingly handsome and tall, slept on a cot in the front display window of the studio, where they had hung curtains to shield their sleeping guest from passersby.

I had also become close to Jane Neylan, the most glamorous, interesting young woman friend I had ever had. Jane, the daughter of Hearst's lawyer and close associate John Francis Neylan, was far more worldly than anyone I had known, and I was more serious and work-oriented than most of her circle. We became friends almost instantly and have remained friends all our lives. I also saw a good deal of my friend from Madeira, Jean Rawlings.

Many Sundays, Aunt Ro and I went to Stern Grove for concerts and picnics. Aunt Rosalie had given the city this hillside grove of eucalyptus trees, which formed a natural amphitheater in which a concert stage was built and where she funded free Sunday-afternoon concerts. There were jars discreetly placed around the Grove for donations if you felt so inclined, and Aunt Ro used to stay after the concerts and count the contributions, which were a tangible measure of public appreciation.

In a funny way, I kept in touch with the world outside San Francisco through my parents. My father asked me to send him all my stories, even the most inconsequential ones, and urged me to keep writing him letters as another way of learning to write. It was also my father who kept me up on both domestic and international politics—he was especially worried about the growing anti-Semitism in Germany. One of his ways of helping to deal with the horror was to support a great friend of his, the psychiatrist Marion Kenworthy, with a legislative scheme to permit the adoption of twenty thousand refugee children.

What was more important for my personal future than his review of the domestic and international scene was my father's appraisal of what was happening at the *Post*. Although all the papers in Washington were down in linage, the *Times* and the *Herald* were suffering the most and the *Post* the least. Still, the *Star* had more than double our share of the advertising field. Dad was optimistic about circulation growth, as well he might have been with the *Post* making significant gains after a rather stationary period. We were at 117,000, and hoping to reach 125,000 before the rise abated. Although I rarely had time to read the whole paper, the *Post* did look better to me all the time.

My father's worries about the *Post* no doubt escalated in February 1939, when Cissy Patterson created one big all-day paper by combining the afternoon *Times* with the morning *Herald*, though first she had to settle a costly strike threat precipitated by all the people she was firing. Mother reported to me that Cissy was ill in bed and said, "I don't think she will last much longer"—a comment that I wasn't sure referred to Cissy herself or reflected Mother's wishful thinking about Cissy's newspaper.

Mother's life went on in its usual fashion. Her latest spiritual conquest was DeWitt Wallace, owner of the *Reader's Digest* and her next-door neighbor in Mount Kisco. She had met Anthony Eden and described him as a slender reed for democracy to lean on; in fact, she was struck by the lack of virility on the part of a number of the world's supposed leaders and concluded that if democracy was going to be saved, the United States would have to save it. She, like my father, was working hard to help get Jewish children to Palestine, or at least out of Europe. She was busy lecturing to women's clubs and actively speaking out against fascism.

Meanwhile, Thomas Mann remained the focus of much of Mother's energy throughout the late 1930s and early 1940s. Mann awed her, but she felt she surprised him a little, too. Somebody once asked him if my mother was German, to which he replied, "Oh, yes, very. She is a Valkyrian type with something else—a mixture of Valkyrie and Juno." She was so pleased with this description that she thought it ought to be put in writing for her grandchildren, so here it is.

The Manns often visited my parents in Washington and Mount Kisco. I met him on one of the early visits, in 1938, and was disappointed, for I thought him cold, unfeeling, and hard to talk to. But Mother worshipped him. She wrote me: "He is the biggest thing I ever met bar nothing." Though my father lived fairly amicably, and generally uncomplainingly, with most of my mother's male friends, he got rather tired of being left with Mann's wife while the two spouses went off into intellectual discussions, most often conducted in German.

She adored Mann openly, but he returned her adoration diffidently. Nonetheless, she still had the "feeling I am one of the few people and one of the *very* few women he has ever liked." In truth, the real passion seemed to be on her side only. Mann has been described by one of his biographers, Donald Prater, as a "cold nature" with a "complete lack of interest and of real feeling for others." According to Prater, Mann tended to exploit people for his personal convenience. He may well have cold-bloodedly maintained the relationship because knowing Mother—and taking advantage of her resources—proved of great help to him.

Indeed, Mother came to his rescue time and again. Over the years of their friendship, she did an immense number of favors for Mann and his family. She tried to make him more understandable to the American public by translating some of his essays and writing long reviews of his books, many of which appeared in the *Post*. In one letter to her he referred to the plethora of honors showered on him in the United States but said, in essence, that what he really needed was financial sustenance. Mother's immediate response was: "If my intellectual efforts are at your disposal, why not then every material resource I possess?" She swung immediately into action. Having already helped smooth the way for an academic berth for him at Princeton, a position that entailed little work and gave him time to write, she now got the Library of Congress, on whose board she served, to make him "Consultant in Germanic Literature," with a yearly stipend of $4,800. There were endless other courtesies, including help in acquiring passports for some of his children.

Prater describes my mother as wanting to become too much a part of Mann's life, and therefore becoming a burden and an irritant to him. Mann wrote at one point that he felt an "almost uncontrollable desire to give this woman tyrannizing me a piece of my mind"—which is just what he seems to have done in a frank letter he wrote her later, saying that he had "served" their friendship faithfully and with care:

> Serving is the very word. For years I have devoted to it more
> thought, nervous energy, work at the desk, than to any other rela-

tionship in the world. I have let you participate as well as I know how in my inner and outer life. On your visits I have read aloud to you for hours from new work no one else has seen. I have shown the most sincere admiration for your patriotic and social activities. But nothing was right, nothing enough. . . . You always wanted me different from the way I am. You did not have the humor, or the respect, or the discretion, to take me as I am. You wanted to educate, dominate, improve, redeem me. . . .

Theirs, like all of her relationships, was clearly a complicated one.

THREE THEMES dominated my own letters: the anguish of the impending war in Europe, my work, and my play. No matter how immersed I was in the latter two, it was hard to forget that so much hinged on events in Europe, even though Europe seemed much more remote from California than it had from the East Coast. I listened one morning to a speech by Hitler and wrote afterwards that "the broadcast sounded a little bit as though you had gotten the zoo by mistake—that rasping voice punctuated by roars that sounded like a pack of insane animals." The more serious the situation abroad became, the more I thought it important to work terribly hard to learn the game well. Not that I thought I or any individual could make a difference, but I thought I'd go mad if I wasn't doing as much as I could in my own little rut.

As the labor story wound down, I looked forward to writing again. The routine activities involved in being a legman and getting kicked around were lots of fun after the highly theoretical existence I'd been leading in Chicago, but I was ready to start becoming a reporter. Initially, I covered sob-sister stuff—a little girl whose Christmas tree had burned and to whom the *News* sent presents, a suicide off the Golden Gate Bridge, an interview with a woman who, in a fit of despondency because her husband didn't love her anymore, tried to choke her baby.

The news from Europe was crowded out of the San Francisco papers by a first-class sex murder with a beautiful blonde corpse. One brush with crime reporting came when I was sent out with a photographer to cover a distinctly unglamorous incident: a garbage truck emptying its contents at the city dump had turned up a corpse, a man who had been dead at least a week. My prayers were answered when the undertaker arrived just before we did, made off with the corpse, and saved me from the grisly spectacle. Not my story but that of another reporter was the discovery of a lady brutally murdered, her breasts cut off; across her torso, with her lipstick, had been written, "Honey, I love you." My mother sympathized with my assignments, deploring the way ugly things rest in the mind. In her inimitable fashion, she suggested I apply Schopenhauer's rule of objectivity: unhinge the will until you feel neither hate nor fear.

My progress at work was uneven, a series of ups and downs. Every once in a while I thought I was catching on to the art of writing a news story, yet, even when I felt I might be getting the hang of it in terms of speed and efficiency, the top still seemed so terribly far away. Efficiency was my special bugaboo. Every time I did something stupid, I could hear my French governess's voice resounding through the years, saying "*Etourdie, veux-tu mettre les accents?*"—"Scatterbrain, will you put on the accents?" Here I was, years later, still forgetting to put the accents on.

I feared getting scooped, but so far it hadn't happened. I went on worrying that I might be "hanging on," that I mightn't have been kept on if it hadn't been for my name, but then, thinking back to my first day, I remembered the hour it had taken me to write a three-line item and felt encouraged by having in just one day written two half-column stories, covered a wool growers' convention and a fire, and written the weekly church column that always got foisted on some poor sucker. The *News*, chronically short of staff, was particularly so while I was there, and I was always tired by evening, when I rode home on the cable car.

My final story for the paper was the opening of the Golden Gate International Exposition on San Francisco's Treasure Island, celebrating the new Golden Gate Bridge and the Oakland Bay Bridge. I covered the Exposition all day and went out at night with an architect friend, Bill Wurster, who had designed the Arts Building for it.

In the spring of 1939, my father came out to visit and reminded me that I had said I was going to come back to work on the *Post*. In fact, his visit came at a propitious moment. The *News* was going through yet another of its economy drives, and it seemed clear that someone would be let go, in which case I, the junior person, was the likely candidate. Besides, I was worried about taking someone's job who needed it. So I agreed with my father that I would return to Washington, not exactly reluctantly but not without mixed feelings and a certain sense of loss. I loved those months I spent in San Francisco as I have loved few times in my life.

On April 24, 1939, my photo appeared in *Time* magazine on the personalities page, with the brief story, "To Washington, D.C., went comely, 21-year-old Katherine [sic] Meyer, daughter of publisher Eugene Meyer, to handle for $25 a week the 'Letters to the Editor' department of her father's Post. Said Father Meyer: 'If it doesn't work, we'll get rid of her.' " Some of my San Francisco friends, with Kagel in the lead, sent me the clip with a note: "There are no ifs in California. Come back to us."

— *Chapter Seven* —

COMING BACK TO Washington after nearly five years away—at college and in San Francisco—I found a new city. I had no idea how much Washington had changed since I'd left for Vassar. There was an intellectually exciting atmosphere, a sea-change from the Washington I had left behind in 1934. I was happily surprised—indeed, thrilled—by this new city, alive with energetic, dynamic young people. From the stodgy town I'd known, where a small group of older people were the "establishment" and saw each other constantly at very formal dinners and the young people were set in a different but equally boring routine, there had sprung a young person's ideal place.

There have been two periods in my lifetime when the excitement of government and of public issues drew to Washington many of the bright young people graduating from colleges and law schools. These were essentially the Roosevelt and the Kennedy years. In the time I'd been mostly gone, large numbers of these able, idealistic young men and women had come to town ready to help institute reforms, to get the economy working again, to guarantee certain benefits to those without jobs, or Social Security to those in retirement, or minimum wages to those with low-paying jobs. It was a moment when youth could accomplish a lot, when ideas percolated up and were listened to by those in authority.

Against this backdrop, in April of 1939 I went to work on the *Post*. I felt it unwise to try to be a reporter back in Washington, since it would be awkward being the publisher's daughter, so it was agreed that I would become an editorial-page employee—work that was very different from what I had been doing in San Francisco. I now worked for the editorial-page editor, Felix Morley. The editorial team, with me quite the junior member, met every morning to discuss the issues of the day. Assignments were made based on an individual's particular expertise, Morley saving the biggest domestic and international issues for himself.

By 1939, the president's energies were concentrated on uniting the country on events abroad. This meant abandoning most of the New Deal programs except for those already in place, so the *Post*'s editorials and news began to be more in sync with the administration. The paper fiercely backed preparedness in this country. As early as April 1939, when Roosevelt casually said as he was leaving Warm Springs, Georgia, "I'll be back in the fall if we don't have a war," the *Post*'s editorial page led with: "In using the collective 'we,' the President told Hitler and Mussolini . . . that the tremendous force of the United States must be a factor in their current thinking." Roosevelt told reporters that this so represented his thinking, "he had almost fallen out of bed" when he read it.

On September 1, 1939, the day the German Army invaded Poland, Barnet (Barney) Nover—one of my editorial colleagues—and I went together to President Roosevelt's press conference in the Oval Office. The fact that he *could* take me, an unaccredited journalist, to the White House now seems amazing. At that time, the president's press conferences generally consisted of a small group of (mostly) men standing around the president's desk listening to him talk, bantering, and asking a few questions.

On this day, it was a larger and more solemn group. Barney and I were there early and so were fairly close to the president's desk. In his diary, Barney noted the tone of the meeting:

> There was a tense feeling of sobriety and solemnity at the conference. The President made a very good impression. When we left Kate said she couldn't help being impressed by him and I said that whatever his faults, Roosevelt was superb in an emergency.

By this time the strain between Morley's view that we must stay out of the war, and my father's opposite view that we had to help the Allies and, if necessary, get in, reached a climax. Morley resigned the following spring, and it was announced in August that he would become president of Haverford College. My friends and I were all exultant that the rift had finally caused Morley to depart—so committed were we all to helping the Allies. Being young, we couldn't understand why it had taken my father so long to see the light.

The transition, however, was fairly smooth. My father first tried to hire Elmer Davis, a popular news-radio broadcaster, but in the end he settled for a recommendation of Morley's—Herbert Elliston, financial editor for *The Christian Science Monitor*. As Morley had done, Elliston carried the page to greater and greater strength.

IN MY FIRST year or so at the *Post*, I began to write with some frequency on the least important issues—so-called light editorials. The titles themselves are revealing of just how light: "On Being a Horse," "Brains and Beauty," "Mixed Drinks," "Lou Gehrig," and "Spotted Fever." I wrote about folk songs inspiring American soldiers; about women mobilizing for defense work; and defended Archibald MacLeish, Librarian of Congress, from accusations of being a "fellow traveler." I wrote a book review of a book by Klaus and Erika Mann, *Escape to Life*, and was unmercifully teased by my friends for the bromidic opening phrase "It is no easy task Klaus and Erika Mann have set themselves. . . ."

I also edited the "Letters to the Editor," made up parts of the page, which involved numerous trips to the composing room on the floor below our offices, where printers put the hot-lead rows of type into page forms on dollies as I watched. One of us proofread the page each night, as well as the opinion page, which contained syndicated columns along with some contributed by *Post* reporters and editors. I took my turn at this. Around the time of the changeover from Morley to Elliston, I moved over to the "Brains" section—today's "Outlook"—and worked for a year there.

I soon began to meet many of the *Post*'s reporters and to deepen my friendship with others. We occasionally left our dingy, run-down, but picturesque building to lunch at Childs or other little neighborhood restaurants on E Street. I quickly fell in with two young reporters whom I hadn't previously known, John Oakes, nephew of Arthur Sulzberger, then the publisher of *The New York Times*, and Hedley Donovan, a young, bright Minnesotan, handsome, soft-spoken, and very funny. He had been a Rhodes Scholar, then returned from England and got a job with the *Post*. John, also a Rhodes Scholar, later became editorial-page editor of *The New York Times*, and Hedley became editor-in-chief of Time Inc.

Because of my friendship with *Post* reporters like John and Hedley, my work world spilled over into a social life that grew lively and rich in very short order. There were legions of young men in Washington who grouped together to live in houses, which proved to be cheap, attractive, and advantageous to all those rooming cooperatively. Most of these men were on modest government salaries, but by pooling their resources they lived like kings. Hedley lived at one of these bachelor houses, located on S Street near Connecticut Avenue, where I went to a party one night in the fall of 1939. We all went to a nearby restaurant for dinner, and a few of us got back to S Street before our fellow diners. I was looking out the window, calling to the others, when the screen fell out, right onto the heads of those returning, one of whom was Philip Graham, whom I met for the first time that night when he looked up to see me staring down with my mouth agape.

Later that same evening, I went to a bathroom upstairs and there ran into a girl named Phyllis Asher, who said she was going to law school, which at that time was very unusual for a woman. I exclaimed with admiration, saying that I couldn't possibly do it and asking how she managed the difficult work. "Well," she replied, "it's made easier because I'm engaged to Phil Graham." She said Phil would come by for her at night and, over a milkshake, they would discuss anything that was on her mind, and this helped. "Oh, how wonderful," I replied, thinking only that he was the one I had just nearly maimed by dropping a screen on his head.

When the S Street house became too crowded, a second house was found into which some of the S Street residents moved, together with some others. This second house was in Arlington, five minutes away from the Virginia end of Key Bridge. It was essentially those with automobiles who moved to this house.

Hockley, as the house was called, belonged to Admiral and Mrs. Theodore Wilkinson, whose daughters were friends of the boys. When Admiral Wilkinson left Washington for the duration of the war, the Wilkinsons bravely rented the house for very little money to twelve young men. John Oakes and Deering Danielson, a wealthy young man who worked in the State Department and whose family owned *The Atlantic Monthly*, were the only nonlawyers among the Hockley boys. The lawyers included Graham Claytor, who had been Louis Brandeis's law clerk; Adrian Fisher, known as Butch, a Tennessean who had clerked for both Brandeis and Felix Frankfurter; gentle, sweet Bill Sheldon, who was the most beloved by us all; Quinn Shaughnessy, who became a friend of mine that fall; Edwin McElwain, one of Chief Justice Hughes's two law clerks; the star, Edward Prichard, known to all as Prich, Felix Frankfurter's law clerk that year, a brilliant, talented, funny, fat, witty storyteller and mimic, as well as a marvelous conversationalist; and Prich's great friend Phil Graham, then clerking for Supreme Court Justice Stanley Reed while waiting to clerk for Frankfurter the following year. Two of these boys—Graham Claytor and Phil Graham—together with Ed Huddleson, who had stayed behind at the S Street house, had successively been editors of the *Harvard Law Review*, then the most prestigious collegiate job in the country, closely rivaled only by the editorships of the *Yale* and *Columbia Law Review*s.

Hockley itself had probably been built at the turn of the century. It was made of red brick and had four white pillars on a veranda overlooking a lawn that rolled down toward the nearby Potomac River. The house commanded a magnificent view of the river and the city just across it. It was like a secondhand Tara from *Gone With the Wind*. There was a huge living room, and a dining room that could seat about twenty people that was almost always full. There was also a library on the ground floor, and there were at least six bedrooms upstairs.

Because they pooled their resources and the rent was low to begin with, the boys almost certainly would never again live so well for so little. They had a gardener and a full-time cook and a maid and, most important, they had Johnson, the all-American equivalent of a major-domo. Johnson and his wife had worked for Dean and Alice Acheson for at least twenty-five years, until the day Alice discovered they had never actually gotten married and sent them packing, much to Dean's dismay. This happened just when Hockley was being rented, and the boys were able to snag Johnson, who ran this new chaotic household with aplomb.

Life for me fell into a glorious pattern, largely centered on Hockley. An extraordinary assembly of guests gathered there, including Dean Acheson, Archibald MacLeish, Felix Frankfurter, Ben Cohen, Francis Biddle, and various other New Dealers, Harvard professors, and judges and justices, sometimes even for breakfast.

Four of us spent so much time there we became known as Hockley's "house" girls: Alice Barry, Anne Wilkinson, Jane Acheson, and myself. There were many others, but we became natural adjuncts of the house. Sometimes we would all meet at Hockley and move on to my parents' country house, farther out in Virginia, or we'd go en masse to the Edward Burlings' log cabin for Sunday brunches.

No topic was taboo at Hockley. Everything from FDR and the New Deal to communism, Hitler, the rising tide of Nazism, civil rights—all issues and events were discussed in great debates that often went on for days on end. Graham Claytor recalled that in arguments they could manage to get two or three, sometimes even four sides to any issue on the table. Insults were hurled as a matter of course. It was understood that the abuse and indignities, even *ad hominem* attacks, were fair weapons in arguing for your position, but in truth there were no real feuds or solid dislikes, despite the wide variety of political opinion. John Oakes and Prich, for example, stood at opposite ends of the scale of social decorum and belief about rules of the political game. John, a journalist, believed in impartiality as the correct approach to an understanding of the issues. He was, of course, accused by the ultraliberals of seeing both or all sides of everything.

Prich and Phil, in a perverse mood of ultraliberalism, at one time during that winter defended the Russians for invading Finland, cause for very violent continuing arguments, in the course of which even their liberal housemates abandoned them. Prich and Phil were, indeed, very liberal, but they also enjoyed espousing unpopular causes. They had sympathy with the Soviet Union, but in the case of Finland they were essentially pushing the argument more for the exercise than from belief. They were in no real sense procommunist.

There were also many moments of wild hilarity at Hockley. Among his other skills, Johnson made excellent mint juleps, an art that was exercised plentifully at a party one spring. A properly made julep tastes deceptively mild, but it is more or less straight bourbon, weakened only by mashed ice and mint. If it's a hot day and you toss off several, you're headed for trouble. At this party, a Harvard Law School professor, at that time an older man—by our youthful standards—of thirty-three, was a guest. He was planning to return to Boston that night and asked if someone would give him a ride to the station in time to catch the ten-thirty train. We agreed to do just that, but by eight-thirty no one could find him—he had disappeared. The professor was known to be one of those who hadn't been adequately warned about the juleps, and it was established that he had innocently downed about six of them and had last been seen wandering around the grounds of Hockley calling "cheers" to everybody. Sometime after he came up missing, screams were heard from the parking lot and one of the young lady guests came rushing back to the house distraught. She had gotten into her car only to find a naked man in the back seat. Everyone hurried to the rescue, to find the professor, five feet six and two hundred pounds with little muscle, out cold in the back seat without a stitch on. He was revived with a bucket of water. His story was that, as time passed, he thought, "Gee, it must be time for me to be getting on the train," so he wandered out to the parking lot, climbed into the back seat of the nearest car, decided he was in his sleeping berth, and promptly undressed and sacked out. Things like that seemed to happen all the time at Hockley.

MY YOUNGER SISTER, Ruth, was being given a tea at Thanksgiving that year as part of her debut. I was trying to help her manage, because she was still somewhat young for her age and very shy, and suggested inviting all the boys from Hockley and S Street to the tea dance at my parents' house. Bis had turned up for the event, carrying with her the glamorous aura of New York as well as her own innate spark. She was a star at the party, of course; all the boys thought she was wonderful, particularly Prich, who was captivated. In fact, he developed a crush on Bis and began rushing to New York to see her.

I viewed this development with no small measure of concern. I had considered this wonderful group of young men "my turf," and here was Bis stepping onto it—the sister who always left me feeling inadequate and envious. In the crowd at the party, I bumped into Phil Graham, whom I hardly knew, and complained facetiously about all the excitement created by Bis. "I think I'll begin to introduce her as, 'This is my sister Bis, who is four years older than I am,'" I said.

"Yes," he responded, "and of course you'll add, 'And *I'm* getting along.'" It was typical Phil repartee, and I thought he was pretty funny. By this time Phil had parted company with Phyllis Asher and had moved on to my friend Alice Barry. She was from an old Washington family, brought up to take certain traditional steps in society: have a debut and get married, which she later did to the wealthy Oakley Thorne. In the meantime, there were lots of jokes about Phil and Alice, who had become a twosome and, indeed, had simultaneously developed cases of poison ivy.

Actually, through Prich's friendship with Bis I came to know Prich better, too. After he stopped chasing my sister in New York, he and I became closer friends, and he even developed a minor and very temporary interest in me. My relationship with him always remained a great privilege, but with sad overtones. Prich was well known throughout Washington and even beyond. He was widely talked about and written about as a future governor of Kentucky, or even president, so great were his political acumen, understanding of public issues, and sense of people. In the end, he may have had too much charm and talent for his own good. Along with all his assets, he had fatal liabilities. He had no discipline or self-control. He left his work undone, his bills unpaid. His friends—and Phil was one of the closest—even finished his work for him on occasion. One weekend during the time when Prich was clerking for Frankfurter and Phil for Reed, Prich went to see Bis and overstayed his leave. Phil completed his work for him on the Court.

Prich accepted endless hospitality, seldom reciprocating. When he did take friends to a restaurant, he often found he had forgotten his wallet, and someone else had to pay the bill. Bill Sheldon once lamented that Prich's friendship at Princeton, where they were undergraduates together, cost him about $900 a year—a large sum for those days, when few young people had any money—but, added Bill, it was worth it. Even my parents were charmed by Prich, but ultimately they, too, became impatient with his constant acceptance of their hospitality without ever writing a thank-you note or displaying normal civility.

Bis decided to give a New Year's party at my mother's Virginia house. She told me I could invite a few of the Hockley boys, including the "flat-faced" one, referring to Phil Graham. The party was a great success, with lots of laughter and the usual loud, raucous arguments. At one point, I found myself seated on a bench next to Phil, whom I knew probably the least of all the boys, and was startled when he turned to me, looked at my sister Bis, and asked, "Are we for her?"

This question was typical of Phil in several respects. It was instant penetration of the human armor. It cut through formalities and reached you directly. It created a sort of charmed circle, enclosing you and him in an intimate association. And it asked a central and real question. Typically, his question elicited a frank answer in which I said everything I felt about Bis, including the ambivalences—the admiration and the envy—but the bottom-line answer was, "Yes, we are for her." Suddenly, with just one question asked and answered, Phil and I knew each other. The last of us to leave the party piled into the remaining car, and I found myself on Phil's lap the whole way to town, getting to know him even better.

A couple of weeks later, early in the new year of 1940, I was invited by Prich to Sunday lunch at the Ritz Carlton. There were several of us, and after we had lunched as long as we could, someone suggested driving to the scene of the happy New Year's party, the Cabin, and we spent the afternoon there. At the end of the day, everyone except Phil and me had engagements, so he asked if I wanted to have dinner. We went to a little-known restaurant, had a long dinner, talked and laughed a lot, and drank until quite late, when he took me home. I enjoyed it, but I also realized that we had been the only two without dates, and that he had asked me for that reason. So I still felt a reserve.

Phil called me once or twice, and carried on in his usual irreverent, breezy way. I found him captivating. By then, Alice Barry and he had gone their separate ways. I've always thought she was too proper to have ever considered Phil seriously, but in the earliest days at Hockley she asked me if I knew him. When I said no, not really, she said, "You ought to; he's the best here."

The second week in February, Phil called me at work late one afternoon suggesting we have dinner with one of his college roommates, George Smathers, and his wife, Rosemary. I said I couldn't, for several reasons. It was my night to proofread the editorial and op-ed pages, and on top of that I didn't feel well and feared I was getting the flu. In addition, I wasn't dressed for dinner. I looked as rotten as I felt, in a simple brown wool dress, cotton stockings, and loafers. So I was firm in my regret.

Phil was equally firm in his insistence. He pointed out that we would eat at Harvey's, a famous old seafood restaurant next door to the Mayflower, where we could buy the early edition of the *Post*. He would help me proofread the pages and we could call in the corrections. It didn't matter how I looked, he persisted, and no doubt this dinner would chase away all my symptoms, which, in any case, were not preventing me from working. So I gave in and joined him after making up the pages, embarrassed and discomfited when I walked in to find George and Rosemary Smathers looking incredibly handsome and impeccably dressed for the occasion. The evening, however, was fine and fun. Phil drove me home, and we talked for a long time. He told me that he loved me and said we would be married and go to Florida, if I could live with only two dresses, because I had to understand that he would never take anything from my father or be involved with him and we would live on what he made.

My breath was taken away. I was, to put it mildly, startled. This was a little ahead of where I was, but not that much ahead. I agreed that it sounded like quite a good idea, but perhaps a bit rash, and that we should put the idea of marriage on hold for all of a month or so while we deliberated and considered. Phil agreed to the month's delay.

It all seems so odd in retrospect. A fast month of deliberate hesitation passed, and in reality it hardly occurred. It seemed to be a given to both of us that, although we were trying to be discreet, things were moving forward. In fact, the night of the Smathers dinner, Phil, whistling happily, had returned to the room at Hockley he shared with Prich. Prich, already long in bed, turned over, looked at Phil, and in the throes of his momentary crush on me, said, "You son of a bitch, you've got her." Prich went into a month-long pout—a real anger, during which he once threw his drink at us. He finally emerged as our best man.

Despite my hesitation, the fact is I was charmed and dazzled. And I was incredulous—this brilliant, charismatic, fascinating man loved me! Even in my excitement over the sudden and unexpected development, and quite apart from his magnetism, I saw at once that the combination of qualities I had hoped for in any possible man had surprisingly and actually come together in this one. Here was someone who combined for me the two parts of my life that I thought were inescapably separate. For the first time I had found a man who was that right mix of intellectual, physical, and social charm, and warm and funny on top of that. Phil was bright, issue-oriented, hardworking, witty, and, to me, amazingly good-looking, with his leanness and angularity making him much more interesting and appealing to me than classic good looks. He loved me, and I loved him. It was incredibly exciting.

The morning after our proclamations of love, my worst flu fears were realized: I had a roaring temperature and was unable to get out of bed. The doctor was called and told me to stay quiet. It was Valentine's Day, and Phil sent a funny bouquet of yellow daffodils and red tulips with a Cupid and an arrow, followed by a phone call, asking, "Has the vet been there?" Although the vet had ordered solitary confinement, the sender arrived in the late afternoon and sat on my bed for hours as we talked and talked.

That month my mother was away with Bis in Nassau. Phil came and went, either visiting or picking me up often enough to cause my father to be suspicious about us. He and I were traveling to New York, talking about young men and what their current interests were. I told him that the young men I knew were mostly lawyers, many of them doing government work. He asked me who was the most interesting of these, and I naturally began describing Phil, without altogether considering what I was doing. I must have made quite an impression with my characterization, because my father asked, "Are you serious?" The agreed-on month was not over, but I said yes, I thought I was. My father promptly said that in that case he would like to know Phil and asked me to invite him to dinner. I was surprised I had waded into this, but didn't blame my father for his natural curiosity. I called Phil, confessed the conversation, and asked if he minded being looked over. With some trepidation he agreed. He made no bones about regarding my father as a wealthy ogre who might want to entangle an unsuspecting young son-in-law in his tentacles. He had never before encountered this kind of wealth and power and was darkly suspicious.

I asked two other friends to dinner also, to make things impersonal and less intense. Phil arrived, and one of the first things my father did was to show him an old cartoon by the *Post*'s talented cartoonist, Gene Elderman. It had to do with Justice Hugo Black, who in the course of his confirmation hearings had been revealed as once having been a member of the Ku Klux Klan. There was a figure of Black on the Court in Klan robes, with the title "Reform of the Judiciary." Phil's response was, "Well, that's a very good drawing and a clever one, but I disagree with its message. I happen to think Justice Black is one of the ablest and hardest-working members of the Court and one of its finest minds."

The room was almost enveloped in smoke. My heart sank as the arguments grew louder and longer, continuing most of the evening. When the guests finally left, I said morosely to my father that it seemed to have been an unfortunate occasion. "What do you mean?" my father inquired. "I had a wonderful time and liked him fine." I breathed a sigh of relief and informed Phil that he had passed.

My mother returned from her trip a few evenings later and joined the family in time for dinner. She was describing her trip when my father interrupted her to say, "We are having champagne for dinner." "Fine," she replied, and went on talking. "Don't you want to know why we are having champagne for dinner?" my father persevered. Without a moment's pause, she looked up and asked excitedly, "Cissy's gone out of business?"

"No," said my father. "Kay's engaged to be married."

"Oh," said my stunned mother, "to whom?"

This whole whirlwind romance had essentially occurred while she was gone. Typically, I had told her nothing about Phil. Equally interesting, my father hadn't picked up the phone and called her. She had met Phil only in large crowds of young people and didn't remember him, so we had another "look-me-over" lunch with my mother, after which I saw Flo in New York. She asked, "Who is this guy you are marrying? Mother says he has a fine jawline."

One important thing didn't happen. There had been a lot of parental disapproval of both my older sisters' suitors at various stages. I felt hopeful that my parents would like Phil, but it never occurred to me to be influenced by what they thought, whereas both Flo and Bis had been dis-suaded from marrying people they loved.

WHO WAS this young man who had so suddenly entered all our lives? Where had he come from? His father, Ernest Graham, was born in Croswell, a small town in northern Michigan. He was the heart of integrity and can-do earthiness—a man with a gruff, appealing quality, hardworking and de-termined, interested in public issues and politics. And he was shy, hiding his emotions beneath a stern exterior.

Phil's mother, Florence Morris, was born in Lincoln, Nebraska, and had been a schoolteacher in South Dakota, despite not being a college graduate. "Floss," as she was called, was by all accounts an extraordinarily charming, strong, intelligent, and sensitive partner who stood up to Ernie even at the cost of angry rows that ensued when she did so. These affected Phil strongly; he couldn't bear anger or arguments or confrontations. His father had once, he told me, thrown a lamp at his mother in the course of a battle. In one of the first quarrels we ever had, during which I slammed a door, he said he couldn't deal with that kind of scene, because of ones he had witnessed as a child, and pleaded that we never fight like that, so I didn't. This wasn't a good idea and led to many unresolved issues. Having a "no-fight" rule meant that I didn't bring up things that disturbed me, and neither did Phil—an unhealthy situation in which things that upset one or the other of us didn't get aired.

Floss was loved and admired by all who knew her. She made friends, always reaching out to the world, even in the impoverished and almost pi-oneering circumstances in which the Grahams lived during the depths of the Depression in Florida. It was very much to his mother that Phil re-lated and to whom he felt most close. Phil was in some ways a mother's boy. He was nurtured and enriched by Floss—she was the cultured one, the reader, as well as the social, friendly one.

Phil was born in 1915, in Terry, South Dakota, where his father was then working as a gold-mining engineer. He was the second child born to Ernie and Floss, two years after his sister, Mary. The Grahams lived in a house on the side of a mountain in the Black Hills until Ernie went into the army in 1917. The war had caused the price of gold to drop until the mine was no longer profitable to operate, so when Ernie got out of the army, he returned to Croswell and operated a couple of dairy farms there for two years. Through a friend, Ernie heard about an attempt by the Pennsylvania Sugar Company to grow sugar cane in the Everglades. George Earle, Sr., the company's owner, had gone to Florida after the war and bought several hundred thousand acres of land in or around the Everglades from outside Miami to Lake Okeechobee, envisioning draining the swamps and ending up with rich usable soil. He wanted his company, Pennsuco, to grow sugar cane on it for its refinery in Philadelphia. The Florida project was costing a lot and producing nothing; this friend of the Grahams, who was the general manager of Pennsuco, wanted someone with an agricultural and engineering background to come down and look it over, and he asked Ernie to take the job. Ernie went to Florida and was asked to stay on the plantation as the resident manager. So in 1921 the Graham family moved to the Everglades, about fifty miles outside Miami. The area was still a wilderness, with no houses and only a few shacks. The only other inhabitants were Seminole Indians.

The Grahams built houseboats on a couple of barges moored to the sides of one of the main canals that laced the Everglades. They lived on one and used the other as a guest house, and there they stayed until 1924, when Phil's brother, Bill, was born. Bill was actually born on the houseboat, but Floss had said that if she was going to have a baby she needed a house, so about six months later the family moved to a solidly built rock farmhouse.

Phil's memories of his early childhood were romantic. He described alligators sunning themselves on the ropes that anchored the houseboat, and portrayed himself and his friends as jumping overboard to swim in the canal. His best friend was Charlie Tigertail, a Seminole Indian whose brother was killed by a white man. The Indians would often take Mary and Phil in their dugout canoes up and down the canal. Charlie and other Seminoles taught Phil to hunt and fish—two passions that remained with him throughout his life. Years later, at our farm in Virginia, he would go fishing late and early and sometimes even all night. He had quail patches and bird dogs, and relentlessly pursued groundhogs with rifles that had telescopic sites.

There in the Everglades the Grahams hung on and eventually triumphed over the wilderness, the hurricanes that then regularly swept through, and the 1929 Crash. First, however, it was discovered that the experiment with the sugar cane was not working. After a hurricane struck in 1926 and flooded the entire area, the company gave up on sugar and, under the name Pennsuco Farming Company, took up large-scale truck farming, investing millions of dollars over the next few years, before Mr. Earle got discouraged and retreated completely, leaving Ernie with some of the land as a sort of severance.

Ernie looked around for a way to earn his living and decided to develop the small dairy that had been set up on the place to serve the Pennsuco employees. By early 1932, the Grahams were delivering two loads of milk a day to a friend with a small chain of grocery stores. Ernie had made a deal to supply milk for two cents a quart under the home-delivery price. From that he began to build some routes, and the dairy grew. His trucks went into Miami every day to buy and bring back blocks of ice, and Phil was taken to school by the ice trucks—if the ice house moved, Phil moved too, to a school nearby. Because of his precocity, he had started school in the third grade in Hialeah. When the teacher found out he couldn't read and was going to put him back a grade, his mother taught him to read so quickly he was able to stay on. Phil was always the youngest and smallest in his class, and therefore socially behind the others. Mrs. Graham worried about his friends when he was young. One was the son of a wealthy Cadillac dealer and had too much money, while another was the son of a "decoy," a lady who sat on the back of a rumrunner knitting, to make it look like a pleasure boat or yacht.

Mainly, the Grahams were poor and had a difficult struggle. The Depression had hit Florida particularly hard. At Christmas, Phil's mother saw that every child in the area got at least one present. She would go to a local store and spend a dime for each present; these gifts were all that many of those children had. Phil recalled that it was a good week when his family saved a quarter for the Saturday-night movie. His brother Bill remembers that the common wages they paid were twenty cents an hour for a ten-hour day. Until World War II, "we worked a seven-day week in the dairy. No days off and no vacations. We'd feed the cows early on Sunday so we'd get off early Sunday afternoon." Eventually, the farm employed about fifty young single men, but even with the low wages and endless work, there were all kinds of people working there—including one Rhodes Scholar and several other college graduates.

With the farm operating fairly successfully, Ernie got involved in politics and spent years in public life, first on the State Road Board, later as state senator—years in which he campaigned for taxing the racetracks and using the funds to subsidize aid for older citizens. He wound up running for governor in 1943–44, suffering a narrow defeat. No one had ever been elected to state office from Dade County, which includes Miami and was unpopular with the rest of the rural state. Ernie almost beat the odds.

From school in Hialeah, Phil went on to high school in Miami. Years later he told me he had developed his wit and humor as a way to deal with his younger-boy social and athletic disadvantages and compete with boys in his class who were older and more sophisticated. His high-school yearbook notes his selection as the wittiest in the class. Toward the end of his life, he acknowledged to me that he used humor as a weapon with which to keep people at a distance.

Phil went from Miami High School to the University of Florida, where the boys with whom he roomed were athletes and politicians, including George Smathers, who later became a U.S. senator. In college Phil enjoyed fraternity life, and girls, and he drank a good deal of bathtub

gin before Prohibition was repealed. He ran Graham's Dairy in the summers, when his family went on vacations to Michigan, which Ernie still
thought of as home.

In 1934, when Phil was nineteen, his mother died of cancer—one of
the great tragedies of his life. He was devastated; he had loved her deeply
and was dependent on her love of him. He was so reluctant to talk about
her that it was years before I realized this. He later confessed that he had
cried himself to sleep night after night in college after she died.

Phil was kept out of school to work on the farm the year his mother
was dying, and this year driving milk trucks, plus the summers running the
farm, undoubtedly taught him how to get along with all kinds of people,
those who worked for him and with him as well as the customers whom he
had to please. He was also influenced by the battles that resulted from the
differences between him—with his pleasure-loving gaiety and tendency to
drink—and his hard-driving, teetotaler father.

Another great influence on Phil was an older man, a friend of his parents—one of several mentors in Phil's life. W. I. Evans was a lawyer who
was also involved in politics, and during her final illness, Phil's mother had
discussed with Mr. Evans, who was also the Grahams' lawyer, her desire
that Phil go to law school. In response to Floss's question about the "best"
law school, he said it was Harvard, so her dying wish, expressed to Phil
and, more important, to Ernie, was that Phil go there.

When the time came, his father said he couldn't afford to send Phil to
any law school. But at the last minute he changed his mind. Since it was
so late in the school year, Phil tried for the University of Michigan Law
School, which turned him down. His father then turned to Claude Pepper, already in Florida politics and a graduate of Harvard Law, and Pepper
succeeded in getting Phil admitted. It was easier in those days, when Harvard had a simple method of winnowing out its students: it took one-third
more than it had room for and dropped the lowest third around Thanksgiving. In fact, when the new first-year students arrived, the faculty and
administrators said to the freshman class assembled, "Look to the right of
you and look to the left of you, because by Thanksgiving one of you won't
be here." A young man named Philip Norton, later a friend of Phil's, said
he turned to the left of him and saw this young guy in a badly cut country
suit, looking as though he had straw hanging out of his rather large ears,
and decided that Phil was the one who wouldn't be there.

Harvard Law School was a unique institution at that time. The boys
there—and they were all boys then, with one or two exceptions—were either the brightest brains from the Ivy League or the brightest from
CCNY, the New York City public college that had graduated Felix Frankfurter. Phil fell into neither category, but his unusual qualities and brains
continued to serve him well. He always had an astonishing memory, an

ability to read quickly and remember what he'd read, and he used all that to good advantage. Phil never changed his basic ways—he went on hanging out at the races and in bars. Even so, he did well and thrived in the new environment. At the end of the first year, he was afraid that the all-important final exams had done him in. He told his father he had let him down after his sacrifice in sending him to law school: he thought he might have flunked. When his marks arrived, his father said, "I guess you didn't flunk. It says here you were third in your class."

From that position Phil made the *Law Review* and, at the end of his second year, became its president. This was undoubtedly one of those crucial events that make all the difference in a person's life. It brought him a new intellectual stimulus, it taught him a lot, it raised his profile from fairly invisible to very visible, and it introduced him to Felix Frankfurter, one of the great influences on his life.

Two young men were ahead of Phil as potential presidents of the *Review*. Their rivalry succeeded in defeating both of them and creating a deadlock, so in the small hours of the morning the editors turned to Phil, who was relatively unknown and belonged neither to the grinds nor to the Ivy League elite. Prich later said they went and hauled Phil out of a bar and made him president of the *Law Review*.

Soon after this, Ed Huddleson, the previous year's president, told Phil he had to meet Felix. As they were leaving for the meeting, Phil was puzzled to see Huddleson racing through the pages of *The New York Times* and asked what he was doing. Ed said he was preparing himself to reply to "all the questions the little so-and-so will want to discuss."

So much of Phil's life flowed from the year as president of the *Law Review* and from his relationship with Felix Frankfurter. Felix adopted Phil as one of his "boys" before he was appointed by President Roosevelt to the Supreme Court in January 1939, the middle of Phil's last year in law school. It was with Felix and with new friends from the *Review* that Phil entered the world of great minds, ideas, and books, stimulating conversation, and above all an interest in current events. Phil had always loved politics and had spent years campaigning with his father, so he had developed an interest in public issues, but now he'd met a man obsessed with the national and international scene, with the uses of power and ideas, with people and politics and political theory.

— *Chapter Eight* —

T HE SPRING OF 1940 was spent in a haze of excitement and romance. It was a wonderful time for both of us, but it was also quite crazy to think about getting married so quickly. I suppose I had the usual nervousness about marriage. Phil and I knew each other relatively little, and we were both very young—not quite twenty-three and twenty-five. We came from such different backgrounds but had so much in common—humor, friends, interests, enthusiasms, and political views. There was a great deal going for us, even though the complexities were not understood or addressed, really ever.

Since Phil was going to be Justice Frankfurter's law clerk the following Supreme Court term, he drove the justice home from the Court one night and told him of our decision to be married and even asked his permission, for there had been an unwritten rule that the law clerks remain single, so as to be at the complete service of the justice, day or night. By this time that tradition had broken down, but Phil still felt the need to ask. Phil later told his father about Felix's reaction, saying that Frankfurter was, in fact, the only one "who could effectively disapprove . . . so I talked to him first, and instead of disapproving he was (since he, unlike you, knows the gal) heartily in favor." Indeed, Felix had been a friend of my family's—and therefore had known me—for years. According to Phil, Felix reminded him that "the apple never falls very far from the tree."

Telling his own father about the upcoming marriage proved to be more difficult than telling Felix or my father—and more painful. Phil wrote to his father on March 17, 1940, inadvertently and in his nervousness dating the letter 1939 and misspelling my name:

This should be a very interesting letter for you to read. . . .

When the Court's work is over, May 27th, or soon thereafter, I am going to get married. . . . I know you'll be in favor. Her name is Katherine Meyer and I've not a doubt in the world that you'll love her. You probably have heard of her father, Eugene Meyer, who is now publisher of the Washington Post, and has been in the past such things as head of the Federal Reserve. . . . He is a Jew, a Republican, and rich as hell. For the last two factors I am not especially fond of him—the first seems immaterial to me, but I pass it on to you. Her mother happens to be a gentile; she was one of the first newspaperwomen in this country, is credited with being quite brilliant, and I find her rather unattractive. . . . Before we get around to discussing Kay (Katherine), this is about enough to mention about the family except possibly to reemphasize the terrible fact that they are lousy rich—for instance, they live in an absurdly huge vulgar castle here, have another in NY, have a ranch in Wyoming, etc. Now we shall get around to Kay.

. . . she really is about as wonderful a person as you'll ever hope to see. Of course, I can't write you why this is so, but I'll just jot down a few very factual things about her—then when we drop in on you this summer you'll begin to catch on to what I meant. . . . We've known each other since last fall and finally decided the hell with it all we were going to shove off this summer. As I said before I can't write you why, yet I've no doubt you'll understand. Naturally, there were a few problems. But I think we've dealt with most of them.

In the first place I thought there might be a problem about Florida; I, of course, want to go back and, though you may not understand this, there are lots of girls who have been raised around here who wouldn't consider this. In any event this turned out to be very little of a problem, for she is quite willing to test Florida's willingness to feed me. Next, and a little tougher, is the problem of her dough; and I think we've got that worked out. It happens that she has a pretty horrible hunk of it in her name and we have worked out this solution: we'll live in the sort of house, have the sort of furniture, eat the sort of food, go to the sort of places, that young people making salaries like mine can afford. If she wants to spend some of hers on special clothes or special trips, etc., for *herself* she will do so, but none of it will go for the sort of joint expenses that ordinary young husbands pay. Mainly, we hope, she'll use her gold by way of helping things and projects she believes in. About the only problems we could possibly have besides these are FF, you, and her family. FF we have already taken care of; I hope this will line you up on our side; and we don't expect any trouble from her family that we can't handle. This I think just about winds up all I can write about Kay and why we're, come what may, going to get married this summer.

Ernie upset Phil at first by resisting the idea of his marrying me.
There was some talk of my being Jewish, and Ernie mentioned having
seen a man on Miami Beach one day who wished he wasn't Jewish. Phil
was protectively indignant. The other issue that concerned Ernie was my
family's wealth. Whether there were letters between the one Phil wrote
and the one his father wrote him in mid-April I'm not sure, but Ernie did
write Phil then, saying he understood that Phil was getting "considerable
advice on the coming marriage," and thought he'd "pass you on some."
He wrote:

> In the first place you and the young lady are the people who are
> getting married and I have always felt that the contracting parties
> should do as they please.
>
> I might retell how your mother and I got hitched. We eloped
> or drove off with a team of broncos with our red setter dog as a
> witness, guardian, or companion or what. We were married at
> Sturgis by a Presbyterian minister. Left horses and dog and went
> to Rapid City (20 miles) by R.R. for one day and got back to Terry
> with about $2 but the knot tying stuck which is the main thing.
>
> Boy, I wish you all the joy and success in the world. I am anx-
> ious to meet Katherine as we all are. . . . You tell [her] I said to
> keep you in the middle of the road. . . .

Ernie eventually wrote me a sweet letter saying Phil "has displayed
the best judgment that he has shown so far. I hope you can keep him in
line and I will just turn him over to you and quit worrying. You know how
it is when a farm boy goes to the city, paw and maw are always worrying
that some of the wild women and so on may get him."

In the end, Phil didn't invite his father to the wedding, but said we
would drive down to see his family afterwards. In part, he was angry over
Ernie's early objections to our marriage. I believe, too, he was concerned
about his father's seeing my parents' large house and number of servants
and the way we lived, all of which, indeed, would have shocked him. In
fact, I believe my father and he would have overcome that; they had many
things in common. I came to know and admire and, finally, to love Ernie
Graham, Phil's two-fisted, rough-hewn, upright father.

AFTER WE PUBLICLY announced our engagement, by which point
many people already knew, we were caught up in the excitement and in
being celebrated. There was one bad week when the engagement was almost broken. We went to a dinner dance with my brother, Bill. Phil had
had a great deal too much to drink, and for the first time I saw a quite

frightening side of him. He was more than ordinarily drunk—there was a sort of out-of-hand, frenzied quality to him. The evening worried me a lot. Bill asked if I had seen Phil like this before. When I said no, Bill said, "Well, you better think about it right now."

In fact, I decided I had to pull back to think it over, or even to break the engagement. I had a date to meet Phil the next night, and I was primed to have this talk, but when he appeared to pick me up, he had brought Prich with him—as always, he was a step ahead of me. Naturally, the talk didn't take place, and got postponed indefinitely. I cooled down, the fear went away, his charm took over, and that was that for the time being.

Phil and my family were getting to know and like each other, but Phil went on worrying about my money. I was still working and, in fact, kept working until just before the wedding. I was also busy, with my mother, buying an enormous trousseau of everything I thought I'd need; since I had promised to live on what we both earned, I wanted to have to buy as little as possible later and as much as I could then. This trousseau saw me through for quite a long time.

There was some discussion about *how* we would be married. We were both painfully self-conscious—Phil to the point where he wanted us to be married in New York's City Hall by Mayor Fiorello La Guardia, whom we both admired. And I was to wear a gray flannel suit. I countered with two nonnegotiable demands—I wanted a slightly religious ceremony in a long weddingish dress, and some sort of small, informal, friendly gathering at home. The compromise we arrived at was the garden at the farm at Mount Kisco, which I considered more home than the Washington house. Neither one of us was religious in the formal sense, but I wanted something more religious than a judge, and through Mother we found a very nice low-key Lutheran minister.

We were married at Mount Kisco on June 5, 1940. The guests were the two justices for whom Phil worked and their wives, the Reeds and the Frankfurters, as well as some of our Hockley friends, my family, and a few other close friends, among whom, luckily for us, was Edward Steichen. Phil and I would never have brought in a photographer, but Steichen had his camera along with him and didn't have to be asked. We were delighted to have his photographs, which I still cherish. My dress was designed by me and made to order at Bergdorf Goodman. It was long, as I had wanted, and austerely simple but beautiful, made of heavy eggshell silk, with a scarf edged with my grandmother's lace. I carried orchids and wore orange blossoms in my hair but no veil. My sister Ruth was my attendant, and Prich was Phil's best man—as Phil said, the biggest best man anyone ever had.

At lunch before the wedding, Phil, Prich, and Butch Fisher started arguing with Felix about a case that had been handed down by the Supreme

Court just two days earlier, which Joe Lash later described as the "first wartime civil liberties case." It was a case on which the young men differed violently from Felix, who had written the opinion of the Court in *Minersville School District* v. *Gobitis*, saying that the state could require public-school students to salute the flag even if it was a violation of their religious beliefs. The Gobitis children in the case were Jehovah's Witnesses. Phil and Prich particularly were deeply disturbed—even shocked—by Felix's position. Steichen was also a vocal participant in the argument. He and Bis and I and others—I'm sure my brother—all took part. Felix loved and encouraged loud and violent arguments, which everyone usually enjoyed, but this time the argument went over the edge into bitter passion. Felix deeply believed in the obligation to salute the flag. The fight grew so intense that at one point great large tears rolled down Prich's reddened, rotund cheeks. Everyone was upset. The argument went on and on, with Felix at another point saying, as Bis recalled, "Everybody always talks about me as a liberal, but I never was one." Finally, the butler came in and announced that the minister had been waiting for an hour, and Felix broke up the argument by grabbing my arm with his always iron hand and saying, "Come along, Kay. We will go for a walk in the woods and calm down." And we did.

We then proceeded with the ceremony, after which we had a slightly larger reception to which my aunts, uncles, and cousins were invited. Then Al Phillips, the much-loved family chauffeur, drove Phil and me to the Carlyle Hotel in New York City. Originally, we had planned to stay at the Essex House, but Phil found out there was a strike there and felt we should not start married life by crossing a picket line. I agreed. We tried to look nonbridal entering the hotel, managing somehow until Phil extended his arm to register and out fell a lot of rice.

My mother had filled our room with fresh flowers from Mount Kisco. We stayed in New York a night or two, seeing a few friends. My sister Flo, who had married the character actor Oscar Homolka, came to see us in the Carlyle and was announced via the room clerk—"Mrs. Homolka to see Mrs. Graham," my first public encounter with my new name, which I very much enjoyed having.

After a few days, we sailed on a steamship for Bermuda, with me taking along an absurd amount of luggage, including, incredibly, a trunk. We stayed at the Horizons on Coral Beach, where we had a room with a small porch attached as a sitting room. I had taken along *War and Peace*, and Phil had equally heavy reading. One day we lent our room to a young army couple, also on their wedding trip. When we got back from a day's bicycling, they said, "My, you have a lot of books in your room. Nothing but a slap and a tickle in ours." Phil wrote his sister, Mary, while we were there, congratulating her on the birth of a baby and telling her of the joys of Bermuda: its unbelievable flowers, the color of the sea, the distinctly not-of-this-world quiet. He added: "She-who-is-wife looks every day more like Health. . . ."

Despite our concerns about the fall of France, we went on doing very traditional things—bicycling, playing tennis, swimming, and reading. Tennis together had certain tensions built into it, which emerged only later. I had played a little all my life, but liked it increasingly, especially after escaping Bis's shadow. Phil had played less, but since it was something I enjoyed he gamely entered into it and in time grew better, always compensating for any inadequacies on the court with his wit, which began lovingly but often ended up with a sharp and upsetting edge. We had one hilarious exchange while still in Bermuda that remained in our lore. We were playing doubles and Phil missed an easy shot. I said, "Oh, well, they say he has a fine mind." Shortly afterwards, I missed one. Phil retorted, "And they say her family spent millions on her game."

After the honeymoon and a short stay at Mount Kisco, we went down to Washington to see about our new house, which we had rented for the coming year, and then set out for Florida in the Buick convertible I had inherited from my brother. I had only the dimmest notion of Phil's family, never having met any of them. Nor had I much sense, from having lived in Washington, Chicago, and San Francisco with Mount Kisco summers, what the South was like or what the country outside cities was like. As we entered Florida, I saw a sign in front of an apartment house that read "No dogs or Jews allowed," and was deeply shaken, never having seen or experienced anything so ugly.

We drove down Route 1 and arrived at the stone house that Phil's parents had built when Bill was born. The farm itself looked large and prosperous, but flat and sandy, where the Everglades' swamps had been developed and drained into ditches and canals. We stayed at the house with Phil's father; his stepmother, Hilda, whom Ernie had married in 1936; and his very young half-brother, Bob, their somewhat spoiled only child.

It was not an easy meeting for them or for me. Hilda was charming, warm, and welcoming. Ernie studied me over the top of his newspaper. He was shy but did his best to be jovial and affectionate. One day, when I was lying on the couch in the living room writing thank-you notes, I was startled to be spat on by the three-year-old Bob. Phil's brother, Bill, later told me that this was, alas, Bob's habit at that point in his life. I thought, in my paranoid way, that there must be a message there. Bob outgrew all this, of course, and developed into a highly successful, natural, and excellent politician, very different from the older three children but extremely able. He became governor of Florida and is now senator, a strange fulfillment of both his father's and Phil's ambitions. He has all the Graham family brains and charisma, and a great deal more stability than Phil had.

Miami was difficult for me for many reasons. It was Southern, and no one had ever suggested to me that the South was still significantly different from the rest of the country—certainly more sexist in atmosphere. Women lunched with each other and talked household problems, which I was still unaware existed. I was tremendously reassured at lunch with my old Washington friend Mary Cootes Belin, whose husband was in Florida working for Pan American Airlines, when she told me that she, too, knew nothing about vacuum cleaners and washing machines.

I tried, and Phil's family and friends tried, but the reality was that I knew nothing about farming or about Florida politics, which were the bonds between Phil and his father. Still, I worked hard at being interested as we drove around the farm looking at the cows and the crops.

Phil's college friends seemed unlike anyone I knew, and I didn't know how to relate to them. One of our more traumatic evenings was spent on a Chamber of Commerce boat ride with some of these old friends. This was a double cultural shock, for I had never encountered a Chamber of Commerce group before, much less the one in Miami, then still a comparatively small town. We played a game called "sniff" in which a cigarette-wrapper paper was passed from nose to nose—you had to keep it up by inhaling until you passed it on; if you let it drop, you had to kiss the man with whom the catastrophe occurred. It was a modified version of the kids' game of post office. This strange game reduced me to total pulp. I didn't know whether to laugh it off or engage in it. Today, of course, I see that I was ridiculously uptight and shy, but then I couldn't help wondering if I was going to be spending the rest of my life playing sniff with the Chamber of Commerce. I wept on the way home out of worry and fear that I couldn't cope. Phil stopped the car, hugged me, and told me not to worry—these were his old friends, but he too had grown away from them; he loved them but no longer saw much of them, and we wouldn't be doing this kind of thing forever. I recovered and we survived the rest of the three-week visit, and eventually some of the main figures from his Miami youth became my good friends and stayed so.

While we were in Florida, I also met Mary, Phil's sister, who adored him. Mary had a needlessly hard life. She was very gifted and bright but not beautiful. She had wanted to go north to a dress-design school and was not allowed to go. She also had a much older beau whom she loved but wasn't allowed to marry. I suppose it might have been different had her mother lived. Mary was difficult about her stepmother, Hilda, who was not much older than she, and whom Ernie had met on a bus trip shortly after his first wife's death. Mary fought the idea of the marriage and fought with Hilda. Phil had his own reservations, but as usual was the peacemaker in the situation and supported Hilda, who was awfully nice. Ernie needed her, and I got along well with her.

While we were in Florida, Phil received a birthday letter from my mother, telling him how happy she was that he and I were married and how she had never dreamed she could accept someone so "spontaneously into our mystic circle." She also wrote:

When I think how useful you and Kay will be in the making of the new world that lies in wait for us, I almost envy you both such an opportunity and such a life. Let me add one word about the conversation on money which we began on the terrace of the cabin but never completed. You were just saying when we were interrupted that money is a danger because it makes people soft. That is true especially if they grow up with it, but for people like you and me who had our own way to make during our most formative years, there is also another danger. I have driven myself mercilessly all my life first out of fear of getting soft and later from habit. This has been so intense an obsession that I fear it affected Eugene and the children almost too much and created an almost restless ambition in everybody. You are so strong and sensible that you need not fear softening, need not even fear the opposite effect which it had on me. But I thought it worth mentioning so that you and Kay will feel free to use what you have to good purpose without complexes of one sort or the other.

When you left you said "You can trust me with your daughter, Mrs. M"—Let me reply as my birthday message that I never trusted anybody more—in any and all respects.

We started back north on August 1 and arrived in Washington a few days later. We stayed at Crescent Place until the furniture I had so carefully chosen with my mother arrived at our new house at 1814 37th Street, and then, in the late summer of 1940, we began our married life together in our first home.

— *Chapter Nine* —

W E QUICKLY AND EASILY settled into our little house, which we rented unfurnished for $80 a month. The house— just outside Georgetown, behind Western High School— was in a pleasant, convenient, unpretentious neighborhood of row houses called Burleith. It had a tiny living room into which you walked immediately on entering, a dining room, and a small kitchen. On the second floor was a nice bedroom over the living room and two little rooms that became studies for each of us. There was a daybed for guests in Phil's study. At the back of the house was a screened-in porch and a postage-stamp yard— taken up mostly by a small tin-roofed single-car garage.

The house was furnished sparsely in classic modern furniture, reflecting my taste at the time. Since the furniture was a gift from my parents, it was all made to order—luckily, Phil was blissfully unaware of how much things like that cost, so he didn't protest. We bought living-room curtains from Woodward and Lothrop.

This little house helped us to accomplish what Phil and I both wanted—to live as our contemporaries did. Because of Phil's insistence, and my agreement, that we live on our combined salaries, and because mine was so little to begin with, my first inclination was to stop work and be a stay-at-home wife—learn to cook and keep house. Phil was horrified by the idea. He said it would be terrible to be working late and have me anxiously waiting at the door with a lemon pie. Furthermore, he really wanted me to go on working and decided we could pay a maid with what I earned. So the superb Mattie Jeffress entered our lives. A friend of my mother's laundress, Mattie came each day before breakfast and stayed through dinner, with two half-days off, if I remember correctly. She did the cleaning and personal laundry, as well as the cooking. For this, I blush to admit, we paid her all of $15 a week.

Phil was earning $3,600 a year as a law clerk, which he pointed out was far from a sacrifice, since at that time this was equal to or somewhat more than the beginning salaries in law firms. I was earning about $1,500 a year. We had one small cushion, a $500 wedding present from an aunt, which I thought I could use for extras like theater and travel tickets. In a sense, Phil was almost as spoiled and unaware of finances as I was, having gone straight from law school into the luxurious arms of life at Hockley.

I began to learn how to live on a different scale. The enormous trousseau I'd bought spared me from worrying about clothes, but it was clear that I hadn't the remotest idea about the particulars of domestic life. And, given the hardworking Mattie, there was still a great deal I didn't have to learn. A hamburger or scrambled eggs on her nights off were almost beyond my competence, for instance. There are still odd lacunae, I confess. I have never in my life pressed a dress.

I was driven to a frenzy of small economies, doing ridiculous things to save money—like taking the laundry to Tolman's, the local cleaner, rather than having it picked up, because it saved ten cents a pound. Of course, Tolman's also ruined the linen monogrammed sheets my mother had given me for my trousseau, but I had no idea that these were very special, since that's what I had slept on all my life. When we moved into our house in September 1940, I began keeping a little accounts book, dutifully noting every penny spent, including the cost of gas and oil for the car, stamps, groceries, even our personal allowances, which were $9 each per week. The entries taper off in October, and there are no more after November, so obviously I quickly tired of this kind of accounting, but except for the $500 wedding present I never used a cent of my own until two years later, when Phil went into the army. Even when I got pregnant, I wore borrowed clothes to supplement my inexpensive department-store maternity dresses—and looked very dowdy, I'm sure, out of a driven desire to live up to our agreement. Yet, despite my overdoing it, it was good for me and for us both to live on our salaries. In fact, most of what Phil decreed and I assented to *was* good for us. And we were having a great time.

Our friends continued much the same that year, with the Hockley boys—especially Prich, Bill Sheldon, and John Ferguson—being among our closest. At the same time, several new people entered our lives. Prich started taking out a beautiful half-English girl named Evangeline Bell, who was Attorney General Francis Biddle's secretary/assistant. I grew even closer to Evangeline later, after she married David Bruce. Joe Rauh, one of the great fighting liberals, and his wife, Olie, became our great friends during this time. We also got to know Joseph Alsop better. He was not that much older than we were but seemed at least a generation ahead in his social life and experience.

Also important to us that year were the Romillys, Esmond and Jessica, or Decca, as she was known; Decca was Jessica Mitford, one of the famously eccentric Mitfords. The very young Decca met Esmond Romilly, her second cousin and a nephew of Winston Churchill's, at a dinner party and asked him, if he was going to fight with the International Brigade in Spain, to take her with him. He agreed, and off they went together, fell in love en route, and created a terrible public storm, during which Anthony Eden, then foreign minister, sent a destroyer to retrieve Decca.

In February 1939, Decca and Esmond came to America, and it was sometime that year that I met them, was charmed, and invited them to Mount Kisco for the weekend. They were surprised to find the atmosphere there so congenial and my parents so warm and welcoming, remarking that such open warmth didn't exist in England.

The Romillys took off on a tour of the United States, heading south to New Orleans, but they took a wrong turn somewhere and wound up in Miami where they got a job in a bar whose owners needed $1,000 for a liquor license. Esmond flew up to Washington to ask my father for a loan. He had a big argument ready, complete with a list of assets in England that could be used as collateral. My father gently said, "You don't need to explain foreign exchange, Esmond," and promptly lent him the money, for which Esmond procured a half-interest in the bar.

When the war intensified Esmond volunteered for the Canadian Air Corps and, tragically, died in a bomber not long afterwards. Decca stayed on in Washington for a while, remarried, and later became a famous investigative journalist. She remained my dear friend until her recent death.

Another key figure who entered our lives was Jean Monnet. In late 1940, Monnet arrived in the United States, an unknown but vitally important figure in the world and in the war. He had been in England when France fell, and arrived here not only unknown but with no official title, no formal portfolio, and no platform except his own brain and personality. Monnet had been nominated by Churchill to be part of the British Supply Council in Washington, and his mission from the Free French and the British was to get supplies built up and moving.

Monnet was proof positive that if someone is brilliant, political, and concentrated, he can make a power base where none exists. And he went on doing it all his life, after the war working on his idea for a united Europe. His mode of operation was to know the right people—those who had the knowledge, the power, and the will to move things—then to learn what made things move and to be constantly pushing the levers of power. He was very selective about whom he saw and how he used his time. He never made small talk, and he always kept to the point in his discussions, at meetings, or even at dinners. Phil hero-worshipped him. At one Sunday lunch on our terrace many years later, with just the three of us together, when Phil and I were praising him, Jean shook his head modestly and protested, "I've only had one idea, but that was a good one."

But the overwhelmingly dominant influence in our lives that first year was Supreme Court Justice Felix Frankfurter, for whom Phil was now clerking. Felix and his wife, Marion, were friends of the Biddles, the Achesons, the Bob Lovetts, and later the Jack McCloys, the Jean Monnets, and the French ambassador, Henri Bonnet, and his wife, and we were lucky enough to get to know them all. Though Phil and Felix had become close when Phil was still in law school, their mutual interests and bright, quick natures now brought them even closer together. Phil's love of politics met its match in Felix Frankfurter.

The year Phil served as Felix's law clerk can only be described as rollicking—it definitely had a Rover Boys quality to it. Our friend and Hockley co-dweller Edwin McElwain was clerking with Chief Justice Charles Evans Hughes, Ed Huddleson was with Justice Frank Murphy, and of course Prich was always around, even though now working for the executive branch of the government.

Felix being Felix, our lives were intertwined. He was all-enveloping. That year there were more or less continual phone calls or visits to our house or his, and constant gossip and jokes about people on the Court or what was going on there.

Our mornings always got off to a slow start. Phil had a lifelong inability either to get up in the morning or to go to bed at night. I am a morning person and a dormouse at night. The phone would often ring in the morning and Felix would say, "Where is Phil?" "On his way, Judge," I would respond, using the title we always gave him, while simultaneously kicking Phil out of bed and helping him rush out.

Phil had bought a secondhand Oldsmobile, painted a weird shade of green by some previous owner, in which he would pick up the justice at his house in Georgetown and drive him to work and home again. They would talk, argue, and gossip nonstop. Felix often dictated to Phil, who typed while the justice strode up and down composing. When Felix's prose occasionally turned elaborate, purple, or bromidic, Phil, disapproving, simply stopped typing. If they disagreed about an opinion, arguments would go on and on until Felix was either influenced or simply decided. Felix was so tolerant that at times his original opinion would simply not get written, but when strong emotions were involved, the arguments could go on for months. During one case about which Phil and Felix disagreed strongly, Phil, looking disgruntled, came in after dropping the justice at his house on 30th Street. Apparently they had argued all the way home. As soon as he walked into the house, the phone rang, and the argument continued unabated until—to my surprise—I heard Phil say, "Well, I don't care what you do, Judge. I just don't want to see you make yourself look silly!"—with which he banged down the phone. I don't remember what the case was, but I do remember that they kept delaying writing the decision while the argument raged on. Finally, they worked all night to finish writing the opinion at the very last possible moment before the Court adjourned, and then returned home in the early morning in a cab, Felix so tired he didn't focus on the driver's asking for his address. Phil quoted the taxi driver as looking back at this exhausted man and saying, "What's the matter? You stupid or something?"

Another day, the justice came into our house with Phil, grabbed my arm very tightly as he often did, sometimes so tightly that it hurt, and asked, "Kay, did Phil tell you what Hughes said on the Court the other day?" "No, he didn't, Judge," I replied. "Phil, why didn't you tell Kay? You should have told her. Holmes told his wife everything."

Felix had boundless energy and ebullience and a tremendous *joie de vivre*. He was cerebral, of course, but he was also emotional. He loved engaging in verbal dueling over issues. And he loved certain kinds of people—particularly those whose ideas of right and justice jibed with his own. But he also liked people who disagreed with him and stood up to him, if they were very smart and were within his mental spectrum; it wasn't enough to be intelligent if you bored him or were pedestrian or had a literal mind. Because the Frankfurters were childless, Felix seemed to adopt as his intellectual sons the young Harvard law students who interested and amused him, hence the fullness of the relationship with the law clerks and their families. He loved laughter and gossip, and he encouraged the extreme irreverence of his favorite students and liked to be challenged by them. To an outsider brought up with old-fashioned manners, the boys seemed breathtakingly rude, but Felix didn't see it that way; the shouted arguments and insults were simply his preferred form of communicating. Prich was particularly irreverent. Someone reported that at a law clerks' dinner Prich sat slumped over a conference table, drumming his fingers with his eyes half shut, while the arguments raged. Suddenly Felix looked down the table and said, "Prich, what are you doing?" Prich looked up and said, "Counting the digressions in your argument." Felix roared.

Since Phil was spending long hours at the Court, I went back to work on the *Post*, writing stories for the "Brains" section of the Sunday paper, now called "Outlook." This was a much more intense writing experience than any I had had, and was sometimes hard for me. Once Phil found me at two in the morning, hunched over my typewriter, pecking desperately away; I was stuck in the middle of a story, unable to go on. He asked me a few questions, wrote out a few paragraphs, unstuck me, and went back to bed.

I wrote on such subjects as the broadcasters' fight with ASCAP, propaganda groups and the America First Committee, Mrs. Roosevelt's beginning her third term, the Harry Bridges trial, the D.C. Juvenile Court, the Cherry Blossom Festival and spring in Washington, Pan American Day, and one piece entitled "Brain Trust Gone, but Professors Are Still Here." I joined the Women's National Press Club, recommended by Casey Jones, who wrote a letter in my behalf saying I was a "thoroughly competent reporter."

The *Post* was still operating from its plant on E Street, several doors away from the National Theater. The entire building was perilous and problematic. Everything in it was old, except some of the people. The small, dark lobby housed a cashier and a counter where back copies of the paper were sold and the public was dealt with. There was a small cagelike elevator run by a man who had to manage the old-fashioned gate, and a dangerous ride in it took you past the city room on the second floor to the editorial offices, women's department, and the editors' and publisher's offices in the front of the building on the third floor.

The local newspaper war was heating up. Cissy Patterson's merging the *Times* and the *Herald* made the *Post* third in circulation behind her combined circulation and the *Star*. My father often complained that, while the other Washington papers were first in advertising and in circulation, the *Post* was first in operating expenses. The Scripps Howard afternoon tabloid, the *News*, was still much read at lunchtime.

My father continued to run the *Post* with zest. He enjoyed being the publisher, and his employees enjoyed working for him. They had begun to refer to him affectionately as Butch—at least behind his back—which he loved and considered a term of respect. Although the *Post* ran a deficit in 1940 of three-quarters of a million dollars and even more the next year, he was working hard at winnowing down the loss. In the summer of 1941, he proposed sharing the "progress" of the paper—there were no profits—with his employees, by offering to divide two-thirds of any improvement over the previous year's results among them. The advertising linage of the *Post* was less than one-half that of the *Star*, but circulation was up to 130,000, compared with the 50,000 in 1933 when my father bought it.

Also in the summer of 1941, *Time* magazine did a piece on the *Post*, calling it "the Capital's sole big-league newspaper. . . . It has become a journal of national importance, a reading must on Capitol Hill, an institution of high character and independence, a force for good in its bailiwick." In a wonderfully hick response that appeared on page one, the *Post* said, "There can be no stretched headbands around the Post; this newspaper has just started to grow." Whatever the response, this must have been an exciting accolade for a paper so new in its regeneration and still so far behind the dominant and wealthy *Star* in local prestige. The progress made was a tribute to my father's tenacity in the face of great difficulties and what at times seemed a hopeless case. He would moan and groan over his breakfast tray, brought to him at my mother's bedside, exclaiming, "I think I'll sell the *Post.*" She always succeeded in encouraging him and bucking him up at the low moments.

PHIL AND I were both ardent Roosevelt partisans, although, since the District of Columbia had no vote, our support was just talk. My parents, like many other District residents in 1940, were passionately pro-Willkie. Mother, in her usual style, became a friend as well as a supporter of the Willkies. I suspect, with hindsight, that Willkie was a fine candidate, although we related to Harold Ickes's condescending description of him as "the barefoot boy from Wall Street."

Our first Christmas together we spent in bed with the flu. First I collapsed; then Phil, on Christmas Eve. We had to turn away our two guests and spent the day on the second floor with a little artificial eight-inch Christmas tree and a few visitors and phone calls—the saddest one being from my brother on his way to Boston to be married to Mary Adelaide Bradley, a research student whom he knew at Johns Hopkins and who had been a year ahead of me at Vassar. The flu kept us from going to the wedding. The little tree remained for years, sentimentally, among our Christmas decorations.

By this time, as the war in Europe went on escalating, English children were pouring into the United States to seek refuge from the falling bombs. The Frankfurters had added great excitement to their house by taking on the three young children of Gilbert Murray, the famous Greek scholar at Oxford, who was a friend of Felix's. My father took on an entire nursery school of fifteen children and their teachers, rented a large country house near Warrenton, Virginia, furnished it hastily, and lodged them there for the duration of the war. It was called Clover Croft School.

When France fell, my father brought over to America two families of his French relatives, who, being Jewish, were in danger. He supported them, helping the men get jobs and providing money to help educate the children here. Unfortunately, his cousin Léon Zadoc-Kahn and his wife, Suzanne, declined my father's invitation to help them leave Europe, and eventually died in Auschwitz. Their son Bertrand, a doctor who was head of the American Hospital in Paris, had shot himself when France fell. Under the shock of his loss, they didn't want to leave. Bertrand's sister Jacqueline stayed in France also and was hidden in what was originally Free France by a very brave Catholic family. She and her husband, Jacques

Eisenmann, were close to my father and are still close to me. They are now well into their nineties and immensely gallant.

AS THE COURT'S term drew to a close in the late spring of 1941, Phil began to think more and more about what to do next. He still thought he would return to Florida to practice law and eventually go into politics, and we had made a trip to Tallahassee during which he had been interviewed and had got a job in the state attorney general's office. But back in Washington the threat of America's getting involved in the war seemed too real for us to move to Florida. Phil concluded that we would eventually be fighting and that he would go. In the meantime, he didn't want to abandon the effort to gear up for war; he wanted to be involved. As talk of war intensified, Phil's after-hours work turned to politics, and he cast around for the place where he could be most useful.

In late May, he had lunch with Robert Lovett, then assistant secretary of war for air, who told Phil he should stay working in Washington "until our need for soldiers and sailors shaped up a bit more." Because his own office bureaucracy was too dominated by army colonels, Lovett decided that Phil's abilities could best be used by Harry Hopkins in the White House, where Hopkins—FDR's closest adviser, but in failing health—was living. Lovett felt there was a bottleneck in the White House and that a good young fellow could take enough of the work off Hopkins to enable him to prepare really important things for the president.

Frankfurter and Lovett both talked to Hopkins, who saw Phil one June morning in his combined bedroom and office. Phil went in weak-kneed and scared. He later wrote his father an account of the meeting:

> HH looked up, grunted, "good morning," and then growled: "Why the hell aren't you in the Army?"
>
> . . . [I] answered that I wasn't sure I shouldn't be, that you rather thought I should be . . . but that the best advised man I knew (the head of Naval Intelligence) had told me to wait a few months and that I had followed his advice. He seemed to give me a passing mark on that and then knocked out a few more balls for me to field: "Why should he use me?" "There were hundreds of guys like me around," etc., etc. I began to wonder what was up when he quieted down and told me he did need someone who could read reports, talk to people for him etc. Then he said he had difficulties because there was no place to put me in the White House, but that if I could get Oscar Cox to hire me at the Lend-Lease administration and give me an office he'd like to have me work with him three days a week. Cox is a fine young fellow of 35

from Maine who, when assistant general counsel in the Treasury, thought up and drafted Lend-Lease, and for whom I had been about to work anyway. So I left the White House to tell Cox of events and he told me I ought to start in for him on Wednesday, the 11th. So I did and I've been there since.

And as yet I've seen no more of HH. Cox—who is terribly wise—told me at the start the Hopkins thing probably wouldn't work. He said HH was a peculiar cuss, worked very irregularly, and probably would never get a real assistant. But he said I'd be just as happy and useful with him because he's in the heart of getting stuff across to England as counsel for the Lend-Lease Administration. . . .

The year that began with Phil's going to Lend-Lease, in June of 1941, and ended with his going into the army the following summer, was one of the most exciting of our lives. Oscar Cox attracted able people to work for him; they in turn related well to each other and to people in jobs with access to higher-ups. In this way, they could constructively pull the levers of power and make government work more effectively than it otherwise would have. Oscar was himself one of those superstars secure enough to want the best around them and to give people a lot of authority and then back them.

One of the great influences on all of those who worked in Lend-Lease was Ben Cohen, a good friend of ours, then a minister without portfolio who in early 1942 was part of a self-constituted group of men who were making sure arms production was on target. Ben never would acknowledge that a thing was illegal, he would simply rationalize it in one way or another.

In trying to understand where the country was starting from, it's helpful to consider a meeting this defense-watchdog group held in early June. Someone brought along the current *Time* magazine, which contained a footnote revealing the Russian losses of planes and other machines of war. The men figured out that these losses were greater than this country even had *on order*. While the military blamed everyone but itself for not having realized how big the war would be, this group of lawyers was able to demonstrate to the powers in charge, including the president, how bad the situation really was and how little the United States was doing to prepare for war.

The competition for the few supplies we were producing was fierce—from our own army, navy, and air force, as well as from the British, the Free French, and the Russians. Roosevelt had spoken the year before about "clouds of planes," and of becoming the "Arsenal of Democracy." One day Phil and Joe Rauh were looking at the top-secret statistics, for which they had clearance, of the Office of Production Management. When they read that only one four-engine bomber had been delivered to the army during August, they saw their chance to push for the importance of doing more and wrote a memorandum to be sent to the president.

Three hours later, a hot memo came back from Hopkins saying, "You shouldn't bother the President with things like this and besides it isn't true." The very young men—Phil was twenty-six at the time and Joe just three years older—felt that the world was coming to an end. They'd misled the president—they'd have to leave Washington! They rushed down to see Bob Nathan, director of research in the Office of Production Management and the originator of the book of statistics from which the memo had been drawn. Nathan got out his yellow backup sheets, while Joe and Phil sat there preparing to die. Nathan kept looking at his papers and making marks with a pencil. Finally, he said, "I made a mistake." Just as Phil and Joe were about to collapse, Nathan said, "There wasn't one four-engine bomber delivered in August. There were *no* four-engine bombers delivered in August. The one I counted was delivered after August 31."

One Sunday we went out to have lunch at the log cabin owned by the Edward Burlings in the nearby Virginia woods. That day one of those present was the undersecretary of war, Robert Patterson, and the arguments on preparedness were being waged at the top of everyone's lungs. Of course, I worried that Patterson was unused to this mode of discourse and would think that everyone arguing was insane, and when we got home I told Phil that their manners in front of this august figure had been appalling. When Phil came home the next day, he said, "I guess we didn't offend Patterson too much. He called me today and asked me to go to work for him." Phil didn't, but so much for my nervous nanny-bred worries.

Soon afterwards, on another Sunday, in early December 1941, my parents had some guests to lunch at their own Virginia cabin. I was there, but Phil and Joe Rauh were at their office working on the report to Congress that Lend-Lease had to make every three months. In the middle of lunch someone from the *Post* called to say the Japanese had bombed Pearl Harbor.

Phil and Joe had gone out to a late lunch, and on the way back, Larry Fly, head of the Federal Communications Commission and of the War Communications Board, spotted them and stopped his car, shouting to them that the Japanese had attacked Pearl Harbor. Joe said, "Thank God." Phil said, "Shut up." "I was so depressed we weren't preparing for war," Joe told me many years later, "that my reaction was 'Thank God' and Phil, whose reactions were always the quickest, realized that there could be an anti-Semitic kickback and the last thing any Jew should say is 'It's good.'" They both went immediately to try to enlist but were rejected for a variety of reasons, all later dropped.

Pearl Harbor was followed quickly by Roosevelt's solemn declaration of war. With the realization of what Pearl Harbor meant, Congress was flooded with requests from the different services, all competing with each other and uncoordinated. Bob Nathan was called on to ensure that there wouldn't be airplanes without wings or tanks without armor. In order to be more effective in moving the country to a wartime footing, some of this group of young men, including Phil, who were already working through Lend-Lease and other agencies, started meeting regularly at Bob Nathan's apartment. These men, calling themselves the "Goon Squad," were all trying to do the same thing in different agencies, waging a magnificent battle against bureaucracy and red tape, at times amazingly successful at getting things done. There was such dispersion of authority in the government until the War Production Board was created that this informal group of mostly quite young men with absolutely no formal authority was actually able to step into the vacuum and compensate partially for that lack of a center.

This chaos was finally resolved when Jimmy Byrnes went to the White House in overall charge. He had a small staff, of which Ben Cohen and Prich were a part. If the Goon Squad recognized some problem, Ben and Prich would tell Byrnes, who could get it fixed. Until that time, one art the Goon Squad developed for making known its concerns was that of leaking information—partly to Al Friendly, who had come to the *Post* from the *Washington Daily News* early in 1939 and who was reporting on the defense buildup, and partly to Drew Pearson, who was writing his very popular and widely distributed national column with Bob Allen.

Prich was thought by the group to be leaking too much and too often to Drew Pearson, who was a personal friend, so one evening he was told that he should stop, that his leaking was doing more harm than good. Two weeks later, the group decided that something *ought* to be leaked to Pearson and asked Prich to leak it. "Are you sure?" asked Prich. "Yes," said the group. "Well, all right, then," Prich said, "I've already done it."

Phil seemed to wear one hat in the Lend-Lease Administration and another in the Office of Emergency Management. Although nominally he was based in these agencies, practically he was all over the place. Wherever he worked, he acquired a reputation as an expediter. He was gone from his office so much that his friends said his secretary spent her time knitting sweaters. For several months in the spring of 1942, he was detached from the legal division of Lend-Lease at the request of Bert Evatt, who was foreign minister of Australia and had been chief justice there, and who asked him to work for Australia as liaison to Lend-Lease. So he worked full-time with the Australians, particularly after the Japanese invaded the Australian territory of New Guinea.

Later, when Phil went to the *Post*, eight of his friends wrote a highly laudatory letter about him to the *Post*'s editor, a tribute that best describes

some of what Phil was doing in the year between his clerkship for Frankfurter and the time he enlisted:

> As much as or more than any single person, Graham was respon-
> sible for the increased production of high octane gas early enough
> to make the strategic bombings and air operations of 1944 and
> 1945 possible. It was he who played a major role in generating and
> executing the measures necessary to put the V-loans in operation
> so that much of our war production could in fact be stepped up.
> Sub-contracting and the enlisting of smaller firms in the manu-
> facture of war supplies were materially increased by his efforts.

The V-loan legislation, which allowed for the loan of money to small
businesses to help them convert to the war effort, was typical of Phil's ability to cut red tape. He worked on it for many months, and finally it was
completed but had to be signed by certain officials before it went to Congress. To reduce the bureaucratically mandated time it would take to pro-
cure all of the required signatures, Phil got in a taxi, carried the bill from
one individual to another, had it signed, and took it to the Hill himself.
Under this legislation, hundreds of millions of dollars were loaned.

BY LATE 1941, having had a miscarriage just a few months earlier in
the initial stages of pregnancy, I was pregnant again, with the baby due in
May. The miscarriage had been profoundly upsetting, as though my
whole physical being had begun to move toward a goal that was suddenly
wrenched away from me, leaving me bereft, so I was deliriously happy to
be pregnant once more. Phil, who had been rejected initially by the army
because of eyesight problems and because he was married, had decided to
wait for our baby to be born before doing anything more about the military, despite his determination to join. In one exchange between us, I had
deplored the fact that we had the bad luck to live in a world with Hitler, to
which Phil responded, "I don't know. Maybe it's a privilege to have to fight
the biggest son of a bitch in history."

By May I was experiencing a lethargy even greater than usual. Pregnancy seemed to dull my mind and sap my energy—perhaps just from the
sheer exhaustion of carrying that much extra weight around. My listless-
ness was interspersed with bursts of activity on the cooking, entertaining,
and shopping fronts. I wasn't working any longer and, as I wrote to my
friend Sidney Hyman:

> I resigned myself quite contentedly to the life of a vegetable. I
> went to cooking school in the morning, had lunch with friends,

sat in the sun with other pregnant ladies, talked, gossiped, did everything in short that's in the books including laying out my husband's slippers and smoking jacket. (I'm serious I assure you.) And the funniest part of all is that I liked it.

I had bought the things we needed for the baby, including three rubber sheets with the crib, although Phil protested that no child of his would need them. And I had gained a lot of weight and was quite uncomfortable, particularly when it started to get hot in Washington.

We were beginning to think the baby was overdue, so I suggested to my doctor that he induce labor, which he did, but it was too soon and the baby wasn't ready. When after three days it finally began to be born, the cord was around its neck, a situation that ordinarily could be dealt with. Apparently, that night, with wartime help shortages, the doctor was delivering several babies at once, and by the time he got to my problem it was too late. We lost the baby boy.

When I came to after the long ordeal, I looked at Phil and groggily asked, "Is the baby all right?" When he said no, I couldn't believe it. I had never heard of anyone losing a baby and was so disbelieving that I was sure it couldn't possibly be true. But it was all too real. I was devastated. I will never forget getting back to the house, where Phil had removed all of the baby's things so that it wouldn't be even more painful. I began to realize not only that there was no baby but that Phil would now be leaving to go into the army and I would be alone. It was a terrible anguish, compounded by a desperate feeling that we'd never have children and an even greater fear that something might happen to him—all the worst dreads combined. Phil was wonderful to me, and we both were helped by my father. My mother was so upset I don't remember seeing her until several weeks afterwards.

So Phil did enlist in the army, and before he was to leave we had a reunion at Mount Kisco that included my brother, Bill, who was going into the Medical Corps, and his wife, Mary.

One night, while we were all at dinner, my mother, still very Republican, started picking on the "young New Dealers," who, of course, were not only our friends but by then were all either gone to the military or working in defense. I was still emotionally vulnerable, and her barbs and gibes about these young men as draft-dodgers were like a match thrown onto a gasoline-soaked bonfire. She and I had an enormous and horrible set-to. I knew that she was still spending her time on her book about Dostoyevsky, Tolstoy, and Mann. In addition, despite the war, Mount Kisco was continuing to operate on its normal luxurious scale—for example, I knew she had laid in a great deal of sugar, which was in short supply or already rationed. So I demanded to know what she herself was doing to help the war effort, writing this remote treatise in a house full of servants and hoarded sugar. She retorted by asking what *I* was doing about it. Since I had just lost my baby and was about to lose my husband to the army, I exploded into tears. We were separated by Phil and Bill, who took me upstairs.

They then talked to her in forthright terms, acknowledging that I shouldn't have attacked her so emotionally, but stating that in fact she really should do something more constructive than what she was doing. They suggested she turn her attention to reporting on America's war-impacted areas and, to her great credit, she took their suggestion seriously, and began an earnest and constructive career as a traveling correspondent on the war and the home front.

THOSE FIRST FEW years of marriage, before the war interrupted all our lives, Phil and I had a very happy time. I grew up considerably, mostly thanks to him. What he did for me was more than helpful, it was essential. He began to liberate me from my family and from the myths they had propagated, eventually leading me down very different paths from those I had known earlier. He counterbalanced my ingrown resistance to new and different ideas, to people with whom I didn't agree politically, to not having to hew to anyone's standards but my own. Phil also brought into my life more laughter, gaiety, irreverence for rules, and originality.

At the same time that he freed me in many ways from my family, Phil also grew quickly to appreciate both of my parents and got along with them better than most of their own children did. Despite his early apprehensions about my father's wealth, politics, and possible impulse to control, Phil gradually grew very close to him, ending up by becoming one of the two or three closest friends of his lifetime. He loved staying up with my father, listening to him reminisce about his life, his experiences, and his successes. Perhaps we children had all got too jaded by my father's growing habit of speaking in a monologue rather than inviting an exchange of any kind; we found ourselves almost involuntarily clicking off our minds. But Phil would respond, question, remember, and enjoy. Their blossoming relationship gave both of them great pleasure.

Phil and my mother also got along well. She adored him from the beginning and was closer to him in many ways than to me, emphasizing to the rest of us in the family that she and Phil—and only they—knew what it was like to grow up poor. He admired her but remained far more ambivalent about her than about my father. Indeed, he was very realistic about her, and at times quite tough and critical.

But though Phil was a great help to both my parents, he always insisted that we lead our own lives. He would always go to their aid if they were lonely or sick or in trouble, but he refused to be used, particularly by my mother, or to be dominated by her. When she insisted on our coming to dinner because she felt Phil should meet so-and-so, he would respond that he would be glad to keep them company when they really wanted us, but we wouldn't be just another two seats at her dinner table. Unaccustomed as I was to thinking of declining her invitations, it gradually dawned on me that he was right.

Although he was much the stronger, Phil also learned from me to some extent. What I brought to him was a greater knowledge of the world's ways, an appreciation of art and music and beauty, and, of course, the world of my parents—the *Post* and Washington—all of which he loved. I also brought him some stability.

But, always, it was he who decided and I who responded. From the earliest days of our relationship, for instance, I thought that we had friends because of him and were invited because of him. It wasn't until years later that I looked at the downside of all this and realized that, perversely, I had seemed to enjoy the role of doormat wife. For whatever reason, I liked to be dominated and to be the implementer. But although I was thoroughly fascinated and charmed by Phil, I was also slightly resentful, when I thought about it, at feeling such complete dependence on another person.

As the war came to rule our lives, I was amazed that we could continue to be so happy despite the condition of the world. What I remember most from those first years of marriage was our fun with each other, the constant growth and learning, and always a lot of laughter.

— *Chapter Ten* —

EARLY ON THE MORNING of July 27, 1942, Phil left for the Army Air Corps as a private, going first to Fort George Meade, the neighboring army installation in Maryland. The dreadful moment of our parting came at the Greyhound bus terminal in downtown Washington, already a depressing place but made more so by the sight of nervous recruits huddling together. Although I knew I was going to join him wherever he was shipped, the unknowns of the parting got the best of me and I embraced him, turned, and fairly dove through the door of the terminal as he joined the group of jittery inductees. I happened to look down just as I fled, discovered that my slip was showing, and decided that once more I had failed in a crisis.

Phil wrote me from Fort Meade the very next day, describing in great detail his first impressions of army life: the barnlike reception center, the primitive cafeteria with surprisingly good food, the physical inspection, and the un-air-conditioned barracks, in which he sat on the edge of his cot using his toilet kit as a lap desk on which to write. The thirteen men from D.C. had stuck together, with Phil sitting next to the only black man among the recruits on the bus ride from Washington. Phil had quickly noticed that the man was being ignored and readily established that Jim Crow was very active in the army, with the one "Negro" being pointedly cast out of the group.

After a short time at Fort Meade, Phil was sent for basic training to Atlantic City, where I joined him and began my life as a camp follower. I found a room in a boarding house not far from the Boardwalk, where we shared a nightly two and a half hours. Much of the rest of the time I spent watching the men marching up and down the Boardwalk in the humid heat.

In some ways, going to Atlantic City meant getting started on normal life again, but it was depressing for me in almost every way—from the rooming house to the damp heat to the all-too-brief visits with Phil. After a few weeks, he was hospitalized with the flu or pneumonia, and since I was not allowed to visit him, I went back to Washington to wait to hear about his next assignment. Phil wrote touchingly from the hospital:

> . . . my afternoon sleeping was rather dozing off and on and all through it as all through the morning I thought of us—I was going to say you but that isn't accurate for I never think of anything but the two of us together.
>
> It is strange and wonderful and strengthening about us. More and more every day for two years we have become the single most important fact for me. Today—reading back magazines— I thought how horribly fakish Washington was run. And then I thought how much of this army was boarding school sadism passed on blindly, by rote. And then I realized that, though those were things of importance to me, they were dwarfed by something I feel sure only you and I have. I don't know how it happened to come to us, Katringham, but I know we must treasure it and I know we do treasure it. Sitting around now I get funny little thoughts all the time—about how I'll get to a phone the minute I land at my new post and tell you to start on at once; about just when I may be able to squeeze a three or four-day pass so we can go off together; about how after the war all other considerations about employment must be secondary to my need of several hours a day to be together with you.
>
> . . . I love thinking all those things. They don't come to mind out of sadness from being a little bit apart now. I think them because they are part of the knowledge of our inseparability—a beautiful piece of knowledge, Kate.

Phil was always ambivalent about the army. On the whole, it was much as he expected, and he liked it more than not. What he didn't like was its illogic. He would get frustrated by the straitjacket of the bureaucracy, the stupid, constant yowlings of the noncommissioned officers, the mix of efficiency with inefficiency, ineptitude, incompetence, waste, and negligence. "Fucking" was the universal adjective. It seemed to apply to everything and everyone—the "fucking chiseler," the "fucking sergeant," the "fucking camp." On the other hand, Phil loved the all-American men, among the best of whom was a young Pole from the steel mills of Pittsburgh who said it was important to trust the men, no matter what they might seem like: "These are good fellows here. I was afraid they'd be toughs but they're not. You can trust 'em. Christ, you gotta trust 'em on the battlefield, why not here?" Phil liked the men from whom he could get honest and useful information—how to make a bed properly, how to avoid the morning rush by shaving at night. Knowing these men gave us both a great pride in America. Many of them, although married and already parents, had enlisted because they believed in defending their country. Most of them had a peculiar mixture of gentleness and toughness. I was moved particularly by the patriotism and sacrifice of the boys from the South, who always seemed most heroic to me.

At the end of six weeks, Phil was shipped out of Atlantic City. We knew only that his destination was one of three communications schools run by the air force. By chance, the schools were one, two, and three days away from Washington. When Phil called at the end of the third day to say come right away, he was in the farthest and most remote radio school, the one in Sioux Falls, South Dakota.

At first I was worried about what life in Sioux Falls would be like, but then my father said he had "saved the town" in 1923 when he headed the Farm Loan Board and thought that he still had enough contacts to help me if all else failed. In fact, I was really pleased about the posting, because I felt I would rather be in a small and unexpected place than somewhere like Atlantic City or even St. Louis.

I arrived in Sioux Falls in early September and settled in within a few weeks. What we found there was a warm and friendly town, with lots of pretty little white houses with service flags in the windows. The clinging odor of John Morrell's meat-packing house shared the atmosphere with the coal smoke from hundreds of barracks stoves. We never saw the supposedly picturesque falls that gave the town its name and, in fact, could hardly imagine anything falling anywhere in such a great expanse of flatness. A reclaimed swamp just a mile northwest of town, flat as Florida, provided a superhighway for prairie gales. The camp was located right there, with the school buildings spread down its middle like an assembly line—the men went in one end the first day to learn the fundamentals of electricity and emerged from the other end as radio operators and mechanics several months later.

The military camp itself had a population of forty-five thousand, the town originally having fifteen thousand residents. Crowding was severe, and living quarters for the families of the servicemen were difficult to unearth. There was no possibility of my getting a decent apartment, and though a room in a house was just possible, I opted for a hotel, where I could have my own bath and telephone and privacy.

One thing we both quickly learned was not to believe anyone or anything about the army. Rumors flew around constantly—for example, that the men would all go on to gunnery school from Sioux Falls, and that the average life of gunners on bombers at the front was four minutes. Another rumor was that the whole air corps would be required to have new and different uniforms, which would cost every man $85 apiece.

The truth amid the rampant rumors was much harder for us than I was admitting, even to myself. We really felt for the first time in our spoiled lives what it was like to be at the bottom of the heap and miserable. It seemed as if an unseen hand was involved in a constant plot to make our lives unhappy. The world we lived in was run by half-mad civilian reserve officers recently called to duty, who appeared to respond to their whiff of power by specializing in a peculiar kind of mindless brutality toward privates. Men's leaves were canceled for no reason, and the men were often punished en masse for minor infractions committed by one or two individuals. Weird things happened, like the men being ordered down on their hands and knees to smooth out the dirt for a general's visit.

Hoping to master a useful tool while waiting for Phil to be off duty, I enrolled in typing and shorthand courses at the local business college, but found them hopelessly difficult. I missed some classes because of a cold and would have had to start over had Phil not gone on the day shift, allowing me to give up the courses altogether. I must admit I was relieved, especially in light of the young high-school graduates who whizzed by me with their prowess. I also did some work for the Red Cross, rolling bandages with the ladies. I intended to submit stories for the Sunday *Post*, but somehow life in Sioux Falls grew too busy, what with movies, concerts by the draftees, church suppers, lectures, and other social events. All of this was new and strange to me; I had never observed, much less lived, life in Middle America or a small town, or experienced the great kindness of people in such a place toward strangers.

A typical entertainment at a Kiwanis dinner consisted of welcoming the new members and wives (naturally not members), a short talk on some potential amendments to the club rules, a song by a young man from the local high school, and a speech by the chaplain of the Air Force School on the famous Sergeant Alvin C. York, World War I hero, whom the chaplain had once interviewed. I sat next to one of the town's oldest inhabitants, who had received a medal the year before for being a good citizen. He kept remarking on how much I could eat.

Besides going out to other clubs' meetings, I joined one myself, "Mrs. Private." This was a club formed by the privates' wives to help each other, especially the lonely and homeless. Its slogan was "Happier Lives for Privates' Wives." Every conceivable type of private's wife was there, a good many of whom were pregnant and most of whom had jobs—as waitresses, as salesgirls, or in the meat-packing house. Some local girls married privates, though others just "got in trouble." One local mother found herself with two unmarried pregnant daughters. When she complained to the colonel, he asked her how he could control thousands of men if she couldn't control her own daughters!

Much of my life in Sioux Falls, and elsewhere later on, consisted in

waiting for the hours a few times each week when Phil and I could be together. I wanted so much to have a baby, and very quickly again became
pregnant—my third pregnancy, counting my early miscarriage. True to
form, I started to miscarry and was quite sure that I'd lost a baby again. A
general practitioner advised total bedrest, which I dutifully accepted, except on days when I could get up and visit Phil at the camp. After a while,
when my troubles persisted, the doctor said it looked pretty hopeless and
suggested I go about my business and just let nature take its course. I got
up and began to lead a normal life, and eventually, to the surprise of both
me and the doctor, things got better. I told the doctor I thought I was still
pregnant—and I was.

Phil applied for Officers' Candidate School. He had a 97-percent average and had worked up to twenty-five words of Morse Code a minute,
which helped get him accepted. At the same time, the camp officer asked
him if he would like to remain in Sioux Falls to teach, which made Phil
even more eager to get to Officers' School.

I was thrilled with the idea of a stay at home in Washington while Phil
was at OCS training, but our momentary euphoria was brought to an
abrupt end. An X-ray of Phil's lungs brought to light seven or eight calci-
fied spots that, typically for the army, would bar him from OCS but permit him to remain as a private in the subzero weather of South Dakota.
Tiring of the straightforward approach, Phil decided to obtain letters of
recommendation for OCS, and asked Oscar Cox and Felix Frankfurter,
among others, for help on a waiver for this minor but normally disquali-
fying defect. While waiting for the hoped-for waiver, we settled down for
at least another six weeks in South Dakota and had Thanksgiving Day together when a new commanding officer let the married men off early,
which stunned us both with joy. An unexpected gift like that from the U.S.
Army was an exciting and important event in our lives. A kind friend invited us to spend the night at her house and have a late breakfast—a lovely
idea that resulted in a happy but sleepless night in a too narrow bed.

In January 1943, Phil graduated fifth in his class of five hundred, a
radio cadet with a waiver in hand for Officers' Candidate School. Soon
we left for the East, and within days of leaving Sioux Falls, we were both
restless and lonely at not being together, nostalgic for the proximity to
the camp of Room 611 at the Carpenter Hotel. The consolation of those
months in Sioux Falls was that we were together. I wouldn't have traded
being with him and sharing that experience for anything in the world. And
despite all its minuses, we had liked Sioux Falls.

On the other hand, I was looking forward to seeing everybody in
Washington and getting a taste of home life, as well as a meal I didn't have
to fight for. Since by this time it was definite, I *was* having a baby, and it
looked more and more as if I would be able to carry it through to term, I

decided to live at my parents' in order not to be alone while I was pregnant. Phil, now doing basic training for officers in Wayne, Pennsylvania, was happier in his work than he'd been for months. He liked the town, his hall, the officers, and the men. Then, in the middle of February, Phil left Wayne for further training at Yale, where he was pleasantly ensconced for six weeks in Farnum Hall, happily supplied with the East Coast's usual array of newspapers and magazines, and with a PX just fifty yards away. Our weekends in New Haven were wonderful, spent in a room at the Taft Hotel, only half a block from his hall. Phil worried about the long trip for pregnant me, but I was glad of the opportunity.

Phil graduated first in his class from the OCS program at Yale and was temporarily assigned, now as a second lieutenant and communications officer, to General "Wild Bill" Donovan's Office of Strategic Services, headquartered in Washington, where we finally had real time together. After ten days of OSS, however, which Phil found political and full of "white-shoe" boys, he decided he was miserable and asked to return to the air corps, which was not accomplished without considerable embarrassment.

Around May 1, his orders came to leave the next day for an air-force assignment center in Salt Lake City. This time I was too pregnant to think of going with him. Though I knew I would have to have the baby without him there, I comforted myself with the assurance that it was better to have had the glorious month of April together while I was still fairly mobile. We again went through a departure at the train station, accompanied once more by the dreadful uncertainty about where he was really headed.

I busied myself in moving to my old single room at my parents' house. I was almost undone by Phil's possessions left behind, especially his pennies, which all his life he took out of his pockets and stacked on a dresser or tabletop. One note of comic relief was that he had left my framed photo behind on the mantel.

THE SECOND AIR FORCE had an awesome array of places to which Phil could have been sent from Salt Lake City, with Boise, Tucson, Galveston, Sioux City, and El Paso being the choicest. On May 7, I heard that he had left for Ephrata, Washington, from which he wrote that his own worst expectations had been met.

Ephrata, near Yakima, was a combat-crew training school in the middle of nowhere, made from old huts left over from the New Deal days of the Civilian Conservation Corps. The camp was terribly organized for living or for leaving, situated as it was near a town of nine hundred people and offering few, if any, escapes for the men. It was a cold and barren place, and Phil was already a bit depressed by the time he reached it. His time there was probably the nadir of his military life, marked by constant bad weather, heights of inefficiency, and depths of loneliness.

My letters to Phil and his to me were like long, continuing conversations—mine about whom I'd seen, where I'd been, some national issues, and the frequently discussed baby, always referred to as Petunia; his about the difficulties of life in Ephrata. I felt unapologetic about confiding any low feelings I had, because I knew how I'd feel if Phil didn't tell me how *he* felt. I didn't see why there should be added to the strain of a relationship by correspondence the false burden of pseudo-gallantry. In truth, I was worried about the real reason for Phil's gloom—whether he was unhappy about the long run or the short. Was his mood, like mine, affected by the weather and not being together, or was it the lack of congenial company, or what was it?

In September 1942, my mother had made a tour of Britain's war centers to report on how the citizenry there was focused on production. She and a friend, Ruth Taylor, journeyed for a month visiting hospitals, children's nurseries, schools, factories, workers' canteens, social centers, and occupational clubs. Her conclusion was that the United States had yet to learn what she considered her major impression of that trip—that this was "a people's war," and that the maximum war effort in Great Britain had "set a social revolution in motion." Her observations of life on the home front in England propelled her to set out early in 1943 on a four-month trip around the United States, visiting factories, shipyards, tenements, schools, day-care centers, reporting on America's home front and the social effects of the war.

In Mother's absence, I enjoyed the relative calm. I kept my father company and helped him at the "smokers," or off-the-record stag dinners and seminars he often gave to bring together administration officials and foreign dignitaries with the *Post*'s editors and writers, so that they could exchange views on how the war was going and what needed to be done by businesses to help the effort. But the dinners I remember most were the quiet ones when just he and I were together. We rarely talked intimately—neither of us had a great capacity, at that time, for intimacy—but without acknowledging it, we had grown very close and very dependent on each other.

During this time, he was as pleased as a little boy because the *Post* was going to break even for the first time. By the middle of the war, the paper actually moved into the black, though not making in 1942 as much as it had lost in 1941. The *Post*'s reputation had grown immeasurably. It had gained substantial prestige and was showing the positive effects of all the efforts and money spent in the ten years since my father bought it. Although he was wary of being too optimistic, nothing could conceal his intense excitement. He and I spent a great deal of time talking about the *Post* specifically and newspapers in general. At one point during the war, he gave me a part-time job reading and comparing newspapers for news play and ideas. I was very enthusiastic and added *PM* and *The New York Times* to the list of papers he wanted me to look at, rejecting payment of any kind so that I could retain the right to leave the job if and when I could join Phil.

In 1943, Herbert Elliston and my father hired Alan Barth from a small Texas newspaper. Barth, more liberal than either of them, was a fighting voice for civil rights and civil liberties and became both a great distinction and, at times, a political problem for my father—and, later, Phil. But he was an ornament to the editorial page, whose contents had markedly improved.

The business side had improved, too, though less spectacularly and more unevenly than the editorial. The circulation department was still in its predevelopment stage and had no adequate managers or professional expertise. Early in 1944, the home-delivery price was increased and the street-sale price went from three cents to a nickel. We were running fifteen million lines of advertising, or two and a half times the original 1933 linage.

On the minus side, the *Post* lacked coherence and consistency and had inadequate local coverage. At the time, Washingtonians still had no vote and the city was governed by a triumvirate of commissioners appointed by the president. The city was also segregated; black citizens and black crime were not considered news. John Riseling, the night city editor, had a map of the District in his head, and when something happened in a black area, no one was sent to cover it.

Patterns were set that influenced the paper for years to come. The editorial page was independent of the news section. It was also independent of my father's views, yet enough in sync with them that he was pleased and proud of it. Campaigns of all kinds were waged by Casey Jones, the managing editor, and others—against congressmen abusing parking privileges, on child-welfare issues, against the sale of babies for adoption, on a subversive propaganda group in league with the office of right-wing Congressman Hamilton Fish. The *Post* also raised a lonely warning voice opposing discrimination against Americans of Japanese descent in the name of national security. Occasionally, Casey Jones would get wrought up enough to write a front-page editorial, causing great consternation for everyone, but especially for those on the editorial page.

A very important role was played by women on the *Post* during the war years. Elsie Carper, just out of college, joined the paper and was able to move up quickly; many women were taking over the jobs of men who had gone off to war. Marie Sauer, always a stalwart on the women's pages, was one of the key reporters and editors. I remember worrying about my father's reaction when Marie joined the Waves—I knew how much he was relying on these women. Unfortunately, like all publications, the *Post* sank back into its old ways after the men returned. A nucleus remained, however, although largely on the women's pages and in what were regarded as women's issues: welfare and education.

Despite all the evident improvement in the paper, however, it was in no way certain that the *Post* would survive. The Washington newspaper scene was very chaotic, particularly for a town its size. No other city of half a million had so many papers, none of which was a fly-by-night. The struggle for survival was omnipresent and at times a discouraging burden to my father, who was nearing seventy. Seeing him as I did each day, I was constantly worried about how tired he seemed and how hard he was working. These past ten years had taken a tremendous toll.

Given his concerns, my father turned his attention more and more to thinking about the future of the *Post*. The first inkling I had that he might have begun to look at Phil as a white knight came just two years after our marriage. In the fall of 1942, Dad and I were on a train coming back from Mount Kisco, and naturally we were talking about Phil. I remember his commenting on how well Phil wrote and how much he'd love to have him on the paper. I told Phil in a letter, "You better watch out if you don't want it is all I can say. You may find it in your stocking Christmas morning."

Shortly after this, my father seems to have brought up with both of us the possibility of Phil's working at the paper after the war. Certainly he saw his whole endeavor as useless unless he could project a future for the *Post* in the family. In those days, of course, the only possible heir would have been a male, and since my brother was in medicine and had shown little or no interest in the business, my father naturally thought of Phil. Far from troubling me personally that my father thought of my husband and not me, it pleased me. In fact, it never crossed my mind that he might have viewed me as someone to take on an important job at the paper.

Although the impending war had prevented us from moving to Florida after Phil had finished his year as law clerk with Frankfurter, he still had plans to follow Brandeis's admonition to young Harvard Law School graduates to go back where they came from and become part of grassroots America. Given his love of politics and natural affinity for it, this was Phil's plan and his desire. He wanted to do public service and to deal with societal problems, as did many of the best and the brightest of our generation—or at least most of those we knew. And despite their mutually respectful, affectionate relationship, Phil had always said he would never work for my father.

But now he was faced with the actual possibility of working on the *Post*. It was an exciting idea, though with a lot of risk involved. It would be a tough struggle in an area in which he had only a passing, indirect knowledge through talking to my father. Phil had to weigh the offer against not only his ambition to go into law and politics in Florida but his own father's wish that he come to Florida to be part of the dairy business there.

Phil was in Officers' Candidate School in New Haven when most of the talks between him and my father took place—and between the two of us. Phil and I sat on the beds in my room at the Taft Hotel for many hours discussing my father's offer. I loved the idea but didn't try to persuade Phil. When he asked me what I thought, I ducked, saying I loved Washington, it was my home, but I knew I could be happy other places as well. I also knew I loved the *Post*, but he was the one who would be working, and it really had to be his decision; this was his life, and he had to decide what he wanted to do with it.

After much talk, consultation, and soul-searching, he finally decided to accept. Agreeing with my father's philosophy, he saw that he could be involved in public issues through the paper as well as through politics. He concluded that the *Post* was a great opportunity, albeit a risky one.

BEFORE HE LEFT for overseas, my brother had suggested that I check in with a new obstetrician at Johns Hopkins Hospital in Baltimore, whom he and my sister-in-law wanted me to go to for the baby. I was so traumatized by what had happened before that I wanted to return to my old doctor, probably as a way of reassuring myself that the loss of the first baby was an inevitable accident. I went on denying that anything wrong had been done, attributing the tragedy to fate. Bill pointed out that a teaching hospital like Johns Hopkins would keep good staff longer. His advice led me to go there for the birth of all four of my children.

As Phil whiled away his time in Ephrata, this baby's due date neared, and all appeared to be well. I had been warned by my doctor that, in order to circumvent the problem of getting to Baltimore in gas-restricted wartime, I should move there on June 5, just to be safe for the June 15 due date. In a fit of well-meant caring, Bis and Pare Lorentz, whom she was just about to marry, persuaded me to go even earlier, so on June 1 I took up residence in Baltimore. Needing someone for company in this strange town, I turned to my sister-in-law, Mary Meyer, who agreed to come with me, leaving her six-month-old son, a deeply generous act (at least to me). We lived together in the Belvedere Hotel in the June heat. Spending any extended time in a hotel, even if it was the best hotel in Baltimore, is difficult; but this was a hotel in wartime in a strange city in which I had no real friends, waiting for a baby to come who didn't seem very anxious to get here. I quickly became nervous, edgy, and vulnerable.

Phil sympathized with my two years of pretty constant pregnancy and suggested that "in 10 or 15 years it'll all be over and there'll stand the 8 or 12 grinning little bastards tearing up the furniture, spilling our liquor, drooling on your new dress, yowling too early in the morning, and generally proclaiming the solidarity of the home"—an old-fashioned view of life, which we shared completely.

Whether we had miscalculated or whether the baby was just late, we waited restlessly for four weeks, by the end of which Mary, whom I'd quite worn out, had to leave. Bis was getting married to Pare and my family were all at Mount Kisco. I asked a friend from Washington, Rosamund Burling, to come and wait with me for what would be the final few days.

I was lucky to have not only Rosamund in the fathers' waiting room but a friend who was a pediatrician, Mary Goodwin. She was the one who lay the baby across my stomach and said, "It's a girl, and she's fine."

Elizabeth Morris Graham had finally arrived on July 3, safe and sound. I remember my father's coming to see me and his new grandchild. My mother was at Mount Kisco, but she didn't seem to enter the picture much. Fortunately, Phil's class had graduated in Ephrata and he himself arrived back east on the very day Elizabeth was born, so he was in on the excitement and was there to bring us home. Needless to say, I was terribly happy to have the baby safely here—after the nine long months and after my earlier losses—and to be together with Phil as well.

I had looked for a nurse to help for the first few weeks, but had decided that I wouldn't—as my mother had done—keep a nurse permanently. My intention was to do it all myself—a resolve that broke down almost immediately. During the first week, while still in the hospital, I struggled to nurse the baby. After a futile effort, which set both me and the baby on edge, I abandoned the attempt and put her on a formula, and everything went better.

The new baby nurse, Mary Bishop—a Scots lady of great warmth, good humor, and devotion—came to help us temporarily, but, just like Powelly with us Meyer children, Mamie, as we came to call her, stayed, becoming part of all our lives, a real friend. The whole arrangement with her worked so smoothly that she didn't leave us until the fourth young Graham outgrew her and she retired to Scotland.

Having a nurse to take care of a baby, except for its visits to its mother twice a day, was not, at the time, so odd an arrangement as it would seem today. But the presence of Miss Bishop undoubtedly impeded my learning how to cope. Gradually I took more care of Elizabeth, but I never learned to be truly at ease with small babies, although I got better with each one.

IN RESPONSE TO an air-force memo stating a need for combat intelligence, Phil switched from communications and was accepted at the Air Intelligence School in Harrisburg, Pennsylvania, which is why he was able to be with me after the baby's birth. After life in the shadows of lethargy at

Ephrata, he was cheered by what he found in Harrisburg, a pervasive competence that lifted him back onto a plane of enthusiasm.

After my six-week checkup, I visited Phil in Harrisburg for his last week there. Again, he was high up in his class at graduation and was asked to stay on to teach. He decided to stay, and for the first time in six months we would be together again.

We set up housekeeping in Harrisburg, taking things from our 37th Street house (which we had sublet to the Steichens). Luckily, we inherited a beautiful apartment from San Francisco friends, Gay and Jack Bradley, who in turn had succeeded Jock and Betsey Whitney. For two months, we led an ideal and spoiling life—fairly normal hours and luxurious living. While Phil taught, I went to work as a volunteer at the Ration Board. Mamie took care of the baby, and Mattie took care of all of us. But at the end of these two glorious months, the owner reclaimed the apartment, and we met the cold breeze of reality when I started looking for another place to live. All we could find was a small apartment in a recently (and badly) built housing complex with paper-thin walls and an electric stove with the maddening habit of dying right in the middle of a roast.

The day we actually moved, Phil was recovering from a farewell party we'd hosted, so I packed up everything—the last object being an inert Phil—and got us to the new apartment. I didn't think much about it at the time, but this was the beginning of a pattern that I can see now was quite unhealthy: I was expected to perform all the pulling and hauling; Phil gave directions and put the fun in my life and the children's. Gradually I became the drudge and, what's more, accepted my role as a kind of second-class citizen. I think this definition of roles deepened as time went on and I became increasingly unsure of myself.

Another development seems to have surfaced way back then—Phil's increasing ill-health and drinking. He was extremely vulnerable to afflictions, which affected him powerfully. I was constitutionally much stronger. If he got a cold, he went to bed. If we both ate bad seafood, it affected him twice as much as it did me. Often he seemed to have some incapacitating kind of "flu."

Shortly after we moved to the new place, Mattie got ill and had to be hospitalized. This is when I was forced to learn some semblance of cooking, but I had no idea how to organize a meal. Phil's admonitions to "keep it simple" were wise but only succeeded in irritating me and making me more desperate as I struggled with *Fanny Farmer*, not to mention my new stove's penchant for suddenly expiring. I always tried to do too much, ending up with frequent failures and several notable disasters. Mamie was as helpless in the kitchen as she was helpful with the baby, having lived all her working life in large, wealthy households with lots of servants who took care of such things as meals.

On Mamie's days off she usually returned to Washington, so I also had the baby to care for. On these days, there was twice as much work as necessary because of darling Mamie's old-fashioned notions of things like hand-squeezed orange juice and beef juice as necessities. My own extreme nervousness, born of my inexperience, seemed to result in instant tears and screaming from the baby. Naps were few and far between, except when I pushed her in the baby carriage for miles up and down the streets of Harrisburg.

Army life, too, was a series of ups and downs—living together followed by another painful parting, living luxuriously and then in relatively difficult circumstances. Relief from the downside of Harrisburg arrived in late January 1944. Phil had maneuvered to jump over to a more exciting and challenging milieu in the Special Branch. So, after another month-long school program on intelligence training, he was transferred to Washington to go into the Special Branch, a super-secret part of Intelligence, run by an ex–Cravath, Swaine & Moore lawyer, Colonel Al McCormick, who had commandeered many of our friends, as well as many others who were to become friends. I never knew, and probably none of the spouses knew, what Phil and the other men did. Only much later, when we learned that early in the war the secret codes used by Germany and Japan had been broken, did we understand that Special Branch had been engaged in reading messages being sent back and forth from the field.

When we returned to Washington, we reclaimed our little row house on 37th Street from the Steichens and resumed a somewhat normal Washington life. Many of our friends were scattered around the world in various parts of the armed services, but still there were old friends like Prich and the Frankfurters, as well as my family. Then, in October 1944, after almost nine months of back-to-normal married life, Phil, as expected, was assigned to the Pacific and had to leave suddenly. The rush of departure again had been so great that the familiar low feelings that always accompanied these leavetakings only hit us after we were separated. Letters between us flew back and forth every day, more or less, for the whole year that he was gone—so many that most of mine were destroyed by him, because their bulk was too great for him to carry around. Phil's are almost all preserved. He left for the Pacific by way of San Francisco, Hawaii, and New Guinea, winding up in the Philippines with the Far East Air Forces. Having just been promoted at the end of September, he was finally beginning to look around when someone yelled "Captain."

PHIL WAS TO spend most of the rest of the war in the Philippines in an important job. He started off reporting to his own boss in Special Branch and also to the regular intelligence officer under General George Kenney, commander of the Allied Air Forces in the Southwest Pacific. Kenney was essentially MacArthur's air commander. Eventually, Phil again rose to the top and worked closely with General Kenney himself. When Kenney later wrote a memoir, entitled *General Kenney Reports*, he inscribed a copy to Phil with the note: "To Phil Graham, the only really intelligent intelligence officer I had . . ."

From the beginning of his overseas duty, Phil talked in excited terms of what was going on out there and the fine team of people he was assembling. He spoke movingly about all those with whom he worked, describing them in detail and bringing them to life. He constantly praised the enlisted people—how hard they worked, how much he counted on them, and how much he appreciated what they did: "Every day one of them rocks me back on my heels by turning up with some complicated job they have dreamed up on their own initiative and done beautifully. They are all terribly eager, in a decent non-bucking sort of way, and they love us and we them. . . ."

I always wondered where Phil's natural affinity for people in all walks of life came from. Perhaps it was growing up on the farm, or dropping out of college to drive the milk truck and relating to his customers as well as to the people on the farm. Wherever it came from, his ability to cut through formalities and talk to both men and women almost immediately in an intimate and connected way was an invaluable asset throughout his life. I learned a lot from him in this respect, but never developed that almost political connection he had with most people.

The *Post*, or at least clippings from it, which he received somewhat irregularly, provided Phil with a continuing window on the way Washington viewed the war and the world. He also went on writing to my father about his reactions to the *Post*'s coverage and editorials, criticizing this or that, praising something else. In one letter, after complaining about the *Post*'s reaction to Henry Wallace, then vice-president of the United States, and disapproving of an emphasis on trivial stories (like a dog getting a ride on an air-transport plane) when he felt there were more important things to worry about, Phil added: "Those are all really minor matters and as long as you keep sending such cigars as those that have arrived I shall bow to your every decision. . . ."

Phil worked hard while in the Philippines, and, typically, the harder he worked, the more he seemed to like what he was doing. Meanwhile, life in Washington went along for me fairly routinely and comfortably. By this time, Elizabeth, or Acey, as Phil then called her—she was later called Lally—was over a year old and I was again pregnant. I wanted to work, in part to help fill the hours while Phil was away, but I needed a job that would keep me busy, teach me something, yet not be draining. I went back to the *Post* at a pedestrian and undemanding but instructive job in the circulation department, responding to complaints. My job fit the bill of keeping me busy without being too exhausting. I caught the bus outside the house and worked regular hours.

We were only a handful of people who answered phones, took down information, and forwarded it to the appropriate office. The department was a mess, riddled with backbiting and intrigue. It was here that I encountered the disagreeableness of seeing things being badly run, with everyone complaining—most of all, the customers—and not being able to do anything about it. The job taught me how to deal with enraged subscribers and how hard it is at times to get a simple situation resolved. One caller said he was a friend of Eugene Meyer's and would go directly to him if we couldn't fix the problem. I promised to do our best, then added that I was Eugene Meyer's daughter and had never had the pleasure of meeting this caller, nor had ever heard his name mentioned by my father. A more important thing I learned was how terrible a confused and poorly managed department is for those who work in it.

Most of the winter went by quietly and quickly for me—I was busy with the routine of working and coming home to Elizabeth. Phil wrote to my mother, saying, "I suppose Kay is still as mother-hennish as ever and bristles when you bust in on the Ace at some crucial time; I love Kay's bristles." I recognize myself in Phil's references to my too-great passion for order and routine—a boring affliction I have carried most of my life, even though Phil did a lot to free me of it. I wish he could have done more.

BECAUSE OUR LIVES had been shaped socially by our New Deal friends and then wartime in Washington, Sioux Falls, and Harrisburg, I had been to dinners such as my family gave or those given by our few older friends, but I myself had never given "a dinner." I was particularly inept at doing things like that because I had grown up in such a large household, where everything happened on a different, huge scale. What I was used to was having a few friends over to share Mattie's very good but simple food, which she both cooked and served.

My first attempt at entertaining has stayed indelibly with me for half a century. Jonathan and June Bingham, young friends who had moved back to New York when the war broke out, were visiting for the weekend, and I decided to have a few friends over, including Prich and Isaiah Berlin, a relatively new but close friend who was in Washington at this time as an information officer in the British Embassy. The other couple I invited was Donald and Melinda Maclean. Donald was something like third secretary at the British Embassy, and through Isaiah the Macleans became friends of mine. The two of them seemed like attractive, intelligent, liberal young people—in short, much like our own circle of friends. None of us could remotely have suspected that Donald would later emerge as a communist spy. Even now it's hard for me to comprehend that both Donald and Melinda were Soviet agents.

The night of my dinner, conversation went well enough during the meal, which was perfectly peaceful except that both Donald and Prich got rather drunker than I realized. After dinner we moved out of the dining room into our front room, a small area with only space for a sofa, four chairs, and a bench in front of the fireplace. No sooner had we settled down there than the conversation got edgy. Prich and Donald began to tease Isaiah about his social life, which they portrayed as being too conciliatory of right-wing or isolationist people. Everyone teased hard in those days, but that night the teasing gradually slid into acrimony and became unpleasant, exacerbated no doubt by Prich's and Donald's alcohol consumption.

Out of the blue, Donald said to Isaiah, "The trouble with you is you hunt with the hounds and run with the hares. You know people like Alice Longworth; that's disgusting. One shouldn't know people like that. If I thought you knew her out of curiosity, I wouldn't mind so much. But I'm told you actually like her company. That is dreadful."

Isaiah asked why Donald thought it was dreadful.

"Because she's fascist and right-wing. She's everything that's awful," Donald spat out.

Isaiah, totally taken aback, summoned up his courage and replied, "Well, you know, we're supposed to be fighting for civilization. Civilization entails that we're allowed to know anybody we wish. It's true that in wartime or during the revolution one may be prepared to shoot them, that I concede, but so long as one doesn't have to . . . Of course, one must be judged by one's friends. I don't deny that either. That is my defense." Donald immediately pounced, saying, "That's wrong. What you say is absolutely false. Life is a battle. We must know which side we're on. We must stick to our side through thick and thin. I know at the last moment, the twelfth hour, you'll be on our side. But until then, you'll go about with these dreadful people."

Isaiah claims that I then said, "He's absolutely right."

Donald kept battering Isaiah: "The trouble is you're a coward. You know what's right and you know what's wrong and you will not cut out in time to defend the right cause. You know perfectly well what I mean."

The poor Binghams were flabbergasted. They didn't know what it was all about and shuffled around nervously. At one point I went upstairs and looked out the window to see Donald Maclean relieving himself on the front lawn. The nightmare evening seemed completely out of control. Finally, everyone decided at once that it was time to go. Melinda offered Isaiah a lift, to which he responded, "No, certainly not." Donald, still pursuing his line, added, "Oh, you wouldn't take a lift from us, oh, never."

So ended my first dinner party as a single hostess.

Prich and I called Isaiah separately after the dinner, apologizing for what had happened and asking him what to do to heal the wounds. I found him angry and bruised. His response to me was, "Prich has no manners anyway, so he doesn't know any better, and I will forgive him eventually. But Donald Maclean does know better, and I'll never speak to him again."

Years passed, and Andrew Boyle, interviewing Isaiah for a book he was writing, asked, "What made all those young men in Cambridge go left-wing?" Isaiah then told Boyle about this dinner. In describing it, he said he felt like Douglas Fairbanks in one of those old films, fending off several of the enemy at once. The first edition of the book added an untrue but funny touch to the drama of the evening by solemnly reporting, "Donald Maclean turned upon his stockier colleague and attacked him for his political views. He would have struck him but Douglas Fairbanks, Jr., thrust himself between them." That bit was removed from the second edition. What actually happened was dramatic enough for me.

As the spring of 1945 approached, I realized I would have to move—our lease was about to expire and our cozy little house, which we had been in off and on for almost five years, would be too small after the new baby came in April. I had hoped to rent, but there was little or nothing to be had, so I faced buying a house, which worried me without Phil around to consult. He was supportive, however, saying that he thought my judgment was sound, agreeing that I should rent if I could but buy if a bargain or necessity forced me to. By "bargain" he meant "something irresistible rather than something for half price." He also felt that eventually we would want to live farther out than Georgetown, particularly if the time ever again came when there was sufficient gas to move around freely.

In early March, as I was in the throes of looking for a house and nearing the due date for the baby, I got word that Phil would be coming back to Washington with General Kenney for a few days of meetings. I went out to the military airport to welcome them when they arrived on March 14 in a C-54, the first four-engine plane I had ever seen. Their mission, which I certainly wasn't aware of at the time, was to argue that Japan was through. Special Branch knew that the Japanese were weaker than General Marshall and many others thought. The meetings also had to do with the need for an immediate invasion of Japan. "I didn't believe it was necessary to wait for Hitler to fold nor did we need help from the Russians to beat Japan," wrote General Kenney later. General Marshall didn't agree, believing the Japanese still had a lot of fight left in them, and certainly a large army that would have to be defeated. Initially, General Kenney was not going to be allowed by the top brass to see the president, but Phil, through his friends in the White House, arranged a meeting. Kenney reported that FDR looked tired and gray and that his hands shook when he held some photos of Corregidor. Roosevelt told Kenney he had lost twenty-five pounds and had no appetite.

Though the visit was exciting in many ways, it was also frantic, and a very strained reunion for Phil and me. I was feeling the pressure of looking for a new house. At the same time, I was laboring under the usual stresses of being eight months pregnant. I always seemed to carry my babies right out front, and I produced big babies. And there was an early heat wave, which made me more miserable than ever.

Phil was already strung out and exhausted from the long trip back to Washington, on top of which he was busy the entire week, working about fourteen hours a day. He spent a large part of his nights phoning the families of his colleagues back in the Philippines, so we didn't have much chance to see each other. I was dispatched with a shopping list and spent my days running around town gathering gifts and necessities for him to take back—cigars for the men; housecoats, bobby pins, and even cotton panties for the WACS; sardines and whiskey for everyone. I then had to sit down and tape the cork tops of the liquor bottles so they wouldn't pop under the poor pressurization of the plane on the return trip.

Toward the end of the week, I begged Phil to look at a house I had found and settled on buying, a sort of solid, unimaginative, but adequate gray stone house behind a Sears, Roebuck store in a rather nondescript neighborhood. Phil, his mind on Kenney's mission and not on house-hunting, walked through the house in a dazed and uninterested way, saying it looked fine to him and agreeing to it without enthusiasm.

Phil and General Kenney were to take off at eight the next morning, and as I was driving Phil to the airport, he told me that the real-estate agent had called him, very embarrassed, to say that the house turned out to be in a restricted area—meaning it was zoned against sale to either Jews or Negroes. It took me totally by surprise. The issue of my Jewish identity had never arisen in a discriminatory way except for the incident about clubs at the University of Chicago, so I was more or less oblivious to the problem. Phil said that it was totally illegal and we could sue, but he didn't think I'd want to do that on my own. He then said, "I don't much like the house anyway. I'm afraid you'll have to go on looking." The thought of extending the search still further added an extra pall to his departure.

So, with the baby only a few weeks away, and without a house for us to move to, Phil flew back to the Pacific. In desperation, I bought the next house to come along—one at 33rd and O Streets in Georgetown, a very odd house with two living rooms on the ground floor and a kitchen and dining room in the basement. I wrote Phil that we had bought a house I didn't much like.

For the first time I faced paying for a house and furnishing it. I worried whether I could make such a purchase without dipping into capital; in fact, I didn't really know the difference between capital and income, or that there was such a thing as a mortgage—a typical example of my ignorance about handling money. In my parents' zeal not to discuss money, they neglected ever to explain what you could and couldn't do with what you had. Nor had I ever asked my father about financing a house; and he didn't offer to tell me how much I could or should sensibly allot.

I was also entirely at sea about decorating or how much it was appropriate to spend. I found a decorator, a nice woman who ran an antiques store a few blocks away from the new house. She asked if I liked English or French furniture and what I could afford. I replied blankly that I had no idea what she was talking about—I didn't know there was a distinction between English or French, much less what either would cost. I still have remnants of some of the furniture I acquired then, but it took many decorating experiences and corrected mistakes before I knew how I wanted things to look.

I moved into the new house that summer. Though it was considerably larger and harder to run than the old one, at least I had a place to live.

ON APRIL 12, 1945, the world got the news that FDR had died. None of us realized how ill he had been, so we were stunned. It seemed as though we had suddenly lost a father figure in whom we had the greatest confidence and were confronted by an unknown, relatively inexperienced, and seemingly uninspiring Midwestern former senator, Harry Truman. With an overwhelming sadness, I went down to see the funeral procession that brought the president's casket from the train to the White House. A week later, I went back to the Belvedere Hotel in Baltimore, my mother accompanying me, to await the birth of the new baby. Donald Edward was born three days later, on April 22.

Don was quite unexpected-looking to me and seemed to resemble no one I knew of in either of our families, although his mouth was slightly like mine. He was light in coloring and had not much hair of any kind, but such as there was was light brown. I thought he was quite a character from the beginning. To commemorate Phil's thirtieth birthday, my father wrote him an account of how he viewed our two children. His letter was amazingly prescient: "Lally is getting more important to me weekly. . . ." He called Donald "Judge" because:

> . . . his reaction to his observations is calm and quiet and seems to be balanced in a sort of judicial manner. I even think I detect in his eyes an expression of humor reflecting his judgement on what he observes. . . . I don't think anybody is going to get him excited if he can help it and I think he thinks he can. If you think he is go-

ing to be a torch bearer for any of the isms that you want to hand him or try to instill in him, I feel it my duty to tell you I think you are going to be disappointed. On the other hand, if you have anything to say to him on a factual basis, with good evidence and perhaps a witness or two, I believe you may interest him in your presentation.

THE WAR IN EUROPE ended on May 7, but the war in the Pacific went on, culminating on August 6, when the atomic bomb was dropped on Hiroshima. The letter Phil wrote me the next day contains his appropriate reactions to the concept of the bomb but no indication that he realized it had been dropped on a city filled with civilians:

> Donald—if they permit him—can always point with pride to the fact he got here just a little ahead of the atomic bomb, or the "greatest achievement of our scientists, industry, labor and military" as someone aptly put it. If it is but half what is claimed for it, then clearly it is the final triumph and there would seem to be no reason at all for so much as a turnip to survive the next one.

But on August 11 he wrote again, saying that the first bomb had "scared the living hell out of me."

Most of September passed with rumors of Phil's being sent to Japan, but he thought there was nothing substantive for him to do there, and by that time he wanted nothing more than to come home. Under the system by which the men and women in the armed forces overseas accumulated points that put them in line for returning home—Don had added six points to Phil's total—he received his orders on September 27 and was on a waiting list with the Air Transport Command, with a good chance of leaving within ten days. He was close to being embarrassed at getting away so easily, but he was grateful. And so was I.

— *Chapter Eleven* —

B ACK IN WASHINGTON lay an uncertain future. Despite his earlier agreement to work at the *Post*, Phil still seemed undecided about what he was going to do. Al Friendly had written to him, talking about his own desire to return to the *Post* and pleading with Phil to "go Postward." At the end of August 1945, Phil told Al that there had been a general agreement with my father the year before but nothing had been said since. In addition, Phil's father, Ernie, was persistent in urging that he come to Florida to help run the dairy business. Even as late as September, Ernie had written Phil about what he called "the set-up out here," referring to the farm at Hialeah, which Ernie said was "too good a thing to be turned down without thought."

Somewhere along the way, Phil made up his mind. On December 28, there was an announcement that he would join the paper on January 1, 1946. The next day, a letter from Phil's friends and associates at Lend-Lease—Oscar Cox, Joe Rauh, Al Davidson, Buster Stoddard, Lloyd Cutler, Winthrop Brown, Louis Hector, and Malcolm Langford—appeared on the editorial page praising the appointment, listing his achievements, and congratulating the *Post* on hiring him. His friends obviously wanted to tell *Post* readers that this was more than the publisher's son-in-law— that he had a demonstrably distinguished track record of his own.

And so the year 1946 was the beginning of a new and drastically altered era for us. We went from young, fun-loving people with few responsibilities to the other extreme. The day-to-day changes were gradual, so at the time I didn't see how different our lives were becoming, but in fact we had taken an enormous step into a new and more serious life.

After a terminal-leave vacation in Phoenix, Arizona, Phil started his postwar work at the age of thirty as associate publisher of the *Post*. My father had said that he himself was too old to let Phil take an entry-level job and work his way up through different departments, so Phil came into the paper as deputy to my father and had to learn an entirely new and very competitive business, starting essentially at the top.

Because he had to work so hard, I took more than ordinary charge of our private lives. And I, too, had to work very hard at learning a variety of things—mostly domestic, some social. My life was centered on shifting gears from the camp-following of the war years and my times alone. Everything seemed new to me, including life in a family with a husband and children.

On a morning newspaper, at least, no one really gets started until ten or so. Lally was our alarm clock. Most mornings at eight she came thundering in, full of cheer, shouting, "Wake up, Daddy!" This was my wake-up call—at which point Phil would grunt and go back to sleep for another hour.

Although we had Mamie Bishop as our children's nurse, I was more actively involved in the care of the children and the running of the house. After Mattie, who never got well enough to return to work, we had a cook, Bessie, and a laundress, Ethel Beverley, who managed to tear up everything. Phil said her husband must be called Peg Leg Beverley, or else why did he possess only one sock out of every pair? Alas, I was never able to fire anyone—a problem I had to face years later, when I went to work—so she remained, and the sock problem stayed with us.

The children were fast developing into individuals, but my own maternal skills were developing more slowly. Despite the help, every day seemed hectic, and Mamie's days off often sent me into a tailspin, in which I seemed more than ever all thumbs. One week when she was away, Donny fell out of his crib because I had left the side down, and out of his swing while I was weeding the yard. He ended up looking like Donald Duck, with his swollen upper lip sticking out an inch. That was the same week I put the nipples for his bottles on to boil and forgot them while I took time out to call people for a party. When the smell of burning alerted me, I found flames a foot high shooting out of the pan, threw it into the sink to put out the fire, and turned the water on, only to have the pot explode glass all over the place. I couldn't help wondering how the children would fare if I took care of them all the time.

At times, Donny was a difficult baby. He took a great deal of patience, and I had very little. From the age of six months to a year, he alternated between violent activity and ensuing exhaustion and crankiness. It was often hard to get him to eat. One day, when he had thrown his entire dinner on the floor, I was so desperate that I asked Lally what to do. With total common sense, she suggested, "Try him with a sandwich." I must say it worked quite well. After that she became my able and enthusiastic assistant.

Even as a three-year-old, Lally was beginning to make a good deal of sense. She loved being "grown-up," accompanied me everywhere, and was a marvelous companion, with plenty of humor and sympathy. I was quite silly about her and scared that I was spoiling her. Lally and Donald both seemed indefatigable, and once we acquired a Springer-spaniel pup the three of them together managed to keep Phil and me, as he put it, "in a constant mood of subdued fatigue."

Despite the occasional calamities, however, my practical knowledge was growing—of how to run houses, bring up children, and relate to them as a parent. Most of all, I had to learn how to relate to Phil himself in a very different environment from what we had experienced previously. He was overworked from the start, and grew tired from the pace and the increased responsibilities, but he also thrived on them.

Our social circle was expanding, and even though some of our prewar friends had left town, we remained close. Prich was one of these. He had turned down several job offers in Washington, including assistant attorney general for civil rights and leader of the liberal group the Americans for Democratic Action, and moved back to Kentucky to start a law firm, but he made frequent visits to Washington on behalf of all kinds of clients.

It was in these immediate postwar years that we entered into our life-long friendship with Joseph Alsop, who was writing a popular syndicated column with Robert Kintner for the *Herald-Tribune*. Joe was a prominent figure around town by this time, so he entertained a great deal and went out to dinners on nights when he didn't entertain. Joe always lived well beyond his means—partly on his expense account, but more because he knew so well how to live. Someone once said of Joe that he was the only person who liked his friends better than they liked him. In the beginning that may have been true, but not as the years passed.

Phil and I were also developing another and very different group of friends. This group included the columnist Walter Lippmann and his wife, Helen; Massachusetts Representative Joe Casey and his wife, Connie, and her brother, Drew Dudley, who worked for the World Bank and was a single man, very much on the town; Joe Alsop's younger brother, Stew, and his young British wife, Tish; Marquis Childs, the columnist, and his first wife, Biddy; Bill and Betty Fulbright; Arthur and Marian Schlesinger, and the *Post*'s editor, Herbert Elliston, and his wife, Joanne.

Walter was the most widely read political columnist of his time. He was very intelligent, but he was also a prima donna. He had married Helen in 1938, after stealing her away from Ham Armstrong, who was Walter's best friend and whose wife she had been. She was tremendously protective of Walter, who led a carefully controlled existence. He wrote his column by hand in the morning, during which time he was not to be interrupted, while the house was kept tranquil and quiet by Helen. Afternoons were for interviewing, reading, and walking their two beautiful poodles. Helen's solicitude for Walter was legendary. Once Robert Schuman, who had been the French prime minister and foreign minister, was their guest of honor at dinner. When the wine was passed, Schuman interrupted something Walter was saying to discuss the origins and vintage with the waiter, as Frenchmen are apt to do. When he finished, Helen leaned over and said to Walter, "*Et tu disais?*"—"And you were saying?" We played tennis frequently with Walter and Helen on my family's court. Little boys from the neighborhood used to stand outside the fence, shouting, "Mista, give me a ball." Once when this happened, Helen turned to them and said, "Shush, boys, Mr. Lippmann is serving."

Other people we got to know better in those first years after the war were Avis and Chip Bohlen—he was the new counsel for the State Department and had interpreted at the meetings of the Big Three during the war—the Bob Lovetts, and the John McCloys. Bob Joyce, also in the State Department, and his wife, Jane, were friends, as were the David Bruces. These four couples, together with the Alsops and Frank and Polly Wisner, made a group of which we gradually became a part.

Two others who remained friends for life were James (Scotty) Reston, then a star reporter for *The New York Times*, and his wife, Sally. Scotty was on his way to becoming the most influential reporter in Washington, later a columnist. About them I can only say that Phil and I willed them our children. At a time when we were traveling a great deal, we had to decide whether we would fly together or separately. Since we traveled so much, it didn't seem practical to take different planes, so we decided against it. However, we thought it irresponsible not to have made firm arrangements about the children. We believed Scotty and Sally would most nearly approximate our values and our love; in addition, they knew the children and the children knew them. The Restons performed the ultimate act of friendship by agreeing to this arrangement.

My best new friendship was with Polly Wisner. She and Frank had moved to Washington from New York right after the war. Polly's spirit was always erupting with fun and laughter, and she was constantly hatching ideas for things that the four of us could do together. She and I became the closest of friends almost immediately, and stayed so for life.

At some point soon after Phil went to work at the *Post*, we gave a dinner for Cissy Patterson. Relations between Mrs. Patterson and our family naturally had ceased after the "pound-of-flesh" incident relating to the comics, but Phil had been head of the negotiating committee trying to work with the craft unions on behalf of all the papers in Washington, so my father said, "If you are in this position, you really should know Cissy."

My memory has always been that, despite the turbulent history between Cissy and my father, he himself took Phil to call on her at her home at 15 Dupont Circle. I only recently learned from Frank Waldrop—the editor of the *Times-Herald* at the time, but really Cissy's top aide, who gave himself the title of "hired gun"—that it was Phil who called Frank suggesting that they collaborate to get the two old rivals back together. Frank protested that it would be an interesting spectacle, "something like two scorpions in one bottle," but in planning the maneuver Frank said, "You handle your man, I'll try to handle mine."

Frank arrived an hour before the allotted time of three in the afternoon and found Cissy completely flustered, rushing around, "dripping her handkerchief off her knee, which was always a sure sign of trouble for somebody," and giving orders right and left. Finally, she ordered the butler to put all the liquor away, saying, "I don't want Eugene to go away from here saying I'm a drunk." So the booze went into the cabinet, Phil and my father arrived, everyone sat down, and they all behaved in a perfectly grown-up fashion. According to Frank, after a short time my father said, "Cissy, have you got anything to drink around here?" She pressed a buzzer, called for the butler, and said, "Get it out," and out came the booze.

Phil's and Cissy's charm led to an immediate rapport, and she said, "Oh, Eugene, you're so lucky to have this charming son-in-law; think of the son of a bitch I got"—referring to the columnist Drew Pearson, who by that time was a great friend of ours and had divorced Cissy's daughter, Felicia, and married Luvie Moore Abell. Right after his divorce, Drew had remained friends with Cissy, but Cissy and her paper had been violently right-wing and isolationist, whereas Drew was a Quaker, a liberal, and pro-Allies. They parted company, and the *Post* gained a great asset with his column, by then the most widely read of any.

In any case, Phil and I decided it was time to resume relations with Cissy, so we gave a small dinner for her. By that time I had a couple working for us. Not realizing that cooks need a little notice, I only notified them that morning that we would be fourteen for dinner. I also hired the one available roving waiter I knew of, who went from house to house helping at parties. That evening he reached into the icebox, grabbed a wine bottle, and poured. To my dismay, he had pulled out a bottle containing leftover martinis. Cissy was extremely gracious, despite the sketchiness of the arrangements, and sent me a huge bunch of violets and a warm thank-you note and asked us back for something at her house.

BECAUSE I WAS developing a "pot" from several pregnancies, several of us started an exercise class, meeting in the mornings at Joey Elliston's large house near the corner of 29th and R Streets. One day Joey told me that the house next door was for sale and that Phil and I should buy it. Although we'd been in our O Street house less than a year, we had begun casually to look around for one better suited to a family with small children. I had always liked the house Joey was talking about, which belonged to

General "Wild Bill" Donovan. The outside looked very much like the El-listons' house, an imposing cream-colored brick structure, but I thought of it as much too big and grand for us, and certainly well beyond our means to buy or to run. "It's not as big as it looks," Joey persisted, "and you should look at it." I did, and it was love at almost-first sight. It looked like a comfortable country sort of house that the city had grown up around—it was oblong, with simple lines, and had a large expanse of front lawn, a long pebble driveway, an old-fashioned back porch, and a big slop-ing back yard with lots of trees. At the foot of the hill was an old stable that served as a garage with an apartment over it.

With some trepidation, I asked Phil to look at it. I knew that if its size and the amount of land on which it sat worried me they would worry him more, but I told him that in an ideal world this was the house in which I would live. One Sunday afternoon, we walked up from O Street. As we passed the high stone wall that marks the property, the wall seemed to loom larger and longer than ever, taking up most of the block. When we finally got to the flight of stairs up to the house from the side, Phil blurted out, "Are you mad?"

"Wait until you look inside," I muttered nervously. "It's much less grand inside, and it's not as bad as it looks." And, indeed, when Phil saw the whole house, he too fell for it right away. After talking as if it were al-ready ours, discussing where children and furniture would go, we agreed to try to buy it. I asked our agent to make an offer of $115,000, slightly be-low the Donovans' asking price of $125,000. This offer, which was more than twice as much as I'd paid for the house we were leaving, seemed as-tronomical to me.

My father had been keeping an eye on the houses I was looking at, and I'd shown him one or two I thought of interest. Here, at last, was a Georgetown house he considered worthwhile—it was brick and therefore solid, it stood alone, and it had some space and land around it. One day while my offer was still outstanding, my father came over to see me and said, "Well, you've bought the house."

"What do you mean?" I asked indignantly.

"I saw Bill Donovan at dinner last night and asked him how much he really wanted for the house. He said, 'I want what I'm asking, because that's what I've got in it.' I then said, 'All right, Kay will pay it.' " When I asked him why he had interfered with my bargaining, since I was the one who was going to be paying, he responded, "When it's where you want to live, don't bargain."

So we bought the house and were always happy that we did. It was and still is our family home, a lovable house with character; it was great for the large family, and it works for me alone. But from the start I quaked at the thought of running it—not to speak of furnishing it. In the beginning, the house was casual, to put it mildly. One of the two front rooms had been a sitting room for the Donovans' staff, and the room opposite was a formal living room. The two rooms at the back were a library and dining room. The library was the room we lived in most, perhaps because it's square and has a beautiful fireplace. As time went on, I realized that there is a magic to square rooms. People are comfortable and can talk easily, but the room is also fine when you're alone.

It took me years to fix up the front living room so it both looked good and sat well. The other front first-floor room became the children's dining room, playroom, and storage for baby carriages, roller skates, baseballs and bats, and later on rock-band equipment. Because I ate breakfast there with the children, Phil referred to it as the Shredded Wheat Room.

FROM HIS BEGINNING at the *Post*, Phil had been working full-steam. Though he knew nothing about the newspaper business—or any business, for that matter—his brains and abilities served him well. At once he became my father's close collaborator, both inside the paper and outside. He joined my father at the Advertising Council, which Dad had inspired to secure the cooperation of the large agencies and advertisers on public issues for the war effort. This helped Dad, but also helped Phil, who knew no one in the newspaper industry or the business world, either locally or nationally.

They also assumed public obligations together. Early in his presidency, Harry Truman had asked the nation to focus on the problems of hunger in postwar Europe. In response, my father proposed to the secretary of agriculture a volunteer program to enlist public support for famine relief. His plan became the one essentially adopted by Truman when he appointed the Famine Emergency Committee. My father, along with members of the *Post*'s staff, then worked to get newspapers and the public behind the idea of helping meet the needs of the world's hungry. The committee was an interesting example of a cooperative effort between government and the press—one that would be more difficult today, if not impossible. In general, the press now sees its role as covering an issue like world hunger and commenting on it editorially rather than being a participant in trying to alleviate it. I wonder if this isn't journalistically right but, still, a loss to society.

Because his responsibilities multiplied quickly in the first few months, Phil was making decisions even while trying to learn. It was clear that my father loved having him there. He was already a terrific help with things that somebody else should have been doing long before. Then, in June 1946, President Truman called and asked my father to become the first president of the World Bank. That night my parents and Phil and I dined together to talk it over. Dad was somewhat reluctant to assume this large, complex job at the age of seventy, but he thought it vitally important that the international bank be launched on a sound basis. And he couldn't understand why other men were running from "the outstanding banking opportunity for world service in world history." Having been an astute businessman and government official for years, Dad understood the situation—the job would be a strenuous full-time one, requiring all his energies. He also knew that if he accepted it he would have to make Phil publisher of the *Post*. He put it up to Phil, saying, "This has always been my primary interest, but if you don't want me to go, I won't go." Of course, Phil encouraged him to take the job. He felt it was the right thing for him to do, even though, as he wrote to his own father, "He undoubtedly deserves a little rest at this point." He assured my father that both he and the *Post* would be all right.

So, on June 18, 1946, the *Post* announced that my father was withdrawing from active direction of the paper and would have no control or responsibility over news or editorial matters, although he did retain ownership. Phil would be publisher in title and in fact. He had been there only five months and was one month short of his thirty-first birthday, the youngest publisher of a major newspaper in the United States. My father's confidence in Phil was evident in his comment at the time of the announcement: "Under those who today take the responsibility of its affairs, I know that *The Post* will be true to its trust. *The Post* will not only carry on; it will go forward."

Although our friends and the press seemed to view Phil's rise to publisher positively, we knew things would not be easy. He had come into a job for which he was ill-prepared, and at once he was responsible for figuring out how to make the paper a viable enterprise. He was in charge of a losing newspaper in what was rapidly becoming the capital of the world.

Indeed, the paper itself was still struggling for its life. It had made profits in most of the war years, but was sliding right back to losses. The *Post* was certainly a marginal paper, and it felt like that to us. Even though the *Star* was the big money-maker, our biggest competitor, because it was our direct morning rival, was the *Times-Herald*. The *Post* had continued to improve in editorial quality and advertising volume and general prestige, but there was a great deal of rebuilding needed after the war. The competition for good people was intense, and it was a competition in which the *Post* had little strength. The paper was quite a small organization and, of course, the company was private and family-owned. Once my father left for the Bank, Phil had to learn even faster, but he had grasped the overall picture, so he focused on finding the right people to carry the paper forward editorially and financially.

Some of the personnel decisions my father had already made had a positive effect on Phil and a lasting effect on the paper. For example, Gene Elderman, the *Post*'s editorial cartoonist since 1932, had been imperceptibly drinking himself out of his job. From the beginning of 1943 until the beginning of 1946, the *Post* had no cartoonist, and my father had been on the lookout for someone. He heard about a man just coming out of the army who, before the war, had drawn cartoons for the *Chicago Daily News* and in Cleveland for the Newspaper Enterprise Association. When Herbert Block and my father met for the first time at the Yale Club in New York, Dad asked to see some of what Herb had done before the war, since in the army he hadn't been doing political cartoons. In return, he sent Herb a subscription to the *Post* so that he could see "how you like us," which Herb found interesting and inviting. Herb was hired and arrived simultaneously with Phil. As "Herblock," this amazing man has been drawing cartoons for the *Post* for over fifty years. His creative genius remains as strong as ever after all these years of solid performance, even at the age of eighty-seven.

In 1946, Herbert Elliston was still the editorial-page editor. My father's old associate Charles Boysen was business manager. There was an experienced advertising manager in Donald Bernard. Wayne Coy, Phil's friend and wartime associate, was assistant to the publisher. There was no one reliable in either production or circulation, or in labor relations.

Phil had his work cut out for him. Under him, as managing editor, was Casey Jones, who had helped my father so much from the time he came to the *Post* in 1935. But after working with Jones for only a short time, Phil decided the paper needed a more sophisticated approach. Casey Jones had done a great deal, but he was an old-fashioned *Front Page* type of character, and Phil was more ambitious than that; he began looking for a managing editor with whom he might be more comfortable. He heard about a man who had been working as editorial writer, managing editor, and Washington correspondent for the *St. Paul Dispatch–St. Paul Pioneer Press*, so he and I went out together to Minnesota to meet him. Phil was drawn to Russ Wiggins, a dynamo who had completed only high school but was extraordinarily well read, and he offered Russ the job of Sunday editor, I suppose hoping to bring him up through the ranks gradually. After much anguish, Russ, being in the enviable position of having two good offers, turned Phil down, understandably choosing to become assistant to Arthur Sulzberger, then the publisher of *The New York Times*.

Phil was also focusing on the news side of the paper. Believing that much of the postwar world would be shaped by decisions that were then being made at the peace conference in Europe, he himself left for Europe in August with Herbert Elliston, while I stayed at the farm in Mount Kisco with the children. This was Phil's first journalistic tour and his first trip to Europe. One of the great perks of journalistic life, whether one is reporter, editor, or publisher, is a trip of this sort. If you love learning as much as Phil did, and I do, these trips bring endless satisfactions. At the same time, you can occasionally do some good for the publication you represent—and for the governments involved—by reporting what you see and learn. This was just such a trip for Phil, one that made a deep impression on him; Isaiah Berlin always claimed—with some justice, I believe—that it contributed mightily to Phil's evolution away from the extreme liberalism of his law-school days and the first few years after graduation.

When we got back to Washington in the fall, Phil was not only running the paper and working to improve it but also lending moral support to my father, who was finding the presidency of the World Bank even more burdensome than he had imagined. Phil worked hard to bolster his morale, helping him in every way he could, from advice to writing speeches.

Trouble at the Bank had arisen for my father almost immediately. The twelve directors had been named earlier and had been working together before his appointment. Many resented someone's coming in really to impose order, and would rather have had a figurehead. And the job was difficult enough without the political infighting. Dad knew that if he stayed and fought he could probably win, but he felt too old and too weary to try.

Toward the end of October, he began thinking of the long-term future of the Bank—five, ten, or fifteen years ahead. He realized that he wouldn't be there to carry out his own plans and that the person who made them should be. "I made up my mind," he said, "that what the president and Jimmy Byrnes had asked me to do, I had more or less done—launched the Bank by organizing it." On December 4, 1946, he tendered his resignation with only two weeks' notice, not even having the energy to stay until a successor was found. Ironically, his resignation succeeded in bringing about some of the reforms needed so that his eventual successor, John McCloy, could function effectively.

By the time Dad returned to the *Post*, in January 1947, a transition had occurred. The six months of his absence had given Phil the chance to establish his own authority, and he was clearly in charge. By the end of his first year, he was omnipresent and involved in everything. My father took the title of chairman of a nonexistent board and had the generosity and wisdom to leave Phil as publisher and not try to take back the responsibilities he had ceded to him six months earlier. What he essentially did was to back Phil in all that he was doing. So there began a complicated but overall happy working relationship between my father and my husband—and another between Phil and me and my parents. The Bank interlude simply brought about the transition overnight instead of gradually.

Phil's respect for my father's experience and knowledge, and his genuine belief in Dad's sound judgment, meant that he gladly included him in major decisions and events in connection with the paper. In turn, my father's recognition of Phil's abilities and talents, particularly his facility with people, reinforced his inclination to support Phil's efforts and to back the paper financially.

My mother, meanwhile, also required some of Phil's attention. She had gone on traveling, reporting, speaking, and writing on various issues after the war. One series of twenty-four articles on postwar problems resulted from four months of travel throughout the United States and was published in the *Post* during April and May of 1946. Phil thought the whole series was first-rate.

At the same time, Mother was intensifying her efforts on the social and welfare front, testifying before Congress on her conviction that the government's administrative machinery to deal with health and education had to become more efficient on every level, and stepping up her efforts in behalf of a bill sponsored originally by Senators Taft and Fulbright for the creation of a Cabinet-level department of health, education, and security. Presaging a much later concern, she charged the radio and film industries with using their resources for "a progressive vulgarization of the public mind and for the debasing of public morals." Somehow she also found time to be president of the Social Legislation Information Service and a member of the President's Commission on Higher Education, the Federal Hospital Council, and the District of Columbia Planning Committee. In 1947, she helped found the National Citizens' Commission for Support of the Public Schools, in which she remained active until her death. At sixty, she was still choosing to be, as *Newsweek* called her, not just "a roving reporter" but also "a one-woman reform movement."

Her pieces for the *Post* were almost always long, frequently too long for a daily newspaper. She thought highly of her own writing—rightly so—and may have created, if not demanded, a hands-off approach on the part of editors. Casey Jones always claimed to have wielded his blue pencil fearlessly when it came to her pieces, but other editors quaked at the idea of editing her copy. Several true stories about her reactions to attempts to edit her work, as well as her conflicts with the *Post* over substance, took on the weight of legend. Once, when she sold an article to *Collier's* magazine, she was alleged to have flaunted her check in front of Jones, boasting, "See? Some people will actually pay me for writing for them." Casey gave her high praise by being quoted as saying, "That gal is a good reporter. She's no trained seal."

The first conflict she had with the management of the *Post* in which Phil became embroiled took place in 1948 and involved an incident in which Herbert Elliston felt she had interfered with his work. He protested to Phil—noting that it was the only occasion he'd had to complain in the eight years he'd been at the paper—that she had corrected a proof of an editorial of his on secularism and sent it directly to the composing room.

Herbert felt, justly, that she had overstepped her bounds, and that she had undermined his responsibility for the editorial page as well as his authority with the editorial staff, not to mention his reputation in the eyes of the men in the composing room.

My mother was apologetic but wounded. She wrote to Herbert at once, saying that she was "horrified by the impression my unfortunate stupidity made upon you." She had her own version of what had happened, explaining it away as "open to misinterpretation," but adding:

> ... dear Herbert, what hurts me more than my own stupidity is that you didn't trust me enough to take me aside when we met at dinner and say to me frankly and firmly: "Look here, that's not the way to do things." Then I could have explained to you at once that I meant no offense and apologized on the spot. Please tell Phil how it all happened and please don't bother to answer this.

Her true feelings came out the next day when she wrote Phil, ostensibly about a speech she was giving on the "Modern Curriculum and Released Time" but throwing in these words:

> ... I shall never again have any dealings whatsoever with any Post employee on any matter whatsoever.
> ... If I do any more about this, the wires are sure to get crossed and it will be my fault. I refuse ever again to be exposed to the humiliation of lectures either from the staff or from you. ...

Naturally, Phil had to take the time to assuage her hurt and smooth relations for the future good of the paper and all concerned.

Phil's diplomatic skills and tact in dealing with this and so many other situations with my mother saved us all. He often ran interference on conflicts I had with her and took the lead in working out the personal relationship he and I developed with her and my father as my parents, as well as with them as the owners of the *Post* and my father as his boss initially.

During this period, Phil continued to want me with him most of the time, but it was he who determined where we went. He hated most formal evenings, especially embassy dinners. Sometimes I begged to go somewhere that sounded glamorous, but he made the decision and I complied. What I hadn't learned was to be more independent of Phil himself.

Paradoxically, my mother should have been a role model, since she didn't operate under any constraints, but she had made her own daughters feel inferior to her, preventing us, in some ways, from viewing her as a positive example. Yet even she, with all her independence and ego, articulated the importance of being—and to some extent lived the life of—a wife whose primary obligation was to her husband and children.

AFTER DON'S BIRTH and Phil's return from overseas, I had not gone back to work. When Phil went to the *Post*, I made a unilateral decision not to, because I thought it would be too confusing for both of us to be there at once. Phil was less sure that this was right and even encouraged me to come back. Early in 1947, his concern for what my life was becoming led him to suggest that I start writing a weekly column that would be a review and digest of what was interesting in the magazines. Its goal, as I described it in a letter to his sister, was "to make me a little less stupid and domestic than I have been of late." My guess is that he thought up the idea to keep me working for the paper but independent of its organization.

Actually, ever since Phil had started on the *Post*, I had been thinking about taking a part-time job, but feared they didn't exist. This was a great one, about which I felt semi-apologetic because I thought maybe it was make-work. In fact, Phil had picked up the idea from another paper, and the column still runs in the *Post*. It was called "The Magazine Rack," and I began writing it for the Sunday paper in April 1947, paid the magnificent sum of $15 per column. It took me only a day to do, but invariably the writing fell on a difficult day, and I was often in a panic about finishing it. To my private surprise, however, I enjoyed the work, and I kept it up for several years, even picking up a subscriber along the way—the *Louisville Courier-Journal*, courtesy of our friend and its editor, Barry Bingham. About a year after the column first appeared, Barry wrote to Phil saying that his paper wanted to add a small amount of feature material. He had been watching the magazine column and thought it was just the kind of thing he would like to have once a week. Phil wrote Barry that his inquiry had made my day and that the *Post* would be delighted for the *Courier* to have the column, right after a few weeks' maternity leave for the birth of our third child. He added:

> I will let you decide what this expensive addition to the *Courier-Journal* will cost you. Mr. Meyer saw your letter and prevented my being more specific by saying: "It is impossible for a publisher to put a price on his own wife." The best level is one a bit below the nominal and just a bit above peonage. . . .

Around the same time as I started the column, I increased my involvement in civic affairs. In 1947, I was appointed to the National Capital Sesquicentennial Commission, of which President Truman was the honorary chairman. It was during these immediate postwar years that I

also got involved in welfare work, doing my share of fund drives, especially for the Community Chest and the National Symphony. I then went
on the board of the Children's Convalescent Home. I hadn't known much
about boards or volunteer work until I was approached to join this one,
and I was upset when it turned out to be an old-fashioned social board.
The very first meeting, held at the exclusive Sulgrave Club, was entirely
occupied with where to put a plaque honoring a lady who had given funds
for a bathroom. The board had been taken over by the second generation
of the quite correct Washington families who later did convert this home
into a really useful institution, at which time I participated more happily.

I was also preoccupied with dealing with our small children. In those
days and in our situation, there was no sharing of duties between parents.
I did absolutely everything domestic—found the schools and supervised
the children's activities, kept the social calendar for all of us (once Phil had
decided what he and I would attend), and decorated the houses. I also was
the one who had to see to repairs and renovations. In 1947, when Lally
was four, I got her into a nursery school which I described as "veddy,
veddy modern," whose application process presaged something of what
today's parents go through. I was asked all sorts of odd questions, such as
did I think my home training had been successful. I roared with laughter
and said I didn't know but I supposed not. They also asked me what I
wanted her to get out of nursery school, which I couldn't answer successfully either. I was never sure why they admitted her—certainly not on the
basis on my responses—but decided it had to be the result of the "test"
they gave her, in which she successfully put blocks together.

WHAT TO DO in the summers was something I struggled with during
these years. Usually I took the children to Mount Kisco to visit my parents,
but my feelings were invariably mixed about going to Seven Springs Farm.
I knew the children would love it, as, indeed, they always did, and as I had
as a child, but I didn't like the idea of leaving Phil in Washington, to commute there for weekends. And since he worked all week with my father, I
thought he might need a break from my family on weekends. I was also concerned about my mother's relations with my children, and how she viewed
their upbringing. She acted as though they had never eaten so well in their
lives as when they were at her house. And there was also an unending comparison between our children and my brother's children, who were often
there, too, in those years. This set up a tense competition between the families. But worst of all, my mother developed favorites among the grandchildren at different times in their lives—a favoritism she displayed with an
astounding lack of sensitivity. Once, she came into the dining room, where
the children were having an early dinner, and said, "Lally, I brought you a

flower." I will never forget Donald, two years younger, saying quietly, to no one in particular, "I guess Grandma couldn't find a flower for me."

Although the children were the center of my life at this time, the main focus of Phil's attention—and at the center of our life together—was the *Post*, where he was working on all fronts at once. His early memoranda to his executives are stunning in their detailed outline of problems, potential, and objectives in business and editorial areas. He looked at and analyzed everything, from making better use of editorial space to obtaining more newsprint; doing a more thorough job of research in order to improve the editorial content; preventing a street-sales drop in summers; decreasing payroll costs; keeping expenses down; minimizing typos, misprints, and mechanical-department problems; promoting the paper; and beefing up suburban coverage for Maryland and Virginia (part of a constant drive by all publishers of the *Post* to maintain a deep penetration of our local market). After only a year on the paper, Phil was thoroughly knowledgeable and totally in charge. As his secretary, Charlie Paradise, wrote a friend, "[S]ince Phil joined the organization . . . he is doing his best to make things hectic around here . . . which meets with my thorough approbation."

Phil became one of the *Post's* best ad salesmen, often writing letters to company executives around the country giving forceful evidence for why the *Post* was a logical, cost-effective choice for their advertising dollars. He was so totally immersed in the paper and was spread so thin, having only a very fragile, if developing, organization under him, that he was undertaking his own labor negotiations—a poor idea even for someone more experienced. He faced labor problems from the start, especially with the printers. After a particularly grueling period, he wrote Isaiah Berlin in January 1948 that he had just made "an unsuccessful attempt to throttle the poor printers with the Taft Hartley law." He also engaged in serious negotiations with the *Post's* circulation people, an area where costs had, as Phil put it, "simply been killing us."

He pushed for using the paper for educational purposes in schools throughout the area. He restored the comics to their prewar size. He even undertook some extensive redecorating of the newsroom, which he described to a vacationing Casey Jones as not unlike childbirth, "in that you get great results but only at the cost of significant pain."

Phil focused a lot of his attention on the people who worked for the paper and those he wanted to work for it. He knew everyone in the building, always taking on the problems of people who worked for him—worrying over someone's sick child, unmet mortgage payment, health crisis. He began actively recruiting young people with potential, as well as more established reporters and editors with proven abilities. And he was very interested in ensuring that women were working on the paper as well as reading it.

One of the biggest changes for the paper took place in early April 1947, when Russ Wiggins came as managing editor. Phil and my father had gone back to Russ a year after their first offer, and this time he accepted, preferring to return to the writing-and-editing end of newspapers. Just before he agreed to come, my father asked him if he wanted to see a financial statement for the company, to which Russ replied, quite typically, "No, Mr. Meyer, you are enough of a financial statement for me." In what no doubt was a move upstairs, Casey Jones was given the title of "assistant to the publisher" and stayed on for another three years before leaving to become executive editor of the *Syracuse Herald Journal.*

Russ's relationship with the *Post* was a happy and constructive one for the next twenty-one years. He immediately instituted several changes, which had a significant effect on the quality and integrity of the city room. He announced a new set of rules, one of which ended the practice of routine racial identification in the paper. No longer would the *Post* write such lines as one identified by Chal Roberts in his history of the paper: "Sam Jones, 24, Negro, was arrested for larceny yesterday." Overnight, he eliminated "freebies"—trips paid for by the government and free tickets for anything. Also, after just a few weeks on the job, he called in the police reporter, Al Lewis, to ask if he was having parking and other tickets fixed for people in the building. Al's prompt response was, "Yes, sir." Russ then asked, "For whom?"—to which, much to Russ's consternation, Al replied, "For everybody." "What do you mean, everybody?" demanded Russ disbelievingly. "Well, people in the composing room, the advertising room, the newsroom, circulation. I just take them to the station and give them to the chief." Russ put an instant stop to this practice by saying, "Starting today, this minute, there is to be no more ticket fixing at police headquarters. We might have to be in a position to write some critical stories about the police department, and I don't want you or the *Post* to be beholden to the chief of police or anybody else."

This new policy proved important right away, because one of the first editorial ventures undertaken by Russ and Phil was a crusade against crime—local and national. The local story led to a bitter fight with the Washington police, and in particular with Police Chief Robert J. Barrett, a veritable guerrilla war that began the year Russ arrived and went on for at least four more, until finally, in 1951, the *Post* supplied to a congressional committee convincing evidence of corruption, and Barrett "retired" amid charges that remained unresolved because he had invoked the Fifth Amendment.

IN THOSE SAME YEARS, cosmic events were developing abroad, starting with the Truman Doctrine in the spring of 1947, and followed by the

Marshall Plan. The *Post* had just acquired Ferdinand Kuhn to report on foreign affairs but had no one abroad, so it used wire services and occasionally free-lancers. Prior to Russ's coming on board, Phil even let reporters take trips paid for by the military, all in an effort to beef up reporting of foreign news.

Among the campaigns the *Post* took on was support for the Marshall Plan, which the paper featured regularly on the front page, and to which it devoted a special section in November 1947. This supplement, spearheaded by Phil and written by top *Post* reporters, won the National Headliners' Club award for outstanding public service and was reprinted widely throughout the country. In fact, the paper was more and more being recognized. The Newspaper Guild, in the course of giving its Heywood Broun awards in early 1948, said of the *Post*: "In these days when playing it safe and treading softly is so general, the record of *The Washington Post* in 1947 is truly extraordinary. It is a vivid demonstration of what an outstanding newspaper is like and what it can do in serving its readers, its community and the country."

On the downside, negotiations with the printers dragged on for months. Plans were made in case of a strike. "Very complicated business, a newspaper," Phil noted in a letter to my father late in 1947. It was a hard winter, one in which, as Phil said, "every damn possible thing seemed to go wrong." Finally, by spring, the effects of Russ's coming to the paper, along with some other new top people, were beginning to be seen, and when the seemingly endless Newspaper Guild negotiations finally wound up, Phil and I took time out for a much-delayed vacation. We set off for Nassau at the end of March, by which time I was eight months pregnant with our third child. Knowing the pace of life that we would soon return to, I clung to the sun and the sand with renewed intensity, feeling fine and fat and sunburned.

While we were in Nassau, Phil had a call from CBS President Frank Stanton, who supervised the radio stations then owned and run by CBS. For several years, Phil had been worrying over what to do with WINX, a small radio station my father had bought in 1944, hoping to create some profits to ease the effects of the *Post*'s accumulated losses. Dad had actually wanted to get a network station at the time, but when he couldn't, he bought this tiny independent 250-watt station, which could be heard within a radius of about two blocks—on a windy day. It did make a little money, but my father quickly learned that what it made came from broadcasting the daily "number" for gamblers and racketeers. He had the station management substitute classical music for the race results, and the bottom fell out of the profits.

When Stanton called Phil in Nassau to ask if he'd be interested in purchasing a majority share of CBS Radio in Washington, with the understanding that they would make an effort to acquire a television license later, Phil replied facetiously, "Not much, but I'll take the next plane up." He was ecstatic. We cut short our trip so that he could hurry north to begin negotiations, and for several weeks he shuttled back and forth to New York.

Years later, Frank told me that he had earlier held conversations with Sam Kauffmann at the *Evening Star* about their possible affiliation with CBS. Kauffmann had expressed great interest in the opportunity, and the deal was nearing completion, when, at the end of a lengthy talk in his office, Kauffmann, an eminent leader of Washington's WASP establishment, said, "By the way, Mr. Stanton, how much of CBS is Jewish-owned?" Frank immediately replied, "All of it, Mr. Kauffmann," put on his hat, and left the room. His call to Phil came soon after this.

The negotiations between CBS, whose chairman was Bill Paley, and the *Post* were easy and quick, in large part because they were conducted by Frank and Phil themselves. Phil was a very able negotiator; he had the figures in his head and knew how to operate in this kind of situation, no doubt greatly helped not only by his law-school training but by what he told me was the most valuable course he took at the school, accounting.

A month after the whole thing began, the baby was due, and I was resting. Phil woke me and asked me to talk to Frank's wife, Ruth, on our back porch while he completed the negotiations in the library with Frank. I had never met Ruth Stanton before, but we chatted amicably for a couple of hours. Frank and Phil concluded the deal, which was announced with great fanfare on May 17, 1948. The *Post* and CBS would co-own the fifty-thousand-watt Washington station WTOP, with 55 percent owned by the *Post* and 45 percent owned by CBS. Privately, Phil was delirious with excitement. It was the real moment of the *Post*'s entry into a new business world and into the electronic world.

On the evening of my talk with Ruth Stanton on our back porch, we went to a cocktail party in honor of Margaret Truman. There was the usual amount of standing around, and I began to feel contractions starting and told Phil I thought the baby might be coming. When he asked how I knew, I realized that this was the first time he was really involved with a baby's birth. It was his third child and he still didn't know what happened.

I didn't want to leave for Johns Hopkins and find out I was mistaken, but when the contractions grew stronger, we set out, having reserved a hotel room in Baltimore in case this was false labor. About halfway there, I suggested that the hospital was indicated, Phil sped up, and we made it with only twenty minutes to spare before things got serious. I had asked my doctor about natural childbirth, which had begun to be in vogue, and when he insisted that it wasn't for me, I took this as a challenge. Even though I hadn't had any of the training involved, I made a resolve to have this baby without anesthesia if I could, but not to say anything in case I couldn't.

There are certain experiences—childbirth is one; moving is another—that nature and time definitely draw a curtain on, so you forget in between times how painful they are. In this case, after four hours I was about ready to give up when the doctor said, "If you can stand one more contraction, you can have the baby." Although I was convinced I was exploding, I did, and our second son was born. It was indeed traumatic, and I kept reliving the sensations for some weeks after, but I was pleased at having done it this way. I was even more pleased with the reality of William Graham, whom we gave the middle name "Welsh" after Phil's grandmother, who regarded Phil—or at least so he claimed—as her favorite grandchild.

The baby and I returned home six days later to a haven on our third floor, where we were quarantined against chicken pox, which Lally had caught. Phil surprised me by having installed our first television set. People were just starting to buy them, and there was a good deal of intellectual snobbery in Georgetown about having one at all. Our first evening home, the Restons came over and we all watched a baseball game until I wilted into bed next door with the baby.

BY MID-1948, the *Post* was still a rocky, if lively, paper, whose eight hundred employees were a proud, generally hardworking lot. In the fifteen years since my father's purchase, circulation had risen from 50,000 to 180,000 daily, while advertising had gone from four million lines to twenty-three million. The *Post* had been awarded numerous prizes, including five major awards for reporting, three for editorials, one for cartooning, and three for public service.

Around this time, my father decided to pass the paper on to Phil and me. At the same time, he wanted to ensure that the *Post* would forever serve the public interest. In effect, what he and Phil did was to set up a kind of trust based on an English model that protected some of the newspapers there. According to a page-one article in the *Post*, to ensure its continued independence and a responsible ownership in the event the paper ever had to be sold, my father appointed "a self-perpetuating committee of five persons who will hold full power of approval or veto over the disposition of voting shares in the *Post* subsequent to the control now exercised by Mr. and Mrs. Philip L. Graham. . . ." The committee—originally made up of James Conant, president of Harvard University; Millicent MacIntosh, dean of Barnard College; Judge Bolitha J. Laws, chief justice of the U.S. District Court for the District of Columbia; Colgate Darden, president of the University of Virginia; and Chester Barnard, president of the Rockefeller Foundation—had absolutely no authority over or responsibility for the policies or operation of the paper, but had "absolute discretion" to approve or disapprove potential owners subsequent to ownership by Phil and me.

The press release that announced these moves went through a number of drafts that were edited by both my parents. It still moves me in its honest expression of my father's beliefs about what he had tried to do with the *Post* over the previous fifteen difficult years:

> To survive, a newspaper must be a commercial success. At the same time, a newspaper has a relation to the public interest which is different from that of other commercial enterprises. This is more than ever apparent in these days when our free institutions are under their severest trial and closest scrutiny.
>
> The citizens of a free country have to depend on a free press for the information necessary to the intelligent discharge of their duties of citizenship. That is why the Constitution gives newspapers express protection from Government interference. . . . It is also possible for the public interest to be defeated by the way a newspaper is conducted since the principal restraint upon a newspaper owner is his self-restraint.

Phil and I both signed a formal letter to my father that read:

> You have discussed with us your ideas concerning The Washington Post and we are, of course, familiar with the provisions of the amendment of the Certificate of Incorporation of The Washington Post Company that is to be made in order to insure, as far as possible, that those ideas shall be perpetuated.
>
> We are very gratified that you have decided that it will be consistent with your hopes for the future of The Post for us to be the owners of the voting shares of the Company, and that you have, therefore, agreed to sell your holdings of Class A stock to us.

On his birthday that year, just before this announcement, Phil received $75,000 as a gift from my parents. Though my mother sent it with a note saying she was giving it to him as a birthday and wedding-anniversary present "with all my affection," it was really to help him buy his share of the stock in the *Post*. Phil and I each already had 175 shares of Class A common stock of the company, which had been given to us by my mother in November 1947. We bought the other shares from my father, at $48 per share. In effect, 3,325 shares were transferred to Phil, and 1,325 shares were transferred to me, giving us a total of 5,000 voting shares. Phil received the larger share of the stock because, as Dad explained to me, no man should be in the position of working for his wife. Curiously I not only concurred but was in complete accord with this idea.

Two years later, the transition to us was completed with the gift of the rest of the shares to the Eugene and Agnes Meyer Foundation, which had been set up in 1944. The foundation had been a very small one, made politically and economically much larger by the acquisition of the B shares. It was set up very carefully to be independent in its administration, and not a tool for the family's use. This was carried out perhaps overly zealously, to the extent that my father could not get the foundation to do anything even remotely connected to his interests. By now there is no connection at all between the family and the foundation, but it has been an effective force in the Washington area.

In order to make things equitable for my siblings, who would not be gaining ownership of the paper, my parents gave an equal amount of money to them at this time. There were a few tense moments when my father told them about the arrangement, but nothing like the difficulties that were to develop in other newspaper families. My brother had some second thoughts, but decided to stick with his decision to pursue his medical career. Bill was asked to invest when we bought the *Times-Herald* and at other times, and though his advisers at Morgan Guaranty constantly warned him not to buy any more stock when we went public, he obstinately kept adding to his position. When he died of a combined stroke and lung cancer in 1982, with the stock still in the $30s, he left some very wealthy children and a large foundation.

Flo, who was already estranged from the family, was, with some difficulty, reassured by my father that she and her children were being fairly dealt with. Bis and Ruth, who had every right to feel unevenly treated, have remained generous, loyal, loving, and supportive in every way. They were left secure but not affluent compared with my brother and myself. They were never given the opportunity to buy *Post* stock, largely because it was worth very little in the beginning and was regarded as risky. Later, Morgan kept them out, even after one sister wanted to buy stock as a sign of support of the paper during Watergate. With true conservator instincts, the bank wouldn't sell appreciated and, they thought, valuable standard stock, such as IBM—this was even after Warren Buffett had taken a big position in the Post Company. (They were still denigrating our stock—and me—to my brother's heirs after he died.)

On my part, in order to help Phil pay back the debt he incurred in borrowing to buy the stock, even with my mother's gift, I volunteered to pay for all our living expenses—houses, cars, schools, entertainment—and did so. Everything except Phil's personal expenses was carried by me from the modest trust started for each of the Meyer children by my father the day we were born. This arrangement was never an issue; it didn't bother either one of us. I never thought about it, and we never talked about it. Only fifteen years later, when things were very bad, did I look at the situation ruefully. I recall my brother-in-law Bill Graham gently telling me it had been wrong from the start.

Two days after the sale of the *Post* to us was announced, when much of the family, including Phil and me, was at Mount Kisco, we received word that Cissy Patterson had died suddenly of a heart attack, at the age of sixty-three. It seemed impossible that this colorful, dynamic, strong, but sad and lonely person was gone. She had been in increasingly poor health, and there were plenty of tales around town of drugs and other habits that increased the danger to her life, but still she was a Washington institution and seemed destined to be here always.

Most important for Phil and me as the new owners of the *Post* was what would happen to our competition, the ever-present, widely read *Washington Times-Herald*, which Cissy had owned, edited, and published. Speculation began right away. Rumors were rampant—Cissy's more liberal and estranged daughter, Felicia, would inherit and revamp the paper, for example. But Cissy left the paper to seven of the *Times-Herald*'s executives, the principal ones of whom were the general manager, William Shelton, and editorial-page editor, Frank Waldrop, the operative figure, the closest to Cissy.

When Phil heard of Cissy's death, he left Mount Kisco almost immediately to start talks with the seven heirs about their intentions. Because of estate-tax considerations, the inheritors felt they had only a year in which to decide whether to keep the paper and continue to operate it or to sell it. We all knew there were too many papers in Washington, and we also knew that only one of the morning papers was likely to survive. It was with this knowledge that Phil began to cultivate his relationships with Shelton and Waldrop. Their conversations continued throughout the year.

In any case, we—at thirty-three and thirty-one—were now the owners of the *Post*. The paper was then incorporated—my father would no longer pay its losses, which increased Phil's already heavy obligation to make the paper viable. It was another of those crucial moments, another big step in the evolution of our lives. Overnight we became adults with a huge but exciting responsibility.

— *Chapter Twelve* —

EVEN RECOGNIZING how far the paper had come from the wreck my father bought in 1933, what we owned in 1948 still looked pretty fragile. As Phil said, "We were sitting in a leaky boat. The paper . . . had practically no assets and had begun to repeat a familiar pre-war habit of losing money." Our hold on the *Post* and its future was precarious.

The *Post*'s dilapidated, roach-ridden building was a fixture on E Street in downtown Washington. One *Post* reporter described the building as "faithful as Man O' War but ancient feeling as Caesar's bones." The front steps opened into a dark, shabby, small vestibule, large enough for the bottom of a long flight of wooden stairs and the creaky, rickety elevator that people wisely avoided. The city room, located on the second floor, was a small town of constant activity. Clouds of smoke hung low over men, still in their hats, hunched over typewriters at their desks. Russ Wiggins, who had been in full charge of the news department since he had come in 1947, had done, as Phil said, "a most amazing job of developing our news coverage and news writing," taking the paper to a much higher level—astounding, really, since he was on a rigidly tight budget.

Together, Phil and Russ created a national staff that was still thin but beginning to be professional—in great part because Russ's standards of professionalism were high. Russ was once described by Phil as someone who "does not lose his Pollyannaish enthusiasm easily." Early on, he was involved in a flap with Molly Thayer, a reporter who often used Washington social gatherings to pick up important news bits. Russ's memo to Phil about her reaction to his changing her copy is typical of his attention to detail and concern for the facts:

> Molly's suggestion that her copy be left strictly alone is the most colossal impertinence I ever heard. It takes an hour a day to check the spelling and addresses of persons named in her column and to

check up to find out if the persons named are dead or alive. She has resurrected more people than Jesus Christ. . . .

It was in 1948 that Ben Bradlee came to the *Post* for the first time, and largely by chance. He had returned from the war and started a newspaper in New Hampshire, which did pretty well, but in the end, as with many such ventures, it folded, leaving Ben without a job. He had two reference letters introducing him to editors at major papers—one to the *Baltimore Sun* and one to the *Post*. When his train arrived at the Baltimore station, the weather was gray and depressing and so was the station. Ben took one look through the train's window, said, "The hell with this," and didn't get out. The train rolled on to Washington, where he arrived at the *Post* and was eventually sent to Russ Wiggins. Before Ben was hired, Phil had to approve, since he oversaw every empty job slot in order to assess whether we should fill it at all and, if so, ensure that it was filled with the best. Ben was hired, and came on board at $80 a week.

Only three years later Ben went to Phil and said he'd like to be a Nieman Fellow, which meant going to Harvard for a year under a special program for journalists. To which Phil retorted, "Why? You've already been to Harvard." Ben quit and took a job as information officer in the United States Embassy in Paris, but it was too stultifying for him, and soon he went to *Newsweek*'s Paris bureau.

In many ways, Phil was at his very best as a publisher in these years. He sparked ideas, praised and persuaded, criticized and cajoled. As he went about his more than full-time chores of administration and policy-making, he worried constantly about the difficulties that confronted him as owner and publisher. He was acutely aware of the dilemma that arose from the fact that "a newspaper must be a successful commercial enterprise in order to survive. Yet, the publisher must realize that he has obligations which transcend any commercial interest." He believed that, "despite the difficulties involved, it is best for the publisher to have an ownership part in a paper, and not merely represent absentee ownership as a hired man"—now almost completely a thing of the past.

Phil was always trying to stimulate the press in general and the *Post* in particular to better performance. He insisted that newspapers should not "brush off our defects by blithely saying that people can cancel their subscriptions if they disagree, since in many cities there is no choice. . . ." He worried continually about basic news reporting and how to do a better job of bringing news to readers. In a speech he gave at the University of Michigan in December of 1948 he said:

The necessary haste with which we operate in the production of a daily newspaper at times leads us, despite our best care, into unavoidable errors. Critics often read into these errors entirely non-existent malice, magnifying them as further evidence of our sins. Responsible newspapers stand ready to correct any errors as zealously as they seek to avoid committing them.

On the advertising front, he was constantly writing advertisers like General Motors and Procter & Gamble about campaigns that broke in the *Star* or *Times-Herald*, explaining why they should have been in the *Post*: "We are especially equipped to sell Ivory for you—witness our first place in local grocery linage in the U.S. (only morning paper in a metropolitan city to have leadership). . . ."

Recognizing the difficulties in trying to change old habits but knowing the inherent cost-effectiveness of automation, Phil began the conversion of the *Post*'s accounting department to machine operation, installing IBM machines as early as 1946. And in an important move on the personnel front, the *Post* became a pioneer in the city on initiating a policy of hiring reporters on the basis of merit alone.

Phil often involved the *Post* in righting wrongs, as he saw them. Apparently, he had always had in mind the idea of a congressional investigation into organized crime. In May of 1949, he met with Senator Estes Kefauver, whom he thought of as "a decent man with a lot of guts," to broach the idea of Kefauver's taking on the chairmanship of a special crime committee to investigate the connection between organized crime and politicians around the country. After a second meeting, Kefauver declined the idea as lacking public interest—to which Phil exclaimed, "Jesus, Estes, don't you want to be vice-president?" But after Phil ran a few front-page stories about crime, the senator expressed a fervent interest in getting started on the hearings that were to rocket him to fame and national recognition. When Kefauver eventually closed down the hearings, Phil said to him that he understood he was going to write an article for *Look* or *Life*, and he would appreciate it if Kefauver gave the *Post* credit for helping get the investigation started. To which Kefauver replied, "Well, Phil, old man, I'd be glad to do that, but tell me, just what did *The Washington Post* have to do with starting the investigation?"

Another wrong that Phil was willing to use the *Post* to right was segregation in Washington. In the late 1940s and early 1950s, particularly prior to the Supreme Court's decision in the *Brown* v. *Board of Education* case, Washington was a highly segregated city. Phil's entire childhood and adolescence had been spent, as he conceded, in the Southern tradition of white supremacy, and he was fully aware of the difficulties in bringing about the necessary change.

In his first, brief tenure at the *Post*, Ben Bradlee was deeply distressed by the side of Phil that used the paper to achieve his political purposes, however worthy. In 1949, riots were taking place, as members of the left-ist Progressive Party, which had fielded Henry Wallace as a candidate the year before, led black children to swim in Washington's previously all-white public swimming pools. The violence grew steadily into pitched battles. In one case, there were two hundred whites arrayed against an equal number of blacks—with park police on horses in the middle. Ben, with another reporter, was on the site for thirty-six straight hours. Emotions ran high, including those of the reporters, who had witnessed the use of clubs with nails embedded in them and had seen several people sent off to hospitals as well as one woman trampled by a horse. The reporters returned to the *Post* to write the story, expecting, of course, that it would be on the front page. It didn't even make the front page of the local news section; instead, it appeared buried in the paper, on page B-7. As Ben later remembered, "The whole thirty-six-hour adventure was called an 'incident,' and the word 'race' was never mentioned."

In the process of blowing his stack, as only he could do, Ben felt a tap on his shoulder and turned around to find Phil, tuxedo-bedecked, who said, "Okay, buster, come with me," and led the way to his office. Around the table in Phil's office sat Secretary of the Interior Julius (Cap) Krug, Undersecretary Oscar Chapman, President Truman's special adviser Clark Clifford, and two or three others. "Tell them what you just told me," Phil ordered Ben, after which he asked Ben to leave. Phil then cut a deal. The story would run on the front page of the *Post* unless the people with the power to do something about it integrated the pools. They agreed, shutting down the pools in the middle of that hot summer but promising to reopen the following summer on an integrated basis, which they did.

This was a typical example of the way Phil used power, in this case the paper's, to accomplish something good. It worked, but at the same time it hurt the paper. It isn't—and probably wasn't even then—the way to run a newspaper. To keep a story out of the paper to achieve a purpose, even a fine one, is neither appropriate nor in the spirit of my father's definition of the duty of a newspaper: "To try to tell the truth. To find it out and tell it. To have a competent editorial department to interpret that truth."

FROM THE TIME of Cissy Patterson's sudden death in 1948 until the following summer, the most important activity in which Phil was involved was his unrelenting attempt to buy the *Times-Herald*. We believed that our lives—or, rather, the company's life and the life of the *Post*—depended on our acquiring it. Others we knew who were interested included William Randolph Hearst, Jr., the ever-eager Samuel Newhouse, and the Scripps-Howard organization, which owned another one of our competitors, the

Washington Daily News. Phil felt he had a real chance, because Cissy Patterson's cousin, Colonel Robert McCormick, the editor and publisher of the *Chicago Tribune*, showed no interest in the *Times-Herald* at the time, and it was worth more to us than to any of the others.

From the beginning, Bill Shelton, the *Times-Herald's* general manager, agreed that we were the ones who ought to get it. But he also felt that Frank Waldrop, who had been closest to Cissy and was most loyal to her memory, was likely to be a "fly in the ointment"—how big a fly I never knew until recently. Waldrop had not only worked for Cissy Patterson but respected her—indeed, loved her. He felt he owed her everything, and he admired her "guts, the fact that she was really trying all the time, trying right up to the day she died." Shelton and Phil, sometimes with Waldrop, held regular negotiations until summer, when the year of decision would be up. When the heirs decided to sell, Phil and my father made a secret written proposal to the seven executives, offering $4.5 million. In addition, my father put up another $1.05 million for the *Chicago Tribune* stock that was in Cissy's estate, with the understanding that he would help the executors liquidate it—something Shelton and Waldrop had asked for—taking whatever Colonel McCormick didn't want.

That summer we rented a house in Narragansett, Rhode Island. Phil commuted on the weekends, always tired and nervous over the negotiations on top of all his other work. I often would remove the children from the small house so he could sleep. I remember taking them outside on one cold, rainy Saturday for what I described to them hopefully as "a picnic breakfast"—just to make sure we wouldn't wake him.

On the weekend before the negotiations were to become final, just before Phil was to leave for Washington, he and I sat on the beach alone, talking and dreaming. I vividly recall his saying, "I know getting the *Times-Herald* would be too good to be true. It's too much to hope for, but just let's shut our eyes for a moment and pretend we have it. The first thing I'd like to see is Sam Kauffmann's face when he hears the news." After we'd indulged ourselves this way for a while, he realistically and soberly said: "If we don't get it, I'll die for a week. Then I'll try to think of doing it another way." We were cautious, but we couldn't help hoping that this would be the end of the long, hard struggle.

Phil called me early the next morning with the news that Colonel McCormick had stepped in and bought the paper. He asked me to break up the house there, take the children to Mount Kisco, and come down to be with him. Weeping, I sat at breakfast with the children before I began the move to join him in Washington.

What we didn't understand at the time was that we might have got the paper at that point if not for Frank Waldrop's loyalty to Cissy's aims and aspirations. Yes, we were willing to pay the most for the paper, which pleased the other six heirs, but Waldrop believed it would frustrate Cissy's intent. He felt it would have been a "betrayal and surrender"—a sentence of death for the *Times-Herald*—so he told the other heirs, "Do as you wish, but I'm not going to sign it."

Waldrop made sure the colonel heard about my father's willingness to take care of the *Tribune* stock. Unfortunately, McCormick interpreted this not as something helpful but as a threat to his total control of the great enterprise, and he stepped in and bought the *Times-Herald* for just what we had offered. Phil and my father tried to raise their offer. Mother, always magnificent in a crisis and wanting to ensure the future of the *Post*, called from Mount Kisco to say that, if the sale hinged on the amount we were offering, then she didn't need to live so elaborately. "Eugene, throw in the house. Nothing else matters." She really meant it. We all had our hearts and souls in this deal. However, the *Tribune* and *Times-Herald* people actually hid from our lawyers to prevent being presented with our higher bid, and we never really got the chance to up the ante.

When I arrived in Washington, I found Phil in a great despond. We both thought the future much dimmer, if not hopeless. Now we were faced with the great, rich, highly professional, and profitable Chicago Tribune Company as our competitor, with the colonel, whose business acumen was widely known and respected, having seemingly unlimited assets to pour into opposing us. More than ever, we thought in terms of a battle for survival—now against Goliath.

One night, a week or so after the takeover, I woke up at two in the morning to find Phil smoking and finishing a book he had obtained from the library on the lives and careers of newspaper magnates Colonel McCormick and Captain Joe Patterson. Phil said, "You know, they put the company together when they were in their thirties. Now they're in their sixties and I'm in my thirties. I think we can make it another way." With that simple conclusion, Phil got over the terrible blow of being defeated in a deal on which we thought our life depended.

And so the struggle for survival continued, absorbing all Phil's energy and attention. The *Post* continued to grow in quality and influence and even in some important business measures, like circulation, but lost ground on others, like advertising. These were lean years, yet we moved steadily forward.

Our competition was formidable and fierce. Various members of the families that owned the *Star* served on the boards of the most important banks and businesses throughout Washington. The paper also appeared to have a heavy hand in running the government of Washington, D.C.: John Russell Young, who was chief of the city's three commissioners, was the former White House correspondent for the *Star*. The offices of the city's

Board of Trade were actually located in the *Star*'s building. Judges were appointed only with the approval of the *Star*. At least on the surface, the *Star* was all-powerful and omnipresent.

Almost everyone in the top management of the *Star* was a member of one of the three families that owned the paper. With the exception of a few fine professionals, most drew a paycheck and did little real newspaper work. (The editor, Ben McKelway, was an outside professional, a nice man with fine credentials.) Members of the family tended to live not in the city but in Chevy Chase or the Maryland suburbs, where they rode to the hounds. Many were snobbish and WASPish. My father actually included as one of his assets the twenty-seven members of the owning families on the *Star*.

The *Times-Herald* also continued to be a force in Washington. Bill Shelton and Frank Waldrop remained on the paper, but shortly after he bought it, Colonel McCormick appointed his niece Ruth Elizabeth (Bazy) McCormick Miller as publisher. The colonel had remarked that he intended the paper to be "an outpost of American principles" and called Bazy and her husband, Maxwell (Peter) Miller, Jr., "missionaries to print these principles." He said that, after trying for so many years to bring Washington to the United States, he was now "sending the United States to Washington."

The fourth paper in Washington, the *Daily News*, was still perking along in its own niche, which was largely lunch-counter and street sales.

What we tried to do at the *Post* was to reach the average reader, in contrast to the *Star*, which was geared to the city's power structure and a middle- and upper-income readership, and to the *Times-Herald*, which appealed to blue-collar, downscale, and upper-crust lovers of scandal and gossip. Phil obviously kept an eye out for the competition, but he felt, as did my father, that improving our own paper was the surest way to improve our chances of survival. As Russ Wiggins remembered, "We didn't really get into slugging matches in the old partisan newspaper tradition. We covered the news in competition with them, but we didn't get into vituperative disputes," and this attitude of honest competition played an important role then and later.

On the business side, Phil succeeded in hiring a first-class circulation manager, Harry Gladstein, from Hearst's *Los Angeles Examiner*. This position had been a revolving door of incompetence and amateurism, so Gladstein's arrival late in 1949 helped solved a problem that had been a sore spot from the beginning. But Phil's most important business recruit was John Sweeterman, who came as business manager and eventually became publisher, the only non-Meyer-Graham-family publisher of the *Post* to date. He had been general manager of the *Dayton Journal-Herald*, and when that paper was sold to Cox Newspapers, he temporarily published a group of "shopping" newspapers, and was president of a publishing company that printed circulars.

Phil courted John assiduously for a few months, but, looking at a paper that was losing money and was still third out of four papers in Washington, John declined the offer, holding out for a higher salary and some stock participation. Phil asked me to listen in on one of the crucial phone conversations in which John spelled out his terms. Phil was so anxious to get him that he offered John the same salary that he himself was making at that time, $30,000. When John said he simply couldn't come for $30,000, Phil raised his own salary to $35,000 and offered John the same.

One of John's first visits to us was at home, where I was in our yard with the children, all of us barefoot in the summer heat. My being barefoot made a deep impression on John, which he often recalled as culture shock. He finally accepted Phil's offer, arriving at the *Post* in mid-1950, and almost immediately Phil and others felt they were in good, sure hands. And so the case proved. There was a great deal of mutual respect between Phil and my father on the one hand and John on the other. John later said, "I was so impressed with your father, with his wisdom, his manner, his strong personality . . . and the same with Phil. I put my future in their hands, really." For his part, Phil was certain we had "found ourselves a prize package," and felt, as he once said, "Aren't I a lucky son of a bitch? This guy could run General Motors."

After a short while, Phil gave John great autonomy—in effect saying, "You run the business side of the paper and I'll back you up." John immediately set to work redesigning parts of the paper and cleaning up the organization. He brought in a great production manager, Harry Eybers, and a fine classified-advertising manager, Jim Daly. This was the nucleus of the team—together with Don Bernard and Harry Gladstein—that brought us such success later.

John was very strong and dominating. At times he was at loggerheads with various editors or executives on the news side, particularly Russ Wiggins, who wanted to do some things that required money—which John basically didn't like to spend. He was famous for focusing on cost-cutting measures, which many others looked on as mere penny-pinching. But in the end, it was John's single-minded pursuit of cost-cutting and revenue-generating moves that helped turn the situation around. Indeed, under John's direction and because of his introduction of more professional business management, we started to make very real gains in circulation and in advertising. He also focused on building the Sunday paper.

One of the results of losing the *Times-Herald* in 1949 was the immediate plunge my father and Phil took with the decision to build a new plant. When Dad bought the *Post*, someone asked him if he was going to build a new building, a natural question given the look of the *Post*'s home. His response, however, was: "No, I'm going to try to build a newspaper first." Having done that, he was ready to move on to provide a better operating environment for the growing paper. At the time, the *Post*'s eight hundred employees had spilled out of the fifty-six-year-old E Street home into three other buildings. The paper was handicapped by the inadequacies of both its building and its equipment, and there was no room to expand production capacity. Land had been acquired in another section of the city—on L Street, between 15th and 16th, with additional space behind. The new building, which Phil considered the most important step affecting the paper since 1933, as well as a testimonial to our faith in its future, was made possible financially by loans from my parents for the $6-million cost of the project. We are still there—with expansions—more than forty-five years later.

When the new building was halfway up, Phil called in my mother and me to more or less sign off on the interior design. Consulting us on decor was not a great idea, since neither of us had a very good eye or track record in this area. Even so, I had definite opinions about what I saw and said I thought it was hideous. Phil, expecting quick approval, was understandably irritated. He said, "All right, if you don't like it, then do something about it; find someone to do the interiors." I got the name of an interior designer, Mary Barnes, who made a great impact, rectifying some of the worst mistakes and putting a presentable look on the building. Because many of the colors she chose were muted, people on the *Post* referred to her as "the gray lady."

Groundbreaking took place late in 1949, and the first full paper was printed at the new L Street site in November 1950. There was a very alcoholic, emotional party as everyone finally left the old E Street building behind. The party—more of a wake, actually—was, as someone put it, to "mourn the death of a building" which, with all its inconvenient horrors, was still much loved. In fact, many longtime employees were less than enthusiastic about moving from the dingy but bustling E Street plant into the spic-and-span newness of the quiet L Street building. The new building doubled our press capacity, while providing modern conveniences like air-conditioning, soundproofing, and a clean environment, but it looked cold and impersonal in contrast to the old. One *Post* old-timer was quoted saying, "It'll be all right once we get to spitting on the floor again."

At the same time that Phil was working on plans for the new building and expanding the *Post* editorially, he was working hard to build the business. For years my father had simply subsidized the paper's losses out of his pocket, but after the A shares were passed to us, we couldn't do that any longer. Luckily for us, the losses had greatly declined, and the radio station we owned with CBS was profitable. Phil always thought of radio and television not as rivals of newspapers but, rather, as another form of journalism. And very early he recognized their potential for bringing profits to offset any losses the paper might incur.

In 1950, again with CBS as a partner, Phil took the company into the television field by buying a station in Washington, WOIC, whose call letters were later changed to WTOP. Since there was $800,000 cash in WTOP, we had to come up with only $330,000, or 55 percent of the remaining amount of the $1.4-million purchase price, of which CBS paid the other 45 percent. My parents loaned us the money for our share of this purchase. Phil wrote to his father at the time: "I think our timing was just about perfect, for it looks as though television here will move out of the red ink this fall. We were anxious to get in because it is going to have great effect on all other media, and especially on radio."

Since 1948, when he had drawn us into radio, Frank Stanton had become a close personal friend as well as a business associate. Late in 1952, Frank told Phil that the three owners who had started the only television station in Jacksonville, Florida, WMBR, wanted to sell. About a month before the election in 1952, Phil set the wheels in motion that led to his purchase of the station. Ten days after the election, we left on vacation, stopping first in Jacksonville, where he completed the deal and met Glenn Marshall, one of the original owners, who was staying on to manage the station. Glenn remembered that when WMBR went on the air originally, in 1950, there wasn't a television set in the whole of Jacksonville, and the station owners would call dealers daily to see if any sets had been sold that day.

The price Phil had agreed to—$2.47 million—was the highest ever paid for a television station at that time, I believe. This was the first time Phil was out ahead of my father, who was slightly nervous about the proposed purchase. It took a call from Don Swatland, Dad's friend and a lawyer at Cravath, the corporate law firm in New York, to reassure him that it was a good idea. Actually, it turned out to be a *great* idea. Phil always referred to WJXT—WMBR's call letters were changed in 1958—as his rabbit's foot. The station built up enormous strength while it was alone in the field. In fact, it was the only VHF station between Atlanta and Miami. The newspapers in Jacksonville, owned by the railroad, were second-rate, so the town came to rely on WJXT as the principal source for news, and this remained the case for many years, until NBC went on the air with a station that had twelve owners, providing negligible competition. Even today, with massive competition, WJXT remains dominant in the market.

AFTER JOHN SWEETERMAN came and began to take hold of the business side of the company, Phil was freer to turn his attention to news and editorial. On the news side, he would have liked to have correspondents overseas and felt the *Post* wouldn't "be doing a proper job in the capital until we manage that." Many of the editorial issues with which the *Post* was dealing had to do with the increasing anxieties about communism in those years after World War II. The political right kept manipulating America's fears in a demagogic way, and the atmosphere grew more poisonous as the Cold War grew more intense. The fear of communism, on which Joseph McCarthy and the political right fed just a few years later, was palpable everywhere, and the *Post* took strong stands from the beginning, which wasn't easy for a paper operating on the economic fringe and fighting for its life. The attacks on us for being liberals or even reds began then, and rarely ceased over the next several years, adding greatly to both our financial problems and our distinction.

There were, of course, genuine, strong reasons for anticommunism, both at home and abroad. At home, the party had succeeded in establishing a surprising network of infiltrators and even spies. Abroad, the Soviets were being very aggressive all over Europe, especially in Berlin, and in 1948 the communists took over in Czechoslovakia. Obviously, there were real concerns, but the political exploitation and misuse of them were shameless.

The *Post* had begun to cover the House Committee on Un-American Activities, or HUAC. By the end of 1947, we were under fairly constant attack for our attitude toward the committee's activities, and the editors felt the need to respond to those attacks. One editorial put the *Post*'s position succinctly:

> This newspaper's criticism of the committee has been directed consistently at its methods rather than at its aims. . . . Because the committee under successive chairmanships has equated loyalty with conformity, has concerned itself with opinions rather than activities, has disregarded the most elementary rules of fair play in dealing with witnesses, its conduct has seemed to us to be more dangerously un-American than that of any of the groups or individuals it has investigated.

An article that appeared in March 1948 in a conservative publication called *Plain Talk* attacked the *Post* as a "Trojan Horse for totalitarianism," following the Communist Party line on most major issues, and assailed Phil especially as "a constant apologist for the paper's editorial policy." The piece also censured Herblock and charged Alan Barth, "unmistakably the ideological guide of its editorial page," with "adherence to the party line." Phil was so enraged that he considered legal action, dismissing the idea only when he learned that *Plain Talk* had no capital. Instead, he wrote an eight-page memo to the *Post*'s staff explaining that the diatribe had been written by a disgruntled *Post* employee who had been let go, and laying out facts to "show the complete absence of any basis for the opinions expressed in the article."

When we were assaulted as communist sympathizers or even dupes, our competition in Washington was only too happy to jump on—or even jump-start—the bandwagon of censure. Both the *Times-Herald* and its relative in Chicago, the *Tribune*, attacked us relentlessly. The *Tribune* called the *Post* alternately a "defender of the Reds" and a spokesman for the Truman administration. They were hoping to undermine us with our readers and advertisers. Backing the reporting and commentary as well as Herblock's strong cartoons, while trying to protect our economic lifeblood, took a lot of courage and judgment on Phil's part.

In August of 1948, the *Post*'s Mary Spargo reported that HUAC had summoned Whittaker Chambers, a former member of the Communist Party but then associate editor of *Time* magazine, to testify. Chambers said that he had once belonged to but had quit the Communist Party, and in his testimony he named some U.S. officials as acting for the Soviets, among them Alger Hiss.

The Hiss affair ignited controversies on every side. Late in 1948, he was indicted for perjury after having denied passing secret documents to a communist spy ring, the statute of limitations precluding the stiffer charge of espionage. After a very public trial with passions running high, he was convicted in a second trial and sentenced to a five-year prison term. The *Post* had editorially noted that Hiss had threatened to sue if Chambers's charges were repeated off the floor of Congress. They were, and we challenged him to sue Chambers, which he did—hence the trials.

The *Post* was attacked from both sides for its coverage of the Hiss affair. Many of our friends criticized Phil and the paper for being too timid and less than objective. Our friend Jim Rowe, for example, wrote Phil several scathing letters, including one in which he said:

> . . . for pure snide newspaper writing the Post is the equal of the Times-Herald in its news columns. I think Alger has a lot of explaining to do. Why not let him make it in the forum of the Baltimore Court—and keep your bias out of the piece until then. . . . All I suggest is objectivity. I don't know the answer. But neither does the Post—and I expect more of the Post than other papers. . . .

Phil responded, agreeing that Rowe had "caught us with our objectivity down," but adding, "There were no bad intentions involved, just some silly judgments, and we are wistfully hoping that we shall learn from experience."

On the other hand, we were attacked for a moderate editorial comment by Merlo Pusey to the effect that

> Hiss had the misfortune of being tempted to betray his country in an era of widespread illusions about Communism and of being tried for perjury in connection with his offense in a period of cold war when the pendulum of public sentiment had swung far in the other direction. That does not excuse him or minimize the enormity of the crime of which he has been convicted.

Merlo was referring to the era of the Popular Front, when liberals viewed the communists as allies in the world's struggle against fascism, which appeared to be and was then the major threat.

When Secretary of State Dean Acheson was asked to comment on Hiss's conviction in his second trial, he made his famous comment, "I do not intend to turn my back on Alger Hiss," whom he had known well for years. The *Post*, in an editorial entitled "Conflict of Loyalties," was critical of Acheson's statement, saying: "Mr. Acheson has played right into the hands of the yammerers in our midst who are trying to rend our society with the Alger Hiss conviction as the instrument—has, indeed, given them a handle. . . . Judgment was obscured when Secretary Acheson decided to yield to a personal sentiment."

Two things followed, both indicative of Phil's dilemma over dealing with these delicate issues for the paper. Some Acheson supporters who were good friends of ours—Paul Porter, Joe Rauh, Oscar Cox, and Thurman Arnold—wrote a letter to the editor of the *Post* supporting Acheson's statement "as an act of personal courage and a declaration of principle rare in past history and virtually unprecedented in these times." Felix Frankfurter also wrote to Phil on the very day the editorial appeared:

> A free society implies a free press and a free press implies a free editor. Feeling these truths very deeply there have been instances in the past, as there will doubtless be in the future, when I have vigorously defended you against the charge of responsibility for editorial views that for one reason or another aroused criticism on the part of friends of yours.
>
>   The occasion for these remarks is, of course, the editorial in this morning's POST, "Conflict of Loyalties." You do not need to be told that the views which it expresses run counter to many deep convictions of mine, not the least my conviction about the duty

of the press. To worry lest uninformed people will disregard "weighed words" or that "yammerers in our midst" will make a misuse of them and therefore to deplore a manifestation of moral clarity, is to join the misinformed and the yammerers. I had supposed that the press enjoys its constitutional status because its duty is to enlighten and not to submit to darkness.

The Hiss case dominated all our minds; it was all we seemed to talk about. One night, Scotty and Sally Reston came to dinner, and as they sat down in our library and reached for a drink, Scotty said, "Shall we talk about something else for five minutes or shall we get right down to business?"

So, contrary to the perception of those attacking us from the right that the *Post* was a liberal, left-leaning paper, we were being assailed by those on the left, who felt we were too conservative and not vigilant enough in speaking out against right-wing excesses and in defense of civil liberties. In fact, there was a mixture of views on the editorial page, but Herbert Elliston and Phil were the deciding voices. The *Post*, indeed, had sympathized with Alger Hiss during the early stages of his trials but, as more and more evidence came to light, had come to the conclusion that he was a "cool and cynical perjurer."

THE YEAR 1948 was the first election year for Phil and me as controlling owners of the *Post*, and we went together to both political parties' conventions that summer. Conventions are fascinating to attend as journalists, and certainly as publishers—more so then than now, when everything is decided in the primaries. To find out what's going on behind the scenes you have to know people and be able to maneuver in crowds, to meet and exchange views with politicians and journalists from all over the country. In 1948, we were still young and the *Post* was still relatively unknown. Everyone else looked important to me, and Phil and I went around with my father, but even he was somewhat at a loss. I remember seeing Henry and Clare Booth Luce come into a restaurant in Philadelphia and thinking how important they looked—and indeed they were. I was very excited to be there but felt very new and small.

In the Truman-Dewey election, the *Post* maintained its tradition, begun under my father's independent ownership, of not endorsing a candidate for the presidency. Rather, the paper commented editorially on both major candidates. We criticized Dewey's statements indicating that he would turn over a large measure of control of atomic energy to private industry, and praised his statements about the Berlin blockade. We criticized

Truman for suggesting that Dewey was a "totalitarian" and agreed with a great deal of his denunciation of the Congress.

The last Gallup poll published before the election gave Dewey a five-percentage-point lead over Truman. When it became clear that Truman had indeed fooled the pundits and pulled off a political miracle, Phil, having spent much of the night at the office, sent off a telegram to the president, which he printed on page one of the morning-after paper:

> You are hereby invited to attend a "crow banquet" to which this newspaper proposes to invite newspaper editorial writers, political reporters and editors, including our own along with pollsters, radio commentators and columnists for the purpose of providing a repast appropriate to the appetite created by the late election.
>
> The main course will consist of breast of tough old crow en glace (You will eat turkey).
>
> The Democratic National Committee has agreed to furnish the toothpicks to be used by the guests who (it is feared) will require months to get the last of the crow out of their teeth.
>
> We hope you will consent to deliver the address of the evening. As the dean of American election forecasters (and the only accurate one) it is much desired that you share with your colleagues the secret of your analytical success.
>
> Dress for guest of honor, white tie; for others—sack cloth.

The president was highly amused, responding:

> I received on the train [back from Independence, Missouri] your very handsome invitation to me to attend a "crow banquet." I know that we could have a good time together, but I feel I must decline. As I said en route to Washington, I have no desire to crow over anybody or to see anybody eating crow, figuratively or otherwise. We should all get together now and make a country in which everybody can eat turkey whenever he pleases.

Truman also added, quite magnanimously, "Incidentally, I want to say that despite what your commentators and polls said, your news coverage of my campaign was fair and comprehensive."

WHAT WAS MOST important for us personally about the 1948 election was the terrible trouble in which our great friend Prich found himself. In the Kentucky Senate race that year between the Democrat, Virgil Chapman—for whom Prich didn't even particularly care—and the liberal Republican John Sherman Cooper, whom he liked, he did an incredibly wrong and foolish thing that ruined his life. Someone came to him and asked him to sign some ballots with faked names, and Prich did.

In April of 1949, Prich and his law partner, Al Funk, were indicted under the criminal code and charged with "conspiring to impair and dilute the effect of the votes cast for the Republican candidates for President, Senator and Congressman in Kentucky" in the general election the previous year. Prich pleaded "not guilty," but though Funk was ultimately absolved, Prich was sentenced to prison for two years.

Phil and other friends of Prich's tried to help as best they could. They collected and sent money, which was always in short supply with Prich, but particularly so as his lawyers prepared appeals and his own source of income—his law practice—ceased to exist. But the appeals—on which Joe Rauh and others had worked tirelessly—failed. When the first judgment was affirmed by the United States Circuit Court, the case was appealed to the Supreme Court, which affirmed the lower court's decision for lack of a quorum on June 5, 1950. Prich filed a petition for executive clemency, asking for a pardon or commutation of sentence, but he went off to prison and served five months of his sentence before being pardoned, just before Christmas of 1951, by President Truman, largely at the behest—ironically—of the very decent Senator Cooper, who had won the race against Chapman, for whom Prich had stuffed the ballots.

Our hearts were broken for our friend. We were dumbfounded. Here was the man among us most destined for greatness; yet now he'd been found guilty of so stupid and irresponsible an act, and was off to prison. It was hard to understand how such a distinguished mind could have done such a shocking thing. As Prich told a reporter in 1979, "I got to feeling, perhaps, that I was bigger than I was, that the rules didn't apply to me." My own inclination is to believe that, flawed as he was in character, Prich let his desire to be "one of the boys" overcome his intelligence and his judgment. He had perhaps been too successful at too young an age and had lived a pattern of permissiveness and laxity, which had always been the despair of his many friends. Even after he got out of jail and began to make a scratchy living, he occasionally neglected to finish work that had been contrived especially for him. Some of his old habits of not always fulfilling his part of any bargain endured. Yet still we loved him. Somehow one couldn't help it.

He wrote Phil from prison that "while I have many moments of bitter self-reproach, I cannot afford the excess baggage of feeling sorry for myself or plotting revenge against those who may have treated me badly (though I hate them plenty)." He found the prison to which he was assigned to be "as good as one could hope for: mild in its discipline and a comfortable enough stopping place." In the end, he regained his influence in Kentucky as head of an education commission appointed by Governor Ned Breathitt, which succeeded in implementing important education reforms. He regained his life and died, in 1984, the heroic figure we had envisioned, enduring his many afflictions with great courage and continuing to function, despite being diabetic and becoming blind.

FROM THE TURN of the new decade, politics seemed to heat up. On February 9, 1950, Senator Joseph McCarthy launched his campaign against a so-called Communist conspiracy to subvert American life. Phil's first response was to dismiss McCarthy's tirades and the senator himself. A few months after the beginning of McCarthy's invective, Phil said of the senator, "McCarthy is causing a lot of noise here and doing a lot of harm, but I am hopeful that he will eventually end up on his backside."

Phil had to tread a fine line in this very difficult time. He had been an ardent liberal, but in this period when he was fighting for the life of the paper he was clearly becoming more conservative and more anticommunist—mostly, no doubt, in response to events in the real world, but also to some extent in response to the constant attacks on the paper and on him personally.

Outsiders didn't realize that Phil had many problems with the internal politics of the *Post* during this period, some of which stemmed from the increasingly differing political views of Phil on the one hand and Alan Barth and Herblock on the other. For example, a real brick fell on Phil's head one day in the spring of 1950. He and I were returning together from New York by train, and he was going through the *Post*. Suddenly, reading an editorial he knew to be written by Barth, Phil went ballistic. In this editorial, Barth had commended Earl Browder, the former secretary general of the Communist Party in America and the communist candidate for the presidency in 1936 and 1940, for defying a special subcommittee of the Senate Foreign Relations Committee that was trying to compel him to disclose the names of his former associates conspiring against the United States. Barth was a brilliant and brave defender of civil liberties and constitutional rights, but in his appropriate concern for the right of privacy he tended to minimize the real dangers of communism. All the paper's top editors and managers were alarmed at the stick we had handed our enemies with which to beat us. And, of course, beat us they did. The *Times-Herald* dubbed us "Browder's organ."

Phil was so deeply upset that he wanted to fire Alan immediately. Luckily, during one of our Sunday-morning visits to Frankfurter, Felix quietly but firmly persuaded him not to, but several days after the editorial appeared, a note was printed in the paper regretting it.

The tensions between Phil and Barth remained. Several months later, Phil wrote to my father that he had been changing or killing a lot more editorials than usual—almost entirely Barth's production—and he was worried that Elliston would think *they* were having differences. Phil met with Elliston outside of the office to review the general situation and philosophy of the editorial page, explaining that he was extremely concerned about Barth. As he wrote to my father and as he told Elliston, he did not "want to slip into being a namby-pamby paper like the N.Y. Times, but at the same time I did not want to throw away the prestige and the power of the paper by getting in trouble on minor fronts through sloppy work." Eventually, however, Phil calmed down and lived with Alan Barth, who went on to be a great adornment to the page and to the *Post*. Joe Rauh later said of the terrible strain between Alan and Phil:

> I think Phil was really quite frightened in the McCarthy period when the *Post* was losing advertisers, by the possibility that he, an outsider, might lose the paper. . . . I think he didn't really analyze some of the problems with Alan, like whether Alan was right or wrong. . . . Phil felt a responsibility for the *Post* over and beyond the normal responsibilities of life because it wasn't his. I think he had been given this thing and he damn well was not going to let it go. He was not going to let it die.

I'M NOT SURE exactly when Phil began to think in terms of Eisenhower as a possible presidential candidate, or even whether he came to this himself or was influenced by someone, possibly my father. In one letter to Prich, who preferred Dewey to Eisenhower but was convinced the Republicans would win in 1952 no matter who the candidate was, Phil urged him not to be "too anti-Ike," admitting that he himself had been until Eisenhower's last visit to Washington, when Phil met him at a small private lunch for newspapermen and began to change his mind.

By the summer of 1951, Phil was so disgusted at the idea of more leadership on either the Truman or the Taft level that he joined my father in becoming a strong Ike man. Dad was convinced that Eisenhower "has the one thing that we have been looking for in recent years. . . . It is generally described as character." Although "independence" was the watchword at the paper, the editorial line clearly began to back Eisenhower, and on March 24 the *Post* endorsed him over Taft for the Republican nomination. Herbert Brownell, Ike's unofficial campaign manager, close friend, and later attorney general, called the endorsement "the most effective journalistic blow that had been struck for Ike."

The endorsement caused waves everywhere, not least within our family. My father's health and strength had begun to fail, and he was feeling "out of the loop" and insufficiently consulted, despite Phil's best efforts to keep him involved in the paper and the company. Apparently, in the case of the endorsement Phil had neglected to bring my father, who was in Florida at the time, into the decision and in on the timing of the editorial. Dad was understandably unhappy at not knowing in advance that the *Post* was going to endorse. My mother wrote Phil that something had to be done to build up my father's ego and restore his self-confidence, that he was feeling fairly useless. On the very day the editorial appeared, Mother followed up with a private, anguished letter to Phil, saying she was worn out trying to keep my father on an even keel, and chastising Phil for not having included him.

There is no record of Phil's response, but clearly he must have taken her words to heart. Following this letter, he wrote Dad several times in great detail about various issues involving the paper, consulting him on different matters, from a proposal to revise the format of the editorial page and the women's section to the idea of a rotogravure section for the Sunday paper. I was concerned about my father's hurt feelings, but I confess that I identified completely with Phil and with the pressures under which he operated—even though I differed with him about backing Eisenhower.

Phil and I went to the conventions that summer, both of which took place in Chicago. Eisenhower was nominated, and Phil was of course happy with the victory. I see now that we all regarded Taft as too much of a right-winger and an isolationist—the latter he was, but his political views were really moderate, farsighted, and decent. Our fears at the time were very real, however, and seemed very valid.

I was slightly more skeptical than Phil about Eisenhower. I suppose, somewhere deep inside, Phil was seeking recognition as an independent, in contrast to his liberal history. My own political views never changed much, and usually made me support the Democratic candidate, although I was and am a centrist. When, in 1952, the candidate turned out to be Adlai Stevenson, I had no doubt where my allegiance lay. Like many people of my general persuasion, I was swept away with excitement by Stevenson. I well remember the impact of first seeing him at the convention: I thought he was marvelously charismatic, and was immediately enthusiastic about him. His acceptance speech—made in the late hours of the night and with its rather pretentious Biblical quotation about the cup passing from his lips—was electrifying. The *Post* editorialized that, for Stevenson, "The office chose the man."

Phil, of course, knew how I felt. In a letter to a friend at the end of the summer he wrote, "I confess that my wife (since seeing Adlai the adorable) has shown signs of being a Crypto-Democrat." Despite my excitement about Stevenson, however, I was under no illusion about the possibility of his winning. Adlai's ambivalence about the presidency—both wanting it and not wanting it—was his Achilles' heel. For a politician to equivocate about his desires regarding the presidency disqualifies him, I later realized, but in the summer of 1952, like so many of us, I was overwhelmed by this extraordinarily articulate, witty man.

Phil, on the other hand, was fervently embracing Eisenhower and the Republicans. That summer he got to know Richard Nixon, who had been taken on as Ike's vice-presidential candidate. Phil was impressed with him and thought he would be a big help in the campaign. Nixon had lunch in midsummer with Phil, Russ Wiggins, and my father, and Phil reported to a newspaper friend that "the three of us all felt that he is obviously a person of major talents," whereas I and most of my friends were deeply concerned about his red-baiting victorious early campaign against Helen Gahagan Douglas and about his pronounced right-wing proclivities and seeming sympathy for McCarthy.

Throughout this campaign, Phil was constantly having to defend both the *Post*'s endorsement in the primaries of Ike over Taft and his own surprising political views. To those who chided him about his strange bedfellows, his comeback was to suggest "they might shake up their own sheets and take a look under the covers." Yet even though the paper was supporting Eisenhower, Phil tried, as he said, "as carefully as is humanly possible not to be prejudiced or blind to the qualities of Stevenson or some of the weaknesses of the Republicans." Among the weaknesses of the Republicans was the failure of Eisenhower to speak out against McCarthy and the excesses of the right wing.

As far as I was concerned, the last straw was added against Eisenhower in the now well-known incident involving General George C. Marshall, whom McCarthy had been viciously attacking. Ike's decent instincts came to the fore, and he had apparently decided to defend the general in a speech on one of his campaign swings through Wisconsin in early October. Wisconsin Republican leaders, however, leaned on Eisenhower's political counselors to dissuade him from making the favorable and supportive comments. Ike, still relatively new to politics, gave in to his advisers and eliminated the paragraph, but did this so late that the whole affair became public.

I had remained open-minded until then, but now I was solidly for Stevenson. Although Phil, too, was shocked at Ike's lack of strength in standing up to McCarthy, my views didn't worry or influence him—nor his me. Our political differences didn't come between us personally; we each understood where the other one was.

Phil's direction of the *Post* during the campaign stirred up some resistance and problems from within the ranks of the staff. At some point, several staffers wanted to run an ad in the paper declaring themselves for Stevenson, but Phil apparently talked them out of it. Most important, he and Herblock had quite a struggle. Herb's cartoons had always been searing and powerful. He had first drawn Nixon in a cartoon on May 16, 1948, in which Nixon and two others, all dressed as Puritans, were pictured building a fire under a chained Statue of Liberty and saying: "We've got to burn the evil spirits out of her."

As the campaign heated up and Eisenhower wasn't speaking out against McCarthy, Herblock drew cartoons that were clearly at odds with the editorial support the *Post* was giving Ike. Phil was incensed by many of these cartoons. One that he refused to print depicted Eisenhower saying "Naughty, naughty" to Nixon and McCarthy, who were drawn as two smear artists with buckets and dripping brushes in their hands. Finally, during the last weeks of the campaign, Phil had the cartoons dropped from the paper altogether—the last time I believe this ever happened. Instead, he used reprints of earlier cartoons. Since the cartoons ran elsewhere in syndication, this ploy was not only ineffective but embarrassing. In late October, the *Washington Daily News* carried an article headlined "Where's Mr. Block? One of D.C.'s Top Draw-ers Is Missing." On the other hand, it's easy to see why Phil felt he had to take action. It's hard for a publisher trying to espouse a certain cause in the paper to have such powerful cartoons running on the same page and dominating print. Even so, Phil later acknowledged to Herblock that he had been mistaken.

Phil became more and more actively involved in the election itself, so much so that he actually campaigned for Eisenhower a few times. On October 30, he served as master of ceremonies for a "Citizens for Eisenhower Rally." To keep Phil company, I went with him to at least one Eisenhower rally, including one where Phil spoke but I sat silently. I can't justify Phil's actions, but publishers did this kind of thing more often then. For instance, John and Mike Cowles, publishers in Des Moines and Minneapolis, were big contributors to, as well as activists in, Ike's campaign.

On Election Day, November 4, we watched the returns at the Rauhs'—ironically, probably our most liberal friends. Phil was thrilled by the result. However, he wrote Stevenson a few days after the election:

If you'll permit an expression from a black soul of the one-party press, I would like to say that yours was a campaign you and your sons can be proud of. In any event, even in opposition, I was proud of you from your first remarks on Astor Street to your closing comments in Springfield.

My wife—over whom you have control superior to mine—

joins me in wishing you (a) an immediate rest and (b) a fruitful future.

By now, McCarthy was growing even more sinister and more powerful. Playing on fears stemming from the Cold War, he made outrageous charges, many within the protected confines of Senate or congressional hearings, or just before newspaper and television deadlines so that all that got on the front page or the air was the charge itself. After a while, we in the media learned to carry the other side and to put his charges in perspective, but he was a new phenomenon with which the press had to learn to cope, and it took a while to catch up with his methods.

Much of Phil's time was taken up with the McCarthy menace. The fear of communism remained pervasive, and attacks on people for being sympathizers or liberals even, much less genuine communists, continued to stir up serious trouble. Editorially, the *Post* was highly critical of McCarthy's positions and attacked him regularly. Most effective of all probably was Herblock's series of cartoons depicting McCarthy and his various outrageous activities. It was Herblock who had coined the word "McCarthyism"—on March 29, 1950—using it as a label on a tar barrel. Taken together, the *Post*'s comments against McCarthy represented a very clear—and brave—position, and the paper took a lot of heat for its coverage. In fact, the war between McCarthy and the *Post* was vicious and frightening.

We were helped to a certain extent by Joe Alsop and his brother Stewart, whose column had become important to the *Post*, and whose anticommunist themes helped soften the perception of the *Post* as somehow sympathetic to the communists. Perhaps, too, some of the criticism was blunted because of the paper's support of Eisenhower. This was offset, however, by criticism from the left that we were not doing enough about McCarthy.

Once Eisenhower was president, he became one of those who Phil felt was not speaking out enough, and he became more and more disenchanted with the president's lack of response to McCarthy and the climate he was nourishing. Walter Lippmann had been an enthusiastic supporter of Eisenhower, but his wife, Helen—like me—had been a renegade for Stevenson. Sometime soon after the election, the four of us were together, and Walter asked Phil, "What are we going to do?" At the same time he turned to Helen and me saying, "And you, shut up." We laughed at the two men's dismay over White House passivity. Phil was constantly badgering Sherman Adams, the president's chief aide, to try to get Eisenhower to take stronger stands.

Since the *Post* was still fighting for its life economically, Phil felt very pressured by forces he couldn't control. One of the principal forces over which he had little control at this time was my mother. Like Barth and Herblock, she was unrelenting in her condemnation of McCarthy and his reckless charges. She despised him vigorously and publicly, calling him variously a "perpetual adolescent who has never matured," a "warped personality who is now revenging himself upon a society which he feels has never been fair to him," and a "gangster type." In worrying that insinuations and accusations by anticommunists were going to get people thrown out of their jobs without hope of reinstatement, she felt that such behavior put America "on the road to something worse than a Gestapo." Her answer was to look to the *Post* to handle the situation and to pressure Phil to "try to save our democratic freedoms." She argued, not illogically, "What is the use fighting totalitarianism abroad if we are going to imitate its worst aspects here at home?" But, as usual, her passion was excessive and uncontrolled.

Shortly after the inauguration, my mother delivered her strongest blast yet against McCarthy, this time to seventeen thousand school administrators in Atlantic City, warning that the congressional committee investigating schools and colleges threatened not only academic freedom but American democracy itself. In this speech, she called McCarthy "our modern grand inquisitor," a dangerous and ruthless demagogue, a political adventurer, and a psychopath, and compared his tactics to those of the bull ring. An article on her speech, along with her photograph, appeared on the front page of *The New York Times*. An Illinois congressman, the conservative Harold Himmel Velde, counterattacked her as having written a warmly pro-Russian letter to *Pravda*. The charge was false—the letter had been written by a Mrs. G. S. Mayer of Canada. The *Post*, of course, defended her, and Velde retracted his claim but not before the *Times-Herald* had picked up and used the accusation.

Not content with taking on McCarthy, Mother often took on the Catholic Church for its stand on education. She viewed this as a just cause and herself as an intrepid warrior for public education, but it was Phil and the *Post* who paid the price, in counterattacks of a serious kind, such as a boycott—a burden which Phil viewed with some outrage as an unnecessary one in the circulation-and-advertising struggle.

Just as he occasionally pulled back editorials and cartoons, so, too, he had to rein in my mother now and then. One notable time came in 1952, when he disowned a speech she made in Detroit condemning attempts by the Catholic hierarchy to support sectarian schools. He felt the speech would be construed as anti-Catholic. Mother had warned Phil that she would be making this speech: "I hope it makes no difficulties for *The Post*. I have written to Wiggins to write the news report on it himself so that he can play down whatever he wishes to." Among the things she said that raised red flags for Phil:

The Roman Church is building up a Catholic state within the state. It can end only in the ultimate catastrophe of a Catholic political party. . . .

No human being can blindly accept authority in one area of life and become self-reliant in day-to-day decisions in the field of morals, politics and economics. The secular public school trains independent minds for leadership in every area of life; the parochial school trains for obedience to authority. . . .

We must close the door tight against the present attempts of the Catholic hierarchy and reactionary Protestants to force our people to support sectarian schools whose rapid increase would destroy our secular school and tear our nation into irreconcilable factions. The costs of private and parochial education are mounting steadily. Few American girls wish to become nuns. . . .

Phil was so alarmed that he was going to issue a press release stating that my mother's views were her own and not to be confused with those of the *Post*. Following Russ Wiggins's advice, however, he softened it to a statement to be read as coming from her, which he hoped would be picked up by the press: "The views expressed in my Detroit speech are my own and do not reflect the opinions of *The Washington Post*. . . . I do not participate in the formation of editorial policies." The question then arose as to how to reach her, since she was on a night train returning home. Russ knew the editor of the *Buffalo Evening News*, Alfred H. "Kirk" Kirchhofer, and got him to board the train there at a water stop at two in the morning, wake her, and get her to sign off on the statement.

A long, feisty exchange of letters followed between my mother and Phil, all written out by hand. Typically, she depicted her situation as unbearable, and asked rhetorically what she was to do:

> I can't live in Hell at home. I can't worry Butch unnecessarily. I mustn't hurt the stock-holders of The Post, Butch's major fear. But I might as well stop all my efforts to create community solidarity, to strengthen the public schools and to defend my country against a foe no less dangerous than the Communists, if I have to shut up about Catholic political ambitions.

She ended her letter by telling Phil not to bother to reply, but suggesting they "must get together for a good talk." He sent back a fourteen-page handwritten response. Rightly or wrongly, he didn't agree with her analysis of the "urgency of the problems you see arising from the American Catholic Church. I doubt if Freud, Jung and Bill Meyer could find out

whether my position results from fear or objectivity, but I at least am unaware of the fear."

At the same time, he knew that her speech would cause considerable
hostility to the *Post*. He believed there had to be a sense of priorities about
the number of wars the *Post* was willing to engage in, and saw his obligation as defining the priorities with "an over-all, institutional point of
view." So the question for him was "why *The Post* should carry another
burden when it is not one our institutional thinking makes necessary."

Even though he felt his "most odious bias is toward being Pollyanna,"
Phil concluded that "time and tolerance and thoughtful discussion have
worked out many a tough problem," adding:

> If we could simply agree to disagree, it would be easy. . . . But
> we're hooked, which makes it both more complicated and more
> fun. For the fact is that you cannot be only an "individual" apart
> from the Post any more than EM can—or Kay, Elliston, Wiggins,
> Graham, et al. . . . we'll have to compensate our occasional, par-
> tial losses of individuality by recognizing the merits of the over-all
> institution.

So the potentially searing episode was gradually put behind all of us.
When this kind of drama arose I experienced no emotional complications.
I was 100 percent behind Phil and in accord with his views about the fam-
ily tensions—as indeed, most of the time, was my father.

Many emotions flared up in this period of McCarthy's heyday. Friends
fell out with each other. Rows erupted on every side. One notable argument close to home took place in March 1952 at a lunch at Joe Alsop's. Although the details are lost to me now, I recall that it was a small luncheon
party with friends, including Isaiah Berlin, who was here from England.
Whatever the specifics of the argument, at some point Phil exploded with
anger, and he and Isaiah fought loud and long. I believe Phil eventually
stormed out of Joe's house. Joe was furious with Phil and wouldn't speak
to him. Isaiah thought Phil had been incredibly rude and called to tell him
so. Phil wrote Isaiah that the "boorishness at lunch was inexplicable—and
inexcusable. Plain bad manners." He added, in his own way of apologizing, "I only hope that by now you may believe it had nothing more to it
than that I am an occasional sufferer from . . . a tendency to get one's
mouth in high [gear] before one's brain turns over."

Phil and Joe made up as well, but their relationship was not without
further arguments and letters flying back and forth. In mid-1953, for example, they got into another terrible fight at Joe's house, over the issue of
taking the Fifth Amendment rather than testifying. That time Joe followed up with a letter of apology and explanation:

I have searched my memory of our conversation to uncover what might have offended you as, so obviously, you were deeply offended. . . . As nearly as I can disentangle our discussion, you may perhaps have thought I was teasing you because you are now a successful man. Well, in a minor way, I suppose I am too.

Joe's reference to Phil's being a successful man and thus forgetting what it was like to be poor obviously touched a more sensitive nerve than any of us understood at the time. It came out later, when he was ill, that Phil resented the way he had been helped to his successful forum. But his abilities were clearly so extraordinary that none of us suspected the insecurities that lay beneath the surface.

ONE GREAT LOSS for us and for the *Post* was that Herbert Elliston's heart disease forced him to resign in 1953 as editor of the editorial page. In a farewell interview in the paper, Herbert said he had no guiding principle to leave, but if he did "it would be a line from Somerset Maugham: 'If a nation values anything more than freedom, it will lose its freedom, and the irony of it is that if it is comfort or money that it values more, it will lose that too.' " Herbert had been the editor for thirteen very distinguished years.

Phil immediately went after our friend Scotty Reston to be Herbert's successor. Phil's offer to Scotty sent *The New York Times* into action to keep him there. The result was that Arthur Krock moved out of the way to allow the *Times* to make Scotty its Washington–bureau chief. From Scotty's point of view, that wasn't even necessary; his response to Phil was simply to say, "I can't leave the *Times*." At that point, Phil surprisingly turned to the youngest member of the editorial staff, thirty-four-year-old Robert Estabrook, to run the editorial page. At about the same time, he cajoled Al Friendly, whom he considered one of the paper's top reporters, to be assistant managing editor for the daytime. This provided Russ Wiggins with the first real backup he had ever had. For a distinguished reporter to become an editor is one of the most difficult transitions, both for the person and for management; the two jobs require different skills, and naturally some reporters make the transition and become able editors and some don't. There is no good way to know except to try. For too long, the *Post* was not very good at helping people to learn to be managers, but though Al missed reporting, he took up the challenge of management with enthusiasm.

THE PATTERN OF our lives was changing. As the busyness increased, I tried to find ways to give Phil some relief. Because both he and I had had strong negative reactions to the summer of 1949, when we tried to take the children away to New England—Phil to the commute, and I to the life of women and children all week without their men—we decided to look for a summer retreat closer to home. I had concluded I'd take any house no more than twenty minutes away from Washington, and in the summer of 1950 we rented a house in Warrenton, Virginia, a bit farther out, but still acceptable to me. Phil liked it so much that we rented another house in the fall to continue country life on weekends.

I would probably never have done any of this had Phil not insisted. He loved the country, and the children thrived on it. I was less enthusiastic, having never lived this way. It meant a lot of work for me every weekend to pack up the children, the household, the food, and later the dogs, but Phil pronounced it all such a success that we started to drive around the countryside looking for a place of our own. Our dream was a house about an hour from Washington with a few acres around it to protect us. Just before Christmas, Phil remarked that he didn't think I really wanted to find a place and asked whether there wasn't anything I'd seen that I liked. I had indeed liked one place in Marshall, Virginia, but had thought it was too big and too expensive. In addition, it was a working farm, which I didn't want to take on and run. As I set out again on the search after New Year's 1951, the agent told me that the place was still for sale, they'd come down in their price, and the farm part was rented out, so the farming was taken care of. We went back to look at it again, and, as happened with our house in Washington, we fell in love with it—the house and the land.

Glen Welby, as the house was called, is located in a secluded area halfway between Warrenton and Middleburg, Virginia, about an hour and twenty minutes from Washington. The house was set in the middle of 350 acres, about sixty of which were woods. We bought Glen Welby for $87,500—a sum that is ridiculously small when looked at today, but which seemed a really large undertaking for us then, particularly since the house needed a lot of restoration and repairs, and, of course, I had to furnish it completely. The house was a real family house, large and sprawling. The center part probably dated to the early 1800s, and the back room had been added by the time of the Civil War. A kitchen wing followed, and a large living room and master bedroom and porch had been added by the former owners in 1929, just before the Crash.

It was typical of our marital relationship that Phil conceived the idea of a country house for summers and weekends and I did the actual work. Our relationship resembled that of a chief executive officer—Phil—and a chief operating officer—me. He had the ideas and spark; I carried them out and ran things. Despite the extra work for me, I'm grateful to Phil for this idea of buying the farm. It's now a familiar phenomenon for those who can afford weekend country life on a greater or lesser scale, but then it was much less common. My son Donald and his wife, Mary, now own Glen Welby and spend time there with their children in much the same way we did.

On the social front, we were getting to know an ever-wider number of people. I lunched with a variety of women, many of whom were close friends. At one point Phil noticed that there was always a three-way morning conversation among Polly Wisner, Evangeline Bruce, and me. He dubbed this the "nine o'clock network" and said he was going to buy time on it. Yet, despite having a circle of friends, I was still maladroit at managing our social life. Because Phil was consumed with work, he was strict with me about how many invitations to accept for the evenings. At first I rather stupidly told people I would consult Phil about whether we could accept. He insisted that I just tell them no, pointing out how hopelessly awkward it appeared if I hesitated or said I'd ask him. I remember once saying, "Shouldn't we go? I've said no to the French Embassy five times already," to which he quickly responded, "What's wrong with a sixth?" One day he came home to Glen Welby with an invitation from the head of the Joint Chiefs of Staff to go out on the *Sequoia*—then the official government entertainment boat—which he said he'd regretted. "Why?" I asked. "It sounds like fun." His response: "It *sounds* like fun, but think who's going to be there."

Whereas Phil was disinclined to accept invitations, once he got wherever we were going he usually enjoyed it hugely and was reluctant to come home. I, on the other hand, initially would want to go much more than he did, but often felt uncomfortable or shy once we got there. One example during these years was the Dancing Class, an old Washington tradition that had been started by Mrs. Joseph Leiter's mother, known as "Ma" Williams. The Dancing Class was the ultimate snobbish social event, and rules for entry were excessively rigid. Politicians were not among those invited to attend. Truman's Vice-President Alben Barkley and his young wife, Jane, were turned down, for example. Someone once wanted to invite Richard Aldrich, the producer, but this request was turned down because it was feared he might want to bring his beautiful actress wife, Gertrude Lawrence, who was in town with *The King and I*.

I confess I wanted to be included. Janet Barnes, our close friend who had grown up with all those people, proposed us to the committee, and we were accepted. I suppose I may have wanted to be accepted because of my childhood and because I knew that my parents had not been members. I suppose I may also have liked the idea of the Class because the rest of my life during those years seemed so unglamorous—houses, children, boards, and good works. Phil could not have cared less but, typically, rather enjoyed the whole thing once we went. Whereas I was usually overcome by an outbreak of nerves and the old fear of getting "stuck" with a partner on the dance floor. I remember Phil telling me, with some impatience, that it was up to me to take care of myself—that if I got stuck with someone I should just say goodbye, walk away, and find someone else. It didn't do to be passive and feel sorry for myself.

Our public life kept me busier than ever—accompanying Phil on trips, social and business dinners, *Post*-related activities. I kept less careful track of my own activities than I did of Phil's. Yet, although it may have seemed prosaic to those looking on, I really loved the life I led. I went on writing "The Magazine Rack" for the *Post* until 1953, when I just couldn't cope with all that I was doing and—against Phil's wishes—gave it up without really discussing it with him. He said, "I hear you've resigned. Have you gone to the competition?"

What I was doing was a good deal of fund-raising for local groups and serving on several boards dealing with welfare and children's issues. And, naturally, my own children were taking up a great deal of time—the usual endless carpools, mothers'-group meetings, birthday parties, riding and tennis lessons, field days, dogs, doctors' and dentists' appointments.

IN 1951, at a time when Phil was away, I found I was having another miscarriage. (He seemed always to be away on these occasions.) I went over to Johns Hopkins Hospital in Baltimore the next day and, after a minor operation, was sent home sad and depressed, but Phil, following a reassuring call from the doctor, reported to my mother that I was "really in very good shape, both physically and mentally, although the only slightly upsetting thing about the development is that it frustrated our perfect time schedule."

In April 1952, I had our fourth and last child, Stephen. Mother wrote me a note two months later, on my birthday: "35 years ago you gave your parents great joy by coming into the world. And now that lovely baby has four lovely children of her own! May your own astonishing tribe give you as much satisfaction and happiness as you have always given us." And she sent along what she called her "usual little check." She wasn't exaggerating—it *was* a small check, like those she sent throughout my life. In fact, Mother was very unwilling to take any trouble with gifts or to give something sizable, except, of course, for the huge business-related transactions that involved the Post Company. Many Christmases would go by in which she would shake her head about the state of the world and say that things were much too serious to bother about Christmas. Or she would say, "Darling, please buy the children something lovely from me"—usually after I had finished Christmas shopping, leaving me to choose something we were giving and sign it with her name. Unfortunately, she never learned to derive pleasure from giving. In fact, she had a streak of real discomfort at parting with things. I responded in various odd ways to this inheritance: overdoing Christmas and birthdays with a neurotic concern that a child not be disappointed, or giving inadequately myself, until I learned from Phil's lavish generosity and from observing friends.

Our relationship with my mother and father continued to be close yet difficult. The connections among the four of us were no doubt complicated by all the various hats we wore with each other, whether child, spouse, parent, friend, mentor, benefactor, or some mix of several of these. Dad was to celebrate his seventy-fifth birthday in 1950, and my parents had gone to Europe, so Phil and I were charged by my mother with planning some event to mark the occasion. What we came up with was a small party for him with his grandchildren, and then a dinner for over a hundred friends the following night. Mother had commandeered her friend Rudi Serkin to play the piano in Dad's honor. And the speeches were all appropriate and gratifying. In his, Joseph Pulitzer said that, of the many bankers and industrialists who had owned newspapers, Eugene Meyer was the first who turned out to be a natural newspaperman. Bernard Baruch spoke of his acumen, General Omar Bradley about his public service, and Steichen paid a touching tribute to the whole family. It was all a great success.

Because both my parents loved occasions and celebrated them to the utmost, we always seemed to be having these ceremonies for their birthdays or wedding anniversaries, or anniversaries of the *Post*'s founding or of my father's acquisition of it. Sometimes we would return from halfway around the world for these events. There was always considerable pressure to arrange them, to say nothing of attending them.

Rituals in one's life often start accidentally and then perpetuate themselves as a pattern. We developed several happy rituals in those years. Because Phil saw so little of the children, we began to take vacations with them. An early one, in St. Petersburg, Florida, turned out to be my introduction to baseball, since the Yankees trained there and we watched the exhibition games. After that—and because of Don's passion for the game—I learned to enjoy baseball and even keep score, because this was something both Phil and Don liked to do.

After we bought the television station in Jacksonville, we began going to a beautiful beach half an hour from town. For several years in a row, we spent ten days there right after school let out for the summer. Directly on our return from Florida, we would give a party at Glen Welby for *Post* people to celebrate the anniversary of the purchase of the paper; it started with the twentieth anniversary but became an annual event—and a large burden on me at the time, since I still hadn't learned how to organize people to get the work done. The caterer did a great deal, but I used to weed the garden, tidy up the house, get my neighbor to arrange the flowers, and generally run around worrying over all the details, including how many portable toilets to bring in for 150 people. We printed a newspaper about my father's achievements and the *Post*'s progress, which Lally distributed riding astride a tiny mule someone had left with us. Don, displaying a capitalist streak, collected small parking fees at the end of the lane.

GIVEN ALL HIS responsibilities and interests, and despite his native abilities and skills, Phil was stretched very thin, which took a toll on his endurance and his health. He suffered from numerous illnesses, increasingly so as the years went by. There were moments of strain between us, mostly when he drank too much, after which—almost inevitably—a rather violent quarrel would ensue, followed by abject apologies and diminished drinking, or even a temporary period of no drinking at all. Whenever I saw the drinking begin, I started to freeze; dreading the inevitable fight, I grew overworried. Probably I could have handled these situations better if I had been calmer about them, but I couldn't be. He was usually guilt-stricken, especially if there had been a sequence of unpleasant episodes.

One such difficult evening occurred in the spring of 1954, when we were cohosts at a large party we all referred to as the Bankruptcy Ball. Tom and Joan Braden had come to town. Tom, good-looking and attractive in a craggy way, had been in the CIA, and Joan was extremely strong, sandy-haired, blue-eyed, with a mysterious hold on the opposite sex. The party was in a huge but almost empty house across the Potomac, on the Virginia side, where the Bradens were living at the time with the first few of their eight children. The hosts—Stewart and Tish Alsop, Joe Alsop, Paul and Phyllis Nitze, John and Joanne Bross, Frank and Polly Wisner, and ourselves—each contributed $400 toward the expenses. The party was a lot of fun, but for me it was one of those all-too-frequent nights when Phil had too much to drink. On our way home from the ball he told me to stop the car, got out, and walked for a while, fuming, with me driving slowly alongside; finally he got back in and we went home.

The subject of his drinking was never openly discussed. When he was drinking, you couldn't talk about it; when he went on the wagon, I always hoped for future restraint. The fights were never in public—the rage would explode after we had left a place and was usually about nothing substantive, nothing concrete that we could discuss. Rather, he seemed to seize on something as an excuse to vent his rage, which built up because of all the pressure he was under. Certainly these incidents could have been early signs of his later illness, but I never suspected that Phil was either ill or depressed, or that that might have been the reason for his drinking.

Despite these difficulties, I was completely immersed in Phil's life. He always had a strong desire to communicate and hated being alone, so I accompanied him almost everywhere, and at home he liked me to sit and talk to him, even when he was in the bathtub. Consequently, I was very aware of everything in his day's work—whom he had seen, what he'd done, how everything was going. He was particularly good at recounting what took place at his many stag evenings. His memory was so photographic that he could recite whole conversations or re-create entire evenings in minute and fascinating detail—it was almost better than being there, since he had a great sense of what was interesting and funny and a great aversion to what was tedious and boring.

In the early days, I often drove him down to the office or back or both. Many late evenings, I would sprawl out on the sofa in his office while he worked. We did very little apart from each other. One memorable time when I did do something separate was not soon repeated. Barry Bingham, owner of the *Louisville Courier-Journal,* who had become a friend, had invited us to the Kentucky Derby, but just before we were supposed to leave, Phil said he felt fluish and took to his bed. When I called the Binghams to tell them we couldn't come, they suggested that I come alone. I distinctly remember being very surprised at being asked on my own, and I was reluctant to leave Phil when he was ill, but he insisted that I go, so I did. The weekend was an endless sea of parties and races, with the one important race happening so quickly that it was bewildering for someone new to racing. Still, I had a very good time, only to return to find Phil in a fit of anger. He admitted that, yes, he had urged me to go, but of course he hadn't meant it and hadn't liked being left alone in his sickbed.

Again, as with his drinking, I interpreted Phil's delicate health and constant illnesses as the result of the strains on him and the fraught, competitive situation of the company. Looking back, I can see that these illnesses, too, were likely connected with his more basic health problem, of which there was no real sign yet. In retrospect I realize that the more difficult moments were definitely connected with mood swings. But I, and indeed the world, was dazzled by him. His wit, great energy, soaring imagination, and fervent desire for excellence—in himself and in others—were so strong that I ignored the fact that he was frequently using that wit at my expense. Phil was often critical or cutting in his remarks when things weren't just right—either about the house or my clothes, for example, which left lots of room for disparaging remarks. Oddly, what I never perceived at the time was that, though he was lifting me up, helping me in so many ways, he also had a way of putting me down which gradually undermined my self-confidence almost entirely.

Nonetheless, Phil was the fizz in our lives. He was the fun at the dinner table and in our country life. He had the ideas, the jokes, the games. He operated on the theory that it was important to do with the children only those things he himself enjoyed—no dull board games, but hunting, fishing, walking. His ideas dominated our lives. Everything rotated around him, and I willingly participated in keeping him at the center of things. In fact, I agreed with almost all his ideas.

I remember once I was complaining about having injured my knee by stepping on a ball on the tennis court. Feeling rather sorry for myself, in a plaster cast in the hot summer in Washington, I whined about "Why couldn't I have stepped an inch to the right or an inch to the left of that ball?" I will always remember Phil looking at me, smiling, and saying, "Think of the ones you've missed"—not what I wanted to hear at that moment, but a truth that stayed with me for life. He always managed to get right through to the heart of the matter.

I learned such a lot from him, from the way he lived. His energy was infectious. He didn't suffer fools gladly, as evidenced in his failure to mince words. I recall one night at the start of the Eisenhower administration when the new secretary of the Treasury, George Humphrey, and his wife came to dinner at our house. I overheard Mrs. Humphrey telling Phil what a great sacrifice George had made to come to Washington. To my horror, I heard Phil respond, "Would you mind if I told you something frankly, Mrs. Humphrey?" "Not at all," was her reply—quite rashly, if she had known Phil better. "Well, Mrs. Humphrey," Phil said, "making that remark in Washington is like belching at dinner in Shaker Heights. We think it's quite a privilege to be secretary of the Treasury." Needless to say, our relationship with the Humphreys never progressed much further.

AS FOR THE *Post*, all our worrying and all of Phil's efforts and hard work were beginning to take effect. The paper had its problems, to be sure, particularly over labor issues—the late 1940s had witnessed several short strikes and work slowdowns by the pressmen and stereotypers. Nevertheless, we were publishing ever-larger papers, occasionally equaling or even surpassing the *Star*. Important moves had been put in motion to improve further the paper's quality and profitability—a television magazine boosted circulation; better technical resources in the new building allowed us to print a finer paper; experiments in using color on the paper added a new dimension; a broader profit-sharing plan for more employees gave people a real sense of belonging. The paper had come from bankruptcy to break even, more or less, with huge advances having been made in the business area, especially after John Sweeterman's arrival. As Phil wrote to John, "How great are the obligations of this entire newspaper to you! You have done all and more than I ever hoped for, and—wonder upon wonder—you have done it so quickly and calmly that many are unaware you have done it. You can be certain I am not among them."

Despite McCarthy and the whole atmosphere of the times, which jeopardized the future of an independent newspaper, we were experiencing the highest advertising-and-circulation increases in our history. And great gains on the news-and-editorial side contributed to the *Post*'s being increasingly widely recognized. It's a salutary nod to humility to realize just how much progress had been made by my father and by Phil with so few resources and such enormous odds against them. In the end, my father's concentration on the basic principles had paid off handsomely. The year 1953 had been an especially good one for the *Post*, which Phil characteristically played down by saying it "does not mean we are ready for retirement, but at least we are a couple of steps ahead of the sheriff."

What made the outlook even better was a letter my father received in the beginning of 1954—an event that led up to what I still think of as the defining moment for the company: the unexpected acquisition of the *Times-Herald*. The letter was a confidential one from his friend Kent Cooper, former general manager of the Associated Press, who was living in retirement in Palm Beach. Dad arrived at our door that morning, waving the letter in his hand, obviously excited, asking, "Where's Phil?" I explained he had gone to Jacksonville. "I've got to talk to him right away. This is really important."

My father then went to the *Post*, where he threw the letter on John Sweeterman's desk and asked, "What do you think?" The letter read simply: "I am wondering whether you expect to be in Palm Beach any time soon for I would like very much to talk to you about a business matter of importance to you."

Sweeterman replied, "I'm probably thinking the same thing you are." They both knew that Cooper was a good friend of Colonel McCormick's, that he lived near him, and that he was likely talking about the *Times-Herald*.

"Well, why don't we find out?" replied my father, and immediately put in a phone call to Cooper. Cryptically, he asked, "Kent, this 'business matter' to which you refer, is it in the field of journalism?" Cooper said that it was. "Is it in Washington?" my father probed. Again Cooper said yes.

This was the moment we had fought for, worked for, and prayed for since 1933. After the disappointment in 1949, when the colonel had stepped in, our hopes that he would sell at all—much less sell to us—had all but vanished, so the excitement aroused by Kent Cooper's letter was immense.

Several developments had occurred, some known to us, some not. Obviously, the staff of the *Times-Herald* could see that we had improved our financial situation markedly. Their paper, on the other hand, was not doing nearly so well. In the end, Colonel McCormick, with all of his resources and the venerable *Chicago Tribune* behind him, turned out to be not nearly so formidable in Washington as we had assumed he would be.

The *Times-Herald* had gone through some transitions of its own. In 1951, the colonel had fired his niece and the *Times-Herald* publisher, Bazy Miller. Bazy had divorced her husband in January of that year, and a few months later she got married again, to a *Times-Herald* editor, Garvin Tankersley. The colonel, I was told at the time, didn't like the idea of her divorcing a husband he liked and marrying someone in the office. More important, in the midterm elections of 1950 she had had printed at her newspaper's plant an election-campaign tabloid, *From the Record*, which came from Senator Joseph McCarthy. In it, there was a forged picture of Maryland Senator Millard Tydings shaking hands with Earl Browder. Tydings, the incumbent, lost the election and charged that the tabloid helped defeat him.

All of this shocked the colonel, who was both straitlaced and ethical. He replaced Bazy with *Tribune* executives who didn't understand anything about Washington or running a paper in the capital city. They put out a paper much like the *Tribune*, isolationist, right-wing, and with all the simplified spelling that had been used in Chicago: "sherif," "fotograf," and "burocrat." So the problems for the *Times-Herald* began to mount. We had no idea that it had lost thousands of subscribers and was losing half a million dollars or more each year. Moreover, the colonel was getting along in years and his health was failing. His doctor wanted him to cut down his responsibilities, and the Washington paper, with all its headaches, seemed like the thing to let go.

Kent Cooper always claimed that it was he who persuaded McCormick to sell to us. Frank Waldrop viewed it another way—that the colonel, a generous man, had let Cooper be a go-between in order to give him some sort of finder's fee. The truth probably lies somewhere in between. The colonel knew that the *Times-Herald* was worth more to the *Post* than to anyone else. Still, McCormick would have had to overcome his sharp difference of views with my father, as well as his resistance to selling out to his longtime competitor. On the plus side, what it all may have come down to is that McCormick actually had a great deal of respect for my father. Whatever his reasons, the colonel had decided to sell, and Kent Cooper sent the word. My father and John Sweeterman took an overnight train to Palm Beach and went straight to the Brazilian Court Hotel, where Phil met them. Then Phil and John left my father to talk to Kent Cooper alone.

The message was that Colonel McCormick wanted only to get out of the paper what he had put into it, which was $8.5 million. My father said,

"Done." It was a bit lower than the outer limit they had set in their minds. Cooper stressed the need for complete secrecy and said that if there was any publicity the colonel would have to end the discussions. They left it that Cooper would phone my father later that afternoon, as soon as he had had a chance to talk to McCormick.

When Cooper phoned, he confirmed that McCormick wanted to sell but that he could not act without discussing matters with his stockholders. All of this would take several weeks' time, since his doctors had told him he shouldn't leave Florida before March 15; only after that would he meet in Chicago with his directors and stockholders and ask for authority to negotiate with my father. Cooper told us there was nothing to worry about, because we had McCormick's word, which was good, but six weeks of holding our collective breaths seemed a lifetime.

Phil, John, and my father returned to Washington. The goal we had sought so long seemed within reach, but until it was signed, sealed, and delivered it was still only an exhilarating promise, almost too good to be true. The colonel sell to us? We had never dared hope for such a scenario.

My parents had planned a vacation trip to Jamaica and worried that they should postpone it. Phil urged them to go, which they did at the end of February. On Saturday, March 13, Cooper telephoned Phil to say that he would shortly be hearing from somebody representing the *Tribune*. Phil then cabled my parents to come home. At seven that same evening, the telephone rang. I answered it in the library. The caller was Chess Campbell, vice-president of the Tribune Company. When Phil got on the line, Campbell said, "I just can't believe it, but I'm here to sell you the *Times-Herald*."

At nine that night, together with John Sweeterman, we met my parents at the airport and went back to Crescent Place with them; there the three men started making plans. Phil knew he had to work fast and in the greatest secrecy. He called Floyd Harrison, my father's business right hand and also treasurer of the *Post*. He also called Frederick Beebe—or Fritz, as we knew him—our corporate and estate lawyer, who was with Cravath in New York. They all met at Crescent Place at 10:00 a.m. the next day. Phil, accompanied by Sweeterman and Harrison, then went off to meet with Campbell. Fritz, meanwhile, went to the offices of Covington & Burling, our Washington law firm, to begin work on a written offer for the *Times-Herald*, together with Fontaine Bradley and Gerry Gesell, who specialized in antitrust matters.

Essentially, Phil agreed to pay the $8.5 million that McCormick wanted for the paper. In addition, however, he agreed to give termination or severance pay to *Times-Herald* employees who did not move over to the *Post*. This meant another million or so.

After transmitting the written offer to the *Tribune* people, Phil came home with my father and put in calls to the top *Post* executives, gathered them all at our house, and outlined the deal, saying, "If it works, in three days we'll also be publishing in the afternoon." He asked them to think through what this would entail, but not to tell anyone for the time being, including their wives.

The contract was accepted with only minor changes. Phil, always impatient with legal procedures despite being a lawyer, said later—after the whirlwind twenty-four-hour negotiation—that he always knew it could be done. The contract was hand-carried to the *Times-Herald* building, where a meeting of *Tribune* stockholders was in progress. It was only at this point that Bazy Tankersley first heard about the pending sale. One person at the meeting described her as looking as if she had been "struck by a thunderbolt." She asked for time to raise the money to buy the paper herself, but Colonel McCormick, who was presiding, won approval for the sale. They did give Bazy about forty-eight hours—until the meeting of the *Tribune*'s board in Chicago on the Wednesday of that week—to raise the money, but did so with the completely inhibiting caveat that she could not disclose why she was trying to raise it.

On Tuesday morning, the colonel left for Chicago—with more suspense left for us to stew in, lest Bazy succeed in raising the money. Phil and Chess Campbell met again on Tuesday at his suite in the Ritz Carlton. In a suite down the hall, other *Tribune* executives were breaking the news to *Times-Herald* executives, whom Phil then talked to. While Phil was doing this, Campbell entered the room and began to prowl around with a concerned expression, looking under chairs and tables. When Phil asked what he was looking for, Campbell replied, "To tell you the truth, it's the letter of transmittal from you and Mr. Meyer." Phil immediately joined Campbell, both on their hands and knees, ransacking the room. Finally, Campbell called his law firm. "Oh," said one of the lawyers, "we have that. We'd never let go of that." This was just one indication of the confusion and rush surrounding the deal. Phil had completed one of the most important newspaper purchases in history in twenty-four hours—backed by my father all the way, including financially.

Also on Tuesday, Phil called *Post* company executive John Hayes to his office and handed him an American Security and Trust Company check for $1.5 million as the down payment for the paper. In an effort to preserve security, the check, John was stunned to observe, was made out to him personally, and he was dispatched to Chicago to deliver it in person. So anxious was Phil that John get there that he insisted he take an overnight train rather than risk losing the check (and John) in a plane crash.

Meanwhile, *Post* executives set in motion the necessary behind-the-scenes activity that would allow for publication of a joint paper if the sale were to go through. Russ Wiggins let some of his executives in on the secret. A list was drawn up of people on the *Times-Herald* whom they wanted to interview. Don Bernard, our advertising director, took a suite at the Mayflower to talk to his managers. Their first job would be to call merchants and others to inquire whether advertising placed in the *Times-Herald* should be inserted in the consolidated paper.

Probably the most complicated job was discussed by the circulation directors, who would have to deliver the enlarged paper to the homes of both *Post* and *Times-Herald* subscribers. They made plans to use *Times-Herald* men and trucks.

On Wednesday morning, Hayes arrived at the Tribune Tower in Chicago, where a much-agitated right-winger was dashing in and out of Colonel McCormick's office trying to dissuade the colonel from selling to us rather than Bazy. As reported by *Time*, Bazy had called a long list of wealthy, conservative potential backers, such as Sears, Roebuck's chairman, General Robert Wood, ex-Ambassador Joseph Kennedy, and Texas oil man H. L. Hunt. She had raised $4 million and asked for time to raise more. The colonel said no—he didn't want to sell to amateurs. He respected my father as a professional newspaperman.

We—Phil, my parents, John Sweeterman, Floyd Harrison—were in Phil's office, from which we put in a call to John Hayes at the *Tribune* and kept the line open so as to maintain the connection while waiting for news of the board's approval. We all took turns talking to John, to keep the line occupied lest we be cut off. At last the board approved the deal, the check was delivered, and Colonel McCormick signed the agreement of sale. Hayes hurried to our open phone and said to Phil, "I've got it. We're all set. Let me tell you about . . ."

"Goodbye, we're on our way," said Phil, banging down the phone, cutting John off. We were terribly moved, and excited beyond all imagining. After great gleeful shouts, I remember telling DeVee Fisher, Phil's loyal, longtime secretary, that we mustn't appear to gloat, but I must have said this through the smile that I couldn't have gotten off my face if I'd tried. The time was 12:44 p.m., St. Patrick's Day, 1954—a supreme moment in the history of The Washington Post Company. We now had the morning field in Washington to ourselves, daily circulation jumped immediately from 204,000 to 395,000, and Sunday circulation rose from 200,000 to 395,000.

That afternoon and evening, however, before we hit the streets with our combined papers, were a real challenge. With so little advance planning, things were chaotic. John Sweeterman's job had been to stay at the *Post* and plan as best he could, assuming the deal would go through. It was his basic plan that was put into operation and made the whole thing work.

The purchase brought problems for us, of course. As a result of adding all the features of the *Times-Herald*, we were running a more-than-double press run of a larger paper, which created problems in itself. Another problem was the *Times-Herald* employees not absorbed by the *Post*, which created a union/employee situation. Also, any time a community loses a paper, there are tensions, unhappiness, displaced people, and the feeling that a voice has been stilled. There remained three papers in Washington, though, so people didn't feel that they were at the mercy of one voice, as happened later in most cities.

Combining news and editorial on these papers was difficult, since we had two very opposite cultures to meld. The *Times-Herald* had more of a mass audience; ours was more of a class audience. The *Times-Herald* had been loaded with features. It was full of comics, columnists—especially conservative columnists—sports, gossip, sex, and crime. The *Post* was more serious-minded and didn't carry all the fun stuff. What we did to mute the criticism we knew would come was to pick up from the *Times-Herald* every columnist, critic, comic, and feature of any kind—with one or two minor exceptions that Phil and Russ felt unable to swallow—so that *Times-Herald* subscribers would find everything they cared about still there in the paper. We started that night by running two equal-sized names on the masthead—*The Washington Post and Times-Herald*. Gradually, over a period of years, we shrank the size of print for the name *Times-Herald* until finally it disappeared altogether.

When we put the two papers together, we covered the market. In fact, something sparked in the combination. We kept the circulation of both papers minus the overlap, and then started to grow. Much of this was due to Sweeterman's policies. What he had done was continue to deliver the paper to all the *Times-Herald* readers—even if they had tried to cancel their subscriptions. This way, they had time to look through the paper and see that their favorite features were still there. As John said, "They just rode along with us and they started paying their carrier bills after a while." With the *Times-Herald* circulation that we held, we had 70-percent penetration of the morning market in the Washington area.

That kind of coverage and the particular mix of the combined circulation helped to produce volume business for the stores, and the results in advertising started to show immediately. The *Star*, which had relied on advertiser loyalty, was so self-satisfied and complacent that it simply went on doing what it had been doing. Its idea was that the *Times-Herald* circulation didn't draw advertising by itself, so why would it do any better because it was running off *Post* presses?

One of the most important issues—one that actually came up in the few days while we were in the process of buying the paper—was antitrust. Gerry Gesell handled this most sensitive issue with consummate skill. We wanted to buy the assets of the *Times-Herald*, not the stock, since the Clay-

ton Antitrust Act prohibited acquisition of stock but not of assets. Mc-
Cormick, on the other hand, wanted to sell his stock, so as not to have to
deal with the people problems and others he'd be left with if he still held
stock. He just wanted to sell the whole company.

We obviously were not in a position to argue, so Beebe and Bradley
had worked out an immediate purchase and then the immediate dissolu-
tion of the Times-Herald Company and the transfer of its assets. That was
all done, and the bank accounts were transferred. Gesell called Graham
Claytor, later secretary of the navy and head of Southern Railroad, and
had him come up from Roanoke just to handle the principal bank account,
so there was no money left, no anything left, nothing on the books that
could be construed as suggesting there was any kind of company left.

Almost immediately after that, Phil got a telephone call from the head
of the antitrust division at the Justice Department, who said that they had
heard rumors that the *Post* was acquiring the *Times-Herald* and he wanted
to see the *Post*'s lawyer right away. Phil called Gesell, who went alone to
the Justice Department. Gesell recalled later that the division head was in
his private office with nine of his top staff:

> I knew most of them . . . and there were a bunch of stern faces. . . .
> [A Justice Department official] said, "We have a pretty good ru-
> mor that the Post is buying the Times-Herald." I said, "You're ab-
> solutely right. They bought it." . . . And he said, "I want you to
> keep the two companies separate until we investigate the matter."
> I said, "Well, I'm sorry, we can't do that. We've already eliminated
> the company; it doesn't exist anymore." "Well, we're certainly go-
> ing to investigate you," he replied. And I said, "Well, thank you
> very much. I'm sure it's legal."

It turns out that there is a clause in the antitrust laws called the "failing
company doctrine," which makes an exception for companies that merge
if both of them are failing. Although the doctrine had never really applied
to newspapers, because newspapers always had somebody who would buy
them, Gesell had decided to rely on this.

Many conservatives, some in Congress—horrified to think that a conservative voice was going to be taken away by what was, in their view, the
lunatic, liberal wing of American journalism—leaned on the Justice Department to bring an antitrust suit on monopoly grounds. Even Clare
Booth Luce, of all people, told Phil and me one evening that it was too
much power for one family to have. But there was never any prosecution.

One sad outcome of the *Times-Herald* acquisition was a letter from my
sister Florence to my father. Deeply unhappy much of her life and con-

stantly at odds with the family, Flo chose this moment to complain that her absence had caused her and her boys somehow to lose out either financially or in ownership of something valuable. My father wrote back that this was not the case and explained that no one in the family would be any poorer. He later reported to us that Flo had cabled back in an "entirely satisfactory" way and "fulfills our hopes for her better understanding and changing attitude."

One of the more interesting sidelights of this whole thing was that, in the middle of the purchase and merger, the *Post* had published what we regarded as a moderate editorial responding to a televised speech by Vice-President Nixon, in the middle of which he remarked in an aside, "Incidentally, in mentioning Secretary Dulles, isn't it wonderful, finally, to have a Secretary of State who isn't taken in by the Communists, who stands up to them? We can be sure now that the victories our men win on the battlefields will not be lost in the future by our diplomats at the Council table."

The editorial had been moderate at Phil's order, just before he disappeared into negotiations. However, it wasn't moderate enough to suit Nixon. He called up Harry Gladstein, the circulation manager, and canceled his subscription to the *Post*—both at home and at the office. Harry asked Phil, "What do you think he'll do in the morning, when he discovers there's no alternative?"

WHEREAS MY WHOLE memory was that our life depended on our getting the *Times-Herald*, John Sweeterman remembers the time differently and perhaps more accurately. He has said that, if it hadn't happened as it did, we

> ... would have fought it through. We were on the verge of licking the *Times-Herald*. We had them beat really. The odds were in our favor. . . . The *Times-Herald* didn't have enough of a foundation. They were a Hearst-type newspaper, tight operation, and an all-day publishing operation, which is kind of screwy anyway. . . . The *Times-Herald* couldn't have continued publishing all day because it was too expensive.
>
> [They were] losing money, more than we were, so that sometime, sooner or later, they would have gone away from that all-day paper and gone morning. . . . Then it would have been more of a decisive battlefield. . . . It would have been a slower, costlier prospect and operation but I think we would have made it. I don't think there's any question about it.

But the perception Phil and I shared was right in a way. This was the best short route to the future. Why take years of struggle if you can do it an easier way? There is no doubt in my mind that the struggle to survive was good for us. In business, you have to know what it is to be poor and stretched and fighting for your life against great odds. Many of the young people on the paper today tend to think that the franchise was bestowed on the *Post* and to take it for granted. We all had a deep fear that, like the *Star* family, we would someday become self-satisfied. That fear permeates our family, down to Don Graham, who was very much aware of all these events as a child.

We paid a price for our extraordinary and unexpectedly great success—we raised advertising rates but not enough to compensate for the large gain in circulation, so the paper lost $238,000 the first year. But that wasn't important. Twenty-one years after my father had bought the *Post*, five years after Phil had been so disappointed at losing the *Times-Herald*, the *Post* had bought its competitor in what was probably the most successful newspaper merger ever, doubling our circulation overnight and propelling the paper into a much more prosperous future. This purchase is what made us a viable company with a future toward which we could look with some certainty, and a foundation on which we could build. At last, after my father's struggle—which Phil had shared for more than eight years—we could begin to believe that the *Post* was here to stay.

— *Chapter Thirteen* —

P HIL AND I were entering young middle age. For Phil, work, though consuming and demanding, was going along more easily. Except for his increasing physical problems, everything was looking up. The *Star* still led the newspaper scene in Washington, but at last the *Post* had some stability and a clear-cut future. Phil himself was an undoubted business and personal success.

For me, these were successful years in different ways. I loved my life and was happy in the circle of my family—my parents on the one hand and my children on the other. I had a husband who was the center of that circle, around whom we all revolved. We had two large, comfortable houses—the one on R Street and the farm in Virginia. In short, we were privileged; but we knew it and tried to acknowledge it, contributing to the world as best we could.

Our lives were so busy in these years that Glen Welby became our retreat, our R and R, the place where we went to collapse and regroup. It was where we spent the most time together and where the children were happiest, with the possible exception of Don, who would often go to the Friendlys' to be with his pal Nicholas. Don's interests lay in town, and, besides, he had severe allergies.

Our days at Glen Welby were crowded with activities, but they were much slower than those in Washington. Life was easy and extraordinarily low-key. The house was furnished informally and sketchily—partly with furniture bought at auctions, partly with a few things purchased from the previous owner, and only a little acquired with the help of a decorator. The large lawn was mowed by an antiquated machine pulled by horses, all operated by Rob Grant, a charming man who belonged to a large, distinguished family that lived nearby. The farm itself was worked by a farmer from nearby Rectortown, aided by another farmer, Buck Nalls, who lived on the place. When eventually we took over the farm ourselves, Buck stayed on, as did two of his sons, and became a pillar of our lives there.

Reconfiguring Glen Welby for our needs was my job. The house itself required a lot of work. We built a hard-surfaced tennis court on the remains of one we found. We created our own recreational swimming and fishing by digging a pond at the foot of the hill in front of the house, then damming a stream and installing pipes under the dam to feed the pond. Every spring I would have a truckload of sand brought in and dumped on the dam to form a small beach. We built a pier with a diving board, and Phil had the completed pond stocked with bass and bream. This one-acre pond eventually was dubbed Lake Katharine, since several such lakes, built by friends in the neighborhood, were named after wives. A few years later, Phil built a second, much bigger pond below the first, lower down on the stream. This pond was named Lake Philip. In 1957, when Ed Murrow was creating a lake on some land he owned, Phil wrote him to "be sure to name this one for your wife. This will seem generous, but more important you are bound to build a bigger pond soon. That one can then be called Lake Edward." We made a little island in the middle of Lake Philip and called it Ile Sainte-Lally—a takeoff on Ile Saint-Louis in the middle of the Seine in Paris.

Because this second lake was big enough for boating, Phil gradually acquired or built a small fleet of boats of various odd shapes and kinds—a sailboat he sent for and put together himself, a rowboat, a canoe, and a little canvas cockleshell. He also had a shed built to shelter the collection, which he then christened the Lake Philip Yacht Club, and for which we had a gala opening, complete with matchbooks embossed with "LPYC" and a song Lally composed for the event. As the children grew older, he added a motorboat, small yet powerful enough to pull them on water skis.

Our lives centered on these two lakes, where we swam and boated and enjoyed the ducks and wild Canada geese as they came and went in spring and fall. We went walking, played hours of tennis and softball, and hit golf balls into the fields. Phil and the children, particularly Bill, fished passionately in both lakes; occasionally Phil fished all night. He had an arsenal of guns at the farm, and everyone learned to shoot at an early age. Even I learned to handle a shotgun, although I always ended up with a bruised shoulder, since I didn't handle the kick very well. Phil used to hunt groundhogs, and in season quail, and we all shot skeet. Bill was an avid marksman, had his own .22 when he was very young, and, I regret to say, sometimes shot pigeons off the barn roof. One day, after dinner, Phil put some pewter candlesticks we had gotten for a wedding gift on the stone wall that separated the house from the farm's fields, lit the candles, and had the children try to snuff the flames out with .22s. Naturally they missed and hit the candlesticks, which I still have, conspicuously dented.

We kept a World War II–vintage army jeep at the farm, on which each child learned to drive, sometimes circling the fields for hours on end. As

Phil once wrote, it was "Really quite comfortable at speeds up to about nine miles an hour."

Meals were mostly family-oriented. We often picnicked on the beach, using a grill on which I learned to cook steaks, chicken, and even a leg of lamb and corn on the cob. We always had friends out to Glen Welby, which added to the normal ten people per meal, counting the children, the nurse, and whatever college students I might have helping out. Most days, we ate lunch at a long picnic table under two goldenrain trees. We'd bring the food and iced tea down to the trees in the back of the station wagon, and I'd fill the plates and pass them down the table. One Sunday—with guests present, naturally—when I got to Phil, who was sitting at the opposite end of the long table, he told me just to throw the plate, which I did. Miraculously, he caught it—mashed potatoes and gravy intact. Unfortunately, the second time I tried, it didn't work so well.

From the very beginning, Lally developed a passion for and a great ability at riding, and entered one horse show after another. She was often the only hatless and coatless member of the party, and one of her ponies resembled a donkey, but she did well and, most important, had a good time. When she learned to hunt, I would get up at 5:00 a.m. and drive her to the meet, where her pony would be delivered by the deep-freeze truck. I would often follow the hunters for a while and watch, but I gave up on the shows, which I disliked. The other children rode also, except for Don, who hated riding, having tried it for about five minutes. I had thought that all the children ought to learn, but one day I looked at him sitting on a horse, vaguely resembling Sancho Panza, and blurted out, "Get down. You're right. It's not for you." He was a superb athlete and loved tennis and everything to do with balls and ball-playing, but riding, swimming, and skiing didn't interest him.

Phil's energy spilled over to all of us. At dinner, he would play games with the children, asking them history questions, teaching them about the Civil War, instilling a love of the land. He organized frog-gigging expeditions, taking the children to the lake with flashlights—often just when I had announced that dinner was ready. He told stories and made us laugh. One night at dinner, when he thought the houseguests too stuffy, he started a stand-on-your-hands contest with Stevie in which everyone had to participate, with the college girls there to help out with the children trying to be decorous and keep their skirts between their knees.

OUR LIFE AT Glen Welby was only one aspect of this period when all was seemingly right with our world. My parents were still active and involved, although my father was increasingly showing signs of his age. Throughout the 1950s, Mother wrote and lectured extensively and well, and was caught up in various issues of public welfare and education, being awarded a number of honorary degrees and receiving widespread positive recognition for her work. On her seventieth birthday, Harlow Shapley, the astronomer, named a galaxy after her to mark the occasion—not a common tribute.

Her writing and appearances always brought strong reactions, the positive ones of which she was only too happy to share with us—like a clip she sent us from the *Richmond News Leader*, a staunch conservative Southern paper that had reprinted a speech of hers, along with an editorial saying, "Today the Supreme Court instead of following the flag, follows the Washington Post." A Richmond citizen wrote her that her speech was one of the "noblest utterances he had ever read, in the tradition of Jefferson and Lincoln." With her normal breathtaking assurance, she told us: "You ought to read it some day. It is actually one of the loftiest things I have ever written. Strong Emersonian influence."

Tensions between Phil and my mother escalated temporarily in the mid-1950s because of a disagreement over the location of a proposed auditorium and cultural center for Washington. She was chairman of the Auditorium Commission and wanted the center located along the Potomac riverfront in the Foggy Bottom area of Washington, where the Watergate apartments were later built; he thought it should be part of the redevelopment of Southwest Washington, with which he was heavily involved. Conceding that the Foggy Bottom area provided a beautiful Potomac River site, Phil nevertheless believed strongly that placing the auditorium in Southwest Washington was an important step toward discouraging white flight to the suburbs and upgrading a community of 40,000 people in the Southwest.

From Mother's point of view—and that of her commission—the river site was perfect, and putting the auditorium in Southwest would have ended the whole project, since she felt she couldn't raise money to build in a slum. She railed at Phil and at those in Congress who were opposed to her point of view, accusing them of having been reached by real-estate interests, and vowed that if the Southwest area of the city were chosen as the site, she and her whole commission would resign. In a P.S. to one letter to him about the issue, she added, "I would like to write an analysis of the factors involved in Foggy Bottom vs S.W. for next Sunday's *Post*. If you don't want it, I hope you don't mind if I offer it to the *Star*"—incredible, even in retrospect.

Yet Phil could honestly say that after sixteen years he approved of my mother, despite an occasional impulse to "matri [in-law] cide." The two of them had a curious, conflicted, but very deep bond, despite the endless dueling over her relationship to the paper.

During this period my father was more and more removed from the day-to-day operations of the paper and the company, but no less interested than ever. When they were not in the same city, Phil sent him letters and memos recounting meetings, speeches, *Post*-related activities, and so on. Dad was clearly aging, but his mind was sharp and his judgment and perspective were still sought by Phil and others. He turned eighty the year after the purchase of the *Times-Herald*, and he clearly was thinking about the implications of aging. In April of 1955, he sent a memo to Russ Wiggins noting the significance of the deaths of two newspaper legends that week: "Joe Pulitzer died on Wednesday; Bertie McCormick died on Thursday; and I have just left to see my doctor."

For a while Dad had been contemplating the idea of leaving some stock to *Post* employees. Phil suggested to him that it would be nicer to give it to them while he was still alive and have the satisfaction of observing their pleasure. Dad agreed, eventually telling the recipients:

> For some time Mrs. Meyer and I have been thinking about the fine people in this organization. We have a lively memory of the valued service of those of you who over the years have helped bring about this institution's success. We have wanted to find some appropriate way of marking our appreciation. Some people remember their old associates in their wills. But Mrs. Meyer and I both thought that a rather melancholy approach to things.

What he did was to work out the details for giving a half-million dollars of nonvoting stock to 711 of the paper's employees and independent circulation dealers—in essence, everyone with five or more years of continuous service in the company. The gifts ranged from four to twenty shares. The fair market value of each share was worked out by Price Waterhouse to be $59.44. My father wrote to all the recipients explaining the gift and adding that he and my mother hoped they would retain their shares at least as long as they were associated with the *Post*: "We believe the stock is a good investment. With the enthusiastic help and cooperation of everyone in the *Post* organization, it should increase in value over the years." Several people understood the stock's value from the beginning and bought all they could from those who didn't. Many sold to each other, but those who simply hung on or bought five, ten, or fifteen shares were richly rewarded as the company grew and went public. One share became sixty shares when we went public, and since we went public at $26 and split the stock twice, these initial gifts eventually became worth a great deal. The stock-distribution gift was announced in a memorable lunch at the Statler Hotel in June of 1955, an event that also served to commemorate the twenty-second anniversary of my father's purchase of the paper. Eddie Folliard, the *Post*'s White House correspondent, spoke for the employees at the luncheon, beginning his remarks with "Fellow stockholders," and continuing—after the laughter subsided—"Well, you never know. You start out for work as a wage-earner and you come home a capitalist."

DESPITE MY PLEASURE in the life I was leading during these years, I can see now that I was having problems I didn't acknowledge to myself. I was growing shyer and less confident as I got older. I still didn't know how to look my best or how to handle myself in social situations. I was afraid of being boring, and went on believing that people related to us entirely because of Phil.

It's hard to convey how unsure I felt or why, or to explain how I could have been so unaware at the time. At some point during this period, I attended a ladies' lunch given by Lady Bird Johnson for the wives of members of Congress and a few newspaper wives—Helen Lippmann, Sally Reston, and me. After lunch, Lady Bird asked everyone to stand up and say what she'd done the summer before. Most of the women had campaigned for their husbands and spoke about that. I was paralyzed with fear at the thought of speaking in front of this group and was absolutely unable to utter a word; what's more, I refused to try. On another occasion, I did make a speech, following a text, to about sixty people, on a study I had headed up for a year having to do with adoption and foster care and with children taken out of their family homes. This must have been my maiden speechmaking effort, and I was terrified. With Phil's help, I wrote and rewrote it a number of times and managed to get through the ordeal, but the cost to me in anxiety was utterly out of proportion to the event.

Maybe my friends—and I had very good women friends—perceived what I didn't. Early in 1956, led by Polly Wisner, they gave a party in my honor dubbed "Salute to Katharine Graham." I was pleased but puzzled as to why they had done it. It was no doubt to bolster me because they thought I needed it, but I honestly had no sense of needing attention.

My insecurity had something to do with both my mother and Phil. My mother seemed to undermine so much of what I did, subtly belittling my choices and my activities in light of her greater, more important ones. My very eccentric relations with her were exemplified in an incident of these years. I would often call on her when she was in bed or resting. We would endlessly discuss her activities and speeches, interspersed with occasional contributions from me about the children. One day I decided very deliberately that I would bring up my project to get children out of Junior Village, a large shelter in the District, and into foster homes. It took some courageous determination, but I started to say she might be interested in some work I was doing. As I went on, she cut me off decisively, saying, "Oh, darling, I gave up on the District years ago." So ended my abortive effort to talk with her about something that mattered to me.

As for Phil, at the same time that he was building me up, he was tearing me down. As he emerged more on the journalistic and political scenes, I increasingly saw my role as the tail to his kite—and the more I felt overshadowed, the more it became a reality. He always had a very sharp wit and sometimes a cruel humor—I'd seen it used in many social situations, and occasionally friends of ours were the targets. He would utter some harsh truth in such a humorous way that most of the time he got away with it, with even the target of his wit joining in the laughter. Increasingly, however, the wit he had turned on others he now turned on me. I became the butt of the family jokes. Strangely, I was still so mesmerized by him that I didn't perceive what was happening, and even played along with it. Because I had gained some weight, though not that much, he started to call me "Porky." He even gave me a French butcher-shop tole head of a pig, which I put up on the porch at Glen Welby, thinking it was funny.

Another habit of his that emerged during these years was that, when we were with friends and I was talking, he would look at me in such a way that I felt I was going on too long and boring people. Gradually, I ceased talking much at all when we were out together.

I recognized none of this condescension at the time, but one lengthy letter Phil wrote my mother at the end of 1955 reflects it. She had sent him an article about Thomas Mann, and he responded, clearly betraying a superior attitude that he shared with my mother:

> Ever since reading The Education of H Adams and Mont San Michel et Chartres I've been completely at sea about the meaning of unity. Prior thereto I was innocent of the existence of the concept. . . .
>
> You did, however, fail to underscore the single most salient sentence—i.e., "No erudition is needed for the enjoyment of Felix Krull." This atomic thought has even led me to playing with the idea of recommending the volume to my Life's Companion.

Quite an odd remark about someone who had probably read more of Mann than he had, and who had read the two Henry Adams books well before he did and had recommended them to him. Yet, despite all this, I failed to recognize how aggressive his behavior to me had become. I had learned so much from him that I felt like Trilby to his Svengali: I felt as though he had created me and that I was totally dependent on him. Even now I can't sort out my feelings about this; it's hard to separate what was a function of Phil's terrible affliction, which manifested itself only later, and what was more basic. The truth is that I adored him and saw only the positive side of what he was doing for me. I simply didn't connect my lack of self-confidence with his behavior toward me.

Although the pace of Phil's work life was brutal, he still seemed to thrive on it. There were shadows developing, but they were so slight that I didn't see them—or didn't perceive them as shadows. Looking back, I see that his constant physical ailments were a prelude to his mental affliction, to a latent disease of which I—or, indeed, he—was totally unaware. His increasing bouts with viruses meant that he would return to an office piled high, as he told a friend, "with deferred crises and accrued catastrophes." Nonetheless, when he was well, there was still no one who could better tackle these crises and catastrophes.

Phil was now managing the greatly enlarged *Post and Times-Herald*. John Sweeterman played the chief role under him and took most of the responsibility for business decisions, but Phil was very much the chief strategist always. He was more involved in editorial issues with Russ Wiggins and on the editorial page with Estabrook, but John and Russ enabled him to focus on the larger issues, dipping into the day-to-day activities of the paper only as he chose. In this period, he spent almost as much time on his many outside activities as on the paper itself, but he managed to keep everything not only in hand but progressing.

By the fall of 1954, Phil was "busier than eight bird dogs," in large part because of negotiations with CBS to purchase its minority interest in the *Post's* station WTOP. Though the timing of this was a little awkward, given that it was only about six months since the purchase of the *Times-Herald*, we had always been interested in owning all of WTOP television and radio, and this was our chance. The price for CBS's 45-percent interest was $3.5 million. It was a daring move on Phil's part to increase our debt, having just undertaken a major expansion, but it was another one that paid off handsomely in the end.

By 1955, the *Star* was finally finding it necessary to do a little work. Within a year of the purchase of the *Times-Herald*, we had equaled or passed the *Star* in many important categories. Having been the leading paper in Washington for a hundred years, the *Star* now found itself with about 125,000 fewer readers than the *Post*, though we continued to lag behind in advertising. The arrival of Frank Gatewood from the old *Times-Herald* to work on advertising made a great difference. Retail stores were wedded to the *Star*, but Gatewood persuaded some of the big accounts to give us a larger portion than before. Frank was so valuable that my father joked that he had paid $9.5 million just to get him on the *Post*. Once it got rolling, Gatewood recalled, advertising improved very fast, and the *Post* went from having 28 percent of the field to 50 percent in three years.

From 1955 on, *Post* profits exceeded those of the *Star.* Costs were tightly controlled. When we look at the size of the *Post* today and think of the foreign correspondents in bureaus around the world, it's difficult to recall a time when the "foreign" reporting was done from Washington, or when only news services were used, but it was not so long ago. And when Phil sent Murrey Marder to London as the *Post*'s first foreign correspondent in January 1957, what Murrey wrote was to be shared with WTOP, which was paying some of his expenses. Not until five years later were two other correspondents added, and Phil Foisie was charged with editing foreign news, essentially becoming the first foreign editor. Under Foisie, the foreign service later grew to twenty-three people abroad, with many stringers to supplement the correspondents—not all of them first-rate.

As time went on, Phil got increasingly involved with public and political events, and the *Post* began to take less of his time. Some of the things he did made him more visible in the local, national, and business communities, as well as in political spheres, but all the things he did were done because he believed in them. Many of his outside activities had been going on for several years—the University of Chicago board, ACTION (a committee on housing), the Council on Economic Development, the Ad Council, Southwest redevelopment, and D.C. home rule. Others began in the mid-1950s and grew increasingly political.

Despite the intensity of his involvement in electing Eisenhower in 1952, Phil had quickly become disenchanted with the administration and had been developing a commitment of time and energy to Senator Lyndon Baines Johnson. I'm not sure what triggered his relationship with Johnson, but it now seems predictable, even foreordained. Johnson worked actively to cultivate the press, and Phil was always drawn to politics. They both loved power and its use for what they thought of as desirable purposes. They were both from the South. Both were full of humor—with an edge. They had a natural affinity.

As early as 1953, Phil had begun steady exchanges with the senator. In January, Johnson sent Phil a list of Democratic committee assignments for the coming year. He had circled what he viewed as the key new appointments and attached a note reminding Phil of their talks in the past "about the need for assuring a greater representation of your members and of conflicting points of view upon the standing committees of Congress." In thanking him, Phil referred to an editorial the *Post* had just printed titled "Best Foot Forward," which praised the committee assignments made by the Democratic Steering Committee—"under Senator Lyndon Johnson's leadership"—as having "given the liberal Northerners of the party generous opportunities on key committees," as well as signaling "a degree of unity never achieved while the party was in power." "As you can see," wrote Phil, "we thought you had done a fine job."

LBJ appreciated the editorial and wrote Phil to thank him. Some months later, Johnson sent Phil one of his speeches and a note about the vote on his resolution against the spread of communism to the Western Hemisphere. Phil actually wrote back thanking Lyndon "for not bawling me out for the skimpy job we did on it the day it came out. I hope we have made some later amends. . . ."

These exchanges reflect a relationship in which the press is closer to government than journalists ought to be—at least today. However, for those times, for that decade, it was not unusual. The problem was that their relationship grew even closer, and though there were still some constructive ramifications, there were to be certain negative ones for me later on.

IN THE MIDTERM campaign of 1954, Vice-President Nixon, with whom Phil had been impressed in 1952, became highly vitriolic. His tactics led Herblock to draw one of his most famous cartoons—Nixon crawling out of a sewer as a band and an official group greeted him, the head man holding a placard reading, "Here he comes now." Despite Nixon's efforts, the Democrats retook control of the House and the Senate, making Lyndon Johnson the Senate majority leader. From this point on, Phil and Johnson became even closer.

One keen interest of Phil's was clean elections and campaign-finance reform. He took up the study of the role of money in politics early in 1955, speaking out and writing about it in the hope of getting something done. As usual, he was ahead of his time on a problem that was to get dramatically worse. People were not even aware of the true cost of campaigns, he argued; there was a huge discrepancy between what was reported as spent by the national committees of the two major political parties and what was actually spent.

As he saw it, most of the money for campaigns came from three sources: the underworld, special-interest groups, and "the hopefuls"— that is, people who contribute in the expectation of receiving high public office. As he stated it in a speech, Phil saw the problem as "how can we raise enough honest, untainted money to permit our politicians to run for office without becoming obligated to corrupt or selfish forces? And in doing this, how can we help to create a higher regard for the importance of politics in the American future?" His solution was to look to the individual good citizen. A Gallup poll had found that one-third of American families were prepared to give politically. Phil thought an advertising campaign could inform people and persuade both that one-third and others to contribute, in order to end corruption. He argued that if "this thoroughly 'doable' thing is indeed done, it should constitute the single most important political reform of our times."

Full accounts of this speech were carried in the *Post*, and the idea became known as the Graham Plan. The following year, Phil persuaded Lyndon Johnson of the need for legislation. Though the Senate seemed, according to Phil, "scared stiff about the possibility of what might come out if Pandora's Box is opened," Johnson was "seriously enough agitated to be most amenable to almost any reform I wanted to propose!" Phil's work was all behind the scenes, because, as he admitted, "we can be useful only so long as the numerous prima donnas are getting all the credit." After much discussion with LBJ, focusing on a bipartisan program of reform, a bill was drafted and eighty-five senators signed on as cosponsors—which had never happened before in the Senate's history, it seems. Only one voted against the bill, which was, as Phil told my father, "not a completely perfect bill, but a good step forward." But the bill failed to pass the House.

I had doubted, perhaps wrongly, that Lyndon Johnson really wanted the bill, and had told Phil so. My feeling was that Johnson wanted to cultivate his relationship with Phil and chose this route to do it. But Phil's enthusiasm for both the bill and the senator kept growing, and despite the failure of the bill, they undoubtedly became even closer after working together on it.

Unlike Phil, I was still drawn to Adlai Stevenson, though my mother met him before I did. She was undergoing a political transformation, which, like everything she did, was carried to extremes. Her doubts about Eisenhower were confirmed when she had tried—and failed—to interest him and his administration in the social issues that mattered so much to her. She was extremely disappointed in his lack of response. "There's no getting away from it, Phil. He's dumb," she wrote in a letter.

Her acquaintance with Adlai blossomed into one of her highly emotional relationships with prominent men. There were heavy exchanges of letters between them over the next several years. Hers to him were full of advice of both a personal and a political nature. But Adlai really did become her friend, writing equally personal and somewhat emotional letters in response.

In June of 1955, my mother had an operation for cancer of the uterus. Even though the doctors had told her the cancer was localized, she, like anyone confronted with such an operation, had some last wishes in case something went wrong, and decided to issue certain instructions. When I was visiting her the evening before the operation, she asked me to send for Phil. Her instructions to him involved three things: her jewelry was to go to specific granddaughters and to be used by their mothers until the girls grew up; a small amount of money was to go to her friend Ruth Taylor; and—most urgent—she wanted to make an immediate gift of $25,000 to Adlai Stevenson. She had learned from newspaper reports that he had no money for preparatory political expenses for the next campaign, and she thought he ought to be freed of that worry. She told Phil that nothing would give her as much happiness as knowing that this had been done. Phil agreed to arrange it and promptly did.

That fall, Phil was going to be making a speech in Chicago, and wrote to Adlai suggesting that we three get together, which we did. Adlai himself drove us to the suburbs of Chicago, where he had a beautiful farm with a pretty, informal, rambling house in which his family of three sons had grown up and in which he now lived alone. For me this was the beginning of a pleasant but complicated relationship. Phil and Adlai had a less rewarding time together. Phil had known Adlai for quite a while and thought him an obviously able and talented man, but he worried that Adlai couldn't compare as a politician to Lyndon Johnson, and he later came to share the view, held by many, that Stevenson was too indecisive and not tough-minded enough. Nevertheless, Phil took the paper back to a policy of nonendorsement.

As expected, President Eisenhower was re-elected by a wide margin. Stevenson's concession was notable for its high spirits and heartening words. When asked on the night of the election whether he would ever try for the presidency again, he responded: "I'm a candidate for bed."

IN ONE OF his letters to Phil that summer before the election, LBJ had casually invited Phil and me to visit him and Lady Bird at their ranch, to "enjoy a little bit of Texas hospitality." Throughout the fall, he went on urging us to come, and an opportunity arose at the end of the year, when Phil was asked to speak at Texas A. & M. University. Phil accepted, in part so we could head over to the Johnsons' ranch.

The college owned a small plane that flew us, after the speech, to Fredericksburg, the town nearest to the ranch. LBJ was at the end of the landing strip to pick us up, and we were immediately put through the procedures he loved, driving over the fields and through the gates to his land for an extended tour of that lovely West Texas country. We even stopped to see his family cemetery, a ritual for guests.

The next day we set off hunting, in pursuit of deer, which LBJ was most eager for Phil to shoot. Phil—who loved hunting birds, in part because they are hard to shoot, which meant he mostly missed them— couldn't stand the idea of killing a deer. Our host, however, considered it a matter of successful hospitality to have his guests return home with one. When we came across a little group of deer on a hill just ahead of us, Phil took aim, on LBJ's orders. "Shoot, Phil," the senator barked. With his gun on his shoulder, pointed and ready, Phil responded, "I can't shoot him in the ass, Lyndon." When one of the deer turned toward us, Johnson urged him again to shoot. This time Phil responded: "I can't, Lyndon, he looks like Little Beagle Johnson." The Johnsons had several beagles, all with names with the initials LBJ, and Little Beagle was one of Lyndon's favorites. The deer ran off, leaving the senator really cross with his reluctant guest. The next time a deer appeared, Phil realized he had no choice but to comply, and he shot his deer.

The visit was an odd one for me—Phil and Lyndon were completely comfortable with each other, but Lyndon regarded me quite differently. He would look straight at me, separating me from him and Phil, and begin whatever he was about to say with, "You Northern liberals . . ." He hammered points home with me, as though trying to explain to me how the world really worked. On one occasion, he spent a long time telling me the story of how civil rights came to Johnson City, relating:

> They were building a highway that was to go through town. The roadgang had some Negras on it. None had ever been allowed to stay overnight in Johnson City before, but the road came nearer and nearer and finally arrived. The town bully found the head of the roadgang in the barber shop, went up to him, and said, "Get them niggers out of town by tonight." The head of the roadgang took his bib off, got up out of the barber's chair, and those two wrestled each other up and down Main Street until the roadgang head had the bully pinned down on the street, at which point he beat his head on the pavement as he repeated, "Can I keep my niggers? Can I keep my niggers?" Finally the bully said yes. That's how civil rights came to Johnson City.

In truth, I regarded LBJ with mixed feelings at that time. I still believed that to some extent he was using Phil, and I certainly wasn't ready to embrace him entirely, as Phil seemed to have done. One night he and Phil put away a good deal of whiskey, both during and after dinner. In our late-night talk, Johnson started complaining about the press—as will politicians of any persuasion. In the middle of his diatribe, he said, "You can buy any one of them with a bottle of whiskey."

I was much too reticent to enter into the conversation or to object, but when Phil and I went upstairs I denounced Lyndon for saying what he had said, and Phil for letting it go unchallenged. Apparently, Lady Bird had similar words for Lyndon, because he was very different the next morning, urging us to stay over another day, which we did. At lunch before we left, he gave us both presents—a large ten-gallon Western hat for Phil and a charm bracelet for me with a little Texas map, a microphone, and other symbols of the Johnsons' world hanging from it. When it hit my hand, it was so heavy I realized it was gold. The press is not supposed to accept presents, and these gifts troubled me deeply, especially in the context of that conversation, which still rankled. Phil told me to accept the bracelet, he would keep the hat, and we would return a gift of equal value, which we did—a water purifier Johnson had mentioned needing.

As we left the ranch, we were handed a large cardboard box containing Phil's frozen deer and sausage already made from it. The mounted deer head was to follow. As it happened, the whole East Coast was socked in by fog and rain, so our plane circled endlessly above the bad weather and finally landed in Pittsburgh, from where we caught a train to Washington in the middle of the night. Unable to cope with the huge box of deer meat, we simply left it on the station platform. The head, sent later, still decorates the library at Glen Welby.

A few days after we returned from the ranch visit, Phil handwrote Johnson a rough but lengthy memo as the basis for some important general ideas for further discussion. What he was doing was giving LBJ advice on how to improve his image nationally, arguing that the senator needed to counteract the reputation he had as a conservative, sectional, and (oil and gas) interest-motivated politician. Phil believed that this was a false stereotype that had weakened Johnson's national effectiveness, but that it had to some extent been accepted by LBJ and his staff, who seemed only to be concentrating on re-election in Texas in 1960. Phil argued that Lyndon had a role to play in truly national politics, and if he was to do so he had to "remember that the best defense is a good offense" and to begin erasing the inaccurate stereotype by paving the way for a legislative "session marked by a higher order of accomplishment." Phil also contended that Lyndon should announce a legislative program for 1957 in a press conference timed so as not to be quashed by the Republican president's State of the Union address. He then suggested that Lyndon follow up with a major address before "the best possible audience," which would have several principle themes, of which perhaps the most important was to "create and articulate a realistic philosophy on civil rights," which were to be strengthened. As he elaborated it, that philosophy needed to be "not one based solely on Texas acceptability. Rather one which goes a bit beyond Russell and yet far short of Humphrey, and which at the same time is realistically suited to the times and to the possibilities of Congressional action."

In the Johnson Presidential Library there is a memo to Senator Johnson from George Reedy, who was then one of LBJ's staff assistants. Reedy's memo was attached to Phil's and commented on it. He thought Phil's idea was "sound, but I do not agree with his timing." In addition,

Reedy said, "Phil lives in the *Washington Post* atmosphere and that atmosphere has great influence in Washington. I have an idea that out in the country you are much more popular than would be apparent from the Drew Pearson columns and the Herblock cartoons. The *Washington Post* atmosphere is highly specialized and is not reflected in very many other communities." I believe that in this case Phil was closer to the truth than Reedy was.

THROUGHOUT the early months of 1957, Phil was still active on all fronts. One of his significant achievements at this time was exchanging *Post* stock held by the Meyer Foundation, which placed the ownership of the business completely in our hands. He was also constantly involved in labor negotiations, particularly with The Newspaper Guild. A contract that was signed in the spring of 1956 came after eight and a half long months of negotiation but brought with it an unprecedented five-year agreement.

Another important thing he did around this time was to make an extraordinarily blunt speech about the Teamsters' efforts to organize our circulation department as they had that of the *Star*. It was reported to us that Jack Kauffmann, then publisher of the *Star*, had agreed to negotiate with the Teamsters if they came over and got us to do the same. Phil's speech, handwritten on a legal pad, said that if the *Star* is contracted with the Teamsters Union, "You can be sure somebody is going to ask you to join the Teamsters. They will probably tell you that you have everything to gain and nothing to lose. The situation is just the reverse," Phil warned. "You will have everything to lose and nothing to gain." He also told them in no uncertain terms:

> Under the legal law of the U.S., the *Post* does not have to deal with the Teamsters. Under the moral law, we should not deal with them. And as a practical matter we would be saps to do so. . . .
>
> *The Washington Post* is not going to do any business with the Teamsters.
>
> Why? It obviously isn't because we're against unions. We have had contracts for years with 15 or so different unions—all of them honest unions.

And he went on to spell out the crookedness of the Teamsters, concluding by saying that we had the best circulation organization in the country and that we were going to keep improving it and expanding opportunities for the dealers. He said, "We are not going to let you down by having any dealings with that crowd. And I am counting on each one of you not to let us down." And they didn't.

Knowing how things work, I assume people around Phil may have tried to tell him all the reasons why he couldn't make such a speech. It might not be legal today, and I'm not sure it was then, but it is a significant example of his ability to know when to run a risk to make a vital point.

The *Star*'s going with the Teamsters proved to be a crucial mistake. To the independent *Post* distributor, selling one more newspaper meant more money in his (or, later, her) pocket. To the *Star*'s Teamster driver, selling one more paper just meant more work to be done. Preserving our own delivery system turned out to be an important move for the future health of the paper, and as later amended, it became a system widely copied by other papers.

By the summer of 1957, Phil was clearly exhausted and in need of rest. Together, we made the decision to retreat to Glen Welby. It was an idyllic summer, spent playing with the children and just doing nothing. As Phil described himself in a letter to his father in late August, he had become "practically a total refugee from work." He added: "I think I am quite a burden to Kay, but I suppose that is the normal role of a husband." Only later did it become clear that by then something serious was the matter with him; it certainly wasn't apparent to me then. What was obvious was that he was high-strung and had overextended himself. Looking back, I see that he was like a rocket fizzling out—still giving off sparks and even occasional bursts of flame, but steadily burning down.

The biggest interruption to the pastoral life on the farm that summer came at the beginning of August, when Lyndon Johnson asked Phil to come back to Washington to help him win passage of what became the Civil Rights Act of 1957.

"For more than eighty years no civil rights act had passed Congress," President Eisenhower wrote in his memoirs. He had tried to make some modest progress the year before, with a bill that passed the House and died in the Senate, where Lyndon Johnson had helped kill it. In June 1957, the same legislation passed the House with a wider margin of Republicans than Democrats supporting it. On July 16, the Senate agreed to take up the House bill. The following day, the Senate amended the bill, weakening it with a jury-trial amendment that LBJ had added to the bill to satisfy Georgia Senator Richard Russell and prevent a filibuster. Since juries were still all-white in the South, this was an obvious watering down of the bill's strength. However, besides voting rights, the bill provided for a Civil Rights Commission and a new assistant secretary to head a civil-rights division in the Department of Justice.

All of this was in line with Phil's plans for LBJ to take the lead in this field. As a Southerner, Lyndon couldn't go as fast or as far as Phil may have wanted him to, but, given his legislative skills and strengths, he could move the country forward. From the point of view of many political observers, what LBJ did was to take everything out of the bill except the right to vote. Phil's argument was that the only thing that really counted about the bill was the right to vote.

Phil's involvement in the whole matter—besides pushing Lyndon on its importance from the beginning of their relationship—began in earnest in July, when he invited Joe Rauh to the farm. Phil's invitations often came in the form of commands, and this was one. He needed Joe's help because Joe had a solid relationship with the black leadership in the country, especially Roy Wilkins, then executive secretary—in effect, leader—of the NAACP, and because Joe was a liberal influence in general, making what he thought about the civil-rights bill particularly important.

Phil also asked Joe to bring Felix Frankfurter along. Joe later recalled that he didn't divine any ulterior motive in the invitation and certainly didn't connect it with the pending civil-rights legislation. However, as he and his wife, Olie, and Felix drove to the farm, he began to suspect he was about to be worked on. All the way out, Felix was trying to persuade him of the overwhelming importance of voting rights. Both Phil and Felix did indeed work on Joe throughout our dinner, suggesting that he was asking for too much in wanting all the other items on the civil-rights agenda at that time—e.g., real and rapid integration and enforcement of school desegregation. The argument by which Phil and Felix stood was that the most important first step for the 1950s was the right to vote. Now I can see how extraordinary—and out of order—it was for a Supreme Court justice to be stepping over the boundaries to this extent, but I didn't then. It was very much in Felix's nature, and he was dealing with two men—Phil and Joe—to whom he was as close as though they were his sons. And clearly he thought it was important to help Phil persuade Joe that the bill was the best they could get and, therefore, that he should support it.

Sometime after the "brainwashing" party, Johnson urged Phil to come up to Washington to be at his side during the final push for passage of the bill. So Phil returned to Washington, somewhat to my concern, and stayed with Lyndon almost constantly for several days, working day and night. A large part of his role, I believe, was to keep in touch with Joe and the liberal civil-rights group with which Joe was connected. The sticking point was the jury-trial amendment. Negotiations between and among the various groups lobbying for and against the bill centered largely on what would happen to this amendment. Enlisting the help of notable lawyers and legal minds, Phil worked on trying to find a formula that would be acceptable to all parties in order to get the vote to final passage.

In the end, civil-rights activists may have lost on the jury-trial fight but they gained a bill. Joe and his like-minded friends bought Phil's argument that this bill was better than nothing. Roy Wilkins agreed and called a meeting of the Leadership Conference of Civil Rights, which debated for an entire day. Wilkins wrote in his memoirs: "Joe argued for the bill on grounds that after 87 years, the time had finally come for a civil rights bill, even a watered-down bill, and that once Congress had lost its virginity on civil rights, it would go on to make up for what had been lost." Supporting the bill was the hardest decision of his life, Wilkins wrote. In retrospect, he knew it was the right decision. He recalls Hubert Humphrey saying to him in the middle of the struggle, "Roy, if there's one thing I have learned in politics, it's never to turn your back on a crumb."

This was superb politics for Lyndon Johnson. Lyndon was still a Texas senator who had to get re-elected, and the one thing they wouldn't be mad at him for in Texas was voting rights. So the whole strategy of going for voting rights was inspired—the idea for which Phil was the architect. Lady Bird Johnson, in recalling those days, described Phil and LBJ together as a sort of bridge between two very set-in-their-ways blocs of people. Phil could talk to both groups, but Lyndon couldn't talk very successfully to ardent liberals. "He would talk," Lady Bird said, "but they would not believe." Lyndon wrote Phil the day after passage, saying, "You stepped into the breach at the critical hour. That is something that I will never forget and I wish there was some way of telling the country that your contribution to an effective, enforceable bill was decisive."

Phil used the opportunity to press his point with Lyndon about the importance of looking to his political future. He argued that Lyndon shouldn't have overt designs on the presidency: "Your present attitude strikes me as just right. Anyone who works up noticeable and passionate designs on that particular office harms himself in two ways. He begins to lose control of his own judgment; he also gives aid and comfort to the political enemy. So just sit," he advised. "Don't deny or confirm—or even conjecture. Three years is a long, long time. All rushing and panting should be left to fellows from Tennessee and Massachusetts," referring to Kefauver and Kennedy.

THE EFFORT Phil made to push the civil-rights bill for Johnson was enormous, particularly coming at a time when he knew how exhausted he was. Perhaps if the turmoil had ended there he might have been able to rest again at Glen Welby and get his strength back. Instead, just a month later, Arkansas Governor Orval Faubus ordered the National Guard to bar nine Negro students from the previously all-white Central High School in Little Rock. The next step in the battle for civil rights was on.

Since Eisenhower was not very interested, except in theory, and was concentrating on his vacation golf games, there was a vacuum within the administration. On the day that Press Secretary Jim Hagerty announced from Newport that the president thought patience was what was needed, the *Arkansas Gazette* received from a wirephoto service a picture of the president lying down on a putting green, lining up a putt. They played the story on page one and put a caption on the picture, "Study in Patience."

Into this vacuum in Washington, Phil moved swiftly and with great assurance. He was determined to solve the problem—to get the children admitted to the school peacefully, to get Faubus to back down, and, above all, to prevent the federal government from having to send in troops. It was, of course, highly unlikely as a concept—essentially, he hoped to take over the government and pull the strings of policy.

At heart, Phil still felt a strong empathy with the South. He believed devoutly in school desegregation, but he also understood how hard it would be to accomplish in the face of Southern resistance. So he injected himself into the situation with frenzy as well as with conviction. Believing that he knew enough of the key players so that he could solve the problem with behind-the-scenes maneuvering, he kept several phones going day and night, calling, among others, Sherman Adams and Maxwell Rabb in the White House; Bill Rogers (about to become attorney general) in Washington; Harry Ashmore, the fine editor of the *Gazette*, in Arkansas; Brooks Hays, the congressman from Little Rock; Thurgood Marshall, then head of the NAACP's Legal Defense and Educational Fund; and Roy Wilkins, still head of the NAACP. He called Joe Rauh one night at 3:00 a.m., demanding Marshall's home telephone number. When Joe said he didn't have it, Phil ordered, "Well, goddamn it, get it." Indirectly he was in touch with the president, ex-President Truman, and Vice-President Nixon.

When Eisenhower finally sent in federal troops, the violence ceased, but events in Little Rock sputtered on for two more years. However, the act that ended the immediate crisis—the sending in of the troops—was a crushing blow for Phil. He saw it as a defeat not only for the South but for himself personally.

Phil's activities in regard to Little Rock were the first sign for me that something was wrong with him, that his powerful talents could be used in such an idealistic but confusing and irrational way. His health, already frail, was affected physically and mentally. He held on to his activities— and his balance—for only another month after Little Rock before his first major depression set in. On October 28, in the middle of the night, he broke. There is no other way to express it. All of the latent physical and psychological symptoms came to such a sudden crisis that I didn't even connect them in my mind. He was racked with pain and in despair, in a to- tal and overwhelming depression. He wept and wept and couldn't stop. He said that he felt trapped, no longer able to go on, that everything was black. We were both up all night, with me trying desperately but to no avail to be of some reassuring help, to convince him everything would be all right. There was little I could do except stay close to him. We discovered that a hot bath helped, so he took several during the night in an effort to stem the tears and alleviate the desperation.

Early in the morning, I called my brother in Baltimore, who was at that time a psychiatrist on the staff of Johns Hopkins Hospital, describing what had happened and asking him what we should do. He gave me the name of someone at the National Institute of Mental Health who could see Phil for analysis of what was wrong and in turn recommend a psychiatrist. It was a relief to both of us to have some plan of action, with the hope of someone to lean on in this ghastly and incomprehensible crisis. Phil saw this doctor for a time or two, after which he was sent to Dr. Leslie Farber, with whom he began a long, bizarre relationship that in the end did more harm than good.

I had no idea what had happened and didn't recognize what I was witnessing. I couldn't put a name to it, and didn't for a very long time to come. I only knew that Phil had had what seemed like an intense and complete nervous breakdown, which I thought had been brought on by all the activity in which he had been engaged, climaxed by Little Rock—the activity day and night and the ensuing disappointment. It was all kept very private; our one idea was to conceal what had happened not only from the world but from our friends, my family, and even our children. For some reason, beyond my initial phone call I never even talked to my brother about what was the matter or what had brought on the crisis. As a result, I had no one on whom to lean for advice and just concentrated on trying to be of help to Phil. Still, despite my lack of knowledge about his illness and all the unknowns, I believed that we'd get through this—that with enough rest he'd recover and we'd go on. Phil, I thought, with all his self-assurance, his glamour, his good humor, his brilliance, his wit and sagacity, would surely recover his good health, and things would return to normal. There was no need to share the temporary problem with the world, and every reason to conceal it.

Phil's parents at his birthplace in Terry, South Dakota (top)

Phil with his sister and parents on the road (above)

The young hunter (left)

PHILIP GRAHAM   JANIS BOSTWICK

From Phil's 1931
high-school yearbook

Phil with his father and
brother, Bill, in 1942

At our wedding

Phil in the army

With Lally and Don

Tennis

Together at Glen Welby

Phil and me in 1962

At work at *Newsweek:*
Phil, second from right;
Oz Elliott, with the bow tie,
to his right; Kermit
Lansner, next to Oz

Phil dancing with Lally at her coming-out party

— *Chapter Fourteen* —

MOST OF THE year following Phil's breakdown was spent in slow, gradual recovery. He had all the symptoms of severe depression—overwhelming doubt about himself and his abilities, a desire to seclude himself from the world and from people, a deep uncertainty that led to indecision even about which pair of shoes to wear, guilt about whatever he felt he had done wrong, and even occasional talk of suicide.

We escaped to Glen Welby whenever possible—frequently just the two of us, without the children, since sometimes even dinner with them was too much for him. These long visits to Glen Welby were hard on me, because I was his only support system. There was one period of about six months in which he was so depressed he couldn't be alone. We hadn't been out at all, nor had I left the house except when he visited his psychiatrist. At his most depressed, he was completely dependent on me, almost like a child. I was "on duty" a great deal of the time for long talks about what he was thinking. I confess I felt the need to escape at times, to lead a normal life again, to see friends, but being with someone in this kind of severe depression is compelling. And though it was grueling, there was also something strengthening in being needed that much—in being able to help him by talking about whatever was on his mind or, sometimes, whatever I could think of with which to try to reach him. Gradually I learned to say whatever helped him to hear. The experience literally taught me how to talk. If I had any strength later, much of it came from surviving these exhausting months.

What Phil mostly did was go to his psychiatrist, read, and think about the basic issues that someone in severe depression tends to reflect on. The doctor to whom he was sent, Leslie Farber, was heavily into existential psychology, inspired by Dr. Rollo May, an originator of the humanistic psychology school. One thing Farber did was to start Phil, and therefore me, reading existentialist philosophy and, in my case, Dostoyevsky, for whom I had always had an affinity. Farber himself was working on a study of the importance of "will" in life. It was he who instilled in Phil a distrust, fear, and horror of any drugs, not to mention shock therapy, claiming that these treatments reduced people to something less than human—something tranquilized and fishlike. In addition, Farber believed that labeling something, giving a name to a disorder, changed how the patient viewed himself and was viewed by those around him. Because of this, he never put a name to Phil's illness. I didn't hear the term "manic-depression" until some years later. Throughout this period, I viewed what was happening with confusion and very little understanding.

Farber was not a strong individual. Phil, by force of his personality, seemed to have taken charge the minute he walked into Farber's office, when he told Farber he wasn't charging enough and that he, Phil, would pay more. Farber let him do so. From then on, even in his most depressed moments, Phil seemed the dominant figure in that relationship. Every rule of psychiatry was broken. Farber became a personal friend of Phil's, writing him letters, coming to visit us at R Street and Glen Welby, giving Phil some of his research and writings to edit and comment on, even at one time suggesting we visit him in Italy, where we could all drink together—not something I wanted to encourage in Phil.

After each of his sessions with Farber, Phil would come home and essentially repeat all that had been said, seeming to hold nothing back, although I suppose he must have been more selective than I realized. These recappings had the effect for me of indirect participation in his therapy.

At the same time, I was trying to keep the children's lives as normal as possible, and the outside world unsuspecting. As a result of all this, I came close to the breaking point myself. Toward the end of January 1958, three months after the onset of Phil's depression, I found the weight on me more than I could bear, until one morning I felt almost physically paralyzed. But, like many people, I was unable to admit I needed help and thought there might be something weak or wrong about someone not *in extremis* looking to psychiatry for help.

Phil discussed all this with Dr. Farber, and between them they arrived at the bizarre solution that I, too, should begin seeing him. They suggested this as a way of keeping things secure and cohesive, but it was certainly unusual for both Phil and me to be seeing the same doctor. Never did Farber suggest that this might not be a good idea. Incredibly, there was one point in the next few years when I was going to him often and Phil was not seeing him at all. I once asked Farber if I had to keep constantly at Phil's side, if I could take a break from a weekend at Glen Welby, to which he responded that I absolutely must keep it up. I needed and was grateful for a guiding hand at that time, and Farber undoubtedly helped to some extent, but this three-way conversation was very complicating, and I didn't know enough to suggest a different program or to seek one out.

For nearly a year, Phil went to the office hardly at all—occasionally for a meeting or two, or for lunch. He canceled almost all meetings and public events and never made a speech, although toward the end of that first year he participated in a panel of fathers and sons for Donald's class at St. Albans. He played golf with different partners at Burning Tree several times a week. He spent every weekend and sometimes weekdays at Glen Welby. If he traveled, it was mostly by train, since airplanes disturbed him in his depressed moods. We went out to dinner only selectively—mostly with one or two people, sometimes but rarely to larger, more social dinners. Going out at all was risky, for he often drank too much and used unacceptable language.

Phil's position at the paper and in the company was such that people could understand his leading this kind of life. Many *Post* people knew that he was stretched thin and taking a rest, but no one knew exactly what had happened—partly because of his ability to cover up and partly because of my help in explaining away his absences and concealing his excesses. Phil himself was unsure of what he was dealing with. Months after the breakdown, in his correspondence explaining his lack of activity, he said, "I have been taking a sort of sabbatical after several doses of flu and an accumulation of exhaustion . . ." and that he had had a "winter of boringly bad health." In one letter he said he had "pledged to my wife to limit my engagements in the near future so that I may maintain that state of rosy health which is now mine." His secretary wrote to someone that Phil was "out of circulation for several months, resting under doctor's orders."

Luckily, these years of his illness coincided with a period when major achievements at the paper already had been consolidated. Luckily, too, there was a strong national boom in both general business and advertising that year, which helped the paper and the business along—the paper turned a record profit of $2 million in 1957. In 1958, the *Post* was the only Washington paper to show a gain in advertising linage. The *Star*'s lead in total advertising was whittled down to three million lines, from eighteen million just five years before.

BAD AS IT WAS, Phil's depression in 1957 was not as extreme as those that hit later. He was obviously ill, and he had several sieges of normal sicknesses as well—bouts of flu, rounds of viruses—but at this point he could still function a little if he had to. While leading this restricted life, Phil still accomplished quite a lot by means of correspondence, memos, or

the telephone. He also went on working with Lyndon Johnson, occasionally meeting with him, writing him letters of advice, or drafting a speech.
Johnson wrote to Phil saying how much he missed his "favorite coun-
selor," adding, "I certainly want your advice and your suggestions because
this job is so big that I need all the help I can get from the best and most
enthusiastic source."

Phil also turned to writing—perhaps indicating his longing for another kind of life—writing plays, some light verse, and extensive bulletins
for the Lake Philip Yacht Club, extremely convoluted in their humor. He
also did some writing of a more serious kind. In the summer of 1958, he
wrote a highly appreciative essay/book review of John Kenneth Galbraith's *The Affluent Society*, which appeared in the *Post* under the headline
"The Folly of America's Faith in Chain Belt Living."

He became enamored of a book by a French writer, Germaine Tillion,
Algeria, and recommended it to everyone, sending it around to several of
his friends, including Lyndon Johnson and Jack Kennedy. He wrote to
Kennedy:

> I am sending you a little book which you can read in one hour,
> while Jackie should only need fifty minutes. . . .
>
>   I hope you will read it. You may or may not agree with her
> specific ideas on Algeria. But I send it for another reason. In her
> analysis of under-developed areas in general, I think she has great
> wisdom about a major problem of our immediate future.

I know of almost no one in the First World who was then thinking about
the Third World and the importance of development.

DURING THIS PERIOD, we were seeing much less of my parents, but
we still gave the *Post*'s twenty-fifth purchase-anniversary party at Glen
Welby in the summer of 1958. Mainly we spent a lot of time with the Restons, and Phil met with Scotty separately for long talks, during which he
again made a pitch to Scotty to come to the *Post* and again got rejected.
Despite being as close a friend as Phil had, Scotty disapproved of Phil's active involvement in issues on which the paper reported and his use of the
paper to further his own political goals.

It was during this period that Phil got to know Edward Bennett
Williams, the famous criminal trial lawyer. He and Williams had met in
the early summer of 1957, while Williams was defending Jimmy Hoffa,
the powerhouse of the Teamsters, who was accused of bribing one of Sen-

ator John McClellan's staff. Phil was riveted by the Hoffa case, which he thought was hopeless and unwinnable. Ed later recalled that first meeting vividly:

> We began to talk and we had an instant rapport. Sometimes your chemistry flows and you have an instant relationship with someone. You really understand one another, you can almost talk in shorthand. . . . I was intending to go home to work, because I had a lot of work to do for the next day, but he came home with me and we talked almost all night long. . . . By the end of six hours I felt I knew as much about Phil and he knew as much about me as there was. . . .
>
> So we followed up on our friendship, the instant friendship, and then I realized, not too long after we met, that he had periods of depression and he told me there would be times when he just couldn't get up in the morning. He told me one thing very early in our relationship: "You know, if you ever don't want to get up, if you want to pull back the sheet and drapes and not let the sun in, you've got to force yourself. You've just got to force yourself. You've got to drive yourself to go open those drapes and let the daylight in. You cannot stay in that room."
>
> Like all people who are in that kind of depression, they don't know why they are in depression. My feeling always was that he was terribly troubled by a self-doubt—whether he could have been as successful as he was if he hadn't married you. In other words, whether or not he would have hit the heights that he did professionally if he hadn't been Kay Graham's husband, Eugene Meyer's son-in-law, and hadn't had the Post stock given to him. Whether he would have made it as just Phil Graham, out of Harvard Law School with great grades, Felix Frankfurter's law clerk. I used to say to him, "How in the hell can you have doubt when you were Felix Frankfurter's clerk?" Just to be a Supreme Court clerk meant that, in those days, you were probably one of the eighteen best law students in America and out of the best law school in America with an academic record at the very top of that school. It was inevitable that he was going to be a top flight success, but that doubt drove him absolutely bananas.

Phil told me in great detail all about his meetings with Ed, but he didn't bring him home. I remember meeting Ed and his first wife, Dorothy, but a joint friendship didn't develop then; the relationship was between the two men. Ed and I became warm friends only much later. Phil told me about his first meeting with Dorothy, who had been born with a deformed arm. Upon meeting her, Phil did one of those breathtaking things which came to him so naturally. He said, "Hi, kid, what's the matter with your wing?" She apparently loved the honest, benign curiosity, compared with the way many people ignored her arm or looked the other way.

So, despite his continuing lethargy, Phil engaged in various minor ac- tivities, making his usual impact. He arranged for a car to be given to Wal- ter Lippmann for his seventieth birthday, which Lippmann immediately traded for one he preferred. He conferred with Lyndon Johnson, con- vincing him to push the D.C. home-rule bill—for which we had both worked for so long. He spoke to *Post* meetings of stockholders and em- ployees. These little incursions into the world were definite steps forward, and it's hard to reconcile them with the way he was still feeling.

Except for Farber, I spoke to no one about Phil or what was wrong, and this was eating me up. Phil liked me to be there when he came home from seeing Farber, so I always arranged to be at home for him at those times. What I did otherwise, perhaps as part of our cover-up of the real situation, was to step up my involvement in welfare work. I kept meeting with all the organizations with which I was involved—the children's schools, the boards, and so on—and entered a more interesting phase of my work with the Department of Public Welfare, involving an in-depth study of how to get children out of the District's Dickensian dumping- ground, Junior Village.

Although I was trying hard, I certainly didn't understand Phil or re- spond to his needs well enough during this time. I don't know now, and certainly didn't then, how much pressure he felt because of his son-in-law status at the *Post*. It's possible that he really wanted out of our marriage but felt he couldn't get out because of the paper. But by the time I might have acknowledged that, his illness was so evident that it was impossible to sort out what was driven by the illness and what were his underlying feelings.

Throughout these first years of his illness, Phil remained the domi- nant figure by far in the family. Yet I had some say. I was the foundation, the stability. I can't remember exactly when he suggested just picking up, taking the children out of school, and living abroad for a while, but it must have been around the beginning of 1958. I thought this idea was much too out of the ordinary. To leave his job, uproot the children, put everyone in French schools—it all seemed unthinkable. Was he right? I'm not sure, but I know I wasn't able to face the idea at the time. Actually, it may have been a good idea, and was certainly typical of his inventive zest for life. He was undoubtedly feeling pressures from which he wanted to escape, and we might all have profited from it.

In the summer of 1958, after months of going slow, Phil wrote to his father, "I am beginning to feel quite a bit better, but it has been a slow process. I still get tired more than I like and I guess I will have to continue at reduced speed for a few more months. If it were not for that I would grab a plane and fly down for a visit. . . ." Actually, at this point Phil was even less connected to his own family than he was to mine, but he was still explaining his absence as a need to lie low for a while and get his strength back.

By the summer and fall of 1958, Phil was starting to do a little more, but only a little. Yet his business instincts continued to function at a high level. He was in negotiations that continued over a long period to buy the Greensboro *News and Record* in North Carolina—the town's only newspaper and the owner of Greensboro's only TV station, WFMY, a CBS affiliate—at a cost of $7 million. The deal finally fell through because of the reluctance of a member of the family who owned the paper, but Phil had nursed it along for months. He then devoted the same energy to planning new buildings at already existing properties: one for WJXT in Jacksonville and the other a $5-million addition to the *Post* building to be completed in 1960.

MEANWHILE, my own life evolved to accommodate Phil's changed one and the changing needs of my four children and my aging parents. Mother called us a great deal and had her ways of letting us know if we hadn't been attentive enough. She would hint about how much she'd seen of her other children—e.g., "Ruthie is so wonderful, she calls every day"—or make not-so-subtle statements about how thoughtful Bis had been. My visits to her remained mostly one-sided. Actually, after 1957 this was helpful to me: it was easy to keep from her Phil's illness or how I felt about it, since she rarely asked about me and didn't take time to listen when she did ask. Like Phil, she had frequent bouts of colds, flu, or even pneumonia. She stayed in bed most of one winter—I suspect there was some depression along with whatever ailed her—and drank pretty continually, too.

Then, just as Phil began to get a little better, my father began to deteriorate, adding to my deep concerns. In his early eighties, he was declining sharply. He was also increasingly a problem for my mother, who looked to Phil and me to help her with him. She was having a hard time concentrating on her work, because he was often in a dark and difficult mood, and she poured out her heart in a letter to me, saying that more and more she was anxious over Dad's state of mind, and she thought we ought to know "how precariously he is poised between stability and neuroses." She continued:

I actually get frightened about the future. When he was strong, I could fight back. That is out of the question now. He conquers through weakness and I am helpless. The only people who can help me, therefore, are you and let's admit it, especially Phil, who can say anything because he is the one person who can do no wrong.

For the next two years, as she struggled with Dad's increasing debility, she relied on us, especially me, more than ever, keeping up her trips and leaving us in charge of him. One day I was surprised to read an interview with her in a New York paper in which she discussed the role of women—about how a woman could have her own work but always had to take care of her husband first. She actually said that before she left on trips she always arranged to have my father kept busy and kept company. The "arrangement," of course, consisted of calling me and asking me to lay on bridge games and companions. Since I was extremely busy by this time and had no secretary (which she did), not to mention being consumed by Phil's illness, I was indignant.

As Mother became even more absorbed in her work and in herself, we became my father's mainstay, and he too became increasingly reliant on Phil and me. He would come over in search of company, and occasionally lean on us about his problems, often complaining about my mother's drinking. When his adored older sister, Rosalie Stern, died, we told him the news. He was devastated and broke into tears. After Phil's breakdown, it became harder for me to be there for my father always. In protecting Phil, I unfortunately never shared with my father—or anyone else—what was wrong. I wasn't embarrassed; it was just something very private—something we both still assumed he'd get over. And there was the stigma of mental illness. Phil once said to Don, "This means I can never be in the Cabinet."

Dad must have been puzzled and worried by Phil's health, but luckily he died before things with Phil came to a crisis; he was so devoted to Phil that it would have been an unbearable blow for him. I believe there were three main people on whom my father had bestowed his love and affection and respect—his brother Edgar and his partner Gerald Henderson (both of whom died young), and Phil. My father's feelings for me were very strong, but I couldn't fill the role any of those three played in his life. Phil reciprocated his feelings and showed it in almost all of their encounters and relations. He expressed them in a birthday letter he wrote to my father a few days after his breakdown. I can imagine how much strength he would have needed to summon up, just to put pen to paper: "I have no aversion to friends and in fact I have a group, which while not multitudinous is more of a host than I need or deserve. Of all these I want to say that none is as close or as integral as you."

EARLY IN 1959, Phil and I decided to take the children to Europe for a couple of months during the summer. Lally would be sixteen and Don fourteen, and we thought it was about the last time we could take these older two on a sightseeing tour. One day that spring I had seen my father cough up blood, after which he shook his head and said to me, "Not good." I didn't then know exactly what he meant, but he must have known it suggested a tumor on his lung. His condition affected me deeply, for I realized he must be slowly dying. It was utterly shattering and left me with a gnawing grief and constant anxiety. I was terribly torn about leaving him at that time, and still don't understand why I did. The trip had seemed like a good idea in the planning, and I didn't have much will of my own. It was hard to foresee how long my father's decline might go on, but his doctor felt that his condition was pretty stable and that the decline probably would be slow but steady, conceding, of course, a surprise always possible. Even my mother put her imprimatur on my going by writing me:

> Do not worry about me. Dad is so patient, so philosophical that it is exalting to be with him. When Adlai was here and felt sad for me I said firmly, "I am not to be pitied. I am to be envied." That's the way things are, darling. Throw yourself into every experience, knowing that all will be for the best over here.

I was somewhat reassured when Phil stayed behind to finish some business and to be with Dad.

Phil took us to New York and the four children and I set off for Paris on June 24. I thought about my father all the time, particularly when I received a letter from Mother saying that my brother Bill's son would be bicycling in France, and adding: "So the third generation spreads its wings just as the man who, unknown to them, has provided them with security is getting ready to fold his wings forever."

Despite my remorse about not being home, the whole time we were in Europe I felt I had been transported to another world. As I wrote Phil, "I feel so remote that I can't even in my imagination get back to Crescent Place—R Street." Phil, at home, was attending to my parents' needs, relieving Mother of some of the tension of visiting Dad at the hospital, where he had gone when he had taken a turn for the worse. Phil reported on one lunch he had with my mother that "reminded me of some of your experiences. To keep it going I mentioned Lally's asking me about Zen

Buddhism. Wham! It turns out that definitive, seminal, etc. discussion of this is in Aggie's Chinese art book. Thought you'd be glad to know."

One letter Phil wrote to me from Glen Welby in that interlude before he joined us in Europe still gives me profound pleasure and comfort. What followed in the next several years—all the illness and chaos and heartache—left me so confused about what Phil truly felt that I like to think it was this letter from the distant past that reflected his true feelings. It was written at a moment when the depression was subsiding and he seemed to be nearing a balance, when the old Phil emerged again, the one I knew and loved.

This is such a curious curious place alone. All places are but this most and R St next. A couple of hours ago I thought of J Alsop on that Sunday afternoon in our house just a week ago and his saying [about] his loss of not having a family. Then I gave it no credence, that is, none of the heart, and to the mind only that sort of loss doesn't seem so much. When the heart gets working along with the mind then that is when you imagine which is why imagination is probably one of the biggest human capacities.

It's not all clear to me how much J Alsop feels the loss but it is certainly clear that no one can feel a loss who hasn't first had a family as much as the feeling gets to be to one who has. Loss is a pretty inaccurate blown-up word for a few days' absence. Absence doesn't come close to what I'm thinking. What am I thinking? Reminder I believe is the point. A home to reverse the madam's phrase is not a house but a great big store of memories and if that is why a home is good it is also why a home alone is almost un-bearable.

Just before sunset, to take one example, the softing light was ending so surely and so gently that no one could afford to ignore it, to lose it unnoticed in a house. And also there were our friends [the dogs]. So, I tossed me up a large beaker of scotch and ice and whistled them up and banged out the front screen down the gate to the dusty driveway where they headed at once toward Lake K. "No," I called, "No, no" and I whistled them back, "we're going up the drive to the gate as Mummy does." And we swung along, George all tired until on the curve by the woodmill he saw a rab-bit and dashed clear to the bridge with the speed of wind (unsuc-cessful once again). As we neared the dip in the drive near the bridge I could see you heavy and sad the way I saw you over a year ago as I stood down at the barn and watched you walking alone and heavy with cares in a similar dusk. Those cares caused by me. Can I wash them away; can I tidy them up like a month's end bank account by saying, ah, but there were my cares, too, heavy and also having cause. Oh no my memory will not go away nor will it cancel out nor does it bear me down in the facile lament of *mea culpa*. Those cares you walked along so heavily burdened with, they are memory too. Part of the long story. As I knew when we reached the bridge and the three of them hurled their hot selves through the weeds into the cool pool of the run. That bridge was memory too, a thousand memories, and one especially of a dark dark night when I was as dark as the night was and sat on that bridge and talked to my good red dog.

Just beyond the bridge the edge of the woods was bright with the bloom of day lilies and they leaped across the drive and started again around the foundation of the old tenant house where they were joined by brilliant red hollyhocks and just then three separate quail called from the quiet of the woods behind me and I said to myself you must remember every bit of all you saw and tell Kay. . . .

What did we do. Glorious dinner last night—Vicky's and Nicky's [Friendly] 13th birthday—with Erlene's fried chicken, Susiebelle's cake, and your champagne! Then bridge. Then today a bit of baking tennis and then Agnes down for lunch. Really too hot for her to walk to Lake K but she and I paced up and down under the front elms in a great breeze while the F's swam. Then chairs and a drink table under the front elms in the breeze and Jean [Friendly] worked the Waring mixer and rum and we ate a chicken salad the chef sent down and Erlene's hamburgers and more of the cake and ice cream. A good day for Ag till 3:30 and then more bridge till 5:00 when the F's left and then I thought what if Kay did say not to be here alone. I'd rather be lonely here than in town so my pearls and I jeeped to Lake P and tried some dull fishing but too hot and then came back and then as I said saw the sun setting and walked into it. So I'll sleep here and rise early-ish and drive up for breakfast in town.

Next Sunday's sunset I shall see with you in Paris—also from a bridge if you will kindly arrange that.

Until then, my dearest, I hope you will accept this which is meant to be—by God, it is!—a love letter.

Your burden and your sustainer,
And always yours—in love, Phil

THE CHILDREN LOVED the vacation from beginning to end. In Paris, they often explored alone. The four of them went together to the roof of the Arc de Triomphe, took horse-and-buggy rides and bus rides, on one of which Donny got shut in the door, and when she came to his rescue Lally was saved by an Englishwoman from an altercation with the bus driver. The children and I had a warm, familial time, interspersed with raucous moments, like Don going off to the races at Saint-Cloud by himself, returning a big winner.

When Phil arrived in Paris to meet us, he reported that my father had gone home and then back to the hospital. Mother had tried to run a hospital of sorts for him at Crescent Place, but, as Phil pointed out, she had neither the temperament nor the competence for the job. Everyone had convinced her that my father was better off in the hospital. Phil was certain we had done the right thing by carrying on with our trip. Despite some alarms, the situation was the same, he thought—i.e., slow deterioration. Company was now almost meaningless to my father, and Mother had Bis, Bill, and Ruth there to help. I felt, with good reason, horribly torn. Today I can see that the summer was wonderful for the children but wrong for me. I can hardly bear to think that I left my father's side when he was dying.

From Venice, Phil wrote a moving letter to my mother:

At 5:45 this morning I awakened thinking of you and these last weeks and I decided I had from now on to call you by your name, which I think you will understand.

Kay was wakeful too a little later and we talked of you so warmly in the dark with the morning canal noises just beginning as a background below our windows. . . .

It seems to me that love comes very hard for you (it probably does for all of us; and to most of us never comes and never even missed)—has always come hard for you.

And now it is with you, a powerful shaking terrifying beautiful love for that gallant old man. You say poor words about "having a job to do" and "being able to stand anything" and you are right to obfuscate because the true words are too seismic.

But he knows what is in you and it is the fulfillment of his life. His cup runneth over. And mine too in pangs of joy for both of you.

We left Venice for a simple hotel at the beach resort of Forte dei Marmi, and there we received word that my father had taken a real turn for the worse and we should return at once. Phil and I left the children with the college girl who was traveling with us and flew back to New York and on to Washington, which took sixteen hours. The thought of being there at his death disturbed me so deeply that I was torn between wanting to see him and hoping it had already happened. He died two days after we got back, but he knew I was there.

People react in such complicated ways to any death, but particularly to the death of a parent, because a lot of what one feels is about oneself and the sense that nothing now stands between that self and dying. You have now become the older generation. I believe that the closer and more loving the relationship is, the deeper but simpler the grief. Of my father's children, my brother had the hardest time with his death, perhaps because their relationship was difficult to begin with and very ambivalent; through no fault of either of them, they had never been close. My mother was so complicated emotionally to begin with that his death was very hard for her. She had chafed under the burden of his aging, but when he died she sank into a deep depression. It was as if she had been leaning against a door that had suddenly burst open.

There was a private service for my father at Crescent Place, and a more public memorial service at the nearby All Souls Unitarian Church—one he had never attended. I suppose it was hard to hit on an appropriate spot for a nonreligious Jew. My parents' friend Chief Justice Earl Warren delivered a eulogy, which I think was written by Sidney Hyman. Rudolf Serkin played with his quartet. The whole thing was simple and moving. And I couldn't believe he was gone.

A WEEK LATER, we left Washington to return to pick up the children in Rome. In our absence they had all fallen in love with Italy and the mad Italians. The children were good travelers and good sports about every-thing, even helping with Steve, then only seven. By the time we arrived in London, we were having such a good time that we decided to prolong our stay by almost three weeks and to return by steamer, the *Mauritania*. For me, the trip had been wonderful in its way, despite my grief and my guilty feelings about my father, which persist to this day. For Phil, the trip was a forward step in his recovery. He was considerably more active that fall.

His activity was mostly related to politics. He stepped up his connec-tion with Lyndon Johnson. He also accepted some invitations to speak to various groups, an indication of his near recovery, or at least his return to some balance. Although he hadn't spoken publicly for a long time, two speeches he gave—one at the end of 1959 and another in February 1960—were vintage Phil, with the added dimension that they were full of thoughts on the necessity for understanding the meaning of one's life.

In the first, to the American Electric Power Company in Canton, Ohio, he spoke about the "shaking loneliness that a man experiences, whatever his job, whenever he faces up to the meaning of what he is en-gaged in":

Where I get in difficulty—at times almost unbearable difficulty—is when I try to examine the meaning of what I am engaged in.

When these difficulties get too great we in the newspaper business . . . retreat to the ritual of reciting old rules that we know are meaningless.

We say that we just print the objective news in our news columns and confine our opinions to the editorial page. Yet we know that while this has some merit as an over-simplified slogan of good intentions, it also has a strong smell of pure baloney.

If we keep wages too low in some few areas where unions still let us do it or if we neglect decent working amenities as long as we can avoid the cost, we defend ourselves by muttering about our concern for stockholders. As though by announcing compassion for a relatively anonymous and absent group we can justify a lack of compassion for people we spend our working days with.

If we are brutally careless about printing something that maligns the character of some concrete individual, we are apt to wave the abstract flag of freedom of speech in order to avoid the embarrassment of a concrete apology.

If we are pressed even harder, we may salve our consciences by saying that after all there are libel laws. And as soon as we say that we redouble our efforts to make those laws as toothless as we possibly can.

And if we are pressed really quite hard, we can finally shrug our shoulders and say, "Well, after all we have to live." Then we can only hope no one will ask the ultimate question: "Why?"

I certainly have been guilty of all those stupid actions—and a great many more stupid. And I suppose that more than a few of you have done as poorly.

What I prefer to recall are those rare occasions when I have had some better sense of the meaning of what I am engaged in. In those moments I have realized that our problems are relatively simple and that some simple, ancient, moral precepts are often reliable business tools. In those moments I have been able to keep in mind that it really doesn't matter whether I am kept in my job. In those moments I have been able to look straight at the frailty of my judgment. And finally I have been honest enough to recognize that a few—a very few—great issues about the meaning of life are the only issues which deserve to be considered truly complex.

. . . by paying attention to the broader meaning of what we are engaged in, we may be able to join our passion to our intelligence. And such a juncture, even on the part of but one individual, can represent a significant step forward on the long road toward civilization.

THE WHOLE POLITICAL year of 1960 was very exciting. There is a thrill to knowing someone of your generation who runs for, and actually becomes, president. By the late 1950s, we had gotten to know Jack Kennedy. Early in 1956, he had been one of four speakers at the *Post*-sponsored Book and Author Luncheon, on hand as the author of *Profiles in Courage*. According to a *Post* article reporting on the luncheon, the young senator "delighted a largely feminine audience by quipping 'I always used to wonder what the ladies did in Washington in the daytime.' "

Senator Kennedy was one of the people we knew much better than we normally would have because of Joe Alsop, who had decided very rapidly that he was all for Kennedy. Phil and I had seen the Kennedys at big parties, looking glamorous and handsome, but I never took him seriously. I remember exclaiming to Joe when he said—sometime around 1958—that he thought Kennedy would be president one day, "Joe, surely you're not serious. You don't really think Kennedy could be president, do you?" Joe said, "Darling, I think he will certainly be nominated and quite probably be elected."

The Kennedys had recently moved into a house on N Street in Georgetown, and in the late fall of 1958 or early winter of 1959, Joe invited us to dinner with them. Phil had too much to drink and was visibly and audibly out of control. I was embarrassed—probably too much so—but impressed with Kennedy for his cool approach, which ignored it totally and treated Phil as though he were perfectly sober. I admired that and was grateful. After the other guests left, we and the Kennedys, urged by Joe, stayed on. Phil looked Kennedy straight in the eye and said, "Jack, you are very good. You will be president someday. But you are too young and you shouldn't run yet"—to which Kennedy replied, "Well, Phil, I'm running and this is why. First, I think I'm as well qualified as anybody who is going to run, except for Lyndon Johnson. Second, if I don't run, whoever wins will be there for eight years and will influence who his successor will be. And third, if I don't run I'll have to stay in the Senate at least eight more years. As a potential candidate in the Senate, I'll have to vote politically and I'll end up as both a mediocre senator and a lousy candidate." I was thoroughly impressed by this, and each time I saw Senator Kennedy I grew more impressed.

We also got to know Jack and Jackie better through Bill Walton, their painter friend and ours. One night we went to a dinner at Bill's with the Kennedys. Also there was Frances Ann Hersey, an acquaintance of mine from Madeira School and by then the divorced wife of the writer John Hersey. As Frances Ann Cannon, daughter of the wealthy linen manufacturer in the South, she had had a romance with Jack in college. He had apparently proposed to her and she had turned him down, or so she told Bill. Somehow, Jack had gotten back his love letters and Jackie had read them, so, when Bill called Jackie and suggested this dinner, she responded, "Oh, wonderful, I would rather meet her than any other woman in the world."

Bill enlisted our help as neutral parties. We accepted, and arrived with great anticipation, particularly because Phil hadn't then spent many hours with Jack in such a small group. Bill later recalled the evening, remembering Frances dressed seductively in a short and revealing black dress, "switching along to attract." Jack greeted her with kindness but didn't seem to speak to her again; from her point of view, Bill said, it was a disaster. Jack and Phil, however, went to each other like magnets and talked solidly all evening. As Bill said, "They were both at their best and it was a really important evening for both of them. And Jackie was in heaven because she saw her old rival being rejected."

On January 2, 1960, Kennedy formally announced his decision to seek the presidency. Johnson declared only a few days before the convention. What a difference between that and the current process! The *Post* at the time of Kennedy's announcement editorialized that he had "a tenacity of purpose and maturity of judgment . . . an acute awareness of the great issues of the day."

By now, Phil was much better, though he still had moments of depression and at least two periods that year of health problems followed by two-week vacations, or getaways, that allowed him to rest. He was in balance, but only precariously; he was on the edge of a manic period that built with his growing and still-constructive involvement in the political dynamics of that crucial year of 1960. Very early on, Phil predicted that Kennedy and Johnson would be the only candidates to come into the Democratic Convention with sizable blocs of delegates—five hundred for Kennedy and three hundred for Johnson, he thought. He had visions of Kennedy's not making it and Adlai Stevenson's emerging as the compromise Northern candidate.

In June 1960, Kennedy, as had Nixon before him, came to an editorial lunch at the *Post*. At that point, he had entered and run in seven primaries—including the roughest, in West Virginia, where only 5 percent of the population was Catholic. I recall Jackie saying later that Caroline's first words were "West Virginia." Kennedy had clearly demonstrated he was a vote getter. Much of the luncheon talk concerned Nixon, who was regarded as the almost certain Republican nominee. Eddie Folliard, still the *Post's* key political reporter, asked Kennedy if he would debate

Nixon on television if it turned out that both of them were their parties' nominees for the presidency. Kennedy said he would. Reminded of Nixon's reputation as a debater, Kennedy calmly added, "I think I can take him." Asked about the possibility of Lyndon Johnson as vice-president, Kennedy scoffed at the idea, saying he felt sure Johnson wouldn't accept it. Russ Wiggins disagreed, feeling that Johnson would like to broaden his horizon as vice-president. Although the interview was off the record, both these exchanges—about the debate and about the potential running-mate—were of great help to those covering the convention and the rest of the campaign. These days, all such interviews are done on the record and therefore take on an entirely different significance, and are sometimes, I think, less helpful.

On July 5, Johnson held a press conference at which he announced his candidacy. Phil, who had been helping him prepare for this moment for months, was at his side working on his statement. He ended up on his hands and knees, crawling around at the last minute to retrieve one of Lyndon's contact lenses, which had popped out. The announcement got made and Johnson went to New York to meet with the press and do all the ritual things.

Phil and I flew to California early, five days before the Democratic Convention was to open on July 11. I was already committed to Kennedy. Phil remained loyal to Johnson until he lost the bid for the nomination, but he was entirely realistic, and he, too, admired JFK. My mother, a year after my father's death, was beginning to come out of her depression. Like the rest of us, she had geared up for politics in this election year and arrived in Los Angeles still staunchly supporting Adlai Stevenson, who as usual had declined to be a candidate but was eligible for a draft.

On Friday, July 8, Johnson arrived, the first of the candidates. Almost immediately he confided to his office staff, "It's all over with. It's going to be Kennedy by a landslide." Only Kennedy had a sophisticated organization already in place in Los Angeles. It was the first time we saw electronic communications between people working in different places, talking to each other through hand-held intercoms and beepers—now so routine. It was very impressive.

Phil called on Bobby Kennedy and got from him confidential figures on his brother's strength, numbers that showed JFK very close to the number of votes needed to win the nomination—close enough so that the Pennsylvania delegation, or a big chunk of it, could put him over. On Monday, Pennsylvania caucused and announced that the state delegation would give sixty-four of its eighty-one votes to Kennedy, which made Phil and the *Post* reporters write that it would be Kennedy on the first ballot.

At that point, Phil got together with Joe Alsop to discuss the merits of

Lyndon Johnson as Kennedy's running mate. Joe persuaded Phil to accompany him to urge Kennedy to offer the vice-presidency to Johnson. Joe had all the secret passwords, and the two men got through to Evelyn Lincoln, Kennedy's secretary, in a room next to his dreary double bedroom and living room. They took a seat on one of the beds and nervously talked out who would say what, while they observed what Joe termed "the antechambers of history." Joe decided he would introduce the subject and Phil should make the pitch.

When they were then taken to the living room to see JFK, Joe opened with, "We've come to talk to you about the vice-presidency. Something may happen to you, and Symington is far too shallow a puddle for the United States to dive into. Furthermore, what are you going to do about Lyndon Johnson? He's much too big a man to leave up in the Senate." Then Phil spoke—"shrewdly and eloquently," according to Joe—pointing out all the obvious things that Johnson could add to the ticket and noting that not having Johnson on the ticket would certainly be trouble.

Kennedy immediately agreed, "so immediately as to leave me doubting the easy triumph," Phil noted in a memo afterwards. "So I restated the matter urging him not to count on Johnson's turning it down, but to offer the VPship so persuasively as to win Johnson over." Kennedy was decisive in saying that was his intention, pointing out that Johnson could help not only in the South but elsewhere in the country.

Phil told the *Post*'s reporters they could write that "the word in L.A. is that Kennedy will offer the Vice-Presidency to Lyndon Johnson." On Tuesday morning, Kennedy called Phil, who told JFK he was to lunch with Johnson and would get back to him afterwards. But when Phil lunched alone with Johnson, he was unable to bring up the subject.

By clerical error, the Kennedy staff had sent to the Texas delegation a form telegram asking that Kennedy be invited to appear before them. The Johnson staff seized on it and asked for a debate before both the Texas and Massachusetts delegations at 3:00 p.m. that day. Johnson was bone-tired from a grueling morning appearing before three or four delegations but was tremendously exhilarated by the prospect of the debate, which breathed life into his candidacy. At 1:50, Phil, egged on by the Johnson staff, persuaded LBJ to take a nap and, together with the couple from his ranch who had come along to help, got him into pajamas and into bed. While putting him to bed, Phil said, "We're not going to be *ad hominem*, we're going to talk about the world. Walter Lippmann came out for Kennedy this morning, saying you were an ignoramus about the world, and we're going to show him he's wrong."

Johnson fell asleep at once, and Phil scribbled out some thoughts and had them typed. At 2:50 Phil handed a sleepy Johnson his notes, and at

3:00 Johnson appeared at the debate looking rested and well. Kennedy spoke first, then Johnson, using Phil's notes but continuing on ad lib with some thrusts at Kennedy "which he kept within the bounds of propriety," according to Phil.

Later Tuesday, Phil got the wild idea of a message from Kennedy to the convention to be read by Stevenson on Thursday, asking the delegates to draft Johnson for vice-president. Just before he went to bed, he left me a note to call Steve Smith and ask for a Kennedy appointment:

1. Don't think me bereft of my senses. I have a hell of an important idea.
2. Therefore please call MA6-3592, say you're calling for Phil Graham and want Steve Smith, and it is important.
3. Tell Smith who you are and say "I had a 5 o'clock in the morning inspiration as to how to accomplish the substance of the two items Senator Kennedy discussed with Joe Alsop and me. It will take 5 minutes to lay before the Senator but this should be done before the Wed. session, either at the Biltmore or at his house near the Convention. I can arrive either place within less than an hour. I asked you to convey this because I am sleeping owing to early morning inspiration."

I woke Phil at 9:30 to tell him he had an appointment at 10:40.

Kennedy appeared with the increasing aura of a nominee and suggested Phil ride across town with him. As they rode along on Wednesday morning, Phil explained his idea and Kennedy said to leave it with Mrs. Lincoln. He said he might be twenty votes short of nomination—with the nominating session to begin in four hours—and asked Phil if he could get any Johnson votes out of the vice-presidency offer. Phil replied he could think of none, unless George Smathers would try to swing some of Florida's votes—to which Kennedy responded that the trouble was, Smathers also wanted to be vice-president. Phil then assured Kennedy that he'd never miss the nomination by twenty votes; indeed, that afternoon Kennedy was nominated.

Unbeknownst to Phil at the time, the previous afternoon Kennedy had formally offered the vice-presidency to Symington through Clark Clifford. After conferring with his wife and two sons, who were opposed to the idea, Symington told Clark to accept, but added presciently, "I bet you a hundred dollars that no matter what he says, Jack will not make me his running mate. He will have to pick Lyndon." Clark called Kennedy back and accepted for Symington.

Early Thursday morning, Kennedy called Johnson, waking him up

and making an appointment to see him a little later. At that meeting he offered him the vice-presidency—both because he thought he had to and
because he thought that Johnson would not accept. Kennedy went back to
his headquarters and, according to Arthur Schlesinger in *Robert Kennedy
and His Times*, told Bobby, "You just won't believe it. He wants it." Phil
had been right. Johnson would indeed accept.

Everyone around the Kennedys, especially those connected with the
labor movement, was upset. Apparently, they all spent much of the day
thinking how they could undo what they had done. Bobby went down to
see Lyndon twice, once to feel him out and the second time to tell him
that there was going to be a lot of opposition, that it was going to be unpleasant, and to offer him instead the chairmanship of the Democratic
National Committee.

In the meantime, Joe and I and some others arrived at the Biltmore
and entered the Grill for lunch. Phil said, "Order me a roast-beef sandwich and I'll be back." He disappeared, and for the next couple of hours,
people joined us, ate Phil's sandwich, and left, and others sat down. We re-
ordered the sandwich several times, and it kept getting eaten by friends
who came along. Phil never came back.

Finally, we broke up, and as I started down a long hall toward the
Post's headquarters, I met Betty Beale, society columnist for the *Evening
Star*, running toward me. "Have you heard?" she exclaimed.

"No, what?"

"It's Johnson."

"Who says?" I asked.

"Kennedy says," she replied firmly. He had just said it in the Bowl,
which was a small auditorium on the floor below where the press offices
were, used for public announcements. I went on to our offices, where Phil
shortly appeared in a state of high tension, almost trembling all over, and
said, "You can't believe what I've just been through. Let's get out of here
and I'll tell you." At a restaurant in the convention center, he grabbed a
drink and sandwich and told me the story of what had happened.

When Phil had appeared in the Johnson suite at about 1:45 p.m.,
Johnson seized his arm and said that Bobby Kennedy was with Sam Rayburn, speaker of the House and Lyndon's great mentor, offering Johnson
the vice-presidency. Phil said he thought he had to take it. Lady Bird was
somewhere between negative and neutral. The evening before, Rayburn
had called especially to tell him not to take it if offered.

Rayburn entered and said Bobby wanted to see Lyndon. Lady Bird
felt he shouldn't meet with Bobby. Phil agreed, saying, "You don't want it.
You won't negotiate for it. You'll only take it if Jack drafts you and you
won't discuss it with anyone else." Finally, as Phil wrote, "in that sudden

way decisions leap out of a melee, it was decided." Mr. Sam went off to explain the Johnson position to Bobby, and Phil was to phone Jack with LBJ's position.

By this time, Jim Rowe and John Connally had joined the nucleus, and Phil went down the public hall, crowded with press, to an empty bedroom. He finally got JFK on the phone and gave him the Johnson message; Kennedy responded that he was having trouble with people urging him to take Symington—as someone who was trouble-free—and that Phil should call back in three minutes. By this time, Phil and Jim Rowe were in a state of nerves—or, as Phil described it, "as calm as Chileans on top of an earthquake." Each time he wanted to reach Jack, Phil had to go through a telephonic obstacle course—Mrs. Lincoln to Steve Smith or Sarge Shriver, then finally to JFK.

On the phone, Kennedy was calm. "It's all set," he said. "Tell Lyndon I want him." He asked Phil also to tell Stevenson and ask for his full support. Phil called Adlai first, then walked back down the hall to give the message to Johnson, who quizzed him for details. Lady Bird wondered about Stevenson's reaction, to which Phil shrugged and said, "Oh, you know, sort of silk underwear, as you'd expect." Phil then left the room to call the *Post*.

Soon, however, LBJ asked him to return, saying Bobby had been back to see Rayburn about twenty minutes before and had said Jack would phone directly, but there had been no call, and what should he do. Phil volunteered to call Jack, who said he had assumed Phil's message from him to LBJ would suffice. Phil told him what Bobby had told Rayburn, and he said he'd call at once. According to Phil, Kennedy again mentioned opposition to LBJ and asked Phil what he thought. Phil replied that "Southern gains would more than offset liberal losses," and added that "anyway it was too late to be mind-changing and that he should remember, 'You ain't no Adlai.' "

Phil was still trying to reach Bobby shortly after 4:00 p.m. when Bill Moyers, LBJ's appointments secretary, came in and said Johnson needed him at once, and dragged him by the arm through the packed hall to Johnson's suite. Lyndon took Phil into an adjoining room to avoid one filled with some political types, but they found this other room occupied with fifteen Hawaiian delegates. When Johnson called out that he needed the room, "they solemnly filed out bowing . . . in turn to all of us at the door (LBJ, Lady Bird, Rayburn, Connally, Rowe and me) with LBJ loudly chanting, 'Thank you, boys, thank you. Thank you for all you did.' "

LBJ, about to jump out of his skin, shouted at Phil that Bobby Kennedy had told Rayburn and him that there was so much opposition he should withdraw for the sake of the party. As Phil wrote, "There was considerable milling about and hub-bub and finally, Mr. Rayburn said, 'Phil, call Jack.'" When Phil got JFK on the phone, Jack said calmly, "That's all right. Bobby's been out of touch and doesn't know what's been happening."

"Well, what do you want Lyndon to do?" Phil asked.

"I want him to make a statement right away; I've just finished making mine." He had done it in the Biltmore Bowl at five minutes past four.

"You'd better speak to Lyndon," Phil then said.

"Okay," he answered, "but I want to talk to you again when we're through."

Phil, standing between twin beds, handed the phone to Lyndon, who was sprawled out on the bed in front of him, and who said, "Yes . . . yes . . . yes," and then, "Okay, here's Phil." Kennedy then chatted on about the problems—Alex Rose was threatening not to list him on the Liberal Party ticket in New York because LBJ was the running mate. Phil responded, "Oh, don't worry, *we'll* solve that," and then, returning to sanity, he said, "You'd better speak to Bobby," who had just walked into the bedroom looking sullen and tired. Phil said, "Bobby, your brother wants to speak to you," which, Phil wrote, "at once seemed to me the silliest line in the whole play." Bobby took the phone, and as Phil left the room he heard Bobby say, "Well, it's too late now," and half slam down the phone.

In the entrance hall, Phil found the Johnsons standing "as though they had just survived an airplane crash," with Lyndon holding a typed statement accepting the vice-presidency. "I was just going to read this on TV when Bobby came in and now I don't know what I ought to do." Phil, "with more ham than I ever suspected myself of," then blurted out, "Of course you know what you're going to do. Throw your shoulders back and your chin out and go out and make that announcement. And then go on and win. Everything's wonderful."

Phil described this "soap opera thrust" as "somehow wonderfully appropriate" and wrote that "Bill Moyers echoed loud approval while swinging open the hall doors and pushing Johnson out into the TV lights and the explosion of flash bulbs." Phil watched Lyndon and Lady Bird stand on chairs, "their faces metamorphosed into enthusiasm and confidence." At that point, as word spread of Johnson's acceptance, the area filled with people and Phil fled, to meet up with me in the *Post*'s offices.

Phil wrote all of this in a memo for his own files. He kept it confidential until three years later, when he let Teddy White borrow it when he was working on the book *The Making of the President* for the 1964 campaign. To my surprise, White printed the whole memorandum as an appendix to that book, which I felt Phil would not have wanted. When it was published, Bobby was extremely angry and said that it wasn't accurate—

that Phil didn't know the whole story. "What was wrong with it?" I asked. He replied, "My brother and I were never apart."

Even later, after LBJ was president and the strain between him and Bobby had grown great, I was sitting next to Bobby at dinner at my house when I mentioned that I had seen President Johnson at his request just before the dinner, and I noted that that was odd since Johnson wasn't really speaking to me. "What do you mean, he's not speaking to you," Bobby asked, "when Phil made him president?"

"I thought you told me Phil's memo was inaccurate," I responded, incredulous.

"It was," Bobby replied, "but because of what Phil didn't know, his role was more important, not less."

I asked him to tell me what he meant, but he would only say that he would someday; unfortunately, he never got the chance. The explanation, however, can be inferred from various books, especially Arthur Schlesinger's on Bobby. There is no doubt in my mind, from reading these books and from thinking back, that neither Jack nor Bobby Kennedy really wanted Johnson on the ticket. After vacillating for three or four hours, the Kennedys, according to Bobby, "came upon this idea of trying to get rid of him, and it didn't work." When Johnson surprised the Kennedys by accepting the *pro forma* invitation, Jack sent Bobby down to persuade him to withdraw. When JFK realized that Bobby's mission wasn't going to work, he made the disingenuous remark that Bobby was out of touch.

Even a year later, Bobby said they were all too tired that day. He told John Seigenthaler, an editor and a friend, "We were right at eight, ten and two, and wrong at four o'clock." Whatever their real feelings, as Phil and Joe had predicted, they would not have won without Johnson.

BECAUSE THERE WAS only about a week between the conventions, we had planned to go from one to the other without returning to Washington, so Bill and Steve flew out to join us and we had a nice family time with a glorious day at Disneyland. More important, we had a day with my sister Florence, who was now living in California. Previously she had been in Switzerland, near her close friends and mentors, Otto and Maria Halpern. Mrs. Halpern was a handwriting analyst and had several acolytes—wealthy ones—like Flo, whose lives she influenced. Flo had included us in her tensions with the family, and so we had not been in touch with each other in any but formal ways for years. At Phil's prompting, I had called her and suggested getting together. This reunion was a great success, with even the children all getting along. Phil, Flo, and I enjoyed each other's company and were happy to have discovered each other as grown-ups. By this time, Flo had gotten very heavy, but she was still her old self—literate, witty, interesting, intelligent, and sensitive. This visit began a relationship that continued in the two years remaining to her and meant a lot to both of us.

THE REPUBLICAN CONVENTION in Chicago, of course, was entirely different from that of the Democrats. Nixon was the only candidate, but Nelson Rockefeller, who had given up the race in December, acted as a goad to him and to the party. In June, Rockefeller had made a speech saying, "We cannot, as a Nation or a Party, proceed to march to meet the future with a banner aloft whose only emblem is a question mark."

After Chicago, we went home to Glen Welby, where we spent much of August, but politics reached us even there. Joe Alsop visited often, as did others, including Arthur Schlesinger, who brought along his campaign document—a profile of both candidates, favorably contrasting JFK with Nixon—which I remember poring over.

In the midst of all my activities in this busy political year, I had undertaken a major renovation of our house in Georgetown, and we had moved out in June and taken up residence in my mother's house on Crescent Place. Unbowed by the failure of her "Draft Stevenson" effort, and even though she was never a Kennedy devotee, Mother had embraced the Democratic ticket and become a national vice-chairman of Citizens for Kennedy and Johnson. She wrote to Kennedy, asking to see him to discuss campaign strategy in New York State and how she—as a Protestant "who has the reputation of having been anti-Catholic"—could help him fight the religious issue.

I had become a real Kennedy enthusiast and conveyed my excitement for the charismatic candidate whenever I could. Even while still in Los Angeles at the convention, I had been swimming with Marian Sulzberger Dryfoos, the wife of Orvil Dryfoos, the publisher of *The New York Times*, and had told her—while both of us stood waist-deep in the pool—how I had become impressed by Kennedy, and why I was an ardent supporter. That conversation led to a dinner Phil and I gave at my parents' house on August 16 for Jack Kennedy to meet Orvil, as well as to spend some more time with Scotty Reston. We felt they were both uncertain about Kennedy, and we wanted to let Kennedy sell himself to the *Times*. What still amazes me is that Kennedy drove up our circular driveway alone, in a convertible with the top down.

Phil and I had decided that, as publisher, he couldn't contribute to the campaign, but it would be okay for me to do so. We played this game in several other situations, but I now think it was questionable, since we believed in nonpartisanship for a publisher. We were both so concerned about the District and its problems that Phil told me that, if there was a chance to get Kennedy alone before the others came, I should give him my check personally and tell him there *was* something I wanted in return—for him to pay some attention to the District and its problems. I did as Phil suggested, and remember JFK looking a little startled when I delivered the first part of my speech, about wanting something. Although I was embarrassed, I managed to get through the second part, and he thanked me and took the check.

The whole atmosphere in Washington that fall, as well as the real intensity of Phil's highly subjective feelings about Kennedy, was best described by him in a letter to Isaiah Berlin, written on October 9. He told Isaiah he had time to write because he was "lying at home coughing and gulping achromycin pills the size of the new U.S. Embassy eagle." He wrote:

> Your ... friends are in the main riding an upward curve of Kennedy enthusiasm. Joe and I (I lagging three months behind him) are beyond enthusiasm into passion. Kay also has passion (earlier arrived at than mine) but passion marked by an irritating feminine discretion—she sometimes sees warts on the nose, or succumbs to momentary depression about his chances. Joe and I float along on an idolatrous cloud blind to his missteps, confident of his triumph. Curiously enough those closest to our state of mind are, in order of non-detachment: (a) Walter Lippmann, (b) Scotty Reston. Felix is pro-Nixon almost or anyway *dubitante* about Kennedy because of Papa. Arthur is strongly and effectively pro and has published a brilliant pamphlet but is a bit left out in the direct campaigning which is run by Ted Sorensen (32) and Dick Goodwin (an FF law clerk about 30). (The "last generation" definitely now begins at 40.) Kenneth Galbraith is also not directly involved but seems to mind it less and also is idolatrous. ...
>
> One has to make big guesses about candidates and I remind myself my last one was Ike in 1952. There's a lot of pure sawdust in Kennedy's campaign (cf. FDR, 1932) but there's also style, vigor and a show of knowing that this is 1960. He is decisive when that is the order and wonderfully vague and elusive when it is not (e.g., will Stevenson be Secretary of State?). My antennae tell me he is not a "cool cat," not young in a pejorative sense, and not wanting in hope and idealism. My guess is that he will be wanderingly eclectic in his early programs, will often exasperate us of the "last generation" and ultimately may be a political leader of great size.

The other fellow [Richard Nixon] has surprisingly shown almost no style in his moments of truth. He is so artfully and
thoughtfully synthetic that by now pose has become his reality.

Despite his zeal for Kennedy and his worries about Nixon, Phil continued the paper's policy of nonendorsement. Hindsight had convinced
him that it would have been wiser for an independent newspaper in the
nation's capital not to endorse, even in the Republican nomination fight in
1952. The *Post* had commented on the issues as they arose throughout the
campaign, and Phil thought the responsibility remained to comment
freely. In fact, in 1960 our editorials left little doubt about which candidate
we thought preferable. And in private Phil worked hard to bring about the
result he wanted. In late October, he drafted a long statement for Lyndon
Johnson to deliver, asking people to rally behind JFK. He also wrote a
speech for Johnson to use in Texas to appeal to his fellow Texans to vote
for Kennedy.

ELECTION NIGHT CAME at last. Joe Alsop and I stayed in Phil's office
at the paper, while Phil came and went from the newsroom floor. The
election was so close throughout the night that we didn't leave the building until the *Post*'s last edition had been closed, at about three or four
in the morning, carrying the headline "Kennedy Near Victory." Chal
Roberts, in his history of the *Post*, wrote that Phil, remembering the paper's profound embarrassment in the 1948 Truman election, would not let
Eddie Folliard, who was writing the lead story, call the election "for a few
thousand lousy papers."

When the final edition closed, the three of us moved to Joe's house,
where the sleeping housekeeper owned the only television set, but we listened on the radio while I cooked us scrambled eggs at about 6:00 a.m.
Later, when it appeared there would be a hiatus on returns until 11:00
a.m., I told Joe I was going home, to which Joe, in his usual style, said,
"You go home, darling. I may have to sell my house in the morning."

Phil and I retreated to Crescent Place. It was late in the morning before we were reassured that Kennedy had indeed won. The deal that Phil
had engineered in Los Angeles at the convention had helped bring about
the election of our friend as the next president of the United States, and
another, even closer friend as his vice-president.

To calm down from the excitement of the Kennedy victory, Phil and I
spent two weeks in Phoenix at the Arizona Biltmore. When we returned
home, Phil went directly back to politicking. Except for weekends, which
we still tried to spend at Glen Welby with the children, he was immersed
in politics. In fact, he facetiously turned down one invitation by saying,

"We go to the country with the children every possible weekend, as an aid to such limited sanity as I possess."

Right after the election, he started talking to and writing the president-elect about appointments to the new administration. Both Phil and Joe Alsop thought Kennedy ought to appoint our friend Douglas Dillon as secretary of the Treasury. Dillon was a liberal Republican who had served as undersecretary of state in the Eisenhower administration and had contributed to the Nixon campaign, so this didn't seem like a strong possibility. Arthur Schlesinger and Ken Galbraith had dinner with us one evening, and, as Arthur noted in his book *A Thousand Days*, "we were distressed by [Phil's] impassioned insistence that Douglas Dillon should—and would—be made Secretary of the Treasury. Without knowing Dillon, we mistrusted him on principle as a presumed exponent of Republican economic policies." But as Arthur also wrote, "When I mentioned this to the President-elect in Washington on December 1, he remarked of Dillon, 'Oh, I don't care about those things. All I want to know is: is he able and will he go along with the program?'"

What a refreshing thought—if only more presidents felt that way! In fact, the president-elect called Joe about the liberals wanting Albert Gore (father of the Clinton administration vice-president, Al Gore) for the position, but he told Joe that he wanted Dillon. Joe recalls Kennedy saying, "They say that if I take Doug Dillon he won't be loyal because he's a Republican." Joe responded that it would be very hard to imagine a man less likely to be disloyal than Dillon. He also added, "And if you take Albert Gore you know perfectly well, a) he's incompetent; b) you'll never be able to hear yourself think, he talks so much; c) when he isn't talking your ear off, he'll be telling *The New York Times* all." I'm sure this whole conversation with Kennedy was recalled in Alsopian terms, but I'm also sure that some such conversation did indeed take place.

Kennedy agreed with Phil and Joe about Dillon and said he wanted to get the message to Doug. Joe told Kennedy that the man to do that was Phil, not himself, so Phil called Doug, who was giving a dinner, and said he needed to see him. Not wishing to be observed by the dinner guests, Phil crawled in through a dressing-room window, which had been left open for him. The butler called Doug out of the dining room, and Phil and Dillon had a conversation right there in the dressing room, during which Doug assured Phil that he would love to be secretary and that he would most certainly be loyal.

Phil and Joe also recommended David Bruce for secretary of state, advice that the president didn't take. Later, Phil effected David's being sent as ambassador to London, not Rome, which Kennedy had promised; David was so modest that he hadn't told JFK he would actually prefer London. Phil realized the situation, thought David would be just right for

London, and went to JFK to tell him so. David was named ambassador and stayed all eight years of the Kennedy-Johnson administrations. He and Evangeline were an enormous success in London, and David turned out to be one of JFK's favorites, particularly since he not only kept the president in touch with what was going on substantively in Great Britain and in Europe but amused him with London gossip.

Phil also suggested Robert Weaver for a high-level position. Weaver, a black, Harvard-educated, distinguished economist, had become an expert on housing and urban affairs whom Phil had known through the board of ACTION. Among his other credentials, Weaver had advised Franklin Roosevelt's administration and had been in Averell Harriman's New York State Cabinet. Kennedy did appoint him as administrator of the Federal Housing and Home Finance Agency, and Weaver later became the first black appointed to the United States Cabinet, when LBJ made him the first secretary of housing and urban development in 1966.

Phil was involved in a scoop for the paper on the appointment of Dean Rusk as secretary of state. Chal Roberts had narrowed the choices and was prepared to predict his likely appointment when Phil, in Chal's presence, called JFK in Palm Beach. Kennedy confirmed Rusk's appointment, and the *Post* put it in banner headlines. Kennedy was extremely angry and told his press secretary, Pierre Salinger, to track down the leaker immediately. Within two hours, Salinger called the president to say he had tracked down the leaker: "It's you."

"What do you mean, me?" Kennedy asked.

Salinger asked Kennedy if he hadn't spoken to Phil the evening before. Kennedy said he had. "Did you tell him he couldn't use the story?" There was a long silence, Salinger later recounted in his own book, "before Kennedy chuckled and replied, 'No, I guess I didn't.' "

THE BEGINNING OF the new administration was an exciting and very busy time for us. For Phil and me personally the big moment was supposed to come on the afternoon of the Inaugural Gala—January 19, 1961. In the tradition of my family, we had planned a large reception at our R Street house, back into which we had just moved. Phil had written President-elect Kennedy to invite him personally, reminding him that he and Jackie had come to the inaugural reception in January 1957 and hoping he would drop by this time—"unless you are dissatisfied with your progress in the past four years." Both the president- and the vice-president-elect had promised to come, although Jackie, recently having had her second baby, John, had written that she was saving every bit of strength to get through the two days of official activities.

On the early afternoon of the reception, an icy snow started to fall and quickly rendered Washington's streets so perilous that cars slid all over the place and traffic became gridlocked. Some people took hours to get home; others gave up and took shelter. It was an unprecedented mess. The Secret Service descended on us and held out the promise that either Kennedy or Johnson or both would still manage to get to our house, but we could see by the snowdrifts and by the few guests who had managed to trudge through the blizzard that this was not likely. Finally, we were told it was hopeless—even with an escort, cars couldn't move, and the city and the Secret Service were doing everything they could to get the president-elect and Jackie to the gala that night. So, instead of a big party for six hundred people who would drop by for a while and then leave, we had about two hundred who got to our house mostly on foot and wouldn't leave—a jolly gathering of a different sort.

The next day, the streets were mostly cleared, but it was bitter cold. We went to the swearing in and were amused by Cardinal Cushing's long blessing, during which the podium seemed to start to smoke because of some wiring problem. Along with so many others, we were thrilled by the inaugural speech, which had mostly been crafted by Ted Sorensen, helped by Ken Galbraith. Then we watched the parade with families of *Post* employees from a hotel room on Pennsylvania Avenue.

Joe and Phil had planned a dinner at Joe's house to precede the Inaugural Ball at the Armory. I no longer remember who came, except for Mrs. Longworth, the Bohlens, the Joyces, and the Mac Bundys, who were recent arrivals in Washington. I do remember that Bob Weaver was there, and it may have been the first time Joe had a black person to dinner at his house.

Everyone was a little delirious with excitement. Phil had hired limousines to get us all to the ball, and we set out with the Bundys, whom I didn't know well, and Joe and another couple, and a bucket with champagne on ice. When we got bogged down in traffic and held up while the official motorcade whizzed past, someone mentioned opening the champagne. Goody Two-Shoes yet again, I nervously suggested waiting until we got to the dance. Whenever I saw Phil starting to drink in a certain way, I became anxious, having lived a lot with the inevitably difficult and contentious results. But Mac Bundy, the ex-dean of Harvard and new national security adviser, turned around from the front seat and authoritatively and merrily commanded, "Open the champagne."

By this time, Carl and Dorothy McCardle were stopped in their station wagon next to us. Dorothy was the much-beloved society reporter for the *Post*, and Carl worked for the Eisenhower administration. Phil pulled the cork from a champagne bottle and tossed it through the McCardles' window, muttering, "Here, you Nixon-loving son of a bitch."

At the ball, the Kennedys looked very handsome—and regal. Because

Joe had asked Afdera Fonda, the beautiful Italian wife of Henry Fonda, and Flo Smith, an old Kennedy friend from Palm Beach, to come by his house for a drink, he decided to go home early, and tried to get Phil and me to leave with him, but by then Phil was having much too good a time. So Joe found Peter Duchin, who was also leaving, got a ride with him through the still-snowy streets, and arrived in time to welcome his guests. They lit a fire and sat down to enjoy it and quietly reflect on the momentous day. Flo and Afdera, however, had spread word of the after-ball party, and their friends started to arrive.

Eventually, we drove home from the dance with the Bohlens and the Bradens, and as our car passed Dumbarton Avenue, we looked down toward Joe's and noticed that the street was lit up, blocked off, and full of police. Avis said, "Either Joe's house is on fire or the president's there." Indeed he was.

We felt sad not to have left with Joe and shared in the exciting moment when he heard a quiet knock, opened the door, and found the new young president of the United States, snowflakes in his hair and a smile on his handsome face, waiting to come in.

— *Chapter Fifteen* —

E VEN NOW it's hard to appraise how good a president Jack Kennedy was in the relatively short time allowed him in office, but it's not hard to recall the excitement and hope generated by a president who was vibrant, young, eloquent, and committed to solving old problems in new ways. Especially in the beginning, we were electrified by the prospects of this administration. Phil and I had been much closer to Johnson than to Kennedy, but Phil, especially, grew close to Kennedy as time went on. Theirs was an easy relationship. At dinner one night at Joe Alsop's, Phil, typically, was offering political advice when Kennedy teased, "Phil, when you get elected dogcatcher I will listen to you on politics."

Many of Kennedy's appointees were or became and remained our friends—among them, Douglas Dillon and Arthur Schlesinger, who served the president as special assistant and adviser on Latin American and cultural affairs and as his resident "court philosopher." Our old friend Ken Galbraith was ambassador to India, but because he was closer to Kennedy on economic matters than were many others, he commuted frequently from India to Washington for consultations with the president. Kennedy once said to him, "I don't want to hear about agriculture from anybody but you, Ken, and I don't want to hear about it from you either."

Robert McNamara, whom we hadn't known, came into the administration as secretary of defense. He had been a classmate of my cousin Walter Haas at the University of California, and Wally wanted me to meet him right away. Though ours was not an immediately positive relationship, a strong friendship developed between Bob and Margy and Phil and me, a friendship that Bob and I continue to this day.

Bill Walton was made head of the Fine Arts Commission in Washington, which Kennedy thought was a salaried position, but which, to the president's embarrassment, turned out not to be. Bill had a marvelous time, though, despite his forced volunteering, influencing the design of the city, including LaFayette Square, and helping Jackie on matters of renovation and art for the White House.

Part of what contributed to the excitement of the Kennedy presidency for us was that these men surrounding the president, and indeed the president himself, were our friends and, for the most part, our contemporaries. We no longer were the younger acquaintances of the older generation constituting the government. With Phil having become publisher of the *Post* just before his thirty-first birthday, we seemed always to have been the youngest people in the room. Now our generation was running the country. As Phil put it at the beginning of a speech he gave at the National War College, "I have been feeling especially venerable and ancient ever since the moment on January 20 when I first learned that it was possible to be older than the President of the United States."

By EARLY MARCH, 1961, Phil was involved in his old in-depth way with many activities—political and Post Company–related—and he seemed to me to be enjoying himself. I can see today that his activities had become increasingly frenetic, though still fairly constructively so, the most obvious example of which was his purchase of *Newsweek*, then a weak, marginally profitable newsmagazine for businessmen, far behind its rival, *Time*.

The magazine, *News-Week*, had first appeared in February 1933, and in 1937 was renamed *Newsweek*, having been bought by Vincent Astor, with Averell Harriman and a few others as investors. At Vincent's death, the Astor Foundation—controlled by Vincent's widow, Brooke—in effect owned the magazine, and the trustees decided that it should be sold.

As early as January 1961, one of the men on the *Post*'s business staff had told Phil about the magazine's being for sale and Phil had said he wasn't interested. He was then approached by a management group led by Malcolm Muir, *Newsweek*'s chairman, but Phil again dismissed the idea. Then Ken Crawford, a friend of Phil's and Washington bureau chief for *Newsweek*, and Ben Bradlee, Crawford's assistant, began egging him on. The idea must have begun to take hold, because when Ben called Phil one night at home (a call Ben later referred to as "the best telephone call I ever made—the luckiest, most productive, most exciting, most rewarding"), Phil told him to come right over. Ben, reminiscing later, said: "I used to stew about it at night, and it seemed incredible to me that mature people couldn't have some control over their own future." That's what prompted his call. Phil talked at length with Ben at our house and asked him to go home and write an extensive memo on why Phil should buy the magazine, encouraging Ben not to worry about what he said, because Phil would be the only one reading it. Ben went home at 3:00 a.m. and spent the rest of the night drafting a long stream-of-consciousness memo (unfortunately lost), which seems to have been persuasive to Phil.

A few days later, in late February, this time in the evening at our house, Phil met again with Ben, who brought along Oz Elliott, *Newsweek*'s thirty-six-year-old managing editor. Ben remembered the instantaneous rapport between Phil and Oz: "Phil had this way of leaping ahead of himself. He would start out a sentence, switch, and then expect others to know what he meant and where he was going. Elliott was on the same wavelength, and so they hit it off very well." The next day, Phil flew to New York, where he met with the company's lawyers and financial advisers, bringing into the situation Fritz Beebe, who had helped with the purchase of the *Times-Herald*. After Fritz looked favorably at the figures, Phil decided to try to buy the magazine and dove right in.

As active negotiations over *Newsweek* increased to breakneck speed, Phil got terribly frantic and wound up. The deal took only about three weeks from beginning to end, during which time he slept very little and rode a high crest, working feverishly to get it done. The whole idea of buying *Newsweek* and adding yet another huge responsibility to his already too-full plate made me nervous. I wasn't a regular reader of *Newsweek*, nor was Phil at that time, and it had no real emotional appeal for me. I knew the magazine was national press and therefore had an impact, but I wasn't thinking about the business effect so much as the potential personal—and negative—effect on Phil. Having been through so much with Phil's depression, I worried that this would become just another problem for him to deal with, at a time when he was already overextended. On the other hand, some of our long talks over the past few years had made it apparent to me that Phil was worried about being a "son-in-law," about having been "given" the paper and the company by my father. He kept questioning whether this was the reason for his success and his prominence. Could he have achieved what he had on his own? He seemed to be brooding over this question more and more, and by then this had become enough of an issue in my mind that, despite my misgivings, I came down on the side of the *Newsweek* purchase, it so clearly being something Phil would have done on his own.

Once he had decided to go for the magazine, Phil touched every base he knew to influence the people who would make the decision on which bidder would be the victor, the other finalist being the wealthy publishing house Doubleday. He met with Allan Betts, the vice-president and treasurer of the Astor Foundation, giving him an outline of The Washington Post Company's proposal for the purchase. While other potential purchasers had simply announced that they wanted to buy the magazine, Phil took the trouble to write down his ideas for its future. It happened that a few of his ideas coincided with plans that Vincent had made and shared with Brooke, so she was especially keen on Phil's being the victorious bidder. For her, this decision would be based on more than money. She said at the time, "I want Phil Graham to have it because he's the only person who has written down exactly what Vincent was thinking about." Brooke Astor was an important voice in the sale, and she wanted to be sure *Newsweek* would end up in responsible hands. Phil also went to considerable trouble to acquire Averell Harriman's support—without which, Betts later acknowledged, the foundation would have refused to let Phil enter the race for the magazine at the last minute.

Finally, after a weekend at Glen Welby, Phil left for New York with Al Friendly, John Sweeterman, and John Hayes to meet Fritz. I was supposed to go with them but had some things to take care of, so I suggested I come up the following day. After the flurry of departure, I received a telephone call from my doctor, who asked to see me that afternoon. This was unusual, but I was unsuspecting. I had been to see him the previous week for a chronic cough and fatigue, and as a matter of course I had had a chest X-ray, since the doctors were always looking at several healed scars on my lungs, a not uncommon thing. But this time Dr. Felts said to me that he suspected I might have tuberculosis. If I did have it, it was in the very early stages and therefore could be dealt with, but he wanted me to go to the hospital for a week of tests.

I explained to him that Phil was in the middle of extremely tense negotiations in New York and that I was supposed to join him the following day; there was no way I could call him with this piece of news—I couldn't possibly divert or upset him with my own problems at such a moment. Believing that I had to be there for him and support him in this effort, I asked Dr. Felts if we could postpone the hospital visit until I got back from New York. I realized that Phil was fragile and that I could help bolster him. Dr. Felts knew Phil well and understood my predicament and said that it was probably safe to go, as long as I didn't stay up late or spend time in smoke-filled rooms—neither of which I could avoid, of course. His admonitions went the expectable way—none of us slept much, and everyone around me was smoking nonstop.

I felt somewhat like a soap-opera heroine, but not telling Phil at the time was the only thing to do—things were dramatic and tense enough as it was. So I sat in the Carlyle suite with Fritz and Phil and followed the negotiations as a close spectator, watching as they worked together in a perfectly complementary way, enthralled by what was going on and caught up in the excitement. At one point, Betts called to say that although the offers from the final contenders were more or less equal, we had to come up with more cash if we wanted to be competitive—cash we didn't have. At first Phil and Fritz were overcome with despondency. Again, my mother got into the picture, calling me to tell Phil to feel free to spend her money, too, if needed. But instead Phil got on the phone and sold the old *Times-Herald* building to the developer William Zeckendorf. After that, he went into one of the bedrooms alone with a yellow pad and a pencil for about an hour, playing with numbers to make the purchase work out. When he emerged, he said to Fritz, "There are three ways we might do this." Fritz glanced at his pad and quickly responded, "The first two won't work, but the third one will."

The whole thing was very courageous of Phil and Fritz. We were still a small private company without much cash, especially after borrowing for all the previous deals and for the *Post* and Jacksonville buildings, which we were in the process of either enlarging or rebuilding, and particularly when contrasted with Doubleday, which was cash-rich.

We were all on pins and needles on the day of decision, March 9. Ensconced in the Carlyle, Phil had nearly worn a path on the room's carpet, pacing back and forth with worry and excitement. He decided to take a shower to relieve his agitation, and naturally he was in the shower when the phone rang. Allan Betts was calling. Dripping wet and barely covered by a towel, Phil ran out to take the call, turned to us, and said, "We got it." *Newsweek* was ours.

Once we realized we had the magazine, Phil had to come up with the $2 million down payment. He had no company checks with him but did have a crumpled blank personal check that he had been carrying around in his wallet for a year or longer in case of need. He crossed out his name, wrote in "The Washington Post Company," and made out the check for $2 million, letting the *Post*'s treasurer in Washington know, so that he could scramble to cover that amount. The check was later framed and hung in Phil's office, and still hangs in mine. The deposit was a down payment on a total of $8,985,000 to the Astor Foundation at a rate of $50 a share. In the end, Phil had triumphed over about a half-dozen other bidders. Sam Newhouse made a higher bid after the deal was closed, but the Astor Foundation honorably stuck by its word.

The rest of that day was taken up talking with the press, and Phil made an appearance at the *Newsweek* offices. He went over to meet Betts in Malcolm Muir's office but didn't identify himself to the receptionist. Muir apparently knew what was afoot but wasn't aware who the victor was, so told his son Mac (Malcolm Jr.) to go out and see who was in the reception room. Mac, recognizing Phil, reported back to his father, and that's the way Muir learned who had bought *Newsweek*.

Newsweek gathered twenty or so editorial and businesspeople in the conference room, and Muir handled the situation with real elegance, saying, "As you know, I've been trying to raise the money to buy the magazine myself and I've failed, and in that failure I can imagine nobody more appropriate to be the owner than Phil." Others were slightly more cautious. Many of the staff, knowing only of the reputation of the *Post* as anti-McCarthy, wondered who this man was, and ran to the library to study a *Time* cover story on him that had run in 1956.

Ben Bradlee wrote me a note shortly after these days of frenzied activity. It was so typical of him in its tone and stream-of-consciousness style:

> That was a nice day. You were funny. The way you jumped when the phone rang. Your husband was funny, too. The way he jumped when the phone rang. Charlie was funny, too. The way he jumped when the phone rang. And that nice Mister Sweeterman. Boy, was he ever jumpy. It was lucky I wasn't jumpy, or anything. I am never jumpy when someone is trying to buy things. It really is very hard to be jumpy when you are walking on air. . . .

The day after our victory, Phil and I took the train back to Washington, traveling in one of those small compartments in a Pullman car. About halfway home, I felt I had to tell him what was happening to me and what the doctor suspected. It was a tremendous shock to him. His reaction was strange and should have warned me about his state of mind. He simply denied the possibility, saying it couldn't be TB, that was out of the question, of course it was a mistake, he would take care of it, etc., etc. Nevertheless, I went to the hospital the next day and stayed there for a week, during which time it was confirmed that I did indeed have TB. I wonder now about the relationship between my illness and stress. It was very rare in those days for someone in an upper-income bracket to develop this disease. Maybe all the stress of Phil's illness had come to be more of a factor than I realized.

The combination of events—his anxiety over the purchase and my illness—sent Phil into a bad spin of drinking and frantic behavior of every kind. At one crucial moment in the hospital, the doctor and I waited to discuss my diagnosis with him. Phil came in and never drew a breath, talking incessantly, being so witty and so funny that we rocked with helpless laughter, and it wasn't until he had left the room that we both realized no serious word had been spoken, no difficult issues had been dealt with. It sounds incomprehensible, but it was true.

Many people believed Phil had endless energy, but a few of the hundreds of congratulatory letters Phil received after the *Newsweek* purchase expressed concern for his health. One was from Tommy Toms, who had worked for Ernie Graham for years and had known Phil since he was a little boy in Florida, and even in Terry, South Dakota, before that:

> You no doubt have been congratulated and toasted by many great and important people on your last adventure, none more sincerely than by one who has been privileged to sit on the side lines and watch these developments since long ago in Terry.
>
> When I look back now over the many years of tremendous effort your father expended in building his, a land empire, which has now wrecked a fine physical specimen of a man, I cannot but be skeptical of such attainment.
>
> I hope you have learned over the years (which I have not) to cast aside such responsibilities that accompany such business as yours and not follow the footsteps of your father and work at it 24 hours each and every day.
>
> There is no greater wealth than health.

Phil thought this was one of the nicest letters he received, but he sloughed off Tommy's concern by writing, "Just remember that unlike my father and you, I sleep late in the morning."

Phil wrote my mother of his excitement about *Newsweek*, soberly adding, "Now we go slow. . . . [R]eally there are few problems and lots of opportunities. But easy-does-it is the watch-word." Yet, despite his talk of going slow and easy-does-it, Phil speeded up again. He wrote to his friend Harold (Andy) Anderson that buying *Newsweek* "was somewhat like doing the four-minute mile—quick but exhausting. Yet, for someone who believes in the slow and steady approach, I find myself exhilarated at having made the dash." He immediately set to work to get rid of the deadwood at the magazine and start hiring talent, promoting Oz Elliott from managing editor to the top editing job.

Probably the most important move Phil made just after the purchase was persuading Fritz to leave his law firm, Cravath, and join him in running The Washington Post Company as his equal partner. Fritz was to remain in New York, overseeing *Newsweek*, but to have a large role in all the company's activities and business. My father had once told Phil that, when you are operating with a full head of steam and have a lot of responsibilities, you ought to have a partner—not an employee who is your executive officer but a real partner. Phil knew he had found that real partner in Fritz. He made him a handsome offer, which eventually rewarded Fritz well. Still, Phil had to use all his not inconsiderable powers of persuasion. Fritz had to think long and hard, because he obviously was destined for higher things at Cravath—in fact, several Cravath partners never forgave him, regarding his defection as a kind of betrayal.

Fritz's becoming chairman of the board of the company and vice-chairman of *Newsweek* was probably the saving grace for the company in the immediate time to come, and certainly was a key factor in the survival of The Washington Post Company in the decade after I took over. Fritz was an extraordinary combination of qualities. Above all, he was wise and bright and had a great legal mind, always thinking ahead conceptually. He was devoted to our family and to the company, possibly in that order, but there's no way of telling, since the two were so intermingled. He was editorially involved, and the editors at both the *Post* and *Newsweek* became devoted to him. For his part, Phil was so elated that, in responding to a congratulatory letter from Frank Stanton on the *Post*'s getting Fritz, he said: "Now I am completely free of duties! Eureka!"

This, however, was far from the case. While reinventing *Newsweek*, Phil took a renewed interest in the *Post* and attended to his duties there and throughout the company once again. He involved himself in editorial improvements at both places and watched the stations' business closely. He always kept his office door open when he was at the *Post*, allowing reporters and others from throughout the building to come in to discuss anything. He enjoyed arguments and back and forth, and was known for his salty language and loved for his informality. He provided many ideas for news stories and often contributed to the reporting of them as well.

In February 1961, Phil had promoted Russ Wiggins from executive editor to editor and John Sweeterman from general manager to publisher; Phil himself would now use the title of president. But though he was still going into the office, he soon grew less and less patient with the details of the job. Early in 1961, he described his office in a letter to the book publisher Blanche Knopf as "the usual sort of thing: phones and mail and teeming people moved by the unurgent urgency of the day-to-day; a place I go to as late as I can and leave earlier than is at all proper."

In New York, Phil was occupied with the final details of the *Newsweek* deal, with becoming the magazine's leading subscription salesman, as Gib McCabe, *Newsweek*'s publisher, called him in a letter to an advertiser, and with the start-up of the newly formed editorial team headed by Oz with Kermit Lansner and Gordon Manning as his deputies—or, as Oz described it, his equals. Despite differences in background and education, these men worked well together, making a strong contribution to the energizing of the magazine. A nearly ideal political ticket, they were a driven, hard-news, peppy Boston Irish Catholic; a conservative WASPish Protestant; and an Upper West Side artistic, intellectual Jew. The balancing act that this threesome brought to the magazine caused them to be referred to as the Wallendas, the high-wire family, a name still used today to refer to the top editors at *Newsweek*. Oz may have been the driver, but Kermit and Gordon, both more detail-oriented than Oz, were the engine and the fuel. This triumvirate in New York, with Ben Bradlee in Washington, essentially remade the magazine. Oz recalled the excitement at the time—the Kennedy era was dawning and the World War II generation was coming into its own. The magazine was at last challenging *Time*, which was being edited by the fairly reactionary Otto Fuerbringer and which, because it was number one among the newsweeklies, didn't worry much about the second-place *Newsweek*. Gordon remembers those months after the purchase as one of the most exciting ever: "When you got out of bed in the morning, you'd say, 'Hey, the world is my apple.' "

On the business side, Gib McCabe was a man who liked his work and was good at it. He also was very protective of and stood up for his editors, even in the face of threats to withdraw advertising or other such trouble, as happened over a *Newsweek* cover story about the right wing in America, called "Thunder on the Right," which the magazine ran in December of 1961. Thirty years later, a *Newsweek* editor from that time remembers McCabe saying about the advertisers: "Whether it's true or not, let's act like they need us more than we need them." Fritz and Gib both recognized that without a good editorial product there was nothing to sell.

MY CASE OF tuberculosis was an active one, but, on the cheerful side, it was caught very early and hadn't done any harm to my lungs, and I was not contagious. I was never too worried or too ill, but I was ordered to stay in bed for at least six weeks, taking two pills a day for a year and one pill for another year after that. (I was very lucky to have gotten the disease after the discovery of these pills, which was fairly recent, or I would have been sent away to a sanitarium.) I was also told not to drink any alcohol, which was eventually modified to three drinks a week. Phil brought in two consulting University of Chicago doctors whom he had met while serving on the board of trustees of the university. They confirmed the diagnosis and the prescription of the local doctors.

The weeks I spent essentially in my bedroom were a mixed, ambiguous experience. I was a kind of miscast Camille. Being forced to slow down was not an altogether unhappy thing, and I seemed to be the envy of everyone for my enforced weeks in bed. As I wrote to a friend at the end of March: "If anyone discovers what a racket this is there will be a whole series of blossoming lungs from Georgetown to Kalorama Road: bed; books; see whom you want to, not too many; boss your husband around; no good works; no obligations." Even Phil benefited from my illness. As I explained to Drew Dudley: "Phil claims that he is hiding behind my lung and there never has been anything so useful to him. He has fended off a galaxy of events and I am sure he hopes I recover slowly if at all."

I was allowed out of bed only four hours each day. Lally used to come into my room after school every afternoon in her little green jumper, the Madeira School uniform, and have a snack while we visited. One day early in my forced hibernation, she found me reading a mystery, promptly removed it from my hands, and substituted *Swann's Way*, the first volume of Proust's *Remembrance of Things Past*. She was right that I shouldn't waste this valuable time in bed reading trash or light, amusing books. All I needed was her gentle push and I finished all seven volumes.

These weeks were a turning point of sorts for me, as was the purchase of *Newsweek*. I resigned from all my welfare projects and withdrew from my outside work in Washington. Owning *Newsweek* meant going to New York a lot, which Phil did right from the start and I did once my health allowed. We began a New York life while maintaining our Washington one, and I decided to use some of my time there by starting to look at paintings with the idea of learning more and eventually buying a few.

The stresses for Phil accumulated. While I was ill, he seemed to be dealing with a hundred things at once, as well as with the children. He coped with their spring vacations from school, had frequent golfing days with Don, bought a new bicycle for Bill, and dealt with a constant convoy of school friends for Steve. He even took Lally to New York to buy dresses for her coming-out parties that year, enlisting my old Madeira friend Nancy White, by then editor of *Harper's Bazaar*, to help them shop. On one trip, he took Lally to meet Jackie Kennedy at the Carlyle, which thrilled her. He wrote to my mother, who was taking one of her frequent cures at Saratoga, that he had been "damn close to tired," but felt "brought back" by the peaceful interlude in which he was involved with the children. But in fact Phil was stretched too thin, and drinking a lot. And there were frequent erratic moments.

Ben Bradlee remembers Phil's sort of dropping out of sight right after the *Newsweek* purchase but then becoming involved one Saturday morning just after the Bay of Pigs, over a *Newsweek* cover story on the CIA that Phil stepped in to tone down. Since Phil knew the players particularly well—friends of his like Frank Wisner and Tracy Barnes—he was very concerned about this piece and went over the story with a fine-tooth comb. He was acting arbitrarily.

With regard to the Bay of Pigs fiasco, Chal Roberts ascribes the *Post's* failure to send reporters to Florida and Guatemala to the fact that Phil, his editors, and Chal himself saw nothing wrong with such a CIA operation and indeed hoped it would succeed. On April 22, a *Post* editorial declared that events in Cuba were "only one chapter in the long history of freedom, which has encompassed many greater disasters and darker days before men have combined their wit and determination to write a brighter sequel." Only on May 1 did an editorial refer to "the Cuban misadventure" and the next day to an "appalling mistake of judgment." Then Phil pulled a critical editorial by Bob Estabrook out of the paper without telling him, a warning that his mood was deteriorating again. Clearly his being absent from the paper much of the time but occasionally plunging in deeply must have been very confusing and disorienting to the staff.

One of the first people Phil turned on at that time was Estabrook, who had been named editorial-page editor when Russ became editor of the *Post*. Phil's and Bob's personalities were not in harmony, and they had developed various differences on issues over the years. In this instance, Bob had argued that on some editorial issues the paper had to acknowledge when it was changing its position, and that seemed to be the last straw for Phil—he was so angry that he wanted to fire Bob. Russ Wiggins solved this problem by sending Bob off to London to be a columnist for the paper and taking over the editorial page himself, which had the effect of putting Al Friendly in charge of the news operation.

Another change that Phil brought about at this time was a change in the law firms used by the company. When Bill Rogers left the government, Phil tried to get Covington & Burling to take him in as a partner so that he could work for us. When Covington rejected this idea, Phil switched all the company business except for broadcasting to another firm that Bill had joined, in part with the idea of upgrading it. With this move, Bill became general counsel to The Washington Post Company and a close associate of Fritz's, Phil's, and later of mine.

As was typical of Phil during these years, he kept his hand in politics, drafting and editing speeches for Bobby Kennedy as well as for the president and vice-president. He also drafted a foreign-policy speech on unity for LBJ to deliver to the Magazine Publishers Association—which he had gotten the vice-president to agree to deliver in the first place—and accompanied him when LBJ spoke to the group. Immediately afterwards, LBJ and Lady Bird flew to the Far East for an official trip. They had been house-hunting just before leaving and had narrowed their search to two houses. Lyndon left Phil his power of attorney, told him to consult with Abe Fortas and to decide on which one to buy. Abe was worried that the bigger, grander one, owned by Perle Mesta and known as the Elms, would hurt LBJ's political image—it was a formal, large, French-style house with a lot of lawn and grounds around it—but Phil, who was in charge of making the decision, decided in favor of that one, despite Fortas's misgivings. Years later, Lady Bird expressed profound pleasure in Phil's choice, saying she would never have dared set her sights that high. "It was too elegant, too expensive. But that's the nicest house I ever lived in. I loved that house and I loved every day that I spent there."

BY MID-MAY, I was allowed out of my bed five hours a day. I mostly used that time moving around with Phil. And as summer neared, I gradually was up more and more. Lally graduated from Madeira on June 3, and Phil described our daughter at the time in a letter to a childhood friend, evoking the natural love of a proud father: "She miraculously goes to Radcliffe this fall and is as far beyond me in sophistication and general wisdom as you and I once were beyond Uncle George and Ernie."

Several parties had been planned for Lally's coming-out year and graduation. My then friend Bunny Mellon, Paul's wife, had decided to give a dance at their Upperville farm, Oak Spring, for her daughter by her first marriage, Liza Lloyd. Whenever Bunny did something like this, she did it in a major way. She had suggested that I give a dinner for Lally and Barbara Lawrence, Lally's close friend, earlier on the night of the dance, and then bring all of our guests to Oak Spring. Poor Dr. Felts agreed to the idea of the dinner on June 16—as long as it was a quiet family occasion. I nodded agreement. The quiet family occasion, however, turned out to be 120 for dinner—roughly eighty young people, friends of Lally's, and forty adults. This was my first real night out, my own coming out after the weeks in bed.

So, after our dinner at Glen Welby, we all drove over to Upperville, to the Mellons'. Bunny had had a dance floor built and had decorated the dance area to look like the center of a small French village square with a fair going on around it and lights twinkling on the outskirts. A tent city, where scores of young men had been put up, was in a distant field, but looked very pretty, complete with flags flying. Two orchestras played throughout the night, Count Basie's alternating with another of the prominent dance bands of the time. The dancing carried on until the early hours of the morning. Someone said an entire vintage year of Dom Pérignon was consumed that night.

It was the last extravaganza on this lavish scale that my children attended, but it was fun, and I was pleased to have had such a memorable evening for my first party night out.

LALLY'S GRADUATION WEEKEND coincided with President Kennedy's summit meeting in Vienna with Khrushchev. Shortly after the president's return, Joe Alsop—who had recently married Susan Mary Patten, the widow of his close friend Bill Patten and the perfect wife for him— asked us to drive him out to see the president in a house the Kennedys had rented in Middleburg, Virginia. We sat together as the president soberly discussed the drama of the Vienna meeting and Khrushchev's toughness with him. As we sat in his living room, President Kennedy, in an old-fashioned rocking chair that he used for his bad back, sent for the transcript of the meeting between the two leaders and read the exchange that had taken place at the end of it, concluding with his own words in response to one of Khrushchev's threats: "It's going to be a cold winter."

Jackie told me of sitting next to President de Gaulle while in Paris, where she had been so overwhelmingly received and where the French adored her. "*Prenez garde,*" she quoted de Gaulle as telling her, "*elle est la plus maligne*" ("Watch out, she's the wilier one"), referring to Mrs. Khrushchev. When she met Mrs. Khrushchev in Vienna, Jackie decided de Gaulle had been right. The two women went out onto a balcony to respond to the crowds in Vienna, and Jackie said that Mrs. Khrushchev, "with her little pig's eyes, . . . grabbed my hand and held it aloft before I could stop her."

Kennedy had been deeply shaken by his exchange with Khrushchev, confiding to Scotty Reston right after the meeting that it was the "roughest thing in my life." Some people believe that Kennedy was driven to his first steps in Vietnam because Khrushchev frightened him so in Vienna over Berlin and other issues. Murrey Marder told me later that on the plane back from Vienna the president was talking to Marie Ridder, who was along on the flight with her husband, Walter, and who was pregnant, and told her gravely, "You have no right to bring a child into this kind of world." Marie was astonished and pointed out that Jackie was pregnant, too—to which he reportedly responded, "That goes for her also."

The effect on Phil of our visit was immediate and long-lasting. Shortly after this trip, he responded to Kennedy's concerns about the grim situation, especially in Berlin, by calling in his editors and reporters—from both the *Post* and *Newsweek*—and impressing on them how Kennedy felt. Phil also met at length with Ben Bradlee one afternoon, joined by Dick Hottelet of CBS and Larry Collins of *Newsweek*'s Paris bureau. And for hours, late into the night, he talked with Tommy Thompson and Chip Bohlen, both Soviet experts and diplomats, at Chip's home. Phil even suggested some pieces about the threat to Berlin and the possibility of millions of lives being lost in a nuclear war. "We knew he'd been over and got it all from Kennedy," said Chal Roberts, who had covered the Vienna trip. "We knew he was actually asking us to write something to promote Kennedy's policies, which was a legitimate news story, but it made us uncomfortable. . . . I never had a falling out with Phil in any formal sense, but I did think he got too much into politics and the Kennedys."

NOT KNOWING WHAT to do with the summer, to give Phil a rest and me a change of scenery, I was influenced by a friend to return to Cape

Cod. We rented two houses in a family enclave, known as the Bailey Apollonic House, in Cotuit, which had a pier across a small road and a ladder down a cliff to the beach.

The summer was a difficult one. By the time we left for Cotuit, Phil clearly had become depressed again and was also suffering from a very bad back. For the most part, because of the way he was feeling, we led a relatively quiet life while on the Cape. He retreated from involvement with work and from most social events, though he did spend a certain amount of time with the children, teasing Lally about her young boyfriend, whose family was in the arms business and whom Phil christened "Pistols."

Bunny Mellon, who had a house nearby on the Cape, called me one day and said, "You know, the Kennedys go around in this boat and they have the most awful thick sandwiches and canned clam chowder for lunch. I think it would be nice to have them to a picnic, and I'd like you and Phil to be there." I'm sure she didn't need us, but I was excited. I pleaded with Phil to go, and he hesitantly accepted. We were all waiting on the Mellons' beach in Osterville when we saw the president's boat approach with the press boat following. Jack and Jackie jumped off and came in to the beach and took shelter from the press boat, which disappeared after the president had gone out of sight.

Bunny had substituted steamed clams and champagne for the meager lunch she thought the Kennedys usually had on their boat. The president chatted with Phil and me about members of the press corps, giving pretty frank appraisals but being flattering about the *Post*'s two reporters who covered the White House, Eddie Folliard and Carroll Kilpatrick.

At lunch, we all sat around at small tables. The president and Bunny were alone at one, and it was then that he asked her, whose skill at landscape gardening was legendary, if she would redesign the garden outside his office window, complaining that people called the place a rose garden but there wasn't a rose to be seen—that, in fact, there was nothing but crabgrass. Sometime later, when nothing had happened with the garden and Bunny was going through a receiving line at the White House, the president asked, "Where are the plans for my garden?" "Oh, Mr. President, I've been busy and I've been traveling. They are in my head but I haven't had time to get them down on paper." "That's the trouble with the whole New Frontier," the president wryly commented. Bunny eventually got the garden done, and its beauty remains.

One thing Phil did that summer, despite his condition, was to join the board of the RAND Corporation, an independent research organization founded after World War II to advise the air force on public-policy issues, particularly those involving national security. Being on the board put Phil in the position of having yet another connection with an organization closely related to the government. I think it was still marginally acceptable for him to participate, because the criteria for what publishers could and should do were looser in those days. Some years later RAND invited me to become a member, but by then I felt I couldn't do it: the connection with the government created too much of a conflict for me.

Most of that fall, Phil was still feeling low and liked to have me with him; as always when he was depressed, he didn't want to be left alone. Often during this period he would go to the office for only a few hours and then come home. Having fully recovered from TB by then, I started to go along with him to New York most weeks, where we rented a beautiful apartment in the Carlyle Hotel. Occasionally I ventured out—to lunch, with Babe Paley, for example, and sometimes with one or both of her sisters. I was very flattered to be included in their, to me, glamorous New Yorky circle. Despite my own background and actually having been born there, I always felt like a country girl in New York.

Babe became one of my good friends. One day she asked me if I knew Truman Capote. My sister Flo knew him, but I had never met him. Babe said that he was a very close friend of hers and that she wanted to bring us together, so she arranged a lunch for us with Truman and Harper Lee, the author of *To Kill a Mockingbird*. It's hard to describe Truman as I first saw him. He had that strange falsetto voice for which he was so well known. He was very short, perfectly dressed, groomed, and coiffed. And he was a magic conversationalist—his sentences were like stories. We quickly became friends. Harper Lee was different. She later became a recluse, and I saw her only one other time, also with Truman.

AS THE ADMINISTRATION got rolling, Phil and I went to the first of several dinner dances at the Kennedy White House. These parties included exquisite women from New York and Europe, but old friends of ours, too, the Johnsons among them. We danced the twist—or attempted to. I found it impossibly difficult to learn and never really did, although my children tried having me learn by stamping out cigarettes and drying myself with bath towels. Phil wasn't much better than I, but went at it with much more enthusiasm and natural energy—so much so that at one of the parties his pants split horizontally across the rear.

Early in 1962, Drew Pearson reported on the twist parties in his column, headlined "They Twisted at the White House." Pearson said that "the big story social Washington has been buzzing about has not been U-2 pilot Powers, or the astronaut Colonel Glenn . . . but rather who leaked the news about the big White House twist party when even the Secretary of Defense, to the amazement of his generals, twisted and when the President himself danced until 4:30 a.m." The twist was thought to be rather daring, and some people were shocked that it was being danced in the White House.

There was, indeed, a certain unreality to these evenings—to be dancing like that in those historic and elegant rooms. Once, while Phil was twisting with Ethel Kennedy, she used the occasion to ask, "Now that you have a president you can be 100 percent for, why aren't you 100 percent for him?" "Well, I'll tell you, Ethel," replied Phil. "*You* can be 100 percent for him."

A few months later, there was another dance at the White House. Guests were assembling in the Blue Room and Phil said, "Jackie, it's even better this evening to be here. I loved the first time but I felt sort of tense." In her magical voice, Jackie interrupted, "And now you just think it's Hamburger Heaven?"

President Kennedy's charm was powerful. His intense concentration and gently teasing humor, and his habit of vacuum-cleaning your brain to see what you knew and thought, were irresistible. The Kennedy men were also unabashed chauvinists, as were the great majority of men at the time, including Phil. They liked other bright men, and they liked girls, but they didn't really know how to relate to middle-aged women, in whom they didn't have a whole lot of interest. This attitude made life difficult for middle-aged wives especially, and induced—or fed—feelings of uncertainty in many of us in those years. Though the men were polite, we somehow knew we had no place in their spectrum. My ever-present terror of being boring often overwhelmed me in social situations with the president and at the White House, particularly whenever I was face to face with the president himself or one of his main advisers, and my fear was a real guarantee of being boring, since it paralyzed and silenced me.

I only felt secure when Phil, whom the president liked, was with me and could do the talking. Douglas Dillon's wife, Phyllis, who I thought was the height of sophistication, confided to me that she felt the same way: she complained that she was always left on the sidelines with Rose Kennedy at parties in Palm Beach.

One notable exception to the chauvinist tradition was Adlai Stevenson. Women enjoyed Adlai. In the end, my mother, my daughter, and I all had close friendships with him. Clayton Fritchey once told me a story that helps explain Adlai's appeal—and that contrasts it with what many of us felt about other men in the Kennedy administration, including the president himself. About three weeks before Kennedy was assassinated, Clayton saw the president in New York, at a time when Adlai was the ambassador to the United Nations and Clayton was his deputy. The three men were together at a party, and Clayton was helping himself to a drink on the balcony overlooking Central Park when the president came up behind him and said, "We haven't had a chance to talk much tonight, but we've got a good subject in common," meaning Adlai. The president then told Clayton he didn't understand the hold Adlai had over women, commenting on how much Jackie liked and admired him and confessing that he himself didn't have the ease with women that Adlai had. "What do you suppose it is?" he asked, adding, "Look, I may not be the best-looking guy out there, but, for God's sake, Adlai's half bald, he's got a paunch, he wears his clothes in a dumpy kind of way. What's he got that I haven't got?"

Clayton's response hit on what I think women saw in Adlai and what they shied away from in other men of that era. "Mr. President, I'm happy to say that for once you have asked me a question I'm prepared to answer, one I can answer truthfully and accurately. While you both love women, Adlai also likes them, and women know the difference. They all respond to a kind of message that comes across from him when he talks to them. He conveys the idea that they are intelligent and worth listening to. He cares about what they're saying and what they've done, and that's really very fetching."

The president's response was: "Well, I don't say you're wrong, but I'm not sure I can go to those lengths."

I SPENT QUITE a lot of time that fall of 1961 working on Lally's coming-out party, to be given at my mother's house over the Christmas holiday, when Lally was home from college. I adhered to the 26th of December as the night for a big party, because my mother had given annual gala parties that night as each of her four daughters came of age and made her debut. Mother, who tended to deal harshly in her appraisals of others, paid me the first lavish compliment I remember receiving from her. She looked at me one day during the preparations for the party and said, "Darling, you are very good with lists."

At the party there was a happy mixture of our friends, some of my mother's friends, and, of course, a great many of Lally's. Grown-ups wore white-tie; the young wore black-tie. Don, Bill, and Steve wore their best suits, and Steve went through the receiving line several times. Susan Mary Alsop recalled how handsome Phil and Lally looked as "we all stood back and he waltzed Lally from one end of the ballroom to the other. They were the best-looking, most lovely couple I ever saw. And the most dramatic, with Lally's black hair flying and he so fine."

It was, indeed, an enchanting evening, and one of our last really good and happy times.

— *Chapter Sixteen* —

OR ALL THEIR BUSYNESS, the first six months of 1962 had a certain stability and comforting routine to them. Phil still didn't feel very confident and didn't trust his instincts; one day he said he had an idea, but it couldn't be a good one because it was his. A young Otis Chandler had taken over the *Los Angeles Times* as its publisher and had ambitious plans to develop it from a partisan and mediocre paper to an independent one of quality. Phil saw the chance to get together with Chandler and form a news service, with each paper adding to the number of its correspondents abroad and perhaps helping pay for the expansion by selling the combined product to twenty-five or so other big papers.

Otis reacted favorably, and Phil and I went out to California to advance the plan, and the Los Angeles Times–Washington Post News Service was launched successfully that year, with thirty-two initial subscribers. It has since grown and now goes to more than six hundred newspapers, broadcast stations, and magazines here and around the world.

On July 7, Phil and I left with Chip and Avis Bohlen for a week's vacation to the lodge in Nova Scotia owned by Bowater Mersey, which supplied the *Post*'s newsprint. The trip with the Bohlens was memorable in part because Phil seemed well and in balance. Only once during the week did he ask me to take a walk and talk to him because he was a little down. He still needed help, but my main thought was, "How marvelous, he's well again. He's recovered."

What we didn't know during the trip was that Chip had been notified by President Kennedy that he was going to be appointed ambassador to France. Chip and Avis were extraordinarily discreet, not saying a word. Avis was reading Camus' *La Peste* in French, which might have tipped us off but didn't. We had no sooner gotten back from Canada than the appointment was announced. A few days later, we went out on the president's boat for a dinner in honor of the Bohlens. The guests were all on the open fantail of the boat when Kennedy's car pulled up. There was a largish circle of friends sitting on folding chairs, and the only unoccupied chair was one next to me, so the president had no choice but to sit in it. I looked at Phil, silently imploring him to come over and help, but, despite knowing of my nervousness at talking to the president—or perhaps because of it—he just looked at me and smiled sympathetically.

My insecurity was exacerbated by my feeling that the president had been forced to sit next to me. Nevertheless, we began chatting. He wanted to know about the Bohlens' oldest daughter, Avis, who was a very able young woman. (Now one of the stars of the Foreign Service, she has just been named ambassador to Bulgaria.) I told the president that she was an extraordinary girl and that she was writing a book on Peter the Great. "I wonder if she's been around her family too long?" he inquired—referring to their long diplomatic career. I knew what he meant—Avis was somewhat shy and retiring—but I reiterated that she was a terribly nice girl and how much I liked her. He looked at me quizzically and said, "Oh, we like nice girls, Kay."

The day after the boating party, Phil and I left for Florida, taking Steve with us for the dedication of Bill Graham's project, Miami Lakes, the planned development of the original family farm, which eventually became a community of almost twenty-five thousand people. Something very significant happened to me while we were in Florida. I had been feeling that Phil, after five long years, was finally better. His depression seemed gone, and he was growing more interested in work again. What baffled me was my own mood. My emotions seemed to be changing from one week to the next. I was happy in Canada, when we were with the Bohlens, but I found myself in tears much of the time we were in Florida and had no idea why. It was only later that I realized it was Phil's sudden mood change that had so affected me. The little walk we'd taken in Canada to overcome his momentary depression had been the last time he'd been calm. It is clear to me now that the almost-in-balance period was suddenly over, and that one of hyperactivity—with its accompanying anger and vitriolic diatribes—was beginning. I have since learned that manic-depressive cycles, when left untreated, tend to grow more severe and occur closer together. What I was experiencing was a quickening and an intensifying of these cycles.

One thing he did was begin to buy things—some sensible, some less so. In addition to part of the Bowater paper mill—which he had more or less negotiated while we were on the boat returning from Canada, during a shuffleboard game with the head of the mill—the first week in August he bought the monthly magazine *ARTnews*, the oldest continuously published art magazine in the world. Phil considered the purchase "Not a big investment of dough, nor a big bother of time and energy, but considerable fun and prestige—and a reasonable profit. So all very pleasant." Essentially, he bought it for me, thinking I could be involved with it in some way that would fit my growing interest in modern art.

PHIL'S INCREASING NEED to be always on the go resulted in a hastily planned summer trip to Europe with the children, from which we returned in time for Don to head off to Harvard. He had graduated that June from St. Albans, a year younger than his class but close to the top. Phil's advice to him on departure was clear—and unusual for a newspaperman: "Stay away from the *Crimson*. You have lived in a journalistic atmosphere, either at our house or the Friendlys'. You've edited the *St. Albans News*. You ought to study other subjects, to broaden your horizon." Don waited three months before trying out for and making the *Crimson*. From then on it constituted much of his life at Harvard, and he eventually was its president.

Our own routine resumed after Europe, with the difference that we were going out more and Phil was working harder. He pulled off a significant coup by signing Walter Lippmann to write a fortnightly column for *Newsweek* and the *Post*, to be syndicated by the *Post*. This was a stunning development, since Walter's column had been appearing in the *Herald-Tribune* since 1931. Despite his advancing years, Lippmann was still the pre-eminent commentator, and the column was a distinguished asset —much quoted and very influential and a great boon, especially for *Newsweek*. At the same time, Phil signed up Emmet Hughes for a weekly column for *Newsweek*. Oz Elliott, however, had not been told about this arrangement, and was none too happy that Phil had hired Hughes without consulting him.

The pace picked up still further. Phil was pressuring the president on two subjects. For one, he argued that Dean Rusk should be removed as secretary of state and replaced with David Bruce. The other subject—a tax cut—met with a more sympathetic reception. Phil was convinced that there was a need for a tax cut to boost the economy. He made his arguments in a long, well-reasoned letter to the president that makes it clear that his mind was still functioning brilliantly.

From October on, Phil was increasingly given to impatience and anger. Besides working constantly to improve the Los Angeles Times–Washington Post News Service, maintaining his trusteeships at RAND, the Committee for Economic Development, and George Washington University, and keeping his hand on the tiller at the *Post* and *Newsweek*, he had several other balls in the air. He had undertaken a major speech, which he hadn't done for quite a while, agreeing to address the twenty-fifth anniversary dinner of the Washington Building Congress. He spoke of the "full-blown crisis" facing Washington, saying that the Year 2000 Plan for the city was being used as "an opiate by planners and by out-and-out obstructionists to tranquilize us against our day-to-day and year-to-year problems." The speech was positively received. Even the *Star* covered it and editorialized that Phil had "delivered an eloquent and perceptive analysis of the shortcomings plaguing the Nation's Capital." Incredibly, Larry Stern, a *Post* reporter who had helped draft the speech, also covered it for our paper.

One interesting sidelight on this dinner is that the executive secretary of the organization had written to Phil beforehand, inviting me by saying, "One way you can tell that the Washington Building Congress is getting older is that it has decided that the ladies should be invited to share the head table with their husbands. . . ." Phil sent this to his assistant with a note: "Call . . . and say Kay will be delighted and then tell Kay how delighted she is." This peremptory message from Phil says something both about his mood and about our relationship; it also says something about the role of women in those days. It was assumed that I would go where Phil wanted me, and in fact I assumed it, too.

In October, Phil took on a job that changed both our lives and sped us up even more. He accepted an invitation from President Kennedy to serve as an incorporator of the Communications Satellite Corporation, known as COMSAT, with the understanding that he would be elected to head it, and in mid-October he was appointed chairman of the group. COMSAT was a groundbreaking public/private organization, half government, half telephone company. Getting it launched—in essence, translating an exciting vision into a working, financially viable organization—was a full-time job, requiring massive organizational skills, infinite tact and patience, and a huge amount of time and energy. It was not what Phil needed at that time, but it was what he wanted—an irresistible temptation to be engaged in an exciting venture that would, in fact, alter the shape of the world.

SIMULTANEOUS WITH Phil's appointment to head COMSAT, there was an ominous development abroad. Signs of a crisis emerged at a dinner party Joe and Susan Mary gave on the night of October 16, a send-off party for the Bohlens, who were about to leave for Paris. Joe had wanted President Kennedy to attend the dinner to show the French that this ambassador was important to the president. Besides the Alsops and Bohlens, there were only a few guests—the president and Jackie; the French ambassador, Hervé Alphand, and his wife; Isaiah Berlin, who had come down from Harvard, where he was teaching on an exchange program; and Phil and me.

The president had just that morning received the first pictures of Soviet missiles being erected in Cuba, but he had decided to keep his normal schedule and attend the dinner. When he arrived, he barely greeted anyone before he led Chip out to the end of Joe's garden for a long talk. It appeared to some of us who glanced out that they were arguing. Joe began to think they'd never come in and started pacing, but just when Susan Mary was convinced the meal would be ruined if it was held up any longer, they returned and we all sat down to dinner.

The president was sitting on Susan Mary's right. "I felt extraordinary tension," she later recalled. "I've never felt anything like it. It was a physical sensation. I felt I was sitting by a very high-powered motor, which was revved up to its fullest powers." The other thing that struck her was that the president, who so rarely repeated himself, so rarely monopolized dinner conversation, asked the same question twice, first of Bohlen, then of Berlin: "What have the Soviets done historically when their backs are to the wall? How do they behave?"

Joe remembered the president as being "in a brown study the whole evening." When the men separated from the women, as they regularly did after dinner, he recalled Kennedy saying, "Of course, if you think simply about the chances in history, you have to quote the odds as somewhere near even that we shall see an H-bomb war within the next ten years." When the men rejoined the women, the president again took Chip into the garden, where they stood talking. Finally, they came back and the president left, apologizing that he had an early and hard next day, and still arguing with Chip as he went down Joe's front steps.

This was at the start of the Cuban Missile Crisis. Chip was a member of the team Kennedy had assigned to advise him, and the president, it turned out, had been urging him to stay home and remain part of this Executive Committee. But, knowing that a change of his plans might tip off the Soviets, Chip advised the president that he and Avis should sail the next day as arranged. Joe reflected later that this showed what a real pro Chip was—sacrificing his own participation in the crucial event of the decade for what he thought was the greater good.

The president, still keeping up the appearance of normalcy, left for a scheduled weekend of political campaigning. He was in constant touch with the Executive Committee, then pleaded a cold and returned from his trip to preside over the ExComm in its final debate. The course was decided—a blockade rather than a military strike, which had also been considered. By the weekend, the story, kept so tightly secret all week, started to leak. *The New York Times* noted troop movements and other activities and prepared a story by Scotty Reston. When Scotty checked it with the White House, a plea by the president to *Times* Publisher Orvil

Dryfoos got the story killed, on the understandable grounds that, according to Arthur Schlesinger, "publication might confront him with a Moscow ultimatum before he had the chance to put his own plans into effect."

By October 20, the *Post* began to get wind that something was going on. Al Friendly was giving a dinner at his home when Walter Lippmann phoned to say that something serious was up. Friendly called Murrey Marder at home and then went to the office, from where he called Arthur Schlesinger at the White House. Schlesinger said only that everything was "tense and tight." This, plus the fact that the president had returned from Chicago with his alleged cold, was all we had.

Marder then did a brilliant piece of reporting. At that time there was a check-in book at the State Department, which no longer exists because of this very story. Marder observed that two people from the CIA had just checked in. He thought this was odd on a Saturday night. Certain that a crisis was at hand but not knowing where, he raced around the department and found that the only lights on were in the Latin American Bureau and the Bureau of International Organization Affairs, which included the United Nations, and of which Harlan Cleveland was assistant secretary. Running into Cleveland, Marder had to think quickly of a question that might elicit a useful answer, which an open-ended one like "What's going on?" clearly would not. So he asked, "How bad does it look to you, Harlan?" to which Cleveland replied, "Well, pretty bad."

By that time, Marder had eliminated the idea of Berlin or the Middle East and guessed Cuba. Hoping to get Cleveland to confirm his guess without asking him directly, Murrey asked, "Is it going to be like last time"—referring to the Bay of Pigs—"where you're going to be in on the crash landing but not the takeoff? Are you people in the loop this time on this Cuban thing?" Cleveland said, "I think we are."

So, on Sunday, October 21, the *Post* published a story about a crisis that appeared to be centered in Cuba. President Kennedy blew his stack; he had fended off the *Times*, which actually had about half or three-quarters of the story, and here, out of the blue, came the *Post*, to which nobody was paying much attention.

Apparently, Kennedy called Phil that day and asked him to move the paper away from targeting Cuba. Unaware of this, Chal Roberts and Murrey were racing around town trying to put together whatever they could. Phil, in Al Friendly's office, called Marder in and asked him if he was sure he knew what he was doing. When Marder told him what had happened the night before, Phil said, "Oh, my God, is that all it's based on?" Murrey went back to his typing, and Al said we weren't sold on the Cuba angle, so we were going to take it out of the lead. To this day, Murrey says he doesn't know what President Kennedy said to Phil or what Phil agreed to, but clearly Phil wanted the *Post* to stop focusing on Cuba.

The next day's story ran under an eight-column banner, "Major U.S. Decision Is Awaited." Marder, without a byline, began:

> Official Washington yesterday wrapped itself in one of the tightest cloaks of secrecy ever seen in peace-time while key policymakers worked out a major international decision they were forbidden to discuss.
>
> At the White House and the State and Defense departments, officials refused to confirm or deny reports published in The Washington Post yesterday that Cuba is the focus of the extraordinary operation.

That day, Monday, October 22, President Kennedy briefed congressional leaders and spoke to the nation in the evening, revealing Cuba as the locus of the crisis. Bill Walton and a friend, Helen Chavchavadze, who were to dine with the Kennedys, watched the speech at Bill's house in Georgetown and then tore down to the White House to be there by the time the president got upstairs from the basement broadcast facility. Bill recalled telling Kennedy that he had given a very impressive peace speech, to which Kennedy replied, "But right now, we are just listening and praying. We don't know what's going to happen." At that moment a White House aide drew them aside and said, "If there is trouble, you and Miss Chavchavadze will be whisked off with them. And you'll just have to go," which meant going to a protected facility in the countryside built especially for the president. Helen burst into tears, sobbing that she couldn't go because she had left her two small children at home with a nanny. "I can't go; I won't go," she said. The aide quieted her by saying, "In fact, we think it will be all right."

Phil behaved perfectly well throughout the Cuban Missile Crisis, except perhaps for carrying out Kennedy's wishes too literally. But it was a hard call to make in view of what was at stake. My own reaction was one of concern for the world, but I didn't really believe it would come to all-out war and cannot remember feeling any personal fear. The prospect of nuclear war seemed more unreal to all of us than it actually was.

AT ABOUT THIS TIME, Phil made two more significant purchases, accelerating the buying trend so typical of this phase of the illness that no one had yet named; only later did I learn that buying things is a well-known symptom of manic-depression. In the first case, he saw a classified ad in the *Post* for a farm about five miles from Glen Welby, in Hume, Virginia—a farm that consisted of 365 acres and a house, all for $52,000. Phil sent for an aerial photo and, without even visiting, asked his lawyer to take care of everything so that he would only have to sign the final contract. He accomplished the whole purchase in just two weeks, with a $26,500 down payment, $20,000 of which was provided—ironically, as it later turned out—by me. I'm sure I had no logical reason for acceding to the idea of acquiring a second farm. No doubt I agreed to it because I agreed to almost everything. I certainly understood that we didn't need a second farm, but I believed that Phil had to be mollified. I also was fully aware that he'd often bought things about which I'd had doubts that turned out to be good acquisitions in the end. As usual, I thought, "Who am I to question this?"

Phil also decided to purchase a big, expensive plane, a Gulfstream 1. Normally, people ordered this kind of plane months ahead of delivery, but Phil wanted it so immediately that he took the model the Grumman company used for demonstration purposes. It was my mother who suggested we think about the consequences of having a plane at our disposal. She wrote Phil:

> Let me utter one caution about the plane. It is bound to speed up your lives far more than did the automobile in former days. You both need to protect your physical resources more than do other people with duller nervous systems. A great future lies before you which your beautiful partnership will make as joyous as it will be important to your country if you will both keep watch on your own and each other's health.

Mother was still totally unaware of Phil's problems, but was staunchly brave and supportive later, when, alas, she necessarily learned of his illness.

TOWARD THE END of October, the COMSAT incorporators held their first meeting. The need for haste in dealing with the beginnings of COMSAT contributed to the frantic pace of Phil's life and to his anger with anyone and anything that got in his way. He began to look for a chairman for COMSAT and turned to our friend General Lauris Norstad, who was soon to retire as Supreme Allied Commander in Europe. Phil pushed hard to get him to agree to take the COMSAT job, even involving the president and Secretary of Defense McNamara in trying to convince him. Phil also wanted Frank Stanton, his fellow RAND trustee but still CBS president, to become COMSAT's president and operating head.

On November 2, I flew up to Idlewild with Phil to see him off to Europe, where he was going to talk to Larry Norstad about COMSAT. Early the next day, Phil and Larry in Paris both wrote letters to Stanton. Phil felt such urgency about co-opting Stanton that he decided to send a personal messenger to ensure that the letters reached Frank in New York. Late on the afternoon of November 3, Frank's secretary buzzed him to say that there was somebody waiting with a message for him. He said, "Just take the message and I'll get it later," but the secretary insisted, "No, *she* wants to see you." According to Frank, a young woman then came in, sat down, and said, "Here's something Mr. Graham wanted me to give you." Frank thanked her and put the letters on his desk, intending to read them later. She said, "Aren't you going to read these? I came all the way across the ocean with this message. You ought to look at it."

The appearance in New York of this young woman, whose name was Robin Webb, was the beginning of the tragic end. I have only been able in later years to piece together some of what had happened up to that point and what happened in the ensuing months. Larry Collins, then head of *Newsweek*'s Paris bureau and later a well-known author, had received a call from Phil asking to have a secretary on a standby basis for that November weekend. Larry sensed that this was important and that it had to be someone he trusted—that he couldn't just call a secretarial service in Paris. The office secretary's English wasn't good enough for dictation, and he knew that Robin, who was a *Newsweek* stringer, could do the job, so he called and asked her to fill in.

Robin was actually quite an able journalist, Larry recalled. "She was Australian. She was very much one of the boys, a little bit 'matey.' She was fun and very nice. Drank a fair amount in the good Australian tradition. A nice kid is what you would say. Worked very hard and did very well for us." When Larry called her, her first response was, "I'm not a secretary. I'm a journalist," to which Larry said, "Come on—don't be stupid. This is going to give you a chance to know the boss." She agreed reluctantly, but insisted that Larry never ask her to take dictation again.

Phil later told Collins he had "borrowed your secretary for 48 hours" to deliver the letters to New York. He also mentioned he had told Robin that once she got there she could use his suite at the Carlyle and relax and enjoy New York for a couple of days before returning to Europe.

The connection between Phil and Robin had been just that quick. On November 5, Phil himself flew back to New York, where I met him. We came home to Washington, and then he flew back to New York the following day, went to *Newsweek* for an editorial conference, saw Frank (who had never really been interested in the job), and, most important, picked up Robin and flew to Glen Welby with her. And so it began. I don't know how long she stayed in the United States, but when she returned to *Newsweek*'s Paris bureau, she was discreet about the relationship with Phil, though it was clear, according to Larry Collins, that she was on cloud nine.

When Phil came back from Glen Welby on that Friday, November 9, he skipped some scheduled RAND conferences but did attend a meeting at the *Post*. That night we went to the White House for dinner. The next day, Phil and I took my mother in the Gulfstream to Hyde Park for Eleanor Roosevelt's funeral. After their rocky adversarial early relations, my mother and Eleanor Roosevelt had grown very close—a really intimate friendship, involving many mutual interests, both personal and political. They were both in somewhat the same mold—very strong, cerebral, emotionally complicated, and fundamentally lonely. My mother was deeply saddened by Mrs. Roosevelt's death. She had only two tickets to the funeral, so Phil escorted her to the service while Steve—whom we took along with us so that he wouldn't be left alone in Washington—and I waited for them in the Poughkeepsie airport.

PHIL'S BEHAVIOR GREW more and more erratic. Things were getting very bad and much more public, but we all excused his angry, aberrant moods as signs of exhaustion. He *was* doing a great deal—and a great deal of what he was doing was still very good. At the same time, however, he began to turn on everyone around him with incredible explosions of anger. Blowups directed at Russ and Al were particularly extreme and became more regular, but both men covered up, so that others at the *Post* weren't aware of either their frequency or their severity. Max Isenbergh, an old classmate and colleague whom Phil had recruited to work with him on COMSAT, recalled one day when Phil gratuitously turned on him. Nothing had stimulated him; he just wanted to be abusive, Max said— which seems typical of the explosions that were becoming habitual. Max also later told me that, around the time of the embargo of the news on Cuba, they were in Phil's office when Phil got a phone call from the president. Max started to leave, but Phil told him to stay, and he heard Phil "talk to the president as I have never heard two French truck drivers in an accident talk to each other. And the president did not hang up."

Phil was becoming more intolerant and offensive, using foul language to excess. During the summer of 1962, he had started to direct his angry outbursts at me. But there was worse to come. In mid-November, he met with the incorporators of COMSAT on what turned out to be a traumatic occasion. At one point, probably toward the end of the afternoon session, according to Max Isenbergh, Phil turned to him and said, "Moose"—

Max's nickname—"take over, I'm going to the Metropolitan Club to get a massage," and he walked out. That session was adjourned fairly soon afterwards, and everyone went off to dinner at the F Street Club, where Phil rejoined them. It was here that one of the board members, Byrne Litschgi, responding to a press release that had been prepared that afternoon and which concentrated on relatively minor appointments of personnel and consultants, suggested that it was "very important that the public know that you're having stellar personnel and that's a policy of COMSAT, but I think we ought to have a policy statement of some kind very soon."

At that point, Phil became abusive and lunged across the table as if to strike Litschgi. People were aghast, and Phil was escorted out of the room. Everybody was baffled; no one knew what to do. Several of the incorporators stayed there talking until about 2:00 a.m.

Phil came home and recounted the story to me, telling me how this man had pushed him beyond endurance and that he felt he had to go away for a rest and to regain his calm. The very next day, we made hasty plans to leave for Palm Springs, though when we got there he decided he didn't like it in California, so we packed up and left for the Arizona Biltmore in Phoenix. We took with us on this trip Liz Hylton, who had been recruited from the accounting department by Phil's secretary, Charlie Paradise. She had been unhappy in accounting, and Phil had brought her in as number three in his office. Liz remains with me to this day, my invaluable assistant.

After only a few days away, Phil wrote to Litschgi, managing to work in some of his resentment against the man and only half backing off:

> I realize that the conventionally proper form after an outburst of anger such as mine, would be to write a note of apology and to ask you to forget the episode. . . .
>
> But after five days of rest and sun and contemplation I am not going to be so conventional—because to do so would be so patronizing, and inhuman, and insincere. . . .
>
> I shall say this. It is very regrettable for anyone to flare as I did. But I think it is equally (more?) regrettable for anyone to act as woodenly, unimaginatively and frustratingly as you have acted as incorporator. . . .
>
> Enough of that. I have told myself that you are perhaps under strain by reason of being new to being on boards. I have told myself you may simply be one of those unfortunates who utterly lack a sense of humor or a spirit of imagination.
>
> But it is not for me to presume to make such patronizing analyses of you. . . . Don't fight being angry. Emotions are more helpful to useful human actions than they admit in Harvard Law School.

And you are entitled to be angry over my mean and hyper-bolic blast.

I want sincerely to apologize to you—and then go on and work with you—in agreement or in direct, manly, outspoken dis-agreement. Heaven knows, there is room for lots of disagreement in this matter. And direct, open disagreement can let in light and lead to sensible solutions.

And I will apologize to you and work with you—when I have heard a forthright expression of your grievances and any ac-knowledgment of your possible lapses you may care to make.

A couple of weeks later, Phil wrote Litschgi again, this time opening with an honest self-analysis of this incident:

I fear I am like some deep-sea animal, who cannot rise quickly to the surface without excess decompression.

In any event, my rise has been slow.

My first letter to you was just part of the gradual decom-pression.

Now I wish to say that I have thought through the situation. And now I can with complete honesty say:

1) I wish to apologize fully.

2) My behavior was inhumane and unpardonable.

3) I cannot plead mitigating circumstances because I don't be-lieve in them for such bad conduct.

I also want to say that you have behaved yourself in a most gentlemanly way. I hope and believe your example will be conta-gious—as far as I am concerned.

I look forward to working with you.

It's impossible to know whether time or a third person brought about this change in view.

Apart from dealing with some correspondence and business, mostly COMSAT-related, Phil and I had a comparatively quiet time in Phoenix, playing golf and resting. In the middle of the first week, Phil asked me to go with our plane to the Lockheed field in Burbank, California, to tell the people there how to redesign the interior, which was due for refitting in early December. Our "showroom" model plane had partitions with cutouts of dancing girls and "Come to Hawaii" motifs, all of which were to be taken out and replaced, and I was to choose the fabric and design. Phil also suggested that while I was in California I should call my sister Flo and meet her for lunch. Initially I protested, thinking it would be too difficult to arrange and saying that in any case we were supposed to go to

Los Angeles the following week to meet about the news service, so why bother now. "Call her," Phil insisted, "and if necessary meet halfway."

So I did. Flo and I met at the Brown Derby and had a long, touching, memorable lunch. We talked intimately about our parents, with her railing at great length about how much she disliked Mother, who, she complained, had succeeded in breaking up Flo's most important early romances—one with David Grene, whom I had known at Chicago, and one with Drew Pearson, who had been judged not suitable by my mother. Flo viewed that particularly bitterly, given that Mother later became a great friend of Drew's.

Flo was so obviously sad and tormented by all these events in the distant past that I finally said, "Wouldn't you be happier if you put all this behind you? After all, you are fifty and she's seventy-five. Isn't it time?" My question had little effect; she remained adamantly negative about Mother. Ours, however, happily for me, was a close and loving exchange. Except for the unhappiness about the past, she seemed well. When I left her, we were both looking forward to our return to Los Angeles in a week or so and seeing more of each other.

Four days after our lunch, a messenger came and got me in the middle of a golf game to say that Flo had died suddenly. As far as anyone knows, there was no warning. Grief-stricken as I was, I felt and remain grateful to Phil for insisting that I call her for that lunch.

We immediately flew to Los Angeles. Again, Phil rose to the occasion and was the greatest help in every way to Flo's boys—Vincent and Larry—and to me. I was deeply fond of Flo. She was so beautiful and funny and literate—and sad. She adored her boys and had brought them up carefully and closely. I will never be able to appraise the strange relationship she had with the Halperns, who seemed to have such a strong hold over her. After Flo's death, they produced a letter signed by her saying that if anything happened to her they, the Halperns, were to have the boys. Soon after the funeral, the Halperns left for Europe without telling any of us, taking the boys with them. Flo had had a bitter divorce, and the eventual settlement excluded her husband from her boys' lives. He remarried and, I think, took no interest in them. After that it became next to impossible to see or know the Homolka boys until the younger one, Larry, returned home and married his high-school girlfriend against the Halperns' will. Vincent lives in England and relates to Mrs. Halpern. I've seen him only once. He gave most of his money away and lives a spartan existence.

After Flo's funeral we went back to Phoenix, and the night before we headed home had drinks with Harry and Clare Luce in their house, which adjoined the Biltmore grounds. Despite the few weeks of rest interspersed with a certain amount of activity, Phil's mood was agitated. At dinner that night, he removed Clare's plastic shoes, declaring them to be unworthy of her. Then, as we were leaving, he picked her up and carried her to the car, clearly a reflection of his fundamentally aberrant behavior.

ONLY the superficial effects of all Phil's activity—the news-service expansion, the purchase of *ARTnews*, the acquisition of Walter Lippmann's and, later, Joe Alsop's columns, COMSAT, editorial and business decisions at *Newsweek* and the *Post*, buying the airplane and the second farm—were evident to the outside world. The last week of November 1962, *Time* ran an article about Phil titled "The Acquisitor," in which the reporter asked if there were any more columnists to come, to which Phil responded, "Well, I could have had another big one, but I didn't want to seem greedy." The article also quoted Phil as saying, "I'm looking for another TV station or two, and maybe a pulp mill."

December brought with it a quick return to the old heightened level of activity. Phil, still trying to get a team of people to take over the leadership of COMSAT, flew back and forth to New York several times in the next week and had another important meeting with the incorporators in New York on December 10. This time, he received a telegram from Sam Harris, effectively Phil's vice-chairman, saying, "I knew that you could do it. Congratulations. Let us continue to reason together." Phil himself thought this third meeting went quite well. As he wrote to George Killion, a COMSAT incorporator who had not been able to attend, "At least I did not repeat my offer to hit anyone."

At the same time, Phil took part in some important RAND meetings, which he hosted at the *Post*. I've never been clear what he was engineering for RAND, but he received a telegram from its vice-president saying he had heard that Phil's "superb performance saved the day. The country, the Air Force and the people who are RAND all won. I can assure you at least the latter group will not soon forget. We'll strive to merit your success." Here was yet another demonstration that, even in the midst of this darkening scene of hyperactivity, rage, and irrationality, Phil still retained much of his ability and got significant things accomplished.

On December 13, he went to the White House to meet with President Kennedy to report on space-communications issues and a few other matters, and the next day he flew to Europe on COMSAT business. It was on this second trip within five weeks that Phil reconnected with Robin Webb. On the official schedule, she was described by Phil as "Newsweek reporter and temporary personal shopper, tour director and femme de chambre for our group." I had no idea what was going on in Paris, except that I thought Phil was engaged in a very important task. Soon after he came home, we settled in at our R Street house for the Christmas holidays. Phil had grown increasingly to dislike Christmas, and gradually I had taken over everything having to do with it—decorating, planning, gift-buying, parties—especially since his years of mood swings. That Christmas Eve afternoon, the world I had known and loved ended for me. The phone rang and I picked it up, not realizing that Phil, too, had picked it up, in his dressing room, with the door shut. I heard Phil and Robin talking to each other in words that made the situation plain. I waited until he had hung up and went right in and asked him if what I had surmised was true. He said it was.

It's hard to describe my total devastation after my discovery of the affair. This kind of thing has happened to innumerable people of both sexes, but I had never dreamed it could happen to me. I knew that marriages could endure momentary disloyalties, but this was different. It's very hard to understand, even in retrospect, how the possibility of his having an affair had never occurred to me, I was so blinded by the closeness of our relationship and by what we had been through together in the last years. My feeling that something fundamental had been destroyed was a result of my own total commitment and my belief that these feelings went both ways. Also, it was part of my bafflement at what I saw as Phil's increasingly strange behavior. I had no understanding of the context of the terrible depression he had come through or the polar-opposite mood that was dominating him at the time: not even then had anyone bothered to utter the term "manic-depressive." I truly believed that he and I were bound together by time, by choice, by shared experiences, by our family, and by the life of the company that was so important to both of us.

Phil was clearly upset, too. He told me that he wanted to preserve our marriage and our family; he said that he loved Robin but would tell her the affair was over, and that he would stay with his family.

It was a memorable Christmas holiday. I was wrenched apart by finding out about the whole thing, and Phil was torn at having decided to end it. He knew a breakup would be terribly difficult for Robin, so, to help her recover, he sent her on a vacation in the sunshine and even sent along a friend of his to keep her company. The friend turned out to be another girl from his past, about whom I, of course, had never known.

For some reason, in those immediate days after my discovery of Robin's existence, Phil seemed to have a compulsion to tell me much more than I wanted to know about this side of his life, of which I had been happily oblivious—about his past relations with other women, of whom there apparently had been several. I was, of course, shattered, as well as completely stunned to learn of his interest in others, including some of my own friends to whom he had made approaches, and Robin's companion, with whom he said he had had a long, strange relationship.

Of the children, at first only Lally knew that something was wrong. She had planned to go skiing in Aspen with friends over the holidays, but

Phil told her what had happened and asked her to give up her trip and stay home while we all tried to get our bearings, which she heroically did.

A sad, small, but symbolic event took place during this time, which seemed to me to be the nadir. We were at Crescent Place, and my mother gave me some long, pretty paste earrings of hers. It meant a great deal to me; she was not very forthcoming about that kind of thing, and it had never happened before. Phil said, "You don't wear long earrings and Lally does. Give them to her." How could I have simply obeyed? But I did. I handed them to Lally and went out by myself to the pantry, where I burst into tears. I suppose I didn't have the strength to resist and just quietly laugh and keep them, which any normal person would have done. To me, it was symbolic of losing everything. I felt ultimately demeaned.

During the few weeks after I found out about Robin, Phil drank a great deal and there were many problems, overlaid with our attempts to hold things together and keep our lives going. One night before the end of the college holidays, and so before Lally and Don went back to school, I had an especially hard time with Phil. We were at home, and he had had a lot to drink and was saying some wild things, most of which were not very rational. I finally got him to go to bed, but not until around two in the morning. When I came out of our room to turn off the lights throughout the house, I saw Don, looking spectral and drawn, sitting at my desk in the room right next door to the bedroom. "How long has this been going on?" he asked, referring to Phil's drinking and the row. I confessed that it had been for some time. "Why have you never told me?" he asked.

Should I have told him? Who knows? We all try to protect our children, and my natural response was to keep this from them. I don't know that I was right; perhaps it's better to share problems with children as they grow older.

We somehow got through the nightmare holiday season. Phil and I were both trying to make things work, to keep up some semblance of normalcy even as our personal world had fallen apart. We attended some dinners and went out a few times. I remember one evening going to a musicale at the Frankfurters'. On our return home, Phil reprimanded me for looking so dejected and drawn when we were trying to conceal things.

At the beginning of January, Phil went to New York for a meeting of COMSAT, which he was still running, and running well. He had breakfast with Larry Collins, who was leaving for Paris, telling him, too, that he was very much in love with Robin but wanted to get his priorities straight and keep the family together.

We were both just moving numbly through our days. Phil wired Lally at college about a routine matter, but it ended with: "All is very well here. Much love to you. Pa." At some point, however, not quite three weeks after Christmas Eve, the phones started to work again between Phil and Robin.

On January 12, 1963, after dinner, Phil and I had an argument—I can't remember what precipitated it. The upshot was that he walked out of the house holding a blanket, got in the car, and drove away. I had no idea where he'd gone. He later told me that if I had come after him he would have come home. My response was that I hadn't known where he'd gone, and still didn't know.

"Where would I go?" he replied. "The office, of course."

By this time, Robin had returned to Paris. Phil called and told her to come back to America as soon as she could. Evidently she protested, saying that she was just beginning to recover and that he had been right the first time, they should end the relationship. He said that if she didn't come he would come and get her. According to Larry Collins, Robin thought that Phil was in a really bad state and that she was the only person who could really talk to him, so she decided to come back.

Robin Webb behaved well throughout. She was as much caught up in the tragedy—and a victim of it—as the rest of us. She was obviously mesmerized by Phil, charmed out of her mind, and she couldn't have understood the background.

Phil flew to New York the day after he walked out of the house. I sent him a telegram reflecting my own despair:

Mascots are for loving helping and listening. You are stuck with me as a mascot repeat mascot. The moment of happiness you gave me is more help than most people are given in a lifetime. Thank you for it. I'm here if you need me and I love you.

Phil wrote me back a pretty strange letter:

Dearest Kay—

One morning when you were despairing I tried to help you by words. I told you how lonely it had been when I had visited my Far Country and how I could not get near enough to help you in your Far Country. And by the words you came near enough for help and I touched you and we went for a walk and were again in life.

I have now gone. Gone not to my Far Country but to my Destiny. It happens to be a beautiful Destiny and I shall be there while it is beautiful and while it is not.

I did not go to help you. I did not go because I did not want to help you. I went because it was my Destiny. And by not "helping" you I believe and I pray I shall *help* you.

I loved you and I shall always love you and I love you too

much to be false about major matters. And while you need help you will be getting it from me—now and always in this new but loving way. And you shall help me.

Love, Phil.

He added a P.S., saying, "Les will know my plans." Farber again. I wonder still what Farber must have advised Phil.

Lally called Larry Collins in Paris, told him of Phil's departure for New York, and asked where Robin was. Larry called her apartment and when he got no answer checked with TWA and found she was indeed on a plane flying to the United States. And so it all started again.

Phil welcomed Robin with a carload of flowers, and together they flew to Sioux Falls, South Dakota, where Phil and I had been scheduled to go, and where he was to make a speech to the Chamber of Commerce and to talk with the publisher of the local paper, the *Sioux Falls Argus Leader*, about buying it. George McGovern, then senator from South Dakota, flew along on this trip, and he later told me about the flight, on which Phil and Robin sat separately and Phil wept a good deal and spoke of loving me. The three of them were met by the publisher of the paper, who said he had heard great things about Phil, to which Phil replied: "I hear you are a son of a bitch." Naturally there was no sale of the paper.

I had told no one about Phil's departure—not even my mother. Finally, fully two weeks after he had left, I couldn't hide it any longer. I also felt the need for consolation from someone, so I walked down the hill to visit my friend Lorraine Cooper and told her what had happened and that Phil had left. Expecting the sympathy and commiseration of a friend, I was startled when she said, "Good!"

"What do you mean, good?" I replied. "It's terrible."

"No," Lorraine responded firmly. "You'll be better off without him."

"What do you mean?" I asked, incredulous.

"Don't you realize what he does to you? Don't you realize he puts you down all the time, that you are the butt of all the family jokes?" She gave me several instances. Though I didn't agree totally, I got a glimmer of what she meant, but Lorraine didn't understand the other side—that he had also built me up. I literally believed that he had created me, that I was totally dependent on him, and I didn't see the downside at all.

From Sioux Falls, Phil and Robin flew to Phoenix, where many of the nation's most prominent publishers were gathered for a meeting of the Associated Press. Otis Chandler and his wife, Missy, met Phil and Robin at the airport. According to Otis, who told me all of this only much later, Phil was disheveled and spinning out ideas, some of which Otis found interesting and others of which were unintelligible. It was clear to him that

Phil was not well. He said that from the moment he first saw Phil, he began to worry about how he was going to handle the dinner that evening and what he could do to help Phil get through it.

Otis was unsure if it was Phil's mental state or if he was keeping himself perpetually drunk—or both—but certainly Phil was making very little sense. He had even gotten upset over the Chandlers' not staying right next door to him and Robin at the Biltmore Hotel. Also, by this time there were a lot of four-letter words.

At the dinner, when Ben McKelway, editor of the *Star* and president of the AP, rose, Phil stood up and went straight to the lectern, where he began to speak. He started out saying some nice things about the *Star*, but his remarks quickly degenerated, turning into nonsense interspersed with ugly language. No one present that night has ever told me exactly what happened or what Phil said. Reports of his obscene comments have appeared in several books, but at the time those who witnessed this sorry spectacle seem only to have talked among themselves. As with other outrageous behavior by noted or known persons in those days, the incident was hushed up and not reported. Apparently, though, Phil's wild remarks attacked individuals as well as the press in general.

Nobody knew what to do. Finally, Ben McKelway's wife went up and managed to get him off the platform and back to his seat, but not before he had begun to take off his clothes. Otis and some other men got him to his room. From there, Phil actually called President Kennedy and, incredibly, must have gotten through to him at a late hour on Eastern time. Soon Otis had Phil banging on his door saying, "Come and talk to the president." When Otis said, "Phil, you didn't wake up the president, did you?" he responded, "Yes, he's a buddy and I want him to meet and talk to Robin."

Otis called John Hayes, the company's head of broadcasting, who also happened to be at a meeting in Phoenix, and got the message through that Phil needed to be taken out of there and back to Washington. Someone—I've never been sure who—reached President Kennedy, who agreed to the use of a government plane to transport the doctors to get Phil, for the situation was described as extreme.

By then, Phil had made telephone calls all around the country to many people, some close and some whom he hadn't seen in years. One of these calls had been to me. It was the only exchange I ever had with Robin Webb, and was a sensitive one. She said, "I do love him, but you were there first."

One of the most important calls Phil made was to Lally, who adored her father more than anyone in the world, but who was a pillar of strength and stability to me then and throughout all those terrible months at the same time as she was trying to be understanding with her father. She was always loving but firm with both of us. At this point she called me from Cambridge and said he needed her and she thought she had to go.

Since at that point it had been decided that Dr. Farber and a fine Scots psychiatrist, Ian Cameron, whom Farber had brought in to consult, were to bring Phil home, I was reluctant to have her go. I understood her desire but hated her being there for what was sure to be an ugly scene. Her response was adamant: "I'm his daughter and he says he needs me, so I have to go." I couldn't help agreeing.

Don drove her to the airport in Boston and, on an impulse, got on the plane and went with her. The doctors had decided to try to get Phil to return to Washington voluntarily, and if not to bring him back forcibly. I gather that Farber initially tried to read him passages from Martin Buber, and when this failed to work, they forcibly tranquilized him and put him on the plane. Under the strained circumstances, Robin was sent away with too little care and attention.

When the plane landed in Washington, there was an ambulance waiting and another scene in a small, private terminal at National Airport. At this point, Phil simply walked away, and had to be talked back by the children. The three of them then got into the limousine, and the doctors drove off in the ambulance without their patient. He was taken first to George Washington University Hospital and later to Chestnut Lodge, a private mental hospital in a suburb of Washington, selected by Farber. Phil viewed this whole sequence of events, with some reason, as a violation of his rights and civil liberties. As he was being taken out of George Washington, he loudly proclaimed who he was and what was being done to him and that he was a prisoner.

Once Phil was installed at Chestnut Lodge, where I considered him "safe," I wrote to President Kennedy, thanking him for being a "real life saver," and telling him that the hours that the government jet had saved the doctors "turned out to be critical as the situation snowballed so rapidly. No one involved could have lasted that much longer without serious harm being done in some way." I also thanked him for his kindness toward Phil, saying, "He would and will die at the thought that he might have hurt you in any way. I hope he didn't—too much—and was awfully relieved to hear you understood," and concluded that I knew Phil would recover.

The president realized, however, that Phil couldn't continue with COMSAT. He had Clark Clifford work through Les Farber to get a letter of resignation from Phil, which Phil signed three days after arriving at Chestnut Lodge. The president wrote Phil a routine public note saying, "I appreciate very much the devoted service which you have given to this exacting task and with great regret accept your resignation effective this date." He also wrote a more personal note, showing, as always, his sensitivity and concern: "I understand you are back in Washington. I hope that you will rest for a while—get feeling well again and then come back to work—as we need you. Best of luck."

The president answered my note that same day: "All of Phil's and your friends are strongly with you and are hopeful that things will now go better. No two people deserve it more."

Phil was seeing Dr. Farber daily at the hospital and Dr. Cameron when Farber was called out of town to visit a dying older brother. When the two psychiatrists and I were meeting with *Post* executives all deeply concerned about Phil, Cameron threw a bucket of cold water on the group by saying, "I don't understand why you all care so much about this man." As an outsider who didn't know Phil, he was reacting to everything he was hearing about Phil's behavior. I must say, that remark shook us up.

In meetings over the next few days, Farber and Cameron confessed to me that they were puzzled by my refusal just to give up at some point—by my protestations that I was a "one-man dog" and my unwillingness to accept that Phil might have left me for another woman, and my emotional belief that I could never love another man. In a way they were right to ask the questions, but in a way not. It may be unusual to think you can never love another person, and they certainly thought it suspect, but at the time it was true for me.

Phil's brother Bill came up from Florida to be with him and to represent him at this time. He stayed a few days, making an important phone call to Robin, and being enormously helpful to both Phil and me. Phil wrote him on January 27, thanking him "for electing yourself older brother *pro tempore*," and adding, "I am doing my steady best to relieve you of the latter responsibility with all deliberate (and prudent, patient, cautious, thoughtful) speed."

After a few days at the Lodge, Phil began going out to Les Farber's office for visits. Only five days after he had been flown back from Arizona, I saw him for the first time at Farber's office and drove back to Chestnut Lodge with him; I went again the next day. We talked for a long time, and he told me in great detail both how terrible the scene had been at George Washington University Hospital and how kind and wise had been the people at Chestnut Lodge, who had "talked him down" to his present fairly cool state.

Phil told Bill Graham of our talks, saying in his January 27 letter, "Kay and I are having especially good talks—the first free from any lies and deceit on my part in a good many years. She is still—as you know—very tired. And more deeply wounded than you may suspect."

We talked a lot about what had happened. I felt rocked to my foundations by all these events, but I knew I had somehow to endure them, difficult as that might prove to be, and I still hoped—and believed—that we could restore our relationship and keep Phil functioning and the family together. I suppose the repeated experience of seeing him resume his life after periods of depression encouraged me to believe that things would once again be all right.

Phil was also reading and thinking. He reread an article by Martin Buber on guilt and quoted a few passages to Bill, saying:

"No one other than he who inflicted the wound can heal it." And then he says that a man who has done evil must (1) "with a broad and enduring wave of light" find *self-illumination* about the sum total of his guilt; (2) even after he has long passed out of guilt to *persevere* in "humble knowledge" that he is the same man as the man who was guilty; (3) and then proceed on to *reparation* of the wounds he has caused. Those wounds cannot be called back or wiped away. But "the wounds . . . can be healed in infinitely many other places than those at which they were inflicted."

At the moment I am correctly placed to experience (1). And I am getting there not by orders or instructions but by having a quiet time—and the help of doctors and nurses—to permit me to get myself to full confession on my own. It is my first experience with confession. Humbling and strengthening. And I shall, older brother, keep working.

After about ten days at Chestnut Lodge, Phil went to see Dr. Farber three days in a row. I don't know whether I was deluding myself or whether it was some sort of denial, but I actually thought everything was going well and that Phil was once again on the road to recovery. I even wrote our good friend Cy Sulzberger, on January 31, that "things are working out both 'well and quickly' as you fondly hope. . . . You can certainly write Phil anytime and I can get it to him or, in fact, he may be home by the time it arrives as he is very much better."

Clearly unbeknownst to me, almost simultaneously with my naïve letter to Cy, Phil must have been having very different thoughts about the future. On the last day he visited Farber, Farber released him from the hospital. On February 1, Phil came home briefly, and the next day, a Saturday, he went to Glen Welby with Don and Al Friendly. However, on February 4, he traveled to New York with Edward Bennett Williams and Charlie Paradise and went straight to Idlewild Airport, where he met Robin once more. This time Phil saw his departure as final—something he may have been planning all along, since he later wrote to Clark Clifford, thanking him for "your goodness to Robin during our embattled two weeks. Only you and Frank Stanton (and the Commander-in-Chief) seem to have remembered that gentlemen should be kind to ladies—even young and beautiful ladies." He also said that he had "sweated my way out of that jail-sanitarium via a doctor's discharge, although I was tempted to get a lawyer and some quick habeas corpus until I thought of the kids and the publicity. Then I learned there were plans to shove me back in after I had Robin en route to the U.S. again. At that point I called Ed Williams. I wanted to call you—but you will understand I could not involve you because of some other friends and clients you have"—referring to the president.

Phil did engage Ed Williams as his lawyer and firmly stated his intention to divorce me and marry Robin, announcing this in letters to his friends as well. To Jean Monnet, Phil explained his absence at a dinner in New York by saying:

> I would have been at your dinner but for the fact that I was temporarily "jailed." I am now out, and you can tell Sylvia that I am extremely happy and fully back at work.
>
> In addition to my journalistic duties, I am giving considerable attention to a young Newsweek reporter—Miss Robin Webb. It is my hope to get a divorce in the reasonably near future and to marry Robin. Soon thereafter we hope to have a meal with you and Sylvia, if we are invited.

Phil also wrote a patient he had gotten to know at Chestnut Lodge, saying that he missed him and the other patients and would call on them as soon as he could arrange to. He encouraged one of the patients to write to him at *The Washington Post*, explaining, "After 3 days of 'returning home,' and a telephone call to Robin Webb in Paris, I realized what I wanted to do. She came over on February 4th and we are living in New York (in separate apartments on the advice of lawyers) and go for weekends to my funny farm near Hume, Virginia. I hope to get a divorce so that we can marry before too long."

Phil knew that he controlled the *Post* because my father had given him the majority of A shares. He felt he owned it because he had worked for seventeen years to make it a success, so from his point of view the paper was his. He contrived a plan, which quickly got back to me, of paying me off by buying back my stock with *Post* money. He and Robin would then be in charge.

In some ways, this was the bottom moment for me—very confusing, very difficult, and very painful. Not only had I lost my husband but I was about to lose the *Post*. I saw his plan as a logical aspect of his illness, and I knew he was really ill, but by now the effect was real and I was frightened. I was also terrified by Ed Williams's new role as Phil's lawyer. I didn't know Ed very well then, but I was aware of his reputation as a successful criminal attorney and litigator, and I envisioned terrible court scenes and battles.

I had to face facts—Phil was really gone. He had left me for good, and I had to come to terms with this devastating reality. It was almost more than I could bear. My feelings about the *Post*, however, were very clear. My father had indeed given Phil the major part of the stock, and Phil had run the company well, but it was my father's financial backing that had enabled the *Post* to build a new building and later to buy the *Times-Herald* and ensure its future. It was the millions invested in the paper by my father that enabled it to survive the years of losses. It was my paying all our living expenses that had allowed Phil to purchase his stock with his income from the *Post*. So my bitterness about his plans was extreme, and my intention to dig in was total. I was not about to give up the paper without a fight.

I needed a lawyer. As head of the company, Fritz Beebe—Phil's friend and mine—had to be neutral in all this, so the Cravath firm, our estate lawyers, sent me to the respectable and able Whitney North Seymour of Simpson, Thacher & Bartlett who advised me just to sit tight for the moment. Although I was prepared for the roof to fall in on me, nothing actually happened for the next few months. There was no movement toward divorce, despite all Phil's talk about it. Ed Williams told me later that he had advised Phil not to move right in with Robin but to live separately and to wait—that you couldn't walk out of your house one day and ask for a divorce the next.

Although I wasn't directly talking with Phil, I was always aware of his and Robin's whereabouts, either through other people's reports or through his calls to the children, which began soon after he left. He took Robin to Florida to meet his father, who, as Phil reported in a letter to Clark Clifford, "promised Robin he'd live long enough to come to our wedding even if the divorce took two years." Phil and Robin returned from Florida to settle in at the Pearson farm, the farm he had bought in the fall of 1962, with my help. There he began to build ponds and in essence to reproduce the life we had at Glen Welby. It was not unnatural that Phil would want to create a nice farm out of this ramshackle place he'd bought, but I found it haunting that the life he was reconstructing seemed to be a mirror image of everything we had done together—the farm, the house near Georgetown he eventually rented, and even his trips to Sioux Falls, Phoenix, and Puerto Rico, all of which were places where we had been together.

I went to Florida to see Bill Graham, to ask his advice. Bill was a true support for all of us throughout those months. After our talks, Bill flew me up to Hobe Sound to visit Douglas and Phyllis Dillon, two loyal friends. While I was there, I called the *Post*'s switchboard to connect with my house. The operator made a mistake, and before I knew it, I was connected with the farm and Robin was answering the phone. I hung up instantly, but the mistake let Phil know I was out of town. I then got a wire from him asking if he could see the children at the house alone. I was so tense about everything that I left the Dillons at once and flew home early to prevent Phil's coming over. I think now that I may have been too rigid at first about not letting him visit with Bill and Steve. They missed him and wanted to see him, but I was frightened by the unpredictability of his behavior. I didn't trust him or believe him. I didn't have a very clear idea of his condition and just reacted emotionally.

LIFE FOR ALL of us settled into a strained and endlessly painful pattern. I was on my own, trying to hold things together for myself and for the children. I kept working on the Junior Village project and was also engaged in an undertaking to start a modern-art museum in Washington. But Phil still dominated our lives. He wanted to see the children and to have them, particularly Lally, meet Robin. I feared he would even introduce her as their potential stepmother. This wouldn't have been the end of the world, I suppose, but, not surprisingly, I thought at the time that it would be. When Phil telephoned, the boys would go into a room and close the door—with me fully aware that they were experiencing the worst of all worlds, not being able to talk to one parent about the other. It was excruciating for all of the children in different ways, but especially hard on Lally. She showed great wisdom and strength and love for him, but not for what he was doing or the people around him at that time. She agreed to see him in New York, but found herself in a large group, including Robin, and firmly said that she didn't want to be a part of that. Don, too, was very vulnerable and supportive of both of us. We finally worked out times when Phil would take Bill and Steve out by himself, usually picking them up from school to avoid encountering me.

I continued to get reports from mutual friends about where Phil was and what he was up to, or I heard about his activities directly, in part because some of what he was doing was spectacular and quite public. At other times, things were quieter, but I would be aware of what Phil and Robin were doing because of bills or other mundane things that brought their comings and goings into my sphere. They seemed to be settling in together. I got wind of credit cards having been established for Robin, and that Phil had separated our billing in the country, so that everything at Glen Welby was in my name and everything at the Pearson farm was in his. When Phil's secretary, Charlie Paradise, asked me if I wanted to be listed in the phone book as "Mrs. Katharine Graham" rather than "Mrs. Philip Graham"—another small but severe irritation and wound—I said no.

Even during these months when he was living separately from me, I could see indirectly that Phil was doing some things that made sense and others that were puzzling. One of the more bizarre occurrences of this difficult time took place from February 22 to 26, when Phil went up to New York and inserted himself—uninvited and unwanted by the publishers—into the New York newspaper strike with the firm conviction that he could settle it. Here again, Phil involved President Kennedy, calling him to discuss the implications of the strike. In his 1975 book, *Conversations with Kennedy*, Ben Bradlee recalled: "Holding his thumb and forefinger close together, the President said, 'The line is so damn narrow between rationality and irrationality in Phil.' "

On March 1, Phil finally left for two weeks in Puerto Rico with Robin, during which time he again began buying things, arranging to rent with an option to acquire two apartments. Though these were ostensibly for the company, he and Robin intended to use them; he even wrote someone that they might make Puerto Rico their home base rather than the Pearson farm.

A few weeks earlier, Phil had had an argument with Russ Wiggins over an editorial about de Gaulle that Phil wrote and wanted to run in the paper—he had a kind of fixation on de Gaulle, seeing him as a great man standing alone. Phil wanted to fire Russ at some point during one such argument, but Al Friendly said, "If he goes, I go." Faced with the loss of both top editors, Phil had backed down.

Now he sent Russ an editorial he himself had written about the newspaper strike which he wanted printed in the *Post*. He also sent along seven pages he had typed himself that were highly critical of the editorial the *Post* had run on the strike, saying he should have been consulted and even suggesting an apology in print for the earlier editorial at the same time that the paper ran his. Russ not only refused to run Phil's editorial but said he would quit if the piece appeared. Phil backed down again, but it escalated his feud with Russ—to the point where Phil told Al Friendly to take over the editor's post. But Al again refused.

Phil also wrote several articles, including one on Cuba that appeared in the "Outlook" section and generated many positive letters, one of which was from the president, who added a note to his letter saying, "I hope you will come by some day soon." But as Chal Roberts reported later, "[W]hen Graham took to berating Kennedy over the phone, asking 'Do you know who you're talking to?' the President replied, 'I know I'm not talking to the Phil Graham I have so much admiration for.' "

The difficulties, indeed, were constant—for me, for Phil, and for the company and those trying to hold it together. The whole affair, as David Bruce noted in one of his diary entries, was "inexpressibly sad."

— *Chapter Seventeen* —

I SEEMED TO be living on another planet. The most painful moments—the ones that disturbed me the most profoundly—were those in which people reported to me that they had seen Phil and that he appeared to be rational and calm, indeed quite well. Even Fritz Beebe at one point told me he seemed fine. I had begun seeing Dr. Cameron by this time, and he assured me that people in these states could appear very normal for defined periods of time when they wanted to, but that fundamentally Phil was not rational, that he was ill. Even so, despite his assurances, the apparently normal encounters Phil was having with others shook me—about him, and about us. Was this the real Phil? And was this what he really wanted? If so, what did that say about our relationship, about our twenty-two years together? What he seemed to be saying was that whatever was the matter with him was my fault, and here was the girl of his dreams, and all he needed was to be rid of me and to be with her and with the *Post*.

Among my staunchest allies were the Restons. Scotty had seen Phil at two or three critical moments. According to him, "Phil thought my religious faith could help him":

> He thought, inaccurately, as it turned out, that I had this deep faith of my mother and father, which I wish I did have, but I did not have at that time. I did not tell him that. I told him that I thought that there were times in life when you go through all these things and did he have any feelings about religious faith that could help him through this period and he said no he did not. And I don't know what I said to him that time but it obviously was a failure. I was not able to get through to him, probably because I couldn't define it myself in any persuasive way and by then he just went away.

One day during this period when Phil was away, I myself went to see Scotty and Sally in a terrible state of despondency. Scotty remembers thinking that I was giving up, that I didn't seem to have the strength to go on. He said to me, "Kay, you've got to fight for this paper. It does not belong to Phil Graham. Your father created this paper. There is not room in Washington for two Graham families. You and I can't do anything about Phil, but we can start training Donny, and I would like to take him as my clerk this summer"—which he did.

The other person who stiffened my back was Luvie Pearson, who was the closest, most helpful, most ever-present friend throughout all those months. She somehow transmitted to me some of her own extraordinary strength and originality. The most important moment, one I will always remember, took place when the two of us were walking in Montrose Park, across the street from my house. I was talking about hanging on to the paper until the children, especially the boys—since in those days that's how I thought—were old enough to run it. I recall Luvie firmly and distinctly saying, "Don't be silly, dear. You can do it."

"Me?" I exclaimed. "That's impossible. I couldn't possibly do it. You don't know how hard and complicated it is. There's no way I could do it."

"Of course you can do it," she maintained. "Cissy Patterson did it. So can you." And to counter my disclaimers of impossibility, Luvie added, "You've got all those genes. It's ridiculous to think you can't do it. You've just been pushed down so far you don't recognize what you can do."

That was the first time that anyone had mentioned the idea of my running the company, or that I had even contemplated it in passing. The whole notion struck me as stunning and ridiculous, wrongheaded but sweet, coming as it did from my good, loyal friend who was trying valiantly to buck me up but who obviously didn't understand what running the business was all about and what it would take.

Though I didn't think much more about going to work myself, I did think a lot about what Luvie, and Lorraine before her, had said about Phil's attitude toward me, and I began to realize how he had been treating me, especially in the past few years. Jean Friendly later recalled certain times at Glen Welby when Phil was being very peculiar: "He was charming to the children and nasty to you. He was so mean at that point to you, I couldn't get over it." She correctly understood that I always viewed it as a joke and thus didn't see the comments and behavior as put-downs.

After Phil's return to Washington from Puerto Rico, I got a call saying he wanted to meet me at the R Street house to discuss the divorce and to pick up some of his things. I called Luvie and told her what had been proposed. "Listen, dear," Luvie said, "you don't need this. I'll come and pick you up right away and we'll drive out to my farm." I was frightened at the idea of seeing Phil face to face and uncertain how to handle it, so I readily agreed to Luvie's plan. We drove away in haste, spent the day at her farm, and returned to find that he had packed up most of his clothes and possessions and had apparently been angry at my absence.

At one point that spring, Polly Wisner and another friend, Oatsie Leiter, urged me to go to New York with them to see the ballet. I had mostly been staying at home, where I felt comfortable—being in my own house with the children gave me some sense of routine, as if everything hadn't fallen apart. I had particularly stayed away from New York, because that was part of Phil's and Robin's turf. I hated thinking of them in our apartment at the Carlyle and at *Newsweek* and at other spots Phil and I had frequented. Both Polly and Oatsie, however, thought this New York foray would be a nice diversion. On the contrary, it turned into one of those star-crossed occasions when a good idea goes sour by happenstance. Before the ballet, we were having dinner at "21" when Leonard Lyons, the gossip columnist, came up to us and said he'd heard Phil and I were getting a divorce and he was off with another woman, and was that true. I found my food hard to swallow after that interruption. Then we went on to the theater and discovered that our tickets were for the next night. So we bought whatever last seats were left in order to save the evening from being a complete bust.

No one conspired against this expedition—the whole fiasco was accidental. Nevertheless, it gave me a feeling of complete rejection and exclusion. I felt that no one cared, that I didn't count anymore, and that life was passing me by; all the good things were going to Phil. I was certainly vulnerable, ready to be wounded, so that even a petty misfortune like the tickets seemed to be a straw breaking more than the proverbial camel's back. The trip to cheer me up brought me down lower than ever.

M ANY OF OUR friends were caught in a bind. Quite often, they were pushed by Phil to receive Robin. For the most part they didn't, but said they would when things between Phil and me got sorted out. The Friendlys were particularly strong about stressing their love of him and loyalty to him but their disinclination to accept the new arrangement until it was legal. There was one sharp exchange by letter between Phil and David Bruce over David's refusal to have lunch with Phil and Robin, which David had said would be "untimely." Phil testily and angrily responded that there could be only one act that he felt David would really consider untimely, and "that would be the act of being rude to a lady and disloyal to a friend." Several days later, Phil wrote David again, saying he had been hurt and baffled and telling him, "I am *always* your friend. I apologize for stupidly thinking you could ever act toward me out of any motive but the highest kind."

There were very few happy times for me in those months. One was when Pamela Berry came to visit me over a weekend. Pamela was the wife of Michael Berry, later Lord Hartwell, owner of the *London Daily Telegraph*. She was an intelligent, strong, articulate woman, with a great wit—a leading London hostess and quite a political force in England. Though we were all friends, she was known to prefer men, so I naturally thought she was more Phil's friend than mine, but she connected almost entirely with me during this time. It was very reassuring to have her come stay with me and express such solidarity.

During this period, my mother was also very supportive, although she had to be restrained from occasional impulses to write Phil or get in touch with him on the theory that she had a special relationship with him, which in a way was true but in a more important way was not. At one point, she signed a will in which my brother, Fritz Beebe, and I and a bank representative signed an agreement about property going to descendants, from which, I suppose, we omitted Phil. Each one of these moves was its own trauma, reminding me of the painful reality with which I now had to deal. Most of the time, I lived in a dream that we would get past this nightmare and that normal life would somehow return.

New York seemed to be Phil's home base when he and Robin weren't in Puerto Rico or at the farm, but he made several trips to Washington. Once he had dinner with Bob McNamara, and the next day went to the White House to call on the president. Phil had earlier written Kennedy asking if he could stop by, saying, "If there is any chance of seeing you late that afternoon I promise to be on my best behavior."

This is one of the few times he acknowledged that there might be a problem with his behavior; more often than not, he was adamant in his denial that anything was wrong. Whenever anyone wrote him suggesting that he'd been ill, he at once responded testily, writing to one man, "I am not, nor have I been, seriously ill." In response to Hugh Kindersley, an English friend of ours who had written Phil that he'd heard he was ill, Phil wrote: "If the Daily Telegraph said I was 'taken ill' in Phoenix it was partly right—because I was certainly 'taken.' " In a letter to David Astor in England, he spelled out his intentions: "You have kindly written me a note worrying about my being 'ill.' I am not, and have not been 'ill,' but I have managed to start getting a divorce in a rather turbulent manner. When the divorce is through I plan to marry a proper Commonwealth lady—Miss Robin Webb from Sydney, Australia." Phil spread the word far and wide, even apologizing in some of his routine correspondence for being late in responding because "I . . . have also been somewhat occupied in the earlier stages of the unfortunate business of getting a divorce." He wrote to all of our friends in London and Paris, telling them he was planning a month-long trip to Europe and would be coming with Robin, whom he was going to marry.

Evangeline Bruce wrote me from London that our friends were dreading the visit, fearing that, since they had basically decided not to receive Robin, Phil might "try to trap us into lunching with him at a restaurant 'alone' " and then they'd find her with him and there would be some awful scene. She also noted that Isaiah Berlin was "planning to stretch out his hernia operation and recuperative period" to cover the entire time Phil would be in London. Evangeline added that Phil's insistence on taking Robin everywhere led them all to speculate on whether he would find a way to "smuggle the little woman into his interview with the PM." Pam Berry wrote that they were all "dreading the arrival of Phil" and added:

> I don't think she will find London a very social city! I can't believe the trip will be a success compared to all the fun he is accustomed to having—and has had in the past. It is all so sad and horrible I can hardly bear it for you all.
>
> . . . I will write and describe The Visit—that is, if, which seems unlikely, I witness any part of it!

Before going to Europe, Phil, taking Robin with him, flew to California for RAND meetings, where apparently there was vast discomfort over her presence at the business-related dinners. Then, on April 19, they left for London. Evangeline wrote me a detailed report of what she knew and had seen:

> He seemed tense and the contrary of healthy and sad that particular morning (it was the one after he had talked to Stevie on the telephone for his birthday) and sort of volcanically tamped down. Apart from that, hard to tell. We kept off certain subjects like divorce. After 10 minutes or so, Phil asked if I would change my mind, and meet R. I said no, and this was the opening to say why, and what I felt about the blackmail mutual friends had been subjected to in this respect. Took it well, but heaven knows how he really took it, the grapevine will tell. Lots of things he said were so patently UNtrue. Pam can tell you much more of this, since he saw her 3 times for hours. Isaiah too. . . .
>
> Incidentally, brave old Isaiah told Phil what he felt about his financial behavior, the 51%, etc. etc. and appeared to meet with

reasoned arguments, but could see a black rage mounting. He was also treated to many a Zionist argument. . . .

Isaiah, who had deliberately arranged for his surgery to be done while Phil was in London with Robin, wrote me:

Phil telephoned to me and visited me twice in my hospital room. On the first occasion not one word was said about any personal matter at all. This was queer, but I did not bring it up, neither did he. He was acutely nervous throughout, and although he talked quite sanely and even interestingly about the Kennedys, etc., I could see that this was not what his mind was on. However, I did nothing to let him off the hook, and lay back in my exhausted condition and smiled wanly from time to time, and in the end the nurses had to ask him to leave. On the next day he returned and there was a certain amount of personal talk, from which I gathered that he does indeed want a divorce and hopes to see you to discuss it with you, etc. He has an iron control of himself at the moment, but within some kind of devils are certainly still at large. On the other hand, it is quite impossible to say that he is in any respect insane. His own account of his incarceration had a wonderful grim humour about it. I had no idea whether what he said was accurate—it certainly didn't tally with the accounts of others, but I didn't practice any inquisitorial methods. I merely made clear my devotion to you and left it at that. He claimed to harbour no resentment or bitter feeling towards you of any kind. I did not see the lady. Nor was she mentioned, except very glancingly. It was not suggested that I should see her and I behaved as if she did not exist. I have no idea whether any banquets were held or how much entertainment occurred, since I really was absolutely out of everything.

In advance of this trip, Phil had planned for a meeting of *Newsweek's* overseas correspondents. They arrived from all over the world to meet with the editors in London, and he made a speech to this group, demonstrating yet again his ability to function at a high level even in the face of his illness. He began his remarks by describing the company, saying, "I have been responsible for its affairs for 17 years—and for the last 15 years, since it became a corporation in 1948, I have been controlling owner of its voting shares." There was no mention of my father or how this came to be or the existence of me as a minority owner, of course. He ended his re-

marks with some philosophical thoughts, including a phrase about journalism's being the first rough draft of history, which is quoted to this day:

> I am insatiably curious about the state of the world. I am con-
> stantly intrigued by information of topicality. I revel in the recita-
> tion of the daily and weekly grist of journalism.
>
> Much of it, of course, is pure chaff. Much of our discussions
> of how to do it better consist of tedium and detail. But no one yet
> has been able to produce wheat without chaff. And not even such
> garrulous romantics as Fidel Castro or such transcendent spirits
> as Abraham Lincoln can produce a history which does not in large
> part rest on a foundation of tedium and detail—and even sheer
> drudgery.
>
> So let us today drudge on about our inescapably impossible
> task of providing every week a first rough draft of a history that
> will never be completed about a world we can never really under-
> stand. . . .

While Phil was in London, I tried to pick up the pace of my life a little. My mother and I together planned a large reception at her house for
May 7, to which we invited hundreds of people. Mother called it a "Show
the Flag party"—a way to assure people we were still here and still okay,
despite Phil's efforts to take over. It served its purpose.

On May 11, after going to Paris from London and then on to Ravello
for five days of rest, Phil and Robin flew back to the States, and after
taking care of some things in Washington, he and Robin left again for
Puerto Rico.

I went on seeing close friends and going out a little more. One person
I saw was David Bruce, to whom I talked about my plans and intentions
and my resolve not to give Phil a divorce unless he gave up at least enough
of his controlling stock in *The Washington Post* so that I would have the
majority interest. I'm not sure how I came to this conclusion, but I do
know that my determination was total. I was not going to lose my husband
and the paper. And if my husband was firm in his decision to leave me,
then I would fight to keep the paper.

The chain of events and activities quieted down, and an audible
silence was emanating from Puerto Rico. I suspected that my not hearing
much from there meant that Phil had become depressed, and indeed
he had. Being there hadn't cured his exhaustion; instead, the calm and
inactivity seemed to have given him time to think and added to his
depression.

When they returned to New York from Puerto Rico on June 12, Ed

Williams met them at the airport, and it was Ed's view that Phil was the worst he had ever seen him, "really so depressed it was like he was paralyzed, physically paralyzed, with almost an inability to move." It's hard to sort out whether he returned intending to remain with Robin or break up with her, but they did come to Washington and move into a large house on Foxhall Road.

A few days later, on Monday, June 17, Phil consulted both Dr. Farber and Ed and in effect told them that it was all over. He wanted to end the affair with Robin. Farber, typically, was again questioning and indecisive; he asked Phil if he was sure. Ed stepped in and asked Phil three questions: Did he want Robin to leave? Did he want Ed to ask her to leave? Did he want to come home if I would have him? To all three questions, Phil—in an agony of despair and depression—answered yes. Poor Robin took the shuttle to New York, and Al Friendly went to spend the night with Phil in the house on Foxhall Road. The next day, Phil's brother, Bill, again came up from Florida and stayed with him, as did Fritz Beebe.

On that same Monday I got a call from Al saying that Phil wanted to come back if I would agree—which I did immediately. On the afternoon of June 19, Phil returned to R Street and spent the night.

Having Phil back was a tremendous—and tremendously complicated—relief. For me, one of the immediate questions was whether I could go through another black depression with him. I knew all too well what it was like—not being able to leave the house except when he was at his doctor's; hours and hours of intense talk; hearing things I wasn't sure I wanted to hear or know about. All of those years we had labored through together to get him out of the depressions had resulted in his leaving me. None of my efforts had led to a happy ending, and I felt I just couldn't assume once again the heavy burden and responsibility of being his sole support system.

Clearly we needed intensive outside help. Phil, almost pathetically, asked to be allowed to stay at home, not to go back to Chestnut Lodge, which I viewed as the only option. I don't believe any of us thought there might be an alternative to Chestnut Lodge at the time, and in terms of Phil's treatment, I assumed that the psychiatrists knew what they were doing and didn't question whether the Lodge was the right or appropriate place, or whether Farber was the right doctor.

This decision-making about whether to go to Chestnut Lodge or stay at home was horribly painful—made a little less so by Ed Williams and Bill Graham, who both felt Phil should go, and by Phil himself, who in the end went sadly but willingly. Our loyal driver, Tony, drove him to the Lodge late in the day on June 20.

At some point that evening, when several of us were at the Lodge with

Phil, I saw Ed for the first time since Phil's last illness had begun. There was a roomful of people, but on instinct I went up to him and very quietly thanked him for everything he'd done, saying, "I can see you did the best for him." When I later met with him to go over what had happened and how he viewed it all, he told me that his one idea had been to hold on to Phil.

What Ed had done was right. With his ability to appraise people and situations, he had been very aware of Phil's mental state at almost every turn and very clear about his instability. At the same time, he was determined to do the best he could for him under the circumstances. Ed's devotion to Phil was not unlike mine, unswerving and uncompromising, and his behavior at this time created a lasting bond between us.

The day after Phil went back to Chestnut Lodge, Al Friendly wrote him:

> At the rock bottom of despair, and against the hardest opposition conceivable, you made the toughest decisions possible. When every thought was an agony to frame, your mind remained the best and most exciting one I know.
>
> With those resources, how can even you doubt that you will succeed in what you have to do?
>
> There will also be the help from the love of more friends than you know.
>
> I'll see you soon, whenever you'd like me to.

Lally, who was working in the *Newsweek* Washington bureau that summer, wrote about the mid-June events to my mother, whom she was going to be joining in Greece for another yacht trip:

> Last night he went in the hospital, and Donny and I were both so glum about the future. But, this morning, I really feel certain that he will indeed come through it. Mummy seems greatly cheered by the last two days during which he's been at home. I am greatly cheered that despite the fact that he feels there is so little to live for at the moment, he has been so incredibly courageous, strong, and kind. Not only did he get rid of the girl but he also managed to dismiss Farber which I think in ways was even harder; for Farber was really his only ray of hope in the past few days, since he told Daddy that he knew he could pull through his depressions and do it without a hospital and also that although the words "manic depressive" might be a very adequate description of his past behavior, they did *not* necessitate a future cycle. Obviously, giving up Farber meant giving up the hope of going through the

depression without a hospital and also accepting the label of manic depressive. I wince at the thought of the agony he must be experiencing. It must be so frightening to realize that your whole life is governed by cycles in which you are either irrationally happy or just as irrationally depressed. Enough . . . I just hope so much that somehow all this can be cured or at least helped.

Lally's letter suggests Phil's still-positive feelings about Farber, although he himself had dismissed him as his doctor. Indeed, he was attached to him—partly, I think, because Farber espoused ideas Phil agreed with and played down any idea of real mental illness. Perhaps his dismissal of Farber at this point was an indication of just how low Phil was—that he no longer believed Farber and knew the sickness would recur. The letter also reflects that, at last, a name had been given to this illness.

To me, Phil seemed, as usual, to be truly courageous, positive, and hopeful in the face of terrible anguish. In a letter to my mother, he said:

What seemed for some moments an end, I must now turn into a beginning. With Kay's singular love, with that of the children, with yours, with that of my brother and that of friends—I know I can do it. A beginning scaled to decent human values. At least I do so pray.

There was a short interlude after Phil went to the Lodge before I started to visit; then I went pretty much every day for several hours. I often took picnics, and we'd sit outside to eat. Occasionally, we'd play tennis or bridge. Gradually, a few friends started to visit him, but mostly they were from the family or the company. Billy and Steve had gone off to camp. Lally went abroad to visit the Berrys in England before joining my mother's yacht party in Athens. Don and I were alone at R Street, he working all day for Scotty Reston. (Scotty wrote Phil saying that he had had two guys doing this job at the *Times* for him, but that "Don Graham, in his sophomore year at Harvard, is better than either of them. He has come in here very quietly and composed sometimes as many as 60 letters a day and written them simply and quickly and done a lot of other things on the side. Everybody likes him. . . .")

Bob McNamara was very good about visiting Phil at Chestnut Lodge. One Saturday morning I was playing tennis with Bob's wife, Margy, and she told me that Bob had said to tell Phil he was coming to see him later that afternoon. I said I'd ask Phil to see if he was up to it, but Margy replied that Bob, who thought it would be good for Phil, had insisted on just announcing that he was coming. It was so typical of Bob, who was working at the Defense Department at a feverish pitch, to conclude that

that was the best approach and to take time on a Saturday afternoon to drive an hour to Chestnut Lodge. Phil demurred but eventually agreed to see him. Phil and I sat together on a bench under a tree waiting for the long black official limousine, which eventually swung into the driveway. I left the two men alone to talk. Bob's recollection of what he said to Phil was, "Goddamn you, get out of here, come down and help us. We need you." And Phil said he couldn't, in effect saying that nobody would accept him. Bob assured him that he knew more about the Defense Department than almost anyone, and repeated that he should get down there and help out. Bob later told me that he said all this partially because he thought that's what Phil needed to hear, but more because it was basically true. He felt strongly that Phil had an extraordinary insight into the nation and how to deal with its problems. One thing Bob recalled was that, when he asked Phil what he should be doing to help, Phil replied, "Well, the first thing I'll tell you is not to waste your time coming out here."

Although of course it was hard, I was ecstatic about Phil being back, even if in the hospital. Naturally, I dropped nearly all of my activities, including a planned trip to Europe, to concentrate on him. He remained seriously depressed but seemed to me to be already quite noticeably better, even after only a week or so at Chestnut Lodge. I felt he finally had doctors who were treating a real and known illness, and because of that I was able to hope that we could, as I wrote a friend, "surmount the difficulties of the last few years." Although I still naïvely believed that Phil could and would get better, on some level I think even I was beginning to recognize that this was wishful thinking.

I wasn't on sure footing when it came to what to talk about with him, but advised one friend who wanted to write that "he loves love at this point and also any sort of news or political gossip that you can think of." Phil was full of remorse and guilt and sadness. He, who hated to hurt people, had to begin to deal with all the hurt his actions had wrought—for me, for the children, for Robin, for himself. It's hard to imagine his frame of mind—knowing he had left his home and children, had sent for Robin more than once, and then in the end had told her it was over and had come back home to us. Worry about his actions and what he had done to himself, his life, and to all of us was the main thing on his mind—that, plus the thought that not only had it happened but it might happen again.

It had finally penetrated to me that Phil's diagnosis was manic-depression, but the whole issue of treatment—or, indeed, even what manic-depression was—I didn't really comprehend. Although the illness was now named, I didn't know what its outcome usually was if not properly treated with a combination of drugs and psychiatry. I certainly didn't understand something that I learned later from Dr. Kay Jamison, the author of *An Unquiet Mind*, about her own manic-depression. She has written that it is "a lethal illness, particularly if left untreated, or wrongly treated." And, of course, much less was known then. Lithium was only in the experimental stages, being used mostly in Europe; it wasn't in clinical practice here.

Electric-shock treatment had been used routinely with manic-depression for decades and at least should have been considered for someone who was severely depressed or severely manic. Though it had improved considerably since the 1950s, electric shock was still a rough therapy, with many cases of convulsions leading to cracked ribs and broken backs. It might still have been the preferred treatment at the time, but a place like Chestnut Lodge, which prided itself on psychodynamic or psychoanalytic treatment, would certainly not have used it.

In any case, Phil had a deep aversion to both drugs and shock treatment—an antipathy that had been inculcated in him by Farber and reinforced by his having seen the negative effects on our friend Frank Wisner. Phil may have been a victim not only of Farber's peculiar form of psychotherapy, but of the timing of his illness and of his own antidrug attitude. I don't know whether there still exists a branch of psychiatry that treats manic-depression by shunning drugs and relying completely on talk therapy and discussions of existential philosophy, but I hope not. I don't believe you can reach people in the depths of depression or in the heights of mania through mere talking.

It bothers me still that I was so passive about the nature of Phil's illness and so accepting of Farber for so long. I'm not sure why I didn't insist on more of an explanation. Perhaps I was just holding on to the naïve notion that all would be well. I don't think I would have felt so optimistic had I seen something Phil wrote at that time, addressed to Scotty Reston but never sent. It was a little essay on balance and moderation and being "middle-of-the-road," all written out in careful longhand. This turned up later in Phil's papers, and I sent it to Scotty when I found it. It's hard to fathom why he addressed these thoughts specifically to Scotty and why he didn't send them, but they reflect thinking that—had we known of it— might have led us all to a different decision about whether he was ready to have a day away from the hospital. Phil wrote:

> . . . I find it unendurable to believe that "balance" or "moderation" or "middle-of-the-road" represent human approaches to living.
>
> Similarly we are told that all tough questions are matters of degree, of simply drawing a line, etc. What nonsense. It is not just a matter of degree involved in the chasm between freedom and

tyranny; nor just a matter of drawing a line. One is an embracing of life as a holy project; the other is a rejection of all but the finite and temporal and material.

"Balance" or "middle-of-the-road" are blinders and deceivers. That kind of language inevitably carries the suggestion that one can finesse the problem through a sort of vegetable neutrality. That is highly appropriate for turnips but not for men.

Get right down to day-to-day living. How much should one pour into one's work? How much save for one's family? How much for solitary thought? How much for service to one's sovereign or one's God? How great is one's duty to truth? . . .

How do we ration our small supply of energy and talents and character amongst all the claimants?

We know that there is no answer to those questions and there could not be without stripping life of its most valued meaning. We know we have to face these and a thousand other questions again and again, sometimes with vigor, at times with heavy fatigue, now in hope, again near despair, but always so long as there is any life at all, facing again and again and again.

How wrong it is to try to banish all this, to pretend it doesn't exist, by admonishing "balance" as an approach to life. Or the "middle-of-the-road." The man who leaves life by the most violent suicide is still at least more honest than those who choose suicide-while-living by defining away all that is human in life. . . .

Phil very much wanted to go to Glen Welby for a break from the hospital, and had started to work on the doctors to obtain their permission. There was a sharp difference of opinion among the doctors at the Lodge about whether this was a good idea, but no one ever asked me if there was liquor or sleeping pills at the farm, nor did I think to mention the guns we had there. I, who certainly knew the farm was stocked with guns that Phil used for sport, was completely deluded by his seeming progress, lack of visible depression, and determination to get well; in fact, I was optimistic about his ability to do so. One doctor at the Lodge told a friend later, "Phil was determined to get out and really was unbelievably masterful in his ability to manipulate people." He even got the patients to take a vote among themselves—and he went to them to argue his case and get them on his side. Naturally, they voted that he be allowed to go. During one of his hospital stays, Phil had confided to his friend and colleague Jim Truitt that when he was sick he made people dance "the devil's dance." Indeed, Dr. Cameron once remarked to me that someone like Phil, especially in his manic moods, could pull people into going along in some way with his madness, becoming part of it. "When I look back," Anne Truitt said, "I see Phil as a dervish. . . . He's going round and round—dancing himself the devil's dance and pulling into his orbit—nearly magnetically—everyone whom he touched." I see now that we were all enablers, in the long run not helping him in the least in the end.

Even I started asking people what they thought. I asked Ed Williams, among others, and he was very bothered afterwards that he had said yes, Phil should be allowed out. My own doctor, Dr. Cameron, who had an office at Chestnut Lodge, thought the whole idea of Phil's leaving the hospital for a weekend at the beginning of August was definitely premature.

In any event, Phil won. And I must say I was glad. He wanted so much to go to the farm, and I got caught up in thinking how good it would be for him—he loved Glen Welby and was always so happy there.

The night before we were to go to the farm, I had dinner with my neighbor Kay Halle, whose brother-in-law was Dr. George Crile, Jr., of the Cleveland Clinic. He walked me home and asked if Phil was being given drugs. When I said no, he expressed surprise and told me that, according to what he knew, drugs were absolutely necessary for Phil's future. I remained skeptical that Phil would ever agree to drugs, given his feelings about them, but I thought of pursuing this when he went back to the Lodge after our time at the farm.

On Saturday, August 3, Phil's driver picked him up at Chestnut Lodge, and then they came to R Street to get me. One of the things Phil had said he wanted to do was to work on farm problems while he was there, so I had asked Buck Nalls to come up to the house in the afternoon. I remember that Phil expressed surprise at my having asked Buck to come, no doubt having forgotten that he had mentioned working on the farm as one of his reasons for going there.

We had lunch on two trays on the back porch at Glen Welby, chatting and listening to some classical records. After lunch, we went upstairs to our bedroom for a nap. After a short while, Phil got up, saying he wanted to lie down in a separate bedroom he sometimes used. Only a few minutes later, there was the ear-splitting noise of a gun going off indoors. I bolted out of the room and ran around in a frenzy looking for him. When I opened the door to a downstairs bathroom, I found him.

It was so profoundly shocking and traumatizing—he was so obviously dead and the wounds were so ghastly to look at—that I just ran into the next room and buried my head in my hands, trying to absorb that this had really happened, this dreadful thing that had hung over us for the last six years, which he had discussed with me and with the doctors, but which he had not been talking about in recent weeks, when he was obviously most seriously thinking about it. The sight had been so appalling that I knew I couldn't go back in, so I ran to call Buck and our caretaker, William Smith, for help. They had heard the gunshot and appeared immediately.

I finally went back upstairs to my bedroom and used a direct phone to the paper. There was a much-loved phone operator named Molly Parker who had been at the *Post* almost fifty years, and luckily she was there. I told her what had happened and that I needed help. I made a call to Dr. Cameron, and then just sat and waited. The next thing I can remember is the arrival of the local police, whom, I suppose, Buck and William had called. Finally, Alfred and Jean Friendly arrived, bringing Don with them. Don and I walked along the road, consoling and sustaining each other.

What I was agonizing about was that I had let him leave the bedroom alone. I can only say that he seemed so much better that I stupidly was not worried enough. It had never occurred to me that he must have planned the whole day at Glen Welby to get to his guns as a way of freeing himself forever from the watchful eyes of the doctors—and the world. He left no note of any kind. I believe that Phil came to the sad conclusion that he would never again lead a normal life. I also think that he realized the illness would recur. As Kay Jamison has written, "There is a particular kind of pain, elation, loneliness, and terror involved in this kind of madness." However he himself defined his illness, Phil was well aware of the damaging effects of it on others and on him. I think he felt he'd done such harm the last time around that he just couldn't deal with it, couldn't fix everything. It was unendurable to him not only that he couldn't make any of it right but that he might cause more hurt again. I concluded all of this only later; at the time, I could barely deal with the reality of what had happened and begin to handle the shock to all of us.

Essentially I had gone through losing Phil twice. First he left, and there was all the embittering agony of that time since Christmas. Then to have that horror over, to have him back, was an impossible dream come true. But that, too, was now over, and a very different kind of grief consumed us all.

It took most of the afternoon before we could leave Glen Welby. Al took charge—informing authorities, dealing with the practicalities, seeing that family and close friends knew. Someone, I suppose the local coroner, came and removed the body. One oddly distinct vignette in my memory is of a strange man walking into the library where Don and the Friendlys and I were sitting. We looked at him, puzzled, and he said, "I'm from the *Washington Evening Star* and they sent me down to check on the story that Mr. Graham is dead." I just nodded, and Al took him out of the room.

Finally, we got into the Friendlys' car to go back to R Street, with Don and me sitting together in back. About halfway to town, I asked the rhetorical question, "What's going to happen to all of us?" Al turned around and pointed at me without saying a word, distinctly meaning that I had to do it. But the whole notion went right past me, as did most everything else that day.

When we got back to the house, some friends had already arrived, and more and more gathered. Finally, there was almost a wake of people—not one of whom I can remember except for Lorraine Cooper. I went to bed late that night, after everyone had left. Years later, Ed Williams told me that he had come over even later that night—he had no idea at what time—and walked right in the open back door. He had gotten very drunk and was looking for me. Distraught, he walked all around the blackened first floor, found no one, and left.

The next day, the nightmare of the reality began to set in. Phil's death was the most unbelievable and awful shock to all the children, particularly the younger ones. Lally and Don, at least, were more aware of his illness and its implications; Bill and Steve, on the other hand, faced the suddenness of the loss without any preparation for an ending to the difficult months of separation.

Bill, then fifteen years old, flew home from camp. Lou Eckstrand, our housekeeper and sort of sitter, went to get Stevie. Don flew with Charlie Paradise to Idlewild Airport in New York, to meet Lally and Luvie Pearson, who had also been on the trip with Mother, and who accompanied Lally home. My mother wasn't up to the trip and stayed on the yacht. She sent me a heartfelt and sad wire, saying she needed us to come to her and urging me to return with Lally and Luvie:

> I am confused and I hurt all over. What this tragedy must be for you I cannot imagine. I wish only that I were near you. . . . Here you will have companionship but only when you want to. And I need you to help me face life. It is sad that I can offer you only my weakness. But it is the result of my feeling for you and my love for our lost darling. I can only say Come—a different world will distract you. . . .

Don also met Scotty and Sally Reston and brought them back, too, on the company plane. They had come home from Europe as soon as they heard. In one of the many phone calls in those difficult days, I had urged the Restons not to interrupt their trip, assuring them that I needed and wanted them, but later, and begging them not to come then—to which they replied, "We are coming."

THE NEXT FEW days were what everyone goes through even with normal deaths, let alone the suicide of a prominent individual. Letters and telegrams and flowers began flooding in. I think I read very few of the letters then, but I read each of them carefully later. In an odd way, being active and making arrangements have a numbing effect and help get you over the cold realization of what has happened and the loss you are facing. Many people helped so much—especially the two older children—both with arrangements and with emotional problems and issues. Phil's father had had a series of strokes and had been quite ill—I'm not sure whether he was even told of Phil's suicide. He died several months later. Bill Graham was his usual wonderful self, helpful to me in every way.

As difficult and sad as all of this was for us, Phil's family, it was also wrenching for his friends and for people throughout the company, the industry, and the city. The resonance at Chestnut Lodge, of which I was then unaware, was also immense.

A great many wonderful things were written and said about Phil in the days after his death. The *Post* published a collection of his sayings and writings. An editorial said:

> Mr. Graham invested the full capacity of his mind and heart in everything that deeply moved and interested him. He was not a person given to qualified commitments to his country, his enterprise or his friends. It was this quality that precipitated the illness that led to his death. . . . Our sense of loss is total; he was a man neither easily forgotten nor found again.

Herb Block wrote a particularly moving farewell. Al Friendly said Phil "could out-sleuth the paper's star reporters, out-think its fanciest—or most fancied—stylists." Russ Wiggins wrote a personal note to the staff:

> Philip L. Graham has left in our daily care and custody an honest and a conscientious newspaper which I know that all of you are eager to maintain as a daily memorial to his own genius and integrity. And now we must take up the duties he laid upon us, with a heavy heart, but nonetheless with a high hope that we may succeed in doing what he would have us do.

Fritz Beebe was especially a hero in the days immediately after Phil's death. I was only dimly aware of the mountainous difficulties with which he coped. He maintained stability and continuity and some calm within the company, and was there for me as a friend and as an adviser. At the same time, he shouldered much of the heavy burden of dealing with the whole issue of there being more than one will. Phil, during the height of his last manic period, had written a new one. As Ed Williams later said, "Any will lawyer would have been horrified by the way I handled this, but if you just operate simply from your instincts you do better." What Ed had done was extraordinary. Phil had begun pushing Ed to make a new will that would have given a third of Phil's estate to Robin—who Ed believed was not the instigator of this and may never have known how much she stood to benefit—leaving two-thirds in trust to be divided among the children. At the time, Ed thought that the worst thing he could do was to tell Phil that he wasn't going to help him make such a will, that in fact he felt Phil wasn't competent to do such a thing. He knew it would spell the end of their relationship. In trying to hold on to Phil, Ed wrote the will for Phil but simultaneously wrote a memorandum for the file saying he didn't think Phil was competent to make a will and that he was doing it "solely for the purpose of retaining a relationship with him and exercising what influence I could over him to get him back to his old life." Just after this will was executed, Phil went back to Ed and wanted to reverse the percentages, making Robin the recipient of two-thirds of his estate and the children one-third. This one was never actually executed. When Phil finally decided to leave Robin and to come home, he asked Ed to destroy the rewritten will, and it was officially torn up in front of witnesses.

But although the Robin Webb will was invalid, a technical question remained: Did Phil's 1957 will have legal standing, or did he die intestate? This was resolved by a compromise, whereby I gave up part of Phil's estate in favor of the children, which was fine with me. The children eventually had to have their own lawyer, and after the funeral we all had to go to court to deal with the legal issues involved. I will never forget Steve, then only eleven, dressed up in his little suit, straightening his tie and saying, "I have to go to see my lawyer." His remarkable and ever-present wit was with him even in these darkest of hours.

As far as I know, Robin received nothing in the end, nor did she ask for anything—ever. She was carried away by Phil and only slowly must have come to understand his illness. I believe that she called to ask if Phil had left a note, but she never reappeared in the life of my family; and she never gave an interview about her relationship with Phil. She must be a very decent person. I understand that she married an Australian diplomat and seems to live a quiet life. I hope that she, too, eventually recovered.

On the day before the funeral, the board of directors of the company met. Fritz suggested that if I felt up to it I should come to the office to say a few words to the directors, reassuring them that the company would go on and not be sold. I agreed, but was terrified. I thought about what to say, wrote it out, and even rehearsed. When the car arrived to take me downtown, Lally, in her nightgown and robe, hopped in and went along with me for comfort and support. I still have her touching and helpful handwritten notes on what she felt I should say—notes that she placed in my hands and which I relied on in what I said:

1) Thank them—all deeply involved—that gives you confidence.
2) There has been crisis and still is one but you know they will carry on as they have over the past months.
3) never expected to be in this situation.
4) going off to clear mind and think about future
5) no changes or decisions at this time. The paper will remain in the family, next generation.
6) and be carried on in tradition so well set.
7) further thoughts

It touches me still that this young girl, who was, if anything, more devastated than I, could scribble out this simple but correct sequence of thoughts and jump in the car in her nightclothes to put them in my hand.

I recall walking into the room where the all-male board was gathered. To a man they looked almost as stricken as I was. They also seemed to be looking at me hard to decipher what was there. Oz Elliott later recalled what I said better than I could:

> You said you appreciated very much how everybody had handled this very difficult situation with professionalism and you just wanted to say that you knew rumors were around and would be around that the company would be for sale or that some part of it would be and you said that you wanted to make it clear that it was not for sale, no part of it was for sale, this was a family enterprise and there was a new generation coming along.

Knowledge of that "new generation"—my children—was what led me, however hesitantly, to the decision I made then: to try to hold on to the company by going to work.

PHIL'S FUNERAL WAS on Tuesday, August 6, in the Washington National Cathedral, and was so big and so public that in a way it again shielded me from what was really happening. The children and I had all participated in deciding on the nature of the service and the selection of the hymns. President Kennedy attended. He came up the side aisle by himself after everyone was seated. The sun shone through the stained-glass windows, somehow illuminating him as he walked to his seat.

One jolt occurred when we left for the private burial. Others had been to the funeral home to make all the arrangements, but I didn't know the details. I did know from Phil's endless jokes that he had procured a plot in Oak Hill, the cemetery across the street from our house. It was extremely difficult to get in—the Dean Achesons, the David Bruces, and the John Walkers were all planning to be buried there—and Phil had developed an enthusiasm of an odd kind to be buried there, too. One night long before he became ill, he came home from a St. Albans school-board meeting and said there was a man on the board who was influential at Oak Hill and he was sure we could have a plot. He went on joking about it, saying that all I would have to do was to wheel him across the street. I was deeply upset when we pulled up in front of the burial site to find that this was not an exaggeration. His grave is directly in front of a little chapel right across the street from my house, where I can see it every day. I like this now, but in the beginning it disturbed me a great deal.

People came home afterwards—touchingly, people from all over. It's funny how much you care who is there—and even somehow count the house at a moment like that. For friends to care and to come means something.

Two messages came to me from President Kennedy. The one I received on the day of the funeral quoted Prime Minister Macmillan saying that when Phil called on him that summer he had found him particularly attractive and interesting. The president then said, "I thought the service today was appropriate and moving—especially the last hymn. Phil was so helpful to me in so many ways since I have come here. We shall all miss him greatly and I send you and the children my deepest sympathy." Jackie Kennedy wrote me an eight-page letter, one of the most understanding and comforting of any I received. Just a few days after Phil's funeral, Jackie gave birth to the baby boy who died.

These days—from Phil's death through the funeral—that we all endured are as hazy to me now as they were then. If there is one regret I feel, one enormous failing, it's that I was so overwhelmed that I wasn't thoughtful enough or helpful enough with the children, whose trauma was even worse than mine. Phil was the bright, shining light in their lives. Each of the four had been through the months of his absence, only to get him back and then to lose him again.

Lally and Luvie at some point began insisting that what I needed was to get away from everything. They pressured me to go back to Europe with them, as did my mother by cable. I felt it would be impossible—even apart from the children, there was much too much to do, given the will, the estate, the company. Their rejoinder was that they had already packed for me and had my passport, and that I was going. I finally agreed to the plan. Bill and Steve bravely returned to their camps. Don stayed at his job with Scotty, living at home and spending a lot of time at the Friendlys'. I took off with Luvie and Lally the day after the funeral to join my mother's chartered yacht at Istanbul.

That decision may have been right for me, but it was so wrong for Bill and Steve and even for Don—so wrong that I wonder how I could have made it. Would my younger boys have been better off going too? Would it have been better if I'd stayed home for them? This is, for me, the most painful thing to look back on. It's hard to remake decisions and even harder to rethink nondecisions. Sometimes you don't really decide, you just move forward, and that is what I did—moved forward blindly and mindlessly into a new and unknown life.

— *Chapter Eighteen* —

L EFT ALONE, no matter at what age or under what circumstance, you have to remake your life. When I came back in September 1963 from the trip around the Black and Aegean Seas to take up my life again, there was a great deal of painful loneliness, only somewhat dulled by work and by the necessity of tending to the children, my mother, the business, and the task of balancing them all. The cruise had been a reprieve of sorts—it certainly took me into another world—but I experienced it with a mix of emotions. The inner turmoil continued. Always in my mind was the climax of the years of secret struggle with Phil's illness, the shock of the suicide, the loss, and the eternal questions about why and what next. I didn't talk with anyone intimately on the trip; mostly, I kept my agonizing to myself. I couldn't stop reliving the awful moment of the gun going off, my springing up, racing downstairs, and finding him. The scene replayed in my head until I thought I might be going mad. It took a long time to get through that. To this day, a gun going off or any loud bang nearby affects me profoundly.

Yet, on another level, life carried on. The trip was diverting, no doubt serving my mother's purpose, bad as it was for my young boys left behind. For me, this was the first of many such trips in which looking around, observing, and learning became almost addictive.

One vivid moment from the end of this interlude took place at a stopover I made on my way home to visit friends on the island of Spezos. As I was leaving, Chip Bohlen asked me, "You're not going to work, are you? You mustn't—you are young and attractive and you'll get remarried." I said emphatically that I *was* going to work. Chip actually meant what he said flatteringly: for a woman, being married was a goal, a way of life—at that time certainly the most desirable one. But I wasn't thinking about remarriage at the time. I also saw no contradiction between going to work and whatever happened in my private life. I suppose that, without quite realizing it, I was taking a veil.

On September 9, the day after I returned from Italy, I did, indeed, go to work. More formally, I was elected president of The Washington Post Company at a meeting of the board of directors on September 20. Often I have been asked how I had the courage to take over the company, and I've always replied that I never saw myself as "taking over" anything or becoming the true head of the company. I had no conception of the role I was eventually to fill. While recognizing the importance of controlling the company, and having been willing to fight for it, I saw my job now as that of a silent partner, watching from the sidelines as I tried to learn about the company to which I had tragically fallen heir. I saw myself as a bridge to my children and viewed my role before they could take over as supporting the strong men—principally Fritz Beebe for the whole company; Oz Elliott at *Newsweek*; John Sweeterman, Russ Wiggins, and Al Friendly at the *Post*; and John Hayes in broadcasting—who were running things, and learning what I needed to in case some big decision came to me, as the holder of the A shares. I naïvely thought the whole business would just go on as it had while I learned by listening. I didn't realize that nothing stands still—issues arise every day, big and small, and they start coming at you. I didn't understand the immensity of what lay before me, how frightened I would be by much of it, how tough it was going to be, and how many anxious hours and days I would spend for a long, long time. Nor did I realize how much I was eventually going to enjoy it all.

My going to "work"—in the sense I defined it—seemed to be the only sensible step to take and, in some ways, shouldn't have caused much astonishment. The years with my father and later with Phil were years of absorbing from them, and often with them; fortunately for me, they both believed in sharing what they were doing with daughters and wives. One strength I did bring to the company was some knowledge and appreciation of news and journalism. I knew the principal journalists on the *Post* relatively well—I knew Russ, Al, Chal Roberts, and Eddie Folliard as old friends—and had spent my life listening to talk about the news and about the company. I had some sense of whom to listen to. Rightly or wrongly, I felt competent to size them up. On the other hand, I felt awfully new and raw, and the job, even as I had limited it, looked very big. It seemed like the difference between watching someone swim and actually swimming. As I wrote a friend in late September, "I am quaking in my boots a little but trying not to show it."

I felt terrified without Phil. I badly missed his guidance. Even with all the difficulties of the last few years, he had always been there to lean on. Though I had learned a great deal from him, I still felt insecure making my own decisions. What strength I did have derived from the last, grueling year, when I had had to carry the burden at home, but it had never occurred to me that he wouldn't be there at all.

Ironically, at the same time I was wishing he was there, all that Phil had been made my job more difficult. His having done everything so well—and, as it seemed to the world, so effortlessly—made it even more daunting for me. Not only had I mythologized him, but others shared the same idolatrous view, which added to my confusion. Everyone would come in and weep on my shoulder about him. As time passed, I developed more perspective and realized that my image of him was at some variance with the reality. He hadn't been as perfect as I thought. He had been brilliant and had achieved an amazing record, but, of course, there were attendant problems. My job was made infinitely harder by comparing myself not with the real Phil Graham but with my exaggerated idea of his ability and accomplishments. Still, I didn't have as much energy as Phil had had, nor were my interests as broad, my knowledge nearly as deep, or my training as adequate. As I readily admitted, I certainly didn't feel in any way equal to running the *Post* the way he had run it. I wrote to an old friend that having me at the helm of the *Post* and *Newsweek* "isn't like having Phil running them, but I feel like the President of the United States who said to Congress, 'I am the only President you've got.' " I had to come to realize that I could only do the job in whatever way *I* could do it. I couldn't try to be someone else, least of all Phil.

What I essentially did was to put one foot in front of the other, shut my eyes, and step off the edge. The surprise was that I landed on my feet. I did so largely for two reasons. One was Fritz Beebe and the circle of men who had served Phil so well and who remained in place to help me. The other was luck.

Fritz was a life-saving presence to me and to the company. He himself was relatively new at business and at media, having only been at our company for two and a half years, much of which he had spent simply holding things together and trying to counteract whatever damage Phil did or tried to do during his illness. He also had worked hard to steer a path between Phil and me in the last several months, and then had had to pick up the pieces after Phil's death and deal with the legal complications he left behind. Fritz was generous to me in every way, making me feel comfortable, wanted, and regarded. We got along easily because of his understanding—and forgiving—nature.

One of the things Fritz and I had done between Phil's death and my leaving for Europe was to discuss our roles and to decide on titles. He suggested that he should remain chairman and I should succeed Phil as president. The titles themselves didn't bother me or even interest me, but I did see that this might entail his being boss and my being number two, and I wanted to be clear. I suggested that, whatever the titles, we be partners as he and Phil had been. Appropriately, Fritz asked how I thought this would work. "I'm not sure," I replied, "any more than I can tell you at the beginning how a marriage would work, but maybe this will work like a business marriage." I'm not sure how I dared to suggest equality, considering my lack of credentials. And I'm also not sure why he acceded to my position, which most businessmen of his stature would have viewed as unreasonable, even though I was the owner. Maybe he understood—or I may have explained—that I had lived all those months in fear of losing the *Post* and didn't want to end up ceding it away. I don't think our relationship would have worked differently in any case, no matter what our titles.

There was also considerable luck involved in my being able to function at all in this new role. The company was relatively small, and it was private, both of which helped during my first months on the job. The groundwork of stability for the *Post* had been laid with the purchase of the *Times-Herald* nearly a decade before. Revenue at the *Post*, *Newsweek*, and the television stations was growing fast, as were profits. Management at each business was steady. (This, of course, is all much clearer in retrospect than it was to me at the time.) We were editorially visible through the *Post* and *Newsweek*, both of which mattered to various constituencies, especially the government and the president. We had a solid base on which to build, a firm financial footing. If the company had been bigger or public or less secure, I might not have had the luxury of learning as I did.

Personally I was lucky because I had a demanding and difficult but interesting and absorbing job to try to fulfill. I was economically independent and, despite my loneliness, I was not really alone. We were a family unit, with Bill and Steve still home and Lally and Don at college, and my mother nearby. My brother and two sisters were also helpful, along with a core group of friends.

I will never forget the support I felt from Lally throughout these difficult days and weeks. She sent me the most moving letter, which I received as I got home and just as I went to work:

> There is no use my again reiterating my belief that you will do very well with the business—as we agreed not in a Daddy way for who else in the world could run things with his brilliance and imagination—yet in another way, your own, which in a different way will be just as good—your good judgment, great ability to get along with people, earn their respect and discern their strengths and weaknesses and desire to follow things up which Pa was quite unwilling to do.
>
> . . . Do remember that the beginning of anything is the worst (trite but true I think), that we will all make it ensemble and try desperately hard to think about St. Paul's "in all things give

thanks." I find that last bit of advice much easier said than done but j'essaye.

Besides all of this, I had another important asset in my passionate devotion to the company and to the *Post*. I cared so much about the paper and about keeping it in the family that, despite my lack of knowledge and feelings of insecurity, I felt I *had* to make it work.

And so I got down to the job. I had very little idea of what I was supposed to be doing, so I set out to learn what the *Post*, *Newsweek*, our television stations, and the company itself were about. Throughout the first weeks, I felt I was wandering around in a fog, trying to grasp the rudiments: who did what, when, why, where, and how. It's hard to describe how abysmally ignorant I was. I knew neither the substance of the business and journalistic worlds in which I was moving nor the processes through which these worlds operated. Despite my father's expertise and experience, I knew next to nothing about business and absolutely nothing about accounting. I couldn't read or understand a balance sheet. I remember my complete befuddlement and inability in the beginning to follow technical financial discussions. The mere mention of terms like "liquidity" made my eyes glaze over.

I was also uneducated in even the basics of the working world—how to relate to people professionally, how to tell people things that they might not want to hear, how to give praise as well as criticism, how to use time to the best effect. Things that people learned automatically in the workplace or in graduate schools, I didn't know: that there were organizations of headhunters who could help you find executives if you had to go outside the company; that there were well-defined reward and incentive systems, which everyone but me seemed to know about; that there is a system for dealing with people in a hierarchy—that you don't bypass executives but, rather, deal with problems through them, or risk undermining their authority. I stumbled around the *Post* building talking to people, not realizing that I shouldn't always start with the first person I encountered—who often turned out to be the union head—or that people would try to use me for their own purposes. There really wasn't anyone who could take me by the hand and teach me the things I needed to learn and how to go about learning them. I fell into a somewhat mindless pattern of routines and trying to deal with issues as they arose.

Naturally I looked to others for advice and counsel. Two of those who were helpful with specific suggestions were Clare Booth Luce and Walter Lippmann. Clare gave me interesting and useful guidance on how to handle myself at work. Although some of it was peculiar to her and some of it seems dated now, much of it being about a woman in a man's world, I took to heart what she said. Among other things, she warned me not to commit

myself to being in the office a set number of hours each week in case it diminished with time—which it didn't. She also advised me to have a male
secretary, which I did, keeping Charlie Paradise, who had served Phil well
for so many years. Clare also told me to keep in close touch with my correspondence, and that, when I sent mail to some other executive or staff
person to be answered, I should ask to have it back to see how it was handled, so that I would know and learn.

More help came from Walter Lippmann, with whom I had shared my
concern about the excessive amount of reading material I had and how to
sort it all out. Although he thought this troubled me unduly, he wrote me:

> For the time being, my advice would be to devote an hour, or less,
> to the newspapers before you go to the office, concentrating on
> the Post and looking at the Times only for headlines of stories
> that might not be in the Post. Then, instead of trying to study all
> the strange subjects that are reported, make a note of the stories
> in the Post or Times that interest you particularly and that you
> want to know more about. Make a point of calling in the reporter
> who covers it and have him explain it to you. In this way, you will
> kill two birds with one stone. You'll get informed on the news in a
> fairly painless way and you will get to know better than you prob-
> ably would any other way the people who actually write the paper.
>
> I wouldn't try to worry out everything myself. Not everybody,
> by any means, understands everything, and nobody expects you to
> do that.

What I knew was that I was way behind most people engaged with
current issues on a daily basis—in general familiarity with these issues, as
well as in knowledge of specifics. In addition, I am a naturally slow reader,
which made for further problems in getting on top of things. Walter's suggested remedy was a good one, but it would have taken much more self-
confidence than I had to ask reporters to brief me—that would have
required an assurance on my part that I had a right to impose on them to
try to bring me up to speed.

Oveta Hobby, who had also inherited her job as publisher of the
Houston Post Company when her husband died, came to see me at
Newsweek soon after I went to work. She was a personal friend of Phil's and
mine, and of my parents before me. We had a cozy talk about the obligations of a news executive, among which she cited speechmaking. I said that
speeches were going to be outside my bailiwick, that I wasn't going to give
any, because I simply wasn't able to. She responded equally dogmatically,
saying that I had no choice: I would have to learn to do things like that.

She herself hadn't known many things but had learned. I realized, with some dread, that she might be right, and that speechmaking might indeed be in my future.

Feeling that I needed to do some of the things that Phil had done, I created an unnecessarily rigorous schedule, going up to *Newsweek* in New York each week for two days. My intentions were good: the idea being for me to learn, and for the people there to feel I cared about them and their work. Today I'm not sure this was a wise investment of my time and energies, especially since it also left Bill and Steve alone too much.

Newsweek was especially difficult for me because I truly was an outsider. The people working there viewed themselves as an autonomous unit of the company and were happy to be quite separate from Washington. Except for Fritz, whom the executives liked, they welcomed the backing of The Washington Post Company but not its guidance. Having always felt uncertain about *Newsweek*, I was nervous and jittery there. For me, it was the newest and the strangest part of the whole company, practicing what I later called "its own particular approach to journalism." *Newsweek* seemed far from my familiar ground in Washington—literally and figuratively. Because I didn't know most of the people who worked there, nor they me, and because Robin was associated with *Newsweek*, I felt all the more disconnected from it.

On my way to Europe right after Phil's death, I wrote to two men whom I regarded as unfriendly—Ben Bradlee and Arnaud de Borchgrave. I thought of them as Phil's people, Phil's friends, and both of them had stood clearly and decisively with Phil for their own good and separate reasons. Ben felt he owed Phil loyalty for his purchase of *Newsweek*, but I think he, and actually most of the people at *Newsweek*, simply didn't know The Washington Post Company or feel any loyalty to anyone but Phil himself. When they saw things coming apart, they tried to cut a straight professional line and separated Phil from me, naturally taking his side.

Arnaud was a friend of Robin's from *Newsweek*'s Paris bureau, which made me all the more wary of him. But he played a large and useful, if ambiguous, role abroad for *Newsweek*. He was a dashing figure, a charmer of sorts who knew many of the monarchs, rulers, and leaders, and a fine reporter. And he was good for the magazine. (He also lived very well off it.)

What I said to both of them was that the past was past and that I hoped we could all go forward together. Ben doesn't remember receiving such a letter, but I am very clear about having written to both men. I knew enough even then to understand that personal feelings shouldn't enter into professional situations. My later relationship with Ben, of course, became one of the most cherished professional and personal relationships of my life, and one of the most productive. Arnaud remained more or less

distant from me and seemed to feel that I was "out to get him." If I was, it
took me an inordinately long time, since he was at the magazine for seventeen more years, until he was fired by the editors in 1980 over an editorial disagreement. Even then, when Lester Bernstein, *Newsweek*'s editor at
the time, told me that the editors had unanimously decided to part company with Arnaud, I asked if they were certain, stating that Arnaud did
have a lot of talent. Lester's response was, "I came to tell you, not to consult you."

Yet, despite all my problems about the magazine, Miss Dutiful that I
was, I went to New York early every Tuesday morning, stayed over Tuesday night, spent Wednesday at the *Newsweek* offices, and returned late that
afternoon. This allowed me to attend the editorial meeting and conferences on the cover story for the week. I tried my best to learn what made
the magazine work, but I often got quite depressed up there. I was constantly worried about perceived minor slights, or awkward encounters
with people. I couldn't tell which were valid worries and which were not.

It's understandable that I was much more comfortable at the *Post*. Not
only was it in my hometown, on my own turf, but at the *Post* were people
who knew me and whom I knew, especially my dear friends Russ Wiggins
and Al Friendly. I was no doubt more relaxed with the newspaper because
what little work I had done had been on newspapers, and I had lived
through a thirty-year history of having the paper in the family. But even at
the *Post* my road was a bumpy one. The whole start of my working life was
a process of nibbling around the edges, of trying to learn what made editorial and business function and how they fit together. It was a difficult
and lonely process. I made endless unnecessary mistakes and died over
them. There was nothing to do but feel my way. Gradually I put things
into place and began to get used to an office routine, becoming adjusted
to the presence of secretaries, to answering mail, to trying constantly to
relate to people and learn from them or at least to accommodate myself to
them, as they began to accommodate themselves to me. Some people at
work were shy around me, wanting to keep me at a distance, while others
wanted to guard their turf. Some welcomed my presence, but others
viewed me as an ignorant intruder to whom they had to be patient and polite. Most company employees probably went quietly about their business,
not bothering about me at all.

When people were hostile to my arrival on the scene, I took it personally. Some of the executives didn't know how to deal with a woman in
their midst—particularly a woman who controlled the company. I didn't
understand sexism or anything to do with it—nor, in fact, did many of the
men with whom I worked. And I was encumbered by a deep feeling of uncertainty and inferiority and a need to please, to be liked. What people
really want and need is rational, logical leadership, but when I had to de-

cide something, I asked the advice of everyone I could, often irritating those closest to me, who felt, understandably, that I should trust their judgment.

This seems to be what happened between me and John Sweeterman. Tension between us increased from the start, and I wasn't brilliant at handling the situation, to say the least. I seemed to irritate John with all my questions. I may have been welcomed by the news-and-editorial side of the paper, but John and the business side didn't know what to do with me. The feeling was mutual.

I knew it was John who was largely responsible for the paper's success, through his strategies, business plans, and tight-fisted control of the company, which was necessary in those days. John held the purse strings and controlled the budget, so in effect he had his hand in almost everything. Bill Rogers, the company lawyer, always took John's side when I was critical of him. Bill kept telling me that John was doing a fine job and that I should appreciate him. It was a message I failed to get at the time, but Bill was right.

What I see now is that John had been given complete authority by Phil, almost from the time of his arrival in 1950, and that Phil had backed him firmly and completely. His authority had expanded over the years, as Phil grew less involved in the day-to-day operation of the paper, and particularly as he grew ill. From 1961, when he had been made publisher, but especially since the onset of Phil's more pronounced ups and downs, John had been the final decision-maker, consulting no one, conferring with few about his decisions. And here I came along, asking hundreds of questions—Why did he do this? Who was in charge of that? How was this being done? If John had accepted my questioning in the spirit in which it was intended—that I was trying to learn—he might have been able to take me in hand and teach me, and our relationship might have gone better. But he wasn't used to women in business, and particularly one as ignorant as I was. He had a temper when crossed, and we had a few encounters that reduced me to tears and therefore made everything harder.

Yet, despite the strains with John, the *Post* and the company continued to grow. In the years since the purchase of the *Times-Herald*, the paper had in fact flourished, increasing the quantity and quality of news. By the time I went to work, its circulation had reached more than four hundred thousand daily and more than half a million on Sunday, well ahead of the *Star*; in advertising, we were now first in Washington. Our two television stations were starting to grow, too. John Hayes had run the stations in much the same way John Sweeterman ran the paper, having been given the same kind of authority by Phil, but Hayes was more open to me. Perhaps, too, because television was completely strange to me, I stayed out of that business more in the beginning, and therefore didn't get into his hair as I did with John Sweeterman. Also, the stations were doing better than the paper was and didn't face the competitive or labor problems and crises that the *Post* did.

One persistent worry that began as soon as I went to work had to do with rumors that I wanted to sell. Naturally, right after Phil's death there had been numerous offers to buy the whole company. Many people thought I would decide to sell it rather than go to work. Little did they realize that, having lived through the rebirth of the paper from its bankrupt McLean days, having stood by my father and my husband as they built it up with such zeal and devotion, I would never sell; it was unthinkable for me. But I was descended on by people trying to buy. Fritz had received some offers even while I was in Europe, one from CBS through Frank Stanton, which I rejected firmly. Perhaps I overreacted to these overtures. Instead of understanding that we had a desirable and vulnerable-looking property, I regarded the would-be buyers with outrage—more or less as vultures circling around my head, waiting for me, the helpless-seeming widow, to keel over. Because of my insecurity, I was unable to discuss anything to do with purchase offers coolly, and all these feelers had the unhappy effect of adding to my unease. I remember meeting Roy Thomson, the head of a huge Canadian newspaper conglomerate, sometime within the first six months of my being at the company. He took me by surprise by telling me of sending men to scour America to smell out media properties to buy. I actually recall quaking when he said, "There are lots of reasons why people will sell—a paper not doing well, an elderly owner without an heir, a widow. . . ."

The first real offer to buy the company was never formally delivered. It came from Times Mirror through John McCone, then head of the CIA and a friend of the Chandler family. McCone was with Scotty Reston in the back seat of a government limousine, and, knowing that Scotty was my friend and would carry the message to me, he told Scotty of Times Mirror's interest in acquiring the *Post*. Scotty actually answered for me, saying that he knew I wasn't interested in selling but would let me know of the inquiry. The next bidder—and the most persistent—was Sam Newhouse, who offered $100 million for the company. We turned this down emphatically, but Newhouse never took no for an answer and kept reappearing with better offers. Every time I shut one door, he would enter through another. He began to try to approach us through intermediaries, one of whom was Clark Clifford.

The last try during that early period was the most amazing. Four months after I went to work, Ted Sorensen came to lunch with me to explore the possibility of his working at the *Post*, the idea of which appealed to me: he had been a large power in the Kennedy White House and was obviously able. I very much wanted to think creatively on how to attract

Ted. We discussed jobs for him in administration, in editorial, and as a columnist. He was negative about everything until finally he came forward with what was actually on his mind: "The only job I really want is yours," he said. "Why don't you move over and let me run the company for you?" I was startled but managed to say that, if mine was the only job he wanted, there was nothing more to talk about.

A few months later, Ted called and asked if I was going to a particular party. When I said I was, he suggested picking me up before the party, because he had something to discuss. He arrived a little early, and we sat down in my library. Without much hesitation, Ted said, "I am empowered to offer you a hundred million for the *Post* alone. I would run it, and you can keep the rest." I was truly nonplussed. I said, "Ted, is this from Newhouse?" After a brief moment of playing games, Ted said that it was, but the difference was that he would be running the *Post*. Newhouse then operated his papers extremely tightly, with small newsholes and large profit margins. I said, "You don't really think Newhouse would let you run it, do you?" Ted insisted that he would, which was supposed to appeal to me. When I said I was surprised he would participate in such an offer, his response was, "I told you I wanted your job." And in that jolly spirit, we left for the party.

This was the last offer of that kind, although there were several more feelers in later years for all or part of the company, and particularly for *Newsweek*—we must have rejected half a dozen such offers. Despite these adamant rejections, the rumors that *Newsweek* was for sale kept recurring in print and were damaging to morale there. At the end of my first working year, Andrew Heiskell, then one of the three heads of Time Inc., and an old friend, took me to lunch at "21," where he hammered home the point: "What are you doing keeping *Newsweek*? You don't know anything about the magazine business and you shouldn't try to be here in New York." Surprisingly, he didn't really rattle me. I had the same fears he was expressing, but I felt confidence in Fritz, and things seemed to be moving along, not necessarily smoothly but at least in a positive direction. I told him that though I understood his point of view, I thought I'd stay.

My basic reason for hanging on to this admittedly precarious situation was the people on the magazine. It wasn't a business-motivated decision; rather, I thought we had recently bought an institution, involving many people, and to turn around and sell the whole thing a few years later wasn't right. I felt a strong loyalty to those people and to the organization, although I didn't always feel it was reciprocated.

THERE WERE a lot of firsts for me in those early months of my working life. I joined the board of Bowater Mersey as its first woman director. This was my first business board other than being on the company's, but it was to be followed by many others over the years. I also replaced Phil on the board of George Washington University.

I began to have lunches with others throughout the industry and gave my first dinner for a business friend, Otis Chandler, as a way of publicly showing a renewed commitment to our working relationship with the news service. Otis wrote me afterwards, thanking me for the "exquisite party," and adding: "I know it was not easy for you. . . . At least the ice has been broken and things like this will come easier for you from now on."

As part of getting better acquainted with the other divisions of the company, I visited our two television stations. In Jacksonville, I spent time with Glenn Marshall, who ran WJXT there. Glenn was an early enthusiast for cable television, which didn't interest John Hayes, and I recall that, even on this first visit I made in my new role, he spoke about its importance for the future and the possibility of cable's being the gateway to pay-TV. I was too new at my job to be able to participate usefully in the discussion, so we didn't make the leap into cable at this early stage.

I started regularly attending *Post* editorial meetings and lunches, which proved to be the biggest help to me in comprehending what was going on in the outside world. I began to understand journalistic and political jargon, the language in which reporters and editors and government officials spoke. I remember one very early editorial lunch—when I was still painfully unsure of myself—at which our guest was Madame Nhu, the sinister, powerful sister-in-law of South Vietnamese President Ngo Dinh Diem. She was justly infamous for her role in that country and widely feared and disliked. This was the first lunch at which I asked a question, and I almost collapsed from worry as I summoned up my courage to ask it. I have no memory of what I actually asked, but I have a very vivid recollection of nearly dying afterwards from embarrassment and fear that I had looked stupid or ignorant.

I also distinctly recall my first lunch at the White House in my new role, a lunch in honor of President Tito of Yugoslavia. I took with me an election-projection poll, which I gave President Kennedy on my way out. He glanced at it, stuck it in his pocket, smiled at me, and said, "Oh, so that's the way it's going to be."

I got a rapid introduction to another aspect of an owner's or publisher's job. In October 1963, I received a call from Mac Bundy from the White House saying that he was in the office with President Kennedy. They had gotten wind that Russ Wiggins was going to be critical of a trip that Jackie was proposing to take on Aristotle Onassis's yacht—she was going off to recuperate from the birth and subsequent death of her baby, and the president had asked Franklin Roosevelt, Jr., to accompany her. Russ viewed it as a conflict of interest for Roosevelt to be a guest of Onassis, since Roosevelt was undersecretary of commerce at the time and Onassis was doing business with him. I did tell Mac that I'd talk to Russ, but the editorial ran.

This was the first of many, many calls I have gotten over the years, which have given me a lot of experience in being the go-between between complainers, supplicants, and others of all kinds on the one hand and editors at the *Post* or *Newsweek* on the other. The editors are more often right than wrong, and Russ was clearly right this time. He stood by his position and criticized the trip editorially. The trip took place anyway, and life carried on.

Another strange and difficult first experience was being an object of interest throughout the media and being interviewed. This happened a few times during the first year. In one published interview, I said I did not find it difficult to be a woman executive in a field dominated by men, and "after a while, people forget you're a woman." That last was bravura, brought on by my newness and inexperience. Women's issues hadn't yet surfaced, and I simply wasn't sensitive to how people viewed me. Since I was so painfully new and had so much to learn, the unpleasantness of being condescended to and the strangeness of being the only woman in so many rooms got mixed up in my mind. But I didn't blame my male colleagues for condescending—I just thought it was due to my being so new. It took the passage of time and the women's lib years to alert me properly to the real problems of women in the workplace, including my own.

I also had my first experience in a labor situation and didn't do very well. The *Star* underwent a wildcat strike by the typographical union. There was a lot of grumbling about how the paper had fired a union executive, and our union at the *Post* made it clear that it hoped we would not support the *Star*'s management. The Washington newspapers traditionally had negotiated with the craft unions together, and we were just deciding to support the *Star* when, one evening at dinner, I met Jim Reynolds, a distant friend, who was assistant secretary of labor—representing labor, of course, a fact I didn't fully appreciate. "You're not going to support the *Star*, are you?" he asked. I said it looked as though we were. He said how foolish that would be and gave his reasons. I picked up the phone and made the mistake of passing this on to John Sweeterman, who took it, not unnaturally, as my own opinion and therefore my direction, and drew back from his plans to support the *Star*. The whole incident was very upsetting to *Star* executives, who in the end had to give in to the strikers. Crosby Boyd, the *Star*'s president, came over to see me and said he hoped this was not a new policy, since historically we had supported each other. I agreed to continue our old ways. This was a lesson about the weight of my voice—I hadn't understood that I could no longer say something without its carrying a message that I might not want to convey. Later, when our very survival was at stake, the *Star*, under new ownership, chose not to support us.

I also had my first encounter of many with a reporter's getting into trouble with a dictator in a foreign country, usually over the reporter's freedom to report. In this case it was Bob McCabe, who represented *Newsweek* in Hong Kong. He had actually been jailed in Indonesia, and I talked about it with George Ball in the State Department, who promised to keep on top of the matter and, indeed, did make a statement to President Sukarno. This was the first of a series of battles with dictators— which go on to this day—in which it is always important to let the political leaders know that the organization and its executives personally stand behind the reporters.

I made my first business call for *Newsweek* with Fritz, this one on the Chrysler Corporation. Although this kind of visit continued throughout my working life, the amount of good they do is hard to measure. I do believe, though, that in the end knowing a company's executives sometimes makes a difference in large advertising decisions. At the least, it establishes you as a human presence.

A bigger test for me, and another first, was a speech to the *Newsweek* advertising-sales meeting in Puerto Rico. I vividly recall the terror of giving this first speech, but I had quickly discovered that I had no choice— giving speeches was part of the job description. Because my father, mother, and husband had all written their own speeches, I wasn't aware of speechwriters. For this particular speech, I sat down with my pencil and a pad and wrote out some thoughts of a personal kind. When I got to the part where I felt I had to say something about *Newsweek*, I was completely stuck and consulted Fritz, who reminded me that Emmet Hughes, Eisenhower's former speechwriter, who had been hired by Phil as a *Newsweek* columnist, was supposed to provide this kind of assistance. Emmet took my start and completed a speech that we called "I Believe in Individuals," which I delivered on wobbly knees. Even reading from a text took more experience than I had, but the emotion of the moment helped me muddle through, and the speech was actually well received.

Learning to create and give speeches was an agony for a long time. Emmet helped me on one or two other occasions, but finally refused to go on, because I was so hard to work with. I simply didn't know when a text was fine and finished and when it needed more work. For years, I had no one to help me. I went through several speechwriters but couldn't figure out how to formulate with them what it was I needed or wanted to say, or to appraise the outcome. Meg Greenfield, who arrived at the *Post* in 1968, offered to help, and was essential to the speech process for many years. It wasn't until eighteen years later, when Guyon (Chip) Knight arrived at the Post Company, that the problem was completely solved.

In any case, all of these firsts during that first year of my working life added up, and I began to realize that just by putting one foot in front of the other I actually was moving forward. Despite all the inner turbulence and confusion, and despite my feeling unsure that life could really go on without Phil, my days were becoming more endurable and even, at times, interesting again.

ON NOVEMBER 22, 1963, I had invited my old friends Arthur Schlesinger and Ken Galbraith to have lunch with the editors of *Newsweek* to discuss their views of the "Back of the Book" section of the magazine. I stopped by the White House to pick up Arthur, who was working there at the time, and we flew to New York and assembled for lunch with Ken, Fritz, and all the top editors and others concerned. We were having drinks when someone came flying down the hall, stuck his head in, and said, "The president has been shot."

Our reaction was disbelief—either there was a mistake or it would be all right—yet we were panic-stricken. We rushed to a television set, and the reports quickly made it apparent that the situation was very serious. A Secret Service man, Clint Hill, who had accompanied Jackie to India when Ken was ambassador there, was quoted as saying that he thought the president had been fatally wounded. Ken said, "If that comes from Clint Hill, it has to be taken seriously." When the horrifying news came that the president was dead, we moved quickly to get to the airport to return to Washington. Ken later recalled the contrast between the total crushing feeling in the car and the still-exuberant noonday crowds, who hadn't yet heard what had happened.

When we got back to Washington, we went together to the White House. I was reluctant to go, since I was much less close to the Kennedys than either Ken or Arthur, but they both insisted I come with them, so I did. We went into a room full of people in which Ted Sorensen was giving orders. After we'd been there a short time, he looked up impatiently and asked everyone who didn't have a specific job to do and a right to be there to clear the room, at which point I departed, certain the remark was aimed at me, even though a great many other people left, too.

Our sense of loss was enormous—for the country and for so many of us personally. Isaiah Berlin summed it up best when he later said, "I feel less safe." Bill Walton remembered that, after helping make plans for the funeral, he returned to his house, shattered, and my mother phoned him, crying. According to Bill, she was just so straightforward. She said: "We're nothing but a goddamned banana republic," and hung up.

The day after the assassination, I went back to the East Room of the White House, where President Kennedy's casket was lying in state, and then I went to call on Lady Bird, who had invited me to tea. (Liz Carpenter, who became Lady Bird's press secretary, later said that President Johnson suggested that she talk to me.) Like all of us, the Johnsons were in shock at the loss of Jack Kennedy. At the same time, they wer ⌐ having to take on their enormous responsibilities as president and first lady, and to take them on with such heavy feelings. As Liz Carpenter explained, "If you only knew how awful we all felt after the assassination. Not only because we'd lost this golden president, but because it happened in Texas. It was just a hell of a burden to bear." Lady Bird described it this way: "They look at the living and wish for the dead."

She has also spoken about what it was like for her to become first lady: "I feel like I've walked on stage for a part I've never rehearsed." Although this was an apt description for my own new role in life, I felt at a total loss to be of any help to her. We were all so much in shock that it was hard to imagine any other administration and any other people in the roles of president and first lady. I admit that I didn't appreciate at the time that Lady Bird Johnson would do things very well in her own way.

Liz Carpenter also later talked with me on the phone about what kind of program would be right for Lady Bird to undertake, bringing up the idea of "beautification" as one possibility. Because I had worked for so long on the District's severe social problems, I worried that beautification was too superficial. Liz wisely said that Lady Bird had to choose something on which she could have a real impact. Liz was right, and the beautification program was a triumph. Happily for me, Lady Bird asked me to be a member of her Beautification Committee, and I was delighted to serve.

WHOEVER FOLLOWED John Kennedy would have had a difficult time. Certainly a new era had begun. On December 3, less than two weeks after the assassination and before the Johnsons had moved into the White House, Joe and Susan Mary and I were invited to dinner by the president and Lady Bird. As we walked into the entrance hall of the Elms, we saw the portrait of Sam Rayburn hanging just to the left. The president spoke of how much he lamented that Rayburn and Phil weren't there at this moment, when he most needed their advice.

My memory of the evening is spotty. Jack Valenti was present, and I think we four were the only guests. Susan Mary remembered that the president was in a friendly, gentle mood, which she said "was astonishing in view of the fact that he soon told us over cocktails he had been having a very rough day because what he called 'the Kennedy men' . . . had come one by one to present their resignations to him." He also talked about what had happened in Dallas. He described sitting with Lady Bird in a room at the hospital waiting to hear the news from the operating room. He couldn't remember what the room looked like except that it was small and there were a lot of sheets in it. Twice Lady Bird had left to see if she could help Jackie, who was standing alone in the hall, but she had come back and reported that Jackie preferred to remain alone. It was while they were still in the room with the sheets that someone—Susan Mary thought it was Kenny O'Donnell—came in and said, "Mr. President, the president is dead." Then Johnson stopped talking about the events of November 22 and began telling Texas stories. It was an unusual night.

BY THE BEGINNING of 1964, I had got a bit of a start on my job, but on a personal level I was lonely. Life alone had to be figured out—single life is hard to resume after twenty-three years of marriage. I was miserable every time I did another thing alone that Phil and I had done together, or any time I entered a place that flooded me with memories. For ages, I couldn't look at anything of Phil's—especially his handwriting or personal objects. As quickly as I could, I did over his rooms, both at R Street and at the farm. For a while the associations with Glen Welby were so gruesome that I wanted to walk away from it, but I had to remember that the children didn't have that horrible scene in their heads. For them, Glen Welby had no negative associations; they loved the place and everything about it. So I kept going there, although I rebuilt that bathroom so that nothing was in the same place, and changed things around so that I wasn't so spooked every time I walked into the house. For me, always, Glen Welby was the essence of Phil. It was his ponds, his fields, his fishing, his hunting, his dogs—in short, his creation. It was the place where we had spent so much time together, and it was the place that was so inspired by his presence, not to speak of being the scene of his death.

I remained lonely in most places, especially when I went to New York. People were generous about hospitality, but I hated being alone in hotels. At first, I was painfully shy, but, because I found it so hard to be alone, I began going out a great deal. Social life quickly became spoiling and fun for me. I started to see more people in New York, including Truman Capote, the Paleys, and, to a lesser extent, the Jock Whitneys and the James Fosburghs (Babe Paley's two sisters were Betsey Whitney and Minnie Fosburgh), as well as Pamela Churchill Hayward and her charismatic husband, Leland.

In Washington, I also began to see more and more people—advertisers or business types related to the paper, a combination of friends (new and old) in journalism and government, from both parties. It was Washington at its best. Looking back, I am appalled at how much I went out. I had grown up with my own parents going out all the time, so I suppose it was easy for me to slip into a pattern of doing the same, or traveling a lot without the children, first with Phil and then on my own. Somehow, after his death, I didn't think to change the pattern—I didn't realize that I should have worked harder to make more time for the children.

Though my going to work had definitely made it easier for me to resume life after Phil's death, it certainly made it harder for Bill and Steve. In effect, they lost both parents at once. Up to that time I had been a fairly present mother, attending school functions, driving teams to sports events, trying to be back in the afternoons when the kids got back from school. All that was mostly over now, though I tried to be with them as much as possible, at least getting to some of their school occasions. I faithfully attended Bill's and Steve's football games and took the boys with me to events when I could, although undoubtedly not enough. In different ways, they were both having a hard time. Billy led a typical teenage life at St. Albans, but at home he lived very largely behind his closed door. Steve had the hardest time of all—too old to be left with a baby sitter, yet not old enough to be on his own. A gifted boy, Steve was not a jock, as his older brothers had been, and as the St. Albans School formula called for. Like Don, he had skipped a grade, a disastrous idea for both of them, which Don had warned against for Steve when it was suggested by the school. In fact, St. Albans was probably the wrong school altogether for Steve.

In addition, because it was all so painful to me, I had found Phil's illness and death difficult to talk about—even to the children, which must have added to their own heavy burden. At first I didn't talk about Phil at all; I just shut the door, a mistake with an impact on all of us. Lally somewhat assuaged my guilt about Bill and Steve by writing me:

> Yes, of course it's ghastly for Billy and Stevie but I still believe so firmly that they were oh so lucky (moi aussi) to have had him for a father—even if it was only for eleven or fifteen years. Because even if I try desperately hard to be objective I find them both rather perfect and certainly think that so much is due to Pa and above all to you and Pa *together*.

On the social scene, one thing that happened was that I began to be asked out on "dates." My principal suitor was Adlai Stevenson, who turned up increasingly in my life. It's hard to judge exactly where I ranked among all his lady friends. For my part, I was always fond of him and admiring, but I was not at all enamored of him. I didn't share the breathless enthusiasm my mother and daughter—and many other ladies—had for him. I used to get impatient with his indecision. A mutual friend, the British economist Barbara Ward, told me that I had to understand him and be more patient, but I found it difficult. Perhaps Phil's ambivalent attitude toward him had left me with some of *his* annoyance, but I think this was genuinely my own reaction. Nevertheless, I saw a great deal of Adlai. He stayed with me frequently when he came to Washington, and we went out in New York, too. I suspect that this was one of the few friendships he had with women in which there was more enthusiasm on his side.

In the summer of 1964, the *National Enquirer* did a story on the two of us, fueling all kinds of rumors:

> UN Ambassador Adlai Stevenson is involved in a romance that could become the hottest political story of the year. He is courting Mrs. Philip Graham, widow of the late publisher of the Washington Post and Newsweek magazine, and the owner of a chain of TV stations.
>
> If Mrs. Graham should agree to a wedding before the Democratic National Convention in August, friends of Stevenson report that his chances for the Democratic Vice Presidential nomination would soar.
>
> Not only would Stevenson gain an attractive wife but with her would go control of one of the most powerful TV-magazine-newspaper combines in the U.S.

I sent the clipping to Adlai with a bantering note, joking, "I am sure you didn't realize the treat you have in store for you. After all, what could do your Vice Presidential chances more good than to marry a TV-magazine-newspaper combine? I am ready and waiting but we'd better announce before Atlantic City."

THAT SUMMER, Pam Berry came over from London to visit me and follow some of the political campaigning, so she and I and Joe Alsop set out for the Republican Convention in San Francisco on July 10, and Lally joined us as the convention began. I wrote my mother that I knew of "no nearer resemblance to the three witches in Macbeth huddling around the caldron than the thought of Pam and Lally and me in one establishment."

We were all in a high state of alarm about the likely nomination of the extremely conservative—we thought reckless—Barry Goldwater. His views on nuclear issues disturbed us, as did his views on civil rights. In addition, he had attracted all the John Birch kind of Republicans. Goldwater seemed menacing to us at the time, but I realize now that we had a very distorted view of him—and an unfair one.

Memorable for me was a speech that former President Eisenhower made in which he attacked newspaper columnists; convention-goers throughout the entire hall started booing the press. Eisenhower's theme was taken up by every other speaker. One man who was seconding the nomination of the vice-president actually spat out the words: "Walter Lippmann, Walter Reuther, *The New York Times*, and *Pravda*." This brought down the house, with everyone cheering wildly except those of us in the press section, who sat mournfully quiet. I felt we were watching a minority take over a major party.

Still, though I was clearly a Johnson supporter, I was intent on keeping the paper independent and maintaining the *Post*'s basic policy of nonendorsement. Mac and Mary Bundy came down to Glen Welby for a weekend in late July, between the two conventions. Just a few days afterwards, Mac wrote a memo for the president on what we had talked about. I didn't know about this until more than thirty years later, when it was found in the Johnson Presidential Library. The memo is interesting for its insider look both at what Mac and I discussed that weekend and for its insight into Johnson's hopes for an endorsement and the way an administration dealt with the press:

> Mary and I had a delightful weekend at Kay Graham's, in the course of which I told her that it would be a great help if the Post would endorse us openly. I told her that this seemed only a reasonable request in the light of her violent comments on the Republican Convention and on Goldwater himself. She asked me with a smile whether I was acting for you, and I said of course; I asked her whom else she thought I would be acting for. She then told me that if I were a Washingtonian I would know that the Washington Post has never given its formal endorsement to anyone, and she told me that if any of us at the White House can't tell whom the Post is for, then it must be because we can't read. I told her in reply that just because the Post had never endorsed someone, it ought to begin now, when the stakes are so high and the issues so clear, but I got no commitment.
>
> My very strong impression is that Kay Graham needs a little personal attention from you. Not from her but from other people in the Post-Newsweek establishment, I have heard snippy remarks to the effect that Harry Luce, the arch Republican, seems to be more welcome around the White House than people who have supported the Kennedy-Johnson Administration 90% of the time. I find that the parable of the laborers in the vineyard does not do much good with such people (it is not the most persuasive of the parables for most of us).
>
> My suggestion is that you might ask Kay to come for lunch or an informal dinner some day, on the same basis that Harry Luce

came the last time. If you ask her and then ask her to bring any three or four of her people from either the magazine or the newspaper, I think a lot of good can be done. I know that a lot of these individuals are not your favorites, but I cannot help thinking that if we can swing the Chamber of Commerce, we ought to be able to handle the busy liberals—especially as Kay herself is very sensible when she hears both sides. . . .

Mac offered the president three options: work out a lunch, work out an informal dinner, let it wait a while. LBJ chose the last. Someone else had put a handwritten note on the memo before it went to the president saying that Bundy had been shown how many times I had been invited to the White House in the last six months. Those occasions had included a luncheon for Queen Frederika of Greece, a dinner for the prime minister of Denmark, a luncheon for "women-doers" that I'd regretted, and a lunch for newspaper publishers.

As it happens, just two days after Mac's memo had gone to the president, I wrote to Senator Goldwater. In my efforts to bend over backwards to be fair in the paper and in *Newsweek*, I wanted to ensure that we were not giving him short shrift:

I know you knew my husband Philip Graham and regret very much that I don't know you. I would like very much to come to see you on a "get acquainted" basis if you should have a few minutes within the next few weeks. I will call your office to see if this is possible. We would also like to have you to lunch here at the paper or at Newsweek or both if possible, and I feel it would help us in our coverage of your campaign. If you could do one here, I would be glad to have the Newsweek editors down.

In the meantime I want to say to you how very much it has been my desire and will continue to be my desire to cover the campaign as fairly and objectively as we can. Of course I include the three parts of The Washington Post Company when I say this—The Post itself, Newsweek, and the television stations here and in Jacksonville.

When I use the words "fairly and objectively" I realize how difficult this is to achieve at all and how differently too it can be viewed.

I would appreciate it very much if you would send any differences of opinion on this subject to me at once should they arise—or we would also be glad to cooperate with you or your staff in any way you feel we can help insure complete and accurate reporting.

> These are not idle words as I believe very deeply that we in
> control of news media have a solemn obligation to this kind of
> news reporting and that much depends on our ability to fulfill it.

Nor were they idle words. I believed intuitively—and the feeling grew with experience—that the news columns *had* to be fair and detached, even while recognizing that there really is no such thing as "objectivity." The very act of deciding what is news and what is not involves the use of judgment, and editors should use their best detached judgment to achieve fairness in news columns. The editorial page and editorial views are so completely separate from the news columns that they sometimes are not even in touch, and certainly don't influence each other.

The Democratic National Convention of 1964 began in late August in Atlantic City. I took Don around with me a good deal, and he got a lot out of it. A former girlfriend of his was also at the convention, but—somewhat to my embarrassment, I have to admit—she was there as part of the "human chain" around the auditorium, demonstrating on behalf of the Mississippi Freedom Party.

The heat and humidity in Atlantic City were intense, and we were all glad when the week wound down. Hot and tired, we headed for the airport. I had with me my secretary, Charlie Paradise, and Luvie Pearson and Lally, along with a few *Post* reporters and photographers who were going to fly back with us on the company plane. Because of some confusion, we arrived at the airport an hour later than the intended takeoff time, and when we got there, Air Force One was drawn up at the gate and our plane was way off across the field. When it finally pulled up closer, our bags and the photographers' gear were loaded, the nine of us were collected, and we all boarded the plane and sat there melting in the extreme heat while the airfield was shut down because the helicopters with the president and vice-presidential candidate aboard were arriving.

I was gnashing my teeth when Lally said, "Oh, Ma, let's go see the helicopters land." With the temperature at a steaming one hundred degrees inside the plane, I agreed. By the time we had run over to the fence, the president was out of the helicopter with Lady Bird and had started walking down the long line of the crowd gathered at the airport, shaking hands across the fence. Luvie, Lally, and I were at the end of the line, between two parked cars and the fence. I didn't think the president would come down that far, but he did. He wasn't really looking as he walked right past me, shaking hands automatically. I was wearing a bandanna around my sweaty head, a sleeveless cotton dark-blue dress, no stockings, and moccasins, so I wasn't surprised that he didn't recognize me. Involuntarily I exclaimed, "Hi, Lyndon," never having called him anything but "Mr.

President" since November 22. He stopped, looked surprised, and said, "Hello, Kay, what are you doing here?"

"Waiting for you to leave," I replied.

"Do you want a ride?" he asked.

I was so flabbergasted that I assumed absent-mindedly that he was going to Washington and asked if Lally and Luvie could come too. He said, "Sure, but you realize we're going to Texas?"

"Texas!" I exclaimed. "I can't go to Texas." Steve was expecting me in Washington, and I had houseguests already waiting at Glen Welby; obviously I had to get home. Luvie kicked me hard in the shins and said firmly, "Go."

"Come on," the president continued. "Have you got a bag?"

"Yes, but don't bother with it. I don't want to keep you waiting, and I'd love to come." Before I could turn around, two Secret Service men descended and asked where my bags were. Another one, who turned out to be the president's chief agent, Rufus Youngblood, said, "Follow me." Rufus and I became friends, and he told me later that Johnson had said, "Lift that woman over the fence." Happily for me, Rufus had pointed out that there was a gate and ushered me through it. Luvie had heard the whole exchange, but I only had time to say to Lally as I was whisked past her, "I'm off to Texas." Considering my two suitcases full of dirty, smelly clothes worn in the damp heat of Atlantic City, I believe no one ever started out for a state visit so inadequately prepared.

The president grabbed my arm and took me to the stairs of the 707. I hung back, waiting for him to go up, but instead he pushed me ahead of him into the jet. A reporter asked my name as we went up the steps, the door closed, and off we went.

I hastily looked around the small compartment into which I had stepped, which included only the Humphreys—Hubert had just been nominated for the vice-presidency—and the Tom Connallys and the Humphreys' son, Douglas, then sixteen. I fled to the front of the plane, where I found, besides a press pool, every Texas politician I had ever heard of and other important Texans from business and industry. From the White House staff were George Reedy, Jack Valenti, and Bill Moyers, the latter two chomping at the bit, having been suddenly herded onto the plane when they were exhausted from the campaign and the convention and had been promised time off.

I settled down with someone from the governor's staff and had just begun to talk Texas politics when Lady Bird came down the aisle and said, "Kay, there's a man back there who wants to see you." I went back to where the president was, sat down at a table opposite him, and began by congratulating him on the way the convention had gone, the outcome of the credentials fight, the selection of Humphrey, and the manner in which he had handled it all. The president then launched into a description of what had gone on from his point of view regarding his choice for the vice-presidency. "I have never touched so many bases on any issue," he said, enumerating some of the two hundred or so calls he had made. He emphasized that he had wanted the process to get to a point where people were fairly unanimous in their choice and were urging him to take someone, rather than his pushing them to accept his choice. In the end, I gather, the Kennedys and other crucial people were all entreating him to name Humphrey, and that is exactly as he wished it to happen.

The president complained despairingly about his living quarters in Atlantic City: "Will you tell me how I ended up in a two-bedroom un-air-conditioned house fifteen minutes from the center of town with no food? After I changed my shirt once and my pajamas twice, I just gave up. It was right on the street with people outside the window, so you couldn't even open the windows, and there were fifteen people in the two bedrooms. Then, when I wanted to go out, Security had locked the doors. Bird, how did that happen?" he yelled out.

We then went on to discuss various people in the media. Of those at *Newsweek*, LBJ said that he had not trusted Ben Bradlee at first but was impressed with the accuracy of his reporting of the interview that both Bradlee and Jack Steele of *Time* had with him; he was beginning to change his mind about Ben. He said that Eddie Folliard was his favorite *Post* reporter, and maybe his favorite reporter, period.

He then moved on to the newspapers that would be for him, naming the Cowles papers, Tom Vail's Cleveland paper, Oveta Hobby's, and the *Kansas City Star*, the latter two of which did indeed endorse shortly thereafter. He speculated on others and said he thought that Otis Chandler and the *Los Angeles Times* would not endorse. He was obviously hoping for our endorsement, but I wasn't yet prepared to change the policy inherited from Phil and my father. After some remarks about various possibilities for the Cabinet, the president suddenly said he was going back to the bedroom and left, and I returned to the front of the plane.

As I was chatting with Mary Rather, the president's secretary, an air-force major came by and said, "You are to get in the number-one chopper." Lady Bird followed and told me to remember "the Gay bedroom" if someone asked where to put my bags or where I was to go. I took the opportunity to suggest that I just return to Washington from Austin, telling her I felt the president had been carried away and that I had enjoyed the trip immensely but that I really shouldn't be there when she was so tired and he needed to confer with Humphrey. She insisted that I come, but said she hoped I'd understand if she disappeared into bed for about twenty-four hours. She never did, poor thing.

There were several hundred people waiting in the broiling heat at the air-force base near Austin where we landed, and all four of the principals—Lyndon and Lady Bird, Hubert and Muriel—worked the line for a long time. Later, the president mentioned choosing to shake a "colored" hand over several white ones, substantiating something Bill Moyers had said to me when I expressed worry about the quick invitation: "Don't be silly; he's impetuous but he always knows what he's doing."

The hand-shaking and picture-taking finally ended, and a kind air-force major took me to the helicopter at a discreet moment when the wives were entering and before the candidates got there. I was glad to be out of the limelight, having spent a great deal of time jumping around to try to avoid being included in public events or photos with the two families.

I was charmed by the Humphreys, whom I hadn't known very well. I found him truly funny, utterly human and honest, and her the same. During the helicopter ride, there was a marvelous exchange between the candidates, begun by Humphrey, who said he just wished his daddy could have been there at the convention on Thursday night. LBJ said he only wished *his* daddy had lived to see him in Congress, which had been the height of his father's ambition for him. "My dad lived that long," Humphrey responded. "I was elected in January and he had a stroke the following March, but he was there when I was sworn in. When I looked up at him he was in such a glow of pride he looked as if he had a halo around his head."

At one point Johnson said that he would love to make Arthur Goldberg, who was on the Supreme Court, attorney general, but concluded, "I'll probably put Katzenbach in, at least for a while. I'd like Goldberg to do it, but he probably won't want to get off the Court. I started to talk to him about it the other day, but I just started to get my hand up his skirt when we were interrupted"—typical of Johnson's earthy language.

I was momentarily alarmed when LBJ's head fell over in a snooze, but the short nap seemed like a shot in the arm and revived him completely. He woke up just in time to point out the ranch and the swimming pool as we landed in a swirl of dust that blew across the cattle looking up from the surrounding fields. He invited me to sit beside him in the front of an electric golf cart, which he drove. Lady Bird sat on my other side, and the three Humphreys climbed in behind and we lurched away.

Instead of taking us to the house, he started down the driveway, across the Pedernales River, and out the front gate and down the highway. The cars passing by slowed up to look. People waved. The president exchanged greetings. Cameras were hanging out of every car, and he willingly stopped for pictures.

As people got out of their cars to shake hands, traffic stalled. The

Secret Service, used to Johnson's sudden whims, kept things fairly calm and good-natured, but I noticed that they had emerged suddenly from everywhere and were very much on the lookout. Finally, the president turned back to the house, by then talking about boating. Lady Bird firmly but gently got him to rest in bed, while the Humphreys and I went swimming.

The president reappeared after only a short rest and asked if we wanted to go boating. When we agreed, to Muriel's and my utter astonishment we found ourselves back in the helicopter, to be swept across what looked like a brown desert to pick up a friend and then flown back to a huge inland lake where the president's boat was kept.

"Come on, Kay," the president said, "you go in the little boat with me." The rest of the party got in a larger motorboat, while he and I and his young secretary, Vicky, got in a rakish speedboat behind which she water-skied at his request. By now it was dusk and quite cold in the water. The president drove at breakneck speed, occasionally bouncing on the water as if it were concrete, which slowed him down only temporarily. Two Secret Service boats followed us, trying to steer clear of the skier.

He finally handed over the speedboat to a Secret Service agent and we got into the big boat with the others, whereupon he again started reviewing Humphrey's nomination. He mentioned that he owed his own nomination largely to Phil and talked about how Phil had always thought that he, Johnson, was better than other people did. He also confided that many people, especially conservatives, had urged that he take Robert Mc-Namara for vice-president, not realizing, said Johnson, that McNamara was far more liberal than they thought, assuming he must be conservative because he had been the president of Ford Motor Company.

The discussions at dinner were wide-ranging and always political. That first night we talked about the loyalty of Mrs. Earl Long in the Louisiana delegation, at which point—right in the middle of the conversation—the president picked up the ever-present phone from under the table and tried unsuccessfully to call her. Later, he referred to the next year's budget and said that, although it would have to increase, he still wanted to keep it under $100 billion—which, by all sorts of game-playing, he managed to do.

Although we were all ready to collapse from such a long day—not to mention such an action-packed week—when dinner was over, LBJ suggested a walk down the road to call on Cousin Oriole and Aunt Jessie, who lived in a little cabin at the end of the lane. Aunt Jessie was the youngest of the previous generation of Johnsons and the only surviving member. Oriole was almost completely deaf, and the president had to beat on the door and yell like a banshee before they woke up and opened the door.

We waited for a moment while they put on wraps; then we all sat on the porch where Aunt Jessie had been sleeping. The president actually lay down on the bed and went to sleep while the rest of us talked to the old lady, a ritual which the secretaries told us was followed every time he went home. Hubert carried on a conversation with Aunt Jessie, drawing out her stories—one about LBJ's father announcing his birth by saying, "Here is a senator"; another about a birthday party of hers to which many people had brought presents. The president had brought only a cake, but when she cut into it, she was relieved to find a $100 bill inside.

On the way back to the ranch house, Lady Bird turned to me and said, "Kay, I'm afraid I don't know how to tell you to ring for breakfast in the morning. We used to have a real simple system in the house, but it has all been replaced and I don't understand it." She asked an agent walking beside us what I should do. "Just ask the operator, ma'am, and he can get you any place in the world." I laughed and asked if he could get me something as simple as the kitchen.

Saturday was much like the previous day. The two candidates discussed campaign strategy, Humphrey volunteering to go into farm areas, where he felt at home. After another outing on the boat, we got back late for a country barbecue that LBJ had to attend in honor of his birthday. He grumbled all the way, complaining that Lady Bird had gotten him into it. He was so savage about her that I, sitting in the front seat, spontaneously said, "She also got you where you are today." This angered him even more, and he went on blaming her and complaining, until I finally heard myself saying, "Oh, shut up, er ... Mr. President"—after which I was acutely embarrassed. I was half in awe of him and half felt as though I really knew him. There was a brief silence, broken by Hubert being his usual jovial self and making some comment that alleviated the tension.

At the barbecue, the president ended up speaking at great length and seriously about world affairs. When I commented on this on the way back, he said that he didn't want all those reporters to think these were hick people whom he didn't take seriously, but that he had talked much longer than he had meant to. I thought the speech very good.

There were some neighbors in that night for a late dinner. Again, the conversation ranged across a lot of subjects, but, despite his talking on and on, LBJ seemed so preoccupied that I asked him if he was worried about the Vietnam situation, which had not yet been mentioned. "Yes, very," he replied, without elaborating. At one point he turned to Humphrey and said, "God has a funny way of taking care of things. I think it's because I always try to do right."

That night, after dinner, Johnson and Humphrey and some of the staff who were there at the ranch sat up until 2:00 a.m. working on campaign plans. We were supposed to leave at 9:00 the next morning, but our early departure got pushed back, though, when it was decided we would all go to church in Fredericksburg, about thirty miles from the ranch. Even though this was an unannounced stop, there were a number of reporters and cameras. It was such a tiny church that after the Johnsons took communion they had to leave their seats in the front row and stand outside until everyone else had taken communion, when they returned for the end of the service.

As we returned to the ranch, the president was again at the wheel, followed by an increasingly long line of cars, all headed for his old birthplace, which had been fixed up. As we got out, he picked up the intercom and told the Secret Service agents to allow only photographers to follow us. There ensued about an hour and a half of picture-taking, first at the house, then at the old family graveyard, then outside in a field of cattle, and finally at the superintendent's cottage. It was an extraordinary performance, especially Humphrey's remark when he stepped in a cow flop: "Oh, Mr. President, I've just stepped on the Republican platform."

Lunch was ordered by telephone to be ready in twenty-five minutes. Two hours and several telephone calls later, we finally all sat down, fourteen strong, to a Mexican meal of chili and tamales at which the discussion was about getting around the Dirksen Amendment in order to preserve foreign aid.

The plane, which we had planned to board in Austin, was told to come to the ranch to pick us up. Just before we left, I asked for two minutes alone with the president. He took me into his bedroom and sat me on a chair while he lay down on the bed. I then talked in terms I had inherited from Phil and in a way I would never have done later—and that embarrasses me now. I told him I had the feeling that he thought my point of view was different from Phil's, but that in general Phil and I had agreed. I said that, much as I admired and loved President Kennedy, Phil personally had got along with him much better than I had. I also said that I admired the legislation he himself had got passed and was for him and wanted to make sure he knew it. Although we had a policy at the *Post* against contributing to campaigns, it had been followed loosely. Phil hadn't actually contributed to campaigns, but I had. I guess I forgot I was now in the other seat, because I told the president that my mother and I both wanted to contribute to his campaign. Later, I came to believe that the paper had to be completely neutral, and I decided never to make another contribution to a presidential campaign. In any case, the president said he had appreciated our help in the past and added warmly that we must see more of each other. He didn't mention an endorsement, said that he understood I had to run an independent paper, and gave me a goodbye kiss.

Publicly, I maintained my independent stance throughout the campaign, but privately and openly among my friends, I was clearly an LBJ supporter. My support for him actually got me in trouble with Russ Wiggins. Sometime that fall, Russ and I were together with the president. Chal Roberts, in his history of *The Washington Post*, reported that I told the president that the *Post* would not endorse him. According to Chal, "When tears welled up in LBJ's eyes, she added, 'Oh, we're for you 100 percent.' Wiggins was appalled at her remark; he knew his boss still had a lot to learn." That was partly true. Though I had made it clear to LBJ from the beginning that we wouldn't endorse him, I felt he could read between the lines of the paper and realize that the *Post* was positive about his programs. Yet Russ was right to be upset that I had said we were for him.

Despite what he had said to me, our sticking to our policy of nonendorsement actually hurt LBJ deeply. He couldn't understand how he could have won over so many Republican, even right-wing papers, and yet not have received the endorsement of the liberal *Washington Post*. I'm also sure that he assumed that Phil's old paper and his hometown paper, the paper to which he had been so generous, would endorse him. He must have felt that, after all the kindnesses he had shown me, all the extra, special attention, I would surely come round and bring the paper with me. But I not only had inherited this policy of nonendorsement for the paper, I believed in it. Of course, Phil had broken the policy in 1952 for Eisenhower, but that was only for the Republican nomination, not the election itself. I could have changed the policy to endorse LBJ, but Russ didn't want to, and I didn't do much independent thinking yet—nor would I have liked to differ with Russ over such a big issue so early in our working relationship.

THE FALL CAMPAIGN was in full swing when Scotty Reston suggested that I go along on the press plane of each candidate for a couple of days, to experience for myself what a campaign is really like. I decided to do just that, so Chal Roberts and I joined the president's press contingent in Indianapolis. There we met up with Chuck Roberts of *Newsweek*, and the three of us drove to the center of town, where the president was about to speak from a platform next to the Soldier and Sailor Monument. LBJ was on the highest level, and we were on a level below with several other press people. I was walking around enjoying the drama of the scene when I felt a tap on my shoulder and turned to see Agent Rufus Youngblood. I was wearing a shocking-pink wool coat, so the president had spotted me.

"Mrs. Graham, the president wants to see you," he said.

"Wants to see me where?" I asked.

"Up there," he said, pointing to the higher platform.

"I can't go up there!" I exclaimed. LBJ was standing almost alone on the small platform several yards above us.

Gently, Rufus said, "Mrs. Graham, you have to."

I climbed some steps up a ladder and stopped when my head was on a level with his platform and said hello.

"Do you want to ride with me?" the president asked. This was not too long after the weekend at the ranch, and for the paper's sake I didn't want to seem too close to him, so I cautiously replied, "No, Mr. President, I really can't thank you enough for the offer, but I'm out here to ride with the press."

Typically, he teased, "You got a boyfriend on the plane?"

I said alas, no, but I wanted to get the feel of the campaign and of the reporters as they covered it.

"Well," he replied, "come and see me at the hotel in Cleveland."

I carefully climbed back down the ladder and rejoined Chal and Chuck, and we were shortly off to Cleveland. The press plane was great fun, as were the buses that followed the president's motorcade. No doubt the whole thing can quickly get tiresome if you have to follow an entire campaign, dragging yourself from one campaign stop to another. But for me, limited as the experience was, it was constantly stimulating. It was certainly very different from what happens on today's press planes, where reporters have much less access to the candidate and his managers.

When we arrived in Cleveland, I went up to LBJ's room. The president was lying on one of the beds in his suite, and Jack Valenti was there as well. They were talking about how Lady Bird's train-trip campaign swing through the Southern states was going. Something displeased the president while I was in the room, and I became an awkward witness to a scene I wouldn't soon forget. He suddenly turned on Jack and laid him out savagely, the unpleasantness exacerbated by being delivered in front of a relative stranger. It was quite callous and inhuman, something I have never witnessed before or since. I had heard about LBJ's temper but had never seen it in action; Jack, however, was used to these tantrums and remained unflustered while I squirmed. I escaped as quickly as possible.

We went on to Louisville and continued the next day to Nashville, ending as planned in New Orleans, where the president's campaign group was to meet up with Lady Bird and her entourage, who had completed their Southern swing by train.

In order to stay true to my goal of some balance, I also rode along on the Goldwater press plane, flying first to New York and then on to Los Angeles for the night, from where we left for a whistle-stop tour to San Diego. Much as I disagreed with his views, Goldwater himself was a charming man, and it was fun to watch him speak to the crowds gathered for his quick campaign stops.

A MONTH FOLLOWING the first anniversary of Phil's death, Lally came to me in great excitement with her young beau, Yann Weymouth, to tell me they were engaged and wanted to be married in a few months. Yann was in architecture school at MIT, and Lally would be entering her senior year at Radcliffe. I felt that they were both awfully young, but I kept my concerns to myself, deciding that articulating them would do no good and might harm my relationship with Lally and Yann. I even wrote my mother trying to be reassuring about the marriage to a greater extent than I felt. A part of that letter expressed both my anxiety and some of my attitudes about women in those days:

> One of my worries about Lally was that she so adored her father she might not be able to find someone who measured up to him in her eyes.
>
> The good thing about Yann is that she not only loves him, she looks up to him in every way—mentally and morally. He leads and she follows—given the strength and will of our girl—this had to be a rare and lucky thing for her to find.

I spent much of November, after the president's overwhelming election, dealing with company business while at the same time immersing myself in plans for a Thanksgiving-weekend wedding. One interlude was an evening at the White House that didn't seem so funny at the time as it does today. Joe and Susan Mary and I were invited to a small party for the Johnsons' thirtieth wedding anniversary. We were the only three semi-outsiders at what was essentially a party of close friends and associates—the Valentis, Liz Carpenter and her husband, the Abe Fortases, and only a few others were there.

The president was in, or perhaps developed over the course of the evening, a very bad mood. There was a coffee table "smothered in lovely done-up presents," Susan Mary recalled. He looked at it and said, "What's all this trash? Get rid of it, Bird, and let's have something to eat." We had dinner in the beautiful oval family dining room upstairs, with the French wallpaper paid for by the Dillons under Jackie's restoration project. Joe, unfortunately, banged on a bit about Vietnam, which didn't help the president's mood.

After dinner, which hadn't lasted long, we returned to the family living room, but LBJ left early for his bedroom, which was adjacent to the living room, while the rest of us sat around talking. We were in the process of saying good night to Lady Bird when the double doors of the bedroom were flung open and the president looked at me in obvious anger and barked, "Come here!" I glanced hopefully over my shoulder to see if he could possibly be referring to anyone else, but it was clearly me he wanted. "And you come here, too," he called to Abe Fortas.

We went into his bedroom, where on the turned-down bed lay the early edition of the *Post*, with a large headline saying that Walter Tobriner, the lead commissioner for the District of Columbia—in effect, the appointed mayor—had named a new police chief. LBJ was livid. He said he had told Tobriner not to do anything without discussing it with him, because he had wanted to appoint a "super" police chief to address the problem of crime in Washington—the only place a president can get his hands on the issue, since elsewhere it's up to the states.

President Johnson equated me with the *Post* and viewed the article's appearance in the next morning's paper as entirely my fault. The *Post* had endorsed Tobriner, and "this stupid son of a bitch," as LBJ referred to him, had gone ahead and deprived him of appointing the kind of person he wanted. He was ranting at me: "Tobriner was your creation," etc., etc.

As he was yelling at me, he started to undress, flinging his clothes off onto a chair and the floor—his coat, his tie, his shirt. Finally, he was down to his pants. I was frozen with dismay and baffled about what to do. I remember thinking to myself: This can't be me being bawled out by the president of the United States while he's undressing. Suddenly he bellowed, "Turn around!" I did so, obediently and gratefully, and he went right on with his angry monologue until I turned back at his command to find him in his pajamas. He bid the two of us a curt good night, and Abe and I turned on our heels and vanished.

The last big event of the year for me was Lally and Yann's wedding, held in the Navy Chapel in Washington, with the reception at home. Felix Frankfurter had written Lally saying that he felt Phil would have wanted him to give her away, but by that time he was in a wheelchair from a stroke. And so it was Don who walked her down the aisle. She wore a beautiful Mainbocher dress given to her by her grandmother. Although the marriage lasted only a few years, out of it came two marvelous children, Katharine and Pamela Weymouth, my oldest granddaughters.

— *Chapter Nineteen* —

F OR PEOPLE WHO lose a spouse, the year that immediately follows is horribly painful—and so it was for me. After the first year, however, comes a more bearable kind of grief that allows accommodation to the outside world, the world that just carries on no matter what has happened to you.

The difficulties of my job remained enormous. I still had little idea of how to relate to people in a business environment, and no idea how closely I was being watched by everyone. Within the company, whatever I said or did, even my body language, sent a stronger message to people than I realized. In addition, I had spent a lifetime with dramatically impressive people and probably dismissed as unimportant too many quiet, unassuming, but hardworking people throughout the company. It took me a while to learn that certain people may have important skills that are not always blazingly apparent. Gradually I came to realize—slow as I may have been—that what mattered was performance, that sometimes people might have to be helped to develop, and that it takes all kinds to make an organization run properly.

I made mistakes and suffered great distress from them, partly because I believed that if you just worked diligently enough you wouldn't make mistakes. I truly believed that other people in my position *didn't* make mistakes; I couldn't see that everybody makes them, even people with great experience. What I did that I'm certain my male counterparts did not, and which was particularly tormenting, was to lie awake at night reliving events of the day, going over and over certain scenes, wondering how I could have managed whatever it was differently.

Yet, despite all my insecurities and misgivings, I was gradually beginning to enjoy myself. And unconsciously, somewhere along the line, I seem to have begun redefining my job and what it was I was doing. Indeed, within the first months of my new working life, the color started returning to my face, my jaw was beginning to unclench, and what I had once called "my initial girl-scout type of resolve" was turning into a passionate interest. In short, as I said in a speech at *Newsweek*, I "sort of fell in love." I loved my job, I loved the paper, I loved the whole company. As I wrote Frank Waldrop, "I suppose it's odd to speak of loving the Company but all I'm doing is agreeing with Colonel McCormick when he said a newspaper is a living thing. . . ."

Gradually, too, I began to learn. The Montessori method—learning by doing—once again became my stock in trade. One of my greatest learning tools over the years was the trips I took with various editors and reporters from the *Post* and *Newsweek*. These trips—which, more than thirty years later, now number nearly as many as the years that have passed—were among the richest and most rewarding of all the many opportunities available to me as head of a communications company.

Of course, I had been to Europe several times with Phil, but my first trip as the executive rather than as the spouse who often got left out of the most interesting occasions was something altogether unusual. It was an around-the-world venture with Oz Elliott and his then wife, Deirdre, or Dee, and I loved it. The only drawback was having to leave Bill and Steve again—this time for six weeks, far too long.

I may have been the president, but I was still a woman, and I recall being upset when I received a letter from *Newsweek*'s correspondent in Hong Kong, Bob McCabe, asking if I really wanted to be included in stag lunches and substantive briefings during the trip. "Naturally I want to go," I replied, somewhat indignantly. "Since I have been working, I never seem to notice whether I am with men or women. As I happen to be on this job, I obviously want to learn as much as I can."

Some matters specific to women couldn't be avoided, however, as evidenced by the expression of horror on Oz Elliott's face when I met him in San Francisco at the end of January 1965. I was carrying a large, not inconspicuous yellow-and-red box with the name "Kenneth" on it, for the well-known hairdresser in New York. It was the fashion in the mid-1960s to use fake hair or "falls" over the back of your head, with your own hair combed over the front, which both puffed out your hair and eliminated the need to have it done when you were traveling. My box contained my fall, or wig, pinned to a felt head-shape inside. On seeing me, Oz announced firmly, "Don't think I'm ever going to carry that for you." I laughed, realizing how ridiculous it looked, and said, "Don't worry, I'll carry it myself." That settled, we took off.

Our first stop, in Japan, included a visit to *Asahi*, then the largest newspaper in Japan, with a circulation of many millions. Next was one to a large advertising agency, Dentsu, where I was stunned to find a big sign reading "Welcome Mrs. Philip L. Graham" and about eighty people, mostly young women, who applauded as I stepped inside, a startling

Japanese display of manners. We had a brief meeting with Prime Minister Sato, and within the next few days we also met separately with Kiichi Miyazawa and with Yasuhiro Nakasone, both of whom later became prime minister. I am abashed to admit that what I remember of Nakasone from that meeting is that he made the list of sexy men which Dee Elliott and I were compiling as we circled the globe.

On February 1, we had an audience with the emperor and empress. This formal interview with the sovereign, we were told, was the first he had granted to a woman in her own right. Despite the pomp and high drama associated with the occasion, the whole visit had a musical-comedy aspect to it. Before we were escorted into the meeting place, we were briefed by a striped-pants equerry, whom we asked whether we should shake hands with the emperor, bow, or what.

"His Majesty would be very pleased to shake your hand," the attendant replied in a tone, Oz recalled, that suggested we should treat the emperor as we would any "regular god." Once briefed, we trooped into a hideous audience room, laden with overstuffed furniture with antimacassars on the plush brocade coverings. The emperor and empress appeared, and we all sat down stiffly, with the emperor and me on a kind of love seat across from Oz, interpreters close by for all of us. There was a long silence while we waited, as instructed, for the royals to begin the conversation. The emperor had a way of wringing his hands and sort of bouncing up and down, so much so that Oz, who was sitting across the room, recalled that "every time he went up in the love seat, Kay went down."

What the emperor began with was the question, which was duly translated, "Is this your first trip to Japan, Mrs. Graham?" I heard myself saying, "Yes, it's my first trip, and Mrs. Elliott's as well, but Oz was here during the war . . . uh, er . . . I mean many years ago." I could almost feel Oz trying not to laugh. None of the conversation was gripping or important; rather, it was stilted and artificial, painful even. After one long stretch of silence, I actually volunteered, "Well, Your Majesty, we understand you're interested in marine biology," and then told him about Oz's being on the board of the Natural History Museum in New York. That topic, too, went nowhere.

We had worried about how we would know when the interview was over, but quite abruptly the emperor turned to his wife, they arose as one, we all shook hands again—with, as Oz said later, the emperor appearing to be "so unused to shaking hands that he watched his hand go up and down to make sure he got it back"—and it was over. The retainer in striped pants assured us the meeting was a great success.

Everywhere we went throughout Asia, Vietnam was the principal subject of discussion. After a stop in Hong Kong we flew on to Saigon for a closer look at the country that would get so much of our attention over the next decade. We landed at an airfield that seemed equally divided between civilian traffic and military helicopters and fighters—a fantastic jumble of peace and war. Saigon at the time was ringed by the Viet Cong, with very few "safe" roads leading into and out of the city. The Viet Cong came right onto the airfield at times, and just a few weeks before our arrival a bomb had gone off on the fifth floor of the Caravelle Hotel, where many from the American press stayed, and where we, too, were staying. I took some comfort in being on the fourth floor.

This visit, in early February 1965, was in the days when the number of American advisers was mounting but still relatively small. We were not yet directly involved, but *Newsweek* had two or three correspondents there and the *Post* had one. After a briefing by army officers the day following our arrival, we lunched with General and Mrs. Westmoreland. Throughout this trip, I used letters home as a way of setting down my observations and experiences. Of Westmoreland I wrote: "He is an inarticulate soldier-type of a peculiar kind. If he is bright, it is as a technician because he certainly doesn't communicate—is tense and uneasy and almost scared."

Oz and I, Bob McCabe, and Bill Tuohy of *Newsweek* all left right after lunch in a small helicopter for a visit to a nearby—about twenty-five miles away—base not far from the Cambodian border, on the top of "Black Lady Mountain," on the outer edge of a patch of land completely dominated by the Viet Cong but used by the Americans for radio communication with planes in the area. When we got in the helicopter—a Bell UHIB called a Huey—I was startled to find that we were to sit on a bench situated horizontally in the small cab of the helicopter, which had its sides off so that your feet were on the edge of the cab. I was right behind the pilot and tried to look cool, as though this sort of thing was routine for me. When we took off, leaving the sides or doors of the helicopter behind, I held my breath. I was even more startled at seeing soldiers toward the rear of each side holding loaded machine guns.

We flew low, at about twenty-five hundred feet, over rice paddies and fields. The single houses below us, according to the major from the army's public-relations department who accompanied us, belonged to Viet Cong sympathizers. Government people lived in armed hamlets surrounded by trenches and barbed wire. None too soon, we landed on a tiny helicopter pad, big enough for only two helicopters. The mountain was held by special forces—our advisers, mostly marines. We were met by a Steve Canyon–type figure, Lieutenant Saudlin, who felt even then that the relationship between the Americans and the South Vietnamese was frustrating and that it would take at least five years to judge the results.

On this mountaintop there were thirteen Americans and about a hundred South Vietnamese soldiers. The entire area was laced with barbed wire and machine-gun emplacements. Our guide claimed that they were quite safe there, though subject to harassments, and that the area was actually surprisingly peaceful. Around Thanksgiving, just a few months before, CBS had done a broadcast from the mountaintop, bringing in roast turkey for the soldiers. A live turkey had been dropped in earlier, and had been granted a reprieve from the feast, becoming a pet of sorts. The Vietnamese had hung a red Special Services scarf around his neck, and now he wandered around as if the entire zone were his fiefdom.

As we got ready to leave, one of the resident soldiers explained that when we took off from the mountaintop the helicopter would drop sharply before rising. I was grateful for the warning, which was not enough to calm my nerves but helped me understand my stomach dropping as I watched the gunners crouch over their weapons until we had left the ground safely behind us.

Only my extreme interest in seeing more of South Vietnam prevented me—who under normal circumstances even disliked elevators—from panicking during those helicopter rides, but I got back in to visit two villages in the Mekong Delta where pacification was said to have worked. We also went to the provincial capital of Ben Tre in Kien Hoa Province, and then drove on to a nearby hamlet, Binh Nguyen, where we met with an optimistic and determined province chief, Colonel Chou, who talked about how he was building strength in the hamlet. The Viet Cong had been creating infrastructure and developing people for twenty years, we were told, but the American advisers and the South Vietnamese military leaders still felt they were making progress. Only one American colonel cautioned that the Viet Cong seemed to be everywhere and to be willing to pay any price for their inroads.

I was unsure how to react to the things we saw, heard, and did. Certainly our trip was circumscribed by the public-relations officers who took us around. More important, my feeling that I knew very little about the history of the conflict and the issues involved meant that I kept to my normal approach of listening a lot and questioning little. I also tended to accept Russ Wiggins's views on the main issues with which the *Post* wrestled, and I knew how strongly he favored American involvement in Vietnam. My habit of listening to what the men in my life said resulted in my leaving Vietnam with much the same views I had when I arrived—i.e., maybe we shouldn't have been there in the first place, even in small numbers, but we *were* there, and there was no choice but to help the South Vietnamese in their fight against the communist guerrillas.

As Chal Roberts later wrote of Wiggins, he was "not a mindless hawk; he was repelled by the all-out war proponents." Indeed, Russ was never mindless about anything—he thought long and hard about the positions he took. The *Post* gained a reputation for strong support of American involvement in the war, and Russ supported Lyndon Johnson on the war throughout his presidency—not because he blindly went along with whatever LBJ put forth, but because he believed that the United States had to use its power to prevent the usurpation of legitimate authority from taking place around the world. But there was a great deal that bothered Russ about the predicament of Vietnam. He felt strongly that our advance knowledge of the 1963 assassination of Diem, the head of a state with which we were allied, created grave problems and the "spectacle of being a rotten and faithless ally." In fact, he was always looking for an alternative to American involvement in Vietnam that wouldn't destroy the international position of the United States government.

My own position on Vietnam continued to parallel Russ's, changing only very gradually as time passed, until I had a son serving there, which gave me my own private view and inside perspective on the war, and until Phil Geyelin arrived to take over the editorial page and we gradually began to turn the editorial position of the paper around.

We left Vietnam on February 10 and, after brief stopovers in Cambodia and Thailand, moved on to India for a dizzying few days. One of our most astonishing interviews there was with the white-coated population minister—or at least the coat had at one time been white and was now a dirty gray. He sat in a dusty office at his cluttered desk, on which were arrayed a variety of population-control devices, and he kept picking up an IUD inserter and playing with it, swinging it and knocking it against his palm. I will never forget his saying, "Many of the ladies, when they use the IUD, they complain of headaches, but I do not think the headaches come from the IUD. Rather, I think the headaches come from the in-laws."

An all-night flight from New Delhi took us over burning oil fields that lit up the desert, to Beirut, still untouched and beautiful. The Lebanese never ceased arguing about Gamal Abdel Nasser, the Egyptian strongman, during our entire visit. From Lebanon we went on to Egypt, where we interviewed Nasser himself, from which meeting an ugly misunderstanding ensued. Nasser had a reputation in the Middle East for playing the East against the West, with Egypt benefiting from Cold War conflicts. East German President Walter Ulbricht had visited Cairo just the month before, and during our interview we asked Nasser if he had been pressured by the Soviet Union to invite Ulbricht. Nasser said no, although probably it was true. Unfortunately, the issue of *Newsweek* that appeared a few days after our interview reported just the opposite. That piece actually had no connection with our interview and had not been seen by me or by any of our *Newsweek* staff in Beirut at the time of the interview. We had tried to wire ahead a few lines from our interview, but they had not arrived in time to be included. The interview was reported accurately in the *Post* a few days later, but by then Nasser had flown into a rage, calling us "liars seeking only to discredit us." No amount of explaining helped. Eventually, I learned to accept most such unintentional mistakes and confusions with some grace and not to take them personally.

We flew home via Rome and London, where we mostly rested and partied. In Rome I had a passing flirtation with an attractive Italian journalist. Afterwards, Pam Berry encouraged my little fling in Rome by writing me, "Do be female and free and frivolous from time to time. It will be terribly good for you in every sort of way. I'd been worried that you would gradually immolate yourself in work. But when you walked into Cowley Street last Thursday I saw a huge difference though without knowing why."

I worked as hard on this trip as I'd ever worked, but, far from being tiring, the whole experience was strengthening, and I returned with more energy and enthusiasm for my job than ever.

ONE TRIP I took that summer was just for fun—and it was that. Truman Capote had told me that he was going cruising with Marella Agnelli, the international beauty and wife of Gianni Agnelli, the head of Fiat. Marella had chartered a large sailboat for a tour of the Adriatic and through the Greek isles, and was inviting Truman and a group of her friends or relations whom I knew to be in the international jet set. I had come a fair distance in worldliness but not that far, so I told Truman that I wouldn't fit in and would feel ill-at-ease, but eventually I accepted Marella's invitation, though with great reservations.

This trip was different from anything I'd experienced before—and a reflection of my new life. It wasn't something Phil would ever have done, nor would I have done it without him, and the puritan in me worried about it even then. Truman and I decided to get to our rendezvous with Marella via London in order to visit the Bruces and Pam Berry on the way. Adlai Stevenson had earlier suggested that he and I stay with his sister, Buffy Ives, at her house in Switzerland that summer, and I had been relieved to be able to tell him that I couldn't, because of the Marella trip. On our arrival in London, my heart sank a little to find that Adlai was there, too, also staying with the Bruces at the U.S. Embassy in Grosvenor Square. However, the guests were so numerous that week that things were easy and agreeable. Adlai's great friend Marietta Tree was also in London. On our third night, July 13, we all went off in different directions, he to do a BBC broadcast. When I came in from dinner, I noticed him talking to someone in the upstairs study. Since it was late and I couldn't see whom Adlai was talking with and didn't want to interrupt, I tiptoed past the room and went to my bedroom at the end of the hall. I was still reading when the door flew open and in breezed Adlai, full of reproaches about my not having joined him and Eric Sevareid, with whom he'd been talking while waiting for me to return.

Adlai stayed in my room for at least an hour. When he departed, he left behind his tie and his glasses, so I crept quietly down the hall to his bedroom and put them in front of his door. The next day, when I got back to the embassy in the late afternoon, the butler answered the bell looking very glum and immediately asked me, "Have you heard about Governor Stevenson?"

"No," I responded, "what is it?"

"He's dead," was the reply.

I was crushed and disbelieving. He had been walking with Marietta in the rare late-afternoon British sunshine when he just fell to the ground with a fatal heart attack. Eric Sevareid arrived as I stood there, as did Marietta and Phil Kaiser, minister at the embassy, who were returning from the hospital; they had gone there in the ambulance with Adlai. Eric told me that he thought Adlai had looked unusually tired—several times during their conversation the night before, Adlai had leaned back and closed his eyes. Not exactly how I had found him later, I ruminated, thinking guiltily of the glasses and tie at his door.

Adlai had spoken to me, as he did to many of us, about wanting to re-sign from his position at the United Nations to take a rest and then go back into private business, but I had no idea how tired he must have been. In many ways, he was an unhappy man. Eric Sevareid said on the CBS Evening News a few days later that Adlai had told him, "For a while I would just like to sit in the shade with a glass of wine in my hands and watch people dance."

Marella's father had also died while we were in London, and she had to be in Italy a week longer than expected, so our plans changed, and Truman and I flew to Athens and departed in lonely splendor on Marella's beautiful boat, the *Sylvia*, stocked with a great deal of my favorite Italian wine. Truman had with him the galleys of *In Cold Blood*, in the four sections that were to appear first in *The New Yorker*. Sitting for hours on the back deck of the boat in the balmy air, we discussed it all in detail, section by section—why he had done what he'd done, what the murderers were like, what Garden City, Kansas, was like, the characters of the detective and the judge, his own life while in Kansas.

We finally met up with Marella and the other guests and set off on a route based partly on a book by Freya Stark, *Lycean Shores*. Our goal was to go down the southern coast of Turkey, at that time almost undeveloped. The boat wasn't big enough for all of us and on top of that was un-air-conditioned, which made life somewhat difficult in the extreme heat that set in. But Marella herself was casual and generous and uncomplaining, and the entire voyage was a happy interlude of R and R in an otherwise turbulent year.

WHEN I HAD first gone to work at the *Post*, I assumed that things would carry on as they always had. One area that, surprisingly, started to shift under my feet was the *Post*'s editorial quality. I hadn't realized that the *Post* wasn't perfectly okay as it was. I had great faith in Al Friendly as managing editor and in Russ Wiggins as editor, leading the editorial page, and basically believed that all was well. In fact, almost a year to the day after Phil's death I wrote Al a personal letter saying, "You must know, without this word—but I want to say it anyway—that you've done so well for this year, and been so great."

One of the first people to put into my head the idea that the paper wasn't all that it should or could be was Scotty Reston, who, on a visit to Glen Welby, asked, "Don't you want to leave a better paper for the next generation than the one you inherited?" This may not seem like a startling question, but it was to me. I had not considered that we weren't making the kind of progress that we had in the past, or that what we were doing wasn't good enough for the 1960s.

It's difficult to recall how I eventually became seriously concerned about what was happening on the editorial floor, on the news side, but there were many signals, and I certainly was beginning to think about the direction the paper should be taking. The two people I talked privately to about the future were Walter Lippmann and Scotty. In truth, I felt I needed Scotty, who was such a close personal friend, to help me move the paper forward, and in the summer of 1964 I met with him several times to discuss the possibility of his coming to the *Post*. One of the things we talked about was his concern over Phil's overstepping his bounds as publisher, and we agreed that working with me would be different. Finally, with Fritz's help and after consultation with Walter and Russ Wiggins, I offered him the rather ill-defined job of advising the paper editorially while continuing his column. This was completely impractical, but I was unwilling to disturb Russ and Al, to whom I remained devoted and grateful.

Scotty quite rightly rejected this offer, firmly but kindly, and very constructively. We carried on without him, but gradually I had to acknowledge that there was a problem. How could I tell? I certainly didn't have a sophisticated judgment about the quality of our news product, but I was observing a great deal of indecision among the executives, followed by some odd decisions, especially about people. I sensed a certain lack of adrenaline, and through the grapevine I heard talk of stagnation in the city room. One report that reached me said that you could swing a dead cat around the city room after nine at night and not hit anyone.

Then there was Al himself. Bob Manning, who was working for the government, came to see me with the idea that he replace Al Friendly; that he was what was needed to revitalize the paper. I rejected the suggestion out of hand, but that episode, too, left a seed of doubt. By 1965, Al had been managing editor for ten years, and people were commenting on how he was aging. He did seem to be getting tired, and he was clearly growing hard of hearing, which made difficulties for him on the job. He himself must have felt some concern, since he decided he should take two months' vacation every year—he and Jean had bought a place in Turkey and wanted to spend time there. Al was my friend, but the managing editor is a key figure who gets the paper out each day, and the idea of two months off worried me.

All these were clear warning signals, but I was puzzled about what to do about them. Not only had Al done a fine job with meager resources over many years, but he and Jean were such close personal friends that it was unthinkable to upset him. When I tried to suggest to him that the paper could use some energizing, he seemed to dismiss my feelings and obviously didn't take my judgment seriously. So I conceived the idea of asking him to talk with others, particularly Walter Lippmann, to find out what they thought of the paper and what he might do to move it forward. He agreed, but by then Walter had gone to Maine, and they couldn't get together at that time.

In the meantime, I had learned that Ben Bradlee had twice been offered promotions by *Newsweek* which would have entailed his moving to New York, but had turned them down. Although I had gone back and forth to New York with him on various trips for *Newsweek* and had had a few meetings and lunches with him, I didn't know Ben very well. I still associated him with Phil's bad period, when I thought he had taken sides. But I knew that he ran a good bureau, had good people working for him, and was generally well regarded. And I realized that he was eminently hirable and worried about losing him from the company, especially to some television network, which I feared might recruit him since he was good-looking and appealing.

Because I wanted to discover what his ambitions were, I invited him to lunch. I had never done such a thing before. In those days, it was still a little awkward, I felt, for a woman to take a man to lunch and to pay the check, so in December 1964 I took him to the F Street Club, where I could sign for the bill (those were the pre-credit-card days) and avoid a scene about who would pay—so odd to think of now.

Our talk meandered around. I asked him why he hadn't gone to

Newsweek in New York, although I knew that he and his wife, Tony, had six children living with them—four of hers and two of theirs, apart from Ben Jr., Ben's son from an earlier marriage—which would make changing cities difficult. He told me he liked running the bureau here in Washington and was in no hurry to move on.

"But what would you like to do in the long run?" I asked.

"Well, since you asked," Ben responded, with his typical picturesque language, "I'd give my left one to be managing editor of the *Post*."

I was stunned. This was neither the question he expected nor the answer I anticipated—or even welcomed. However, given the context of my concerns, it was certainly a thinkable thought. What I said to Ben was that we could discuss the idea, but not right now or at any time soon. Ben, however, saw his opening and pursued it—hard. I'd see him around and he'd say, "When are we going to talk some more? What are we going to do next?" I was surprised by his tenacity.

I used the time to check out the idea with Scotty, who didn't know Ben personally but thought it might work out. Walter Lippmann, who did know Ben, reacted favorably, saying he thought Ben could do great things for the paper. Encouraged by that, I took the idea to Fritz, who heartily approved, and to Oz, who of course did, too.

Ben and I met several more times in the course of the next few months. He made it clear that he didn't want to give up a job he loved in order to sit around the *Post* waiting for Al to retire in two or three years. He was, however, willing to come to the paper and wait one year. I didn't like that prospect. Part of me thought, "What gall this guy has to be so pushy when he doesn't even have the job," but part of me thought, "Maybe this is exactly what we need and what I'm looking for."

Ben kept pushing and I kept delaying until the early summer of 1965, when I finally brought up with Russ and Al the idea of bringing Ben over from *Newsweek* as assistant managing editor. They both reacted negatively at first. Russ said he should come in as a reporter like anyone else and work his way up. Al was on the ladder to be head of the American Society of Newspaper Editors in two or three years, and he very much wanted to do that, so he wasn't in a great hurry to give up being managing editor and lose the opportunity. Ben actually told Al that he wanted to move up within a year, to which Al responded, "What's your hurry, buster?" Ben finally came to the *Post*, agreeing to disagree.

On July 7, 1965, it was announced by Russ and Al that Ben would join the *Post* as deputy managing editor, with principal responsibilities in the area of national and foreign news coverage. He was young, forty-three, and had been *Newsweek*'s Washington-bureau chief for four years. Mel Elfin was appointed the new bureau chief, and served that office reliably and well for the next twenty years. At the *Post*, Ben Gilbert, one of the last of the first-rate old-timers, was made deputy managing editor for local news and administration.

Ben was to take up his new duties on September 1, but he arrived on August 2, having taken no vacation: he left *Newsweek* on a Saturday and came to the *Post* on the following Monday. I had written him on July 20 saying I had had a nice note from Al telling me that Ben had learned more in spare half-hours than had others in months. Indeed, Ben hit the ground running.

Then and always, Ben was charismatic. He was good-looking in an unconventional way, funny, street-smart, and political—all of which stood him in good stead. What was also always important was how hard he worked. In his determination to learn, he worked into the night and on Saturdays, too, and what he quickly observed was that Russ was concentrating on the editorial page and that Al had indeed lost his energy. By default, Ben Gilbert, by "controlling all the screws and the screwdrivers," really ran the paper. Ben saw Al as not knowing the basics of the paper— the various production departments and the unions, for example—and felt that his lack of knowledge had been to the detriment of the *Post*. From the beginning, Ben saw that, to be a good editor, it was important to know how things came together.

What I hoped was that the issue of timing would slide. I couldn't see my way around the problem of moving Al out and wished the whole matter would quietly go away. But few things regarding Ben are ever quiet. That fall, after Al and Jean's vacation in Turkey, Al and I resumed our talks about the future of the paper. He told me that he had made a lunch date with Walter Lippmann, as I had suggested. Walter called me, too, and asked, "How far do you want me to go?" I said as far as he felt he could at the time, suggesting he "just feel your way." By this I meant—and thought Walter meant—talking to Al about the inadequacies of the paper and what we should do to improve it; I had nothing else in mind. The phone rang after the lunch, and it was Walter, who said, "Well, the conversation went so well I went all the way." Having not heard that expression since high school, I anxiously asked, "What do you mean by 'all the way,' Walter?"

"Well," he replied, "I told him that these administrative jobs wore people out and there came a time when they should think about giving it up and going back to writing."

I was dumbstruck. I had no idea Walter was going to go to that point with Al. Ben had only been at the paper for three months, and I had no intention of dislodging Al that early. I thought that even Ben, who was pushing, was still assuming it would take a full year, while I was assuming even longer. Unbeknownst to me, Ben must have been pushing from other directions, too, and talking about the situation with Al directly. His impatience is reflected in a letter Henry Brandon, correspondent for the *Sunday Times* of London, wrote to his editor, Denis Hamilton, on October 12: "Ben B. told me that the situation with Al still in the chair and him assigned to kill the sacred cows cannot endure, that he will press for a decision within the next two months."

Press he may have done, but I couldn't have faced my old and dear friend and asked him to step aside that abruptly. However, because Walter had indeed gone "all the way," and because I really knew by then that it was best for all concerned, I went ahead with the change. So much for my alleged courage.

I had barely hung up from talking to Walter when Al came into my office, looking stricken and pale, and said, "Is this what you want?" There was no going back. The awful deed had been done for me, so I just said, "Yes, I'm afraid it is." Al, with justice totally on his side, sadly said, "I wish I'd heard it from you." I can't remember whether I tried to explain, but I do remember the pain we both felt.

Even Ben was surprised at how fast everything happened in the end. On November 15, it was announced that he would become managing editor of *The Washington Post*, succeeding Al. There was something in the announcement to the effect that Al had "asked to be relieved of executive duties and to resume an earlier career of reporting and writing on national and international affairs." Al became associate editor of the paper, continuing as vice-president and a member of the company's board of directors.

The strain with Al and Jean was grim, but they both did their best to be polite, even coming to Glen Welby for a weekend. The miracle was that eventually Al rebuilt his life as a stellar reporter. Luckily, he owned a lot of stock in the newspaper and was wealthy, so he was able to buy a flat in London as well as maintain the house in Turkey and his large home in Georgetown. Most important, things becoming too uncomfortable here at home, he eventually went abroad to write and report. There he did some of his best journalistic work and won a Pulitzer Prize for his reporting on the Six-Day War in the Middle East. Eventually our friendship resumed, and for that great credit went to Al and Jean, who might well have harbored a grudge forever but were too large-minded for that. Later, Al wrote me that he had only two regrets about the shift: "One was that I hadn't the wit to have initiated it myself, and the second is that I was awkward in failing to find myself afterwards." I think that's a measure of extraordinary character in a man who had essentially been fired.

Ironically, on November 2, just before the announcement of Ben's taking over, Al had sent me a "Whither The Washington Post" memo that began, "By good luck and good management, all the conditions are present to make The Post the best paper in the world." He had ended this seven-page memo with what he called "a final word": "To move from where we are to becoming the 'best' will require some very tough decisions, the toughest of which, having to do with intentions and goals, and attitudes about spending, must of course be made by you. They will not be easy, or serene, or reachable overnight."

He was right on all counts.

— *Chapter Twenty* —

B EN SET TO work at once to build up the paper. He and his cronies at *Newsweek* had been critical of what they saw as uninspired writing and unassertive managing at the *Post*. He was determined to be different. A great discoverer and developer of talent, he hired some big, well-known bylines, quickly bringing in Stanley Karnow and Joe Kraft, Ward Just and Dick Harwood. Bart Rowen came over from *Newsweek* as financial editor and started to expand what had been a business staff of one. A signal arrival was the star political reporter David Broder, who came from *The New York Times*. Ben also hired Nicholas von Hoffman, who was the first to cover the drug scene at Haight-Ashbury in San Francisco, writing about it so graphically that Ben was inspired to fly to San Francisco to observe this hippie world for himself. Nick, with his eccentricity and originality, required an editor willing to take risks, which Ben was.

The *Post* also benefited from the demise of at least three New York papers after severe labor problems caused a crisis. From the *Herald-Tribune* came Harry Rosenfeld, who became night foreign editor, and later Dave Laventhol, both strong additions to our editing staff. From 1966 to 1969, we added about fifty news positions. Our editorial budget rose by $2.25 million, to over $7 million in 1969.

There were departures, too, during these years, some of which signaled a real changing of the guard. When the longtime night city editor, John Riseling; the head photographer, Hugh Miller; and Eddie Folliard, a brilliant reporter on politics and national affairs, each decided to retire at about the same time, I gave a goodbye party celebrating the 130 years they had together served the *Post*. Other departures later on worried me a great deal. I was deeply distressed over losing good people and was sure they had left because of something I'd done or neglected to do, not realizing they may have had other opportunities too good to decline.

Probably Ben was less capable as a manager than as a finder of talent, but he somehow managed by osmosis. The important thing was that he excited people under him, eventually corrected whatever mistakes he made, and moved on. He rapidly learned the ropes, including how to deal with John Sweeterman about budgets. Because John knew more than Ben did about his own budget, Ben met total defeat the first year. It never happened again. When he went in the next year and dealt with John on more even terms and with my unspoken backing, things began to change. John respected people who knew what they were talking about and who wanted what was best for the paper. Ben was driving to make the paper better, and, of course, that kind of push was expensive.

Ben's arrival changed my life in an unexpected way. He was the first person placed in a major position by me, and the difference between my relationship with him and my relationship with most of the people who had been at the *Post* before me was striking. Despite my controlling ownership, to those who were already there I was still the newcomer, the junior partner. Even though they were mostly friendly and generous, they were almost always the leaders and teachers and I was the follower. Ben and I, however, were partners, very much together in focusing on our common goals. Though some may have viewed him as a bizarre choice, it was the right one for me.

Ideas flew out of Ben. He was always asking important "why" questions—"Why not build, start, or buy a printing plant in suburban Maryland?" "Why does a great newspaper have to lose ground?" He sent me a steady stream of memos on things he felt the *Post* ought to do—some were right, some wrong; almost all were interesting. Ben was tough enough and good enough so that for the most part I not only let him do what he thought was right, I largely agreed with him. When I didn't, his track record was such that I didn't like going head to head with him. As time went on, I learned how to deal with him, as he did with me. There were certain things we'd talk about and others I recognized he had no interest in, and I figured out fairly quickly what he had little time or inclination for. Our friendship was forming over those early years. We grew fond of each other and enjoyed a wonderfully complementary and constructive professional relationship, emotionally uncomplicated. Most important, I saw constant improvement in the *Post*.

The buildup at *Newsweek* was as dramatic as that at the *Post*. Because Oz Elliott had a fine feel for cutting-edge issues, *Newsweek* distinguished itself in the 1960s, becoming a "hot" magazine by recognizing important trends, writing about racial issues and the new sexual mores, and reporting on them before our competition had awakened to their importance. From a business point of view, the magazine was doing less well. Fritz was extremely lenient with the editorial and business managers, allowing them to operate with relative freedom and without having to adhere to strict budgets. I had no idea of what *Newsweek* could earn or should earn, and those in charge tended to resent my questions or to interpret any overtures as interference. The company had almost no corporate staff then, except for Fritz and me and a telephone between us. When one started to grow, *Newsweek* executives mostly disliked the idea and felt threatened.

As long as Oz Elliott was editor and Gib McCabe was publisher or president, the magazine went from strength to strength, both in editorial quality and in advertising. However, several changes of editor, including Oz's leaving and then returning, created upheaval and bad feelings. Chaos ensued for a while, with many talented people departing.

In press accounts and outside gossip, I often became the fall guy who took the hits for whatever mistakes we were viewed as making—whether in personnel or in editorial decisions. I was also the recipient of grumbling whenever *Newsweek* editors were unhappy, so I was the target of complaints from both within and without. This disarray added fuel to the rumors that the magazine was to be sold—rumors that inevitably reached print and understandably shook the staff. I suppose they arose partly because financial analysts—especially after we went public—saw no reason why this relatively less profitable part of our business should be retained by a company with responsibility to shareholders. But I believed then and still believe that *Newsweek* matters.

When I first went to work, the third part of the company, the broadcast division, consisted mainly of two television stations (there are now six)—WTOP in Washington, D.C., a popular and strong franchise; and WJXT in Jacksonville, Florida, which was beginning to make its mark through its investigative reporting. John Hayes had admirably led the operations of the stations, but in 1966 Lyndon Johnson named him ambassador to Switzerland. We tried and failed to find a successor from within the company, so Fritz and I hired Larry Israel, who had been the head of Westinghouse Broadcasting Station Group, and he brought with him a whole new group of people, the most important of whom was Jim Snyder, who became news director of WTOP-Radio, then almost immediately of WTOP-TV. Jim was truly a Ben Bradlee for television news—charismatic, driving, creative, devoted, tough, and skilled at developing talented people.

Larry Israel did certain very productive things. Under him, in 1968, we bought a television station in Miami and renamed it in Phil's honor with the call letters WPLG. And we bought a station in Hartford in 1973. Larry also suggested banning cigarette advertising from our stations before it was mandatory and thought of the idea of donating our FM radio station to Howard University. Although we didn't comprehend the value of FM and we all undervalued the gift, this was a unique action. At the time, there was no broadcast station in the United States owned by a black person or group; this was the first, and it later became, under Howard University's management, the number-one-rated station in Washington. Larry loved broadcasting and held us to extremely high standards in programming and news—the stations were much improved in that respect—but he had little idea of how to run radio, not much sense of business, and even less about how to motivate people. I watched him at several meetings shouting at people, and puzzled over this, but decided it seemed to be working. I was wrong.

As president of The Washington Post Company, I oversaw all three of these divisions, and in doing so relied on Fritz—who spent most of his time in New York and ran *Newsweek*—and on different people within each division. Unfortunately, Fritz and I had one failing in common: neither of us was a manager, and the problems of management seemed endless and intractable.

I was always interested in what constituted good management, both within and outside our industry. In the same earnest way that I attacked many things, I began to do my homework in management. I must have driven everyone around me crazy by studying everything so intensely, but I was compelled to know more. I traveled to several cities to observe newspaper operations. I spent a day at Texas Instruments, which had an excellent reputation at that time for its planning processes. I visited the headquarters of Xerox and NCR. I attended a week-long hands-on production-process school run by the publishers' association, the ANPA.

I also attended IBM's seven-day course designed for heads of companies to learn more about computers and what they could do. It's hard to realize now how difficult it was for executives only thirty years ago to understand this new technology, then relatively simple—how it could help them and how to introduce it into a company. For big-city newspapers, things were even more difficult, because of the stranglehold the typographical union had on us, but I knew it was important and decided to take the course, which was held in an old country house in Endicott, New York. We were a class of ten, and my fellow students included some of the most high-powered, ablest, and brightest executives in the country—all male, of course. There were men who ran large banks in Boston, Chicago, and Charlotte, and two heads of insurance companies, as well as the head of Bamberger's stores in New Jersey, the head of Phillips, Van Heusen Shirt Company, and the head of a large printing company.

My unhappiness at finding myself in yet another situation with knowledgeable men far more experienced than I quickly reached panic proportions, but my worry abated somewhat when I began to grasp that they were nearly as apprehensive as I was and were feeling equally sorry for themselves at being stranded there for a solid week. We rapidly bonded together, like people achieving instant familiarity on an ocean liner.

My favorite memory of the week was of an evening when we students gathered in one of the tiny rooms that served as bedrooms. Alcohol was prohibited on the program, but several of the men—more daring than I—had packed bottles in their suitcases. All ten of us stood around the bed, sneaking a drink before dinner. It was wonderfully ludicrous to see these pillars of the establishment standing awkwardly around, drinking clandestinely out of paper cups. By the end of the week, I realized that I had retained enough of what I had learned at least to joke about it.

There was nothing to joke about, however, in my relationship with John Sweeterman. Some of the difficulties arose because I was more interested in the editorial side of the operation than in the business side. Others, however, had their source directly in the way John and I dealt with each other. I resented his inability to accept me. On the other hand, I never understood how much his position on the paper had changed with my arrival on the scene, and I didn't seem able to get over my fear of him. I deferred to him more often than not, backing down quickly whenever there was the slightest hint that there might be a confrontation.

I still recall vividly the trouble we had over an admittedly minor matter. The *Post*'s chief telephone operator, Molly Parker, was retiring after fifty years at the switchboard. She had known all my family and was close to my children, who, when they were small, often picked up our direct line to the paper to talk to her. She always took time for them. I gave Molly a farewell dinner at my house and bought her a small diamond pin. When I told John about this, he became quite angry and asked if I didn't see that this set a precedent. From my point of view, Molly Parker's fifty years didn't present much of a precedent problem. I am ashamed to admit that, even after several years in the working world, I was reduced to tears by John's anger—an unacceptable response, and one I eventually outgrew, but not for many years.

In some ways, John was a victim of my lifelong tendency to fasten on what is wrong or could be better rather than on what is right. I turned this characteristic on myself as well, being overly self-critical much of the time, but I realize that others only became aware of it when they and their work were the target. I was seen as always finding fault or second-guessing. I'm sure it made me difficult to get along with, particularly for someone like John, whom I later came to appreciate and for whom I have great affection.

I once asked him what he thought was the most important quality a person running the paper should have. "Good judgment," he replied; "don't worry about your experience." I was seen as seeking help or advice from too many people on the outside instead of relying on my own people. That was a justified complaint, but I simply had no idea how differently humans behave in professional situations, and it took me too long to learn. And picking other people's brains was my way of learning. For John, the contrast between working under Phil and working with me was just too great.

While I toiled away at learning about management, I was also busy in other areas. We made a few acquisitions in these years, which helped me feel we were moving forward on the business side of the company. The first one, in 1966, proved to be a fine one, if not a great profit center over the years. In a complicated and sometimes irritating series of negotiations, we became the one-third owner—with Whitney Communications and the New York Times Company—of the *Paris Herald-Tribune*. The *International Herald Tribune*, as it became known, is a great newspaper, with an impact around the world far exceeding its relatively small circulation— only about two hundred thousand. But it is read by government leaders and decision-makers everywhere, and above all, it was of great use to our reporters in becoming known abroad and gaining entry. It also helped the *Post* and the *Times* become more familiar to readers around the world. Even with the headaches involved, it was a significant, if small, step forward for The Washington Post Company.

WHILE WORK WAS constantly demanding, my social life was getting to be more varied. My friendship with Pamela Berry added enormously to this period of my life. She often came to political conventions here, and when I stayed with her in England, we would talk about the political situation for hours. The year that Edward Heath became prime minister, we together followed the campaign for the leadership of Great Britain, attending Labour Party press conferences and spending an afternoon trailing Heath as he campaigned in his constituency, Bexley, a suburb of London. It was exciting to be there when his Conservative Party won the election and, according to the British custom, he moved into 10 Downing Street within twenty-four hours, as Harold Wilson departed.

Ted Heath and I became friends, which later developed into one of those crazy press stories, occasioned by a widely read gossip columnist, "Suzy," who wrote for the *New York Daily News*. She claimed that I had been seeing Heath every night in London and had extended my stay there in order to continue our candlelit dinners. London's tabloids, and even the venerable *Manchester Guardian*, as well as *Women's Wear Daily* here at home, jumped on the story with blazing headlines. Both Ted and I denied it all politely, but not before Don, who was in London at the time, had been amused to read in one of the London papers of his mother's alleged romance with the prime minister.

My dearest and most constant friend in these years was Polly Wisner. Tragedy had struck her in 1965, when her husband, Frank, after a long illness, killed himself at their family farm at Galena, Maryland, in the same way Phil had. It was eerie to find our lives following so much the same pattern. Polly retreated for a long time after Frank's death, finally finding a wonderful companion in her second husband, Clayton Fritchey.

Polly and I—frequently together with Joe Alsop—took many trips together over the years, often in search of some restful cure. Once, on a skiing trip to Switzerland, the two of us were walking across a glacier, talking about aging and making observations about some of our friends—like Alice Longworth and Averell Harriman, who were a couple of decades ahead of us. I told Polly that I had decided how to handle aging gracefully: "We have to read a lot and not drink." There was a long silence from Polly, while the noise of ice crunching kept up its regular beat. Finally she asked, "When do we have to start?"

One of the first of our trips when we were both alone was in 1966, to my mother's favorite spa, Saratoga Springs. While we were there, Truman Capote phoned me to say he was going to give a ball to cheer me up—what he said would be "the nicest party, darling, you ever went to." My initial response was, "I'm fine. It's really nice of you, but I don't need cheering up." But Truman went right on talking of his plans, paying no attention to me. He explained that he'd always loved the Grand Ballroom at the Plaza, and also the Ascot scene in *My Fair Lady*, for which his friend Cecil Beaton dressed everyone in black and white. He had decided to have everyone at his ball dress in black and white, too, and wear masks, which they would remove at midnight. I was to be the guest of honor.

I was puzzled by the whole idea and not sure if Truman was serious, so I didn't think about it much, but when Polly and I joined Truman for lunch at "21" soon afterwards, I realized that this party was more about him than about me. I think he was tired from having written *In Cold Blood* and needed to be doing something to re-energize himself. I was a prop.

In any case, the excitement began to build. Truman's "Black and White Ball," as it became known, was the height of my social life then— in some ways, ever. The gossip columns quickly went into action about who was and wasn't asked for the November 28 event. In the weeks before the party, whole pages of magazines and newspapers were devoted to the young beauties from New York and around the world who would be attending—their dresses, their hairdos, their masks. Truman spent hours developing the list of invitees. At one point, he was quoted as saying, "I decided that everyone invited to come stag had to be either very rich, very

talented, or very beautiful, and of course preferably all three." The list included people from New York, Kansas (scene of *In Cold Blood*), California,
Europe, Asia, South America; from stage and screen and the literary
and artistic worlds; business executives; and the media world—all friends
of Truman's. The guests included Janet Flanner (*The New Yorker*'s Genêt,
correspondent from Paris), Diana Trilling, Claudette Colbert, Frank
Sinatra and his new wife, Mia Farrow, Glenway Wescott, Thornton
Wilder, Katherine Anne Porter, Virgil Thomson, and Anita Loos. I was
allowed to invite twenty couples from Washington.

I had a French dress—a Balmain design—copied at Bergdorf Goodman. It was plain white crêpe with slate-colored beads around the neck
and the sleeves. The mask was made to match, also at Bergdorf's, by Halston, who was then still making hats. The only direction I gave Halston
was to remind him that I was five feet nine inches tall and didn't want
something that would stick up too far. I also told him that Truman and I
would be receiving the partygoers, so I couldn't have a mask on a stick that
had to be held. I had begun going to the salon of the hairdresser Kenneth
when I was in New York, but no one knew me there; I didn't have anyone
special who did my hair, and I had never had makeup put on. I certainly
didn't know how to put it on myself! I was leaving Kenneth's the night before the ball when a woman I knew who worked there said, "We're so
busy, Mrs. Graham, with the hairdos for the Black and White Ball. Have
you heard about it?"

"Yes," I replied. "It seems funny, but I'm the guest of honor."

She gasped and asked who would be doing my hair. I wasn't sure, and
I knew I had no appointment for makeup at all. She swung into action and
insisted that Kenneth himself do my hair. In fact, she led me to him
straightaway, and I was given the last appointment at the very end of the
next day. I sat watching while he pinned curls all over the beautiful Marisa
Berenson's head, one by one. Finally, he got to me, and the wait was worth
it: I wound up looking my very best. Of course, in that company, compared with the sophisticated beauties who blanketed the ballroom, my
very best still looked like an orphan.

Truman had planned everything, down to the last detail. He arranged
dozens of dinners before the ball and assigned everyone to one of them,
thus maintaining complete control. He and I went to the Paleys' for a
drink and then left for the Plaza. We had to get through a crowd that was
already gathering in front, including a bank of almost two hundred television and still cameras set up in the lobby. It was both exciting and terrifying. I had never seen anything like it, let alone been the object of that kind
of attention.

Truman had asked me to arrange only one thing—get the two of us a
picnic dinner that we could have in a room at the hotel while we were

waiting to go down to the ballroom to receive the guests. Knowing that what he mainly wanted was caviar and champagne, I decided to order "a bird and a bottle" from "21." Having never lived this kind of life, I'd never bought caviar before and, when told its price, decided on a quarter of a pound, which was barely a couple of spoons for each of us. In addition, the chicken was dry. I was chagrined, but luckily Truman was so excited that he remained good-tempered.

We went downstairs promptly at 10:00 p.m. to greet the guests, a few of whom had already arrived. By 10:30, they were pouring in. I stood next to Truman, who introduced everyone to me. One of the most stunning moments came and went very quickly, so quickly that I barely had time to speak or look. Truman turned to me and said, with great emphasis, "Here's Jack." It was his friend Jack Dunphy, who was always behind the scenes and never appeared in public with Truman, but had been persuaded to come to the ball.

Curiously, once people managed to get through the press gauntlet outside, they seemed to forget the cameras and the self-consciousness, and the ball became a genuinely intimate, easy, even cozy party. Peter Duchin's magic music and the very good, simple food helped enormously. There were memorable scenes, such as Lynda Johnson, Margaret Truman Daniel, and Alice Roosevelt Longworth meeting—all the daughters of presidents—and Lauren Bacall and Jerome Robbins dancing up a storm.

Truman had invited quite a few young people, including Marietta Tree's youngest daughter, Penelope, then just sixteen; knowing that Penelope was going to be extraordinary, he had defied Marietta by inviting her. Susan Mary Alsop remembers sitting that night with Marietta and Ronnie Tree in the Trees' library before leaving for the ball when in walked this schoolgirl wearing a black leotard, which in those days was staggering in itself, and some sort of a little top, and carrying a black-and-white mask. Susan Mary recalls her looking absolutely gorgeous, and with a beautiful figure. Her governess followed her into the library, in tears, not knowing what to do. Penelope was allowed to go to the ball, and Diana Vreeland, ever the sharp, observant editor, hired her that night, and she became one of the highest-paid models in New York.

Why was I the guest of honor? Who knows? Truman and I were good friends, but we were on a less intimate basis than he was with Babe or Marella, probably the two most famous beauties in the world. In discussing who was more beautiful, Truman once said, "If they were both in Tiffany's window, Marella would be more expensive." He was also great friends with Slim Keith and Pamela Hayward and Lee Radziwill. In the end, however, when he had fallen out with so many of his friends, he never turned on me as he did on most of them. I think he felt protective of me. Truman knew I didn't lead the glamorous kind of life that many of his

friends did; he may have given the party for me primarily so that I could
see it all up close, just once. I also think I was appropriate for the occasion
because I really was a sort of middle-aged debutante—even a Cinderella,
as far as that kind of life was concerned. I didn't know most of these people or their world, and they didn't know me. He felt he needed a reason
for the party, a guest of honor, and I was from a different world, and not
in competition with his more glamorous friends. One of Truman's biographers, Gerald Clarke, conjectured: "She was arguably the most powerful
woman in the country, but still largely unknown outside Washington.
Putting her in the spotlight was also his ultimate act as Pygmalion. It
would symbolize her emergence from her dead husband's shadow; she
would become her own woman before the entire world."

The coverage of the party—here at home and internationally—went
on for weeks after the event, giving Truman enormous pleasure. Mrs.
Longworth said that the party was "the most exquisite of spectator
sports," which *The New York Times* used as the headline for its extensive
story on the event. The *Post*, in an ambiguous position, ran the story on
the front page of the women's section. The day after the ball, I got a call
from Diana Vreeland asking me to have everything put back on—the hair,
the face, the dress—and to pose for photographs by Cecil Beaton again
(he had done some photos of me before the ball), since she thought I
looked so much better fixed up by Kenneth. Arthur Schlesinger wrote a
flattering piece to go with those photos, and it ran in *Vogue* the following
January.

My own reaction to all this attention was mixed. The publicity and
higher profile frightened me a little, and might actually have hurt me—
and probably should have, given the serious, professional person I was trying to be. Oddly, however, the party itself for the most part escaped being
described as Marie-Antoinette's last fling. Perhaps this was because the
women's movement had not yet come to the fore, and it was before the
most serious racial urban problems surfaced and before Vietnam became
the burning issue that so dominated our society. This was the last possible
moment such a party could take place and not be widely excoriated. To a
certain extent, of course, it was. Pete Hamill reviewed it in the *New York
Post* and juxtaposed wisps of conversations from the party with horror stories from Vietnam. My Quaker friend Drew Pearson, who had come to
the ball as my guest because I loved his wife, Luvie, wrote a highly critical
column—this after promising Luvie that if he came he wouldn't comment
negatively—saying that Truman's party "overshadowed the tragedy in
Kansas, which won him fame," and that Marella Agnelli should have donated the price of her dress to flood relief in Italy.

For me, the party was just great pleasure, maybe doubly so because it was unlike my real life. I was flattered, and although it may not have been my style, for one magic night I was transformed.

In 1966, Don Graham graduated from Harvard, magna cum laude, despite having spent most of his time editing the *Crimson*. He had decided to volunteer for the army and not wait to be drafted—a decision that surprised me. I had supposed he would go on to graduate school, which you were still allowed to do and stay draft-exempt. Most of Don's friends were against the war, and Don himself had reservations, but when I asked him about his decision, he quietly replied, "The rich are staying in school and the poor are being drafted. I can't live with that." The possibility—or probability—of his going to Vietnam concerned me, but there was no way to argue with that kind of thinking.

On August 22, 1966, I drove Don to Washington's Union Station early in the morning; we said goodbye and he got on the train, headed for Fort Bragg, North Carolina. It was an awful scene, so reminiscent of Phil's departure for the army twenty-four years earlier. Don's reaction to the military was like Phil's, too—depressed by the nearly complete lack of logic in army routine, the mindless brutality he saw everywhere, and the rules designed to promote fear.

While still in college, Don had fallen in love with a fellow *Crimson* editor, Mary Wissler, and they decided to get married. I questioned this decision mildly, on grounds of youth—they were both twenty-one—and the confused emotions brought on by the army, but he was adamant. Our whole family and Don's and Mary's friends assembled for the wedding in January 1967 in Chicago, where Mary had grown up.

Only six months later, Don was on his way to Vietnam. The war was just beginning to be the searing, anguishing issue it later became, and now it invaded my personal life. Don's letters throughout the year he spent in Vietnam, assigned to the First Air Cavalry, gave me my truest and best view of what was going on there. One of his first, written just two weeks after his arrival in the country, reflected skepticism already:

> . . . though I cringe at the thought of what infantrymen do to the people over here . . . I admire them enormously for sticking it out, for fighting a war they hate in a country they loathe for a cause they neither care about nor believe in.

He wrote to Mary that, whatever the outcome of the war, "the worst will not be for us, but for these poor, poor Vietnamese, who will go on suffering no matter what happens."

In September, he wrote me:

The only thing I can vaguely see from over here is that many policies which seem bad are being pursued because it is impossible for
the Administration to change them without admitting serious
previous error. Suppose McNamara now concluded that the
bombing all along had been doing no good, that it had produced
no substantial results and had to be stopped. Could Johnson turn
around and say, "Well, we have lost a few planes and a few hundred pilots and a few million dollars but we have decided that we
were *in error?*"

In January 1968, he wrote:

I bet this all sounds familiar—probably Daddy wrote home about
the same things. I expect there are a lot of things here anyone who
saw World War II would find familiar. One thing must be missing
though—I've never heard anyone express much concern about
how the war ends or whether it ends, or, indeed, any expectation
that it will end before the expiration of anyone's tour.

"The one-year hitch," he added, "which is responsible for our 'high
morale' and much more, is also responsible for this."

For a while, the *Post* had only one reporter in Vietnam, Ward Just,
who as early as mid-October of 1967 had a piece in "Outlook" about how
hard it was to believe anything about Vietnam. Don read it and agreed,
writing me, "There really is too damned much self-deception going on
among the US military in this country." From what he could see, civilian
casualties in Vietnam were "horrifying," and he added: "It just seems goddamned awful that we are doing such immense damage to people who are
truly innocent bystanders, who never wanted us to fight for them, or the
North Vietnamese. And even if the outcome of the war is somehow positive, I think our treatment of these people will ensure that no government
considered too friendly to the US will endure in South Vietnam."

Meanwhile, as television brought the war right into our living rooms,
the home front was beginning to boil. Many young people felt it was just
as patriotic to protest the war as it was to serve the country by fighting in
it. Don, hearing about the demonstrations across the country, worried
about their effect:

I recognize people I knew as conservative or politically uninterested going through what I did: recognition of the radicals' home-
truths (war is bad; we are acting cruelly and terribly toward the

Vietnamese) and the thrill that comes from participating in something like the protest. At the same time, over here, I talk to people who have had another totally changing experience—they have seen friends die, and they know they are going to die, and they don't want to die now. They could care less about what we do to the Vietnamese.

We will come out of the war so fragmented. I wonder what will happen.

I was seeing and experiencing some of that fragmentation in my own family. My second son, Bill, chose the opposite route of demonstrating and protesting against the war. Both Bill and Steve were of the generation that transformed this country. They let their hair grow, experimented with drugs, and led a new and different kind of life.

That fall of 1967, Bill was arrested for demonstrating in front of the Oakland Induction Center during "Stop the Draft" week. He appeared in a photograph with a raised hand, confronting a policeman, which the police maintained was a threat but which Bill said was an act of self-defense, since he clearly wasn't about to try to hit an armed officer. The judge threatened to send all the protesters to jail. Our company lawyer, Bill Rogers, undertook to defend Bill, working through one of his law partners in San Francisco. I didn't want Bill to have a jail record, and in the end, Bill Rogers saved him from jail. But he got arrested again during his senior year, for a sit-in at Stanford's Scientific Research Institute, which did some defense work. That time, the protesters hired a lawyer to represent them as a group, and I wasn't allowed to interfere.

For me, it was strange—and strained—to have one son in the war in Vietnam and one at home demonstrating against it. To a certain extent, this was a product of their personalities, but even more it was the three-year age difference between them. This difference of opinion didn't affect their relationship with each other or mine with either of them. But their two reactions certainly added to my own doubts about the war and eventually to my feelings about how the *Post* should position itself.

Russ Wiggins, as editor of the *Post*, was overseeing the whole editorial-and-news operation, focusing on the editorial page for the most part, particularly after Ben came to manage the news side. Even though I was still basically following Russ's support of the administration, I was beginning to be concerned about our position on the war and had a lot of questions. Great heat had been focused on me, mostly by my friends Bill Fulbright and Walter Lippmann, and to some extent by Bobby Kennedy, whom I knew less well but saw occasionally. Fulbright had accused the *Post* of "obsequiously" following administration policy, and he invited me to lunch with him on Capitol Hill, to try to get me to turn our editorial policy around. I listened, but I'm not sure with how much of an open mind. I was pretty convinced still that Russ was right about the war.

I was also getting complaints from readers. In March 1966, before I had begun to be more questioning, I wrote one *Post* reader saying defensively, "We do in general agree with the White House position on Vietnam. While there is obviously a great deal of room for differences of opinion on this subject, we are in no way in touch with the White House nor do we talk to anybody in it about our editorials."

I wrote another woman in June 1967:

> We approach our position on Vietnam with the same degree of concern and worry that everyone shares on this difficult and frustrating war. I am sure Russ Wiggins, the Editor, keeps reviewing our policy on the bombing with an open mind. However, as long as we have half a million troops in the South, I suppose they need any support we can give them.

Even so, I was becoming increasingly uneasy about the paper's position. I also saw that the news side and the editorial page were diverging more and more about the war. A 1966 editorial stated clearly, "We are in South Vietnam to preserve the right of a small people to govern themselves and make their own choices." Ward Just, a month later, wrote in a dispatch, "We are here defending freedom as we understand it for people who don't." Thinking about the war in Vietnam consumed much of our time and energy at the paper during the late 1960s and early 1970s—nowhere more so than in editorial-page conferences. Russ himself wrote most of the Vietnam editorials, at least through the end of 1966.

Ben and I both knew that Russ had every intention of retiring at the age of sixty-five, which he would reach at the end of 1968, so we were looking for someone to lead the page after that. Somehow, Phil Geyelin, a respected diplomatic reporter for *The Wall Street Journal*, had got a message to Ben that he was interested in the job. In 1962, Phil Graham had tried to get Geyelin to the *Post*, but he had decided to stay with the *Journal*. In the meantime, he'd grown restless there, and now that his friend Ben had come to the *Post*, he was much more positive about it.

When Ben proposed the idea of Geyelin, I welcomed it. In August of 1966, Phil and his wife, Sherry, came to visit me on Martha's Vineyard, where I was vacationing. He and I took long walks discussing everything about the paper, particularly the role of an editorial page in the nation's capital, his lack of knowledge of local issues, and what our relationship might be. I also suggested to Phil that he talk to Walter Lippmann, who—Phil later told me—gave him simple but great advice for an editorial page: "Beware of predictability."

We spoke at some length about what I called the "no surprise rule." I told him something that I have said to every editor I've ever worked with—that I didn't want to read anything in the paper of great importance or that represented an abrupt change which we hadn't discussed; that I wanted to be in on the takeoffs as well as the landings. As editor, he would have real autonomy; I didn't expect to agree with every specific, but I expected to have a "constant conversation" in which we would each know what the other was thinking. I warned him that I didn't want to wake up more often than not to editorials with which I didn't agree. I recall telling him that, if that turned out to be the case, something would have to give, to which he jokingly said he assumed that wouldn't be the owner.

Most of all, we talked about Vietnam. Phil had made two trips to Vietnam for the *Journal*, as a result of which he had grown opposed to the war, concluding that it was unwinnable. But, to my great relief, he was moderate in his views, and I felt comfortable with his thinking. We agreed that the *Post* ought to work its way out of the very supportive editorial position it had taken, but that we couldn't be precipitous; we had to move away gradually from where we had been. He used the image that changing our policy was like turning a great vessel around—you first had to slow down before you could start to turn.

When Phil came aboard in January 1967 as an editorial writer, but clearly slated to succeed Russ, the tension within the editorial-page staff increased, and the arguments about Vietnam at editorial meetings grew more vociferous. By this time, almost everyone on the page except Russ had begun to change his views on Vietnam. Herblock, who in 1965 and 1966 had kept his pen relatively benign on the war, began to draw cartoons that were much more critical of the administration's policies and decisions. Ward Just's reporting from Vietnam, which I viewed as perceptive, detached, and accurate, became tougher as he grew more disenchanted with the war.

Russ, however, remained uncharacteristically locked into his position. Fortunately, he was always good-tempered and forgiving and never personal in his passions, which made discussion possible, despite the violent emotions Vietnam aroused. The back-and-forth between Russ and Phil resulted in a sort of two-steps-forward-one-step-back movement, but in the end the *Post* did begin to turn around its editorial position on the war. An amusing sidelight is that, when Phil brought Meg Greenfield to the *Post* as an editorial writer in July 1968, Russ—in the throes of our debates over Vietnam—said to Phil, "My boy, you're making the mistake of your life. She's on my side."

There *were* "sides" on Vietnam. What President Johnson seemed to feel as time went on was that he was on one side and I and the *Post*, except for his friend Russ—of whom he once said that one of his editorials was worth as much to him as a division in Vietnam—appeared to be on the other. The war definitely got in the way of my friendly relationship with Lyndon Johnson, but even before the war heated up, I seem to have been on his bad side. He had stopped calling me himself, and by 1966 our relations were definitely somewhat distant. I was no longer asked to anything intimate or friendly, and though I was invited to state occasions from time to time, his greeting in the receiving line was frigid or almost nonexistent. Because I saw Lady Bird regularly in connection with the Beautification Committee, and because I was so busy to begin with, I wasn't fully aware of how the president was distancing himself from me.

The distance, however, was real. I was visited confidentially first by Bill Moyers and later by Bob Kintner, who served a brief stint in the White House. Both Bill and Bob, wanting to be helpful, carried the same strange story: that the president had heard I had "called in my editors" and told them that he was trying to influence me by inviting me to the White House and that they were not to pay any attention to this. The very idea that I would do such a thing was inconceivable to me. I was incredulous, but so impressed at having heard the same story twice that I decided to write the president to straighten things out. On May 16, 1966, I wrote him what I genuinely felt:

> I hear from two of our mutual good friends that the Washington grapevine carried back to you something I was supposed to have said. . . . I was both sad and baffled at how such an erroneous report could have been invented. It's terribly presumptuous of me to take up your time to assure you I would never think anything like what was attributed to me much less say it. Because if I had, it would have been pompous, stupid and rude.
>
> I want you to know that I only think the things I said directly to you at the ranch about being for what you are trying to do for this country and believing very much in your ability and courage to do them. Because I am responsible for two publications, one or the other of them is probably bound in the nature of things to irritate you—or worse at times. And I am always sorry when we add to your problems—whatever reason. I only hope that at other times our support has been of some small pleasure or help.
>
> There are so many worries on your shoulders that I hesitate to bother you about this nonsense. I just decided there was too much in our past to leave such a horrid misapprehension lying around. Phil would not have liked it. Devotedly.

This letter sounds toadying. It wasn't meant to be. I greatly admired President Johnson, even though I eventually differed with him on Vietnam. I had no problem if he was angry about our editorial policy on Vietnam, or even about our more objective news policy as opposed to Phil's. What I minded then, and I mind now, is when misunderstandings get in the way of proper, professional relations. The very real problems between the *Post* and any president are complicated enough without fictitious and malicious stories making unneeded trouble. Johnson had been a friend, but I also knew he was paranoid enough to let something like this weird story anger him.

When LBJ responded the next week, it was with what I considered a slap in the face:

> I was, of course, happy to hear from you in your letter. . . . The spirit in which it was written is most welcome. Mrs. Johnson and I are fond of you, as we were of Phil; he is still very sorely missed by those of us who knew him so well.
>
> There is so much said and written that is untrue that to try to deal with it would be an endless task. Contrary to what some of your columnist colleagues seem to feel, I let most of it pass. But I do feel obligated to try to correct certain untruths that take on larger proportions than others. I owe that to the Office, not to mention my family. A great deal of gossip and opinion winds up in print often under the guise of fact; a great deal more makes the cocktail circuit. It is always good to expose it as such when possible and that should be the duty and privilege of both of us.

Clearly, Johnson found life with the post–Phil Graham newspaper difficult. Certainly, the president was growing more and more discomfited with our reporting, especially about Vietnam. To Johnson, loyalty was everything—loyalty as he defined it. The papers in Texas and their publishers were loyal. Phil Graham had been loyal. Why was I allowing my paper to report and say such things about his policies? From his point of view, according to those around him, Johnson saw me at times as masterminding the paper against his interests and at other times as being too permissive, and he used his aides, especially Jack Valenti and Joe Califano, to approach or reproach me. After one call, Jack went back to him and said, "Well, Mr. President, Kay says that she doesn't write these stories and doesn't command the stories to be written," to which Johnson replied, "Well, by God, if I owned a goddamn newspaper, I ought to have some people around me who are going to do what I want. Hell, I'd just as soon have a pack of beagle dogs out there—at least I can train them." When Jack reminded him that he didn't tell his newspeople at the Austin station he owned what to report, the president replied, "I'm not down in Austin. By God, Kay Graham is sitting there in her office. She ought to know what the hell those goddamn reporters are writing." This is such a classic politician's attitude about a publisher—every politician probably believes publishers sit in their offices doling out orders to reporters about what to write when.

LBJ particularly hated reading stories in the *Post* that predicted what he was going to do. One of the early ones on which he and I crossed swords was when we had heard that he was going to appoint Walter Washington as the "mayor" of Washington, D.C. The president called me himself to say I had to understand that, if we ran the story, Walter wasn't going to be appointed. Califano called Ben several times during the day, pleading with him not to run the story and thereby ruin Washington's chances. It was the good side of Ben—and the obdurate side as well—that there was no way he was not going to run the story. I didn't try to stop him. When we did print it, the president, indeed, held up the nomination for a few weeks, and then announced the appointment as he had planned. According to Jack Valenti, "Those leaks were kind of like somebody dropping carbolic acid on him. He considered them a personal affront."

What the president never accepted, or even clearly understood—as most people don't understand—is the autonomy editors have, and must have, to produce a good newspaper. I used to describe it as liberty, not license. I felt then, as now, that I was never antagonistic to Lyndon Johnson; I was doing my job at the paper as I defined it, and he was doing his.

On a couple of occasions, President Johnson did send for me on matters of business. One of the first was about his wanting to send John Hayes to Switzerland as ambassador. Hayes had helped LBJ with broadcasting problems during the campaign, and this was his reward. Carroll Kilpatrick went in with Russ and me for what turned out to be a fairly leisurely and informal conversation, mostly on Vietnam.

Among other things, the president talked about the recent bombing pause, saying he felt it was a mistake, because Ho Chi Minh could view it as a sign of weakness and vacillation. He looked directly at me and asked how my son would feel if we were walking down a street and someone slapped me on one side of the face and then stepped back and slapped me on the other, and my son's hands were tied behind his back. "Well," the president said, "that's the way our troops there felt during the bombing pause." LBJ believed the net effect was bad: it had prolonged the war, demoralized our side, and got us in trouble on the resumption. He obviously was worried about the war and about our casualties, reporting sadly that we had already lost twenty-five hundred men and were now losing fifty a week, with the enemy losing many times more. When he asked us how we thought it would all end, Russ said he thought it most likely that there would be no formal conclusion to the war, but the president expressed confidence that it would end soon.

IN THE SUMMER of 1967, I went off on a trip to Europe that included a tour through the Greek islands and up the Dalmatian coast on a yacht chartered by Charles and Jayne Wrightsman. My mother, knowing that we would be going to Yugoslavia and having met Tito on a trip she had taken with Chief Justice Earl Warren and Drew Pearson, asked if I wouldn't like to meet with him. She had already written to him that I was coming. Tito hadn't given an interview in two years, and when he agreed to see me, I got off the yacht and went to Rome, where I spent two days preparing for the promised interview.

Because Bill Pepper was *Newsweek*'s bureau chief in Rome, he came along, and my son Bill, traveling in Europe at the time, came too. We flew to Belgrade and from there went north somewhere and were taken by motorboat to Tito's summer-vacation island of Brioni. The moment we sat down in Tito's office, he started speaking at a very rapid pace and obviously on the record. These were the days before tape recorders were routine. A quick glance at Bill Pepper made me realize that I'd better start taking notes, which I did for a solid two hours, while Tito talked over a range of subjects. Once we finished, we returned to Belgrade, where I slogged away, summarizing the interview as best I could, and sent the story off to the *Post*, where they ran it on the front page with my byline. (Unlike the case at many newspapers, the *Post*'s editors really were free to decide whether or not to use the publisher's contributions, and they often downplayed stories I sent back from these trips.)

Having been away from home for several weeks, I returned to find that problems had piled up while I was gone. I set to work and also spent a week of many nights out, after which I went to Glen Welby with Billy, Steve, Lally, and Yann for what I hoped would be a restful family weekend; it turned out to unleash yet another crisis. We were in the middle of a tennis game and I was about to serve when I looked up into the sun and passed out cold with a convulsion. It was actually much more frightening for those who witnessed it than it was for me, who didn't really understand what had happened. I came to with Billy and Yann reassuring me and saying that I had been unconscious, that they had sent for an ambulance, and that I would be taken to the George Washington University Hospital for tests. The doctors tested for everything, including a brain tumor, which was the most terrifying prospect, but after six days in the hospital, I was told simply that I had some sort of irregularity in my brain that could have come from anything, including an injury at birth or scars from the earlier TB. My doctor put me on an antiseizure drug, Dilantin—a strong drug, which no one explained to me. It took me almost a year to get even somewhat used to it, and my body never quite accommodated to it. I would often have spells when I would suddenly feel faint or get palpitations, and was worried that I'd never be able to travel again or even feel completely comfortable about engaging in sports or other rigorous activities.

Later, hoping to get off the drug, since I had had no more seizures, I kept checking with the neurologists, who would do brain scans and tell me the problem still existed, and that I had to keep taking the pills. Finally, after about fifteen years, I found a brilliant neurologist who said, "I can't promise you'll never have another one if you stop taking it, but I'd rather see you have another one than stay on that drug." So I stopped, felt much better right away, and have never had another attack.

Some weeks after the initial incident, I started to go out again. One of my first outings was to a small, informal party at Liz and George Stevens's home, at which, after dinner, Bobby Kennedy started arguing with me about the *Post*'s position on Vietnam, keeping up a steady drumbeat about how hopeless the war was and why didn't I do something about it. He was perfectly pleasant, but my head started pounding and I felt that I might faint. I knew I had to leave, so I quickly said to Bobby, "I'm terribly sorry. This has nothing to do with our conversation, but I have to go," and got out in a hurry. I so much didn't want him to think that I was avoiding conversation about the war that I wrote him a note, saying I hadn't wanted to end the conversation but had been afraid I was going to have some physical problems if I didn't leave. I got a charming letter back saying, "I hope you are feeling better. I often have that effect on people—but they recover rapidly."

THE YEAR 1968 was a crucial one for the country and for me personally. Our involvement in the war was tearing at the society more fiercely than ever. On March 16, Bobby Kennedy announced that he would be a candidate for the Democratic nomination for the presidency. LBJ told Carroll Kilpatrick in an off-the-record interview that Kennedy's announcement neither surprised nor upset him; in fact, he said that he had always believed Kennedy would run, because the senator found something to criticize or object to in every one of his legislative proposals. Johnson still felt he was right about Vietnam, and cited the fact that every Asian leader was telling him to hold on.

Only two weeks after he spoke to Kilpatrick, however, the president stunned the world by announcing—at the end of some televised remarks about Vietnam—that he would not run for re-election. Saying, "I have concluded that I should not permit the presidency to become involved in the partisan divisions that are developing in this political year," Lyndon Johnson, his famous energy flagging, took himself out of the race.

The auction at which my father purchased the *Post*

OPERA

S. F. Society Gathers for
Gala Opening of Season

In San Francisco

The embarrassing picture of
me on opening night of the opera

At an early editorial
meeting at the *Post*

The *Post*'s city room in the 1930s (top) and in the 1960s

President Eisenhower and Phil (center) at a Washington Senators game

At the LBJ Ranch

With Ben Bradlee emerging from a Pentagon Papers hearing

With Carl Bernstein and Bob Woodward

Speaking to newsroom employees during the pressmen's strike

The only woman at a 1975 meeting of the AP's board of directors

At bat

With Meg Greenfield

Wearing various hats: with Mayor
Coleman Young at a groundbreaking
ceremony for our new television
station building in Detroit, 1980;
popping up out of an M-1 tank,
Germany, 1983; and at a surprise
birthday party for circulation
executive Frank Woodard

In many ways, Lyndon had been consumed by the war in Vietnam. He remained bitter about what people thought of him and the extent to which the war obscured many of his domestic accomplishments. Just over a month after he withdrew from the race, Carroll Kilpatrick spent several hours with him, on a flight from Independence, Missouri, where Johnson had visited the Trumans. At one point, as Carroll reported in a memo he wrote at the time, LBJ turned to Ray Scherer, a reporter for NBC, and "began berating NBC as scandalously prejudiced against him. . . . 'The only difference between the Kennedy assassination and mine is that I am alive and it has been more torturous,' he said. . . . 'I think I understand the press a lot more than the press understands me.' "

Political discussions within my family began to heat up as the campaign year progressed. Don, viewing some of this from afar, was amused to talk both to Lally, from her hospital bed—she had just given birth to her second daughter—and to my mother, ill and also in the hospital. "And what did both want to talk about?" Don wrote me. "Bobby Kennedy, of course. Grandma evidently feeling anti, Lally pro. Family gatherings, I can see, will be more fun than ever. Perhaps I'll extend over here until after the convention."

My mother was having an operation for breast cancer. I was very concerned—after all, she was eighty-one and basically wheelchair-bound from arthritis—but she still had a lot of mental energy and her old emotional approach to issues. I sat with her the evening before the operation and tried to chat about things that would keep her mind off it. The question of Bobby Kennedy had become an emotional one for her—Mother disliked him with an intensity that only she could muster. Instead of staying calm, she kept reverting to Bobby, attacking him savagely. I liked him very much, and found it difficult to listen to her tirades against him. Finally, I said firmly that we had to change the subject, and the moment passed. The next morning, my brother was with her as she began to emerge from the anesthesia. Still groggy, she opened one eye and asked clearly, "Why does Kay like Bobby Kennedy so much?"

The American home front was experiencing tremendous tumult and upheaval that spring. In April, Martin Luther King, Jr., was murdered, and the country went up in flames. The situation in Washington deteriorated throughout the night of his assassination. I stayed at the paper, and several of us climbed up onto the roof to look out over the city at the large fires—especially on 14th Street, near the *Post*. Rioting and looting were taking place everywhere. Finally, over fourteen thousand National Guard troops were joined on the streets by the District's full contingent of nearly three thousand police officers. Joe Califano, LBJ's aide, later said that they got one report at the White House that Stokely Carmichael was organizing a mob at 14th and U to march on Georgetown and burn it down. Joe recalled that President Johnson read the report, smiled, and said, "God-damn, I've waited thirty-five years for this day," preserving his sense of humor in the middle of the riots while venting his ever-present disdain for what he viewed as an elitist enclave.

THE PHONE RANG in my bedroom very early on the morning of June 5. Ben was calling to tell me that Bobby Kennedy had been shot, adding, "We need to stop the presses and replate with the story. Jim Daly refuses to stop the presses, and I think you had better get down here." Daly, the *Post*'s general manager, was haunted by the prospect of late delivery and dissatisfied subscribers. I arrived at the plant and found Harry Gladstein, the circulation director, on the back platform and asked him what our alternatives were. We decided that since it was already 4 a.m., beyond our usual delivery hours, we would go ahead and deliver the papers that had been printed and then recover the routes with a special edition. It would be expensive, of course, but if we wanted to tell our readers about this shattering piece of news, this was what we had to do. My decision to proceed caused yet another problem in my relationship with John Sweeterman. I should have checked with him, but I was there on the spot and simply didn't think in that kind of managerial way. In fact, John had been on his way in to the paper, and when he got there he said to me icily, "I hear you've been giving orders on the loading dock." I said I had, and that time we both retreated. I imagine that John would have given the same order, because he was always willing to spend money when it mattered, and it clearly mattered in this case.

Another change in a relationship took place at the time Bobby died—this one not directly connected with me but with the paper. Herblock had drawn a cartoon with a roll of dishonor on it, listing all the senators who had voted against gun control. The caption on it was "Murder." It seemed to Phil Geyelin that publishing Herblock's cartoon on the day of Bobby Kennedy's assassination was just too rough, and he decided to take the caption out and leave the cartoon. Herb was furious and reacted strongly. Not only did the incident result in "no-speak" between the two of them for at least six months, but Herb gradually removed himself from editorial control, becoming more and more independent. He started to—and still does—walk out into the newsroom to check his judgment with a group of people whom he likes and trusts. It was an irritating arrangement for Geyelin, but by that time Herb was so powerful and respected that he could get away with flaunting his independence.

The next day, June 6, I went to "Resurrection City" with the Reverend Walter Fauntroy, a black minister and city leader, to see the muddy, cold area where the blacks and civil-rights leaders who had marched on Washington at that time were camped. On the seventh, I flew to New York for Bobby's funeral the following day at St. Patrick's Cathedral. It was a highly emotional service, followed by an equally wrenching ride back to Washington on the funeral train for the burial in Arlington Cemetery. The memory of that day is seared into my mind, watching the mourners lining the railroad tracks and the weeping people in the stations, and making the sad climb up to the spot on the hill in the cemetery beside where his brother was buried.

To me, Bobby was a complex character. He could be very tough—as he was and probably had to be as JFK's campaign manager. We had occasionally been at odds, and he had once reduced me to tears over a piece on Jackie Kennedy that had appeared in the *Post*. At a dinner at Joe Alsop's, Bobby attacked me and the paper about the article, saying sharply to me, "You have lost your husband, too. You should know better." His comment caused Joe to shake his head and mutter, "It's like a young nephew attacking his rich old aunt." We had both got past that and become friends. Like thousands of others, I saw him grow and change and become a significant political figure, relating to people with a charisma different from but as compelling as JFK's. Though I had some concerns about Bobby's positions on certain issues, he had become a passionate and articulate advocate for many of the things in which I deeply believed.

MUCH OF THE SUMMER of 1968 was taken up with political matters of one kind or another. Without Johnson and Kennedy in the picture, the presidential-election campaign took on a different shape, with Hubert Humphrey, Eugene McCarthy, Richard Nixon, Ronald Reagan, Nelson Rockefeller, and George Wallace all in the running. Having made his famous "you won't have Nixon to kick around anymore" speech, Nixon had returned to political life. He had a number of image problems to overcome and had worked throughout the primary season to accomplish that. In mid-July, he came to an editorial lunch at the *Post*. Among those who attended were Don Graham, safely back from Vietnam only a week earlier, as well as several reporters and editors. Rockefeller had been there the week before, arriving for lunch with an entourage of sorts. Nixon came alone. He began by saying how glad he was to be at the *Post* and welcomed the gathering. I mentioned that I thought he and I had first met in 1946. "No, Kay," he said, confidently, "it was 1947. We met at that marvelous house of your parents. There were a lot of very prominent people there and I couldn't figure out what I, a very poor congressman, was doing in that company."

We sat down to lunch, which Nixon refused to eat on the grounds that he had to watch his weight. I persuaded him to have some iced coffee, which he took but never touched. At least two people made notes after the lunch, and two memos—one from an editor, Al Horne, and one from Ward Just—have survived which recall what we discussed and what Nixon said at the time. He felt confident that he would win the nomination on the first ballot and commented that Rockefeller had even less chance with the Republicans than McCarthy did with the Democrats. He was already thinking about his running mate but knew it would depend on which state he needed to win the general election. He mentioned several possibilities—Spiro Agnew not among them. He offered the opinion that Humphrey would do best if he ran in the opposite direction from the administration's record—which turned out to be accurate, but Humphrey separated himself from Johnson too late to make much difference.

On the Vietnam War, Nixon felt that things had changed a great deal since he was last in a position of power, that the domino theory wasn't as valid in 1968 as it had been. He also recognized that the public clearly wanted to end the war, but that the new president had to hold out for some kind of "honorable settlement."

Nixon handled himself so brilliantly throughout the lunch that we were all truly impressed. Meg Greenfield, who had only just come to the paper, said she'd have to go home and lie down to think over what she'd seen and heard. Geyelin, in reflecting on this episode later, said he thought it was one of those rare moments in Nixon's life when he didn't feel threatened by anybody; he was on top of the world, with the convention all locked up. But as soon as he got to Miami, at the slightest challenge from Rockefeller and Reagan, Nixon began to feel threatened, worrying that those two would somehow get together and stop him. It was then that he turned mean again, according to Phil. I attended the Republican Convention and witnessed Nixon's nomination, an extraordinary comeback from his defeat for the governorship in California.

Later, Steve and I flew together to Chicago, right into the stresses of the Democratic Convention. Humphrey emerged the winner over Mc-Carthy, the peace candidate, but the chaotic convention hurt him mortally going into the fall campaign. Few would soon forget the images of the violence of the demonstrations outside in the streets—which I witnessed close up along with Nick von Hoffman—or the picture, televised nationally, of Mayor Daley signaling to cut the demonstrators off by making a slashing motion across his throat.

At the *Post*, we stuck by our policy of nonendorsement, at least in theory. In effect we supported Humphrey indirectly by saying in our editorials, "If you believe in this or that, then you'll want to vote for X or Y." At the time of Nixon's nomination, the *Post* had carried an editorial saying that he "had shown an admirable understanding and restraint in his public approach to Vietnam; a commendable comprehension of some aspects of the Nation's social ills." However, it also said that in private "he has revealed a disquieting disregard for principle, not to say good sense, in his discussion of the war, of the courts, of open housing and gun control and other things. As well as we ought to know him by now, he remains remarkably unknown."

We had also editorialized about Nixon's choice of a running mate. In an editorial titled "The Perils of Spiro," we said, "Given enough time, Nixon's decision . . . to name Agnew as his running mate may come to be regarded as perhaps the most eccentric political appointment since the Roman emperor Caligula named his horse a consul." Ward Just, then writing editorials, wrote this one and also said, "[Y]ou can view Agnew with alarm, or you can point to him with pride, but for now we prefer to look on with horrified fascination."

My mother, ever the political commentator, wrote me before the election, sending along a form letter she had received from Nixon that had been addressed to "my fellow citizens of the Jewish faith," and extending Jewish New Year's greetings. She appended the note: "I do think that he gives *The Washington Post* more opportunities for humor than the Editorial Department realizes."

Hubert Humphrey had become a friend of mine. I admired him greatly and feel he would have made an ideal president. Humphrey, however, had never been a favorite of Lyndon Johnson's, who considered him gabby, going so far as to remark often to Jack Valenti, "Those people from Minnesota, they just can't keep their mouths shut." LBJ felt Humphrey's gabbiness got him into trouble, because he ended up leaking information that cost the administration. He didn't think that Humphrey leaked deliberately but that he was so effervescent he would talk when he should have been listening.

Of course, Johnson was right about Humphrey's being effusive, but he could also be remarkably eloquent, reducing people to laughter and tears almost simultaneously. He often made off-the-cuff, brilliant remarks, but then would not be able to stop, and would go on and on until the dazzling effect wore off and the audience grew restless instead of mesmerized. Hubert's saving grace was his humor. He was just incredibly funny, and I found him to be a wonderful companion always.

But despite Humphrey's attractive qualities, Richard Nixon was elected, in one of our closest elections. Phil Geyelin wrote the *Post*'s editorial on Nixon's victory, saying he had "fully earned the opportunity to test himself, he has also earned encouragement, cooperation, good wishes and an open mind among those whose security and welfare have been placed in such large measure in his hands."

Even Herblock provided Nixon with a honeymoon—however short.

In his cartoons throughout the campaign—indeed, throughout Nixon's entire political career—Herb had drawn him with a five-o'clock shadow that seemed to grow darker as the weeks (and years) went by, becoming almost a beard at some point. Russ Wiggins had sent Herb a razor, suggesting that maybe it was time to give Nixon a shave. When we discussed the beard at an editorial conference one day, Herb pointed to a picture of Nixon in that day's paper which clearly showed a heavy growth of beard to be a distinguishing feature of the man. He claimed that the dark face was a characteristic like any other—large ears, a prominent nose, whatever—and therefore fair game for a cartoonist. Actually, Herb's cartoon that appeared after election day made it clear he recognized that a president of the United States has to be handled somewhat differently from a candidate for the office. He drew his own office as a barbershop with a sign on the wall that read: "This shop gives to every new President of the United States a free shave. H. Block, proprietor."

Much had been going on at the *Post* while this political year proceeded. Typically and modestly, Russ had notified me in June 1968 that he would indeed retire on his sixty-fifth birthday, "without any undue fanfare or attention," at the end of the year. As Russ explained in his letter to me, he had a "personal distaste for a lot of flap" and also felt that this way would be better for the institution.

I wrote Russ that I literally could not imagine the *Post* without him. Of all the helpful people there when I was new to my job, Russ was the most helpful: "The nicest thing you did was to take me seriously when a lot of people wouldn't have, but not too seriously, which was just right." In fact, Russ left earlier than expected, because President Johnson appointed him ambassador to the United Nations in late September. It had been twenty-one years since Russ's arrival at the *Post*, and it was a wrench for me to see him leave.

Russ's departure caused a series of changes in the structure of our organization and in the management of the news-and-editorial side of the *Post*. Being nonpolitical and nonpartisan, Ben was geared to hard news and never much interested in editorial, so, when he became executive editor after Russ left, we both agreed that the editorial page, which was now under Phil Geyelin, should report to me rather than to him. I didn't know Meg Greenfield very well then, and at first I was puzzled that Phil took her everywhere with him. Meg rapidly made her own place in the organization, and only ten months after she had come to the paper, I sent Phil a note saying I'd been thinking about the necessity for him to have a "No. 2" eventually, and wondered if it might be Meg—"Or do you discriminate? Or would she hate it?" Just a year after she arrived, Phil named her deputy editor of the editorial page. I gave him great credit for appreciating Meg's amazing mind and extraordinary ability both to write and to edit, and her prodigious capacity for work. It was foresighted of Phil to make her his deputy—well ahead of upward mobility for women. For Phil, Meg was a real partner; he once described their working together as being like "two people at the piano playing 'Chopsticks.'"

THESE YEARS WERE filled with executive turnover, the blame for which was often laid at my doorstep, sometimes incorrectly. One instance where Ben did the hiring and the letting go took place when he became executive editor of the *Post* and his job of managing editor fell open. Ben brought in Gene Patterson, the former managing editor of the *Atlanta Constitution*, who had a reputation for the kind of independent-minded, tough, straight editing we all admired. But over a three-year period, a combination of mismatched temperaments, overlapping responsibilities, and newsroom politics convinced Ben that things weren't working out. He aired his doubts to Gene and Gene resigned immediately. When he left the *Post*, Gene summed up his feelings by saying, "Ben Bradlee needs a managing editor like a boar needs tits." This was a quote that amused Ben vastly, but it accurately spelled out what Gene had long suspected: "There was no job there." Miraculously, we all stayed friends, a remarkable tribute to Gene's classy, lovely character.

Howard Simons, then deputy managing editor, moved right up when Gene left and accommodated himself to Ben's personality and Ben's ways. He was willing and able to do the job as Ben defined it—to do the things Ben didn't and wouldn't do, either because they bored him or because his attention was elsewhere. It would have been hard to portray this relationship accurately on an organization chart, but theirs was a partnership that worked well.

Fortunately, Howard had talents complementary to Ben's. He was especially interested in what he irreverently dubbed SMERSH—"science, medicine, education, religion and all that shit"—and he created and headed a group of reporters who began to look more closely at these areas and to report on them more fully. He was a great hand-holder, and he developed many young people whom he spotted, hired, and tracked. And he had a droll, pixie humor which delighted us over the years.

Increasingly I found the confidence to pass along ideas or criticism or praise of stories that appeared in the *Post* or *Newsweek*, and I got great pleasure if a story idea I had passed on to the editors eventually made it into print and had some impact. Howard recognized my gratification in these small things and teased me occasionally with a "Brenda Starr" award for reporting. In true Brenda fashion, I once gave a story to Ben that he later regretted not trusting me on. Truman Capote had confided in me that he knew Jackie Kennedy was going to marry Aristotle Onassis—an enormous story, if true. I called Ben from South America (where I was on a trip) and told him I was sure Truman was right. Ben cabled back, "You're great, Brenda, but I chickened. Source confirmed but everyone else reached—and we reached scores—most skeptical and I decided 'twas too thin a reed to stake the paper's reputation." Of course, Truman was right, and the *Post* missed my scoop. Fortunately, Ben and I didn't hold incidents like this against each other.

Howard was also a constant fount of ideas—some good, some not so good. He kept me well stocked with things to think about for the future of the paper. He sent me countless memos about his ideas for improving the *Post*, never mincing words and once prefacing his comments by saying, "Eat this after reading." It was Howard who suggested exploring the publication of a weekly magazine to be distributed in the Friday-morning *Post*—in essence, the "Weekend" section, which remains an important feature of the paper.

Howard often addressed his memos to me as "Mama," a nickname both he and Ben used, although with Ben it was usually "Mums." It didn't bother me; in fact, I liked it. The team of Ben and Howard functioned smoothly for many years, and only began to unravel after Watergate.

I had lost one old friend and important person at the *Post* when Russ left in the fall of 1968, and toward the end of that same year John Sweeterman told me that he wanted to be relieved of his day-to-day publishing responsibilities—in effect, to retire. Despite my difficulties with him, I was fully aware of all he had done and was doing for the paper, how essential he had been, from his arrival in 1950, when the *Post* was a losing paper, through the merger to our present position of stability and strength. Fritz and I both tried to dissuade him, but he remained firm. Later, he told me that he was tired "and had had it, sort of. I just wanted the freedom."

When I realized he was serious, we named him to the newly created post of vice-chairman of the board of the company, to be concerned with planning for the future development of all of its divisions. I also asked him to help me find someone to replace him. John said that I could and should become the publisher—at the time I was president of the company and held no title at the paper. My immediate response was to say that I couldn't and that we'd have to find someone, but John was adamant. With trepidation, I decided to take the title, which my father and Phil had had before me, and to look for a new business head of the paper, but I hadn't the remotest idea how to organize a search that would evaluate anyone properly. I still didn't know about headhunters, nor did I know the industry. I didn't even know exactly what skills the job called for. After sounding out one or two people whom I knew in the industry, I turned to my friend Bob McNamara. Bob recommended Paul Ignatius, who had been the secretary of the navy and was reputed to have gotten the supplies to Vietnam. The qualities in Paul that were described to me by people he had worked with ranged from "imaginative" to "budget-minded" and "profit-oriented"—in all of which we were certainly interested. He had also been in charge of several building projects, and since a new building for the *Post* was uppermost on my mind, I decided this was a good fit and that, although he didn't know the newspaper business, he could learn it. So I hired him, and Paul came on board as president of the newspaper and executive vice-president of The Washington Post Company in January 1969. Almost from the outset, his tenure was troubled. It was a painful period for both of us. I knew he wasn't going to work out six months into the arrangement, and I told Fritz then that we had made a mistake. Fritz—correctly—told me that I was being too hasty and that I had to give him a chance, and we carried on with Paul well into 1971.

John's departure, in fact, ushered in a very difficult period for me. Problems seemed to arise everywhere, and I found managing the company to be a nearly impossible task at this time. At the *Post*, production was going from bad to worse, compounded by increasingly severe labor difficulties. At *Newsweek*, both editorial and business were troubled. At the stations, there was worry about profits and margins.

None of this was happening in a vacuum. I felt that I could manage one problem at a time if only everything else would hold still while I concentrated on it—but, no, the whole company kept spinning. I fretted that I wasn't up to it, that all the qualities I was lacking added up to an overwhelming deficiency that might very well work to the detriment of the company. I worried that the company might actually fail—and I stayed worried.

I suffered over my decisions and my nondecisions—my sins of commission as well as my sins of omission. Of the many mistakes I made along the way, the ones that tormented me most were those that seemed to be written in concrete—like buildings and labor contracts, which at least *felt* like concrete. One of the most painful episodes had to do with a new plant for the paper. We chose I. M. Pei as the architect, but wasted nearly four years in the process of planning and designing an elaborate building that wasn't going to work for the production of the paper. In the end, not only we but Pei became discouraged. We decided to cut our already great losses and stop working on what certainly would have been the wrong building for us. Except for our undue haste in turning again to the less distinguished firm that had built the original structure and then pushing that group to get started too quickly, I believe that dropping Pei's firm was the right decision for us, despite all the money and time wasted. It was the right decision—but I hated it. Ever since we completed the building, in 1972, I have had the most ambivalent feelings about the structure I work in, which is plain, dowdy, and full of compromises. On too many days, any one of its features reminded me that the decision-making process—and my role in it—had been poor. I still had a lot to learn.

Yet, despite the turmoil and self-doubting, many things at the *Post* and the company were going well. One of the groundbreaking achievements at the paper under Ben's direction was the creation of the "Style" section, replacing what before then was known as the "women's section" and called "For and About Women" in print. The new section was Ben's idea, with Dave Laventhol the chief implementer. Dave had outlined what it should include—people rather than events, private lives rather than public affairs—and to whom it should be addressed: Washingtonians of both sexes, black and white, suburbanite and city dweller, decision-maker and homemaker. Prelaunch, the section was called "Trial Balloon." There were a number of meetings on what to rename it until Ben came up with "Style," an abbreviation for "Life-style," which he thought was a bogus word, and this was adopted.

When "Style" first appeared, I was cautiously optimistic. I didn't like some of what I saw, but was willing to reserve final judgment. Fairly soon, however, I became more and more distressed over the direction the new section was taking, but I was unsure how to criticize constructively something I wanted to improve. I tended to apply a dentist drill too frequently instead of considering things coolly and not constantly complaining. One of Ben's strengths is that he stood by his convictions even if it meant standing up to me, and one of our rare square-offs had to do with "Style." Once he cautioned me: "Give us time. It's coming." Another time he said to me sharply, "Get your finger out of my eye"—a stern directive that shook me up, especially because he had always been so good-tempered. It upset me enough so that I was able to cool down; I realized I'd pushed too hard. I had improved, but I still tended only to see what was wrong and to ignore what was right.

What was right was that we had broken an old mold and were inventing an important and entirely new one—one for the new times that were dawning, in which women's and men's interests were coming together, in which neither one nor the other wanted to hear about women holding teacups around a table, or, as Ben put it: "We had become convinced that traditional women's news bored the ass off all of us. One more picture of Mrs. Dean Rusk attending the national day of some embassy (101 of them) and we'd cut our throats."

Things began to straighten out. "Style" went through a series of editors, each of whom added something to it, until finally, in 1976, we arrived at Shelby Coffey, a charming Southerner who was a born writer and, above all, editor. Writers *loved* Shelby, and "Style" really took off under him, with a group of highly talented people writing terrific stories. One of the *Post*'s finest talents, Tom Shales, was hired and developed by Shelby as a general reporter and moved on to become the paper's television critic.

Ben also hired Sally Quinn, and she began to develop into a first-rate writer. Initially, Sally had been interviewed by Phil Geyelin, who had met her when she was social secretary to the Algerian ambassador. Phil sent her on to Ben, who said to Phil, "She's fine, but she's never written anything in her life." Phil's response was, "Well, nobody's perfect." So Sally arrived—totally inexperienced except vicariously, through a relationship with journalist Warren Hoge of *The New York Times*. She told the story of being paralyzed by having to cover a party on her first day on the job. She called Warren and said, "I'm on a deadline and I'm having a nervous breakdown." He suggested she pretend that she was on the telephone to a friend and just talk about the party. That first piece came out very chatty. As Sally said, "People liked that because it was fun and easy to read. I felt as if I had come home. After the first few weeks, I realized that this is what I'm supposed to be."

Henry Kissinger, in a fit of pique, once said to me, referring to how he felt when his name was mentioned in "Style": "Maxine [Cheshire, the gossip columnist] makes me want to commit murder, but Sally makes me want to commit suicide." What he meant was that Sally had a gift for making people feel free to talk to her and then hanging them with their own words. As she progressed, her profiles of various personalities became the talk of Washington. On occasion she almost destroyed people with the strength of her writing.

In 1983, when Shelby left "Style" for the national desk, he was succeeded by Mary Hadar, who was a big success in a way different from Shelby's. She made "Style" more balanced and easier to read, and at the same time brought along her own writer-stars. Many of the most gifted came to cover parties, did that briefly, and immediately moved on to greater glory. "Style," now under David von Drehle, remains a great developer of skills and talent. Not only was "Style" right for us, but the concept has been successfully embraced by papers all over the country.

— *Chapter Twenty-one* —

WHEN IN 1969 I became publisher of the *Post* as well as president of the company, my plate was fuller than ever. I had partly worked myself into the job but not, except for rare occasions, taken hold. I had acquired some sense of business but still relied on others more than most company presidents did. One article written about me that appeared fully five years after I'd gone to work said, "Mrs. Graham accepts her responsibilities much more often than she asserts her authority." That was true; I didn't always take charge or handle my relationships with people throughout the company in the coolest or best way. My expectations far exceeded my accomplishments. In fact, the years from the mid-1960s to the mid-1970s, rich and full as they were, were depressing for me in many ways.

I seemed to be carrying inadequacy as baggage. When I thought about my uncertainty and nervousness, a scene from the first musical comedy I'd ever seen, *The Vagabond King*, kept recurring to me. There is a moment when the suddenly enthroned vagabond, appearing for the first time in royal robes, slowly and anxiously descends the great stairs, tensely eyeing on both sides the rows of archers with their drawn bows and inscrutable faces. I still felt like a pretender to the throne, very much on trial. I felt I was always taking an exam and would fail if I missed a single answer; a direct question about something like *Newsweek's* newsstand circulation would flummox me completely.

What most got in the way of my doing the kind of job I wanted to do was my insecurity. Partly this arose from my particular experience, but to the extent that it stemmed from the narrow way women's roles were defined, it was a trait shared by most women in my generation. We had been brought up to believe that our roles were to be wives and mothers, educated to think that we were put on earth to make men happy and comfortable and to do the same for our children.

I adopted the assumption of many of my generation that women were intellectually inferior to men, that we were not capable of governing, leading, managing anything but our homes and our children. Once married, we were confined to running houses, providing a smooth atmosphere, dealing with children, supporting our husbands. Pretty soon this kind of thinking—indeed, this kind of life—took its toll: most of us *became* somehow inferior. We grew less able to keep up with what was happening in the world. In a group we remained largely silent, unable to participate in conversations and discussions. Unfortunately, this incapacity often produced in women—as it did in me—a diffuse way of talking, an inability to be concise, a tendency to ramble, to start at the end and work backwards, to overexplain, to go on for too long, to apologize.

Women traditionally also have suffered—and many still do—from an exaggerated desire to please, a syndrome so instilled in women of my generation that it inhibited my behavior for many years, and in ways still does. Although at the time I didn't realize what was happening, I was unable to make a decision that might displease those around me. For years, whatever directive I may have issued ended with the phrase "if it's all right with you." If I thought I'd done anything to make someone unhappy, I'd agonize. The end result of all this was that many of us, by middle age, arrived at the state we were trying most to avoid: we bored our husbands, who had done their fair share in helping reduce us to this condition, and they wandered off to younger, greener pastures.

When I first went to work, I was still handicapped with the old assumptions and was operating as though they were written in stone. When I started my job, I was "inferior" to the men with whom I was working. I had no business experience, no management experience, and little knowledge of the governmental, economic, political, or other matters with which we dealt. I truly felt like Samuel Johnson's description of a woman minister—"a woman preaching is like a dog's walking on his hinder legs. It is not done well; but you are surprised to find it done at all." Since I regarded myself as inferior, I failed to distinguish between, on the one hand, male condescension because I was a woman and, on the other hand, a valid view that the only reason I had my job was the good luck of my birth and the bad luck of my husband's death.

Being a woman in control of a company—even a small private company, as ours was then—was so singular and surprising in those days that I necessarily stood out. In 1963, and for the first several years of my working life, my situation was certainly unique. Even at my own company, there were no women managers and few women professionals—and probably no women within four levels of me. The *Post* was not an anomaly; rather, this was typical of the times. The business world was essentially closed to women. At least through most of the 1960s, I basically lived in a man's world, hardly speaking to a woman all day except to the secretaries.

But I was almost totally unaware of myself as an oddity and had no comprehension of the difficulties faced by working women in our organization and elsewhere. For far too many years I thought my handicaps were entirely due to my being new and untrained, and attributed none of my problems to being a woman.

Early in 1966, I was asked to speak at the Women's City Club of Cleveland. Someone there had written me suggesting "The Status of Women" as a topic for my speech. My response to the president of the club reflects my views about operating in a man's world at that time:

> It may be that I am inevitably saddled with this subject as it has, I must confess, come up before. It is one in which I am honestly not interested nor educated but it may well be that I should become so. My own status is, as you know, a complete accident and I find that I lead a man's life so completely that I do not dwell on the subject much. . . . If you really insist on the status of women I'll try to adjust!

Even more revealing of my old-fashioned attitudes was an interview I did with *Women's Wear Daily* as late as 1969. Overall, the piece reads perfectly sensibly, except on the topic of women in the workplace, about which I was grossly insensitive. The report portrays me with the editors in the unconsciously sexist way then taken for granted:

> . . . Kay Graham joins in the by-play, but does not dominate it, preferring to let the men, an assertive group, play the starring roles. It is a small slice of her life, one in which assertive, strong-willed men have played a major part. . . .
>
> "I rely on Fritz's—and other men's—judgment in every decision." . . .
>
> "I think being a woman may have been a drawback for the job—unless you're a career woman, which I wasn't." . . .
>
> "My generation of women really didn't have the seriousness to work. Girls now are more serious about their careers." . . .
>
> "Would I urge that a woman be appointed to an executive job? I haven't really been faced with that. But I think it's a matter of appropriateness. I can't see a woman as managing editor of a newspaper. . . .
>
> "I guess it's a man's world. . . . In the world today, men are more able than women at executive work and in certain situations. I think a man would be better at this job I'm in than a woman."

The day the *Women's Wear* piece appeared, Elsie Carper, the longtime *Post* reporter and editor, and my friend, marched fiercely into my office and said—in response to the last line—"Do you really believe that? Because, if you do, I quit." That shook me up. I saw her point, but for me, an understanding of the real heart of women's issues surfaced only later, and far too gradually. Professionally, I remained very isolated as a woman and had no one in my work world to talk with about these things, certainly not in the upper reaches of the newspaper industry. The organization that I joined when I went to work, the trade association called the Bureau of Advertising, became the first of many over the years in which I was the only woman. Meetings were especially hard for me as a woman alone, because they took place over several days and often were held at resorts, creating problems of a social nature—whom to join at dinners, what to do if nothing was planned, what to do when the men paired off or went in groups.

One of the most awkward occasions for me was the bureau's annual trip to Detroit for a meeting with officials from the automobile industry—needless to say, a totally male group at the time. For several years I stuck out like a sore thumb. There was always the most acute discomfort and self-consciousness about my presence in a room. One speaker after another used to start his presentation coyly by saying, "Lady and gentlemen," or "Gentlemen and Mrs. Graham," always with slight giggles or snickers. It made me extremely uncomfortable, and I longed to be omitted, or at least not singled out.

At one bureau meeting, a friend of mine was presiding over a discussion of an issue totally new to me. To my horror, he decided to go around the table asking each individual for his view. I was sitting on his right, and he started at his left, which gave me time to try to think what to say while listening to what everyone else had to say. When he got all the way around the table and we had heard from everyone but me, he just stopped and acted as if I wasn't there. Maybe he thought he was being kind, believing I had nothing to add. There was a brief pause, and then we all laughed, I shakily said something, and the moment passed. At the time, I didn't know whether I was more relieved at not having to make a comment or more upset at being ignored.

I often observed that at times women were invisible to men, who looked right through you as though you weren't there. I once mentioned this syndrome to Peter Derow, one of *Newsweek*'s executives. Later I found he was hosting an event for chief executive officers who were or might become *Newsweek* advertisers, a typical promotion—to which I hadn't been invited. I inquired politely why he hadn't included me in this meeting, which was being held in Washington, especially since I was the CEO of his own company. "You remember telling me about the meetings where men looked right through you?" Peter replied. "Well, that's the reason." Oddly, I was still insecure enough to let this pass.

Each time I was the only woman in a room full of men, I suffered lest I appear stupid or ignorant. And yet I have to admit that, as much as I may have been discomfited by being the only woman in most of the meetings I attended, as time went on there was part of me that quite liked it. I actually confessed to a friend at the time that "it's spoiling—and fun—to be the first in the door."

An extreme example of my acceptance of traditional notions of men's and women's roles and realms was a frivolous but basic one. In Washington and elsewhere where large, social dinners were given, men and women automatically separated after eating, the men usually remaining at the dining-room table discussing serious matters over brandy and cigars while the women retreated to the living room or the hostess's bedroom to powder their noses and gossip, mostly about children and houses—"women's" interests, as they were then considered. I remember hearing a story that once Cissy Patterson, on being herded off with the other women after dinner, said to her hostess, "Let's hurry through this. I have no household problems and my daughter is grown." But she, too, accepted this ancient custom, as did I. Long after I had gone to work and was engaged in discussing political, business, or world affairs with many of these same men by day, at night, after dinner, I would mindlessly take myself off with the rest of the women, even in my own house. Finally, one night at Joe Alsop's, something snapped. I realized that I had worked all day, participated in an editorial-issue lunch, and was not only deeply involved in but was actually interested in what was going on in the world. Yet I was being asked to spend up to an hour waiting to rejoin the men. That night at Joe's—he was especially guilty of keeping the men around his table—I told him I was sure he would understand if I quietly left when the women were dismissed. Far from understanding, Joe was upset. Defensively, he insisted that the separation didn't last a full hour but only long enough for the men to go to the bathroom. I maintained that that was nonsense, that I liked early evenings, that I looked forward to my reading, and, further, that I wasn't trying to tell him what to do but only stating what I wanted to do. Joe couldn't accept the idea of my leaving and promised that if I stayed he would let everyone—men and women—remain at the table.

My action didn't come as the result of some major philosophical stance; rather, it simply occurred to me that I could use that after-dinner hour better by going home and reading the early edition of the paper. But clearly my working experience had at last combined with the influence of the increasingly strong women's movement.

I had had no intention of starting a revolution, but my action did indeed trigger a minor social coup, as news of my innocent suggestion spread. Because I was regarded as a conservative on these social issues, my stance was particularly effective. The illogic of expecting women to leave while men held meaningful discussions became obvious, and the practice gradually broke up all over town.

THERE WAS NO single dramatic moment that altered my views about women; rather, I just began to focus on the real issues surrounding the women's movement. However slow I was to learn—no doubt much too slow to suit many women—I finally became increasingly aware and involved. Looking back, I can't understand, except in the context of the times, why I wasn't quicker to recognize the problems.

Thinking things through with Meg Greenfield helped a great deal. She and I came at women's issues from different perspectives but with surprisingly similar attitudes. Meg had "made it" before women's liberation—in her early days at the *Post* she had a sign on her office door that said, "If liberated, I will not serve"—but she faced many of the same prejudices in her office that I did in mine. We tried to articulate our ideas together. She once added a P.S. to a note about something else: "I have been trying to work out a position—any position—on women's lib but I fear that even moving toward the spirit of [the] thing somewhat, I am irredeemably Uncle Tom. Do you suppose there's a book one should read?" (We did indeed get a bunch of books, including *The Second Sex* by Simone de Beauvoir, and read them and improved our attitude.) She went on thinking about these matters and heartily agreed with what was probably the first *Post* editorial comment on women's issues in this era. In August of 1969, under the title "Not Such a Long Way, Baby," we wrote about a sportswriter, Elinor Kaine, who had been barred from the press box at some football stadium. Unable to cover the game, she had taken her case to court. The *Post* editorial read: "[D]espite Virginia Slims, few 'babies,' as the TV commercial would have you believe, have come a long way." After discussing salary and other inequalities, the editorial noted, "The women's liberation movement, which began a few years ago as a fragile feminine caucus, is spreading," and said that "countless women who were previously resigned to their roles—in this case, often as slaves or salves to the male ego—now see that schools, businesses, churches and government all exploit or oppress women in some way." The editorial—written by a liberated man—suggested legal and social remedies but concluded that "perhaps we can begin with the ultra-radical notion that a woman is a human being."

My friendship with Gloria Steinem was also an important influence in my thinking. Being younger, she had been shaped by the 1950s, a very different time from my own frame of reference. I had watched the burgeoning women's movement, of which she was a distinguished leader, from afar at first and was put off by the pioneering feminists who necessarily, I now suspect, took extreme positions to make their crucial point about the essential equality of women. I couldn't understand militancy and disliked the kind of bra-burning symbolism that appeared to me like man-hating. I remember being repelled by a *New York* magazine cover showing young Abby Rockefeller with a belligerent raised fist to illustrate a story on feminism. This kind of thing made me overlook the real issues and think that there was something wrong with the whole movement.

As time passed, Gloria, more than any other individual, changed my mind-set and helped me grasp what the leaders of the movement—and even the extremists—were talking about. I remember her first efforts to talk with me seriously about the issues. My response was, "No, thanks, that's not for me." She persisted, however. I recall her encouraging me to throw off some of the myths associated with my old-style thinking. She said, "That's General Motors passing through our womb—you know, it goes from our fathers to our sons. But there is this kind of authentic self in there that is a guide if it's not too squelched, and if we're not too scared to listen to it." I was pretty certain that whatever authentic self I may have had had been pretty well squelched, but Gloria kept telling me that if I came to understand what the women's movement was all about it would make my life much better. In time it inevitably dawned on me, and how right she was! Later, when Gloria came to me for funds to start up *Ms.* magazine, I put up $20,000 for seed money to help her get going.

More effective even than Gloria was my personal experience in the workplace and the cumulative effect of the many rooms into which I walked, boards on which I sat, meetings I attended, as the only woman. I saw endless examples within our own company of how women were viewed. Both the *Post* and *Newsweek* certainly operated in the old ways, assuming that white men were the chosen ones to run the business and edit the news. Both organizations were totally male-oriented on the business, advertising, and production sides, and predominantly so on the editorial side. To much too great an extent, I accepted this as the way the world worked.

Liz Peer was one of the exceptions who not only survived but thrived. Having just graduated from Connecticut College, she applied to *Newsweek* in 1959 and was told not even to bother if what she had in mind was a writing position. She persisted, however, and took a job on the mail desk, running copy for Oz Elliott on Friday nights as one of what were known as "Elliott Girls." Liz was the *only* woman given a writing tryout at *Newsweek* between the years 1961 and 1969. (Among the talents that

Newsweek overlooked were Ellen Goodman, Nora Ephron, Susan Brown-miller, Elizabeth Drew, and Jane Bryant Quinn, all of whom served the magazine in the traditional woman's role of researcher.) Liz Peer finally became a writer in 1962 and a correspondent in the Paris bureau in 1964. She said later that, when she hesitantly asked if the promotion to the Paris job involved a raise, Oz replied indignantly, "What do you mean? Think of the honor we are paying you." She has told me that what she found most destructive about minority-group psychology "is that one comes to share the conviction of the majority: that one is less able, less intelligent, less educable, less worthy of responsibility." My sentiments, exactly.

To my surprise, all this was becoming very much a part of me. Though I was still simplistic in my thinking, I was beginning to understand the seriousness and complexity of the issue. Obviously I was in a good position not only to think about the problems of women in the workplace but to do something about them. As I began to understand more, I also began to acknowledge my responsibilities. I did try—in some small ways, some larger—to do something about raising the visibility of women and increasing the sensitivity toward matters of particular concern to them.

As a manager, I was aware of the issues but had no clear idea how to lean on male-chauvinist managers to make changes. I felt that I and other women in management positions had a special duty to bury the old prejudices—first by refusing to accept them, and then by refuting them wherever and whenever we encountered them. Attitudes needed to be modified on both sides. Women had accepted the dubious assumptions and myths about themselves for much too long. And men had to be helped to break out of the assumptions of which they, too, were victims.

I worked hard to educate the men around me, to raise their consciousness, even as I myself was in the early stages of consciousness-raising. I circulated among the executives at the company an article that appeared in *New York* magazine, "The Female Job Ghetto." I wrote a note to our personnel director after I had received a copy of a memo he'd sent around introducing some new people at the *Post*, pointing out what I viewed as a subtle example of bias. In his memo, this head of personnel had referred to all the men by their last names and the women by their first names. "Here is an example of the need for more sensitivity," I wrote. "Uniformity of either kind is OK. I prefer first names throughout. Although this seems superficial, attitudes which it reveals are not. No doubt it could have been written by Mary—but she works for Jones."

At the company I often received requests to listen to women's complaints. Elsie Carper told me of repeatedly receiving mediocre assignments. Meryl Secrest from "Style" came to tell me of always being assigned women or wives to interview and never men. After our talk, I wrote her that I'd always be there to listen to her views but I stood by the editors: "I think editors have to decide issues such as how and where to use reporters." I fear I didn't lean on the editors to change their ways.

When *Newsweek* was looking for a "Back of the Book" editor, I suggested the able art critic of *The New York Times*, Aline Saarinen, whom the editors dismissed out of hand, condescendingly explaining that it would be out of the question to have a woman. Their arguments were that the closing nights were too late, the end-of-the week pressure too great, the physical demands of the job too tough. I am embarrassed to admit that I simply accepted their line of reasoning passively.

Although I was head of a company, I had a hard time making change happen under the white males running things. I think I made some small inroads, however. Ben and I were always talking about the language used in the paper. In 1970, which was "the year of the woman," I was one of five women admitted for the first time to the Washington chapter of Sigma Delta Chi, the professional journalism society. I spoke at the dinner on the night of our induction and talked about the way we referred to women in the newspaper, joking that the headline the *Post*'s copy desk might put on the story of my membership in this organization would be "Newsmen's Frat Taps Working Grandma."

Indeed, only the week before, Ben had agreed to several requests made by a committee of concerned women reporters at the *Post* and had sent a memo around the newsroom on unconscious bias creeping into news articles. He cautioned that "Words like 'divorcée,' 'grandmother,' 'blonde' (or 'brunette'), or 'housewife' should be avoided in all stories" where corresponding words wouldn't be used if a man were involved. His memo continued:

> Words like "vivacious," "pert," "dimpled," or "cute" have long since become clichés, and are droppable on that count alone, without hampering our efforts to get good descriptions into the paper. . . . Stories involving the achievement of women . . . should be written without a trace of condescension.

Feelings about women's issues had slowly gathered steam, and by the early 1970s they exploded. Women in professional situations began to assert themselves through lawsuits in behalf of equal opportunity. In March of 1970, forty-six women at *Newsweek* filed a complaint with the EEOC claiming discrimination. Not coincidentally, it was the same day that *Newsweek*'s first cover story on the women's movement, titled "Women in Revolt," appeared. I'm sure the frustration of these women was fueled by the fact that there was only one woman writer at *Newsweek* at the time and she was judged too junior for the assignment, so a free-lancer, Helen Dudar, the wife of one of *Newsweek*'s writers, Peter Goldman, was hired to write the cover.

I was away at the time and got a phone call from Fritz Beebe and Oz Elliott together, telling me about the complaint. "Which side am I supposed to be on?" I asked—to which Fritz quickly responded, "This is serious. It isn't a joke." I hadn't thought it was a joke, nor had I meant my question to be. We then went on to discuss what legal response to take, since the women had hired Eleanor Holmes Norton to represent them.

When I got home and was more involved in the action, I think I became too embattled as someone who was part of management. As the situation grew tenser, fueled by the litigation, I wrote a reader defensively, "I agree that the tradition of newsweeklies has tended to appear to discriminate against women. We were making plans to expand opportunities for women—and are continuing to do so. I think we could have done so better and more easily had the group at *Newsweek* discussed this with us before they filed their legal complaint." Of course, I can see in hindsight that they probably had discussed the issues repeatedly with people at a lower level and unbeknownst to me. Eventually we started to remedy the situation—but not enough. By August 1970, we reached a memorandum of understanding, but two years later we had a whole new round when the editors were accused of not living up to the understanding. This time we were more successful. I don't believe it was bad faith that made us fail the first time but lack of understanding.

The *Post*, too, was sued. In 1972, after earlier complaints had gone largely unnoticed—and little action taken—fifty-nine women at the paper, clearly dissatisfied with management's response, signed a letter that they sent me, Ben, Phil Geyelin, and Howard Simons. The memo let the company's own statistics speak for themselves in terms of our stated policy at the *Post* "to make the equality and dignity of women completely and instinctively meaningful." The women noted that the *Post* had actually gone backwards from the time that policy statement had been issued two years previously. Since the new "Style" section had replaced the old women's pages, women had lost four jobs. Besides me, Meg was the only woman in upper management at the paper.

At one point during all this, Ben appointed a committee in the newsroom to report to him on what to do about equal employment. He endorsed the committee's report, recommending the creation of several new jobs for women and for blacks, who were experiencing a similar yet different bias. I responded rather stodgily but not unreasonably, saying it all needed greater care:

> The tendency of white males to accept other white males coming
> in the transom, while they don't recruit Blacks and women is a

tendency that isn't going to be modified by the sudden compensation of . . . additional people.

It's just the way to do it wrong again, I fear, because it takes time and effort and a change of attitudes to do it right.

Whatever we decided to do, I felt we should commit an equivalent effort to the business side of the paper, where I thought even more remediation was needed than in the city room. We wound up asking Elsie Carper, who had put forth the idea of a petition instead of a lawsuit earlier in the year, to become head of personnel to hire more women and more blacks, and she made a big impact on the paper with her hires.

Like all business and editorial companies, in fact all white- and male-dominated institutions, we had a lot to learn in this period. At both the *Post* and *Newsweek* there was a great deal right and a great deal wrong about some of our procedures and some of our responses to the issues. Prior to the late 1960s, our intention had been good but our accomplishments only so-so. Phil had encouraged black recruiting and he had hired a black reporter, but no system of goals and how to achieve them was ever put in place. When the 1970s brought infusions of blacks and women, neither the *Post* nor *Newsweek* at first dealt with the new employees with much sensitivity, understanding, or skill, but this was also true of almost every organization in mainstream America. Adding to the problem was that our beginning efforts to hire "qualified" women and minorities were carried out inadequately. When saddled with inadequate talent or failures whether women or blacks, we didn't know either how to work with them to bring them along or how to let them go.

Eventually things improved dramatically at both places, but without the suits and without the laws adopted by the country, this would have happened even more slowly. My own reactions to these suits were mixed: I felt that some were unfair and some were not. But you always get pushed when things become confrontational, and that is often to the good. Ironically, at both publications we were doing better vis-à-vis women and blacks than were most other papers and magazines, where there weren't even enough women or minorities to confront the management.

Throughout all the turmoil over women's and other minorities' issues, Meg was my valued adviser. In the middle of the suits and EEOC complaints and various battles, she wrote me a stunning memo speaking against the idea of quotas:

I am doing this rather pretentious thing of sending you a memo because I feel so strongly that it will be a mistake—and that it will not be a small mistake.

Everybody . . . agrees that we must do far more than we have to bring equity and opportunity to blacks and to women at the Post, and that we will be not just a fairer employer but also a better paper for doing so. Nobody, so far as I know (including those who are hospitable to the percentage idea), is particularly enthusiastic or even happy about adopting a so-called "quota" system. As I understand it one principal argument in favor is that such a system should now be imposed because it is evidently the only way in which we can make ourselves take action or get some of the footdraggers on the move.

. . . Are we really to concede that we cannot make ourselves do what we agree is both desirable and fair except by a technique that strips from us the power to act on our best instincts and makes us subject to automatic imperatives that rest in some sort of contract or agreement? . . .

. . . These are, of course, practical concerns. There are, in my judgment, concerns of principle too, which are at least as important, perhaps more so. . . . For we are moving, almost imperceptibly, from a concern to eradicate and compensate for the effects of past discrimination through an awareness that we cannot be entirely "color blind" in doing so to an acquiescence in the reestablishment of race (and sex) as legitimate criteria in determining the way we treat people. . . .

"Forgive the melodrama," Meg concluded, "but I should like to think that *The Washington Post* will be known as one of those rare institutions that perceived the enormous cost of putting sex and race back into law, that resisted the temptation of fashion and convenience—that had the foresight to say no."

BEYOND THE WORKPLACE, in the early 1970s there were also many unenlightened, regressive sanctuaries of male supremacy, among them, in Washington, the National Press Club, the Gridiron Club, and the Federal City Council. The Gridiron held an annual dinner at which the members, who were journalists and editors, performed political skits and songs of a slightly Princeton Triangle quality for an audience of government leaders, business heads, and other well-known people, as well as newspaper people from all over the country. Naturally, it was an all-male affair. Here, actually, as in some other arenas, it was easier for a black to be accepted than for a woman: the columnist Carl Rowan was already a Gridiron member.

By this time, women reporters had begun picketing the annual dinner and giving counter-Gridiron parties and urging government officials not to attend. The club was feeling the pressure and knew it had to change, and in 1972 the leaders decided to invite a few women as guests. Nineteen were asked, of whom I was one. Others included Mrs. Nixon and Mrs. Agnew, Alice Roosevelt Longworth, Representatives Shirley Chisholm, Martha Griffiths, and Edith Green, Senator Margaret Chase Smith, Margaret Mead, Barbara Tuchman, and Coretta Scott King.

Controversy over the invitations immediately arose. Mrs. Chisholm responded in a press release headlined "Guess Who's Not Coming to Dinner!" Several men had also pointedly declined the invitation that year, including Senators (and then presidential candidates) George McGovern and Edmund Muskie. Alice Longworth, on the other hand, had said she wouldn't miss it for anything, adding, "Only real illness could make me miss the dinner. I'll have to be too ill to stand if I don't go."

My first reaction was that after all these years of being on the outside I was excited to be invited, and I was all set to accept when I received a letter signed by many of the women on the editorial side of the paper and from other papers, asking me not to go until the club accepted a woman as a member. But there was no opening at the club at this time, and the gesture of an invitation seemed to me a beginning. Besides which, I really wanted to go. However, I asked several of these women to dinner at my house to discuss the issue. Among those who came were Meg, Marilyn Berger, Liz Peer, Sarah Booth Conroy, and Elsie Carper. They made many valid arguments, but the clincher belonged to Sally Quinn, who said, "If a country club excluded you for being a Jew but said they'd like to have you for dinner, would you go?" That cemented my decision to regret the invitation, which I did.

Meg and I were planning to have dinner together on the night of the big event. She had worked late, and as she left the *Post*'s building, a picket line was already forming across the street at the Statler Hotel. Placards read: "Write On, Sisters," "I'm a Member of the No-Iron Club—Support a Permanent Free Press," and "This Is the Last Supper." Meg saw that Judith Martin—now "Miss Manners"—was already walking the picket line, pushing a baby buggy. She called to describe the scene to me, and we—both too self-conscious to picket—decided that we had to take a look at the white-tie-attired men and the few invited ladies who had accepted make their way through the gauntlet.

Thinking we'd be less conspicuous, we hopped into Meg's beat-up Mustang rather than my more identifiable car and began our cruise, trying to be as casual as possible, circling the block, driving past the hotel to see what we were missing. With all of the media coverage, we were worried about the cameras' catching us in what we knew would be a dreadful photo and could already imagine the caption—but we couldn't resist. So Meg drove and I hunched down as best I could, trying to avoid being seen, while Meg tried to shield the whole car by keeping us partially hidden behind a bus. We had a hilarious perspective on this scene of limousines, white tie and tails, the baby buggy, and the picketers. After many circlings and several sightings, we went back to my house and had dinner and a great laugh, satisfied to have had it both ways. It was not until 1975 that the Gridiron changed its policy and admitted women; that was the first year I attended.

The Federal City Council was another case in point. Ironically, it had been created in large part by Phil, and many *Post* executives had been or were members. I was only vaguely aware of my not being included until one day when I was invited to go along with council members on a tour of the District's subway system, then being constructed. As I looked around our group, it dawned on me that not only were there no other women present, but there were none on the council. I was absolutely sure that there had been women on it when Phil founded it, because I remembered at least one. I asked what had happened and only then realized that no one had ever asked *me* to join. I remember being more indignant than embarrassed—a more helpful reaction for furthering the goals of the women's movement—and insisting that someone make sure the head of the council knew that either they must get some women in the organization or the *Post* was going to write about it. Very soon after our tour I was invited to join, together with a few other women.

Further proof that much of what I was hearing from women everywhere was seeping into me and affecting my thinking was a letter I drafted to Paul Miller, then chairman of the Gannett Company and later head of the Associated Press for many years. I raised a problem I felt was serious enough to bring up at the next membership meeting of the AP—the composition of the board, which was not only all-male and all-white but also business- rather than editorial-oriented. I said I would be personally reluctant to continue to participate in meetings or social occasions that perpetuated such a state of affairs. Obviously I felt strongly, but in the end my native caution took over and the letter was never sent. I regret now that it wasn't. Much later I myself got elected to the board—the first woman—and served three terms. Everything, including the staff that came to meetings, was still the same—male and white. Although I repeatedly brought up the subject when I was on the board, it was generally treated as a cute joke, despite the association's having been sued by its women members—a suit which I, in vain, told them they ought to settle. It took many more years for the situation to begin to change.

I always thought things would grow better with time, that the atmosphere would become more welcoming of women, particularly when there were more women involved and less notice was given to any single one of us, but it didn't happen that way. For one thing, there never were that many more of us—and still aren't, at least not at the highest levels.

The issues relating to women were on my mind constantly throughout these years. Though it took me a long time to throw off some of my
early and ingrained assumptions, I did come to understand the importance
of the basic problems of equality in the workplace, upward mobility, salary
equity, and, more recently, child care. What the women's movement eventually did for me personally was to help me sort out my thinking. Most
important to me was not the central message of the movement—that
women were equal—but that women had a right to choose which life-style
suited them. We all had a right to a frame of reference other than that we
were put on earth to catch a man, hold him, and please him. Eventually I
came to realize that, if women understood this and acted on it, things
would be better for men as well as for women.

IRONICALLY, it was during these particular years of the late 1960s and
early 1970s, while I was anguishing over so many personal and professional matters, that my own profile was beginning to rise. To my surprise,
I was suddenly written about. Essentially it had started with the piece in
Vogue by Arthur Schlesinger. Later that same year, 1967, I was on the
cover of *Business Week*, and still later in the year appeared on the cover of
the *Washingtonian*, profiled flatteringly by Judith Viorst. This was a completely novel and strange experience. Even my mother was impressed and
asked for a dozen copies.

I was unused to being interviewed and very self-conscious about these
articles. In fact, I usually refused requests for interviews, cooperating only
if I thought it would help the company. I steadfastly refused to do television interviews, on the grounds of protecting my privacy. I didn't want
that kind of visibility, but I also felt awkward and nervous about doing it
and wouldn't have been good at it if I had tried.

Yet, despite my apprehensions, it was pleasant having these articles be
so positive. And, indeed, I was doing some things right. For instance, I
formed the habit early, and have kept it up to the present, of answering
letters from readers, whether of praise or criticism. People need to feel
that they can react against what is published or aired and that someone is
listening to their suggestions or complaints. Because of my scrupulous impulse to respond, to explain, even to soothe, there is a paper trail of correspondence from these years which reflects the growing pressures and
tensions of the times. Mostly, my top priority was to back the editors and
reporters and defend them from assault, especially if the complaint came
from somewhere in the government, while at the same time trying to protect the company from undue heat.

Sometimes it was as difficult to deal with a reporter or an editor as with an outsider. Editors tend to develop what Ben calls a "defensive crouch"—a natural reaction that has its virtues, because it's often assumed in support of reporters. They get so many unwarranted complaints that they become hardened, until they will sometimes react defensively against even the most persuasive arguments. As a result, they need to be very certain that they're not rigid, but are listening carefully for those comments and complaints that are on target, and responding to them constructively. Not surprisingly, all of us publishers and editors react as violently as the public does when it's our ox that's gored. I know that reporters who have never been written about are not sensitive enough to the feelings of the people about whom they're writing—often I wish that those writers who seem to delight in savaging their targets could experience it themselves sometime. Having endured my fair share of savagery, I try harder to monitor our fairness and to be sympathetic to rational complaints from readers.

At times I've had to defend things I didn't like or think were fair or in good taste. For instance, my life would have been a lot simpler had Nicholas von Hoffman not appeared in the paper. I remember one column in which he said, in effect, that all used-car dealers were crooks. This piece resulted in a very expensive advertising boycott of the paper and lost us a large amount of money. I recall throwing up my hands at one point and writing a reader that I agreed that a particular column of Nick's shouldn't have gotten into the paper. Nick did have extreme views, some of which were distasteful to me as well as to some of our readers, but he also had a gifted voice and represented a certain segment of the population that needed to be heard. Almost alone among American journalists at the time, von Hoffman was telling us what was in the minds of the young who felt dispossessed and unrepresented by the so-called establishment press. I firmly believed that he belonged in the *Post*.

I also took a lot of heat over the years because of Herblock's cartoons. They inspired a great deal of mail, and I was constantly defending him. Herb has been one of the great—and most relentless—assets of the *Post* for half a century. His cartoons are so powerful that they've sometimes made me gasp. His strong feelings come through in every drawing. I would try to reassure furious readers by reminding them, "The nature of cartoons is to exaggerate to make a point." I also often reminded readers that a great cartoonist is an artist, with all the temperament that that implies. Herblock is undeniably a great cartoonist, and as I wrote to one reader, "It seems to us that he has therefore earned a certain license. He could not continue to be as good as he is if he were subjected to censorship or control by those who do not share his particular genius, by somebody constantly telling him to be more careful, to pull his punches, to do it some other way." To another reader, I summed up the situation by saying: "You either live with him or without him—the latter of which is unthinkable to me."

The war in Vietnam and the *Post*'s and *Newsweek*'s position on the war also caused a great deal of dismay on the part of readers—naturally, from both ends of the political spectrum. Mostly I tried to explain our stance and to remind readers that we didn't dictate government policy or unduly influence anyone. On April 4, 1968, by which time the paper had turned away from its largely supportive position on the war, and after LBJ had announced that he would not be a candidate for re-election, I wrote a *Post* reader, "We simply believe the policy of automatic escalation had been tried and had failed. We suggested rethinking our policy in Viet Nam. I can only deduce that the President too has come to this conclusion. Neither of us, I am sure, did this under any subversive influence."

In 1970, the *Post*—only the second paper to do so—started employing an ombudsman, whose job it is to receive and review complaints about what appears in the paper. Even corrections can be troublesome, particularly when attempting to rectify some egregious error only compounds the original problem. In a sense, we in the media are all ombudsmen, trying to lessen the feeling some people have that they are helpless and without hope of a hearing.

Most of all, what I know I did well in these years was to care about the company. I took an inordinate interest in all that we did, an interest that was once described accurately (if in a sexist way) as "compounded of equal parts of house mother and cheerleader." I tried to create an atmosphere that gave people the freedom to do their jobs, an environment in which good ideas would always be heard. I think I shared the highs and the lows, the failures as well as the successes.

And successes there certainly were. We were barreling forward on the news side and enjoying some success editorially in both publications and at the stations. There is nothing as good for morale as a few victories and the feeling of progress that comes from innovative ideas. Ours was still modest progress, but it was visible.

— *Chapter Twenty-two* —

C OINCIDING WITH CHANGES in the company came further changes in the country, not the least of which was Richard Nixon's inauguration in 1969 and the beginning of his administration. Nixon had a long-standing problem with the press as a whole and the *Post* in particular. Twice, he had angrily canceled his subscription to the paper. But at least at the beginning of his administration things were civil, if not friendly, between us. Basically, I was reserving judgment. After he had been in office only two weeks, I wrote Ken Galbraith, "The Nixon group is still a puzzle, as no one knows what he—or they—are for. Apparently nothing they were discussing pre-election, but that's par, isn't it?"

In March, President Nixon called me to suggest that I invite Henry Kissinger to an editorial lunch to brief us on administration thinking on Vietnam. The very next week, Kissinger came to lunch, a meeting that was the start of a long relationship with the paper and with me. All of the top editors and reporters from the *Post* were there, as well as a few from *Newsweek*'s Washington bureau. We all noted with interest that Nixon sent Kissinger, not Bill Rogers, his secretary of state. (Bill's had been a significant departure for me and for the company, since he had been a friend as well as our legal adviser.)

"We inherited a mess," Henry said, in answering a question about whether the new administration didn't appear to be almost as hawkish as Johnson's. He emphasized that LBJ had sent half a million men to Vietnam with no overall policy. Though Vietnam was the primary focus of the lunch, we also talked about arms control and nuclear proliferation. It was clear that Henry was brilliant, and at lunch that day he was both funny and articulate.

My relationship with Nixon was very different. I went to the Nixon White House twice in 1969, once for the farewell dinner for Chief Justice Earl Warren, who had resigned from the Supreme Court, and the second

time for a dinner for the Associated Press directors, at which local publishers were included. Incredibly, I received a letter from Nixon in June of
his first year in office congratulating me on being one of four women
given awards as "Distinguished Women in Journalism." Nixon's letter, no
doubt staff-written, read: "This is a just tribute to your outstanding career
and example. There are few women in our nation held in such high opinion by their peers. We are glad to count ourselves among your admirers."

This admiring attitude didn't last long. Whatever Lyndon Johnson's
feelings had been about the press in general or me in particular, I began to
realize how much I missed him. The atmosphere between the Nixon administration and the media quickly became embattled. That very fall, the
war on the "Eastern establishment elitist press" began in earnest, and the
Post was dragged into the middle of it. In mid-November, Nixon made a
tough speech on Vietnam, implying that most of the American people
supported him in what he was doing and that only the press was critical.

A reaction to Nixon came in the form of the biggest antiwar rally ever
held in Washington. When asked for his response to it, Nixon said he had
been watching football, a reaction that the *Post* compared to Marie-
Antoinette's "Let them eat cake." The following week, Vice-President
Agnew selected the *Post* for particular attention, saying in a speech that we
were "an example of a trend toward monopolization." He was not recommending the dismemberment of The Washington Post Company, he emphasized, but "merely pointing out that the public should be aware that
these four powerful voices"—he counted our all-news radio station, along
with the *Post*, *Newsweek*, and our television stations—"harken to the same
master." When I first heard his allegation that all the branches of the company answered to one voice—mine—I was flabbergasted at such a lack of
understanding.

My defending The Washington Post Company in these years, and
what we were doing or saying or publishing, was instinctive. Since I believed so much in our mission, it wasn't hard to do. My response to this diatribe of Agnew's was to insist that the various divisions of our company
decidedly did not "grind out the same editorial line." On the contrary,
each branch operated autonomously, and they all competed vigorously
with one another, even disagreeing on many issues. In addition, I pointed
out that by any objective standard the *Post* and WTOP were operating in
one of the most competitive communications cities in America.

Agnew's words had landed on fertile ground in an emotional environment. It wasn't just Vietnam and civil rights that were tearing the country
apart and preoccupying us; there was a social revolution going on. There
is no doubt that he worried all of us—perhaps more than he should have—
by striking a popular chord in a vulnerable area. Once he got a positive re-

sponse, he kept up his harangues, pouring on the heat—egged on, we increasingly felt, by Nixon himself.

Toward the end of November, Phil Geyelin was at a dinner with Herb Klein, press officer at the White House, and sent me a memo afterwards about their conversation, during which Phil had asked Klein if what we were facing was a concerted campaign from the White House and to what extent the president exercised control over it. Klein's reply: "The president tells them which way to go . . . but he can't read speeches in advance." If there was another speech by Agnew, Phil asked Klein, could it be "laid at Nixon's doorstep?" He also asked if Klein conceded that we might have reason to wonder what such an attitude on the part of the administration meant for the renewal of our television and radio licenses. Klein felt that Agnew's speeches guaranteed we'd get our licenses, since so many people would be watching. This was all, of course, before Watergate, and a real foreshadowing of things to come.

Soon after this exchange, on December 17, Newsweek's Washington-bureau chief, Mel Elfin, invited Agnew to dinner at his house, along with certain reporters from the bureau, editors from New York, and me. The main discussion of the night centered on why Agnew had taken after the press—and, alternately, why the press was so much after Agnew. Mel and Bob Shogan wrote up a long memo of what took place that night. "What we all had for dinner," they wrote, "was pure essence of Agnew. It was a typical, predictable performance. It may or may not be reassuring to know that the man doesn't sound or act differently in a semi-private, semi-social situation than he does in public. . . . What made it seem so abrasive—and a little unreal at times—was that we had an unusually intensive dose."

One of the first things Agnew said that night was, "The real trouble with this administration is that it has bad PR." When asked if he cleared his own speeches with the president, he responded, "Except for foreign-policy matters of substance, I don't clear anything with anybody." Reporters responded, nearly in chorus, to the effect that, "if he expected us to believe that, why couldn't he believe that Newsweek, The Washington Post, and our stations didn't clear everything with Kay Graham?" It was the only point all evening, Mel noted, on which the vice-president "seemed to give a little ground, albeit somewhat grudgingly admitting that maybe he hadn't fully understood how the Washington Post Co. ran." But, as Mel wrote, all that had been said throughout the evening seemed only to have been

> . . . preparation for the veep's big curtain speech. Agnew must
> have been rehearsing it in his mind as the rest of us chattered away
> while he glanced continually at his watch. Suddenly there was si-

lence and Spiro spoke. Out of the past Caligula's horse came gal-
loping again, providing a cognomen and a symbol for the evening,
something like Citizen Kane's "Rosebud." "I want you to know
how I feel about things," the veep said, in his most candid manner.
"To refer to me as Caligula's horse is intellectual dishonesty."
Then beaming like a man who has struck precisely the right blow
he pranced out of the room and into the night. . . .

Despite these unsettling strains, there was still a good deal of traffic
between the administration and people throughout the Post Company. I
was trying to keep open the channels of communication, and for the most
part during the first year of the Nixon administration everything remained polite and professional. We had several administration people in
to editorial lunches, including Attorney General John Mitchell. Just after
he had come, the *Post* got into a flap with him because Ken Clawson, a reporter who later joined the administration, misquoted him in a story. We
ran a correction in the same place where the mistake had been made, on
the front page, and the attorney general wrote me a pleased letter, saying,
"Now you can see why I say *The Post* is the best paper in the country." I
should have framed the letter.

I also had professional dealings and even some social relations with
John Ehrlichman. As head of a committee trying to deal with crime in the
District, I had first met Ehrlichman when I went to him to seek aid for
funding more police, at which time I found him helpful and even fun. At
one point early in 1971, in a regular daily column that appeared in the *Post*
called "Activities in Congress," we had, through a typographical error,
mistakenly identified Ehrlichman as a "White Mouse aide." He had
clipped the piece and sent it to me with a note saying, "For a while now I
have suspected that *The Post* thought the President was a rat. Now it appears that you have turned your calumny on the rest of us—oh oppro-
brium! Perhaps there will be a place at Disneyland for me when all of this
is a memory." I responded in kind, saying I understood we had not only
termed him a mouse aide, "but a white mouse aide, thus introducing a
note of racial prejudice," and asking if he intended to "launch a full-scale
fairness investigation."

As time went on, I saw much more of Henry Kissinger. He was still
single and occasionally asked me out to do something casual at night.
Much later, when he married Nancy Maginnes, I worried that he would
go out of my life; I didn't know Nancy, and wasn't sure how we'd get
along. Gradually, however, we three formed a close friendship that flour-
ishes to this day. People have often asked how I handled friends like Henry
insofar as the paper was concerned. It varied with different people, but
certainly no one at the *Post* or *Newsweek* went any easier on Henry because

we were friends—in fact, our friendship may have made things a little harder for him.

Nixon remained puzzling to me. Early in 1970, I had written to Lyndon Johnson saying, "I often think of you. I must say Washington is a very different place. This is the strangest group I can ever remember!" I hadn't communicated much with LBJ since he and Lady Bird had left Washington in January 1969, but whatever had come between us over the years seemed to fall away, and he wrote me back how glad he was to hear from me. When he sent a large bouquet of flowers around Easter, I felt that the time of frost was over. I called him immediately and asked whether he might be coming to Washington soon and, if so, whether I could do something for him—dinner at my house or an editorial lunch at the *Post*. Soon the answer came back that he'd like to do both, and the dates were set.

In April, the Johnsons came to R Street for a dinner, the guests at which included some of his oldest friends and my family. Johnson dominated the evening, holding court in the living room before dinner, talking with Lally and Don at length about their father, reading to them from letters and memos Phil had written him which he'd brought along, and telling them how much Phil had meant to him. It was Johnson at his best and most thoughtful.

But, nice as the evening was, it didn't hold a candle to lunch the next day, when the top editors and reporters of the *Post* and *Newsweek* gathered at the paper. The conversation went on for more than four hours. Two *Post* reporters, Dick Harwood and Haynes Johnson, later wrote about it movingly and in great detail in their book, *Lyndon*. They noted how Johnson had had one of a series of heart attacks only a month before this Washington visit. His hair had turned almost completely white and had grown long because, he explained, the ranch was so far from a barbershop that he cut it himself. Though he didn't look very well, any sign of illness seemed to fade as he began to talk about the problems of the presidency. "Gradually his manner and mood changed," Harwood and Johnson wrote. "He began talking about Vietnam, and suddenly he was more vigorous and assertive."

Because he was writing his memoirs, foremost in his mind was his own place in history. He was very concerned with how he and his administration would be viewed and had actually planned for this luncheon meeting, having Tom Johnson—now president of CNN, then still Lyndon's administrative assistant—bring along some of the most sensitive files so that he could review with us how he had made certain decisions. Tom had brought two briefcases full of top-secret documents about the war in Vietnam, and he later recalled, "There was no other occasion like that that I experienced either inside the White House during his White House years or in his retirement years."

As he talked, Lyndon would reach behind him to Tom, who knew just what paper he wanted and put it into LBJ's extended hand—Lyndon was just like the relay runner who reaches behind him for the baton without looking back and while still running. Meg, who was seated somewhere between LBJ and Tom, had to keep bobbing back and forth to accommodate Lyndon's outstretched hand.

As Tom saw it, LBJ used the lunch as a venue for venting some of his feelings and frustrations about things that had worked against his achieving all he had tried to accomplish while in the White House. He started with a detailed chronology of why he had called for the bombing halt in 1967, and how he came to the decision not to run again in 1968. He spelled out the background of each decision in detail, almost minute by minute, complete with typical Johnson language. He talked about his own love-hate relationship with the press and said he agreed with many of Agnew's criticisms of the press's liberalisms. He reminisced about his childhood and his entire political career. As he got going, particularly on his own background, he became, as Haynes and Harwood said, "more colloquial and more Texan." "He was overpowering," they recalled—a feeling I had, too. He gave us the full Johnson treatment: "He thumped on the table, moved back and forth vigorously, grimaced, licked his lips, gestured with his arms, slumped back into his seat, switched from a sharp to a soft story, and kept the conversation going from the moment he sat down at the table until hours later when Lady Bird called the *Post* and sent in a note reminding him he should come home and rest."

By that time, late in the afternoon, LBJ had become more serious and philosophical. He recounted with pride his domestic achievements and spoke of the three men who had been most influential in his life: his daddy; Franklin Roosevelt, "who was like a daddy to me"; and Phil Graham—omitting Sam Rayburn, who certainly should have been on that list. "Phil used to abuse me and rail at me and tell me what was wrong with me," Lyndon recalled, "and just when I was ready to hit him, he'd laugh in that way of his to let me know he loved me. And he made me a better man."

When, at last, he did get up to leave and we were all standing, he told a final story, filled with friendly feeling. The story was about Sam Rayburn, at the beginning of his political career and still an unknown young man, looking for a place to stay in a small Texas town. Everyone turned him down—all the important people, including the bankers, the newspaper editor, the judge. Only an old blacksmith agreed to take him in for the night. Much later, now famous and powerful, Rayburn returned to the town, this time with everyone wanting him. He told them all no and asked for the old blacksmith. The two of them stayed up very late talking, and when Rayburn finally said he had to get to sleep, the blacksmith said, "Mr.

Sam, I'd just like to talk to you all night." That, LBJ concluded, was "the way he felt about his friends at the *Post*." Everyone in the room—not all of them Johnson fans by any means—burst spontaneously into applause, something I had never seen before and have not witnessed since. It was a highly emotional farewell.

WHILE MY PUBLIC life grew busier and busier, my private life grew even more so. Nevertheless, there were many small and large pleasures in these years, quiet times that I remember still. To some extent, family problems increased. As my mother aged throughout the mid-1960s, she went rapidly downhill physically. Too many years of too much food and drink, combined with too little exercise, had made her overweight as well as arthritic. When a psychiatrist finally succeeded in getting her to reduce her drinking, it was too late for her to retrieve her mobility but not too late to recover her control of her interests and pursuits. She was back again, exercising her authority, criticizing, and arguing. It was quite a comeback, and she was in very good form for the last few years of her life, which she lived to the fullest, with all her mental faculties intact right to the end.

I had gone to Mount Kisco to visit her for the Labor Day weekend in 1970, and was awakened on September 1 by her maid, who told me she was worried because my mother had not rung for her breakfast. I sensed that she knew something was wrong, so I jumped up and ran in to find Mother in her bed, weirdly inert and already cold. Though I had been expecting her death for some time, it was still a profoundly moving shock when it became a reality. My mother was no longer there to love, to resent, to emulate, to rebel against.

It has always mystified me that I am a weeper on other occasions but not at deaths. It seems almost inhuman to cry at superficial books and movies or when upset or angry but not when I'm deeply shaken, as I certainly was not only at my mother's death but at Phil's and my father's, as well as my sister's, and later at my brother's, and since then at too many close friends'. I think that part of my reaction to my mother's death was that I couldn't believe she was gone. She had led a long and extraordinary life and left her distinctive mark in many areas—certainly on her children and grandchildren, and even on the two oldest great-grandchildren. I admire and am impressed by her increasingly with the passage of time.

My brother, having finally broken up his long-term marriage, was another worry for me in these years. He seemed always to be ill and had innumerable back and neck operations, and had started taking pain-killing drugs as well as drinking more heavily. His loneliness was terrible. Later he, too, recovered and led a good life for many years.

My son Steve was still another concern. He was lonely at home, since Bill, four years his senior, had left for college. Steve was a classic member of his generation—his class at St. Albans was the first really to confront drugs in school—and few of us parents knew how to cope with the social revolution that we saw reflected in our own homes. Unfortunately, since our house was the biggest and the least supervised, it became the place where Steve and his friends gathered, and his room became the local pot parlor. I would return home to find the windows all open in an attempt to get the fumes out and cover up the telltale signs of smoking. I begged him to stop, threatening that, if caught, he and his friends would find themselves right on the front page of the *Post*. It had little effect.

My social life was escalating. Some of it had to do with new friends I was making within the industry, some with maintaining a life in two cities—Washington and New York. Much of it was work-related, but part I did from sheer enjoyment. There remained an element within me of disbelief that I would be included by people I thought remote and glamorous. I wasn't pursuing either famous or wealthy people, but my son Bill later told me that he remembered thinking on occasion that there were too many famous people around the house. I suppose that I fell somewhere between the way I had grown up and the way my children now live.

High fashion was certainly new to me. Betsey Whitney and Babe Paley had suggested that I try Halston as a dressmaker—he had set up his own designing establishment after leaving the hat department at Bergdorf Goodman. I did try him, and our relationship was a great success: for fourteen years, until he went out of business, he made my clothes. I felt I looked better than I ever had.

Rudi Serkin was one of my good friends at this time. For a weekend each summer, I went to Marlboro, the music festival and school that my parents had helped him start. I remember watching Casals conduct a Schumann symphony, the most exciting thing I'd ever heard. And we attended rehearsals, much the best part of visiting Marlboro. More important to me, even in our short time together each summer Rudi and I developed a real friendship, which grew over the years. I loved his stories of his youth, his teachers, growing up in the Adolph Busch household and falling in love with Adolph's daughter Irena when he was only fifteen—and she was four! My one weekend every summer at Marlboro was never enough for Rudi. He always lamented the lack of music in my life, shaking his head sadly about the few concerts I attended or records I played, and saying, "How can you live a life without music?" I felt I made up in part for this deficiency by soaking it up so intensely while I was there.

I also saw something of Jean Monnet in these years. He had remained a friend from the time Phil and I had first met him in the early 1940s. The thrill for me of being with him never disappeared as long as he lived. He was energetic and interesting, and I can testify to his virility. I especially loved the way he used the English language and his insightful comments on the American political scene. I recall his once telling me, after he had lunched with Bobby Kennedy, that he had been very impressed, saying, "The president had authority—Bobby has strength."

I also developed a friendship with Clay Felker. We fell into instant conversational rapport. I had never met anyone like him, and I appreciated his ideas, his obsession with editing, and even his preoccupation with New York City and with *New York* magazine, which he had successfully launched. I never got used to Clay's odd estrangement from the human race, but I grew to be and remain very fond of him. He changed my New York life from one of solemn dinner parties to one of great fun, taking me to ethnic restaurants or to the theater. He often came to Washington, and we went to Glen Welby for occasional weekends. On one of these I brought him together with Rupert Murdoch, feeling sure that they would become friends, which they did. But it turned out to be an unfortunate friendship for Clay, since he talked to Rupert freely over that weekend, even about his having badly alienated his own directors on the magazine. Rupert ended up taking over Clay's company.

IN THE SPRING of 1971, Fritz Beebe came to me with a critical decision to be made. He thought our situation was such that we had to take the company public, as some other, bigger companies—Times Mirror and Knight-Ridder, for instance—had already done. If we didn't, he felt we had to sell one of our assets—something big, like our television station in Jacksonville. According to Fritz, we were strapped for cash. Phil had handed out stock options fairly freely, and since we were a private company we were required to buy the stocks back at a valuation determined by Price Waterhouse. By this time, the price of the stock had risen far more than had been foreseen, and we were having to spend cash for these options as people left or retired.

I wish I had understood the whole thing better than I did. My learning paths were more in editorial and management, and I still knew little about business and simply took Fritz's word for the problem and assumed we had only two choices: either go public or sell WJXT. I wasn't sure what being a public company entailed, but I knew there would be obligations and disciplines that were not imposed on private companies. I also knew that we would have to be open with information to shareholders. Yet, thinking that it might be good for us to have to run our businesses in a more disciplined and profitable way, I decided that we ought to go public. All my instincts said we should go forward, not back.

What I didn't understand—since the day of the takeover had not yet dawned—was that there was a risk we might be taken over by any of these larger companies that had sent out feelers and had remained in a friendly, courting kind of stance. Thank heaven, Fritz and his Cravath partner George Gillespie did understand this. They created a situation in which we went public with two classes of shares—the A shares, about one million, which were all owned by the immediate Graham family, and the B shares, of which there were ten million, owned by the public, by my brother, and by the profit-sharing fund started for employees. I controlled the majority of A shares, and my four children owned the rest. People bought the B shares knowing the company was family-controlled.

Warren Buffett, whose company, Berkshire Hathaway, bought about 10 percent of the company's B shares in 1973, later told me he didn't think we really had to go public but was glad we had. In fact, I was glad we had, too, although I still dislike some of the responsibilities being public entails. The advent of Warren was only one of the positive things that resulted from our going public. It gave us some proper discipline about profit margins, although I worry about the overemphasis at times on the price of the stock. It also gave my children who were not working for the paper a certain amount of flexibility in their own financial management.

The date of the stock offering was set for June 15. In a ceremony on the floor of the American Stock Exchange, I bought the first share for $24.75, and we went public at $26 a share. This important step in the life of The Washington Post Company coincided with some heightened tension with the Nixon administration. As it happened, the June date turned into one of the most dramatic times of my life, but not because we went public.

In May of 1971, the *Post* had had another of those dust-ups with the White House which got quite shrill over nothing. Tricia Nixon was going to be married to Edward Cox at the White House in June. We had assigned Judith Martin to cover the wedding and the activities preceding it, but almost a month before the wedding, the White House barred Judith, claiming that while covering Julie Nixon's wedding a few years earlier she had crashed a closed reception at the Plaza Hotel. A spokesman from the White House said, "The First Family, quite frankly, does not feel comfortable with Judith Martin."

Despite my success in maintaining some kind of relationship with a few people in the White House, I had never tried with H. R. Haldeman. He made my blood run cold, and I felt sure the feeling was reciprocated. The only time we ever met on an informal basis was one night at a dinner at Joe Alsop's when I sat next to him. I had suggested that he call me if he ever had problems he wanted to talk about, and the one time he did call had to do with Tricia's wedding. Amazingly, someone had prepared a "talking paper" for him on the points he should go over, which came to light only a few years ago:

> As you probably know, there's been considerable discussion back and forth between your people and our people regarding the assignment of Judith Martin to cover the Tricia Nixon wedding.
>
> I just wanted you to know that the decision not to provide Judith Martin with credentials for the wedding was in no way a matter of the White House dictating who is to cover events, or a punishment of any kind.
>
> It's a matter of principle in the same sense as breaking a backgrounder would be. Out of the 350 some reporters who covered Julie Nixon's wedding, all but two followed the ground rules that were laid out. . . . The two that broke the rules were Judith Martin and the other reporter from the Post. . . .
>
> I'm sure you'll understand the reasoning behind this and will agree that, under the circumstances, it was the logical action for us to take.
>
> I trust that you also will understand the desire of the Nixon family to have the wedding conducted and reported in as wholesome and positive a fashion as possible, since it is completely a personal event, not an official one, and one that means a great deal to all of the family—especially to Tricia.

Haldeman phoned me on May 13. Little seems to have escaped the taping system in the White House, since our extended conversation was taped and a transcript made, which turned up in the Nixon Library. It ends:

> KG: I wonder if there isn't some way we can just cool it. . . . But, if you can think of anything more ridiculous. I'm not even sure Larry Stern knew when he assigned her that—you know, he wasn't here when the first thing—I don't suppose he even thought of it. . . . I just hate to let it get bigger. . . . You know, it doesn't *really* matter to you or to us, does it?
>
> H: No, it probably doesn't, probably doesn't.
>
> KG: I mean (laughter) it *really* doesn't matter. . . . I'm just *really* thinking out loud to see if there isn't some way we . . . usually there's some way of getting both sides off the hook. If we just think about it, unless you just want to leave it stand . . . I'm just afraid it will be the ridiculous [*sic*]. . . .

H: Well.

KG: So, the thing is that they've made an issue and I don't think they can back down. . . . I'll try to calm our fellows down—that's the best I can try to do and I may come back to you pounding the table but I don't honestly care. . . .

It's disconcerting to see all this in print, and I'm sure I would have handled the whole thing differently later, but I was in an embarrassing position. I had grave concerns about some of the stiletto party coverage that "Style" seemed to produce, and, knowing how sharp Judith's pen could be, I actually had wondered privately why we had to take on this battle when we were engaged in so many more serious ones. My view was that Judy was an able, even brilliant reporter, but I wasn't sure I'd want her to cover my own daughter's wedding. She had, for instance, already compared Tricia to a vanilla ice-cream cone. I didn't mind defending us under most circumstances, but when I had my own doubts about the rightness of our position, the situation grew more ambivalent.

In the end, because the *Post* was denied credentials to cover the wedding, the paper had the best coverage of the event, since, as a form of protest, reporters from other papers all gave Judy their notes, placing at her disposal the finest pool of material available to any reporter in town. The story in the *Post* appeared on page one with no byline.

Much more important was a piece that appeared on the same day, June 13, about a study of the Vietnam War that *The New York Times* had found out about and was publishing. Ironically, it was at another wedding—also on that Saturday in June—that I first learned about what came to be known as the Pentagon Papers.

Don, Mary, and I had gone down to Glen Welby for the weekend to attend the country wedding of Scotty and Sally Reston's middle son, Jimmy. The wedding was a casual event, and while we were talking to Scotty, he told Don and me that the *Times* would be publishing, starting the next day, articles about a super-secret history of the decision-making that led us into and through Vietnam, labeled the "Pentagon Papers," but more formally titled "History of the United States Decision-Making Process on Vietnam Policy."

Unbeknownst to President Johnson, the review had been commissioned by Secretary of Defense Robert McNamara sometime in the middle of 1967, before he left the Pentagon. McNamara later said he had started the study "to bequeath to scholars the raw material from which they could re-examine the events of the time."

Don and I were unclear what it was the *Times* had, but we knew that, whatever it was, it was important, and that editors and reporters there had been working on it for some time. And, important for us, whatever it was, *The New York Times* had it exclusively. When we got back to Glen Welby, I called the *Post's* editors, who immediately started calling around, to no effect. Ben had heard rumors, starting in the early spring, that the *Times* was working on some kind of "blockbuster," but was not able to find out anything about it until he read it in the paper himself.

On Sunday morning, I sent to Warrenton for ten copies of the *Times*, since there was a sizable group staying at the house over the weekend. Most of us spent much of the day poring over the six pages of news stories and articles in the *Times* that were based on the Pentagon Papers, and in discussing their content and their possible impact.

What emerged was that the Pentagon Papers had turned out to be in large part just what McNamara had envisioned—a massive history of the role of the United States in Indochina, which he had intended to be "encyclopedic and objective." We learned of a year-and-a-half-long study that had resulted in a three-thousand-page narrative history with a four-thousand-page appendix of documents—forty-seven volumes in all, covering American involvement in Indochina from the Second World War to May of 1968, when peace talks on the Vietnam War began in Paris.

Later we understood that there had been a bitter fight at the *Times* over whether or not to publish these so-called top-secret documents, with Scotty and other editors arguing for publication. Scotty believed always that this was a question not merely of legality but of a higher morality: a vast deception had been perpetrated on the American people, and the paper must publish. The lawyers for the *Times*—Lord, Day and Lord—felt so strongly against publishing that they ultimately refused to handle the case. But the *Times* went ahead and delivered their bombshell on that Sunday morning in mid-June.

Ben Bradlee anguished over being scooped. He had worked so hard to build up the paper, not just to be competitive with the *Times* but to be taken as seriously, to be "out there" with them, to be mentioned in the same sentence. Now the *Times* had landed this big one on us, and Ben, mortified but unbowed, set to work to try to get the Papers for the *Post*. Meanwhile, he swallowed his pride and rewrote the stories that appeared in the *Times*, crediting the competition with their original publication.

The next day, Monday, I was in New York and ended up having dinner with some friends, including Abe Rosenthal, managing editor of the *Times*. When we had settled down with a predinner glass of wine, I congratulated Abe on the publication of the Papers. Soon afterwards, before we had been served dinner, he got word that the government was asking the *Times* to suspend publication. In fact, Attorney General John Mitchell and Robert Mardian, assistant attorney general in charge of the Justice Department's internal-security division, had dispatched the message, with the president's approval, that if the *Times* did not comply the government would seek an injunction. Abe left immediately, and I used the head-waiter's telephone to phone Ben and tell him what was going on.

Meanwhile, the *Times* "respectfully" declined to cease publication of the series, sending the paper on its path through the courts. By an odd co-incidence, when Scotty heard about the government's reaction he and Sally were dining alone with Bob McNamara, whose wife was in the hospital. Scotty asked McNamara what he thought of the *Times*'s defying the government, and McNamara considered the issues in his usual objective way and, despite his distaste for the early publication of these documents, nevertheless encouraged the *Times* to go ahead. He even went over with Scotty the message that the *Times* proposed to send back to the government, responding to Mitchell's message. It was Bob who suggested alter-ing the proposed sentence that the *Times* would abide by the "decisions of the Courts" to read "the highest Court." In fact, a compromise was reached by which the *Times* agreed to abide by "the final decision of the Court." Scotty later recalled that, had it not been for McNamara's inter-vention, the *Times* would have been committed to stop printing by the ad-verse decision of *any* court. So, half an hour before its deadline, the *Times* recovered from a careless and potentially harmful mistake, courtesy of the former secretary of defense.

Deciding to continue publishing the Papers also meant that the *Times* had to scurry to find new lawyers after seventy-five years with one firm. They were lucky to get Alexander Bickel, a Yale law professor, and a young lawyer, Floyd Abrams, to work with him as litigator. On Tuesday morn-ing, the *Times* carried the third part of the series, as well as the story of the government's effort to stop the paper from publishing. Also on Tuesday morning, after an all-night stint by the lawyers, the *Times* went before Judge Murray Gurfein, who was only in his second day on the bench. Gurfein asked the paper to suspend publishing voluntarily, which the *Times* refused to do. He then issued a temporary restraining order, setting a hearing for Friday of that week. This was America's first-ever order for prior restraint of the press.

The last story rewritten from the *Times* ran in the *Post* on June 16, my birthday, which I celebrated at dinner with Polly Wisner and Bob Mc-Namara at Joe Alsop's. That day was also the last on which the *Times* was free to publish, and the day we received the Papers—a tremendous day for the *Post*, and for me as well.

Our editors and reporters had been trying desperately to get their hands on the Papers. Ben Bagdikian, the national editor, had guessed that Daniel Ellsberg was the source for them at the *Times*, and he had been frantically calling Ellsberg. Finally, on the 16th, a friend of Ellsberg's phoned Bagdikian and asked him to call back from a pay phone. Bagdikian spoke to Ellsberg, who said he would give him the Papers that night. He then returned to the paper and consulted with Gene Patterson—Ben Bradlee was away—asking for assurances that if we got the Papers we would start printing them on Friday morning. Gene said we would but felt Bagdikian should check with Bradlee, which Bagdikian did from the airport. Bradlee's response, which may be apocryphal but certainly sounds like something Ben would say, was: "If we don't publish, there's going to be a new executive editor of *The Washington Post.*"

Bagdikian then departed for Boston with an empty suitcase, as per instructions. He returned to Washington the next morning with what has been described as "a disorganized mass of photocopied sheets completely out of sequence and with very few page numbers." The suitcase he'd brought was too small for what he was given, so he loaded the Papers into a big cardboard box and flew back to Washington on a first-class seat, with the box occupying the seat beside him—an additional expense the *Post* didn't mind paying.

Bagdikian went straight to Ben Bradlee's house, rushing past, as Ben later reported, "Marina Bradlee, age ten, tending her lemonade stand outside." Ben Bradlee had already gathered there several reporters—Chalmers Roberts, Murrey Marder, and Don Oberdorfer among them—and two secretaries to help sort out the mess, as well as Phil Geyelin and Meg Greenfield from the editorial page, and Howard Simons. Chal was two weeks short of retirement, but he and Murrey knew the most about the story, and Chal was the fastest writer on the paper. They were joined at Ben's house by Roger Clark and Tony Essaye, our principal lawyers since Bill Rogers had left his firm to become secretary of state.

Sorting out the forty-four hundred pages that we had and deciding what to write was more than a day's chore in itself, and we were also working under the added pressure of knowing that the *Times* had been enjoined from further publication and that The Washington Post Company was about to go public, with all that that entailed.

I was pleased that we had found the Papers and had them in hand, but I spent the day of June 17 in a rather routine way. I had planned a large party to be held that afternoon at my house for Harry Gladstein, a lovely man who was leaving the *Post.* He had come to the paper as circulation director but was vice-president and business manager at the time. The whole business staff of the *Post* was gathered for the party, including Fritz, who had come down to Washington for it but had gone over to Ben's house to check on things there. As it turned out, a fierce legal battle was being waged.

What Ben experienced as he rushed back and forth between the rooms where the reporters were working and the living room, where the lawyers were conferring, was that the lawyers seemed to be pushing strongly for not publishing, or at least for waiting until there was a decision on the injunction against the *Times*. Our situation, however, was very different from that of the *Times*. The court order against them meant that, if we were to publish, our action might be viewed as defying the law and disrespecting the court. Even more difficult than that was the delicacy of our business position. In going public, a company negotiates with its underwriters—in this case a group led by Lazard Frères—and on the day of the offering, everyone agrees on a price and signs an agreement. Our agreement said that in a week the underwriters would buy all the stock from the company and then turn around and resell it to those they'd offered it to in the intervening week. There was a standard stipulation that if any one of a variety of crises—such as a war or national emergency or, more to the point in our case, the company's being subjected to criminal action—were to intervene, the underwriter would be let out of the contract. We were exposing ourselves to just such a possibility if we published while the *Times* was enjoined.

In addition, Fritz had written into the original prospectus a paragraph stating that we would publish a newspaper dedicated to the community and national welfare. He now worried that the underwriters could make a case—as indeed the administration was trying to do—that what we were doing was contrary to the national welfare. Fritz had an extraordinary sensitivity to editorial issues and to the editors themselves, both at the *Post* and at *Newsweek*, but in this case, as a lawyer, he had to worry about the future of the company. Furthermore, he worried that we could be in trouble under the Espionage Act. He thought the government would be most likely to prosecute the corporation or the company, and if the corporation acquired the status of a felon, we would be stripped of our licenses to own and operate our television stations, adding a huge financial issue to the already high stakes.

So, while in one room at Ben's house Chal was banging out his story for publication the next day, Murrey was slowly reading through the material, and Don Oberdorfer was working on installments on the late Johnson years, in another room the lawyers, with Fritz and the editors, were locked in tough and tense arguments. Clark and Essaye argued against publication and in favor of letting the *Times* handle the freedom-of-the-press issue. Fritz seemed to be siding with the lawyers.

Ben was beginning to feel squeezed between the editors and the reporters, who were solidly lined up for publishing and supporting the *Times* on the issue of freedom of the press, and the lawyers, who at one point suggested a compromise whereby the *Post* would not publish the Papers on Friday but would notify the attorney general of its intention to publish on Sunday. Howard Simons, who was 100 percent for publishing, summoned the reporters to talk directly with the lawyers. Oberdorfer said the compromise was "the shittiest idea I've ever heard." Roberts said the *Post* would be "crawling on its belly" to the attorney general; if the *Post* didn't publish, he would move his retirement up two weeks, make it a resignation, and publicly accuse the *Post* of cowardice. Murrey Marder recalled saying, "If the *Post* doesn't publish, it will be in much worse shape as an institution than if it does," since the paper's "credibility would be destroyed journalistically for being gutless." Bagdikian reminded the lawyers of the commitment to Ellsberg to publish the Papers and declared, "The only way to assert the right to publish is to publish."

In the midst of the bedlam, Ben left the room to call his closest friend, Ed Williams, who by now was also a good friend of mine. Ed was in Chicago trying a divorce case, and Ben reached the editor of the *Chicago Sun-Times* and asked him to send a copy boy down to the court with a message saying he needed to talk to Ed immediately, conveying the idea that this was, as Ben later said, "as serious as anything I've ever faced."

Ed was a great lawyer with a lot of political as well as common sense. The two men talked for perhaps ten minutes, according to Ben, during which Ben, as objectively as he could, told Ed everything that had happened to that point and then waited for a response. Ed finally said, "Well, Benjy, you've got to go with it."

Gene Patterson's job that day was to run the newsroom as though nothing were happening. But the people in the newsroom are as good at sniffing out something happening right in their midst as they are at following stories outside. No one could help noticing the absence of Chal, Murrey, and Don Oberdorfer as well as Bagdikian, Howard, and Ben. Certainly something was up. Gene stopped by Ben's house on his way to my party, and then walked up the hill to my house. As I was receiving guests, he pulled me aside and gave me the first warning of what was to come, saying that he believed the decision on whether to print was going to be checked with me and that he "knew I fully recognized that the soul of the newspaper was at stake."

"God, do you think it's coming to that?" I asked. Yes, Gene said, he did.

By now, crucial time was passing. The deadline for the second edition was fast approaching. Jim Daly had come up to me twice at Gladstein's party, worrying about when we'd get the story and be able to put it into print, and asking if I had yet heard from the other house. I was strangely unconcerned and said I was sure they were just finishing and we would get it in time.

It was a lovely June day, and the party for Harry spilled out of the house onto the terrace and the lawn. I was making a toast to him and going full-blast about how much he had meant to the paper and to me personally when someone tugged at my sleeve and said with some urgency, "You're wanted on the phone."

I protested that I had to finish the toast, but the response was, "They want you now." I finally got the idea that it was really important, wound up the toast quickly, and took the call in a corner of the library. I was sitting on a small sofa near the open door, and Paul Ignatius stood near me. Fritz was on the other end of the line. He told me about the argument between the lawyers and the editors over whether to publish the next day, outlined the reasoning on both sides, and concluded by saying, "I'm afraid you are going to have to decide."

I asked Fritz for his own view; since he was so editorial-minded and so decent, I knew I could trust his response. I was astonished when he said, "I guess I wouldn't." I then asked for time to think it over, saying, "Can't we talk about this? Why do we have to make up our minds in such haste when the *Times* took three months to decide?"

At this point, Ben and the editors got on various extensions at Ben's house. I asked them what the big rush was, suggesting we at least think about this for a day. No, Ben said, it was important to keep up the momentum of publication and not to let a day intervene after getting the story. He also stressed that by this time the grapevine knew we had the Papers. Journalists inside and outside were watching us.

I could tell from the passion of the editors' views that we were in for big trouble on the editorial floor if we didn't publish. I well remember Phil Geyelin's response when I said that deciding to publish could destroy the paper. "Yes," he agreed, "but there's more than one way to destroy a newspaper."

At the same time that the editors were saying, seriatim, "You've got to do it," Paul Ignatius was standing beside me, repeating—each time more insistently—"Wait a day, wait a day."

I was extremely torn by Fritz's saying that he wouldn't publish. I knew him so well, and we had never differed on any important issue; and, after all, he was the lawyer, not I. But I also heard *how* he said it: he didn't hammer at me, he didn't stress the issues related to going public, and he didn't say the obvious thing—that I would be risking the whole company on this decision. He simply said he guessed he wouldn't. I felt that, despite his stated opinion, he had somehow left the door open for me to decide on a different course. Frightened and tense, I took a big gulp and said, "Go ahead, go ahead, go ahead. Let's go. Let's publish." And I hung up.

So the decision was made. But later that evening Fritz came over to my house. Roger Clark, still worried, had thought of a new problem: he feared an extra charge of collusion with the *Times* and wanted to know the source of our obtaining the Papers. Bagdikian by this time had gone to the paper, carrying the last of Chal's story to set in type. At first Bagdikian maintained that the source was confidential, but when Clark insisted, he identified Ellsberg, the presumed source for the *Times*, which only increased Clark's concern about collusion. This time Fritz really helped. I had no idea whether collusion made our situation more vulnerable or not, but Fritz said that we'd made up our minds and should go ahead. I was relieved, and agreed.

Our lawyers by then were behind us and very supportive. In addition, Fritz had Roswell Gilpatric of the Cravath firm down from New York, with whom he was informally consulting, as Ben was with Edward Bennett Williams. The two young lawyers in the Washington branch of our law firm—Royall, Koegel & Wells—sent to New York for a litigator, William Glendon, whom we didn't know and who was relatively inexperienced with cases like this.

At about 3:00 p.m. Friday, while I happened to be sitting in Ben's office, a call came from William Rehnquist, then the assistant attorney general for the Department of Justice's Office of Legal Counsel. Rehnquist read the same message to Ben that he had sent to the *Times*. Ben told Rehnquist, "I'm sure you will understand that I must respectfully decline." He also refused to delay the rest of the series pending resolution of the *Times*'s case in New York. The government promptly filed suit against the *Post*, a suit that matched the one lodged against the *Times*, and named as defendants everyone on the masthead of the paper, plus the author of the first article (the one that had appeared on June 18), Chalmers Roberts.

The case was routinely assigned to Judge Gerhard Gesell, a distinguished jurist of a liberal mind. He had helped in the 1954 acquisition of the *Times-Herald*, at a time when he worked for Covington & Burling and had also been a friend of Phil's and mine when we were all young, but our paths had gone different ways and I no longer saw him and his wife, Peggy. In fact, Phil had fired him during one of his bad years, which was what enabled Gerry to take the case.

At 8:05 p.m. on June 18, Gesell ruled for the *Post*, refusing to grant an order restraining the paper from further publication of the series and saying, "The court has before it no precise information suggesting in what respects, if any, the publication of this information will injure" the nation. The court of appeals, to which the government instantly went, ruled for the government at about 1:20 a.m., reversing Gesell's decision. Fritz was at the court with the lawyers arguing that we had several thousand papers on the street and the plates on the presses. So, at 2:10 a.m., the court agreed with us that the injunction didn't apply to that night's paper, and we finished the press run.

Gerry Gesell confided to me after his retirement, "If anybody ever carves anything on my tombstone, they might say I was the only judge out of twenty-nine judges who heard the Pentagon Papers case who never stopped the presses for a minute. The only one. I've always taken a little pride in that." In staying Gesell's order, the appeals court had also told him to hold a fuller, more detailed hearing on Monday, June 21. Over the weekend, he tried to get a handle on what was behind the case, to get it into some kind of shape to be heard. Because the courthouse was under- going construction, Gesell held a meeting at his house with some Justice Department officials, telling them to select the ten most damaging things in the Papers and that he would limit the Monday hearing to that list. At some point, a Justice Department lawyer told Gesell that, of course, the defendants—meaning all of us connected with the *Post* who'd been named in the suit—wouldn't be present at the hearing; it had to be held in secret. Gesell told him firmly, "We don't do things that way," adding, "If that's the way it's going to go, I'll dismiss the case. I won't even hold a hearing." He suggested the lawyer call the White House—or, as Gesell put it, "wherever or whoever it was that gave you those instructions"—and tell them he would dismiss the case if that was the condition. The lawyer did call someone and returned to say it would be all right to have the defen- dants present. Finally, the Justice Department lawyers left, leaving the Pa- pers behind. As Gesell later recounted:

> They hadn't been gone but two or three minutes when there was a knock on the door and here were two fellows all in uniform, great big white sashes, or whatever it is, across their uniform, and guns and all this and said, "We've come for the Papers." I said, "I don't have to give you the Papers. I want to read them." Well, they said, "You don't have any security out here; we can't let you have these Papers." I said, "I've got the best security in the world. I put them under my sofa pillow and you're not going to have them. You can stay here all night if you want to guard the place, but I'm going to have the Papers." They disappeared after that.

On Monday, Fritz, Ben, Don and Mary Graham, and I, among others, went into court for the hearing. There was a swarm of press people out- side. All the windows of the courtroom were blacked out. At one point as the case proceeded, the government put on the stand an ex–CIA man who had been working in the Pentagon who testified how serious the situation was and that publication of some of these papers would reveal certain war plans of the United States. Gesell didn't believe this man and called for the general in charge of the war plans to be sent over to testify. He was duly brought in—the quintessential general, bedecked with medals—and as Gesell remembers it, after taking the oath to tell the truth, he stated, "Judge, if anybody thinks these are our war plans, I sure hope they do, because these are entirely out of date."

The government then tried to hit another of its points on the list, claiming that there was a Canadian diplomat who had infiltrated Vietnam and was passing information to the Americans, which was a violation of Canadian treason laws. The government's point was that, if the information got out, this was a capital offense and the man would be executed. Here is where the skill of our reporters helped us. Not only did they write depositions, but they came up with citations proving that the alleged top-secret items had already been published. Chal Roberts promptly supplied several published books to our lawyers, in each of which the Canadian diplomat was mentioned by name along with a description of what he was doing. So much for that argument.

In the end, Gesell refused to grant the government an injunction against the *Post*, allowing the series to resume. Later that day, however, the U.S. Court of Appeals for the District of Columbia continued the temporary restraining order and ordered a hearing before the full nine-judge appellate court, which heard the case on June 22. I attended the proceedings that day also. The court affirmed Gesell's decision, upholding the *Post*'s constitutional right to continue the series based on the Papers. At the same time, however, the court continued the restraining order to allow for an appeal.

The day *The New York Times* had published its first story, Erwin Griswold, solicitor general of the United States, and his wife were in Florida sunning themselves at a hotel pool and resting after he had made a speech to the Florida State Bar Association the night before. When he read the *Times*'s story on the Pentagon Papers, he immediately turned to his wife and said, "Well, it looks as though I'm going to have a case in the Supreme Court one of these days." Much later he told me that he assumed November would be the earliest conceivable moment the case would be brought to the Court. When he got back from Florida, there was a note for him to call the attorney general. Griswold—who had been a Johnson appointee but was still serving under Nixon—said that, at meetings with Mitchell and other Justice Department officials, he consistently "counseled against going ahead with the case. I said, 'The trouble is you don't have any ground to stand on.' But nobody except me ever had any thought of not going ahead."

On Friday, June 25, the Supreme Court granted the petitions for certiorari from both the *Times* and the *Post*. At the same time, since the *Times*, because of its separate route through the courts, was still prohibited from publishing, and the *Post* was not, the Court—at least until a final decision could be handed down—put both newspapers under equal restraints, marking the first time the Supreme Court had restricted publication of a newspaper article. What the Court's decision to accept the cases meant for Griswold was that he had only twenty-four hours to prepare his brief, still not having seen the Papers themselves. He began to focus on them at once, arranging to see three government people, and asking each of them to tell him what problems might arise if the Papers were published in full. Even after talking with these people, he realized he didn't have a very strong case.

Griswold was back in his office early Saturday morning to finish preparing his brief. With no help in the Justice Department on Saturday, he and his secretary ran it off on the mimeograph machine. They then assembled the pages, stamped them "Top Secret," and went off to court. Griswold had two extra copies of his brief, one for the *Times*'s counsel and one for the *Post*'s. He recalled being taken aback when the guard for the Papers asked him what he intended doing with those copies and when he was told said, "Well, that's treason; that's giving them to the enemy." Griswold nearly had a set-to with the security man, insisting it was his professional responsibility to furnish copies of the brief to the other side. So bizarre were the security and secrecy surrounding the case that officials from the government had taken away our own brief, impounding it as top secret!

On Saturday, June 26, the two cases—that of *The New York Times* and that of the *Post*—met for the first time, in that they were being heard together at the Supreme Court. None of us fully understood the nuances of what was being acted out in court after court—national security, prior restraint, the right to know—until we actually got to the Supreme Court. I went to the Court with Fritz and several others from the *Post* for this unusual special session. The government's case was argued by Griswold, and the newspapers' case was argued by Alexander Bickel for the *Times* and William Glendon for the *Post*.

I was in the *Post*'s newsroom around midday on Wednesday, June 30, when we received word that the Court would convene at two-thirty. Everyone in the newsroom was deadly quiet, waiting for the news. Right on time, Chief Justice Warren Burger announced the decision. Simultaneously, Deputy National Editor Mary Lou Beatty heard the news on an open phone line to the Supreme Court and Gene Patterson heard it in the wire room, then jumped on a desk and called out, "We win and so does *The New York Times*." The newspapers were free to publish.

By a six-to-three vote, the Supreme Court ruled that the government had not met "the heavy burden of showing justification" for restraining further publication of the Pentagon Papers as endangering national security. At the *Post*, having regarded ourselves as doing the public's business, we were gratified by the results and felt that the principle of no prior restraint of the press had been vindicated.

We were also proud of the *Post* and its people. In a memo to the staff I said, "I know I speak for all of us when I say what a great moment this is for *The Washington Post*." Ben Bradlee was equally proud. He told the staff, "The guts and energy and responsibility of everyone involved in this fight, and the sense that you all were involved, has impressed me more than anything in my life. You are beautiful."

We had prevailed, but ours was an incomplete "victory." Basically, we were challenging the right of the executive branch to prevent a newspaper from publishing material we believed should be available to the public. In court, we had challenged the government's contention that the material in the Papers was too sensitive for the public eye. We had strongly argued the case against prior restraint, but we had in fact been restrained. We were disappointed that the Court's decree was both limited and ambiguous. Though the decision was in favor of allowing the newspapers to publish, there was, as I later said, "no ringing reaffirmation of First Amendment guarantees that all publishers yearn to hear."

The Supreme Court's decision had caused enormous rejoicing in the press at large and at the *Post* and *Times* in particular, but hidden away in the details of the separate opinions were some views that were of great concern to us, having to do with possible criminal prosecution after the fact. It was clear to us that Attorney General Mitchell felt avenues of criminal prosecution remained open, and that the Department of Justice was continuing its investigation and would prosecute those who in any way violated federal criminal laws in connection with the Papers. Aspects of this threat were made even clearer to me by two strange messages received over the fence. One came from Ken Clawson, then still a *Post* reporter.

A few days after the Supreme Court decision was handed down, Clawson told me he had had a message from Richard Kleindienst, then deputy attorney general. At one point, we had independently, and in an effort to act responsibly, decided we wouldn't publish those items that had been specified in the solicitor general's secret brief as being those most threatening to the national interest. We didn't even have some of the volumes of the Papers that the government found most objectionable; others we felt had no news value. Kleindienst, however, wanted me to know that it would not be enough to agree not to publish the portions of the Papers that the government felt endangered national security; rather, the *Post* would have to *relinquish* the parts of the Papers it held relating to this kind of information. Clawson emphasized to me that Kleindienst had told him that the *Post* had been the subject of "considerable talk at Justice." According to Clawson, Kleindienst had actually mentioned certain regulations barring ownership of radio and television properties after conviction for particular offenses. He also told Clawson that our stock prospectus would have to carry information relating to our being charged with a federal crime. It was a not very veiled threat that turning over the Papers in our possession would go a long way toward avoiding criminal prosecution. Kleindienst has no memory of sending such a message.

The second, similar message came through Gene Patterson, who had been called by Joe Alsop. I'm not sure why Joe didn't tell me directly, but I think he genuinely believed that I was being misled by a bunch of wild men and was doing me a favor. Joe told Gene that he had spent some time with a high Justice Department official—Mr. X. He wanted to convey to the *Post* Mr. X's feelings, and those of the government. He talked about how grim the situation was, and said that the government was definitely considering proceeding criminally against *The New York Times*, the *Post*, and other papers. He concluded, referring to Nixon and many of those in his administration, "They hate the *Post* like poison. Knowing Nixon, I think he wants to tear out the guts of *The Times*, and yours too. . . . I think there's an even chance he'll proceed."*

On Saturday morning, July 3, Ben and I met in my office with Edward Bennett Williams—not because he was a lawyer but because we both trusted him—to discuss how, if at all, we should respond to what we had heard. We decided to respond indirectly through Bill Rogers, emphasizing to him that we didn't have in our possession the volumes that we understood contained the information Kleindienst was most concerned about. We also told him that, when we published anything from any of the rest of the documents, we would not publish information based on intercepted communications, signal intelligence, and cryptography in general, adhering to this policy as we had in the past. In the end, no further overt action was taken, but we lived under the threat of repercussions and began to feel the pressure increase as the months wore on.

IN RETROSPECT, it's hard to understand why Nixon and his people were so upset by the publication of these Papers, which were essentially a

---

* Recently Henry Kissinger told me he felt that Nixon had always hated the *Post*. Henry said of Nixon, "He was convinced that the *Post* had it in for him. At what point he got that idea, I don't know, but when I met him, he already had that idea. He wanted a confrontation with the press. He really hated the press. As soon as there was an unfavorable article about him, he'd send notes around . . . prohibiting you from talking to the *Post* or to this or that reporter. Nobody ever fully honored it, because you couldn't do your business if you did, but he was antagonistic to the press. It was a big mistake."

history of decisions made before they were in power. Nothing in them was a reflection on Nixon. I believe the administration's reaction was an example of its extreme paranoia about national security and secrecy in general. Certainly, their paranoia was evident early on. Griswold acknowledged as much in an op-ed article for the *Post*, titled "Secrets Not Worth Keeping," that appeared in February of 1989, at the time of Iran-Contra, saying that there was a "massive overclassification" by the government, and "that the principal concern of the classifiers is not with national security, but rather with governmental embarrassment of one sort or another. . . . [T]here is very rarely any real risk to current national security from the publication of facts relating to transactions in the past, even the fairly recent past. This is the lesson of the Pentagon Papers experience." In fact, only a tiny portion of the contents of the Papers was really secret material, and Daniel Ellsberg, the original provider of the Papers, had withheld those portions from the beginning.

At the end of 1971, I discussed the issues surrounding publication of the Pentagon Papers in a speech I gave at Denison University. I still maintain what I said then, which was essentially that we believed from the start that the material in the Pentagon Papers was just the kind of information the public needed in order to form its opinions and make its choices more wisely. In short, we believed the Papers were so useful to a greater understanding of the way in which America became involved in the Vietnam War that we regarded their publication not as a breach of the national security, as the administration claimed, but, rather, as a contribution to the national interest—indeed, as the obligation of a responsible newspaper.

As I concluded in that speech twenty-five years ago, and as I strongly still believe:

> The sobering reality is that the process laid bare in the Pentagon Papers is precisely the process by which most of the business of government is carried forward. We may wholeheartedly embrace the pledge of "No More Vietnams," but until we open up the system and expose its workings to the light of public scrutiny, that pledge will remain in the realm of empty rhetoric.

NEEDLESS TO SAY, the minor irritations experienced between the *Post* and the Nixon administration prior to this, which had slowly ratcheted up the tension in the overall atmosphere, had now turned major. The Pentagon Papers case took the continual, day-to-day sparring between government and the press onto a new level. Rulers and reporters may be natural antagonists, as I said at the time, but the Nixon administration now entered the ring with a particularly deliberate gusto. By sending the Justice

Department into court instead of merely using the vice-president as a mouthpiece, they had changed the character of the fight.

We all began to worry more and more about freedom of the press and about the Nixon administration's imperious attitude that the authority to determine what the American people should know rests exclusively with the government. We also felt, as Ben later said, that if the press was the target "the victim is the public."

The Pentagon Papers may or may not have been the compelling case we all thought it was, but it set in motion certain trends. Although the case came and went, unbelievably, in only two and a half weeks, its ripple effect was great. And publishing the Papers went a long way toward advancing the interests of the *Post*. As Ben later said, "That was a key moment in the life of this paper. It was just sort of the graduation of the *Post* into the highest ranks. One of our unspoken goals was to get the world to refer to the *Post* and *New York Times* in the same breath, which they previously hadn't done. After the Pentagon Papers, they did."

From my point of view, the *Post* and I had been hurled onto the national scene almost unwittingly. For the first time in my professional life, we became major players. Eyes were on us; what we did mattered to the press and to the country. To some degree, I gained a measure of self-assurance. This was my first serious visibility on the national scene. I was very publicly exposed, written about, photographed, and interviewed, which both seared me and to some extent fed my ego. The pressure, the intensity, and the rapidly unfolding developments were another extraordinary learning experience for me.

The whole affair also bound many of us at the *Post* even more closely together, especially Ben, Howard Simons, Phil Geyelin, Meg Greenfield, and me. The editors had been wonderful. From the late 1960s, these people had worked so well together, having a great deal of fun at the same time. There was trust and affection among them, as well as between them and me. Our group was one of the great strengths that kept me going and lightened my life.

I gained even more confidence in Ben. He and I had already created a true understanding between us, as well as a respect and admiration for each other, but until the Pentagon Papers we had never been tested publicly in any way. Ben later said that not publishing the Papers could have been a real disaster for the *Post*, with many people quitting the paper. He reflected that he himself probably wouldn't have quit, "but I would have been beaten and the goals, the aspirations that we were just beginning to see would have been lost."

What Ben and I told each other at the time says a lot about the point to which our relationship had evolved and how much we depended on and appreciated each other. Ben had started a tradition of writing me a letter at Christmastime in lieu of flowers. I always responded in kind, but I wrote him now in the middle of the year, on the very day the Supreme Court announced its decision:

> We always write each other love letters at Christmas—but the paper over the last 2+ weeks is better than Christmas and it's earlier too. There never was such a show—it was incredible. And it was only possible because of that extra 10% of the 110% that you and those under you put into it. . . . It was beautiful and fun too. And it was a trip—a pleasure to do business with you as ever.

Ben wrote me right back:

> Doing business with you is so much more than a pleasure—it's a cause, it's an honor, and such a rewarding challenge.
>
> I'm not sure I could handle another one of these tomorrow, but it is so great to know that this whole newspaper will handle the next one with courage and commitment and style.

Indeed, publishing the Pentagon Papers made future decisions easier, even possible. Most of all it prepared us—and I suspect, unfortunately, Nixon as well—for Watergate.

— *Chapter Twenty-three* —

O N SATURDAY MORNING, June 17, 1972, Howard Simons called to say, "You won't believe what happened last night." He was right. I barely believed him, and listened with equal amounts of amusement and interest as he told me of a car that crashed into a house where two people had been making love on a sofa and went right out the other side. To top that, he related the fantastic story that five men wearing surgical gloves had been caught breaking into the headquarters of the Democratic National Committee.

President Nixon was in Key Biscayne, Florida, at the time. His press secretary, Ron Ziegler, dismissed the incident as "a third-rate burglary attempt," adding, "Certain elements may try to stretch this beyond what it is." None of us, of course, had any idea how far the story would stretch; the beginning—once the laughter died down—all seemed so farcical.

It was Joe Califano, who was then not only our lawyer but also a lawyer for the Democratic National Committee, who had called Howard in the first place. Howard swung into action. Once he'd spoken to me—and tried to reach Ben, who was at his cabin in West Virginia, with a phone that didn't work—he phoned Harry Rosenfeld, then the metropolitan editor, who in turn called Barry Sussman, the one of his three deputies who focused on the District of Columbia.

Al Lewis, the *Post*'s police reporter since 1935, who knew everyone in the whole department, was dispatched to begin to cover the story. As usual, he headed first to the police station to get the names of those arrested—all fictitious, as it turned out. There he serendipitously bumped into the acting chief of police, Charlie Wright, with whom he was very friendly. The two of them went off together to the Watergate, where Al just walked right in with Wright. What he saw was a hive of activity, with people from the mobile crime lab trying to get fingerprints off the front door and others removing tiles from the ceiling to look for wiretaps. Lewis took off his jacket and stayed all day.

The story of the break-in appeared on the front page of Sunday's paper, "5 Held in Plot to Bug Democrats' Office Here," with Lewis's byline. Contributing to the story were several staff writers, including Bob Woodward and Carl Bernstein, who also did a separate report with background information on the suspects, four of whom, Carl discovered, were from Miami, where they had been involved in anti-Castro activities. Phil Geyelin's editorial appearing the next day in the *Post* was titled "Mission Incredible," and began with a quote from the CBS television show "Mission Impossible": "As always, should you or any of your force be caught or killed, the Secretary will disavow any knowledge of your actions. . . ."

What we were seeing, of course, was the legendary tip of the iceberg. And we might never have known the size of the iceberg had it not been for the extraordinary investigative and reporting efforts of Woodward and Bernstein, famous names now but then two young men who had never worked together, one of whom (Woodward) had not even been long at the paper. In some ways it was a natural pairing, since their qualities and skills complemented each other. Both are bright, but Woodward was conscientious, hardworking, and driven, and Bernstein messy and undisciplined. He was, however, the better writer, more imaginative and creative. In other ways the relationship was oil and water, but the end product came out right, despite—or perhaps because of—the strange mix.

Barry Sussman, with only a few details about the botched burglary, knew that he wanted Bob Woodward on the story. Woodward had come to us fresh from the navy. Having been accepted by Harvard Law School, he had chosen instead to pursue journalism as a career. He so much wanted to work for the *Post* that Harry Rosenfeld had told his deputy, Andy Barnes, to put Woodward on for two weeks—without pay—and to look at his copy every night to see what he could do. Not one of the seventeen stories Bob wrote during those two weeks was printed, and at the end of the trial period, Barnes confidently declared that Woodward was a bright and good guy but lacked the skills needed for being a newspaperman—in short, was hopeless, and would be too much trouble to train. Harry told Woodward to get some experience and come back in a year. To Woodward, this was a kick in the stomach but also an inspiration, and he didn't interpret Harry's parting words as a total rejection. It may have been wishful thinking on Bob's part, since for him the point was that, "in failing for two weeks at journalism, I knew I loved it."

So Bob went off and got a job on the nearby *Montgomery County Sentinel* in Maryland, where it wasn't long before he began scooping the *Post*'s metro reporters. After some months, he started phoning Harry again; one day he called him at home, interrupting his vacation and finding him on a ladder painting his basement. Having already been interrupted more times than he felt warranted for a man on vacation, Harry was in a foul temper and complained to his wife, Anne, about this young upstart calling him up all the time and pestering him. Anne quietly asked, "Isn't that what you always say is the kind of person you want, Harry?" She was, of course, exactly right, and Harry finally decided to hire Woodward, who started at the *Post* right after Labor Day in September 1971, the day, as Bob later told me, "unbeknownst to all of us, that Howard Hunt and Gordon Liddy got on the airplane to go to Los Angeles to break into Daniel Ellsberg's psychiatrist's house."

From the beginning, Bob distinguished himself, and there was no question in the editors' minds whom they were going to send to court to cover the break-in. Carl Bernstein, on the other hand, had been at the *Post* since the fall of 1966 but had *not* distinguished himself. He was a good writer, but his poor work-habits were well known throughout the city room even then, as was his famous roving eye. In fact, one thing that stood in the way of Carl's being put on the story was that Ben Bradlee was about to fire him. Carl was notorious for an irresponsible expense account and numerous other delinquencies—including having rented a car and abandoned it in a parking lot, presenting the company with an enormous bill. But Carl, looking over Bob's shoulder while he reworked Al Lewis's notes, immediately got hooked on this strange story and was off and running. It was Harry who saved him when both Ben and Howard wanted to fire him, saying that he was pursuing the Watergate story with verve, working hard, and contributing a great deal. And it was Carl who made the first connection of the crisp new $100 bills in the pockets of the burglars to money raised for the Nixon campaign.

Woodward and Bernstein clearly were the key reporters on the story—so much so that we began to refer to them collectively as Woodstein—but the cast of characters at the *Post* who contributed to the story from its inception was considerable. As executive editor, Ben was the classic leader at whose desk the buck of responsibility stopped. He set the ground rules—pushing, pushing, pushing, not so subtly asking everyone to take one more step, relentlessly pursuing the story in the face of persistent accusations against us and a concerted campaign of intimidation.

Howard Simons, with his semi-independent pocket of authority on the paper, helped move the story along enormously, particularly with his attitude, as Woodward later described it, of "inquisitiveness and 'Let's find out what's going on.' " Harry Rosenfeld said of Howard, "When the kids were running one way or the other, he would—if it was called for—stand up and screw the tide." It was Howard who carried the story in its early days.

Harry himself was an old-style, tough, picturesque editor, and another real hero of Watergate for us. From the outset, he thought of the story as a very big local one, seeing it as something on which the *Post*'s local staff could distinguish itself. He controlled the story before it regularly made page one of the paper, keeping it going on the front page of the metro section.

Barry Sussman eventually was released from his duties as District of Columbia editor to devote full time to directing the day-to-day Watergate coverage. He was just the person for the job. As described by Woodward and Bernstein in *All the President's Men*, "Sussman had the ability to seize facts and lock them in his memory, where they remained poised for instant recall. More than any other editor at the Post, . . . Sussman became a walking compendium of Watergate knowledge, a reference source to be summoned when even the library failed. . . . Watergate was a puzzle and he was a collector of the pieces."

On the editorial side, Phil Geyelin and Meg Greenfield were invaluable. Through their editorials, along with those by Roger Wilkins, they plugged away at the import of what was unfolding on our news pages. The *Post*'s editorials consistently argued the seriousness of the known facts in the first several months, well before the White House had even acknowledged special concern, and at a time when the whole matter was thought to be dead. These editorials played a great part in keeping the issues before the public and had a demonstrable impact on the way people came to think about Watergate.

An even more immediate impact was achieved by Herblock. From the cartoon that appeared a few days after the "third-rate burglary"—depicting a guard throwing one of the burglars out of the Democratic National Headquarters with Richard Nixon, Richard Kleindienst, and John Mitchell looking on, over the caption "Who Would Think of Doing Such a Thing?"—to his justly famous one of Nixon trying to hang on to the ends of two reels of tape on which the words "I am . . . a crook" appear, with a clipped piece of tape with the word "not" on it in his mouth, Herblock kept up his relentless assault. He was well ahead of me and of the news side of the paper. Six days after the burglary, I was in the newsroom when he shared with me a cartoon he'd drawn showing two men investigating footsteps representing the bugging case and the Nixon fund scandals—footsteps that led right to the front door of the White House. The caption read: "Strange—They All Seem to Have Some Connection with This Place." I laughed and said, "You're not going to print that, are you?" It appeared the next day, June 23, 1972. All this was taking place just as the political campaign of 1972 was getting into full swing: George McGovern was nominated by the Democratic Party as its candidate just two weeks after the burglary at the Democratic headquarters.

From the start, Woodward and Bernstein followed the trail of the Watergate burglars with alacrity and skill, and a lot of elbow grease. From the time Bob went to court and heard James McCord say "CIA," he was hooked on the story. When Carl came up with Howard Hunt's address book, and the two found in it the name "Colson" and the phrase "W. House," they, like Herblock, decided there was a connection to the White House. When it was discovered that numerous calls had been made from the phone of Bernard Barker, one of the burglars, to an office shared by Gordon Liddy and another lawyer at the Committee to Re-elect the President, whose acronym, CRP, quickly turned into the unfortunate CREEP, Woodward and Bernstein were off and running.

On August 1, over a month after the break-in, the first big story appeared under the joint byline of Bernstein and Woodward, reporting on the connection of the burglars to CRP. Three weeks later, on August 22, President Nixon was renominated with great fanfare at the Republican National Convention in Miami. The next week, apparently trying to declare the Watergate affair finished, Nixon announced that John Dean, counsel to the president, had thoroughly investigated the break-in and said, "I can state categorically that his investigation indicates that no one in the White House staff, no one in this administration, presently employed, was involved in this very bizarre incident. What really hurts is if you try to cover it up." Again, we learned only later, from John Dean's testimony, that he had never heard of "his" investigation until the president made that statement. Strange, indeed.

On September 15, a federal grand jury indicted the original five burglars as well as two former White House aides, E. Howard Hunt and G. Gordon Liddy. It was on that same day—but this came to light only two years later—that Nixon spoke to two of his aides, the White House chief of staff, Bob Haldeman, and John Dean, making threats of economic retaliation against the *Post*: "[I]t's going to have its problems.... The main thing is the Post is going to have damnable, damnable problems out of this one. They have a television station ... and they're going to have to get it renewed.... And it's going to be God damn active here.... [T]he game has to be played awfully rough." Of our lawyer, Nixon said, "I wouldn't want to be in Edward Bennett Williams's position after this election. We are going to fix the son of a bitch, believe me. We are going to. We've got to, because he is a bad man."

Two weeks later, a seminal Bernstein and Woodward article appeared on page one of the *Post*. They had dug up information that there was a secret fund in the safe of Maurice Stans—former secretary of commerce, but finance chairman for CRP at the time—which was controlled by five people, one of whom was John Mitchell, and which was to be used to gather intelligence on the Democrats. Thus the story reached a new level, involving Mitchell himself, not only in his new role in the campaign, but when he was still attorney general, since Woodward and Bernstein had unearthed Mitchell-authorized expenditures from the fund from the previous year.

CRP denied the story artfully—and graphically. In an effort to check it out, Bernstein, having been told by a press aide at CRP that there was "absolutely no truth to the charges," called Mitchell directly, reaching him at a hotel in New York, where Mitchell answered the phone himself. When Carl told him about the story, Mitchell exploded with exclamations of "JEEEEEEESUS," so violent that Carl felt it was "some sort of primal scream" and thought Mitchell might die on the telephone. After he'd read him the first two paragraphs, Mitchell interrupted, still screaming, "All that crap, you're putting it in the paper? It's all been denied. Katie Graham's gonna get her tit caught in a big fat wringer if that's published. Good Christ! That's the most sickening thing I ever heard."

Bernstein was stunned and called Ben at home to read him Mitchell's quotes and discuss adding them to the already prepared article. Ben told Carl to use it all except the specific reference to my "tit." The quote was changed to read that I was "gonna get caught in a big fat wringer." Ben decided he didn't have to forewarn me. (Later he told me, "That was too good to check with you, Katharine." I would have agreed with Ben's decision.) As it was, I was shocked to read what I did in the paper, but even more so to hear what Mitchell had actually said, so personal and offensive were the threat and the message. I ran into Carl by accident the next day and asked him if he had any other messages for me.

It was quite a temper tantrum on Mitchell's part—and especially strange of him to call me Katie, which no one has ever called me. Bob later observed that the interesting thing for him was that Mitchell's remark was an example of the misperception on the part of the Nixon people that I was calling all the shots and that I was the one who was printing everything on Watergate. In any case, the remark lived on in the annals of Watergate and was one of the principal public links of me with the affair. Later, though before Watergate had ended, I received a wonderful present from a California dentist who, using the kind of gold normally used to fill teeth, had crafted a little wringer complete with a tiny handle and gears that turned just like a regular old washing-machine wringer. And some time after that, Art Buchwald presented me with a tiny gold breast, which he had had made to go with the wringer. I occasionally wore the two of them together on a chain around my neck, and stopped only when a reporter threatened to tell Maxine Cheshire.

IN OCTOBER, the tempo of the whole story picked up, and the *Post* printed two articles that together brought the administration's wrath down on us. The first, which appeared October 10, described the original break-in as part of a massive, nationwide campaign of political spying and sabotage conducted in behalf of the president's re-election efforts and directed by White House and re-election-committee officials. This idea was dismissed by the main spokesman for the CRP as "not only fiction but a collection of absurdities."

Nixon's press secretary, Ron Ziegler, began his morning briefing at the White House charging that "stories are being run that are based on hearsay, innuendo, guilt by association. . . . [I]t goes without saying that this Administration does not condone sabotage or espionage or surveillance of individuals." That same afternoon, Clark MacGregor, who had taken over from John Mitchell as Nixon's campaign chairman, held a press conference in which he took no questions but read a prepared statement. He said that the *Post*'s

> . . . credibility has today sunk lower than that of George Mc-Govern.
>
> Using innuendo, third-person hearsay, unsubstantiated charges, anonymous sources and huge scare headlines, the *Post* has maliciously sought to give the appearance of a direct connection between the White House and the Watergate—a charge which the *Post* knows and half a dozen investigations have found to be false.
>
> The hallmark of the *Post*'s campaign is hypocrisy—and its celebrated "double standard" is today visible for all to see.

This and Ziegler's turned out to be only two of the salvos in a broadside against us.

Naturally, I intensely disliked these attacks and, in fact, found them hard to understand. I kept remembering the moment in *War and Peace*, as I visualized it, when a soldier being pursued by an enemy with a bayonet thinks, "Can this man really want to kill me, me whom my mother loved so much?"

Senator Bob Dole got in on the attack, saying that he considered what he'd read about Watergate to be "a barrage of unfounded and unsubstantiated allegations by George McGovern and his partner-in-mud-slinging, *The Washington Post*." To ice the cake, Dole added: "Given the present straits in which the McGovern campaign finds itself, Mr. McGovern appears to have turned over the franchise for his media attack campaign to the editors of *The Washington Post*, who have shown themselves every bit as sure-footed along the low road of this campaign as their candidate."

Ben, cool as usual, and convinced of the orchestration of the assault on the paper, quickly responded to reporters who called by putting out his own statement:

> Time will judge between Clark MacGregor's press release and the *Washington Post*'s reporting of the various activities of CRP. For now it is enough to say that not a single fact contained in the investigative reporting by this newspaper about these activities has been successfully challenged. MacGregor and other high administration officials have called these stories "a collection of absurdities" and the *Post* "malicious," but the facts are on the record, unchallenged by contrary evidence.

Dole attacked again on October 24, in a speech in Baltimore that contained—as counted by Woodward and Bernstein—fifty-seven references to the *Post*, among them:

> The greatest political scandal of this campaign is the brazen manner in which, without benefit of clergy, *The Washington Post* has set up housekeeping with the McGovern campaign. . . .
>
> The *Post*'s reputation for objectivity and credibility have sunk so low they have almost disappeared from the Big Board altogether.
>
> There is a cultural and social affinity between the McGovernites and the *Post* executives and editors. They belong to the same elite; they can be found living cheek-by-jowl in the same exclusive chic neighborhoods, and hob-nobbing at the same Georgetown parties.

It didn't help that the next day the *Post*'s second seminal article appeared, reporting, based on Woodward's meeting with his main source, that the fifth person who was authorized to approve payments from the secret dirty-tricks cash fund was none other than H. R. Haldeman, the president's chief of staff. When Dwight Chapin, the president's appointments secretary, had been linked by the reporters to the secret fund, they had had to find ways to explain to the American people who Chapin was, and that he saw the president every day; it had been difficult to make the connection between this fund and those in power in the White House. But this second story—with its two-column, large-type headline, "Testimony Ties Top Nixon Aide to Secret Fund"—was altogether different. This was Haldeman, the most powerful man in Washington after the president, the president's alter-ego and right-hand man. This article would move the Watergate story line right through the front door of the White House.

The story noted that Haldeman's participation was known to federal investigators and known from accounts of sworn testimony before the federal grand jury. In this story, with all its high visibility, the reporters unfortunately made one of their only errors throughout the long months of reporting. The substance of the story was true; the error was not of fact but of assumption. Woodward and Bernstein had assumed that Hugh Sloan, former CRP treasurer and former Haldeman aide, had told the grand jury about the secret fund. He had, in fact, told Woodward and Bernstein about it, and the only reason he hadn't told the grand jury was that he hadn't been asked. Sloan, through his attorney, denied the *Post*'s story the next morning, setting off repercussions everywhere, including more denunciations of the paper by Ron Ziegler at the White House, who unequivocally denied the story, accused the *Post* of being politically motivated, and attacked Ben Bradlee for being anti-Nixon.

Some of the strongest reverberations were felt at the *Post*. Harry Rosenfeld, who had worked on this particular story up until deadline, believed that the tie to Haldeman meant that Nixon was really at the bottom of it all. As Harry said, "If Haldeman is doing it, Nixon is doing it. There is no line between Haldeman and Nixon." Harry was apoplectic at the idea that the reporters had gotten the story wrong. He and Howard Simons were discussing corrections and desperately looking for Woodward and Bernstein, who were nowhere to be found. (Ironically, those two turned out to be meeting with a publisher to discuss the book they intended to write about Watergate.) When they were finally located, the reporters, with Rosenfeld, who refused to retract the story until he knew more, went down to the courthouse. The next day we did retract the part of the story that said Sloan had told the grand jury of Haldeman's connection to the fund, but the substance of the story remained.

I WAS FEELING beleaguered. The constant attacks on us by CRP and people throughout the administration were effective and taking their toll. During these months, the pressures on the *Post* to cease and desist were intense and uncomfortable, to say the least. But, unbelievable as the revelations were, the strong evidence of their accuracy is part of what kept us going.

Many of my friends were puzzled about our reporting. Joe Alsop was pressing me all the time. And I had a distressing chance meeting with Henry Kissinger just before the election, at a big reception of some kind. "What's the matter? Don't you think we're going to be re-elected?" Henry asked me, seeming quite upset. I assured him that I could read the overwhelming polls as well as anybody and hadn't the slightest doubt that Nixon would be re-elected. Henry later told me that, although he was never part of any actual discussions that related to threats, he knew Nixon wanted to get even with a lot of people after the election. Maybe this had been his way of warning me. In any case, the implications in Henry's exclamation added to my tension.

Readers, too, were writing me, accusing the *Post* of ulterior motives, bad journalism, lack of patriotism, and all kinds of breaches of faith in our effort to get the news to the people. It was a particularly lonely moment for us at the paper. Other organizations were beginning to report the story, but we were so far ahead that they couldn't catch up; Woodward and Bernstein had most of the sources to themselves. The wire service and AP sent out our stories, but most papers didn't even run them, or buried them somewhere toward the back pages. Howard used to get on the phone to his editor friends around the country to tell them they were missing a big story. Because an exclusive story usually remained so for only about twenty-four hours before everyone jumped on it, I sometimes privately thought: If this is such a hell of a story, then where is everybody else?

Bearing the full brunt of presidential wrath is always disturbing. Sometimes I wondered if we could survive four more years of this kind of strain, of the pressures of living with an administration so completely at odds with us and determined to harm us. As I later wrote to Isaiah Berlin, "The idea of living with that gang in the White House whacking at you for four more years was depressing beyond words." I couldn't help speculating about what condition we'd all be in—including the paper—at the end of it. The best we could do while under such siege, I felt, was to keep investigating, to look everywhere for hard evidence, to get the details right, and to report accurately what we found.

Just as the stresses of loneliness were at their most extreme, immediately before the election, we got a break. CBS, in the persons of Walter Cronkite and Gordon Manning, then a producer and an ex–*Newsweek* editor, decided to run two long pieces on Watergate on the evening news. Basically, the story had not appeared on television. To begin with, it wasn't easy for television to report Watergate in sound bites—there were few if any picture opportunities, and it was an extremely complicated, hard-to-follow story, full of names of people unknown to the public. There were many different threads to the story, and it was difficult to see how it all came together. And then, as I was soon to learn firsthand, television and radio were vulnerable, relying as they do on a government agency for their licenses to operate. The three television networks all owned local radio or television stations from which a large part of their profitability derived, so it took even more than normal courage for them to take on the government. But Cronkite, who was the supreme authority on his show, decided to go ahead. Manning, who knew Ben from *Newsweek*, tried to get his help for CBS's program, and was startled and dubious when Ben told him we had no documents, no paper trail of evidence, and couldn't help.

The first piece aired on the evening of Friday, October 27, and took fourteen of the twenty-two minutes of that night's network news—more time than had ever been given to any single story—filled largely by quoting the *Post* and the government's various replies to the paper's charges. I will never forget my joy and relief to have CBS News behind us, piecing the story together and carefully explaining to a national audience what had happened, what had been proved, and what had not. Cronkite gave us great credit, and the still photos of the *Post* and its headlines in the background helped enormously. The show ran eleven days before the election.

Also watching the CBS Evening News was the White House tough guy, Chuck Colson, who was assigned to oversee the networks. Colson became known for saying that he would walk over his grandmother if it was necessary to do a job. He had gotten wind of the show, called Frank Stanton, and then gone straight to Bill Paley. Stanton had worked hard at CBS to protect press freedoms and the news division, but Paley had not experienced calls from angry presidents or their flunkies, so he flinched at Colson's call and in turn summoned the head of news, Richard Salant, and leaned on him very hard about the evils of the piece that had already been aired and the necessity of killing the proposed second part, to be run the next night. After a fight within CBS News, Salant compromised, and on the grounds of repetition of what had already appeared on the network, the second piece was cut from fourteen minutes to eight.

In the end, the length of the report didn't really matter: CBS had taken the *Post* national—even against Bill Paley's frightened will.

I spent the day after the first CBS story aired at Glen Welby with a large group of guests, including my friend Pam Berry (by then Lady Hartwell), Clay Felker, Dick Holbrooke, and, most interestingly, Peter Peterson, Nixon's secretary of commerce at the time, and his then wife, Sally, a liberal Democrat. Sally was quite vocal in her views, and there were several awkward moments during the weekend, particularly when she announced emphatically that she would be voting for McGovern—which actually was known to the White House—and made remarks openly critical of the administration, at one point saying, "Nixon has no balls." We all squirmed, but it was also noticeable that Pete didn't come to his boss's defense.

In the middle of a tennis game, Pete was called to the phone by a White House operator, who had placed the call for Haldeman. Having to locate Pete at my house undoubtedly was a factor in the administration's later getting rid of him. It was not a winning card to be weekending at Glen Welby, although Henry Kissinger didn't seem to suffer within the administration even though he went on coming to my house—but not to the *Post*—during Watergate.

Pete remained a friend of mine throughout our reporting of Watergate. In fact, he told me that after the *Post*'s late-October stories my name came up in White House staff meetings even more often than before. Having heard plenty of comments that they were going to "get" me, Pete came to my office by himself one day to say, "Kay, I don't know what the truth is, but there is a group of very angry people who feel you are out to get them. I hope you are using rigorous journalistic standards. If you are wrong, it's serious; they will get you." I appreciated the spirit in which Pete courageously came to see me and assured him that I heard what he was saying—and that we were being careful.

Indeed, we were. We always did our best to be careful and responsible, especially when we were carrying the burden of the Watergate reporting. From the outset, the editors had resolved to handle the story with more than the usual scrupulous attention to fairness and detail. They laid down certain rules, which were followed by everyone. First, every bit of information attributed to an unnamed source had to be supported by at least one other, independent source. Particularly at the start of Watergate, we had to rely heavily on confidential sources, but at every step we double-checked every bit of material before printing it; where possible, we had three or even more sources for each story. Second, we ran nothing that was reported by any other newspaper, television, radio station, or other media outlet unless it was independently verified and confirmed by our own reporters. Third, every word of every story was read by at least one of the senior editors before it went into print, with a top editor vetting each story before it ran. As any journalist knows, these are rigorous tests.

Yet, despite the care I knew everyone was taking, I was still worried. No matter how careful we were, there was always the nagging possibility that we were wrong, being set up, being misled. Ben would repeatedly reassure me—possibly to a greater extent than he may have actually felt—by saying that some of our sources were Republicans, Sloan especially, and that having the story almost exclusively gave us the luxury of not having to rush into print, so that we could be obsessive about checking everything. There were many times when we delayed publishing something until the "tests" had been met. There were times when something just didn't seem to hold up and, accordingly, was not published, and there were a number of instances where we withheld something not sufficiently confirmable that turned out later to be true.

At the time, I took comfort in our "two-sources" policy. Ben further assured me that Woodward had a secret source he would go to when he wasn't sure about something—a source that had never misled us. That was the first I heard of Deep Throat, even before he was so named by Howard

Simons, after the pornographic movie that was popular in certain circles at the time. It's why I remain convinced that there was such a person and that he—and it had to be a he—was neither made up nor an amalgam or a composite of a number of people, as has often been hypothesized. The identity of Deep Throat is the only secret I'm aware of that Ben has kept, and, of course, Bob and Carl have, too. I never asked to be let in on the secret, except once, facetiously, and I still don't know who he is.

This attention to detail and playing by our own strict rules allowed us to produce, as Harry Rosenfeld later said, "the longest-running newspaper stories with the least amount of errors that I have ever experienced or will ever experience."

THE IMPACT OF our October stories and the CBS broadcast continued to reverberate—on Nixon and his administration, *and* on us. There was a good deal of evidence that the campaign to undermine public confidence in the *Post* and in any other news medium thought to be hostile to the administration was intensifying. The investigation of such a tangled web of crime, money, and mischief would have been hard enough under the best of circumstances, but it was made harder given the unveiled threats and major and minor harassments by a president and his administration. Chuck Colson was quoted by a *Star* reporter as saying: "As soon as the election is behind us we're going to really shove it to the Post. . . . Start coming around with a breadbasket because we're going to fill it up with news. . . . And that's only the beginning. After that, we're really going to get rough. They're going to wish on L Street that they'd never heard of Watergate."

I particularly loathed reports that personalized the whole dispute, implying that some sort of personal vendetta had poisoned the relationship between the *Post* and the administration. I had already begun to hear a chorus of rumors concerning my own feelings about Nixon, a chorus that warmed up with some help from Senator Dole, who made a charge, picked up and carried all over the airwaves, saying that I had told a friend that I hated Nixon. Dole made the leap to saying that that was the reason the *Post* was writing all the negative Watergate stories.

I detested the assumption and impression that we were out to get Nixon, that we somehow had it in for him and for the Republicans. Many people misunderstood the role of the *Post*, believing that we got some sort of enjoyment "out of kicking the president and the Republicans," or "extracting every last drop of blood," as I heard more than once. Far from its being our aim or purpose, we got no pleasure from it. As I wrote someone, "It's the only government we have and it would be a lot bigger pleasure not to have to report the kind of things we do."

Incredibly, I was still in touch with John Ehrlichman from time to time, so I wrote him on the day before the election:

A short while back you threw me a message over the fence, and I genuinely appreciated it. Here is a message I want to send you.

Among the charges that have been flying over the past few weeks, many have disturbed me for the general misunderstanding they suggest of the Post's purposes in printing the stories we do. But none has disturbed me more than an allegation Senator Dole made. . . . It was that the Post's point of view on certain substantive issues was explained by me as proceeding from the simple fact that I "hate" the President.

There are so many things wrong with this "anecdote," that one hardly knows where to begin in correcting them. But I would begin with the fact that I cannot imagine that the episode ever took place at all or that I ever expressed such a childish and mindless sentiment—since it is one that I do not feel.

I want you to know that. And I also want you to know that the fiction doesn't stop there. For the story suggests, as well, that somehow editorial positions on public issues are taken and decisions on news made on the basis of the publisher's personal feelings and tastes. This is not true, even when the sentiments attributed to me—unlike this alleged and unworthy "hate" for the President—may be real.

What appears in the Post is not a reflection of my personal feelings. And by the same token, I would add that my continuing and genuine pride in the paper's performance over the past few months—the period that seems to be at issue—does not proceed from some sense that it has gratified my personal whim. It proceeds from my belief that the editors and reporters have fulfilled the highest standards of professional duty and responsibility.

On this I know we disagree. I am writing this note because I think we have enough such areas of sharp and honest disagreement between us not to need a harmful and destructive overlay of personal animosity that I, for one, don't feel and don't wish to see perpetuated by misquotation! (My turn, it seems.)

I genuinely meant what I wrote Ehrlichman. I have a faint memory of talking to Stew Alsop once about how, as the months progressed, I was certainly feeling more and more negative about Nixon, but I had no such personal feelings about Nixon as a politician and couldn't imagine that I had said anything like Dole's quote in his speech, much less that my feelings toward the president would inspire the *Post's* editors and reporters.

THOUGH THE editorial-page editor and his deputy and writers were certainly not in agreement with George McGovern's views and policies, the *Post's* editorial page, which didn't endorse, had vaguely seemed to favor McGovern—partly because it was so unsympathetic to Nixon. Candidate McGovern had used the Watergate story only somewhat tentatively. Ironically, he, too, felt that the coverage he received in the *Post* had not been ample enough or accurate or fair—a feeling shared by almost every candidate about almost every paper anywhere and at any time.

To no one's surprise, President Nixon was re-elected by a landslide, with 61 percent of the vote and forty-nine out of fifty states—evidence of how little impact Watergate had had and how very powerful were these angry and vindictive men in the White House and connected with the president elsewhere. However, instead of becoming more secure with his victory in hand and working to unite the country, Nixon immediately turned to vengeance and to strengthening his hold on power. In a speech at his victory dinner with members of the administration, he mentioned *The Washington Post* several times. He asked everyone in the upper echelons of his administration to resign and set out to replace anyone—even "good Republicans"—who might not agree with him implicitly. One of the first victims was Pete Peterson, who was politely fired soon after the election. *The Wall Street Journal* ran an article at the time speculating openly on what had been on all our minds, that Peterson might have been knifed by the White House inner circle. The article quoted someone from the White House as saying, "How can you trust a guy who has dinner with Kay Graham?" Tom and Joan Braden had a goodbye party for Pete, which was reported in the *Post* by Sally Quinn. At the party, Pete, by this time fed up with the treatment he'd received from the administration, gave a highly irreverent response to the toasts. He described being sent for to go to "Mount David" and being quizzed about his dubious friends in a loyalty test. "Finally, Peterson told the guests," according to Quinn, "he failed the physical test. His calves were too fat and he could not click his heels."

Right after the election, with the atmosphere between the *Post* and the president at its most poisonous, the Watergate story dried up. Our having nothing new to report fed the idea that the whole story had been political to begin with—a baseless, biased attack on the president by the *Post* for the sake of influencing the election.

According to Phil Geyelin, that was the only time that Ben actually asked him to think about writing editorials on the subject: "He told me, 'It wouldn't hurt if you just wrote an occasional editorial saying what the hell's happened to this investigation and why isn't it going forward.' "

Editorials did appear. And on the news side, Harry Rosenfeld was nagging Woodward and Bernstein, hounding them to dig even deeper, to keep at the story, which, of course, they did. Later on, I added a note to the file about something Ben said that applied to this period when the story seemed to be going nowhere. His comment reflected his attitude then and always: "Low profiles are a lot of shit."

That fall, after the election, partly in response to the escalating campaign we felt was being waged against the reputation of the *Post*, I began to make more speeches defending the press in general and the *Post* in particular. One of the first big ones was to the San Francisco Commonwealth Club, quite a conservative group. Meg led the team that worked on the speech, which was a strong defense of freedom of the press. I was in something of a panic about the question period to follow the speech, worrying that I would be quizzed on the minutiae of the Watergate story and not know all the players or the various events relating to it. Meg gave me a chronology of the complicated events that had been put together by the Democratic National Committee, and I took it with me to study on the plane on the way out. I settled into my seat for the cross-country flight and began to look over this document, but promptly fell asleep. I woke up as we landed, at which time the man across the aisle from me leaned over to say, "Hello, Mrs. Graham, can I help you with your bag?" I looked up into the eyes of Senator Dole and was immediately frozen with fear that he had seen me studying the Democratic Party–prepared document, since this was not long after his accusations that we were reporting Watergate because I hated Nixon. However, either he hadn't observed it or else he was being polite, but he was very friendly, helped me off the plane, and did indeed carry the bag for me. We talked pleasantly, and I finally worked up my nerve to say, "By the way, Senator, I didn't say I hated Nixon." "Oh, you know," he casually replied, "during a campaign they put these things in your hands, and you just read them." His reaction amazed me, dismissing so lightly something that had had such a powerful effect on all of us at the *Post*, especially me.

At the same time that the administration granted an exclusive interview to the *Washington Star*, it started a boycott of sorts on us—specifically, as an anonymous White House aide told *Time* magazine, "to screw the Washington Post." The thinking was, *Time* reported, "How can we hurt the Post the most?" We were not to have our calls answered, not to be dealt with professionally in any way; administration people were not to come to editorial lunches, and certainly not to my house for dinner. A uniquely ludicrous, petty, and rather weird form of vengeance took place when the administration excluded our charming, much-respected, and even loved senior society reporter, Dorothy McCardle, then sixty-eight years old, from covering parties and made her sit alone cooling her heels in the pressroom, barring her from one social event after another. The strategy backfired, for Dorothy soon became something of a heroine to her colleagues in the Washington press corps. In fact, the *Star* gallantly ran an editorial supporting us and opposing the ban, stating that, if the *Post* couldn't cover the parties, the *Star* didn't want any favors: their social reporter, Isabelle Shelton, would join Dorothy in the pressroom, declining to attend the events as long as Dorothy couldn't. I wrote Newbold Noyes, thanking him "for the nicest, most generous minded statement I can imagine in behalf of the competition. . . ." Moreover, I wrote that I considered it "vitally important . . . in the light of all that's going on, for the powers that be to know that we care about the ethics of our profession, and will stick together. Their divide and conquer attitude . . . seems very determined."

A few weeks later, David Broder reported in a piece in the *Post* that Richard Kleindienst, by now the attorney general, said that "he thought *The Washington Post* had exaggerated or distorted on occasions in its coverage of the case." Kleindienst also said that he had told me that "the administration is being no more unfair to the *Post*"—in barring its reporters from some White House social events—"than the *Post* was to the administration" in some of its reporting on Watergate. Broder's piece quoted Kleindienst as saying: " 'I told her, "Don't get so upset. You've got a great paper. Go ahead and run the . . . thing the way you want. But don't be surprised if the President gets a little upset and does something a little s——y to you in return." ' . . ."

Indeed, the administration was doing something a little shitty in return. It was embarked on a deliberate policy to undermine the credibility of the press, with—as it turned out—very good reasons for needing to do so. And although there was not a lot of concrete evidence, we at the *Post* were well aware of being the target of Nixon and the administration's vengeance.

On November 13, Colson again attacked the *Post*, singling out Ben Bradlee: "The charge of subverting a whole political process, that is a fantasy, a work of fiction rivaling only 'Gone with the Wind' in circulation and 'Portnoy's Complaint' for indecency. . . . Mr. Bradlee now sees himself as the self-appointed leader of . . . the tiny fringe of arrogant elitists who infect the healthy mainstream of American journalism with their own peculiar view of the world." It was just two days after this—we later learned from the Watergate indictments—that Colson had a telephone conversation with Howard Hunt about the need for more payments to the defendants in the trial.

Another thing we found out only later was that at one point Nixon had a plan to get Richard Mellon Scaife—the "right-wing Pittsburgh millionaire," according to reporter Nick Lemann, who discovered the notes Ehrlichman made on a meeting he had with the president—to buy the

Post. The evidence that turned up in the Nixon Archives was Ehrlichman's notes on a December 1, 1972, meeting he had with Nixon: "Post. Scaife will offer to buy it. (Assets.) Suit by public SH [shareholders] if she (60%) [who controls this much of the A shares] refuses. President can't talk to him."

On December 4, Kenneth Khachigian, an aide to Pat Buchanan, then a White House speechwriter, sent Buchanan a memo that was highly specific about what was to be done with the *Post* as a target: "Colson called this morning with a project that the President wants done." The memo went on:

> They want an article, magazine length, on the worst things the Washington Post has said about RN. The ad hominem stuff.
>
> It should go back as far as the fifties to point out their vicious opposition to RN. The story line would be that the Post's 1972 vendetta was the ultimate frustration. After years and years of heaping scorn and abuse on RN, the public was overwhelmingly supporting RN—something the Post simply could not stand; thus the increasing stridency from them and the irresponsibility of Watergate.
>
> . . . Colson says it ought to be a "butcher piece"—perhaps for the New York Times magazine."

Obviously, the negative atmosphere between the *Post* and the Nixon White House had predated Watergate. My heated back-and-forth with Vice-President Agnew in 1969 and 1970 was part of the venomous mood. Several memos from 1970 were to come to light specifically detailing the administration's dislike for the *Post* and its desire to hurt us.

For example, after Nixon's State of the Union message that year, and after the administration had reviewed the unfavorable editorial and columnar reaction to it, someone on the White House staff sent John Ehrlichman a memo saying: "[T]he following newspapers and columnists are individuals who are beyond appeal. He [Nixon] notes that we simply shouldn't have our people spend any time with them: The New York Times, The Washington Post, the Courier, the Louisville Courier-Journal, the Nashville Tennessean, Martin Nolan of the Boston Globe, and Richard Dudman of the Post-Dispatch."

The following month, Haldeman drafted a memo for Jeb Magruder, then his aide, saying: "[W]e have got to move now in every effective way we can to get them working to pound the magazines and the networks in counter-action. . . . Concentrate this on the few places that count, which would be NBC, Time, Newsweek, and Life, the New York Times, and the Washington Post. Don't waste your fire on other things."

Someone else, not identified, sent Magruder a talking paper that spelled out some actions to take against the *Post*:

1. Put someone on the Washington Post to needle Kay Graham. Set up calls or letters every day from the viewpoint of I hate Nixon but you're hurting our cause in being so childish, ridiculous and over-board in your constant criticism, and thus destroying your credibility.
2. Lyn Nofziger should work out with someone in the House a round robin letter to the Post that says we live in Washington, D.C., read the D.C. papers, but fortunately we also have the opportunity to read the papers from our home districts and are appalled at the biased coverage the people of Washington receive of the news, compared to that in the rest of the country, etc. . . .

Two months later, in May 1970, Nixon himself got in on the act. He sent a memo to Haldeman:

I would like for you to have a talk with Klein and Ziegler with regard to some very strict instructions on the handling of the New York Times and the Washington Post. I will make these instructions precise and I want them carried out precisely for the next sixty days.

. . . With regard to the Washington Post I reaffirm the directive I gave two weeks ago but which has not been carried out. Ziegler under no circumstances is to see anybody from the Washington Post and no one on the White House staff is to see anybody from the Washington Post or return any calls to them. They are to be handled as part of the general press corps. This includes Kilpatrick, Oberdorfer, and everybody else. I realize the argument that has often been made that Oberdorfer one time out of ten gives us a good story. I [am] now reiterating the policy that I want followed out—just treat the Post absolutely coldly—all of their people are to be treated in this manner. . . . If there is any exception to this directive you are to raise it directly with me and I will determine on a case by case basis, but under no circumstances will any individual on our staff, on his own, move in other directions. At the same time I want a policy in which the Washington Star, the Washington Daily News, the New York Daily News, the Chicago Tribune, and, for the time being, the Los Angeles Times and others who may be competitive with the New York Times and

Washington Post continue to receive special treatment when Ziegler and Klein may determine it is in our interest. They will not agree with this policy but it is one I have decided upon after long consideration and I want it carried out.

All of this was the background against which Watergate unfolded. The pressures on us up to that point, however, were nothing to those that followed. On the very day of CBS's first report, October 27, Colson sent a memo to another White House staffer: "Please check for me when any of The Washington Post television station licenses are up for renewal. I would like to know what the upcoming schedule is." Coincidentally, but luckily for the administration, renewals for stations in Florida were due in early January 1973, and these licenses, as Colson well knew, were a sure way the government could hurt us. Of all the threats to the company during Watergate—the attempts to undermine our credibility, the petty slights, and the favoring of the competition—the most effective were the challenges to the licenses of our two Florida television stations. There were three separate challenges in Jacksonville and one in Miami, all of which—not coincidentally—were filed between December 29, 1972, and January 2, 1973, leading us to the easy conclusion that the four petitions must have been orchestrated. Out of more than thirty stations in the state of Florida up for renewal, our stations were the only ones challenged— some sort of record, particularly for stations whose news and community service ranked among the best in the United States.

By this time we were so embattled at the paper that I, and most of us at the company, viewed the challenges as entirely politically motivated by people sympathetic to Nixon or even associated with CRP. Did the White House actually encourage or even originate these challenges? In light of all the threats and memos that have since surfaced, it's easy to believe that Nixon and his co-conspirators were behind them, but we never found a paper trail leading to a direct connection. Maybe we didn't have to, so closely tied were many of the prominent figures to the White House or the Committee to Re-elect the President.

No doubt there was a mixture of motives among the challengers—the perception of blood in the water, easy pickings, and understandable thinking that the atmosphere was right given the Nixon-dominated FCC. There was also dissatisfaction, if not real dislike, on the part of some of the challengers for our strong, aggressive news organizations, especially in Jacksonville, to which the conservative nucleus that ran the city was unused. We could see why some groups didn't like the performance of the two stations: both had played a not insignificant role in the passage of Florida's corporate income tax and the Florida sunshine law.

No doubt, too, some of those in the challenging groups also misunderstood the complex FCC process and underestimated the legal costs involved. Few of the challengers had any broadcasting experience. Of course, the groups had ensured that there was the required sprinkling of minorities, who would profit mightily from being given a few shares in order to lend diversity. One common element of the challenging groups was that each tried to depict itself as the local, civic-minded small team versus the large, out-of-state corporation, making the challengers appear valid in contrast to the "outsiders," as we were branded in both cities, even though we had operated in Jacksonville for twenty years and my husband's family had long been prominent citizens of Miami. Though there were plenty of declarations of a high-minded desire to bring the stations under local management, it's significant that no challenge was raised against another station, owned by Rustcraft Broadcasting Company in New York.

In Jacksonville, one challenger was the Florida Television Broadcasting Company, whose big players included George Champion, a personal friend of Nixon's who had been the chief Florida fund-raiser for his 1972 re-election campaign. It also included the powerful Ed Ball, a close business associate of the national vice-chair of Democrats for Nixon in 1972 and one of Florida's wealthiest financiers.

Another group challenging the license, the Trans Florida Television Company, included Glenn Sedam, former general counsel of CRP and deputy general counsel of the 1973 Presidential Inauguration Committee.

The third group, St. John's Broadcasting, consisted of businessmen thrown together hastily and knowing nothing about broadcasting.

Nixon's close friend Cromwell Anderson was one of the leaders of a challenging group in Miami. He had participated in an earlier challenge there against WPLG, late in 1969, one that was withdrawn after seven and a half months, when Post-Newsweek Stations agreed to pay the challengers $67,000 in legal fees under an FCC provision then applicable but now no longer in effect—and he led the fight to mount another challenge now. Anderson had been a neighbor of Nixon's, had sold him his Key Biscayne property, and had introduced him to Bebe Rebozo. Another member of the group in Miami was Edward Claughton, whose home Agnew had stayed in during the 1972 Republican Convention. Anderson began to move against our station in Miami in September of 1972. This happened to be the same month when Nixon (as later heard on the tapes) said that the *Post* would have "damnable, damnable problems" about our license renewals, a phrase that was censored when the tapes were first released by the White House. To my sorrow, Phil's old friend George Smathers and George's brother, Frank, aligned themselves with the Miami challengers.

Norm Davis had gone to WPLG to be deputy to General Manager

Jim Lynagh just as the challenge there had gotten into full swing. These two men decided to meet with the challengers to size them up. What they heard was vituperative and bitter diatribe, much of it focused on me, as reflected in someone's calling me the "Dragon Lady." "They didn't even know you," Norm recalled, "not one of them had met you, but in their minds you were somebody sinister who was pulling the strings."

Much of my time—and certainly a great deal of my energy and emotional strength—was taken up with activities in relation to this threat and in listening to grievances from some of the powerful and influential members of each community who threatened to join the challengers. I flew down to Jacksonville more than once to meet with such people in an effort to mollify negative feelings about the station.

Since I wanted to do anything helpful to the stations, I was pleased when one of my very few friends left in Jacksonville, a moderate Republican civic leader, Roger Main, called me. He was the head of the St. Luke's Hospital Association, which had suddenly lost its speaker for its annual dinner, and to my astonishment, he asked me for help in getting Attorney General Kleindienst to come to speak—and if not Kleindienst, Representative Gerry Ford. Kleindienst was one of the few administration officials who had always been reasonably friendly to me, so I agreed to try, and he accepted. Roger Main invited me to the dinner at the Jacksonville Civic Auditorium, and I accepted with alacrity—an excuse to see the whole group. The evening was not an easy one, however. Only Roger and another friend, Ed Lane, were even polite to me. I somehow got through the reception and dinner, but after dinner the leading lights said good night to me and took Kleindienst off to a party, so I didn't win many points for providing their speaker.

The timing of these challenges made them potentially devastating, coming not only in the thick of Watergate but also just a year and a half after the Pentagon Papers and after we had gone public. More important, Fritz had been working hard to acquire the company's fourth television station, in Hartford, Connecticut. We were naturally concerned that the Travelers Insurance Company, the seller, would get cold feet in the face of the challenges, and that the sale wouldn't go through, but Travelers stayed true to its word and didn't hesitate. That company's relationship with Fritz was solid, and the deal was closed.

From the point of view of Watergate, the challenges came during the time when the story had dried up after the election and we were sweating about where the trail had gone. Others wondered too. The administration's power—and anger—were at their greatest after the landslide election, and we were at our weakest. Our public stance throughout the license challenges was that we were confident of renewal. Indeed, we had reason to be confident: at each station, we had strong local management and we emphasized independent news and editorial judgment. Both Florida stations had impeccable reputations for integrity and programming of high quality. We had met, even exceeded, all of the FCC tests for a good station. One reason I personally felt we ought to be safe was that I didn't see how the FCC could take away our licenses without jeopardizing virtually every television licensee in the country, or at least making them all nervous—including Nixon friends and admirers—so well had we run these stations. But despite our confidence that the challenges were unfounded, we were scared. Among the worst effects was the sharp decline in our stock price that naturally ensued, from $38 a share to $28 in the first two weeks after the challenges, and continuing on down to $16 or $17, decreasing the value of the company by more than half. As for the direct effect on our finances, the legal costs of defending the licenses added up to well over a million dollars in the two and a half years the entire process took—a far larger sum then than now for a small company like ours.

Equally important were the eroding effects on the people trying to run the stations with these threats hanging over their heads and in this hostile atmosphere. We tried to reassure them by telling them to go on as they always had, but decisions are hard to make under such circumstances. At neither station could we recruit people easily, since there was concern about who would hold the license in a few months' time. It was also difficult to air the kind of advocacy editorials we wanted to, knowing they would be used against us.

THE WASHINGTON POST COMPANY had been in the public eye for several months—certainly more than I was comfortable with, and in ways we might not have wished. We didn't seek out the celebrity; it was thrust on us. During a *Newsweek* sales meeting at the time, I said it reminded me somewhat of the old story about the man who'd been tarred and feathered and ridden out of town on a rail. When asked how he felt, he said, "Except for the honor of the thing, I would rather have walked."

By early 1973, I was growing increasingly anxious and thought I ought to meet with Woodward and Bernstein in addition to the editors. Surprisingly, to this point—seven months into the story—I had had hardly any contact with the reporters. So, on January 15, Bob and Howard and I sat down to lunch together (Carl was out of town). Characteristically, Bob went right downstairs to the newsroom afterwards and made extensive notes about what we'd said—even going so far as to write down what we ate, the main course being eggs Benedict, which led to our future reference to this gathering as the "eggs-Benedict lunch."

My apprehensions about the whole Watergate affair were evident. "Is it all going to come out?" Woodward reported that I asked anxiously. "I mean, are we ever going to know about all of this?" As Bob later wrote, he thought it was the nicest way possible of asking, "What have you boys been doing with my newspaper?" He told me then that they weren't sure all of it ever *would* come out: "Depression seemed to register on her face. 'Never?' she asked. 'Don't tell me never.' "

It was also at this lunch that Woodward told me he had told no one the name of Deep Throat. "Tell me," I said quickly, and then, as he froze, I laughed, touched his arm, and said that I was only kidding—I didn't want to carry that burden around. He admitted that he was prepared to give me the name if I really wanted it, but he was praying I wouldn't press him. This luncheon was reassuring for me—or at least I gave the appearance of being reassured—but I remained nervous. Looking back, I'm surprised I wasn't even more frightened.

The period leading up to the trial of the "Watergate Seven," which began on January 8, 1973, had been extremely tense. Colson was talking around Washington about going to our national advertisers or our investors. A Wall Street friend of mine, André Meyer, a man with administration contacts, called me and asked me to come to see him. When I did, he advised me to be very careful of everything I did or said and—just like in the movies—he warned me "not to be alone." "Oh, André," I said, "that's really absurdly melodramatic. Nothing will happen to me."

"I'm serious," he said. "I've talked to them, and I'm telling you not to be alone." André never explained what his fears were based on, and I still have no idea what he had heard or even meant, but I certainly got the point about how serious he was. I lay awake many nights worrying, though not about my personal safety. Beyond its reputation, the very existence of the *Post* was at stake. I'd lived with White House anger before, but I had never seen anything remotely like the kind of fury and heat I was feeling targeted at us now. It seemed at times that we should really be worrying about some bizarre Kafkaesque plot—that maybe we were being led down a road to discredit the paper.

The moments of anxiety increased in quantity and intensity. Naturally, we were worried when our stories were denied repeatedly and vehemently. Even we, it seems, underestimated for a long time the capacity of government to hide and distort the truth. Finally, a series of events began to unfold in our favor. Three days after the beginning of the trial, Howard Hunt pleaded guilty to six of the charges against him. Four days later, the other burglars followed suit. On January 30, Liddy and McCord were convicted, continuing to claim that no higher-ups were involved and that they had not received any money. In fact, Hunt had urged the burglars to plead guilty and go to jail, assuring them he would take care of them.

Toward the end of February, a civil subpoena was served on five of us from the *Post*, and we were ordered to appear in the U.S. District Court to testify on our sources in the Democratic Party's civil suit against the Committee to Re-elect the President. The subpoena required that we produce a whole host of material, including documents, papers, letters, photographs, tapes, manuscripts, notes, copies, and final drafts of stories about Watergate. As Ben Bradlee put it, they asked us to bring "everything except the lint in our pockets." My name was misspelled, but I was subpoenaed, along with Woodward and Bernstein, Howard Simons, and another reporter, Jim Mann, who had worked on a few of the early Watergate stories. Our lawyers decided to give me some of the reporters' notes. Bradlee had reassured Bernstein and Woodward that we would fight this case for as long as it took, adding:

> . . . and if the Judge wants to send anyone to jail, he's going to have to send Mrs. Graham. And, my God, the lady says she'll go! Then the Judge can have that on his conscience. Can't you see the pictures of her limousine pulling up to the Women's Detention Center and out gets our gal, going to jail to uphold the First Amendment? That's a picture that would run in every newspaper in the world. There might be a revolution.

At some point, Woodward had met with Deep Throat, who told him that the subpoenas were part of a response induced by Nixon's rampage against the *Post*, and that he, Nixon, would use the $5 million left over from his campaign "to take the Post down a notch." "It will be wearing on you but the end is in sight," Deep Throat told Woodward.

In the end, the subpoenas were quashed, but not before we had spent a great deal of energy and money. The intervening drama was intense. I wrote a friend, "The outrage of it is lost in the absurdity," also noting that one of the editors on the *Post*, who was not served, was said to be suffering from a case of "subpoena envy."

The administration also struck a tough blow at Ed Williams's law firm in connection with this suit. The firm had only about twenty-five lawyers at the time, five of whom worked at representing the Teamsters. After the suit was filed against the Committee to Re-elect the President, the president of the Teamsters told Ed that the suit represented such bad judgment it reflected on the judgment of the firm. Ed's response was, "Nobody tells us who our clients are." As a result, the Teamsters moved its business.

At the same time, though, we were gathering allies, however unwitting. One of the principal ones was U.S. District Court Judge John Sirica, who said he was "not satisfied" that the whole Watergate story was being revealed in his courtroom. Equally crucial, the Senate voted seventy to zero to establish a committee to investigate Watergate and other alleged campaign abuses.

I was on a trip to the Far East in behalf of *Newsweek International* when an important call reached me in Hong Kong. Howard Simons was phoning to tell me the stunning news that James McCord had written a letter to Judge Sirica charging that perjury was committed at the Watergate trial, that the defendants had been pressured to plead guilty and keep quiet, that higher-ups were indeed involved, and that "several members of my family have expressed fear for my life if I disclose knowledge of the facts in this matter." McCord agreed to tell what he knew about the original burglary in exchange for a more lenient sentence.

What a relief—or, as Ben would later write, "Bingo!" This was the first real break in the case, and in the story, altering the reporting of the Watergate scandal from that point on, as well as changing the nature of reporting for the future. McCord's letter confirmed our stories, making what we'd said sound much more plausible and changing the image of the paper, as well as my own image in some ways. Suddenly people realized there was proof to back up our reporting; there was evidence that what we had been saying was true. We had been through many long months of hanging out there, and now the press appeared in droves, finally lifting the rugs to look for leads. Piling on began. The *Post* was no longer alone, although we were still out front. We began to get more competition in reporting the story, both from other papers and from the newsmagazines, including *Newsweek*, which started to do cover after cover.

So much that followed stemmed from McCord's letter—our increased visibility, my higher profile, more requests for speeches and interviews. All of this surprised me at the time and worried me later. Because I was still on the Asian trip when McCord's letter became public, mine was a baptism by fire, with interview requests pouring in from news media all over the Far East. But since the aim of the trip was to promote *Newsweek International*, I welcomed the increased opportunities to speak out.

By the time I returned from the trip at the end of March, the situation for the administration had started to unravel. Henry Kissinger recalls that it was shortly after this that he began to realize Watergate was real and was not going to go away. Having been unable to fathom that our reporting might be accurate, Henry had worried mostly about the effect of Watergate on the development of our foreign policy and on the administration's "freedom of maneuver" in conducting it. Early on, he had had lunch with Joe Califano and had asked, "What are you Democrats going to do now?"—to which Joe replied, "We're going to get well on Watergate." Henry then went to either Haldeman or Ehrlichman and said, "What's he talking about?" The response: "It's wishful thinking."

But a great deal was going on behind the scenes at the White House, and several resignations were announced on April 30, along with John Dean's firing as counsel. Elliot Richardson, the new attorney general, was given the right to appoint a special prosecutor. Nixon came on television at 9:00 p.m. that night. There weren't many televisions in the newsroom, so several of us, including Woodward and Bernstein, crowded into Howard Simons's office to watch Nixon's speech. It was one of those many times throughout Watergate when I just wanted to be at the paper with friends and in the thick of things. Bernstein and Woodward, who wrote everything down, even reported that when Nixon came on, seated at his desk with a picture of his family on one side and a bust of Lincoln on the other, I said, "Oh, my God, this is too much."

Nixon, in his speech, accepted the responsibility but not the blame for Watergate. He resorted to his old formulas: "The easiest course would be for me to blame those to whom I delegated the responsibility to run the campaign but that would be a cowardly thing to do. . . . It was the system that has brought the facts to life . . . a system that in this case has included a determined grand jury, honest prosecutors, a courageous judge, Judge Sirica, and a vigorous free press." After the televised address, he gratuitously stopped by the White House pressroom and said, "We've had our differences in the past, and just continue to give me hell when you think I'm wrong."

All of this created a huge stir in the newsroom. Howard Simons said to staff members, "We can't afford to gloat," a sentiment that I shared. Though Watergate was no longer a lonely project for the *Post*, we were proud of the part we had played, but it was now on its way to becoming a national tragedy, and we had no impulse to flaunt our role, though every reason to feel relief at vindication.

— *Chapter Twenty-four* —

I N T H E M I D D L E of the worst of Watergate for us, things had deteriorated for me personally, as my beloved colleague Fritz, ill with cancer, declined rapidly. By the last day of April, 1973, Fritz was in the hospital in critical condition. He listened to Nixon's speech from his bed. His wife, Liane, later told me that, at the point during the speech when Nixon accepted some of the responsibility, Fritz raised his arm with his fist pointing upwards and, as Liane wrote me, "his face all one proud grin, 'Thank you, Thank you!' he shouted enthusiastically, 'GREAT! HURRAH!' That was Fritz's last salute to the Washington Post! Yes, he was fully aware of what was going on! He was beaming for a short while there—excited, thrilled about it all and with you all." Fritz died the next morning. For me the simultaneity of these events—confirmation of our reporting and Fritz's death—brought satisfaction and joy mixed with profound sorrow and loss.

At the next day's press conference, Ron Ziegler apologized to *The Washington Post* generally and to Woodward and Bernstein particularly for his earlier criticisms of their reporting. Ziegler's statement surprised us all, and also showed the extent to which he had been co-opted. Bob called him right away and thanked him, to which Ziegler responded, "We all have our jobs to do." I made a statement to newspeople who called, saying we appreciated the apology and accepted it with pleasure. "It was handsomely made; it was handsomely done. I'm happy to accept it."

Only a week after Fritz's death, it was announced that *The Washington Post* had won the Pulitzer Prize for meritorious service for its Watergate reporting. Woodward and Bernstein were cited, and Herblock and Roger Wilkins were specially mentioned. As it turned out, the Pulitzer jurors, meeting weeks before the most dramatic developments in the case, had *not* voted a Pulitzer for the Watergate coverage or for Woodward and Bernstein. Three other *Post* staffers had been named, however: David Broder for commentary; Bob Kaiser and Dan Morgan to share a prize for foreign reporting; and Bill Claiborne for local spot news for his reporting of a prison riot.

After the McCord letter became known, Scotty Reston and Newbold Noyes, who were serving on the awards board that year, pointed out that it would hardly make sense for the *Post* not to be recognized for its Watergate coverage. We had entered the competition in the category of public service, but had not won, or seemingly come close, largely because the regional editors on the prize committee were so incredulous about the whole affair. After Scotty and Newby voiced their opinions, the board asked Ben whether he wanted the paper entered for public service or investigative reporting. Ben chose public service, for which the paper won the award. However, the Pulitzer jury also rescinded two of the *Post*'s three prizes they had already voted on, with only David Broder retaining his for commentary.

But despite Nixon's dramatic speech and the winning of the Pulitzer with its attendant confirmation of our reporting, the whole Watergate affair was far from over. Some of the rejoicing had been premature. Although we had gained credibility when Haldeman and Ehrlichman resigned, we still had an implacable enemy in the White House, albeit a weakened one. Much of the world remained with Nixon and continued to think that the whole affair had been vastly exaggerated. Some of the world still does: many foreigners failed to grasp the significance of Watergate, particularly in Europe and in the Arab world, where people viewed the president as a foreign-policy genius, which in many ways he was.

There was a lot we—and the public—still didn't know, but we were on the road to finding out, helped along in the spring of 1973 by a federal grand jury's indictment of former Attorney General John Mitchell and former Secretary of Commerce Maurice Stans on charges of conspiracy, perjury, and obstruction of justice for impeding an SEC investigation of international financier Robert Vesco, in exchange for a secret Vesco contribution of $200,000 cash to Nixon's 1972 campaign. The televised Senate Watergate hearings and early calls for impeachment, coming from conservatives—including Barry Goldwater—as much as or more than from liberals, also helped.

The continuing efforts of the *Post*, and, *finally*, other newspapers and other media as well, and the Congress and the courts helped expose the size of the iceberg. There began a steady stream of revelations, with more and more evidence of scheming and political chicanery coming to light. Wiretaps of several journalists were revealed. We were told by many people that the *Post*'s building was bugged and even that I was being followed. Some of this was clearly an overreaction in an environment rife with paranoia. We did a sweep of our phones throughout the building and in my office and the offices of key editors, but turned up nothing. I'm fairly sure that my phones were never tapped, nor do I believe I was ever followed, but the atmosphere was so infected that this kind of suspicion didn't seem irrational at all.

In June 1973, Woodward and Bernstein wrote that the White House had maintained a list of "political enemies" in 1971 and 1972, and the disclosure surprised few of us. By that time, many people—several of my friends among them—regarded it as an honor to be on it. The list was yet another sign of the peculiar mentality of the small group of men running the country. I can't remember whether my name actually appeared on it, but it was clear to me that I was on it whether my name was written down or not.

A month later, a seismic Watergate event occurred—the turning point, the pivotal moment. In the course of his testimony before the Senate investigating committee, Alexander Butterfield, another Haldeman aide, revealed that there was a voice-activated recording system in the White House. Consequently, the vast majority of conversations the president had had in the Oval Office were on tape, a fact the president himself had clearly lost sight of; or perhaps he assumed that no one knew and that therefore the existence of the system would never become public knowledge. However, someone had to have installed this thing as well as run it, and that someone was Alexander Butterfield. As Woodward later said, it was yet another "incredible sequence of events, and luck for us and bad luck for Nixon. Wrong decisions, wrong turns. But full disclosure of it hung by that fragile thread that could have been cut hundreds of times."

Without the tapes, the true story would never have emerged. In fact, I believe that we at the *Post* were really saved in the end by the tapes and the lucky chance that they weren't destroyed. After the discovery of the tapes, people actually began waiting in the alley outside our building for the first edition of the paper, giving additional meaning to the phrase "hot off the presses." Everyone was now following the story.

Who knows why Nixon didn't destroy the tapes? He seemed to think that they were valuable and that he could defend their privacy, which for a long time he tried to do. On July 25, the president announced he would not release the tapes to Special Prosecutor Archibald Cox, who had been appointed by Attorney General Elliot Richardson, because it would jeopardize the "independence of the three branches of government."

Unaccountably, during this time I was still attempting to maintain relations even with Vice-President Spiro Agnew, which in retrospect seems to me undignified, considering the awful slamming we were taking from him. I think my behavior was a combination of a rational idea—that it was better to be talking to people who hated us or disapproved of us than not—and that good old-fashioned encumbrance of mine, the desire to please. Someone had sent me a funny photograph of an old shed some-where in New York on which had been painted "Ted Agnew likes Kay Graham. Pass it on." I thought it was hilarious, and did just that, passed it on to the vice-president, saying, "I thought this sign . . . might amuse you as it did me. The man who sent me the snapshot of the 'graffiti' told me that the shed later burned—thus destroying the evidence! I guess things in life—or in graffiti—often come full circle. I promise to keep it a secret."

Even more peculiarly, Agnew wrote back: "I can find no fault with the sentiment of the graffiti. It is difficult to admire a newspaper that char-acterizes one as Caligula's horse, but I think you are charming." How embarrassing!

A separate drama began unfolding around Agnew. Only ten days after I had written him the sniveling little note, Agnew announced that he had been informed he was under investigation for possible violations of crim-inal law, and two days later, on August 8, he held a press conference to trot out the usual denials of wrongdoings.

As the investigation continued, the *Post*, on September 22, wrote that, despite his statements that he would never quit, the vice-president was plea-bargaining. Agnew's lawyers tried to learn the source of certain dam-aging leaks by issuing subpoenas to *Post* reporter Richard Cohen and oth-ers who had been running stories about him. I later used quite plain language to describe what Agnew was trying to do: "Freed of legalese, he wanted to know who in government was fingering him, so he could deal with them personally or have the President fire them."

The strategy our lawyers worked out to protect Cohen and the paper was to put all of his notes relating to Agnew in my possession, and in my affidavit to the court I asserted that I had ultimate responsibility for the custody of the notes. In fact, I was prepared to go to jail if need be to de-fend the notes and the source. This time the possibility of jail seemed more realistic. I was traveling, and called between planes to hear, with re-lief, that Agnew had pleaded no contest to one count of income-tax eva-sion while governor of Maryland, which meant that I was off the hook. On October 10, Spiro T. Agnew resigned as vice-president.

Meanwhile, President Nixon's troubles continued to mount, not helped at all by the Agnew crisis. On August 15, he had made another tele-vised speech, delivering his fifth major statement on Watergate, calling it a "backward-looking obsession" and trying to deflect interest away from it by suggesting that the nation let the courts deal with it and turn its atten-tion instead to "matters of far greater importance."

A week after that, on August 22, the same day Nixon made Kissinger secretary of state following the resignation of Bill Rogers, he also accepted the blame for the White House "climate" that led to the break-in and the cover-up. Events were proceeding apace. On August 29, Judge Sirica ordered the president to turn over to him for his private examination the tapes involving Watergate. Nixon and his lawyers appealed the order. The battle was joined in earnest when the U.S. Court of Appeals for the District of Columbia upheld Sirica. Nixon then came up with the peculiar idea of providing tapes to the federal courts and Senate investigators with a personally prepared summary to be verified by Senator John Stennis. Special Prosecutor Cox, rightly, rejected the idea. The next day, October 20, Cox defended his decision not to compromise with the president about the tapes.

That night the Buchwalds had arranged a tennis party for Art's birthday. Several of us were either already at or on our way to an indoor tennis court when we heard the stunning news of what became known as the "Saturday Night Massacre." Attorney General Richardson had been told by the president to fire Cox; when he refused, he himself was fired. Richardson's deputy, Bill Ruckelshaus, also refused to fire Cox, and he, too, was fired. Finally, the third-ranking officer at the Justice Department, Robert Bork, consented to and *did* fire Cox. By that point, every journalist had left Art's party to head back to work.

So dramatic and unexpected were the events that night that we were all really shaken. It's hard to realize now how fast everything was unfolding. With Leon Jaworski succeeding Cox as special prosecutor, the House Judiciary Committee met to consider impeachment proceedings against Nixon. Eventually, the many impeachment resolutions that were introduced in the House of Representatives seemed to induce the president to release the tapes Cox had insisted on.

Yet the *Post* remained under attack—and the attack was becoming much more public. By this time I had warmed up to a degree of toughness of which I probably wouldn't have been capable the year before. I am not a good combatant. Generally I hate fights and would like to run from them, but when there is no choice, I feel able to take action. I was much more willing to go on the offensive than to be defensively polite, particularly in my letters to readers and others who wrote complaining about our coverage. For example, whereas earlier I may have been somewhat sympathetic with readers who wrote about the sharpness of Herblock's pen, in the later stages of Watergate I had no patience with those who complained that he was being unfair to the president. To one scathing letter, I responded, "We have been heavily attacked for biased reporting by many individuals, who, when confronted with the facts, have since resigned from the government." I wrote to a man in Florida in October 1973, facetiously thanking him for sending me a copy of an ad from the Miami paper suggesting that we belonged in jail and asking him, "If we are exaggerating minor peccadillos, why has the majority of the White House staff had to be unloaded?"

At some point, I even engaged in a behind-the-scenes back-and-forth with Clare Booth Luce. Personally I admired her, but I was not in accord with her extremely conservative views. She sometimes overdramatized things in speeches. In a major address to the Newspaper Publishers Association convention, she said she had written a speech but was troubled about it and thinking about it as she went to bed. That night, she said, the spirit of her late husband, Henry Luce, came to her and told her to tell the truth about Watergate. She then attacked the *Post* for our reporting and for hiring "enemies" of the president. After the speech, I told a friend that Phil Graham had appeared to me in the night and told me to tell her to "shove it."

ON DECEMBER 28, I was lunching outside the building—a rare occurrence—with Meg and Phil Geyelin at an Italian restaurant when I got called to the telephone by Alexander Haig, who was then White House chief of staff. He was calling from Nixon's California home—or the "Western White House," as it was called, since the president spent a great deal of time there. I vividly recall sitting on the stairs in a dark, narrow passageway where the phone was located, furiously scribbling notes on a scrap of paper I'd hastily grabbed from my purse.

Haig heatedly complained about two page-one stories by Woodward and Bernstein. The first had said that "Operation Candor," the name that had been given to the president's attempt to defend himself, had been shut down, and that two of the president's closest advisers, who had stuck by him, no longer believed in him. The second story said that the president's counselors had been supplying lawyers for Haldeman and Ehrlichman with documents and evidence that the White House was submitting to the special prosecutor's office. Haig was outraged, calling the articles "scurrilous and untrue" and referring to the second piece as "a patchwork of thievery."

Late in January 1974, I went to a dinner at the Clark MacGregors' for the new Vice-President and Mrs. Gerald Ford, which says a lot about where MacGregor was, at least by then. It's interesting, too, that the Fords were willing to have dinner with me even though he was Nixon's new vice-president. Also, I was seated at dinner next to Haig, who seemed to be feeling more friendly toward me with each new revelation from the White House.

The following week, on February 6, members of the House of Representatives voted 410 to 4 to proceed with the impeachment probe and to give the Judiciary Committee broad subpoena powers. Trying to keep all his hatred of the press, and particularly of the *Post*, within the confines of the White House proved too much for the president. He attended Alice Roosevelt Longworth's ninetieth-birthday party and told reporters waiting outside that she had no doubt managed to keep young "by not being obsessed by the Washington scene," adding, "If she had spent all of her time reading the *Post* or the *Star* she would have been dead by now."

Later in February, Haig invited Meg, Ben, and me to lunch at the White House—clearly a kind of reaching out. The whole feeling in early 1974 was the opposite of what we had experienced during the preceding months of strain, worry, and anguish. By this time, we were all undoubtedly on a high because we had been vindicated. Still, our satisfaction was to a large extent vitiated by dismay at the extent of what really was going on in the Nixon White House.

After I'd been to the country for the weekend, Meg asked me, with just the right note of incredulity in her voice, "Have you heard the latest?"—and then proceeded to tell me of the backdating of the deed for the papers Nixon had given as a gift to the National Archives for the proposed Nixon Library. The deed had been falsely backdated to before the effective date of a law curbing tax deductions for such gifts. Nixon had claimed deductions of nearly half a million dollars over four years. I also remember that my reaction then was "How wonderful." I realize that sounds vindictive, but the fact is that, after we had been under assault for so long, it naturally felt good to have such revelations unfolding one after another, far beyond our reporting or even our wildest imaginings. Meg said, "The next time you make one of your speeches saying, 'This certainly gives us no satisfaction. We are only doing our bounden duty,' God will strike you dead."

Again, we were happy to have everything corroborated further when, on March 1, 1974, indictments were handed down by a grand jury for seven former Nixon-administration and campaign officials for allegedly conspiring to cover up the Watergate burglary.

What next? On May 9, the House Judiciary Committee began formal hearings on the possible impeachment of Nixon. Though some of my friends, including André Meyer, suggested that the *Post* was trying to "extract every last drop of blood" from the president, I believed that we were following and reporting the impeachment process in a reasoned and dispassionate way, and replied to André, "I hardly see how anyone, no matter how ill-intentioned, could pervert this . . . to 'extracting every last drop of blood.' . . . It really has more to do with what is best for the country now and in the future, than it has to do with this president—who no longer matters, whereas the country does." Privately, I felt that impeachment was right, but my personal opinion didn't get mixed up in the paper's ongoing reporting.

In mid-May it was revealed that Nixon's talk with Haldeman and Dean about economic retaliation against The Washington Post Company's television-station licenses had been cut from the tape before its release. This was widely reported in the papers, including our own. As a result, I received a contrite letter from Joe Alsop, who, on the whole, had continued to stick by the president and with whom I had had a serious argument about whether the administration was connected to the license challenges. Joe wrote me:

> You're dead right and I was nearly dead wrong. This was my first reaction to the extraordinarily interesting story by Bernstein and Woodward on the President's threat of retaliation against the Post. I cannot tell you how much I admire the enormous courage that you have all shown, particularly you and Ben. Whether the final outcome will be happy, I cannot possibly say, and I sometimes have my doubts. But the fact is that a very dangerous system had grown up in the White House, which would have threatened this country if it had continued. It was destroyed by you and the other leaders of the Post and the Post reporters almost singlehanded. . . . So I send you all my warmest congratulations, and also my apologies for giving our miserable President the benefit of the doubt—which now turns out to be a completely wrong thing to do.

It was a generous letter from Joe, one I'm sure he wrote with a great deal of sadness and lamentation for something irretrievably lost.

Watergate continued on its way toward an ending none of us could have imagined two years earlier. Even as late as the summer of 1974, amazing as it may seem after all that had been revealed and all the constitutional processes that had taken place—the grand juries, the courts, the congressional committees—Nixon was still blaming the press for his predicament, saying at one point that, if he had been a liberal and "bugged out of Vietnam," the press would never have played up Watergate. Despite Nixon's protestations to his supporter Rabbi Baruch Korff that Watergate would be remembered as "the broadest but thinnest scandal in American history," it went on being revealed as anything but.

On July 8, the United States Supreme Court heard arguments in a historic special session in the case of the *United States* v. *Richard M. Nixon*. What was at stake was whether the Court would order the release of the White House tapes. The next day, House Judiciary Committee Chairman Peter Rodino divulged many of the differences between what the White House had released and what the committee had found on certain tapes, indicating that Nixon had played an active role in the cover-up, which was still going on.

On July 24, 1974, events moved inexorably forward as the Supreme Court ruled unanimously that Nixon had no right to withhold evidence in criminal proceedings and ordered him to turn over the additional White House tapes that had been subpoenaed by Jaworski. On July 27, 29, and 30, respectively, the House Judiciary Committee adopted three articles of impeachment, charging President Nixon with obstruction of justice, failure to uphold laws, and refusal to produce material subpoenaed by the committee.

Editorially, the *Post* did not come out for resignation, as many other papers did. We believed, as an independent paper, that people would behave wisely and judiciously if given the information necessary to make their decisions, and that the process should be allowed to work.

Finally, on August 5, the long-anticipated "smoking gun" turned up. Three new transcripts were released by the White House, recounting conversations between Nixon and Haldeman on June 23, 1972, six days after the original break-in. The tapes showed that the president had personally ordered a cover-up and that he had directed efforts to hide the involvement of his aides in the break-in through a series of orders to conceal details about it known to himself but not to the FBI. This was such a dramatic and obviously final development that I left Martha's Vineyard, where I had gone for my August vacation, and flew immediately to Washington.

Nixon initially said that he would not resign, that he believed the constitutional process should be allowed to run its course. All ten Republicans on the House Judiciary Committee who had voted against impeachment then announced they would vote in favor of at least the obstruction-of-justice article. We led the paper with the possibility of Nixon's resignation, but made no predictions, despite speculation on every side.

On August 8, President Nixon announced that he would resign the next day. I stayed at the paper all that day. Together, many of us watched Nixon's television appearance about his decision to resign. Phil Geyelin had dinner at the Madison Hotel, across the street from our offices, and wrote on a napkin a rough draft of an editorial on the resignation. When it was typed, he sent it to me with a note: "This is one you probably would want to take a look at."

On August 9, the *Post* produced a twenty-two-page special section on the Nixon years. Along with a few people in my office, I watched the weird speech Nixon made before leaving the White House, fairly incoherently talking to his staff in the East Room about his mother, who seemed to be on his mind a great deal. The unreality of the whole thing hung all around us. After the long months that had stretched into years, it was so strange to be watching what none of us had ever imagined happening. It all seemed both world-shattering and confusing. A miracle of sorts had taken place—this country was about to change presidents in an utterly democratic way, with the processes that had been put into place two centuries before working in this unprecedented situation.

At the *Post*, we received a lot of unpleasant phone calls, many readers expressing the sentiment that they imagined we were all popping champagne corks to celebrate the result we had wanted from the beginning—in short, the "I-hope-you're-satisfied" school of thought. What I mostly felt was relief, mingled with anxiety. Until the smoking-gun tape had turned up, nothing had been certain; right up to the last few days of his presidency, it seemed possible that Nixon could hold on. Now the unease about where all of it was leading was over.

Immediately after watching Nixon's speech and before he'd left Washington, I returned to the Vineyard to continue my vacation. When I got back to the quiet of my house there, on the island that always gives me a sense of peace and remoteness from everyday life, I turned on the television and heard a voice referring to President Ford. It was quite shaking. Then and only then did I experience pure relief. I actually felt a weight leave my shoulders. It was over. Nixon was gone, Ford was president, and, indeed, "our long national nightmare" was over. The relief came from having a *nice*, open, honest, and nonthreatening president.

One of the final touches to Watergate occurred just after Nixon had left Washington. Bob Woodward came to my office with the most wonderful present—an old-fashioned wooden laundry-wringer. It was signed by the six men who had worked throughout those years to keep the story alive: Ben and Howard, Bob and Carl, Harry Rosenfeld and Barry Sussman. I loved having this symbol, so indicative of the pressure we had felt during Watergate. An antique dealer had called Bob to say he would be willing to sell the old wringer in case he wanted to consider giving it to me. Ever cautious, Bob had asked how much. "Ten," the man replied. "Ten what?" Bob asked. "Ten dollars," came the answer. Bob snapped up the deal, and I received the much-cherished wooden wringer that sits in my office still, over twenty years later.

WHEN I RETURNED to Washington in September, I thought life might finally get back to normal after two solid years of constant stress over Watergate. Little did I realize that the "normal" I was thinking of had wholly changed. What I wanted was to be out of the limelight, and I wanted the paper to be out of it, too. But that was far from what happened. To begin with, we still had the challenges to our stations hanging over our heads. The denouement finally came at the end of 1974. The Miami challenge was withdrawn November 26, and one of the Jacksonville ones in January 1975. The other two were denied by the FCC in April and July 1975, the judge ruling that because of "overt deception practiced in the filing of the St. John's application no finding could be made that the grant of its application would be in the public interest." Again, we were fortunate that the challengers seemed so sure of winning through their political connections that they really never made any kind of a case.

More even than Nixon's resignation, this was the end of Watergate for us. By then we had been fighting this battle against venality for two years in the case of two of the challenges and two and a half in the latter two. We had paid a heavy price, not only in money but in concern, distraction, and erosion.

On December 5, 1974, both Ben and I were invited to a dinner at the Ford White House, where I was seated at the table with the new president—an exciting symbol that the whole sad affair of Watergate was over. (An amusing sidelight on Ford's elevation to the presidency came when tee shirts were printed with his picture on them, together with the caption, "I got my job through The Washington Post," a slogan also used by our classified-ad department.) By then, Ford had granted a full, free, and absolute pardon to Nixon, which I thought premature, believing that he should have extracted at least some sort of admission of guilt for it. I suspected that more awful deeds lurked unexposed—now likely never to surface. I'm sure Ford was under a lot of pressure to get the whole disastrous affair "behind us." But Nixon's associates paid an even higher price than he did. Resigning the presidency was a high price indeed, but his associates mostly went to jail, whereas he was able eventually to work his way back into being some sort of elder statesman, even contributing to thinking about foreign policy in the presidencies of Ronald Reagan and George Bush.

By the end of 1973, we—the paper and certain individuals on it—began to get a number of awards. As I wrote someone, "It is a happy problem." I picked up two of the biggest press awards, the John Peter Zenger and the Elijah Parish Lovejoy. I think some of these awards should have gone to others, particularly Ben, which I believe didn't happen because a kind of reverse sexism was at work.

Fortunately, who got what award didn't cause any kind of problem in Ben's and my relationship. In fact, when, early in 1974, a media-industry newsletter named me "outstanding newspaper executive," with Ben as runner-up, I found it especially ironic since I was still having nothing but travail as a newspaper executive. I realized, however, that Watergate was on everybody's mind at the time, and the editors of that report didn't look at the overall picture.

In fact, my relationship with Ben was solidified forever by Watergate. I relied heavily on him throughout. More than ever he was the gung-ho, charismatic leader, remaining cool and courageous no matter what we were hit with. As Woodward later said, "There was always a sense that Bradlee's our leader. He's the guy who's planting the flag." Ben's personality was and is so "up" that I would go to see him sometimes just because a visit was reassuring. In addition, I almost always learned something new from him.

Rumors swirled around us that I was going to get rid of him, that he had gone too far in reporting Watergate. When this kind of rumor circulates, denials win you nothing; the rumors get recycled even though the person stays on and on. There were also numerous sexist comments on our relationship. Somehow it always seemed to be depicted in exaggerated ways. For example, I wrote Tom Winship after a piece had appeared in the *Boston Globe* on Ben Bradlee and Abe Rosenthal, complaining, "[W]hy is it if a female publisher and a male editor get along, he is accused of stroking and she of being susceptible to manipulation?" The fact is, I always loved working with Ben, and this period—even with its many strains—was probably the most rewarding time of all.

In keeping with our established tradition of writing each other end-of-the-year letters, I wrote to Ben at the end of that momentous year of 1974. This letter summed up many of my innermost feelings about what we'd been through together:

> This year I'm not going to wait for yours—because I began to think while dressing about the past year and by the time I got to my shoes I had to grab the pad and begin—as I thought of your remark yesterday afternoon that it was that time of year.
>
> The first thing you and I have to do is separate myth from reality because after this year the myth will start to grow and reality will start to diminish even in our minds.
>
> The reality is so much less pretentious but so apparently impossible to describe. And it really is much nicer because it's human. You are now supposed to be a hero and I a heroine by many and the opposite by many. I think heroes and heroines are both vulgar and boring and usually lead that kind of lives. But when you tell people you were just doing your own thing in an admittedly escalated situation, they say, Ah, yes, etc.
>
> So what are the realities?
>
> They are so complicated of course because we have known each other and our lives have impinged on each other with almost Proustian coincidence, both closer and more distant than they'd think.

Closer because I am thinking of the shared Walter and Helen Lippmann type memories, the first tour at the Post, Phil and me seeing you and Jean in Paris, leading up obviously to the drama of Newsweek, followed by the horror years viewed so differently at the time and then Phil's death. You have to remember at that time we hardly knew each other and certainly not in reality or very favorably either.

How could the rest have happened? It couldn't ever again. We were still small enough as a company, still private, and so the impossible happened. . . . I with nothing more than a family feeling, a passion for newspapers and this newspaper in particular, (not the slightest clue about business, broadcasting or Newsweek— only negative vibes about the latter which was associated only with madness in my mind) took over this peculiar and charismatic entity.

Two years later you knocked—typically brashly, intuitively, humorously, rudely, perceptively, farsightedly, ballsily, and pushy as Hell. And because this was a not unfamiliar syndrome to me— and one whose merits and drawbacks I knew—I nodded a feeble assent (I guess that's slightly exaggerated I say hastily for all those future fucking Columbia Journalism Review stories). But there's a kind of core truth to the scene.

Then came another—the years of learning, of stumbling, of fun, of some achievement, progress, mixed with big smelly eggs on the floor—laid and cleaned up or just shoved under the rug until the stain soaked through. The fascinating thing—and the thing to remember, is that if you have enough going for you in the way of momentum and luck, everyone looks at the developing pattern on the rug whether it's an Oriental design or the stain from the egg, and says, "What a beautiful rug." And pretty soon we're telling ourselves, "It's a hell of a rug we've made"—and even funnier, it is. But let's always remember the stains, the unfinished work, with the total effect and the fun—my god, the fun. It's unfair, who else has fun? And that's my Christmas thanks to you, kid—more than even the Watergates, although that, too.

The things that people don't know—that I know—are style, generosity, class and decency, as well as understanding of other people's weaknesses. . . .

It was out of all these many things that Watergate evolved for you and for me and for the way it worked.

If there was one thing I thought of at the time it was a high wire over a canyon in which I almost couldn't pull at your coattails and say "Are we all right, because if we're not, look below." It was sort of like trying to talk to the pilot during a hairy landing. Not that I didn't—and that you didn't respond to the feverish "are we all rights?" and "whys?" . . .

And maybe one of the things it's easy to forget in 1974, is that the answer was, we were not all right—we were righteous but mercifully stupid. We were only saved from extinction by someone mad enough not only to tape himself but to tape himself talking about how to conceal it. Well, who could have counted on that? Not you and not me.

Thank god for the reality, it will never be in any book or any cruddy movie. It's much too good for that. . . .

Ben's letter to me at the end of that year concluded: "We probably won't live to see another year like 1974." He was quite right.

EARLIER, in the spring of 1974, at a time when the story had advanced considerably but was still months short of its dramatic conclusion, Woodward and Bernstein had published *All the President's Men*, their first book on Watergate. The paperback rights alone sold for $1 million. Ironically, the million dollars came their way at the time of a strike by The Newspaper Guild. I vividly recall watching a news broadcast that showed the two of them leaving the building with their files, and I caused a stir with a rather acid remark about their being the only two people ever to have made a million dollars while on strike.

From the beginning there had been talk of a movie. Once Woodward and Bernstein sold the movie rights to *All the President's Men* to Robert Redford, who intended to play Bob Woodward, there was a great deal of fun and funny speculation, both in the *Post's* newsroom and elsewhere, about who would play whom in the movie. I jokingly told a group of circulation managers at an association meeting that I had been assured by the editors "that my role will be played by Raquel Welch—assuming our measurements jibe."

In many ways, the idea of a movie scared me witless. Despite Redford's assurances that he wanted to make a good movie about the First Amendment and freedom of the press, I was naturally nervous about having the image and reputation of the *Post* in the hands of a movie company, whose interests did not necessarily coincide with ours. I couldn't visualize how he and his producers would deal with as complex an issue as press freedom in a dramatic story on the big screen.

Someone had to set the ground rules for what they could and couldn't do. I was particularly concerned about the effect of the movie—and our portrayal in it—on the political scene. As public people, which by then many of us at the *Post* were, we had no control over the use of our names, but there was a great deal of discussion in the beginning among all of us, our lawyers included, about whether the name of the *Post* should be used. Many of those on the business side of the company said no. Ben's argument in favor of its use was one with which there was widespread agreement in the newsroom: "Whatever we're going to get, we're going to get whether they call it the *Post* or the *Bugle*."

To help calm my nerves and provide some assurances that the producers had every good intention, Bob and Carl brought the Redfords to breakfast at my house in May of 1974, just as plans for the movie were getting under way. I should have been pleased and interested to meet Redford, but we didn't get along, thanks partially, I'm sure, to my own defensive crouch—the result of all my concerns, however real or imagined. He knew how much I wanted to keep a low profile both for me and for the paper. On the other hand, Alan Pakula, the director, and I became great friends and have remained so.

Redford later gave an interview describing our meeting at breakfast:

> It was brittle, that's the best way I can describe it. She was gracious but tense. There was a definite tight-jawed, blueblood quality to Graham that cannot be covered by any amount of association with Ben Bradlee or other street types. . . . She said she did not want her own name or that of the *Post* used. I told her that was impossible. She was a public figure and in its own way so was the *Post*. I respected her for not wanting her privacy invaded . . . but we weren't interested in her personal life. And I was puzzled. If she wanted to maintain so low a profile, why did she keep making speeches and accepting awards?

Ben sent me a copy of this acerbic interview, to which I responded, "I don't want to be too neurotic but it reinforces paranoia, no? . . . He's got a point about my ambivalence, which was and is real."

I was already worried about the effect of the use of the *Post*'s name when I opened a magazine one day and read that the movie would be filmed in the *Post*'s city room. Within minutes, I was on the phone to Bob Woodward, to whom I exploded with outrage at the idea of our newsroom as a backdrop for the movie. Among all the evils I was imagining was how little work would get done under such circumstances. Bob told me he'd never heard me so angry. In the end, we didn't allow filming in the newsroom; Redford's people had arrived independently at the conclusion that it would be too disruptive for them as well. Instead, an exact duplicate of the *Post*'s newsroom, including the stickers on Ben's secretary's desk, was created in Hollywood (for a mere $450,000, it was reported), and in the interests of authenticity, several tons of assorted papers and trash from desks throughout our newsroom were shipped to California for props. We did cooperate to the extent of allowing the filmmakers to shoot the entrance to the newspaper building, elevators, and certain production facilities, as well as a scene in the parking lot.

At one point, I got a message from Redford that they had decided not to shoot the one scene in the movie in which I was to be portrayed. I was told that no one understood the role of a publisher, and it was too extraneous to explain. Redford imagined that I would be relieved, which I was, but, to my surprise, my feelings were hurt by being omitted altogether, except for the one famous allusion to my anatomy.

The next I heard from Redford was a phone call saying he was sending a preliminary print of the film for us to see, and that we could still ask for changes, which I felt was a charade. In March 1976 several of us went to the viewing in Jack Valenti's screening room at the Motion Picture Association. Because we were all so nervous, we sat in pockets around the room. When the movie ended, there was dead silence. Finally, Redford got up and said, "Jesus, somebody say something. You must have some reaction to it." Then there was a lot of nervous babble.

In fact, I loved the movie. I wrote Redford afterwards, sending the letter via Woodward:

> I suddenly realized that the impact of the movie as we saw it, with you and with each other, was so great and we were all so tense, that I have never told you what I thought of it. It's just extraordinary in every way.
>
> You really did what you told me you were trying to do—and I thought impossible—but you did it. It proves a lot of things that defy reason. My reasoning was that the story couldn't be laid out straight, because if you did, it would bore people. And if you had to hype it, it would hurt the paper. My other concerns for the paper and all our lives were no doubt overdrawn but real. I'm only sorry about them because I'm afraid I let them interfere with the kind of simple, direct relations I usually enjoy and value.
>
> So I want to be very sure you know that I deeply admire what you did in creating "All the President's Men."
>
> It pictures Carl and Bob almost, eerily, as I perceive them. They are tenacious, able, complex, intelligent and wise beyond their years, funny and nice. Incidentally, they have also withstood fame sensibly and decently.
>
> It really does tell people what a newspaper is like—the important thing I thought you couldn't do.
>
> . . . We are grateful for the vision you had, for all the incredi-

ble hard work, financial investment, passion for your profession, consuming attention to detail—all those things we all strive for—and most of all the love and care that makes the movie one of which we will all be proud always.

To pile one irony on another, the world premiere of the movie took place in April at the Eisenhower Theater at the Kennedy Center, next door to the Watergate, and President Ford sent me tickets for the presidential box, along with the key to the refrigerator in the box, which contained champagne for me and my guests with his compliments.

The movie's effect on us at the *Post* was electric, yet a little like a bite from the apple of discord. Maybe it wasn't just the movie but, rather, the outcome of Watergate itself. Sometimes the gods give us too much and then exact a price. I suggest this discord because the portrayals in the movie of the roles various people had played had a negative effect on several real-life relationships. The movie gave everything to Ben, largely because that made for a simpler story line and because he was played by Jason Robards, but of course that wasn't Ben's fault. Howard Simons was made quite bitter by the movie. He was poorly treated—all for the sake of clarity and simplicity. Much of what he had actually done throughout Watergate was divided up in the movie between Ben and Harry Rosenfeld. Barry Sussman was left out altogether, which must have hurt his feelings even more than mine were hurt by having been omitted. Alan Pakula later justified my exclusion by pointing out that I figured only marginally in the book as well.

Although Ben's and my relationship had been strengthened by Watergate, others were not so lucky. The relationship between Howard and Ben, which had been so generous and fruitful, was never the same again. Meg described it best later when she said: "We had had a lot of fun together. There was trust and affection among us. . . . That came apart in many complicated ways. . . . People got on each other's nerves. Everybody would claim a different reason for it. Each of us would claim we were without sin."

As a story, Watergate was in many ways a journalist's dream—although it didn't seem that way in those first months when we were so alone. But the story had all the ingredients for major drama: suspense, embattled people on both sides, right and wrong, law and order, good and bad.

Watergate—that is, all of the many illegal and improper acts that were included under that rubric—was a political scandal unlike any other. Its sheer magnitude and reach put it on a scale altogether different from past political scandals, in part because of the unparalleled involvement of so many men so close to the president and because of the large amounts of money raised, stashed, and spent in covert and illegal ways. This was indeed a new kind of corruption in government.

Even today, some people think the whole thing was a minor peccadillo, the sort of thing engaged in by lots of politicians. I believe Watergate was an unprecedented effort to subvert the political process. It was a pervasive, indiscriminate use of power and authority from an administration with a passion for secrecy and deception and an astounding lack of regard for the normal constraints of democratic politics. To my mind, the whole thing was a very real perversion of the democratic system—from firing people who were good Republicans but who might have disagreed with Nixon in the slightest, to the wiretappings, to the breaking and entering of Ellsberg's psychiatrist's office, to the myriad dirty tricks, to the attempts to discredit and curb the media. As I said in a speech at the time, "It was a conspiracy not of greed but of arrogance and fear by men who came to equate their own political well-being with the nation's very survival and security."

The role of the *Post* in all of this was simply to report the news. We set out to pursue a story that unfolded before our eyes in ways that made us as incredulous as the rest of the public. The *Post* was never out to "get" Nixon, or, as was often alleged, to "bring down the president." It always seemed to me outrageous to accuse the *Post* of pursuing the Watergate story because of the Democratic bias of the paper. A highly unusual burglary at the headquarters of a national political party is an important story, and we would have given it the same treatment regardless of which party was in power or who was running for election. I was often asked why we didn't cover Ted Kennedy's debacle at Chappaquiddick as fully as we were covering Watergate. The point is, we did, and the further point is that the Kennedys were probably as angry at us then as the Nixon administration was. Throughout Watergate, I was amazed at the regular allegations that somehow we had created the agony of Watergate by recklessly pursuing certain stories and thereby causing the turmoil that the president was in. How could anyone make this argument in light of the fact that the stories we reported turned out to be true?

In the end, Nixon was his own worst enemy. The *Post* had no enemies list; the president did. Nixon seemed to regard the *Post* as incurably liberal and ceaselessly antiadministration. In fact, the *Post* supported a great many of his policies and programs, but his paranoia, his hatred of the press, his scheming, all contributed to bringing him down—helped along by the appropriate constitutional processes, including the grand juries, courts, and Congress. Woodward and Bernstein were critical figures in seeing that the truth was eventually told, but others were at least as important: Judge Sirica; Senator Sam Ervin and the Senate Watergate Committee; Special Prosecutors Cox and Jaworski; the House Impeachment Committee under Representative Peter Rodino. The *Post* was an important part—but only a part—of the Watergate story.

My own role throughout Watergate is both easy and hard to define. Watergate no doubt was the most important occurrence in my working life, but my involvement was basically peripheral, rarely direct. For the most part I was behind-the-scenes. I was a kind of devil's advocate, asking questions all along the way—questions about whether we were being fair, factual, and accurate. I had a constant conversation with Ben and Howard, as I did with the top two editorial writers, Phil and Meg, so I was informed in general. As was my habit before Watergate, I often attended the daily morning editorial meetings, where the issues were regularly discussed and where editorial policy was formed.

What I did primarily was stand behind the editors and reporters, in whom I believed. As time went on, I did this more publicly, defending us in speeches and remarks to groups around the country—indeed, internationally as well. My larger responsibility was to the company as a whole—beyond the paper—and to our shareholders.

I have often been credited with courage for backing our editors in Watergate. The truth is that I never felt there was much choice. Courage applies when one has a choice. With Watergate, there was never *one* major decisive moment when I, or anyone, could have suggested that we stop reporting the story. Watergate unfolded gradually. By the time the story had grown to the point where the size of it dawned on us, we had already waded deeply into its stream. Once I found myself in the deepest water in the middle of the current, there was no going back.

It was an unbelievable two years of pressured existence, which diminished only a little as other publications joined us and as the separate investigations and the court cases spawned by Watergate began to confirm and amplify our reporting. When it was perfectly obvious that our existence as a company was at stake, we of course became embattled. Watergate threatened to ruin the paper. The *Post* and The Washington Post Company survived partly because of the great skill and tenacity that our reporters and editors and executives brought to bear throughout the crisis, and partly because of luck.

In fact, the role of luck was essential in Watergate—and luck was on our side. One has to recognize it and use it, but without luck the end result for us could have been very different. From the first incident of the guard finding the taped door at the Watergate building, to the police sending to the scene of the crime a beat-up-looking undercover car that was cruising in the area rather than a squad car that might have tipped off the burglars, to the sources willing—some even eager—to talk and help, we were lucky. We were lucky that the original burglary took place in Washington and was a local story. We were lucky that those under investigation compounded their own situation by further mistakes and misassessments. We were lucky we had the resources to pursue the story. We were lucky that both Woodward and Bernstein were young and single and therefore willing and able to work sixteen- and eighteen-hour days, seven days a week for months on end, at least with fewer repercussions than married men might have had. We were lucky Nixon was eccentric enough to set up a taping system in the White House, without which he might have completed his term.

We were also lucky that none of us went over the precipice under the staggering pressures. During the summer of 1973, the strain on Ben was so great—his responsibility for all the people under him, for being right, for being accurate—that his eyelid began to droop. A doctor told him it might be a serious symptom, indicating a brain tumor or an aneurysm. After ten days of torture from the suspense, it turned out to be a nervous condition. The calmer people look and act under extreme pressures, the more likely they are to pay the price with physical symptoms.

WATERGATE WAS a transforming event in the life of *The Washington Post*—as it was for many of us at the paper and throughout journalism. Anything as big as Watergate changes you, and I believe it changed not only the *Post* and me but journalism as a whole. There were both positive and negative effects.

At the *Post*, Watergate tested our whole organization: our talents, our skills, our ability to organize and mobilize resources to handle a long-term major investigation while still covering the daily news. Ultimately, Watergate showed what could be done by reporters arduously and painstakingly pursuing investigative work, by editors remaining skeptical and demanding and as dispassionate as possible under the circumstances, and by editorial writers helping to keep the questions foremost in the minds of our readers.

More important in terms of its effect, Watergate catapulted the *Post* to true national and international prominence. The paper became known throughout the world because of it. On one level, the changed image of the *Post* was flattering; on another, it was both "disturbing and distracting to getting on with other things," as I wrote Denis Hamilton of the London *Sunday Times*. The positive press we began to get was heady and head-turning stuff, but the world, fortunately, has a way of keeping one humble. If the world didn't do it, I was determined to remind all of us of the need, as I said in a letter to Carl and Bob, to keep "the demon pomposity" in control: "The sound of our own voices, while listened to by us with some awe and even some admiration, is receding. And if it isn't, there are all sorts of stark realities before us to restore balance and defy hubris."

I came to be talked about and written about more and more. I was especially bothered by being talked about as "powerful," often referred to in one headline or story or another as "The Most Powerful Woman in America," making me feel like some kind of weight-lifter or body-builder. Actually, I was amazed at this perception relating to power, and confounded by how absurd it was to be singling me out as more "powerful" than Punch Sulzberger or Bill Paley, for example, who controlled more powerful companies but were men.

I was also concerned—for the paper and for all of us, including myself—that if your profile gets up too high it will be a target. Someone or something will bring you down. Accordingly, I did only interviews that I thought were professional, and tried very hard to avoid the personal ones.

I was fairly confident that the work of *Post* reporters and editors would withstand critical scrutiny. I once said to Truman Capote that it looked as if "either I'm going to jail or they are." On the other hand, I have to admit that I was frightened. I was frightened of the power of a man and his minions, of a president who thought he had the power to wrap himself in the cloak of national security. I was frightened for the future of The Washington Post Company, and, particularly after Fritz died and I became chairman as well as publisher, my responsibilities weighed heavily on me.

Watergate also changed the way journalism and journalists are viewed, and in fact the way they work. During the Watergate affair, we—at the *Post* at least—had developed certain habits that were hard to break. John Anderson, an editorial writer, insightfully discussed this in some notes he made on the editorial page at the time:

> We had become accustomed to a high degree of tension and drama. Morning editorial conferences had become obsessive, as we went back and forth for hours over each day's events. Quickly they came to take up the entire morning, as we sat around Phil's [Geyelin] office with the papers spread out before us. The Post's triumph in Watergate is well known, but we paid a large price for it that has had little attention. When it finally ended with Nixon's resignation, life for all of us was suddenly less interesting. For a long time afterward news coverage was eccentric and spotty because half the staff, particularly young Metro reporters, were off chasing mini-scandals. It was a matter of years before we got back to consistent, orderly coverage of school boards and county councils. . . .

Young people flocked into journalism, some for good reasons and some hoping to be Woodward or Bernstein. Certainly, Watergate provided a great deal of evidence that the national media do indeed shape events. Clearly, press reports contributed to Judge Sirica's doubts about what he was hearing in his courtroom, to congressional questions, to public concern. But we don't set out to have such a major impact. No one—least of all the press itself—thinks we are free from errors and faults or completely without bias. I never once have believed that we in the press do everything right, but we try to keep our opinions confined to the editorial page.

The natural adversarial relationship between the press and the president was subverted in the case of Watergate, and that, too, affected journalism. I was somewhat alarmed by certain tendencies toward over-involvement, which I felt we should overcome as quickly as we could. The press after Watergate had to guard against the romantic tendency to picture itself in the role of a heroic and beleaguered champion, defending all virtues against overwhelming odds. Watergate had been an aberration, and I felt we couldn't look everywhere for conspiracies and cover-ups. On the other hand, I don't believe we "overcovered" Watergate, as some Nixon supporters claimed to the last.

As astounding as Watergate was to the country and the government, it underscored the crucial role of a free, able, and energetic press. We saw how much power the government has to reveal what it wants when it wants, to give the people only the authorized version of events. We re-learned the lessons of the importance of the right of a newspaper to keep its sources confidential.

The credibility of the press stood the test of time against the credibility of those who spent so much time self-righteously denying their own wrongdoing and assaulting us by assailing our performance and our motives. In a speech I made in 1970—before the Pentagon Papers and before Watergate—I said: "[T]he cheap solutions being sought by the administration will, in the long run, turn out to be very costly." Indeed, they did.

— Chapter Twenty-five —

I F I'D EVER had an inclination to let Watergate and the concomitant fame for the *Post* go to my head, management problems throughout the company generally and labor problems, particularly at the *Post*, at which I was failing dismally, kept me rooted in reality. The problems were entrenched, burdensome, and all-absorbing. I had hoped to get some real help from Paul Ignatius, but that had not happened. Paul was a thoroughly nice, well-intentioned man, but he came from a very different culture and never really learned the communications business.

When I decided that we needed a new president of the *Post*, and when we announced Paul's resignation in October 1971, I viewed it as a failure of all of us in management who had erroneously placed someone in an inappropriate position. Though I never made any major move by myself—particularly changing a top executive—and though much of the criticism I received over the years was deserved, the decisions were always publicly viewed as being *only* my mistakes. Because of the new conspicuousness of the company and the fact that I was a woman, I got overly lionized for our editorial victories and overly criticized for *correcting* my mistakes rather than for making them in the first place, both of which I resented. At that time, if a woman fired a man, everyone assumed the woman was at fault. Indeed, I was viewed—and publicly pilloried—as a difficult, whimsical, tyrannical, tempestuous woman. The man was perceived as a victim. Newspaper executives suffer from press criticism, too—at least I did.

In any case, having grown to know the industry and to have slightly more knowledge of what I was looking for, I went outside the company again and hired John Prescott as the new president of the *Post*—in effect, as the general manager. (We had upgraded the title to "president" for Paul because he had been secretary of the navy.) On paper, John looked perfectly qualified. He had had a distinguished newspaper career, starting at the *Baltimore Sun* twenty years before, and he had spent four years on the

Detroit Free Press as labor-relations manager—which was especially important for what he could bring to bear on our desperate labor situation—as well as two years at the *Miami Herald*, a well-run nonunion paper. He had also been general manager of the Knight-Ridder papers in Charlotte, North Carolina, and in Philadelphia.

Before starting work at the beginning of 1972, John visited the paper and met with the executives, after which he wrote me a fairly accurate appraisal of what he'd seen and what he felt should be done immediately. Since I was more than ready to move us off the mark, I was delighted with his action-oriented approach. I had become more and more aware of the difficulties we were in and was worried about problems on several fronts: the poor labor contracts that seemed to keep us in a straitjacket, the further disintegration of production, the constant crisis management. Getting the paper out each night, as I described it to John, was "one last minute, hair-raising rescue after another take[ing] place averting either minor or major disasters in breathtaking succession."

Despite minor problems, John started to take hold. Although I was puzzled and concerned about certain things he did, I was pleased by a great deal of what he accomplished, some of which had a lot to do with our success in the long run. Within six months, he had moved decisively on organizational changes, putting people into more appropriate slots and identifying areas of trouble—all a departure from the past. John brought in Jim Cooper, a young production expert who knew the technicalities of how the machinery worked. He had worked at the Southern Printing and Production Institute (SPPI), an organization that helped train executives to publish in case of a strike. John also brought us Larry Wallace, an able, tough labor negotiator who took the lead in beginning to turn our contracts around. And John replaced our production director with his assistant—a less astute move, but it was hard to find outsiders willing to step into our well-known hornets' nest.

With Fritz's death, one learning curve had come to an end—the first ten years of wading in, of feeling my way, responding to circumstances and problems as they arose. I didn't realize how protected I had been by Fritz. I was now alone again, but in a different way. I became chairman—it never occurred to me to change the gender of what I considered a neutral title—of the board of this growing public company, while remaining publisher of the *Post*. I was now the person with ultimate responsibility at The Washington Post Company, with all that that entailed. A whole new learning curve faced me: how to be chief executive officer of a public company with obligations to shareholders, how to apply what little I'd learned about management to the business of the company, how to maintain editorial quality while exercising financial responsibility. I felt as though I were lying on a nice bed of nails, inadequate to all of the problems I faced.

An affidavit about the hours I was putting into the job would have attested to my good intentions, but results were what I cared about. I didn't know how and when to think about growth, how the job description of a chief executive officer would read, how much profit we should be making or should be aiming to make. Perhaps my standards were unrealistically high: I was judging myself by the ease with which Phil at his best had seemed to deal with his problems, or by some other imagined ideal of what was expected of me.

Because I still had vast problems with self-confidence in public situations, I feared dealing with the industry and with Wall Street, especially the excruciating ordeal of speaking to financial analysts. Because we were a public company, if I hashed things up now the mistakes were all going to be visible. In truth, I didn't even know how much I didn't know, or the complexity of what lay before me. What I did know was that I wasn't at all sure that I could do what was going to be required of me.

Good luck was again on my side, coming just when I needed it. It was my great good fortune that about a month after Fritz's death, Warren Buffett bought into the company, beginning a whole new phase of my life. Warren's arrival not only launched me on my new learning curve but also marked the beginning of a friendship that has gone well beyond the relationship of an owner to a large stockholder.

Warren had actually made a cameo appearance in my life in 1971, when he and his business partner, Charlie Munger, came to see me about a possible partnership with them to acquire *The New Yorker* from Peter Fleischmann. The project died, and I didn't see Warren again, or even particularly remember him, until he wrote me a letter two years later. This letter is still jokingly referred to by us as the "Dear Mrs. Graham" letter.

Under SEC regulations, anyone buying as much as 5 percent of the stock in a company is required by law to notify the officers of the company about such a purchase. Warren informed me that through Berkshire Hathaway he had bought more than 230,000 shares of the Class B shares of The Washington Post Company and intended to buy more. The letter helped explain why he'd bought the stock:

> This purchase represents a sizable commitment to us—and an explicitly quantified compliment to the Post as a business enterprise and to you as its chief executive. Writing a check separates conviction from conversation. I recognize that the Post is Graham-controlled and Graham-managed. And that suits me fine.
>
> Some years back, a partnership which I managed made a significant investment in the stock of Walt Disney Productions. The stock was ridiculously cheap based upon earnings, asset values and capability of management. That alone was enough to make my

pulse quicken (and pocketbook open), but there was also an important extra dimension to the investment. In its field, Disney simply was the finest—hands down. Anything that didn't reflect his best efforts—anything that might leave the customer feeling short-changed—just wasn't acceptable to Walt Disney. He melded energetic creativity with a discipline regarding profitability, and achieved something unique in entertainment.

I feel the same way about The Washington Post. The stock is dramatically undervalued relative to the intrinsic worth of its constituent properties, although that is true of many securities in today's markets. But, the twin attraction to the undervaluation is an enterprise that has become synonymous for quality in communications. How much more satisfying it is going to be to watch an investment in the Post grow over the years than it would be to own stock in some garden variety company which, though cheap, had no sense of purpose.

I am additionally impressed by the sense of stewardship projected by your communications to fellow shareholders. They are factual, complete and interesting as you bring your established newspaper standards for integrity to the newer field of corporate reporting.

You may remember that I was in your office about two years ago with Charles Munger, discussing the New Yorker. At the time I mentioned to you that I had received my financial start delivering the Post while attending Woodrow Wilson High in the mid-1940's. Although I delivered about 400 Posts per day, my record of loyalty is slightly tarnished in that I also had the Times-Herald route (much smaller—my customers were discriminating) in the Westchester. This was perhaps the first faint sign to keenly perceptive Washingtonians that the two organizations eventually would get together.

I should mention that Berkshire Hathaway has no radio or television properties, so that we will not be a complicating factor with the FCC. Our only communications property is the ownership of Sun Newspapers of Omaha, a group of financially (but not editorially) insignificant weekly newspapers in the metropolitan Omaha area. Last month our whole organization, seventy people counting printing, went into orbit when we won a Pulitzer for our reporting on Boys Town's undisclosed wealth. Incidentally, Newsweek and Time used approximately equal space in covering the story last year, but Newsweek's reporting job was far superior.

You can see that the Post has a rather fervent fan out in

Omaha. I have hopes that, as funds become available, we will add to our holdings, at which time I will send along amended 13-D filings.

Cordially, Warren E. Buffett

I knew nothing about this man who had just bought a significant chunk of the company. Warren was the same person then that he is now, but he was a relatively small investor at the time, and mostly unknown. I knew that he had bought into the company because it fit his "rules" for investment and because our stock was so cheap: at that moment all stocks were selling below their value, thanks to a recession, and ours was selling below other stocks, since we were relatively unknown in the business world and because of the challenges to our Florida television-station licenses—and possibly, too, because of Fritz's death and my succession. But I knew nothing about Warren personally.

I also knew so little about the operations of the stock market that it took others to alarm me about an unknown investor buying such a big piece of the company. I had no idea about takeovers; I felt safe with the system we had in place of the family-controlled A shares as opposed to the B shares that Warren was buying. Warren assumed I felt safe and so didn't see the need to assuage any fears, but so great were the alarms that came from men around me and from the few business people I knew, including André Meyer, head of Lazard, that I grew concerned. Their message clearly was: "He means you no good."

I tried to find out whatever I could about this man. Research turned up only one highly flattering chapter in a book titled *Supermoney* by "Adam Smith," which was read voraciously by several of us at the *Post* shortly after Warren's letter arrived. And when I called everyone I knew who might know Warren directly or indirectly, no one I spoke to had anything but positive reactions: he had never done anything hostile, he was straight, brilliant, fine. One of Phil's major influences on me was the idea of reaching out to different kinds of people. He had encouraged me and the children to be curious about people, not to assume things about them and their motives without getting to know them. He emphasized the importance of not believing in stereotypes, not only because they don't hold true to form but because you miss so much if you allow them to dominate your responses. I followed this impulse with Warren and answered his letter telling him how totally committed I was to effective business management in our enterprises, thanking him for his confidence in us, and saying I hoped we could live up to the flattering comparison to the Disney company—a hope not exactly fulfilled.

By this time, I was curious and even nervously eager to meet him.

When I realized I would be in California that summer, I wrote him to suggest our getting together out there, since I knew he would be at his vacation house in Laguna Beach. I was going to be meeting with the *Post*'s news-service partners at the *Los Angeles Times*, and the *Times* offered us a room in which the two of us could talk. When we met in Los Angeles, Warren's very appearance surprised me. He resembled no Wall Street figure or business tycoon I'd ever met; rather, he came across as corn-fed and Midwestern, but with that extraordinary combination of qualities that has appealed to me throughout my life—brains and humor. I liked him from the start. As I later wrote a friend, "If I would ever bet on someone being Mr. Clean, it's Buffett."

At our meeting, Warren persisted in analogizing between Disney and the Post Company, because at the time it looked as if no one cared about our company. He told me he had a feeling not only that Wall Street didn't see the value of the Post Company but that even I and the group from the *Post* didn't appreciate how valuable it really was. He said that someday the market would recognize its value, although one couldn't predict when.

At that first meeting, Warren saw that I knew nothing about business and finance, and, further, that I thought people like Otis Chandler and others knew much more. He later told me he had the impression that my perception was, "There are all these 24-foot-high people around who are going to eat me alive." I didn't feel as though I knew him well, but I instinctively trusted him, and invited him with his wife to lunch both at *Newsweek* in New York and at the *Post* in Washington, as well as to my house for dinner, when he came east. He accepted, and we set a date.

I was fascinated by this man. Shortly after our meeting, I wrote to Bob Abboud, then with First National Bank in Chicago and a fellow trustee of the University of Chicago, and also one of those who had been warning me away from Warren:

> I have met the threat . . . and was conquered, unfortunately. You've got to keep warning me about how they always charm you at first. He has.
>
> Don't worry, I'm not charmed into doing things we shouldn't do. I don't want to be taken over—even by seductive corn-fed Nebraskans. But if he isn't OK, I'll eat and digest my hat—or your hat since I don't wear them any more.

There followed a getting-to-know-you period with Warren, during which we began a correspondence—always encouraging and invariably instructive—that has continued to this day. He told me that our meeting had deepened his feelings about *The Washington Post* as his "favorite investment." He consistently renewed the promise of recognition someday by the stock market, saying that he knew it must be "discouraging to management to have poured the efforts that you have into profit improvement—with terrific results and an obvious momentum which promises more to come—only to be greeted with a big yawn in the stock market. It won't be permanent."

Warren wrote me, too, about Don Graham, who had been with me in Los Angeles when Warren and I first met:

> You have one more thing going for you long range that I didn't know about when I first bought the stock. It looks to me like the Meyer genes have moved along 100% intact for three generations. Don has the makings of a first-class manager and, since he is about fifteen years younger than I, that takes care of my lifetime. Which is far enough ahead for me.

Warren's confidence in the company was obvious, since all the while he was buying more stock himself. By September 1973, he had around 410,000 shares, worth more than $9 million.

MY BIGGEST WORRIES had to do with the *Post*, where management issues and labor problems most interrelated. Production was still a mess, and the unions were at war with us about who was going to run the building, since they knew only too well the nature of our weaknesses and their strengths. Our production problems went back so many years and involved so many people and circumstances that it was difficult even to explain them, much less solve them.

Big-city papers, with only a few exceptions, were heavily unionized. We had thirteen unions at the *Post*. Different blue-collar ones dominated the "crafts"—printers, pressmen, photoengravers, stereotypers, mailers, machinists, paper-handlers, and so on. The largest of the crafts was the printers, or typesetters, represented by the International Typographical Union. Most of our labor troubles, and certainly our greatest expenses, were centered on the composing room, where the printers worked. As early as the mid-1960s, the printers had begun slowdowns, which increased in number and intensity into the early 1970s, especially at contract time. Slowing down was a belligerent action by which the printers purposely delayed the paper in any number of ways: by setting type at a snail's pace, dropping whole set pages on the floor, inserting obscene or anti-management messages in the middle of the classified ads or anywhere else, and generally conducting a kind of guerrilla warfare against the management and the editors, who had to go down to the fourth floor—the printers' turf—to make up pages. If the printers slowed down, the presses ran late and readers got their *Posts* late—sometimes very late. The slowdowns were aimed directly at our circulation, at a time of intense competition.

Because the *Post* was growing and trying to get ahead of the *Star* throughout this time, we had put up with these slowdowns to a degree that was extremely shortsighted. During the 1960s, union incomes at the *Post* had risen greatly, through wage increases and huge overtime pay, which put additional pressures on the whole collective-bargaining process.

We had negotiated an amazingly lucrative contract with the printers that included a category called "reproduce." In those days, advertising arrived from most large national advertisers already set; the paper received a kind of mat, a cylindrical cardboard from which a lead plate could be made. Unfortunately for us, however, a decades-old clause in the union contract decreed that the type had to be reset by our printers, proofed, corrected, and reprinted. Hard as it is to believe, this would happen, and then the whole redone thing would be thrown away. These pages had accumulated exponentially, since no one had the time or inclination to do this silly work. It was correctly named "reproduce" or "bogus," and was referred to as accumulating "on the hook."

Naturally the union fiercely resisted letting us set up a plan to deal with this and refused to let us buy out this "bogus," because it gave them control of the composing room and meant that we had to hire *any* printer, no matter how many, who showed up and wanted a job—on the theory that there was work to do. This was their gravy train, their guarantee of jobs forever. As long as we had reproduce on the hook waiting to be set, any printer could arrive at the *Post* and declare he was going to work for us. We could do nothing to stop the influx of unneeded typesetters and had scores of these printers who just stood around and drank or played the numbers. One man went around all day sucking an orange—full of vodka. Another regularly wore a Nazi uniform to work. Morale in the composing room was terrible, and performance was even worse. There were many printers who cared about their craft and about the *Post*, but things had clearly gotten out of hand, and putting the paper out was a vastly onerous task undertaken largely by a saint, Neil Greenwald, an assistant production manager, and a composing-room foreman, Earnie Smith, who was both tough and able but was hated by the union.

Worst of all, when the *Star* bought the *Daily News* in 1972, four hundred printers came over to the *Post*, demanding work, which they got because of the reproduce clause. Overnight we went from four hundred to eight hundred printers.

There is no question that we had run the composing room badly, but we were coming into an age when the industry was in midpassage between one technology and another. Specifically, we were in a state of transition from hot type to cold type, or photo composition. Hot-metal printing was a direct descendant of the techniques Ben Franklin had used to set *Poor Richard's Almanack* in the eighteenth century. But whereas Ben put his raised letters together one at a time, our printers used Linotype machines, a wondrous late-nineteenth-century invention now on its last legs. Hitting keys on a complex keyboard, the printer assembled letter-molds into a line of type—hot lead poured into the molds to form the line. The stories were proofread, and when corrections were needed, individual lines had to be replaced one at a time—a spectacularly labor-intensive process. As long as this system was in place, it was impossible to function during a strike, because the whole process of setting type with hot metal was so complex. The arrival of computers and photocomposition, which set type about 150 times faster than the old way, made it possible to set type automatically, thus making the whole process simpler, safer, and less costly. Now management could run production without the craft unions in case of a strike. The balance of power was shifting. It was the heavily unionized big-city papers, however, that found it the hardest to convert to cold type, because the typographical union, stronger on large papers, resisted the change, knowing what it portended for them.

So the problem of what to do about the thousands of pages of reproduce haunted us. Most of the debate about it focused on the question of whether we should eliminate the backlog by making a one-time payment to the union or by finally setting it. Of the Washington papers, the *Post* had the most substantial backlog of reproduce by far; dating from 1962, it had accumulated to more than twenty-two thousand pages. The *Star* had only 580 pages of backlog. In 1971, the three Washington newspapers—the *Post*, the *Star*, and the *Daily News*—had proposed to buy the backlog for nearly $1.7 million, the *Post* offering to pay $1.5 million of it, or nearly $70 per page. When the union turned down this offer, we actually set up a separate room to try to work through the enormous backlog, but it kept pouring in. The printers, of course, had no incentive to work through it.

Though the printers remained our principal problem and the main focus of our attention, we were having a difficult time with other unions as well. The pressmen were a tough, blue-collar union, all white (with one exception), and all male. The union had obtained overtime provisions that enabled the pressmen to get large salaries, especially when they purposely delayed the pressruns by sabotage of one sort or another—throwing tiny darts into the newsprint, breaking it, and causing delays while rewebbing the press. Sometimes they left the presses running with only a handful of men in attendance while the rest took naps, went out for drinks, or even worked at the *Star*. Yet pressmen's income at the *Post* had more than doubled in ten years, and our wage scales were the highest—or, in some crafts, next to the highest (after New York City newspapers)—in the country, with liberal fringe benefits. Overtime was a large proportion of all the wages we paid, and was growing.

Again, as with the printers, there were many good, hardworking pressmen, but the *Post*'s pressroom was overmanned, and the union had been infiltrated by thugs who had arrived from cities like Newark and New Haven and Kansas City, where the papers had been on strike and the pressmen had been replaced by nonunion people. Our contract gave the *Post* little discretion over whom we hired—so on they came. They had come to cash in on the rich provisions of our contract, and unfortunately, they began to gain control of the union.

The pressmen were led by Jim Dugan, a tough, able leader in the early days, whose sense of his power had no doubt been inflated by previous wins in contract negotiations—not to speak of the consistent small wins whenever minor altercations took place. The little deals got made by *Post* managers with union officials at the water cooler, with winks, nods, and handshakes on the side. Our record of giving in was so extensive and so bad that Dugan was always confident that the pressmen could keep what they had got from management over the years, and get still more. Our pressroom had gone from bad to worse under his strong influence and because of our weak responses. Why did we give in time and again? Because the need to get tomorrow's paper printed, not to lose competitive ground to the *Star*, was always so great. Dugan had no reason to think our weakness wouldn't last forever. Clearly we were not headed down an easy path.

The stereotypers, who cast the metal plates that fit on the presses, formed a separate blue-collar, all-white, and all-male union, and they were very concerned that their skill would no longer be needed by papers going to photocomposition or cold type, and plastic plates. The stereotypers were led by Charlie Davis, a rough, unbending character, and they aligned themselves with the pressmen, later becoming affiliated with that union.

Oddly, both Dugan and Davis were sort of friends of mine. In many ways, I think, we were misled by them—or at least I was. In walking around the building, I would talk with both of them. They could be charming, friendly, and funny, and they communicated with us much of the time. But neither Charlie Davis nor his friend Jim Dugan meant us any good.

Throughout the production areas of the *Post*, we were trying to encourage our supervisors, whose positions were complicated because they were also members of the union, to manage. The unions resisted more and more. When Jim Cooper arrived in 1972, many of the unions seemed to view his coming as an act of war on the part of management. The pressmen stopped the presses if Jim, or indeed anyone from management, entered the pressroom. Hard to believe—but true.

The Newspaper Guild had been at the paper since 1936. Its local group was the white-collar union that oversaw all the rest of the building. It was one of the largest and strongest unions in the building, representing a wide range of people from the highest-paid reporters and editors and ad salesmen down to clerks, circulation and classified personnel, programmer analysts, and people in a department then called "detail," who collected ads and brought them back and forth to be set and proofed. These subgroups, each with widely diverse interests, were all represented at the same table. Worse still, they were represented in negotiations by union executives from outside the building whose interests lay in getting the biggest settlement in the country and who, at that time, cared little about the specific concerns of people at the *Post*.

The *Post*'s unit of the guild had the highest or second-highest pay scale in the country and was confined by ridiculously restrictive rules. It was also almost impossible for us to fire someone short of proven lying, cheating, or stealing—and even then it wasn't easy. Just plain incompetence was not a valid reason, much less mediocrity or laziness. In one instance, a women's-page reporter, under time pressure to leave on vacation, plagiarized her article, lifting an entire story from a Fine Arts Commission publication. We tried to fire her, but the guild took the case to arbitration, claiming that this was a common practice. After a long hearing, we actually were able to let her go, but this example shows the lengths to which we had to go, even in the face of proven, flagrant violations. At this time the guild was led by Brian Flores, who consistently asked for—and received—big and unprecedented increases in salaries and benefits over a period of years.

On the management side, we were hopelessly bad at dealing with the guild. At one point in the fall of 1971, after the guild contract had expired, there were endless meetings at which Fritz and Paul Ignatius and I would talk with Jim Daly, who was ostensibly running the negotiations, about some far-reaching proposals he wanted to make. There were others present also, and everyone felt free to chip in and offer suggestions. The whole process had become a kind of endless free-for-all. I believe the one person not there was Larry Kennelly, the actual negotiator with the guild.

During these negotiations, we were having trouble responding to various demands for paid leaves, four-day weeks, vacations, and so on which were on the table. What followed was complex and interesting and by no means easy, despite the lighter moments. We sat for long hours in a smoke-filled room—both Fritz and Paul smoked cigars continually. Finally, because we felt that the city room was not hearing the management side of the story, we decided to enlist the help of the top editors to write a statement that could be presented to the guild stating our position. We tapped Ben and Howard, Phil Geyelin and Meg, all of whom were known to possess great authority on the news and editorial floor, as well as some knowledge of what might be the management side. We also asked them because they were our friends.

The four of them agreed, and retreated to a bar in the nearby Pick-Lee Hotel, an old-fashioned and favorite watering hole called the Old Corral. There they wrote a statement on long yellow paper, literally saturated with martinis as they labored over it, plus what Meg described as some "boilerplate stuff." The three men then asked her to type it all up, which—this being pre-liberation—she did. Single-file, they then came into the board room, where several of us were gathered, trying to work on our problems. I looked up as they filed in and could see instantly that they were all four totally plastered. As Meg remembers, I got a huge grin on my face and said, "Meg's drunk." She said the others were coming in behind her and burst out laughing, at which I said, "Jesus, they're *all* drunk." Phil Geyelin got terribly indignant and tried to sober up quickly. He handed the statement to me. I began reading it, stopped right away, thanked them for their effort, and sent them on their way.

Ben always hated contract time. The inevitable tensions and altercations often tore the city room apart and interfered with his plans for progress. Since he was focused on pushing the paper forward, he tended to get impatient with the business side, seeing these periods of tension as roadblocks to progress and the source of ill-will in the city room. When management became determined to turn things around, the leaders of the guild tried to drive a wedge between Ben and the business side of the paper. For too long my sympathies were with the editors, with whom I had always related more easily than with the business executives. As time went on and I understood the problems better, I saw that the editors had to learn to become managers, which in our earlier burst of growth they had not been asked to be and, indeed, weren't.

The only nonunion area of the *Post* was the circulation-delivery organization. There, Phil, Harry Gladstein, and Jack Patterson under him had installed distributors who handled different areas of the town and suburbs and who made more money by selling more papers. There had been repeated efforts to organize the dealers, but these had so far been successfully warded off, though there was constant background noise from a nucleus of dissident dealers trying to organize the others.

One thing I knew was that the life and future of the *Post* depended on fending off a circulation union. I knew that, in case of a strike, if we were ever able to get to the point of printing without the craft unions, we could not succeed if we had no way to distribute the paper. We knew that at the *Star*, where the Teamsters had organized the delivery trucks, incentives for carrying and distributing additional papers had been eliminated, which, of course, frustrated attempts to grow the *Star*'s circulation.

We fought hard against unionization of the dealers, but it was difficult in the face of increasing slowdowns from the printers. The dealers suffered greatly because of the lateness of papers. I frequently went out to the alley late at night and stood there talking with and listening to them while they waited for the papers. Mostly, I let them dump on me as a way of letting them know that I cared. I remember one middle-of-the-night vigil when one of the men I knew and liked, who was driving furiously out of the alley, stuck his head out of the window of his truck and said, "Well, if it isn't the Mother Superior. Come here, dear." He let me have a good piece of his mind.

FROM THE COMPOSING room to the pressroom, the *Post* was entirely out of control. After John Sweeterman left, we didn't have the strength and know-how to address labor problems at the top. Complicating things was the fact that all the Washington newspapers used to negotiate together. In dealing with the unions, John Prescott and his *Star* counterpart, Bin Lewis, had met with the union leaders and laid out the situation frankly—our costs were too high and we were headed for trouble. Bin was a decent and able man, a member of the *Star*'s enormous family, and he shrewdly let John do all the talking, so the *Post* became the focus of union hatred and attacks, leaving the *Star* less vulnerable. Prescott, Larry Wallace, and Jim Cooper were constantly harassed, or, in Jim's case, tormented by silence, since the union labeled him a "notorious strike-breaker" and fined people who spoke to him, although this silent treatment was lifted some months later, after Cooper had improved conditions in the stereotype department.

I was beside myself with worry. Night after night, the questions were: how could we get tomorrow's paper out, and how late would it be? Costs were escalating, profits diminishing, and at the same time a large part of the work force was deeply dissatisfied and hostile. Knowing we had to begin to manage, to regain control of our own production departments, I tried to consult various people about what to do. I met with Sam Kagel, my old friend from my San Francisco days, whose business it was to negotiate for unions. I also invited a labor economist from Harvard, Professor John Dunlop, to come down and meet with us to assess our situation and help develop some long-run strategy. Dunlop suggested setting up ongoing discussion groups to talk about issues of concern and interest to both sides on a continuing basis, so that when contract negotiations began, anger over secondary issues would not impinge on the bargaining of the moment. He also suggested the need for better communication generally, so I invited all the union heads to lunch with us to discuss peripheral issues—the new building, for instance.

Many theories were propounded by the so-called experts I consulted, but the basic truth was that we didn't have the thing that matters most: competent, alert managers who know what they are doing. Without that necessary ingredient, we weren't going to make much progress. While working toward improved management, I decided—with John Prescott—that we had to begin to prepare to publish in case of a strike by the production departments of the paper. Accordingly, as early as 1972 we set in motion a plan to train nonunion *Post* personnel to run certain equipment necessary to print the paper. This was not unprecedented, having been done by several other newspapers. What we were trying to do was gain some sort of parity at the bargaining table by being able to print the paper without union labor—in effect, to take a strike if we had to.

John Prescott, Ken Johnson—a young night editor who had crossed over into production—and I from the *Post*, and Jack Kauffmann and Bin Lewis of the *Star*, agreed: each paper should be prepared to publish in the fall of 1973 if a strike proved unavoidable. John then planned and implemented a training program, with Ken Johnson's help. He set up an "emergency-procedure committee" that met weekly in 1973, and sometimes twice a week. We sent several people to the training center in Oklahoma City, SPPI, where Jim Cooper had once worked. We rented a large space in suburban Washington, where we set up a course in production training.

All of this was by way of learning to walk before we could run, and it was all background to what was to happen that fall. As we entered the time of year when advertising traditionally grew to its heaviest, meaning larger papers, we also headed into the time for the usual disasters, when there were more opportunities for the composing room or the pressroom or the mailroom to hold up the papers to harass management. Slowdowns grew even more common, which meant that our distributors were waiting three and four unpaid hours, our carriers were quitting, complaints were pouring in from subscribers—and the printers and pressmen were seen flaunting their overtime paychecks in the faces of the dealers.

We had been trying to negotiate a contract with the printers, who had been slowing down more than ever. After Larry Wallace arrived, our negotiations with the ITU took on a new and firmer tone. John Prescott had recently issued a letter threatening disciplinary action, including discharges and firings, for anyone caught in a work slowdown or obstructing the printing of the paper. Things got increasingly tense and confrontational after that letter. It wasn't easy to prove a slowdown, but one of the supervisors finally did. A printer named Michael Padilla was "marking up" an ad. When, after eight hours of work, there were only two marks on his copy, he was fired. Padilla was not one of the usual troublemakers but an experienced printer who was normally okay.

This action on our part triggered a major confrontation with the union. The other printers refused to work but stayed in the composing room until the next two shifts arrived. We were then faced with a milling mass of printers, hundreds strong, none working—in fact, refusing to work until Padilla was rehired. Federal marshals were called in to evict them. Everyone left at that point in a wildcat strike, except twelve printers who were promptly arrested and held in contempt.

I was in San Francisco at a meeting when all this started but flew right home. Faced with what we considered an illegal work stoppage, we felt we had no choice but to try to produce a paper. We decided to put our "emergency procedures" to the test and to attempt to print without the unions, using our newly trained executives and exempt people.

We were all there at the *Post* on the night of November 4. It was a dramatic moment, with rumors of printers and pressmen carrying guns. Coincidentally, Warren Buffett and his wife, Susie, were right across the street from the paper, staying in the Madison Hotel, having come to town for their close-up look at The Washington Post Company and for a dinner in their honor at my house the next night. They were looking out their window all night at the commotion, the lights, and the television cameras. It wasn't a very auspicious beginning for this new stockholder to observe what was happening at *The Washington Post*.

Inside the building, we set to work, Jim Cooper and Ken Johnson in the lead, and, to all of our relief, we got through the complicated process of creating a newspaper, ending up with a forty-page photocomposed paper. As we were getting ready to print, Dugan and the other union heads were meeting. Dugan kept calling John Prescott, asking when he was going to run the presses and asking for more time, saying, "Maybe I can work on these guys." At a certain point, Prescott and Wallace were invited to meet with the unions in the Statler Hotel. This could have been when John first started waffling, because when those two returned Jim and Ken came to me and said, "John is thinking of pulling back. If he does he'll break our hearts."

The trucks were waiting patiently in the alley, so I went to John and said as firmly as I could that he was on the end of a diving board and had to go ahead and dive. Finally, John gave Dugan the hour when we would start the presses, and we carried on successfully until a self-imposed disaster ensued. In the course of walking around the building, John met Dugan and his pressmen at the back door of the *Post*. Dugan had kept careful track of our progress inside and knew we had prepared the presses and were ready to run them.

"What are you doing here?" John asked.

"Well, these are our presses," said Dugan. "If anybody's going to run the presses, we're going to run them. We want to come in."

Dugan persuaded John that the union couldn't stand the idea of strangers running "their" presses and that the men wanted to come back in to run them. John believed him and let the pressmen in. They invaded the pressroom, screaming and yelling about scabs. The terrified people—executives and advertising salesmen who had been working the presses—naturally fled at the sight of the tough pressmen, who immediately sat down and refused to let anyone run the presses. They slashed a lot of the blankets that surround the rollers on the presses and tore out all the webs, stopping the whole night's work.

John sadly said to Dugan, "You told me you were in here to operate these presses."

"Well, I lied," was Dugan's simple response.

They had us. Our whole evening's efforts were lost. In effect, we had to surrender, with only a slight face-saver. We agreed to reinstate Padilla with just a letter of reprimand in his file. Earnie Smith, our tough, devoted composing-room foreman, burst into tears when told he had to take Padilla back. In return, the pressmen eventually ran off a hundred thousand or so of the nonunion-printed paper, after the stereotypers had scratched out the first paragraph in the story describing our achievement and what we had accomplished.

We had made a serious mistake in letting the pressmen back into the pressroom, but, amazingly, they had printed a paper totally prepared by nonunion labor and cold type. The wildcat strike had taught both the unions and management quite a bit. Nevertheless, when the printers came back to work, they resumed slowdowns and production disruptions.

I went home that morning at about six, tired and depressed, and only then did I remember that I had forty people coming to a black-tie dinner that night at my house for the Buffetts. Since I had been up all night I thought of canceling, but it seemed easier to go ahead with it. Warren still recalls his introduction to Washington life, sitting between Barbara Bush and Jane Muskie.

We had scheduled a lunch at the *Post* the next day so that Warren could meet with various people on both the business and editorial sides of the paper. There was some talk of acquisitions, and someone mentioned the problem of amortization of goodwill being a disadvantage in a company like ours, because of its accounting impact. Howard Simons, always a delightful but mischievous goad, looked at me and said, "Now, Katharine, how does that amortization of goodwill work?" The conversation stopped for a second, Warren recalled, and "I could see this look on your face like he'd asked you to explain Einstein's theory of relativity with several corollaries. Here was my chance to be a hero. So I jumped in and explained in a fairly succinct way how it worked." When Warren finished his explanation, I looked at Howard and said, "Exactly."

I think this was the real beginning of my knowing how much Warren would mean to me. After lunch he and I spent an hour together, during which he offered to stop buying our stock because he perceived it was worrying me. He described his "bite" of the company as "baby teeth," but added, "If they look like wolf's fangs, I'll take them out." I didn't even know how to respond—and after some little time, I agreed I would like that. Charlie Munger, Warren's partner, had suggested he wait one more visit, but Warren was anxious not to appear as a threat, particularly since he was hoping for an invitation to join our board.

Warren wrote me a few days after the lunch, saying, "When you can obtain total participation by talented and intellectually diverse people without diluting authority—and at the same time enjoy yourself immensely—you are achieving something." With the note he sent me a box of candy from See's, another company he owned, and a memo on amortization of goodwill.

DESPITE OUR DEFEAT in the wildcat strike, which disturbed me considerably, the results were not all negative. We had finally started to address the nagging problem of the slowdowns, and we had built up our confidence about our ability to print without the unions. We knew—and they knew—that we could print. We also ran stories saying exactly what had happened, showing a new candor with our readers and the unions. Still, it remained a defeat. The unions had won a considerable victory in getting Padilla reinstated and in preventing our running the presses. Very significantly for the future, Dugan, with some reason, saw himself as the hero of the occasion and got the idea that his power was very great—that he could call the shots—because he was responsible for defeating our effort to publish. The lesson seemed to be that, if kicked hard enough, we would give in—a dangerous lesson. Dugan never stopped testing us, testing me. Later, we ran a story on unions that he considered unacceptable and he called me to say that his men wouldn't run the presses. I told Jim there was only one editor of the paper, and it was Ben Bradlee, and he'd better print what Ben edited. I must say it ended there.

The aftereffects of the twelve printers being arrested and charged for staying in the building also caused a lot of grief. There were bumper stickers all over town: "Save the Washington Post 12." I responded at great length to all of the letters I received, many of which implied that we were embarked on some sort of irrational war and that we were "uncaring." One of the printers piously suggested that we were equating money with success. I wrote him an indignant reply:

If the management of *The Washington Post* did not equate profits with success, neither of us would be here to discuss all the other

marks of success, such as the excellence of the newspaper we produce and how we produce it nor the welfare of all the people doing it. . . . [T]he paper's profit margins have come down steadily
each year since 1969 to the point where we have had to make a
concerted and determined effort to turn them around. . . .

As the months wore on into 1974, I was besieged by angry advertisers
on the one hand and unhappy, petulant union members on the other.
When we put out the company's 1973 annual report, I sent a letter to all
Post employees saying 1974 was a pivotal year for the company and that we
had "to turn the tide and begin to increase our profit margins." Some of
the employees wrote me that they found my letter offensive. In a speech
to security analysts, I mentioned a goal of around 15-percent profitability
as the norm for the paper to get back to—not a particularly lofty goal, especially since other companies routinely had profit margins of 20 percent
or more. The unions called this greedy, and people in the city room, most
of whom had little idea about business or profits in those days, posted car-
icatures of me as Justice with scales on one side weighted down with gold.
Meanwhile, the printers continued their slowdowns, and in late March
they rejected, by a vote of 740 to 18, our contract offer: guaranteed lifetime jobs in return for freedom to automate.

The guild, too, was beginning to boil up over its impending contract
negotiations. We had had some disastrous negotiations with it, some of
which had little to do with the specifics of any labor contract and more to
do with grievances of minorities and women on the staff and with feelings
of insecurity among young reporters as they competed for space in the paper and attention from their editors. Both sides approached the early-
April contract deadline with trepidation. Brian Flores had been enraged
by Larry Wallace's firm but patient method of negotiating, something
he'd never encountered before. Basically, Larry had said, "We'll give you
an economic package of $35 a week, and you decide if you want it in wages
or benefits." Flores responded, "We will not be 'packaged.'" When
we made our final proposal, which was both generous and fair at a time
of wage and price controls and high inflation, the guild's bargaining
committee didn't communicate our offer—including a cost-of-living increase—to its membership. Since Brian had the strike vote in hand, he
simply called the strike.

I was in Detroit giving a speech when the guild struck. I got back that
evening. We decided to go on publishing, again using news executives and
guild-exempt people, this time doing the writing and editing. The crafts
all stayed in and performed their duties—however reluctantly, and, in the
case of the still-negotiating printers, with worse attitudes than ever.

Quite unorthodoxly, the guild stated that it would not put up a picket line, which its leaders felt would protect the craft unions from our publishing the paper without them. Bob Levey, then head of the *Post*'s guild unit, said that "the 'absence of [editorial] excellence would be so noticeable' that it would ultimately become an economic sanction itself." I believe that the real reason the guild omitted the picket line was the fear that they would then have to stay out until the typographers settled, and this might cause a much longer strike for them.

But the guild had pulled all its members out of the building—about nine hundred employees walked out. For the duration of the strike, we—including the editors and others who were guild-exempt by reason of their jobs—filled the paper with wire-service copy and photographs, and we all wrote whatever we could. Since "Style" was the place where wire-service copy was the least available, even I wrote two stories that went in. One was about the Iranian ambassador's sister, Homa Homayoun, who was a member of Parliament. I interviewed her and pecked the story out on my typewriter. Then Meg and I together interviewed Nancy Kissinger, Henry's new bride, who had just come to town. We sat talking with her on my back terrace, and afterwards, as we started to write up our piece, neither of us could remember what she had worn, in order to describe it. Ben needed our copy quickly and came up to my office and began grabbing pages from Meg's typewriter and rushing us on. We did manage to finish it in time, and it appeared on the front page of "Style."

We all filled in in other capacities, too. The work for the exempt executives and their staffs was hard and intense and long. I spent some days taking complaints in the circulation phone room. Together with Ben, Howard, Meg, Liz Hylton, my longtime assistant, and some others, I learned to take classified ads and spent hours at it—a skill that became even more useful the following year. We were stunned at what hard work it was, with no letup. You took an ad and hung up, and the light was already on with a new caller. Electric typewriters were then used to fill in the complicated classified forms, but since my typing wasn't up to speed, I took the ads by hand and gave them to someone else to type. I tried to avoid the callers who had long, complicated ads—used-car dealers calling in to advertise several cars, for example. But one day toward the end of the strike, I got a Mercedes dealer on the phone, and everyone else was busy, so I had no choice. I told him, "Look, I'm new around here, so please go slow." We struggled through his list of six cars for sale and then he said doubtfully, "I think you'd better read it back." "All right," I said, and reread the ad swiftly and accurately. "Well," he said, "you sound overqualified. You could be anyone. You could be Katharine Graham." I was startled for a second before I replied, "As a matter of fact, I am." I later met the dealer in person, and we laughingly recalled that odd moment.

During one of our long mornings in Classified, I heard Ben ask Meg,

"When is it piss time around here?" After a pause, she replied, "I don't know. I think Wednesday."

I remember taking an ad at 9 a.m. one day from someone calling in with a pony for sale for $100. Lally's girls loved riding and occasionally came to the farm, so I called Lally and said, "I've just taken an ad for a pony for sale. Should I buy it?" "Mummy," Lally exclaimed, "have you gone mad? Where are you? What are you *doing*?"

Despite our amateur standing, we weren't all that bad at ad-taking. Phil Foisie, the foreign editor, was overheard taking one in Japanese. One of Warren Buffett's associates and friends, Bill Ruane, came down during the strike to look over the company to determine whether he, too, would invest in the *Post*. He wrote me after his visit:

> If there are those who have doubt about your determination to make profits, I only wish they were with me last evening. Your satisfaction in achieving an extra page of classified in the face of the battle you are waging proved to me that you are after the prizes Wall Street has to offer as well.

For every lighter moment in the strike, however, there was an equally dark one. In the composing room, the hostility to editors turned physical. Men there dropped large pans of metal behind the editors to make them jump and flipped the lead so it hit them on the head, all the while inserting type excruciatingly slowly while constantly looking up to ask, "What next?," using crude language in the hopes of shocking women editors. They would also replace type, so instead of "Staff Writer" a byline might read "Washington Post Staff Rat."

After two weeks of grinding work, we were all really tired. I believe there were only seventeen guild-exempt editors at the time. The paper was being put together by them and a few other exempt but not regular writers or editors, replacing the eight hundred guild members who were out and who luckily were getting tired of sitting at home unpaid. There had been a lot of talk by the guild reporters about "removing their excellence." Unfortunately for them—and for me, who cared so deeply about editorial importance and quality—their excellence was remarkably unmissed. During the guild strike, a majority of *Post* readers, according to a *Star* survey, said there was no change in the paper. Of those who noticed a change, a majority thought the *Post* was better! Despite some of the inferior material and wire-service copy with which we necessarily filled the paper, many people didn't realize the paper was on strike at all, a rude awakening for both the guild and us. The guild had genuinely thought we couldn't get the paper out without them, but we proved that we could, and we did. Editorially we had produced a paper each day—without the guild's "excellence," but a perfectly acceptable paper nevertheless. The Sunday paper on the day the strikers came back to work turned out to have the *Post*'s largest classified section ever.

The guild had sent out a letter from its chairman saying to hang tough: "Many members are saying they don't understand why the 'good old Washington Post . . .—and particularly Mrs. Graham—doesn't move to make us a fair offer. The answer is that the GOWP doesn't exist any more." He went on to urge them to ask their friends and neighbors to cancel their subscriptions to the *Post*. The guild leaders also sent letters to advertisers accusing us of being politically liberal while not providing "decent wages, hours and working conditions."

To counter this kind of propaganda, we sent our offer directly to the guild members' homes so that we could be assured that they and their spouses would know what it was we were offering. When people read it, they were furious with Flores for saying that there was no cost-of-living increase. Negotiations were resumed after the offer was sent out. Finally, on April 24, after an intense all-night bargaining session, the guild accepted—by a vote of 347 to 229—a contract not substantially different from our original offer, and agreed to return to work the next day.

We were all exhausted but happy to have the strike over and the guild returning. Every afternoon around six throughout the strike, there had been a gathering in my office for a drink before dinner, which we were serving on the ninth floor of the *Post*. As the news of this opportunity had spread, the numbers of drinkers had grown, so there was a huge gathering of relieved people on the night of the guild vote to return. Before I knew it, we had all formed a big circle in the outer office. Lou Limber, one of the great advertising executives, was Greek, and he led us in a pathetic version of the dance from the movie *Never on Sunday*, with Lou and me in the center of the circle—I with a handkerchief grasped tightly between my teeth. Knowing we had to put out one more paper, most of us finally repaired to the dining room, though a few stayed behind and carried on drinking. In the middle of dinner, Mary Lou Beatty, national editor, approached me hesitantly and said, "Mrs. Graham, I'm sorry to tell you that Buddy Humphries fell straight over into your ficus tree, which exists no more." The evening was well worth the sacrifice of the ficus tree, and Bud is still an excellent ad salesman.

Certainly there were those who resented Prescott and Wallace—and me—and the drive to make the paper profitable. Many of the young guild members were just beginning to mature at that time and had little comprehension of either management or business. To a lot of them there was something dirty about profits and something greedy about those seeking profits. They had no idea of what was needed to maintain and grow a business healthy enough to pay their substantial salaries and benefits. This attitude, encouraged by the union leaders, distressed me profoundly. What I myself saw as the underpinnings of the strike was that people were being well paid but poorly managed and poorly communicated with.

THE END OF the guild strike *was* gratifying for us, but not to be enjoyed for long. Just as it was occurring, Joe Allbritton arrived in town to buy the *Star*, striking fear in my heart. For quite a few years, the *Star* had been going downhill. As early as January 1970, a lengthy article had appeared in the *Washingtonian* magazine entitled "The Evening Star: The Good Grey Lady Is No. 2, and Not Really Trying Harder." But in April of 1974, Allbritton, the wealthy Texan known then—and now—as a brilliant dealmaker, bought the paper from Jack Kauffmann and the three families who owned it. Jack also sold him a valuable television station in Washington as well as two others in Charleston and Lynchburg. The paper, to be sure, was losing money, but the stations were immensely valuable.

Though The Washington Star Company was clearly ailing, Joe represented an infusion of vitality into our principal competitor—not to mention an equally important infusion of new money and resources with his vast wealth. Joe had brains and great charm as well. In true Southern tradition, he called on us at the *Post* right away. Although the reinvigorated competition worried me, I actually believed it was healthy. Joe was a rival to be respected and feared, but I tried to and did remain on friendly terms with him. I wrote a friend, "Joe is the best thing that could have happened. . . . I know he is able, dedicated, and decent—and that we will have lots more competition than we've had in the past."

Indeed, Joe did give us some tougher competition, at least for a while. I was so nervous about it that I would show Warren *Star* boxes on certain streets in the suburbs—more numerous to my nervous eyes than *Post* boxes. Warren often teased me about my hysterical worries. Why look at Audit Bureau of Circulation figures showing the *Post* ahead, Warren would ask, when we can worry about the number of *Star* boxes on this street?

Happily for me, Warren was more on the scene now and, far from a threat, was turning out to be a good friend and valuable adviser. He gave me added assurance about so many things that worried me, and he gave me broader vision. By the spring of 1974, Warren was sending me a constant flow of helpful memos with advice, and occasionally alerting me to problems of which I was unaware. In the beginning I didn't realize how fortunate I was to have this mentor, but I grew very dependent on his advice, and liked it. In effect, he was beginning to teach me the fundamentals of thinking about business, for which I had so longed.

Warren was always very patient with me—particularly since, as time went on, I started to call him two or three times a day, sometimes worrying him with the smallest details of my life as well as with the largest issues of the company. Nonetheless, he was invariably kind, wise, funny, and helpful. And he was always there for me.

We were getting to know each other better all the time, and we enjoyed each other's company enormously. As Warren and I started to spend more and more time together, people's eyebrows shot up, and I was young enough then for our relationship to become quite an issue. And, indeed, he was eternally interesting and fun to be with. At Glen Welby, over one weekend when he and Susie came to visit, Warren and I took long walks through the farm's fields. In crossing the back field, I inadvertently found myself nearly knee deep in a bog that had collected from the rain. Warren later sent me a Boy Scout manual with a note saying it didn't cover such advanced subjects as exactly how far one should march into a bog before reassessing one's position—"a rather severe oversight in what purports to be a definitive work."

In late June 1974, I combined an analysts' meeting in Los Angeles with a visit to Warren and Susie at their house in Laguna Beach. Warren's family was convulsed with laughter about my visit, because Warren, who theretofore had never been known to go near the water despite having vacationed in Laguna since 1962, actually bought a beach umbrella and swimsuit so as to make my visit more enjoyable. He later said this was the "source of enormous merriment in our house . . . because of this incredible—compared to what my family was used to—standard of flexibility I would show around you."

The visit was an intense and happy two days, during which he and I talked about many things, including the possibility of his coming on the board of The Washington Post Company. Earlier that year, Tom Murphy—the very able chairman of Capital Cities, a broadcasting-and-print company, then probably the best-run in the business, and a friend of Warren's—had asked why I hadn't invited Warren to be a member of the board, noting that he wanted him for his own board but that Warren was holding out to be asked by the *Post*. The very idea was like a bolt from the blue to me; it was the first clue I had that anything of the kind was on Warren's mind. I felt dense for not having understood myself that Warren wanted to be on the board, but I was unsure of how to go about it or even if it was desirable, and if it was, how it would be viewed by the other directors. My reaction reveals how truly at sea I was and how little I knew about my new job as chairman of the company.

When the issue of the board surfaced during my visit, I said I wanted it to happen but was waiting for the right time, to which Warren, uncharacteristically impatient, replied, "What *is* the right time?" It was then that

I realized I had been afraid to cross the bridge and needed to do it, so I suggested that the next meeting of the board, in September, would be a good time, and we agreed.

As Warren was driving me back to the Los Angeles airport, I told him something very important to me. I said I would welcome anything he wanted to tell me if he told me gently, but that I didn't respond well to sharp rebukes, which made me curl up in an angry retreat. So I hoped that any criticism from him would be delivered accordingly. I need not have worried. He understood me totally by then.

After the visit, I wrote him a letter that expresses the relationship we had grown into by the end of the first year of our friendship and clearly registers the beginning of Warren's direct influence on me and on the company:

> . . . I feel strangely as though we had been together several weeks—we talked so much, covered so much ground on the one hand—and on the other we laughed so much and had so much fun. To start with the latter, I loved getting to know you both in that special way that comes only with seeing people on their own terrain. Up until now, it's always been in my native habitat—I tremendously enjoyed the role change. . . .
>
> You are both so different from any two individuals I've ever known that I've been quite discombobulated until now. When Phil and I were first married, my sister asked him a series of questions—where was he born? (South Dakota), where did he grow up? (Florida and Michigan), where did he go to school? (Miami public schools and the Univ. of Fla.) "My God," she said, "you're the backbone of the country."
>
> I don't necessarily place you on the backbone, but you are such singular products of this country—you could only have happened here in all the world. It's what I love about the US of A and the life in general—the surprising, the unique, the individual.
>
> Not to get too goopy—if I have a religion it's this—the Judeo Christian civilization is founded on that sanctity of the individual. It leads to all sorts of other things—it led for beginners to democracy and to the shape of this kind of democratic society. And it led to some sort of rationale I can live with about the goal of each individual being to fulfill the unique potential within—and do it to the utmost. . . .
>
> This is what you do, Warren—or you are in the process of doing. Your intensity, concentration and drive almost scare me, but

are luckily and happily relieved by those other things you also possess—decency, gaiety, enjoyment and warmth.

So many moments occur to me as the best, but I have to come down on breakfast as the big winner. It was also strangely symbolic. The first morning everyone was on their company manners. Susie was flipping eggs around (or into the sink) as if she had never done anything else in her life. You were making excessively fake gestures about eating them—as though you rarely missed a good hearty send off to the day. Thank God we only had to go through one charade before Susie made no bones about sleep walking, you reverted to Ovaltine by the spoon and I plowed my way happily and undeterred through several courses, reciting endless biographical chapters in between slices of delicious fattening bacon. . . .

The long hours of talk started so many new trains of thought, altered some I already had and redirected others. I long to resume it in September and hope I'll be rested and renewed and have some of my own.

. . . I'm going to stop because—you won't believe it, the pilot said that to our left was Omaha, Nebraska. Okay?

Love—O Kay

In his response, Warren promised to be helpful in any way he could, which meant he would be honest with me. As he said, "If that requires criticizing how you handle q and a or anything else I will be critical—always in private and very gently."

On September 11, 1974, both Warren and Don Graham went on the board of The Washington Post Company. No two people were of more help to me over the next several years. And I needed all the help I could get. With most things regarding the business side of the company, I still felt uncomfortable, fragile, and vulnerable. Here, Warren really went to work on me. My business education began in earnest—he literally took me to business school, which was just what I needed. How lucky I was to be educated—to the extent possible—by Warren Buffett, and how many people would have given anything for the same experience. It was hard work for both of us—Warren admitted I needed what he called "a little remedial work"—but absolutely vital for me.

Warren saw that I was uncomfortable with the nomenclature and language of business. He later told me that I had a kind of "priesthood approach" to business, and seemed to feel that, if I "hadn't studied Latin and all that, I couldn't make it into the priesthood." He didn't ask me to take anything on faith, but took out his pencil and explained things clearly. He

saw that it would be helpful if we demystified a lot of what we were talking about, so he brought with him to our meetings as many annual reports
as he could carry and took me through them, describing different kinds of
businesses, illustrating his main points with real-world companies, noting
why one was a good business and another bad, teaching me specifics in the
process of imparting a great deal of his highly developed philosophy. He
told me that, whereas Otis Chandler collected antique cars, he himself
collected "antique financial statements . . . [because] just as with geogra-
phy or humans, it is interesting to take a snapshot of a business at widely
different points in time—and reflect on what factors produced change as
well as what differentiates the specific pattern of development from others
also observed."

Warren is a great teacher, and his lessons "took." I told him it seemed
really possible that I might end up "able to add"—in which case "the empire might either collapse altogether or I might really get to be the most
powerful woman in whatever-it-is. Trilby with Svengali lurking close behind. . . ." Though I didn't learn as much as I would have liked, I was coming from such a deficit of knowledge that I nevertheless learned a great
deal. Among other things, he impressed upon me that it is better to be a
bad manager of a good business than a good manager of a bad business.
Actually, what Warren favors is good managers of good businesses, but I
got his point.

One day, some weeks after we'd started on my course of study, Warren mailed me the back of an annual report from the Disney Company,
which pictured a child in a stroller at the end of a day at Disneyland, obviously completely wiped out, his head to one side, fast asleep. "This is
you after the 10th annual report," Warren had scribbled on it. I think I
was a dutiful and diligent student, but, as Warren said, "I didn't feel that
I'd hit the Mother Lode in terms of interest forever on it. It was more like
someone from a strongly religious family going to Hebrew school or
something because one felt it had to be done."

Warren's taking me under his wing was difficult for the top executives
in the company, who had their own problems and possibly were a bit intimidated by the new kid on the block—and how much attention I was
paying to him. I may have viewed Warren as Pygmalion in terms of his
having seen in me underdeveloped resources, but others, at least initially,
considered him a Rasputin trying to manipulate me, or perhaps trying to
run the company through me. There was some sexism in this attitude, too.
Tom Murphy could consult Warren and no one questioned him, but if I
consulted him, it seemed to be something threatening and sinister.

I have always had a compulsive plainspokenness, but I soon realized
that the words "Warren thinks" were pure poison. On the other hand, I
knew it was transparent that on subjects having to do with Wall Street and

finance my views had to have derived from talks with him. But the longer Warren was on the board, the more everyone grew to like him and accept him. Several other directors went to him for advice, and several became friends of his as well.

To me, Warren was a man who loved business, especially the newspaper business. He was a friend who didn't have a lot of spin to put on our relationship. He and his style were exactly what I needed. I was learning but having fun at the same time—learning and laughing, my favorite combination.

Once, on a trip he and I took together to Nebraska, he handed me a blank sheet of paper and told me to draw a map of the United States and put Omaha on it. I began bravely with Maine and got as far as Delaware, and then it started to get a little vague. However, I got my contours all down and then tried to place Nebraska inside. It looked like one of those maps of America drawn at the time of Columbus. Warren started to pocket it, but I knew better than to leave that around and grabbed it back.

On this same trip, we stopped in for a more or less spur-of-the-moment visit to the *Omaha World-Herald.* The pressure of seeing Warren and me together started such wild rumors of sale that Peter Kiewit, the owner, immediately publicized the arrangement he had already made for tying up the newspaper in a trust in order to prevent any such takeover.

I also have gotten great pleasure from Warren's partner, Charlie Munger, who came from Omaha originally, too. His voice and superficial mannerisms are amazingly like Warren's. He founded the law firm of Munger, Tolles & Olson but has spent more time as an investor and as Warren's partner. To the intense amusement of both of them, I made an enduring and pleasing impression on Charlie by solemnly taking notes, like a schoolgirl at the feet of the great professor, when I went to talk with him about investments, since, among other things, I now had the responsibility for family trusts. One of Charlie's typical bons mots is his saying that he frequently reminds Warren "that the main risk we face as we scrabble on is not going broke but going crazy."

Warren's family has always been amused at the clash of our two cultures. Our lives had progressed along almost polar-opposite lines, yet we have so much in common. In many ways, we have influenced each other deeply, although Warren's effect on my life is central to everything that followed, while mine on his is largely peripheral. Fairly early on, I wrote Charlie Munger about this mutual influence:

> Who is going to influence whom in the new association? Warren may have entered the ocean in California, but I am sitting down in Virginia with Ben Graham's beginner's book and "How to Read a Financial Report" by someone called Merrill, Lynch, Pierce,

Fenner and Smith. I am told I have to finish Ben Graham very soon because Warren is unwilling to pay the small fine involved in having the book out of the Omaha public library too long.

I believe my effect on Warren has mostly been limited to his life-style. I like to think that I had something to do with his improved eating habits, as well as his attire. Before he met me, junk foods, peanuts, ice cream, or ham sandwiches for breakfast were the norm; hamburgers and steak constituted nearly the entire range of his other tastes. Dinners at my house helped him to venture a little further afield. Warren later said, "You handled me at the dinner table like I handled you at the accounting books." We both recall with great mirth one dinner when he bravely attacked a lobster, the likes of which he'd never seen before. He did a bit better when I tactfully suggested that he turn it over and try it from the right side. He later admitted that, "but for your help, I might still have been there weeks later, trying to go through on the totally impenetrable wrong side of that sea creature." I introduced him to the possibility that a steady diet of fast food and cherry Cokes might not be the best for him, or even a steady stream of all-white shirts. I may also have influenced his spending habits to some extent. He was parsimonious in the extreme. Once, when we were together at an airport, I asked him for a dime to make a phone call. He started to walk some distance to get change for a quarter. "Warren," I exclaimed, "the quarter will do," and he sheepishly handed it over.

Beyond acquainting him with a few new foods and slightly more varied clothing, I also introduced him to a wide variety of people in journalism and government. In my early years of knowing him, I was convinced that Warren's gifts were so extraordinary that he, like my father and my husband, would eventually tire of making money and want to perform public service and be engaged in world events. In this I misjudged him. What he loves is business—thinking and reading and talking about business. He is acute about public issues, but I can't imagine him in government. Warren is only happy when he is unconstrained, totally in control of his own life, not forced to go to meetings or dinners he doesn't want to go to or see people who don't interest him or do things he doesn't enjoy.

Warren has done so many things for me, but among the most important are the inroads he has made on my insecurities. Just as Ben had always reassured me on the editorial side of the *Post*, Warren, with his store of analogies and anecdotes—"Buffettisms," I call them—and his constant bolstering, was very comforting to me. Early in our friendship I wrote him that "I didn't know when I heard from you that you had become a large holder of Washington Post stock, that although your dividends might not make you rich, my dividends in psychic income would triple." Warren not only knows business but he knows the communications business in a way that I didn't then and don't now. He never calmed me down by false optimism but, rather, by shedding the light of reality as he saw it on whatever it was that was haunting me. He was always accessible—almost like having a personal business psychiatrist.

Warren is humanly wise, too, so naturally I began to share with him things in my private life. His comments always helped. One day I called him because I had been hurt by a friend. "Don't forget," he told me, "she has zero-based affection," meaning that you always had to start from scratch, with no reservoir of goodwill or of love.

He knew me so well that he instinctively knew what might work with me. He once told me that someone in a Dale Carnegie course had said to him, "Just remember: We're not going to teach you how to keep your knees from knocking. All we're going to do is teach you to talk while your knees knock." That's what he then turned around and passed on to me: he helped me learn how to talk while my knees knocked. Warren summed up our learning relationship by suggesting that I seemed to go around as though I were seeing myself through the distorting mirrors of a carnival fun house. He saw it as his task to get me a better mirror that could eliminate the distortions. He later told me that he subscribed to Charlie Munger's "orangutan theory"—which essentially contended that, "if a smart person goes into a room with an orangutan and explains whatever his or her idea is, the orangutan just sits there eating his banana, and at the end of the conversation, the person explaining comes out smarter." Warren claimed to be my orangutan. And in a way he was. I heard myself talk when I was with him and I always got a better idea of what I was saying.

AT ABOUT THE same time that Warren came on the board, several things heated up within the company, particularly on the labor front. We had experienced a nightmare spring when the *Star* had decided to conduct separate bargaining meetings with the printers and had arrived at a separate settlement with the ITU, which was a serious break in our unity and one that very much disturbed me. Our summer had been as bad as our spring, with work stoppages and problems from both the pressmen and the printers. Negotiations with the printers had broken down in the face of many of their frivolous demands—like asking for a holiday for my birthday and then claiming we weren't bargaining in good faith if we wouldn't discuss it at the table.

Eventually, on September 22, 1974, after fourteen months of agonizing on-again, off-again tough bargaining, the *Post* and the printers finally signed a six-year contract. This was a watershed document that permitted gradual automation in the composing room and gave seven hundred *Post* printers lifetime jobs; we had the right to reduce that number through at-trition and buyouts. Most important, the contract ended the practice of reproduce, which by this time had mounted to the point where the per-page cost accrual was $84. We paid about $2.5 million to members of the union to get rid of the bogus. Ominously for the future, John Prescott reported on a conversation he had with Charlie Davis of the stereotypers' union, who said that if he had been a printer he would never have given up reproduce. The rest of us, however, were ecstatic.

It was a landmark occasion, and another essential—and giant—step forward. John Prescott deserves great credit for the final settlement with the ITU, which we had been striving for for years. It was expensive in that we had to guarantee hundreds of jobs which had no reason for existing in the first place—the New York papers had set this precedent—but it was fair to both sides. Most significantly, it got rid of the worst problem that confronted us and the worst running sore in our sides—the constant confrontations with, animosity from, and slowdowns by the printers—which in turn helped us allay the potentially disastrous discontent brewing with the circulation dealers. Most of the dealers liked our system of their being independent businesses—the system paid them well and there were healthy incentives, as long as they didn't have to cope with the problems of the long waits resulting from the slowdowns. But now the dissidents among the dealers created a new threat for us: they wanted to set their own prices for the paper. We met this danger by working out a deal that converted the dealers to an agency system, whereby they got paid for distribution of our paper, which we, not they, owned. The incentives remained good in a way that was both fair and profitable for them. This practice, too, was accepted, and the agency form of organization was actually picked up and copied by other papers.

Given these successes, it would seem as though John Prescott had a solid record, but in fact it was mixed. I continued to think that we were not making enough progress, and there was still a lack of firmness with the unions. With some reluctance, together with Larry Israel, who had been president of the company since Fritz's death, I decided that we needed a stronger hand at the helm at the *Post*. With the acquisition of the *Trenton Times*, which we had made earlier in 1974, and the hoped-for acquisition of other papers, we "promoted" John Prescott to head of the newspaper division, which we established to include our share of the *International Herald Tribune*, our newsprint manufacturer, Bowater Mersey, the news service, and our newsprint warehouse. We also brought Mark Meagher down from New York, where he had been based since mid-1970, serving the company as vice-president for finance and administration. He now became executive vice-president and general manager of the *Post*, reporting directly to me as publisher.

Our timing couldn't have been worse, coming as it did on the very day we were to ratify the new contract with the printers' union. I got a fair amount of flak over the decision about Prescott, but it was made, as always, with enough consensus from those whose judgment I trusted that I felt it was right.

So Mark Meagher took up the reins on the business side of the *Post*. What he found was ill-will throughout the building and low morale among the middle managers because of personnel changes. On the whole, the unions regarded management as incompetent yet able enough to try deviously to set them up as scapegoats for all of the problems that could more clearly be laid at management's own door.

Mark was relatively new to newspapering but learned fast and did a fine job, beginning right away to get things in better shape. He worked hard on labor issues and trusted Larry Wallace to keep a steady hand on the rudder. Larry was a first-rate negotiator, but for years he took incredible heat for being tough and fearless in bargaining sessions. Mark did very well, too, in both labor relations and in equal employment—in promoting and hiring women and minorities, and bringing a renewed vigor to the business side of the paper.

But the pressmen, particularly, were giving us a lot of problems. What it came down to was that, after years of concessions to their union, of deals made over the water cooler, of surrenderings in order to avoid a strike at all costs, we were no longer in control of our own pressroom. We knew that to move forward we had to regain control, and in order to do that, we had to eliminate some of the more excessive clauses and featherbedding that reduced productivity, tied our hands, prevented us from managing the future of the paper, and threatened the economic well-being of the *Post*. Accordingly, early in 1975, we informed the pressmen's local that in our negotiations toward a new contract we would insist on revision of those practices.

As 1975 wore on, we retrained executives in all the production processes needed if we were ever forced to publish without the craft unions. Many of those who had gone to Oklahoma City for the original training had not taken it very seriously; now we sent several people down to the *Miami Herald* to brush up on their production skills.

On September 17, Mark and I went to call on Joe Allbritton, who by then was acquainted with the lay of the land at the *Star*. We hoped he would understand the importance of sticking together for the pressmen's-union negotiations. As I put it to Joe in this meeting, if we had to settle with the pressmen, it would undoubtedly affect the *Star*'s situation in the long run. Not surprisingly, Joe turned us down, saying he could not afford to spend another fifty cents. With the *Star* losing a million dollars a month at the time, he was probably right, but it seemed shortsighted to me.

After this, I thought about our undergoing a strike while the other paper was publishing and concluded that we couldn't "win"—largely because no one ever had. If the other paper published, advertisers had a way to reach people, and the struck paper simply would wither on the vine—unless, of course, it could continue to publish. I concluded that we would be operating at such a tremendous disadvantage that we couldn't possibly take a strike at this time without endangering the paper's existence.

It certainly was a bad time for a strike. The *Star* was gaining momentum. Allbritton was a fast learner, and, as Warren Buffett recalled, a strike at the *Post* was his sole hope, really. "If you owned the *Star*," Warren suggested, "the way you were going to win was to have the *Post* shut down. If not, you were going to lose. . . . If Allbritton prayed for anything, he prayed for you not publishing for a considerable period of time, while people developed different reading habits."

In my discussions with Mark in the late summer and early fall of 1975, I told him not to get us into a situation where we risked a strike. I was clear in saying that perhaps it would be better to extend the contract for a year or make yet another short-run deal than to take a strike alone. Mark pointed out that we were not negotiating with the union over strike issues, but that we had asked our supervisors to start managing and we had to back them up with measures that would permit them to do that. We agreed to live with most of our contract rules a while longer—to settle for a single contract change or two in order to show that change was coming, but to try to avoid a strike.

Contracts with nine of the craft unions—including the pressmen, who by now had combined with the stereotypers—were all scheduled to run out on October 1, 1975. We approached that date fully expecting a tough time and long negotiations. What we got was the unexpected.

— *Chapter Twenty-six* —

VERY EARLY IN the morning of October 1, 1975, I was awakened out of a sound sleep by the loud ringing of the phone next to my bed. Groggily I looked at the clock as I reached for the phone, and was mystified. It was about 4:45 a.m. What could it mean? We had feared the midnight deadline when the contracts between *The Washington Post* and its unions were set to expire; in fact, I'd been so worried that I had returned early to Washington from meetings in Florida. I phoned Mark Meagher when I got back: Should I come to the paper? No, he replied, everything was quiet; all the executives would be there in case anything happened; there was every indication that the negotiations would continue beyond the deadline. So I went to bed thinking that, if midnight came and went with no problem, both sides would carry on with the back-and-forth bargaining.

My phone call was from Mark. The pressmen had "Pearl Harbored" us, running the presses past midnight to throw us off about their intentions, and then, at about 4:00 a.m., just before the end of the pressrun, disabling all seventy-two printing units of the nine presses. Having done severe damage in a variety of ways—including setting fire to one press and brutally beating the pressroom foreman, Jim Hover, who had come out of his office to see what was slowing the presses—the pressmen, Local 6 of the Newspaper and Graphic Communications Union, walked out, taking with them the other craft unions, and started picketing.

There was no time to think. I dressed hastily, jumped in the car without waking my driver, who lived nearby, and drove myself down quiet, dark Massachusetts Avenue to 15th Street. When I rounded the corner to the *Post*'s building, I witnessed a frightening sight: the street was ablaze with lights and action, with fire engines, police, television cameras, and hundreds of pickets massed around the building.

A policeman stood in the middle of the street blocking traffic from entering. I pulled up, explained who I was, and said that I needed to go in but hesitated to drive alone into the parking lot next door to the building. "Leave the car right there," he told me. "I'll watch it." I pulled over, got out, and began walking down the middle of the street, where the picketers saw me coming. For a moment I was worried that they would try to prevent me from entering or, worse, hurt me, but I suppose I assumed they would not hurt a woman—which later turned out not to be the case. As it was, I put my head down and plowed through the picket line into the side entrance.

Once inside, I experienced a sort of reverse drama—a quiet, empty, dark building with no one in sight. Almost all of the executives and managers had gone home at about 2:00 a.m., when everything seemed quiet, and when Larry Wallace had reported that negotiations would continue. Mark had called them to come back in, but they were upstairs conferring.

I went downstairs to look at the deserted pressroom; what I saw shocked and saddened me. Clearly there had been a riot of sorts. A foot of water covered the floor. The smell of smoke was everywhere. Ben later described the place as looking like "the engine room in a burned-out ship's hulk." I don't remember seeing a soul in the entire area, maybe a remaining fireman or two. It was eerie, standing there looking at the damage.

I went up to the seventh floor, where I found Mark and the assembling executives. Mark explained to us what had happened. When the previous night's negotiating session had ended at about 9:30, Dugan had handed Wallace a letter saying that his men were terminating the contract but were willing to continue to work under its terms "only as long as meaningful negotiations continue." Because a federal mediator had scheduled more negotiations, and because Larry had had conversations with several union representatives to the effect that the other unions were willing to forgo scheduled negotiating sessions with the company for a few days while the negotiations with the pressmen continued, both he and Mark had assumed that those negotiations would carry on. The first Mark knew that this was not to be was when Jim Hover, bleeding profusely from a head wound, walked into his office.

Our gathering in Mark's office soon after 5:00 a.m. that first day was the beginning of what turned into several months of high drama and intense challenge. I never wanted a strike and had definitely told Mark and our managers to avoid one if possible. And once it began, I agreed with Mark, who said at the very beginning, "We don't want this strike to last one second longer than is necessary." However, none of the preparations we had made for publishing in case of a brief strike (which was the most we feared) had included the possibility of trouble such as had occurred. We were stunned by having the presses so badly damaged—electrical wiring had been ripped out, essential operating parts removed, oil drained out to strip the gears, and newsprint rolls slashed—and by having almost all the craft unions in the building out on strike together.

The first thing we had to deal with was the reporters who started to come in to work, unaware of what had taken place. We set up tours of the pressroom for anyone who had come into the building through the picket lines. These tours were Ben's idea. Once he saw how extensive the destruction was and how premeditated it had been—for example, fire extinguishers tampered with, and fires then set—he was convinced that the reporters needed to see for themselves what had happened, to get the facts, so that they could make an informed choice. Most of these Newspaper Guild members were as shocked as the rest of us. That afternoon they held a boisterous meeting at which many of them criticized the damage and violence. Brian Flores and the rest of the paid hierarchy of the guild strongly urged them to support the pressmen and denied that much damage had occurred. The guild, however, in a voice vote, voted overwhelmingly against a motion to honor the picket line—except for the very small union representing those who worked in building services, the guild was the only one of the *Post*'s unions to cross the picket line. Some guild members decided to honor it, but most stayed in. The great majority of them were troubled and torn, but they were at work, for which we were grateful—although we knew that their presence was tenuous and might grow more so as time passed.

The battle of public relations started immediately. Luckily, we had hired Ted Van Dyk to take care of our PR in case of trouble, so we were able quickly to release a statement explaining what had happened and then to keep up a steady beat of bulletins throughout the strike, explaining the position of the *Post*'s management and the rationale for our actions. The pressmen's union put forth its own public-relations effort, accusing the *Post* of being responsible for the frustration of its members. Their party line was that the *Post* was outrageously trying to eliminate important clauses negotiated in previous contracts.

THE FIRST FEW days of the strike were particularly wild, punctuated by court procedures and attempts on our part to get organized. October 1 was taken up with *ad hoc* planning. All but about fifty thousand copies of Wednesday's issue of the *Post* had been printed, and those were distributed. While we were assessing the extent of the damage and whether the worst-hit presses were permanently ruined, we announced that there would be no paper the next day and had no guess as to when we would be able to resume publication, but Mark added that the editorial staff was going about its normal work and that we intended to publish soon, "somehow, somewhere."

One of our first concerns was the personal safety of those who were working and would be daily crossing the picket line. This worry led us to

seek a temporary restraining order that would restrict the pickets from violent acts, in part by limiting the number of pickets who could be outside the
building in any given period. We managed to get a court order about twenty-
four hours after the initial violence, but despite this a smoke bomb was
thrown through a window in our photo studio, and there was indiscriminate
swinging at people going in and out of the building. Kathy Sawyer, a
reporter, was struck on the head with a chunk of wood, and Vee Curtis, a
circulation manager, got punched. Unfortunately for the union, so did
Maurice Cullinane, D.C.'s chief of police, who was coming into the building in civilian dress. The police made more than twenty arrests, most of
them for disorderly conduct, but one of someone carrying a gun.

At the same time that we were addressing safety concerns, we moved
quickly to make sure we could publish as soon as possible. Someone had
previously been in touch with several small nonunion suburban papers
about printing parts of the paper in the event of a strike. By 7 a.m., we
were already on the phone to these papers to see what could be done.

On the morning of October 2, Mark and I went to see Joe Allbritton
to propose the idea that the *Star* print the *Post* on its presses, which would,
of course, have resulted in that paper's being shut down, too, in solidarity
with us. Knowing that Joe had refused to negotiate with us in the first
place, I realized that he probably wouldn't agree, but I felt I had to try. As
I assumed would happen, he refused to help us.

Meanwhile, at the *Post*, Roger Parkinson, one of Mark's young assistants, a Harvard M.B.A. newly arrived from *Newsweek*, got to work trying
to find a way to move the pages—*if* we could set them—from our building
to the outside small plants for printing. Having been in a Green Beret unit
in Vietnam, Roger thought of helicopters and had the wit to look under
"H" in the Yellow Pages, where he found a company willing to contract
for the flights. Then he turned his attention to where the helicopters
might land. The parking lot was dismissed as being too close to the picketers; the roof was chosen as being safer. Immediately, John Tancill, one of
the *Post*'s old guard, who was in charge of the building, said it was impossible—the roof wouldn't hold the weight.

When it was decided that Tancill could be proved wrong only by a test
landing on the roof, Roger swung into action, checking first with the District police, who gave us permission, and then with the White House, because of regulations forbidding flights near it. Permission was granted,
though with the stipulation that since Emperor Hirohito was in town we
couldn't fly south of K Street, just one block away from our building, which
would take us too close to the White House. Then the State Department
had to be called, because the Embassy of the Soviet Union was right behind
the *Post*'s building. State said that we couldn't do it, to which we responded
that we had to. At one point, the pressmen went to the Federal Aviation Ad-

ministration to try to stop the helicopters. I argued our case to Bill Coleman, then secretary of transportation, and the FAA stuck with us.

Once all the pieces were in place, we flew in a test helicopter. John Waits of Production ran up the stairs to the roof with the film that first night and handed it to Roger, who in turn handed it over to the pilot. We all cheered as the helicopter took off. I was on the roof, watching in amazement, and in my great excitement, realizing this would work, I hugged everyone in sight. From then on, I held my breath each time a helicopter came in or took off. I wasn't the only one frightened by the risks involved. In the early days, when we needed electricians and engineers to help us repair the presses, at least one man said that crossing the picket line was less frightening for him than being helicoptered into the building via the roof.

WE HAD MISSED one day of publishing the *Post* and didn't intend to miss any more. We had identified six plants that agreed to print the *Post*. Don, pale with fury, appeared in my office later on that second day, the very day that I had gone to see Allbritton, to say that not only was the *Star* not going to help us, but it was going to publish the name of one of the plants that would be printing our paper—almost an invitation to the picketers to start beating up people there as well. I called Joe immediately and suggested that if this was so it might get someone killed. Joe replied that he was unaware this was happening and asked who could possibly be doing it. I exploded, "I don't know, Joe, but if you can't find out who in your goddamn paper is doing it, I can't help you." This was an unneeded outburst of temper, but we were all very tense. The *Star* didn't print the name of the paper at that time; some of the plants that helped us actually revealed the fact themselves.

Working out helicopter landing sites at each of the small plants was highly complicated. Sometimes there was only a football field lit with the headlights of cars. At the other end of the process, the circulation department had to work out inconceivably complicated routes to pick up the papers at each of the plants for delivery back to Washington and its surrounding suburbs. Because different papers' production centers would get tired—they were printing their own paper as well as parts of ours—some would give up or take a break, which meant that each day our planners had to start virtually from scratch, replanning landing sites and delivery schedules.

Despite all the logistic difficulties, on October 3, with only one day of not publishing, the *Post* printed and distributed to our readers—late but nevertheless there—a limited, twenty-four-page edition of five hundred thousand that had been printed in the six small plants ringing the Washington area. It was a halting beginning, but a real and significant triumph.

Knowing that we couldn't ask these plants to print their own paper *and* ours indefinitely, we set to work to try to get our presses up and running again. To complicate matters further, the Goss Company, which made the presses we owned, was on strike, so parts were hard to obtain. I personally called the international president of the machinists' union, who was in San Francisco, where the AFL-CIO was having a national meeting, and asked him to let union machinists fix our presses. I pleaded with him that we had to fix the presses and told him that we hoped to stay with union labor but that, if the union machinists couldn't come into the building, we would have to bring in others. He remained adamant, so other newspapers—mostly nonunion, but a few union—lent us machinists, particularly electricians and engineers, to begin to repair the damage.

We hired guards to establish better security around the plant, which had the desired effect of encouraging more people to come in to work. Though more guild members came in, the guild issued a bulletin calling on both sides to resume negotiations, criticizing Larry Wallace's tactics, and appointing a three-member committee to monitor negotiations and report back to the membership in one week. The guild forbade its members to perform any work other than their own, essentially preventing members from helping us in any way; a few brave people did so anyway.

Throughout the long months of the strike, but especially in those first few wild days, there were fervent discussions, heated arguments, vituperative bulletins, and repeated meetings among guild members, with the guild officers threatening and cajoling while the members continued to vote to stay in, although the margin of votes grew increasingly narrow. Two days after that overwhelming voice vote on the first day of the strike, when the guild voted again to stay in, the vote was 244 to 186.

On October 3, I went to a meeting of publishers at the headquarters of the American Newspaper Publishers Association in Reston, Virginia. I knew they had invited Joe Allbritton and me separately to talk to the members. I gave the publishers a full account of what had happened to date and where we stood in negotiations and in continuing to publish. I took with me photographs of the pressroom, evidence of what had taken place. Basically, my fellow publishers asked me if this was the time to get together in a joint operating agreement with the *Star.* Answer: no. They also asked if I intended to go all the way, by which they meant, did I intend to "bust" the union and never let its members back? My response to this was that I didn't know how things would develop, but that we expected to publish while trying to negotiate with the union; we would do the best we could under the circumstances. I consistently refused to promise to get rid of the union, because I wasn't going to risk the paper over something we might not be able to achieve. Some of the publishers said that, if I didn't promise to go that far, they wouldn't help. I said I was sorry if that was the case, because we obviously badly needed all kinds of help, but I couldn't promise to do something that might not be possible to do. At that point, I was less focused on ultimate goals—not even being sure what our goal should be—and more resolved on getting the presses fixed and publishing the *Post* temporarily without the craft unions but from our own plant.

After I had finished my presentation and was on my way out, a good friend of mine, Frank Daniels, publisher of the *Raleigh News and Observer,* jumped in the car to keep me company on the ride back to Washington. Frank spoke with a strong Southern accent, and I'll never forget his words—or his inflection and meaning: "Watch out, sugah, they want you to bust the union." Despite the warning from Frank and the one issued at the meeting, much of the industry was extremely helpful, and several papers supported us valiantly throughout.

By Sunday, October 5, we were still publishing a clearly curtailed—and money-losing—newspaper, printed by the remote plants, which of course we were paying. On October 6, I met with those people who were still working so that I could tell them what we intended to do. The first thing I did was to address the union charges of bad-faith negotiating and "union-busting" by stating firmly my own belief in the value of unions:

> I do not expect that all our outlooks will be exactly alike. In the normal and healthy tension that exists between unions and management they could not and should not be. That tension, peacefully and lawfully expressed and peacefully and lawfully resolved in contract negotiations, is one of the great goads to the constant improvement of our paper. It keeps us moving toward a better, sounder, more stable and securer enterprise. That tension, in short, is good for all of us. It is good for The Washington Post.
>
> Because I believe this so firmly and because this conception of the value and importance of unionism has been so firmly a part of the tradition of my family and of those who have worked to make this newspaper great over the years, I hope you will bear with me while I address the general charges that have been made.
>
> We have been accused of an attempt at union-busting and of bad-faith negotiations with a view to union-busting.
>
> I realize that these accusations are often merely part of the rhetoric thrown about in a period of labor-management strain. But they happen to be charges that I take very seriously and—yes—very personally.
>
> They are false.
>
> I believe in the right to organize, to bargain, and to strike.
>
> I believe also in the right to publish.
>
> But I do not believe in the right to vandalize, frighten, de-

stroy, and assault. I do not believe in the right of any union to create conditions under which members of other unions would have been unable to work *even if a negotiated settlement had been reached.*

Some of us in this room—let us not pretend otherwise—have had our severe differences in the past over what is desirable and what is just in a contract settlement, and we shall no doubt have them in the future. But we do not disagree on this: we say no to violence, no to brute intimidation, no to the calculated destruction of other people's and other unions' opportunity to work—or even to choose whether to work.

I especially addressed guild members, saying how much I appreciated and didn't take for granted their presence in the building. I honestly felt that those who were there had made a hard choice and a brave decision. I also told them that I knew they, too, would strike if they felt the management was being unfair vis-à-vis the pressmen. I assured them that the channels of communication in our building, though imperfect, were nevertheless open, adding, "When you think we are doing something wrong, we will listen. Within our walls, as at the negotiating table, we are trying to do what is morally right and what is humanly right before we are trying to do anything else."

Mark then spoke, and he also said that we were willing to resume negotiations with the pressmen. The violence, of course, complicated the negotiations immeasurably. We sued the union for damages, and a grand jury began investigating the violence.

By that evening, one press was fixed. We had a crew ready to run it—a group of advertising executives and others, including a woman, which was quite a historic breakthrough in itself. This special press crew was led by Joe Arcaro, a much-beloved figure, who was head of retail sales. The crucial moment had arrived, but could our amateur and barely trained executives really run a press? The press looked so huge and complex and forbidding that it was almost impossible to believe it could work.

Many of us—Ben and I included—were in the pressroom that night watching to see what would happen. "Go, Joe, baby," Ben yelled out, and, incredibly but surely, the press roared into action. We printed a hundred thousand papers that very night.

The next and even greater drama took place on the platform, after the papers had made their way through the mailroom, where they'd been bundled by another crew of executives and sent down the chutes to the waiting trucks. The back platform was all lit up, and the whole alley was electric with tension and excitement. Don Graham was there to help load the first truck, which was to be driven by an extremely brave distributor, with another one riding "shotgun," in a nearly literal sense. Meg and I were both on hand, waiting and watching. There was a police car ahead of the truck, and one behind. To loud jeering from the picketers, the trucks left the alley and were escorted safely to the District line. It was an electric moment, filled with symbolism for those of us watching.

The Newspaper Guild was steadily putting out bulletins to the *Post* unit. One that first week said that many of its members were not going to work because they couldn't cross the pressmen's picket line and "because they bitterly resent management's efforts to intimidate Guild members who are still working inside the building and those who have chosen to stay out." The guild reminded its members that the situation was fluid and could change at any time. On October 7, the guild voted a third time to stay in, but this time by an even smaller margin, 270 to 251. Oddly, the pressmen actually managed to help us in our efforts to keep the guild working. Whenever we were extremely nervous, they would pull some stunt that outraged guild members and helped keep them in. One such occurred when Jules Witcover, a popular and star reporter, was beaten up as he walked to the garage to get his car, chipping his teeth and requiring several stitches close to his eye.

Also on October 7, we held our first bargaining session with the pressmen, under the auspices of the Federal Mediation and Conciliation Service. It was an all-day session that Mark characterized as "helpful and constructive." A second negotiating team, also under the supervision of Larry Wallace, was to begin meeting the next day with the machinists' and electricians' unions. In the meantime, Joe Arcaro's crew had more than doubled their output, printing over two hundred thousand papers that night. And with sixteen nonunion engineers from newspapers around the country working to repair our damaged presses, we hoped to have a second press running soon. We did so by October 9, when we ran 280,000 copies of the paper in our own plant and anticipated phasing out the use of the satellite plants as more of our presses were repaired.

Still, we estimated a daily loss of $300,000 in advertising revenues compared with our normal linage—linage that was going into the *Star.* Once the presses were fixed, we principally needed able electricians and machinists, workers with skills that were difficult to acquire by amateurs, and which our executives lacked but without which we couldn't publish.

The *Post*'s three hundred circulation dealers were absolutely instrumental in all of this, since it would have done us no good to be able to print but then not distribute. The dealers were spirited and courageous, not to mention patient and resolute—despite all kinds of violence against them personally. Within a week, we were delivering to homes and newsstands at a near-normal level. The only papers not going out in the first few weeks were the ten thousand mailed copies and those leaving town by bus, train, and airplane. For these, Jack Patterson, vice-president of circu-

lation, decided he needed help and proposed to hire outsiders. Don's naturally cautious nature made him resist this request; he felt that the pressmen might use the opportunity to smuggle someone into the building to
hurt us. After listening to Don for a while, Jack, with all his independence
and drive, ignored him and hired the outsiders.

Preparing the mailing for the large Sunday papers was time-consuming
and dirty. For that, Jack recruited volunteers. Meg, Howard, Phil Geyelin,
Liz Hylton, and I responded to his call, as did many others, and we worked
in the mailroom on Saturday nights throughout the strike, as well as on several other nights during the week. We went on duty when the presses
started to run at about 9:30 p.m. and at first didn't finish until 3:00 or 4:00
a.m. It was a tough job that left us filthy, sweaty, and covered with paste. We
had to roll up each individual paper in a brown wrapper, paste on an address
label, seal the whole thing shut, and throw the finished, wrapped package
into the big, smelly, heavy, and unwieldy canvas bags at the side of the work-
table, which we then dragged over to another station from which they were
finally hauled off to the post office. This was the only time in my life that I
regretted the substantial circulation the *Post* had outside of Washington.
The whole job was so tedious and interminable that we came to look on it
as our supreme service for the cause, the ultimate sacrifice. Warren Buffett,
who spent several Saturday nights in the mailroom with us, said it made him
rethink the price of the Sunday paper—no price was sufficient.

FOR THE FIRST ten days of the strike, we operated at an extraordinarily high level of activity and in a state of particularly high pressure. There
were constant meetings of top management. The tensions for all of us
were indescribable, and the strain on me was the worst I have ever experienced. The uncertainties, the difficulties, the violence against the people
who were working, the fear that the *Star* would use the opportunity to
turn the tables, were all overwhelming. I felt desperate and secretly wondered if I might have blown the whole thing and lost the paper. I didn't really see how we were going to manage. The only way I can describe the
extent of my anxiety is to say that I felt as if I were pregnant with a rock.
Yet, despite my inner turmoil, I had to appear calm and determined and to
come across as optimistic in order to convey that attitude to others.

One of the toughest pressures that was brought to bear on me came in
a meeting with Ed Williams and Ben, together with Mark and Don. I
know that Ed and Ben thought they had the best interests of the paper at
heart, but Ed, at least, clearly thought we were committing suicide by not
giving in to the pressmen's demands. Ed was a lawyer with superb judgment about almost everything, but I felt he didn't understand the issues in
this case, or all that lay behind the strike and how important it was that we

not give in. On top of everything else, he told us in no uncertain terms that we seemed to be operating under some delusion that we were actually putting out a paper. He said, "I read it in the car coming to work. It takes me five minutes and then I throw it on the floor. Joe Allbritton is eating your lunch. You have to give in and take the unions back."

I'm not sure what Ben's view was at that moment, except that I know he always cared above all for editorial quality, so it must have pained him to hear Ed say this about the paper he had worked so hard to build. I also know that he was worried about the people who worked for him—the reporters and editors—who remained deeply distressed. And perhaps he had been persuaded by Ed that we were wrong. But Mark, Don, and I had no doubts; we just shook our heads and said we had no choice but to go forward and carry on as best we could. The meeting with Ed and Ben bothered me because I loved and valued them, and continued to do so, but it didn't shake my conviction—or Don's or Mark's—for a minute.

One day during those particularly agonizing first few weeks, I was sitting in my office brooding when Meg came in and quickly realized how sunk I was. I knew I could discuss my real feelings with her, because I trusted her discretion, and I told her I literally thought I couldn't stand the tension; I was paralyzed with fear, and thought I might break. She said something that sounds strange, but in fact gave me comforting relief. "Don't forget, there is an alternative," Meg said. "You can give up. You are in control of that decision. And keeping that in mind can help you stay in as long as you want." Neither one of us thought this a serious alternative, but the very idea relieved my desperate sense of being trapped. Somehow, acknowledging that I had an alternative, however horrible, lessened my dread.

Another tremendously helpful friend was Warren, who arrived within the first week and came to stay with me periodically throughout the strike. He later confessed that he came almost at once because Mark Meagher and Don had realized what personal tension I was under and had suggested he come. Warren was at my house on the second Sunday morning of the strike when the *Post* was delivered. We were like two children, standing at the door, amazed to think that we had printed nearly 650,000 copies of the paper in our own plant, only about fifty thousand short of the normal press run. As an eighty-eight-page paper, it looked fairly respectable, too—although less than one-fourth of its normal size.

Our satisfaction and pride were short-lived, however, because the *Star* arrived a few minutes later, while we were still smiling, so thick with advertising that we could hardly lift it. It was 192 pages, more than twice the size of its Sunday paper on the week before the strike. "It was a whopper," Warren recalled. "There was no question about it."

In addition to being constantly supportive, Warren offered substantive advice. "Look," he said, "I'll watch it for you. If I ever think you are in danger of losing and have to give up, I'll tell you." That was a great comfort: I knew that his judgment on this, as on so much else, would be right. He was watching for what he called the "tipping point." As he later explained it, "When you're down for one day it doesn't change anything. If you're down for a year, you've lost your whole enterprise. Where in between do the lines cross?" What he was watching for was that line-crossing point. Looking back, he admitted, "You didn't come near that point where you were in serious danger of losing the company, but it's like looking for a cure for cancer; you either find the cure or you die in six months. And if you find one in the fourth month, you say there was nothing to it."

Warren told me later that he knew it was, for me, "life or death. Yet at the same time you can't look to the troops or do anything as though you aren't in control of yourself. But if you really understand the situation you know you shouldn't be in control of yourself, so you face that terrible dilemma." That expresses better than I can why, even though the pressures on me eased as we grew in capability and pages, the basic tension never receded.

Another pillar on whom I knew I could rely was Jack Patterson. He had been ill with a blood clot in his leg and was not supposed to be on his feet too long, much less lifting heavy bundles, but he was in charge of the very complex problem of delivering the papers from all the small plants, and later from the mailroom, to the waiting trucks of the distributors, in the face of all kinds of violence against the drivers, including being shot at.

My son Don also helped me—not to mention the paper—enormously. Mark Meagher bore the overall responsibility for the company's planning in the strike, and did so superbly. But, needing to look at the larger picture and having his hands more than full planning our strategy, our negotiations, and our outside public relations, he had handed to Don the very difficult job of running the paper day to day. It was a heavy obligation for Don—at the age of thirty—to have thrust on him, but he rose to the occasion magnificently, and getting his hands on the actual machinery used in putting out the paper taught him a lot.

Finally, the people inside the building working to get out the paper were heroic. However, they added to my pressures by saying, "We don't mind doing this, but don't let us down"—meaning, "Don't let the pressmen back, don't give in," as the *Post* had done too many times in the past.

By October 12, nearly two weeks into the strike, we were able to print our entire pressrun from our own plant. We now had four presses fixed, but were still printing only a forty-page daily paper. Probably because we were beginning to get back on our feet sooner than I had thought possible and to an extent that I would not have believed when I first saw the damage to the presses, I began to be more hopeful. Clearly there was progress on some fronts, however gradual. Our press crews were doing an amazing job. There were small milestones. For the October 15 paper we had replated the front page for a later edition, giving readers news about the World Series and an automobile accident President Ford had been in.

By October 16, we had gone to forty-eight pages, the most we could publish without using a kind of printing called a "collect run," which requires more people and longer pressruns. We made a big leap forward when we started running "collect." The advertising executives were on the presses and knew we were having to turn down advertising because we couldn't go up in pages. At first Don was reluctant to let them do it, because it was trickier to pull off, and even dangerous for amateur press people, but they prevailed.

By Sunday, October 19, our final edition had nine sections and 206 pages. We had eight men working in the stereotyping operation. For the October 23 paper, these eight men made nearly six hundred plates for the presses, including three replates for a story on Franco, who was ill and assumed to be dying. The usual nonstrike stereo staff consisted of forty people.

Other than meeting constantly with Mark and Don and others to assess how we were doing, I spent most of my time working at various jobs in the classified department, taking circulation complaints, and keeping up in the mailroom. Many women were working in the reel room, making the "flying pasters" that permit newspaper presses to keep running when one of the huge newsprint rolls runs out. This, as we said at the time, was very likely "the first time in modern newspaper history that women have been in this job." If you didn't prepare the new roll just right, the paper tore and stopped the press automatically. The process required a great deal of dexterity, and I was leery of the responsibility for breaking the web, which was extremely onerous to reweave. To my shame, I was unskilled enough to be reduced at times to picking up accumulated trash. But on the whole we were growing really proficient at all our additional jobs, and the process of putting out the paper was getting more predictable.

Over the months we settled into a certain routine, more or less holed up in the building, with many people camped out, essentially living in their offices. Morale was high—especially in the first weeks, long before we ever thought the strike might stretch on as it did—and we did whatever we could to keep it that way. We served food on the ninth floor three times a day. After the pressrun at night, we also had food and light drinks available, and there was always a large gathering at which those who had produced the paper could get rehabilitated. The hired caterers, as part of their normal operation, wore black-tie uniforms at night, and it introduced a note of incongruity when they appeared amid the din and confusion of the pressroom with juice and milk and sandwiches.

Upstairs, we had a piano, and several people played. Jake Lester, one of the electricians, often played his banjo while people sang along. Whatever entertainment we had was a way to release all the tension, but the *Star's* gossip columnist attacked us savagely, accusing me of entertaining strikebreakers with music and waiters serving gourmet food. I deeply resented people who didn't understand what we were going through or how much people were sacrificing to get the paper out. Staying in the building was no picnic. Conditions were difficult and exhausting. Every person was doing at least two jobs: his or her own regular job during the day, plus helping to put out the paper at night. Spouses were under great strain trying to make do at home alone—and often receiving threatening phone calls. Those living at the *Post* rarely saw their husbands or wives or children. Some shaky marriages broke under the strain of having people live in the building, and—it has to be admitted—some romances started there as well.

Many people came and went in their efforts to help us. My brother, Bill, more or less moved into the Madison Hotel across the street from the paper and worked at various jobs around the building, as did his daughter Ruth and her husband. Lally came down from New York with my granddaughter Katharine, then nine years old, who stood on a box one Saturday night in the mailroom, helping to wrap papers.

But though certain activities had settled into a kind of routine, the worries remained constant. One of the biggest was whether we could keep the guild working. The guild leaders attacked us for a statement I had made earlier that the company's profits should rise to 15 percent, pointing out that we were the area's largest business and Washington's only corporation in the Fortune 500. Brian Flores called the company a "wealthy conglomerate." They kept up a steady drumbeat on their members, trying to get them to honor the picket line. Only a handful of guild members had gone out for reasons I respected. One was John Hanrahan, a good reporter and a nice man who came from a longtime labor family and simply couldn't cross a picket line. He never did come back. Living your beliefs is a rare virtue and greatly to be admired. As for most of the other guild members who didn't work during the strike, I must confess that I would have been happy to see them never come back.

Flores said that the guild would attempt to fine all its members who crossed the picket line 125 percent of everything they earned during the strike, and he threatened to expel those who had—this at a time when a majority of his union members repeatedly voted not to honor the picket line. The guild leaders worked hard to influence various organizations around the city toward its position. For example, Flores sent a telegram to the Washington Redskins urging the players not to talk with *Post* reporters—with notable lack of success.

Flores also attacked me personally. In a citywide bulletin issued on the day I was to receive the Profiles in Courage Award (for the *Post*'s reporting of Watergate) from the John F. Kennedy Lodge of B'nai B'rith in Chevy Chase, Maryland, he said, "One can't help but feel that any portrait of Kennedy should be turned to the wall while an award is presented to the commander of the forces which seek to wipe out labor unions at *The Washington Post*," adding, "Enjoy your dinner, Ms. Graham, while 2,000 of your employees are on strike or honoring picket lines. They too have the courage to fight for what they believe in and back it up with great personal sacrifice for them and their families. If JFK were alive I am sure he would rather have dinner with them than you."

At the same time, he stepped up the pressure on guild members inside the building to come out, which, indeed, five members of the foreign desk agreed to do. Other guild members, however, actually resigned from the guild to protest the position the guild's executive board took toward the strike.

The pressmen, too, stepped up their attacks, including personal ones on me. In one flyer they circulated toward the end of October, titled "*The Washington Post* Cover-up," they said that the owners of the *Post* hoped to "get away with the biggest cover-up this town has seen since Watergate." I was accused of having hired Larry Wallace, whom they tried to depict throughout the strike as some sort of union-buster and described as "fresh from his vicious attack on the workers at the *Detroit Free Press*." They alleged that he then presented me with a Gordon "Liddy-like plan to destroy *The Post*'s unions," which I, according to them, had approved.

We also worried about the constant threat of violence. At one point, three holes were made in the fifth-floor glass windows of several editorial offices, evidently caused by a powerful air gun firing metal pellets. Roughness on the picket line became habitual. Many people who drove their cars to work found them with flat tires caused by nails and large tacks spread across the alley entrance. Others were followed to their cars and harassed. Finally, with the idea of safety in numbers, we began to use a large van to transport people to other locations throughout the city where they could pick up their cars or get a bus. Spouses were regularly called and threatened violently and obscenely. One employee's wife was actually told, "We're going to kill you and the baby if we see you on the street." An older woman, a union-exempt employee, was told that she had better sleep with her eyes open, and, on another occasion, that she was going to have her head blown off. Once when Jimmy, my driver, was at the wheel of my car, several picketers stopped the car as we were crossing the line and rocked it back and forth.

The pressmen also increased their efforts on other fronts, including picketing our advertisers, for which we filed an unfair-labor-practice charge alleging a secondary boycott. Among the other negative things the union was doing were passing out handbills for a consumers' boycott and trashing the stores of advertisers by dumping goods off shelves. In one case, several striking pressmen poured oil into a store's fish tank, killing all the fish.

In addition to the constant threat, if not reality, of violence, we had several other worries as the strike dragged on into November. The city room began to get even more edgy. Many reporters were suffering deeply from pangs about crossing the picket line. I received two communications then from guild members who were still working. One, addressed to both Larry Wallace and me, was signed by forty-one people. They were writing to ensure that their presence in the building wasn't taken as blanket approval of the *Post* management's conduct of its labor relations and demanding reassurance that we were continuing to bargain "in good faith." I assured them that we were, and that we wanted all the unions back with the exception of those pressmen who had engaged in the violence.

A few days later, another letter arrived, from about eighty members of the *Post* unit of the guild. This letter included twenty specific questions to which they wanted answers. They acknowledged the damage done to the pressroom but pointed out that this issue was now in the legal justice system. The signers felt that, more than a month having passed since the beginning of the strike, there should have been further signs that the company was acting to settle the dispute. They added:

> ... we have subjected ourselves to punitive action by our own union and possibly split our ranks beyond repair.... While you may choose to think kindly of us when Guild negotiations come up next year, we would prefer not to have to rely on your benevolence but to go into contract negotiations as a strong union. ...
>
> Your response to the following questions will help us make up our minds. It is our feeling that through your response you may make a demonstration of good faith that would help rebuild the crumbling management-labor relationship at the Post.

Obviously my replies were going to be extremely important. The answers to the twenty questions were drafted and worked over at great length by Don, Meg, and me. From my point of view, some of the questions were irrelevant and silly—such as the reason for the amount of severance paid to Paul Ignatius when he left in 1971. Even so, this was a good chance for us to communicate our views. One important statement was this:

There is one crucial aspect of all this, however, that your letter leads me to believe you have failed to take into account. It is that the violence, both in the pressroom last month and in various episodes since, has profoundly altered and complicated our good faith search for a settlement. Before October 1, we had the luxury of being able to seek a gradual, phased solution to the problems in the pressroom. . . .

When I say we do not have the luxury now, I mean that it would in my judgment be the ultimate act of irresponsibility on our part to permit the pressmen to return under the old conditions. I could not myself in good faith preside over a building or an enterprise in which people who had worked faithfully and to the point of exhaustion for the company were in continuing physical danger from fellow employees, in which those who control a whole section of our building while those who had worked to repair the damage to the company and to get the paper out had to be transferred elsewhere to get them out of harm's way, in which hiring and manning practices permitted not just the same kind of featherbedding, but also the same importation of men likely to commit the same kinds of violence should they be crossed. The pressmen in the early morning hours of October 1 made it impossible for us to set it as some future desirable goal that we should be allowed to have management supervisors present in the pressroom. . . .

We need a contract that is fair to our pressmen; we also need a contract that is fair to us. I would deceive you if I said this result would be easy to achieve or that it is a sure thing that it can be achieved at all. But we are trying. I want you to understand that.

I went on to answer each of the long technical questions: how the pressmen would be paid, what the *Post*'s new position on collective bargaining was, why I had set a profit goal of 15 percent, why we had trained management employees to operate the presses in the first place, why we let guild people help us, whether we were leaning on other publishers to get the pressmen blacklisted, what our position was toward indicted or convicted pressmen. We finally got our responses completed and sent our answers out, as well as posting them around the building on bulletin boards, where clusters of people immediately gathered to read them. One reader was overheard to murmur, "There is one question missing." When asked what it was, he replied, "Mrs. Graham, how is your sex life?"

Guild members who were not working met together outside the building and called themselves the "rank and file strike support committee." They issued at least fourteen pamphlets during the weeks of the strike, trying to get the *Post*'s other guild members to come out with them. It seemed particularly ironic that we were questioned about whether we were negotiating in good faith but that they never asked the pressmen the same question.

THE *Star*, understandably, took every advantage there was to take. At one point, we learned that some of the pressmen who ordinarily worked at the *Post*—possibly as many as forty—were working at the *Star*. It didn't make us feel better when we heard that the pressmen's union said that most of the money these men earned there was being contributed to a central strike fund.

Yet, despite all that our competition was doing, we overtook the *Star*—at least in terms of pages published—on October 23, only three weeks after the strike began, and during the last week in October the *Post* became profitable again for the first time since October 1, a remarkable accomplishment. But also by the end of the month, the *Star* had gained $2 million in revenue over the year before and was up in advertising by two million lines—much had poured into the *Star* because the *Post* couldn't print it. The *Star* ran in the black that October for the first time in sixty months. Its operating losses, according to an article in the *Post* at the time, had been running at a rate of nearly $1 million a month, so its advertising increase was certainly helping to offset the losses. We knew that the *Star*, despite its current surplus of revenues over expenses, had a more than $20-million debt, but we also knew that Joe Allbritton had deep pockets.

I felt we were being lambasted in the press for being Goliath to the brave little David, partly through what I thought were stories planted by our competition. I certainly believed that the *Star* was doing everything it could to hurt us. Nevertheless, because we had to live together in the same town—and, in fact, had helped each other in many ways over the last forty-plus years of my family's ownership—I also believed in maintaining civil relations. Consequently, on December 3, I rushed back from New York, where I'd been for an ANPA meeting, to attend a reception at the Mayflower in honor of Joe Allbritton. I made the effort to go through the receiving line and tried to say something nice to Joe. However, on my way out, my breath was literally taken away when someone showed me a cartoon being circulated around the party. It was drawn by Oliphant, the *Star*'s cartoonist at the time, and used the famous Mitchell quote to depict me brutally with my breast caught and drawn out at length in a wringer, this one from a press. I found it terribly wounding, said nothing, and left.

One group or another started leaning on us to "be reasonable." In mid-November, Mark, Don, Larry Wallace, and I went up to Capitol Hill to meet with the local members of the House whose constituents were most affected. These representatives, two from Maryland and two from Virginia, and Walter Fauntroy from the District, wanted to offer their services to find out what the strike was about, and to step in. When they found out that the pressmen's union was all-male and all-white (the one black pressman had been hurt and left the paper before the strike), their enthusiasm for supporting the union subsided somewhat.

I ran into Arthur Goldberg, the windy, prolabor "expert," at the home of a prominent civic leader in Washington, at one of the few dinners I attended during the strike. He assured me that in a strike everyone had to give and that it had to be settled; he had arbitrated an airline strike and would be glad to step into ours. I responded rather sharply that we were doing fine, and I saw no need for his intervention then or ever.

Other worries abounded. Though the paper was growing and we were printing from our own plant, fourteen of our circulation "route dealers" filed a class-action suit against us, complaining about our transition from independent contractors to an "agency system" of distribution. The Maryland attorney general's office launched an antitrust investigation of the paper.

The strike had occurred just four years after we had gone public, and we were still a relatively small company. Pending the outcome of the strike, industry analysts were withholding their assessments of our financial performance as a company—at best—or, at worst, reducing their estimates of our per-share earnings for the year, which clearly affected stock purchases. Larry Israel, Mark Meagher, and I told a New York financial analysts' meeting that the strike would cause the first earnings drop we had experienced since we'd gone public.

TIME WAS AN odd factor throughout the strike. If someone had told me at the beginning that four and a half months later we would still be working at our regular jobs while helping out in departments everywhere in the building to produce a daily paper, I wouldn't have believed it. I would not have thought we could endure. Sometimes it's better not to know. I remember the first time I heard someone mention Thanksgiving; my immediate thought was, "That's impossible; we can't still be here by Thanksgiving, doing what we're doing under this strain and uncertainty." But Thanksgiving came and went, and the first time someone mentioned Christmas, I thought the same thing.

As we began to experience more and more success and to settle into the routine reality of putting out the ever-growing paper, the early euphoria diminished, a process helped along by fatigue and even boredom, both of which contributed to an erosion of spirits and morale. One editor on the presses said he began to understand what blue-collar workers felt like, constantly performing a tedious and thankless yet difficult job while the white-collar executives upstairs made decisions that affected their lives and their work.

Although the pressure did decrease a bit as we became more successful, there was still no way to tell when it would all end and how it would turn out, so the anxiety and the grinding quality of life remained. I worried incessantly that the total exhaustion of our small work force—particularly because it was getting harder to obtain the extra help we were using in small but essential quantities—would force us to give up in the end.

Certain industry friends, especially Frank Batten, chairman of the private Landmark Communications Company, and Stan Cook of the *Chicago Tribune*, came in periodically to talk the situation over with me. I remember Stan encouraging me to stay the course: "You just have to keep up the steady pressure, like leaning on a gate to gradually shut it."

And despite everything there actually were some lighter moments. Phil Geyelin sent me a note in early December saying that he was so pleased that Natalie Panetti—the manager of employee services for the *Post*, who had become the *de facto* assigner of jobs—had just informed him that, in addition to his regular duties on B press, he had been designated an Assistant Supervisor of Stuffers. His note said, "This is just to tell you how honored I am by this assignment and the expression it conveys of your confidence and trust in me. Upward mobility is the hallmark of a great newspaper. I will do my darndest to be worthy of this latest opportunity you have provided me to serve you in new and interesting ways."

As time wore on for those of us doing the dirty and seemingly interminable tasks in the mailroom, in order to divert ourselves from the tedium, we started writing notes to people on the front page. I believe it is illegal to write notes on second-class mail, but that didn't occur to us—or, if it did, we didn't care—as we scribbled away to whatever name turned up who might be a friend or even an acquaintance. Who knows what these people thought when they got their Sunday *Post* along with a message: "Help, I'm a prisoner in *The Washington Post* mailroom."

Through all this time, of course, negotiations with the pressmen's union were continuing. From the beginning, as Mark said, we were willing to maintain their high incomes, even counting the overtime they had earned in the past due to absurd work rules, but what we wanted was to bring under control those featherbedding practices that were severely affecting our capacity to produce a quality paper. In short, as Larry Wallace summarized, we were trying, through collective bargaining, "to regain some measure of control over the operation of the pressroom in order that there will be a more efficient, more productive, less costly and less wasteful operation."

Our earlier offer was on the table, and at one point in mid-November

a meeting was set at which the pressmen were scheduled to make a coun-
terproposal. When the session convened, they said they had changed their
minds and would not produce one. We were astonished, since by this time
we were publishing marginally profitable newspapers and were surprised
that the pressmen still seemed to think that no movement on their part
was required. Talks were recessed until the mediation service believed
they could be useful. In the meantime, we tried to negotiate with the other
unions, but they gave precedence to a settlement between us and the
pressmen, so we were stalemated.

During this period, those who had been charged with the violence and
damage in the beginning of the strike were called before a grand jury.
Every one of them pleaded the Fifth Amendment, as did Dugan, who said
he had no personal knowledge of the violence in the pressroom. From the
beginning, he claimed that the riot was unplanned, "a simple emotional
outburst by craftsmen who felt frustrated and were overwrought." Prosecutors were considering granting selective immunity in exchange for information and threatened to prosecute the pressmen for contempt if they
continued to refuse to testify.

We were now in December, with virtually no movement, although we
had put forth another offer which the pressmen had ignored. The strike
had been going on for nine weeks, during which we had made several offers of generous benefits and certain job guarantees and securities in exchange for modification of unacceptable work practices. Finally, the
pressmen made their first offer—orally, not in writing—proposing only
one minor change in work practices, for which they asked an additional
$37 a week. Obviously we were still far apart.

The next day, December 4, was important because we made a final offer. To keep the whole thing from dragging on, we had decided to make
what Mark called "the comprehensive, definitive and final settlement offer." This was an offer that I believe was generous. A pressman's base pay
would have gone immediately to $17,318.60, higher than that of any
pressman at any other newspaper in the United States at that time. It gave
pressmen the opportunity to earn as much as the then-current average in
the pressroom by working more reasonable hours (only five days a week),
and more if they chose reasonable overtime. The contract would have
ended the practice of back-to-back shifts. We promised job security
and noted that any de-escalation in manning the presses would be by at-
trition, not through firings. There were other add-ons—overtime, holiday bonuses, and a $400,000 package to divide up. It was an offer the
pressmen could have accepted—and would have done well to—and one
that we could live with, which the final offer had to be.

There was a secret meeting on the eve of the final contract offer, but
nothing happened. Dugan, as usual, was both arrogant and personal. He

called Mark Meagher and Larry Wallace liars and told them to "tell Katharine Graham . . . to take her contract proposal and shove it."

We had warned the union—it wasn't a threat or a ploy—that we thought this offer was the best we could come forward with. We re-emphasized, as we had steadfastly maintained throughout, that we considered the return to work of those pressmen who caused the destruction in our pressroom nonnegotiable and outside the bargaining process. Local 6 voted 249 to 5 to reject our offer.

Why didn't the pressmen accept the contract? I'm sure there are as many answers as there were individual pressmen. Perhaps they were holding out, hoping we would cave in—and remembering that we always had. Jim Dugan himself was certainly a factor, as was Charlie Davis of the stereotypers, Dugan's first henchman. Dugan had always been an able leader, but had undoubtedly gotten an inflated ego from his perceived victory over John Prescott the night of the wildcat strike in 1973. He seemed to believe that he was the strong man in the building and could always make management back down in the end. He projected the attitude that he was going to fix us, to show the management of The Washington Post Company who was really in charge. Not only would there be no concessions but, in fact, he was out to make further gains. From this the union never wavered, through the entire strike. To some extent Dugan was a prisoner—of his power and successful past and of the people who did the damage. He had to ask us to take back the men who damaged our presses. We steadfastly refused.

After the overwhelming turndown of our final offer by the union, it was a question of when, not if, to announce that we would start hiring replacement workers. This was the most sensitive and frightening moment of the whole strike. I had no idea what the reaction might be on the part of the guild, the pressmen, or the many strikers. We talked about the upcoming guild meeting and whether we should tempt fate by making our announcement just before or waiting until just after. But there was no perfect moment. Finally, Mark made the decision to move ahead as quickly as possible and set the date for the eve of a guild meeting, which worried me considerably but which proved to be a wise and gutsy judgment.

Three days after the pressmen's union's rejection of our final offer, December 10, Mark and I walked down to the fifth-floor newsroom, the biggest available place, to a meeting of all those still working. There I announced our intention to hire replacement workers, outlining our attempt to negotiate the terms of the final offer. I then described the alternative to not hiring new pressmen as the continued publication of the paper by an already exhausted crew for who knew how many months, emphasizing that, based on past patterns, there was no indication that ten more weeks—or even ten more months—of bargaining would change any attitudes. Continuing to negotiate seemed likely to lead only to more sterile debate, and, as I said to someone at the time, "unjustified hopes and added delay in reaching settlements with the other unions. The truth is that as far as the pressmen are concerned, it is just too late."

I told those gathered in the newsroom that members of Local 6 were being informed by letter that, if our contract offer was not approved by midnight of the next Sunday (four days later), we would begin hiring permanent replacements. I added that the pressmen as individuals—with the exception of those who had been known to participate in the violence— could return to their jobs in the pressroom. I also tried to speak directly to members of the other craft unions, emphasizing that we wanted to reach agreements as speedily as possible with all those unions whose contracts had expired on September 30.

I knew this action was legal but, as I told those gathered there that morning, it was more important for me to think about whether it was humanly right. In the end, I said to the gathering:

> Like the decisions made by each of you who continued to work in the strike, my decision was neither simple nor easy; and like your decisions it required me to weigh the claims of a variety of responsibilities. My conclusion is that I cannot in conscience permit a situation to continue in which men and women in our trade unions, many of whom have worked here for many years, are faced with a bleak future because they must honor the picket lines of a group of men who are the highest-paid craft union workers in the building. These members of our other unions have already forfeited many hundreds of thousands of dollars in wages for the sake of striking pressmen who continue to draw pay for their work at other newspapers . . . who created this situation by their irresponsible and violent acts . . . and who have rejected out of hand an offer which would have made them the best paid and most financially secure members of their craft working at any paper in this country.

I concluded by saying:

> It is a sober moment for this place and for all of us. The consequences of what we have been forced to do have been thought about hard. I believe we have done what is responsible and right— for the paper, for the 2000 union people who work here, for the honor of the institution itself and for the community we serve.

My statement was greeted by tense silence. Mark followed up. The two of us took a few questions and then left. The next day, the *Post* ran a full-page open letter from Mark, titled "Why *The Washington Post* Has Taken Action to End the Strike and Return to Normal Operations," which was Ted Van Dyk's work. We also ran an ad in the classified section of the paper for "Immediate Openings" for "Experienced or Inexperienced" production personnel for the pressroom. To our amazement, early the next morning there were about seven hundred people lined up in front of the building to be interviewed. In the end, we had a thousand applicants, from whom we hired very carefully, and at first very slowly, a cross-section of people right off the street and some who had worked at the paper during the strike. Our first hire was a black man who had stood on the line in silver platform shoes dressed in a long fur coat. One of the first of the new "pressmen" was Diane Elmore (now Patterson), formerly from advertising sales, who had worked on the presses throughout the strike, liking it so much that she chose to switch jobs. She is now an assistant superintendent for the mailroom at our Springfield plant. There were several Vietnamese men who had worked around the building in various temporary capacities who were hired and became star performers.

One of the fine things Jim Cooper had done was to meet at my farm in Virginia with six of the pressroom supervisors who were union members, inviting them to return to work. They agreed to come back in, which they did only after we went to impasse and had started hiring, and eventually helped with training the new people. Their return was a great step forward for us but a difficult one for them; they were all visibly shaken, pale, and frightened in their first days back on the job.

We brought in two people to begin training our new pressmen in a rigorous two-week training program. We had to lower our standards a little to go faster, but we found such highly motivated and qualified people that they rose rapidly through the ranks. I had been concerned that there would be violent confrontations between the pickets and the applicants. To my surprise there were none. "You might have had two hundred press operators picketing out there who were fearful for their jobs," recalled Jim Cooper later, "but you had seven hundred people—many of whom were black—out there hoping for jobs that blacks hadn't even been allowed to think about. It would have taken a very stupid person to try to oppose them."

Pressures rose on us after the announcement about hiring. Mark, Don, and I were called to go before the D.C. City Council to answer questions. Dugan had asked for a meeting with the council and had actually said, "I used to live in D.C., for whatever that's worth," to which Council Chairman Sterling Tucker had said, "That's not worth anything." Again the racial issue helped counteract the general pro-union sympathy,

With Truman Capote at the
"Black and White Ball"

In *Vogue* magazine: story by
Arthur Schlesinger, Jr.,
photograph by Cecil Beaton

Katharine Graham
New Power in the American Press

BY ARTHUR SCHLESINGER, JR.

N o one has been more astonished by her own emergence as a personality in Washington, New York, and London than Katharine Meyer Graham. She had always been a member of the supporting cast. Now circumstances have thrust her into the lead. She not only plays it well, but she is beginning to enjoy it.

Kay Graham spent most of her life as the daughter of two powerful figures and the wife of a third. Her father, Eugene Meyer, was a bold and successful banker who served from time to time as a government official and in the early thirties acquired *The Washington Post*. Her mother, Agnes Ernst Meyer, has long been a force in public affairs, bearing down like a galleon in full sail, all guns firing, on the enemies of education or civil rights or free speech. They were a formidable couple—Eugene Meyer, emphatic and imperious; Agnes Meyer, copious and volcanic.

Kay grew up in a Washington household awash with public personalities. She went on to Vassar, which she found a little pretentious and self-involved, and happily finished college in the hard-working anonymity of the University of Chicago. After a year on a newspaper in San Francisco, she returned to Washington and a job on the *Post*. It was 1939, in the sixth year of Franklin Roosevelt, and the town overflowed with brilliant young men. One of the most brilliant of all was Philip Graham, a young Floridian who had just come down from the Harvard Law School to become law clerk to Mr. Justice Frankfurter. He was a man of penetrating charm, restless energy, and dazzling intelligence, and Kay Meyer, after a fling as a belle of the later New Deal, married him in June, 1940.

Then the war: and, when Phil Graham arrived back from the Pacific in 1945, Eugene Meyer asked him to take over the *Post*. In the next fifteen years Graham made the *Post* the centre of a communications empire. By buying the *Times-Herald*, Kay's father and husband established an impregnable base in Washington; by buying television stations in Washington and in Florida, they prepared for the TV age. Eventually, after her father's death, Graham acquired *Newsweek* and, in association with the *Los Angeles Times*, began to build an international news service. There was much else—*Art News*, paper mills, and, always and inevitably, politics. Two of his close friends were John F. Kennedy and Lyndon B. Johnson. It was an audacious, tense, draining life, and it told fiercely on (Continued on page 153)

(Continued on page 153)

Attractive, gentle without necessarily yielding, soft without mental flab, knowledgeable without aggressiveness, a woman with a woman's smart mind, a mother of four—that is Katharine Graham who has more power than any other woman has ever had in publishing. She runs a sizable empire and is the acknowledged boss. She owns not only The Washington Post, which every American politician and statesman reads every morning, but also Newsweek, Art News, two television stations and one radio station, plus forty-five percent of the Paris edition of the Herald Tribune. To do that, with grace, she listens long and makes reasonably quick decisions. Her stamina and her brains and her good looks come from both her parents. Eugene Meyer, her father, was a New York investment banker who bought The Washington Post in 1933; her mother is Agnes E. Meyer, a free-wheeling thinker, an expert on Chinese art, an authority on social problems, a writer. Mrs. Graham worked for six years on The Post until 1945, returning only after the death of her husband, Philip L. Graham, in 1963. An extraordinary man, Graham started on The Washington Post in 1946, six years after his marriage to Katharine Meyer. Graham did not begin on the lowest level, for his parents-in-law transferred all the voting stock in The Washington Post Company at that time to Mr. and Mrs. Graham. In that way Eugene Meyer thoughtfully allowed Graham to make his own mistakes and for his daughter to be a part of all future decisions. Katharine Graham manages the intricacies of her life partly because she takes two steps at a time. She likes it that way.

CECIL BEATON

Phil with President Kennedy
on the Cape

On the Goldwater campaign trail

With Bobby Kennedy

With Jackie Kennedy

With President Nixon

With President Johnson

With Margaret Thatcher

With Henry Kissinger

With Indira Gandhi

With the Prince and
Princess of Wales

With President and
Mrs. Reagan

With President Bush

With President Clinton

The family at my seventieth-birthday party: left to right, Steve, Lally, Don, me, and Bill

With Warren Buffett

At the Vineyard

because when we informed Tucker that there were no blacks in the union, he concluded it was a racist union and decided not to help the pressmen in any way.

The president of the Greater Washington Central Labor Council asked me to meet with Mayor Walter Washington and Jim Dugan, accusing us of importing strikebreakers. By this time we had had to borrow a few pressmen from other papers, and I explained by letter why we had had to do this, noting that we never brought in relief pressmen until we went to impasse in December, when our people were exhausted. I added that I couldn't see that the mayor's presence would change a situation of basic wide disagreement between the *Post* and Local 6, especially since the mediation service had participated from the beginning. There never was a meeting.

Just at this time, more than fifteen hundred demonstrators staged a rally parading past the building to show solidarity with the unions. Several of us inside the building were clustered, discreetly hidden at an upstairs window, to watch the approaching parade. I was dismayed to see Charlie Davis at the head of the group with a sign that read, in big letters, "Phil shot the wrong Graham." I cringed and ran from the window. I couldn't believe that Charlie and I had once been on friendly, jocular terms.

Oddly, the pressmen still didn't seem to feel threatened—not even after our hiring began; they acted as though they believed it was only a matter of time before they'd be coming back in. In many ways, this attitude may have been a reflection of how unreal Dugan's perspective was. From the beginning, he appeared not to think that we could actually be running the presses. Even when the picketers heard the noise of the presses, he would insist we were somehow faking it. As we got stronger and stronger, he kept denying our successes. As late as the end of December, Dugan claimed on radio and television that our statements about the *Post*'s circulation were misleading and way off base, asserting that we were dumping thousands of copies of the daily paper. In fact, by this time daily circulation was down by only about twenty-five thousand copies, and Sunday circulation by just twelve thousand. We had reached 98 percent of expectations for this time of year.

Despite their seeming to believe that time was on their side, the pressmen appealed to George Meany, AFL-CIO president, for help. He in turn called me and said, "Katharine, the pressmen have called and want me to talk to you." I confess that my heart sank at his call. Meany could have seriously hurt us by starting boycotts and applying other political pressures—in essence, by getting behind the pressmen's union. He asked me if I wanted him to come to the *Post* to talk. I knew Meany through my father, who had served with him on the War Labor Board. I respected him and liked him and knew that he couldn't possibly cross the picket line, so I told him I'd go to him, which I did on December 17, taking Mark along with me to Meany's office, only a couple of blocks away. When we were seated, George got right down to business, asking, "Would you take the pressmen back if they paid to fix the presses?"

"No," I replied unequivocally. "The presses are fixed. We have already hired half the people we need. It's too late to take them back. We can't have them working side by side with nonunion people."

"Would you take them back if—" George kept raising the ante, in one question after another. I kept explaining that we had crossed the bridge, they hadn't responded to any invitations to negotiate, and now we were launched on another path. Finally, he posed the ultimate difficult question: "What would you do if they accepted the contract?" Legally, of course, if they had at any time accepted the final contract, they would have been eligible for the remaining jobs. I took a deep breath, let my intuition take over, and replied, "I guess I'd slit my throat from ear to ear."

There was a deafening silence for a moment while George stared at me and Mark went limp, looking as though he were going to slide right off the couch on which we both were sitting. But I knew George, and I thought I could level with him, and that was the truth. I also knew that he would understand what I meant; he was very political, with sensitive antennae. Finally, he reflected sadly, "Well, I offered to help the pressmen when this strike first started. I sent them a wire and they never replied. Also, I just can't imagine people who would destroy their tools. I've never approved of that. That would never have happened in my day." We talked a little longer; then Mark and I rose to leave. Meany walked with us to the elevator slowly and sorrowfully. As we were getting in, he said to me, "The *Post* is a great newspaper, and I knew and loved your father."

JUST BEFORE CHRISTMAS, we had our first big break when the paper-handlers—who pushed the huge and heavy newsprint rolls to the presses, a job that was then being done by Don Graham, Mark Meagher, and others—settled their contract, the first union to do so. To the public, this didn't quite count as a breakthrough, however, because the pressmen's and other unions condescended to them. The paper-handlers, being all black and lower-skilled, were slightly different from the other crafts, but from our point of view it was a break, and it relieved us considerably.

At the same time, the regional director of the National Labor Relations Board refused to issue a complaint filed by the union accusing us of delaying or stalling tactics and refusing to bargain in good faith.

Still, the tension was high. The pressmen's wives started to write me. Christmas Eve—a day I never dreamed would find us still in this strike situation—was hard for all of us. Ben's annual letter to me was especially poignant and understanding. He acknowledged that he felt I would "never do anything more difficult." He was so right. He also said that his own New Year's wish was to have the "turmoil ended, so that we can return to our task of putting out the best paper in the world without compromise and without menace." I think the strike was especially difficult on Ben. He himself admitted later, "I have never been comfortable in or with the labor movement." Whereas I had been living through these months with people who were of one mind, he had had to live each day with people who were tormented by what they were doing in not supporting the union, reporters who had to be calmed and reassured constantly. I also recognized that what I was doing in trying to change the labor situation was something I had been working on for years, whereas for Ben the strike was nothing but a mammoth interruption of what he had been trying to do for the past decade.

In responding to Ben, I shared with him my view about how it would turn out: "I know it's going to be good—better than you think from every point of view. I pray it's over before too long but it would be fatal to try to push it faster than it can go."

On New Year's Eve, to my great distress and anger, the *Star* ran an open letter from a group called the "executive committee of the Committee for a Fair Settlement." The letter urged round-the-clock bargaining to be mediated by the Federal Mediation Service, and if that failed, binding arbitration. It was endorsed by George Meany and signed by a hundred people, including many civic leaders and liberals, among them Reverend Walter Fauntroy; Monsignor George Higgins of the Catholic Conference; Leon Keyserling, former chairman of the Council of Economic Advisers; Reverend John Walker, bishop of the Washington National Cathedral; Senator Hubert Humphrey; and Representative John Brademas, who later wrote me that his name had been used without permission.

I believe that *all* the signers were being used, although many of them didn't realize it. They thought the position was a neutral one: that we had won the strike but should now submit to an arbitrator what we had already won. They had little idea what the real issues were but had simply let themselves be duped by the union. In fact, the ad was paid for by the Newspaper Guild, which was made clear at a press conference the same day the ad appeared, called by the members of the committee that had placed the ad.

I sent letters to several of the signers whom I knew, including Hubert Humphrey, saying I was disappointed that they had let their names be used without at least asking to hear our side. Hubert wrote back immediately saying he had thought the open letter was nothing but an appeal to both the *Post* and the unions to try to settle the dispute and he still didn't think it took sides. He added, however, "On second thought, it would have been better if I had kept my nose out of the dispute. . . . It was one of those hasty decisions and, I suppose, one that I would have been much better off never to have made," apologizing if it had caused me distress, which, indeed, it had.

I wrote John Walker, too, sending him a package that was being mailed throughout the Washington metropolitan area by a group called Post Unions United, containing a reprint of the ad along with a postcard addressed to the *Post* canceling a subscription and a prepaid subscription card addressed to the *Star.* There was hardly a need for fact-finding, I wrote, "nor is there any justification for arbitration of an issue that rightly belongs to the collective bargaining process." Bishop Walker replied that he was profoundly disturbed by the subversion of the purposes of the open letter and that he was withdrawing his name from the committee.

My great friend Joe Rauh, who had also been a signer of the ad in the *Star,* contributed to my worries by coming to me to say that he feared my obstinacy vis-à-vis the union was effectively acting as "a wedge being driven between essential allies"—the liberal/labor coalition. We spent three hours one afternoon at my house while he argued the necessity of taking the pressmen's union back and I tried to explain why that couldn't happen.

My differences with Joe reflected one of the ironies of the pressmen's strike. It was difficult to find myself being viewed as antilabor, and it was strange for me to find in my camp many people who normally would have been on the directly opposite side of the mat—and the reverse as well, with many of my friends taking a position contrary to mine. This strange switch was reflected in various situations throughout those long months of the strike. For example, Pat Buchanan—never one to support *The Washington Post*—wrote at the time that, although the company was a media cartel which ought to be broken up, and although the paper's "editorial policies have encouraged the shift of economic power toward Big Labor," "its fight with Local 6 is a fight it has to win." He managed to add about the company: "It probably deserves what it gets."

BY JANUARY 6, 1976, we had hired 107 people as permanent replacements for the pressroom, with a white-nonwhite mix of about 50-50 and with almost 10 percent women. Beyond starting to train these new hires, the issue now was to get the other craft unions back. Not much progress was being made. The paper-handlers, though they had voted to return, were not yet back at work, because of a glitch with their international. A few individual craft-workers had returned on their own initiative, but the overwhelming majority of them were still on strike or were respecting the picket lines of the striking unions. And in mid-January, the local pressmen's union filed a $20-million countersuit against the *Post*, claiming the newspaper had conspired to "ultimately destroy the union entirely."

Just a few days into the new year, the *Star* ran four articles on the strike, purporting to tell the full story—the story from management's side, from the union's side, and from the guild's. In reply to a reader who had canceled the *Post* after reading the *Star*'s articles, I said, "I will ask the Circulation Department to stop your paper if you request, but if you are doing it as a result of reading the *Star*, this was the most outrageous, deliberate knife job any paper has done to another. I would cancel *The Post* myself if I depended on the *Star* article. I enclose my own view of the issues. If you still want your paper canceled, I will do so."

The emotional stress of the entire strike and the losses on both sides were epitomized on February 10 when one of the pressmen, John Clauss, committed suicide. The Coordinating Committee of the Alliance for Labor and Community Action wired me immediately, saying, "You are responsible for the death of *Post* pressman John Clauss."

> When your greed for more profits made you decide to break the unions [you] accepted the moral responsibility for all the inevitable human consequences which flowed from this decision.
>
> Your yellow attempt to lie your way out from this moral responsibility by printing in your paper, "He was afraid to cross the union's picket lines," was the lowest insult you could have made to a man and his family who have been strong unionists for over 30 years—19 of them at *The Post*.
>
> All your and your cohorts money, lies and paid flunkies will not let you hide from this fact that is burning into the souls of working people: John Clauss's blood is on your hands.

I drafted a response that I never sent, perhaps because I was trying to be rational in what was an emotionally charged environment. I wanted to point out that the reason the news story that had appeared in the *Post* said John Clauss was afraid to cross the picket line was that that is what his suicide note had said. In the end I saw no point in responding to what I viewed as intemperate and unfounded accusations.

FEBRUARY 15 WAS possibly the key moment in the denouement of the strike. The mailers finally voted—129 to 58—to accept a new contract, and reported for work the next night. On February 17, the *Post*'s chapel of the photoengravers' union voted to accept our contract offer, and returned to work a few days later. The typographers, who were observing the picket line but were not on strike since they had a contract, came back in with them. We were still negotiating with three groups: the engineers, who held out until March 1; the machinists, a majority of whom were back at work; and the building-services union.

At the end of February, Bob Kaiser, who had been covering the strike, wrote a long piece about everything that had taken place, which took over much of the "Outlook" section of the paper. Because it was a remarkably detached piece of reporting, it was widely applauded. I didn't agree with all that Bob wrote, but I believe newspapers have to let themselves be written about and have to live with it.

Naturally, there had been a lot of press reaction to the strike during those long months. It ranged from very positive to the other extreme. One of the worst stories ran in the beginning, by Eliot Marshall in *The New Republic*. Marshall had been a classmate of my youngest son, Steve, at Harvard, and was about twenty-six at the time. I called him and said that some of what he'd said was demonstrably wrong and I could prove it. He said he was so sorry but he had it from an impeccable source—the *Star*—and every good wish. I did not call his publisher.

In January there had appeared in *Washington Monthly* one of the last in a series of outrageous press pieces about the strike, this one by an ex–national editor of the *Post*, Ben Bagdikian, who since leaving the paper had made a cottage industry of criticizing us. His article was entitled "Maximizing Profits at the Washington Post." I sent a copy to Don, with a note: "This literally takes my breath away it's so insane—the conclusion being that newspapers need more Davises and Dugans." I memoed Ben Bradlee separately, and intemperately, "I am really embarrassed to think this ignorant biased fool was ever national editor. Surely the worst asps in this world are the ones one has clasped to the bosom."

The public got in on the act also, writing me and others at the *Post* with a range of opinion on the strike. Someone even wrote to ask: "Haven't all you magnificent geniuses over there figgered out yet how to blame your press room sabotage on NIXON?"

By March 1, the strike was essentially over. We had had a difficult balancing act to manage, and in the end we had stayed on the tightrope and reached the other side. All the unions, with the exception of the pressmen, were back at work. When it was over, twenty-two pressmen (including supervisors) came back—as individuals—out of more than two hundred members of the union, and twenty-eight out of forty-three stereotypers returned. Some pressmen didn't come back for philosophical reasons and loyalty to the union; some were no doubt afraid to. I know that one of the supervisors who did come back, Hoot Gibson, was frightened at first. When I asked him what he thought might happen, or what the union could do to him, he responded, in his slow, West Virginia drawl, "Anything, anything at all. Why, they could kill your dog or your horse." Hoot and I had a long talk the morning he returned—a talk on which I've never ceased to reflect—about what had brought us to this dreadful mess. Hoot recalled the early days of the *Post*, in the old E Street building, when "We all enjoyed our work and each other." "We used to come in fifteen minutes early just to visit before we went to work," he remembered. And he emphasized how much easier it was to relate to each other when the paper was smaller. It's interesting that on one night we had twenty-three amateurs running the mailroom, and the very next night there were sixty-nine people manning the same equipment.

We handled the return to work very carefully, not pressing people who were slow to come back. We wanted to bind up wounds, not create more. We tried to welcome everyone back into the building. We tried not to gloat. Although there were many uncertainties at the *Post*, including the cost of buying out some of the printers and getting back some of the linage lost during the strike, we had begun to resume normal operations. Despite the three months of the strike at the end of the year, we had actually finished 1975 with an increased share of the Sunday field in Washington and with total *Post* linage down less than 2 percent.

We still had to come to work through what was an increasingly forlorn picket line, which was awful, and pressmen's wives and children picketed my house in Georgetown every Sunday for months, so I had to drive in and out past their sad line, which bothered me more than anyone will ever know. The picket line at the *Post* wasn't called off until May of 1977.

The pressmen kept resolutely harassing us. They had picketed the opening of the movie *All the President's Men*. And in July 1976, when I spoke at a bicentennial program at the Washington Monument, pressmen hidden in the audience emerged hooting and yelling and drowned me out. I made a few attempts to keep going, realized they were futile, and suggested we all join hands and sing "God Bless America," which had been scheduled for the conclusion; this we did. It was, of course, somewhat nerve-racking to have them suddenly appear from the dark night, and I left as soon as I could.

In June, there was one sign of vindication for the actions we had taken. Superior Court Judge Leonard Braman issued a "Findings of Fact and Conclusions of Law" in response to a five-day hearing on our request for a permanent injunction against Local 6. The judge came down hard on the union, saying essentially that in the case of Local 6 the First Amendment's freedom of speech by picketing had gone "beyond the pale of protected communication, and coercion has been mingled with speech."

In July, seven former *Post* pressmen were indicted by a federal grand jury in connection with the opening riot. Four were also charged with assaulting Jim Hover, the foreman. One was alleged to be a minor hit-man for the Mafia. A week later, eight more were indicted on charges of destroying property. In April 1977, a year and a half after the opening salvo, these fifteen former pressmen pleaded guilty to misdemeanors ranging from simple assault to disorderly conduct, and were sentenced in May by Judge Sylvia Bacon, who said that their actions during the strike were "planned, purposeful and unjustified. These events did not erupt spontaneously." Six were jailed and the rest given suspended sentences and fines. Plea-bargaining helped make the sentences fairly mild, but I was happy not to have to go through re-arousing all the old passions in a trial. Dugan had been handed a real defeat, but he, too, was a victim in some ways—of his past successes and his own intransigence. In June 1976, he had been defeated in a re-election bid for the presidency of Local 6.

Brian Flores, who had masterminded most of the guild strategy and run its meetings, had also met his Waterloo. The local guild leaders tried to bring disciplinary action against members who had crossed the picket lines, not even allowing these people to have their own lawyers; they were to be union trials. In protest, there was a movement to get rid of the guild, and about a third of the eight hundred members resigned and formed the Washington Newspaper Union, mounting a challenge to the guild as the bargaining representative. The independent union only narrowly lost, but it did succeed in getting the international union to realize it would lose the *Post* unless something was done. Leaders of the international persuaded Flores to resign as administrative officer and replaced him.

We had weathered a strike we hadn't asked for and didn't control. The *Post* had survived this crucial test, but there was no "clean victory"—it was a painful one for the *Post*, for its guild and craft-union members, and for the Washington community. It divided the paper, creating a false atmosphere of "us" versus "them." Nearly two hundred people lost their jobs; one committed suicide. There were many sad consequences for far too many people and their families.

I never wanted the strike. I know that many people believe I deliberately set out to destroy a union, but that was certainly *not* the case. And if it had been the case, it would not have worked. Certainly I and everyone in the building who was interested in putting out an on-time, quality paper were fed up with the tyranny which the pressmen's union had imposed on us over the years, but I never dreamed it was possible to replace the pressmen, nor did I feel it was desirable.

Most people at the *Post* are still represented by unions. As I said early on, "*The Washington Post* has lived long and honorably with its unions." Mark and I both said repeatedly throughout the strike that we believed the *Post* benefited from "strong, healthy trade unionism." I believed that then, and I believe it now. I felt this as the publisher as well as personally. My father was the only publisher ever made an honorary member of the pressmen's Local 6. I myself had come to maturity in an age of strong labor. I was a believer in the labor movement. One of my earliest aspirations had been to be a labor reporter. Yet I also feel that the unions have to stay productive, and that there are areas that need not be unionized.

What I stand by unequivocally is that we had no other choice but to do what we did, to take the actions we took: the future of the *Post*, as well as of the Post Company, hung in the balance. I knew that we had to have a well-run production department—all of our jobs depended on it. I knew that we had to retrieve management rights that had eroded over the years. I have always thought that blame is divisible, and I take responsibility for some of the management problems that led to the eroding of our rights to run the pressroom; others I inherited. But wherever the source of the problems lay, I knew they had to be corrected.

I was also convinced that we set about doing this in an enlightened and decent way. I believe that we offered a generous resolution from the beginning and throughout. We wanted to settle with the union, but we wanted to settle responsibly. Our aim was always the same: we were asking for the reasonable right to retrieve some of the bad practices that had built up over the years. We tried to be fair—which I know is something many of the pressmen and their families will never believe. We weren't asking the pressmen merely to surrender the outmoded practices to which we objected; we were prepared to give for what we got. We would have willingly bought back what we had earlier given away. The pressmen's union was not prepared to give up anything. The union—or at least its leaders, Dugan and Davis—seemed to be saying, "What's ours is ours, and what's yours is negotiable."

Ironically, it was the pressmen themselves who made it possible for us to achieve what we had longed for. I view the strike as a great tragedy that could have been avoided with wiser union leadership. I believe, as I wrote someone at the time, that "Local 6 killed the goose and its golden eggs with their unbending determination to keep it all."

Dugan could see that unions and management at other papers were arriving at contracts that met the needs of both sides at the table. He could also see that some of the best papers in the country at the time—the *Los Angeles Times, Newsday*, and the *Miami Herald*, for example—were almost completely nonunion. But he remained adamant, refusing to bargain reasonably and act responsibly. Many fine and able pressmen were caught in a bind of having to resign from the union or remain with the leaders who had led them so poorly and had done such harm.

There is undoubtedly a tendency to think that unions must be victims and therefore right, and that employers are probably brutal, powerful, and therefore wrong. I felt this was a particularly serious misperception in our case. I understood people who felt loyal to the union and not to the company when forced to make what I knew was a very hard choice—and said as much in letters to the wives of a few of the pressmen—but I also understood that it was a choice these men had made. I felt that the philosophy that any union is right no matter what it does was an odd cause for which to sacrifice one's career. I wish the pressmen had influenced their union leadership to be responsible in the first place. Failing that, I wish they had returned as individuals. Unfortunately, many followed Dugan over the cliff.

IN SOME WAYS, we obtained by accident what is given to few in their lives—a new chance. Though this was a strike that was not looked for, it was one that was desperately needed. As I told Ben at the time, in an odd sense the strike was "a business-side Watergate that fell on our heads but then had to be pursued." We had wanted to accomplish gradually over many contracts what we were not only enabled but forced to do in one blow as a result of the strike. After years of defeated hopes at contract times, after the agony of concern about how to turn around a seemingly impossibly difficult mess in production, we were given that rare and unexpected gift we all dream about—a clean slate on which we could begin to rebuild. We now had settled our two worst labor problems—the ITU and the pressmen—in different ways. We could begin to address, in a more orderly way, the rest of them, including the mailroom, where there was still featherbedding and inefficiency.

Most important, we had gained the opportunity to deal more professionally with our unions—and the right to upgrade the quality of our production management as well as the ability to manage. We were able to bring in enlightened modern managers—particularly Don Rice and, later, Tom Might, who together brought production from the worst-managed department in the building to the best. The fine current production vice-president, Mike Clurman, was the last apprentice printer we hired.

It's sobering to look back at the strike and realize that, as with Watergate, one reason we survived is that we were lucky. Granted, we had the strong will of the people inside and outside the building who helped us, the leadership of Mark Meagher and Don Graham, as well as the dedication and ability of the nonunion circulation department that distributed and delivered the paper. But we also needed some extraordinarily lucky breaks—and we got them.

The initial deliberate destruction of the presses, which seemed at first sight like such an overwhelming catastrophe, turned out to be a blessing in disguise. The damage—and the unforgivable acts of violence throughout the strike—helped greatly with public opinion, with other newspapers that came to our aid, and, above all, with keeping the guild working. The rampage that some of the pressmen went on straightened our spines on the management side. It made us very determined to come to terms with the arrogance that it reflected.

At the time, I was both angry and baffled about the violence. Why did they do it? Only in hindsight did I come to understand it to a certain extent—although never to accept it. Dugan and Davis knew that in order to prevail they had to shut off either our means of distributing the paper or our means of producing it. Because our distributors were independent operators, the union had no other option than to focus on our means of production—the presses. Also, there had been a strike at a newspaper in Kansas City, and that paper had replaced its striking pressmen the day after they struck, and the union had never gone back. In August 1975, just over a month before our own strike began, the head of the Kansas City pressmen's union made a speech to our Local 6 at the *Post* saying that their error had been leaving the presses intact and ready to run. I suppose Dugan and Davis decided not to make that same mistake. Larry Wallace suggested that Dugan possibly "thought he had figured out a way to succeed where [other] pressmen had failed." I believe that it was the roughneck out-of-town element of the union who mapped out the damage and sabotage rather than longtime *Post* pressmen, the majority of whom I don't think even knew that the damage was planned. In fact, Everett Ray Forsman, a union official who played no role in the violence, left the room in tears after seeing the extent of the damage.

Even the weather was on our side. Whereas Washington had experienced some torrential rains in the late summer and early fall, the days remained fairly clear throughout the strike, which allowed the helicopters to fly in and out regularly without being grounded.

Though the strike at *The Washington Post* ended for the most part in February 1976, its reverberations are felt to this day. We learned a lot of necessary, albeit painful, lessons about the need for strong and compassionate managers who are knowledgeable about the tasks at hand, about labor relations, and about communications. And we put what we learned to good use. There were extraordinarily positive outcomes for the company in greater efficiency and flexibility and in the ability to manage. Our increased productivity was evident in the pressroom, where we went from seventeen pressmen on each press before the strike to eight-to-ten-person crews afterwards. Press speeds increased; for us, it was the equivalent of buying another press. Our pressroom began functioning again the way a pressroom should, and the atmosphere improved throughout the building.

As a manager, I had learned the hard way that, when management, for whatever reason, forfeits its basic right to manage, only trouble can result. The strike made me more determined to establish better communications within the company. And the result was a better, stronger newspaper. Without the groundwork laid by the strike, we would not have been able to build and to grow. We bounded back from the trauma of the strike because the *Post* was a good newspaper to begin with, one that people liked, and because our regained control over the pressroom meant that we could print and deliver the paper on time, something we hadn't been doing for years.

It is ironic that I, who have never liked confrontations, should have been faced with this major one. My mother rarely did things tactfully or in a low-key way; she loved and thrived on strident confrontations. Perhaps for that reason, I always ran the other way when it came to a showdown. I hated fights, which I always found unpleasant and invariably feared losing. On the other hand, in this big one, when I was cornered, I had no choice but to become embattled. I know that I risk sounding pretentious or sanctimonious when I say that, at bottom, I regarded the actions we took as fulfilling our obligation to our readers. But I'll take the risk and say that, for me, it was true.

Yet even when it was over, I had mixed feelings. "It's an awful thing," I wrote a friend in February 1976, "to find yourself engaged in and curiously emotionally worse in victory than in battle." It was, as I also said, "equally awful to meet people who believe the propaganda emanating from a coalition of enemies, that I have suddenly gotten money-grubbing and heartless."

I emerged from the strike with a higher profile than ever before. Though at the *Post* and in the community some people may have had mixed feelings about me, within the industry my star had risen. Even those publishers who denounced the so-called liberalism of the *Post*'s news and editorial pages applauded our actions on the management side.

To say that I was grateful to many people is a supreme understatement. I was indebted to Mark Meagher for his strength and his many abilities throughout those long months. Don made me proud—as a publisher and as a mother. Larry Wallace proved himself to be a man of great competence and common sense; he had my confidence throughout the negotiations. People in the industry—although they may have helped for the common good—were still extraordinarily generous to take on our problems. Those 125 *Post* people who worked so hard at their own jobs by day and other jobs by night, doing work normally done by nearly fifteen hundred full- and part-time production people, earned my undying respect and affection. I have always considered the daily paper a miracle of sorts, but never more so than during the strike.

— *Chapter Twenty-seven* —

I N CERTAIN WAYS, the defining period of my working life was over. During the turbulent years from 1971 to 1976, we had been through the major public dramas of the Pentagon Papers, Watergate, and the pressmen's strike. Ironically, it was the next five years that were the most difficult work years I ever lived through. I sometimes felt as if I were being made to pay for having survived those earlier events relatively unscathed.

I still saw myself as an inheritor who had been very lucky. But, fortunately, after the years of public trauma, I had a fairly steady platform on which to operate. The company's primary businesses—the *Post*, *Newsweek*, and Post-Newsweek Stations—were all generally progressing, but I still tended to exaggerate the things that were going wrong. Despite the recent successes, my confidence, never solid, was shaken, particularly as I began to be written about more and more for my real and perceived mistakes.

Warren's advice and steady communication with me were critical to a number of actions I took in these years. Crucially, he persuaded me of the benefits of buying in our own stock. I had been suspicious of the idea. Repurchasing stock is a commonplace today, but only a handful of companies were doing it in the mid-1970s. I felt that, if we spent all of our money buying in our own stock, we wouldn't be able to grow. Warren went through the numbers with me, showing me what this action could do for the company in the long run, or even in the short run. He re-emphasized how low the stock was compared with its real value and how this was a better business move than many we were contemplating. He gradually made his point: if we bought in 1 percent of the stock in the Post Company, everyone owned a larger share of our stock at a bargain price. I decided we should do it.

My natural caution, however, was such that I thought I had to convince the people around me of the importance of such a move. So I set about persuading the top executives, including the company's legal counsel, of the rightness of this decision. Finally, we agreed and took it to the board, who okayed the stock repurchases. In fact, the board quickly saw what a good idea this was, and didn't want to stop. Over the next twenty years, we bought back 45 percent of the stock.

My management troubles may have derived mainly from my lack of business experience, but they were multiplied by not having a real partner to help me run the company. By the time of the strike, it was clear that Larry Israel, who had been president and chief operating officer of the company since Fritz's death in 1973, was not working out. When I concluded after a great deal of consultation that this situation just wouldn't get better, we made a decision to part ways and announced Larry's resignation in January of 1977. When he left, I took back the title of president, retaining the chairmanship of the company as well, until we decided what to do about a new COO. The announcement of Larry's departure was greeted with a batch of negative stories of which I was the target. *Time's* piece on the move was titled "Krusty Kay Tightens Her Grip." After describing me as difficult to get along with, mercurial, impulsive, manipulated by an "eminence grise"—meaning Warren—*Time* concluded by acknowledging, "Whatever the problems, Graham's company will show record profits and record revenues."

I particularly detested the sexist implications of stories like these—always being depicted as the difficult woman, while whoever left the company was the victim of my female whims. I was still a curiosity, a woman in a man's world. Men like Bill Paley, Al Neuharth, Mort Zuckerman, and Joe Allbritton fired executive after executive, but no one attributed their actions to their gender.

Also at this time, I had some grave concerns about the quality of the paper and of the editing. I felt that the national staff and the metro staff had let down, that we were doing things superficially. Ben didn't agree with me, but Bob Woodward did, putting it succinctly one day: "The paper is going down the shit hole." It is to Ben's great credit that he and I survived the difficult times and all my questioning. I could still come on like a dentist drill at moments like this, but he hung in, and balance would get restored. Sometimes he would do things despite my views, and sometimes he was right to do so. If he was mistaken, he would correct the mistakes in time, as soon as he agreed that something wasn't working. Not listening to me—and to others—was both Ben's strength and his weakness. However, as I wrote him at the time of this disagreement about the quality of the paper, "No superficial problems either of us may have at any particular moment matter compared to the basic trust and rapport with each other. Because if that's there—and it is there as far as I'm concerned—all else flows from it."

Another area I was worried about at the *Post* was the editorial page.

Phil Geyelin seemed to go into a prolonged slump after Watergate. I tried to assure him that, though I felt the page needed revitalizing, I had confidence in his ability to do it. I talked to him about how the complexity of my job and the pressures on my time had left me out of touch with him somewhat; I no longer participated to the extent I had earlier in editorial and management meetings at either the *Post* or at *Newsweek*. I assured Phil that I would try to remedy the situation and help in any way I could.

There were also problems at *Newsweek*. The magazine was doing well in operating revenue, and the business was remarkably good. On the editorial side, however, 1976 was the beginning of some high-level management turnover that affected both the magazine and me personally. In October of that year, after leaving and returning to the magazine, Oz Elliott, who had been *Newsweek*'s editor-in-chief and board chairman, suggested a sabbatical so that he could help save New York. Convinced that his mind was on other things, I had to let him go, and not just on sabbatical. Our mutual affection withstood the trauma, and I have nothing but admiration and gratitude for Oz, who left to become deputy mayor of New York City. Ed Kosner, who had become editor in September of 1975, remained responsible for the general editorial direction of the magazine.

When Oz departed, Bob Campbell, who had become *Newsweek*'s president in 1975, assumed Oz's title of chairman and was succeeded as president by Peter Derow, who had come to *Newsweek* straight out of Harvard Business School in 1965. Peter was, I thought, an able, ambitious, attractive young man who knew his business. I saw him or talked to him frequently, believed in him, thought of him as an associate I could lean on, and viewed him as the promise of the future.

Although I considered myself inadequately educated and experienced for the role I was playing, I did think I was pretty good at appraising people and their performance. In fact, Peter's performance was fine in many ways, and he had smoothly worked his way up to the number-two position under Bob Campbell. I had realized that he was highly political, never a healthy sign, but I was stunned one day in the middle of 1977 when he told me he was leaving to become an administrative vice-president at CBS. I was disappointed by that, but he didn't stop there, going on to tell me that he wanted to be in a healthy, vibrant, well-run company, as opposed to the poorly run one I was operating. He said that he felt I was a hopelessly inadequate leader and that he had little choice but to leave for the dynamic CBS. He touched a raw sensitivity when he assaulted me for not being a professional manager, and I must confess that I wept on and off for at least two days. I didn't acknowledge to myself that his was a highly irregular way to leave a company in which he had achieved success and that had done well by him for twelve years.

Embarrassed as I am to admit it, I worried so much about losing this man that I actually offered him the presidency of the entire Post Company if he would stay. Peter was determined to leave, however, and told me it would take too much out of him to take on the job—he was thirty-seven at the time, I believe. The issue, he said, wasn't a specific position or a title at the company but, rather, "Do I want to spend the next ten years educating myself and educating the family as to how this business ought to be run?" He added that to stay at The Washington Post Company "would take someone with much more patience than I have."

A few weeks later, he departed with encomiums from us—elaborate speeches from me about how wonderful he was. Privately, I knew that I wouldn't soon forget the personal verbal lashing I had taken from him, and I worried about how right he might have been.

In one of the more bizarre events of my working life, just six months later Peter and I had lunch together in New York, and he sounded me out about returning to *Newsweek*. Unaccountably—stupidly—despite the powerfully deflating effect of all he had said to me, I said yes right away and welcomed him back, especially since we had not yet found his successor. In another month, he was once again president of *Newsweek*.

At the company, in corporate, from the time of Larry Israel's departure in February 1977 until close to the end of that year, I was essentially alone as both chairman and president, and was still the publisher of the Post. But Warren was supporting me, figuratively at least, on one side, and Don Graham was growing increasingly important on the other, and at the end of 1976, we had promoted Mark Meagher to president of the newspaper division. Simultaneously, Mark named Don executive vice-president and general manager of the Post, responsible for its day-to-day operation. In November 1977, we promoted Mark to president and chief operating officer of the entire company. Mark was young and, in some respects, short on experience and maturity, but he had done a good job for us, especially during the strike, and, not being quite sure what I was looking for, I thought it better to stay with a known quantity.

IN THE MID-1970S, my focus was on how to grow the company. The question of growth and acquisition had never been addressed in an orderly way. Neither Fritz nor I had known how to go about it, and in fact had rather unqualified people passing judgment on important issues. We had little more than a hit-or-miss strategy, with no logical point of departure, no consistent way of analyzing possible purchases, and no experience with negotiating targets we were aiming at. Of course, at least in the early seventies, our debt was still considerable, and our profits were not large enough to give us much leeway to grow, so in some ways the point was moot, but I wanted to be poised for growth when the opportunity presented itself.

Basically, I was baffled even about how to organize a group to think about expansion. As it was, one person might make a suggestion and the idea would lie on the table while several of us chewed on it in mostly unanalytical ways. At one moment in mid-1979, Joel Chaseman, president of Post-Newsweek Stations, and Mark Meagher, among others, were pushing for us to undertake a cable news network. I disapproved of the idea for us, but there was such a head of steam that I let them present it to the board, which turned it down. Although their memories and mine are at odds about the chronology of all this, I thought that the idea had not only already been conceived by Ted Turner, but had begun to be implemented; he was very determinedly barreling ahead, even though his network was not yet launched. There clearly wasn't room for two such enterprises, if there was room for one—a real concern of mine at the time. In fact, it took many years for Turner's Cable News Network to become a success, and only now are several other companies entering the field.

I started to look into properties that I'd hear were available. Warren was of especial help on acquisitions, knowing to some degree about almost every deal that was taking place or had taken place in the previous ten years. One potential acquisition we considered was a television station in Buffalo. Warren advised me that the newspaper, which was also for sale, would be a better buy, and if we didn't want it, he did. Although dominant in its market, the paper had strong competition, strong unions, and no Sunday edition. When we decided not to pursue it, Warren bought it and after considerable struggle managed it to great success. I still feel we made the right decision for us.

How ill-prepared we were to manage another, smaller paper was amply demonstrated by the problems we were having with the *Trenton Times*, which we had bought in the spring of 1974. I had shared with Warren a memo describing and evaluating the deal and using some valuation parameters that caused him consternation, though he didn't mention it at the time. Obviously, we hadn't done sufficient research into the market. Nowhere in the memo, according to Warren, was there any indication that Trenton was not a single-newspaper town, the competition being a lively morning paper; in evaluating the deal, the memo used illustrations from monopoly cities. Warren apparently went into orbit at the oversight, but was restrained since he wasn't yet on the board.

We offered $16 million for the property, probably about $4 million too much. I had enough sense so that when, at the last minute, one of the sisters in the family selling the paper wanted more money and it looked as if the deal might be held up, I said, "Good, let's can it. If they want more money, just say no. Let's use this opportunity to walk away." I had reacted instinctively, but everyone else in the meeting—including Larry Israel, Mark Meagher, and Ben—rose up to say, "What's the matter with you?

Don't you want this company to grow? Don't you want to make any acquisitions?"

I certainly did, but I didn't want to buy trouble. Unfortunately, with the *Trenton Times*, an afternoon paper in an era when we knew what was happening to our afternoon competition in Washington, that's what we would be getting. Nevertheless, I relented, and we took possession of the *Trenton Times*, adding another worry to my list of concerns.

Indeed, we never learned to manage the paper, and we ran it abysmally. (It's true that we also were in the throes of a bad economy.) There were circulation and advertising-linage setbacks right from the start. We hired some excellent people and some who used the job as a springboard to the *Post*, but we overloaded the paper with people more appropriate for Washington than for the *Trenton Times*. We made every management mistake in the book, including offending and alienating the local establishment with a particularly savage "Style"-like report on one of the city's main social events, criticizing people's clothes, bibulous behavior, and so on. We had a succession of mostly inappropriate publishers who, with one exception, didn't understand the community. We edited the paper well by our standards but poorly by theirs. Instead of thinking about what was the right paper for this particular community, we seemed to edit the paper as though we were thinking of what the community *should* read. I think there was some arrogance involved: we were going to bless them with a minor version of *The Washington Post*. Some people derisively referred to it as *"The Washington Post, North."*

In the meantime, the *Trentonian*, a feisty morning tabloid owned by Ralph Ingersoll in partnership with Mark Goodson, was giving blue-collar Trenton what it enjoyed. It was a clever paper, produced inexpensively and inoffensively, with an emphasis on amusement. We started a Saturday-morning newspaper to try to go head to head with the *Trentonian*, which countered by starting a Sunday paper to compete directly with ours. We may not have been losing money, but we weren't near the profit goals we'd set or been led to believe were possible.

This was our first newspaper acquisition after the *Post*, but it was layered away from me and continued to be mismanaged most of the time we had it. Because The Washington Post Company now had a much higher profile, particularly after Watergate, how badly we were doing in Trenton became a big deal. We were widely written up, and our troubles were highlighted. At one time, I made the foolish statement, which was how I felt, that it was our Vietnam: there seemed to be no solution and no way out. This was not our shining moment.

However, by now we were in a position to add to the company, and we kept looking for compatible properties throughout the communications industry. Among the businesses that we approached or that approached us were *New York* magazine, *The New Yorker, The Atlantic Monthly*, Random House, and Simon and Schuster, but the first three didn't work out, and the two publishing houses were just too large to bite off, or so we thought. We also missed on the newspaper in Wilmington, Delaware, and we declined to bid on the *Denver Post*.

An important deal that we did make was prompted by our concerns about having the number-one newspaper and number-one television station in Washington, and being viewed as a media monopoly at a time when the FCC was looking hard at situations of cross-ownership. The Supreme Court was soon going to be deciding a case relevant to this issue—whether a company that owned a newspaper could also own a television station in the same town or market. Companies in these situations were worried about the outcome.

Our communications lawyers advised me to consider trading WTOP for a similar-sized station elsewhere that was also facing a cross-ownership situation. They were concerned that The Washington Post Company had too much dominance in Washington, D.C., right under the eyes of Congress, and that a decision against cross-ownership would come at a moment when we were in the midst of a license renewal and therefore not in a position to try for a station swap at that time.

Warren and I made the rounds of all the possible comparable stations: in Los Angeles, Dallas, Houston, Atlanta, Detroit. Only Peter Clark, head of the Detroit News Company, which had both a newspaper and a television station in a depressed area, was interested in talking. Detroit was nearly the same size market as Washington; at the time we were the eighth-largest broadcast market in the country, and Detroit was the seventh. The major difference was that our market was growing and theirs was stagnant. However, in some ways Detroit was a better television town than a newspaper town, so there was some hope of ending up in a profitable situation.

The decision of whether to trade WTOP for WWJ in Detroit (later renamed WDIV) was mine, and I was enough worried about the political climate and the weakness of our newspaper competition in Washington that I decided in favor of it. Warren and I together initially negotiated with Peter in Detroit. He wanted $6 million cash plus WTOP, because his station was bigger and more profitable than ours. We said that was too much. Peter came to see me in Washington, and I asked Warren to be there, but he said I could and should do it on my own, and we finally settled for $2 million. The deal was done—the first time I had negotiated by myself.

But still I was not very happy. We were giving up our oldest station— one with connections back to Phil and my father, one which I knew and loved, and which we'd built up to number one in the market—for Detroit, a strange town, unlike any I had known. When the actual changeover

came, people at WTOP were so devoted to Jim Snyder, our news director who was going to Detroit for us, that the anchors burst into tears when
they signed off for the last time under our ownership.

The situation in Detroit was worse than my worst fears. We had traded
a top-flight station in a dynamic market for a mediocre station in a market
that was mired in a recession. On top of that, the station was an NBC affiliate, and NBC at that time was a network in trouble. We had our usual new-
in-the-market problems: we wanted to run a better station, but resistance to
change was endemic, and Detroiters were used to having their news delivered in a certain way, no matter how bad it may have been. Again, as in Trenton, we were painted as the out-of-towners. Any time we made a mistake or
tried something new, critics at the other stations or at the newspapers leapt
on us. It was so bad that Jim Snyder had a serious heart attack and had to
leave. I suffered acutely at having decided to make the trade, particularly
after the Supreme Court handed down its decision, grandfathering those
companies who already had stations in cross-ownership towns. Little by little, the Detroit station improved and became very successful, but that didn't
happen before I had spent an inordinate amount of time blaming myself.

As part of the larger plan to acquire several smaller newspapers which
never materialized, in 1978 we also bought the *Everett Herald*, a small paper located in a city north of Seattle, Washington. As with the *Trenton
Times*, the *Herald* was acquired after poor appraisal. We paid a monopoly
price for a paper that was in a somewhat competitive situation with Seattle and then proceeded not to run it well until recently, when it has been
vastly improved. We also participated with Dow Jones in a start-up
newsprint mill at Bear Island in Virginia.

A little later, under *Newsweek*'s aegis and at its urging, we made another start-up—a monthly sports magazine called *Inside Sports*. This was
spearheaded by Peter Derow and the business side of *Newsweek*. Again, we
conceived it poorly, tested it poorly, and ran it poorly, despite a clever editor, John Walsh. It, too, lost larger amounts of money than we expected
and drained talent, energy, and time from *Newsweek* itself.

IMPORTANT CHANGES WERE taking place at the *Star*, which in the
short run created some worry at the *Post* and in the longer run caused us
even more concern before the end came, when the *Star* finally folded. Joe
Allbritton had worked hard to turn around his staid and failing newspaper.
When he first came to town, he had put in as editor Jim Bellows, a great
talent who didn't try to compete with us where we were strong but went
under, around, and beside us. The paper became livelier, more interesting,
and scrappier. Jim started a gossip column called "The Ear," which specialized in tweaking the *Post*, which the *Star* referred to as the "O.P."—or

the Other Paper. The most intimate details of the lives of many of us at the *Post* became grist for the mill of "The Ear." In particular, it was savage about Ben Bradlee and Sally Quinn, referring to them as the "Fun Couple" and reporting on their every activity, no doubt with some help from reliable sources in our own city room. We all came in for attention, some of it accurate, some of it half accurate, some entirely fictitious.

But despite the good things that were happening, the *Star* was in a real decline, which, of course, had started long before Allbritton entered the picture. There is no question that its longtime dominance and success had bred self-satisfaction and lack of drive; it never seemed to occur to the ownership that the world could change.

Even so, the extended *Star* family wasn't the main reason why we started to gain and the *Star* started to decline. A societal change in the country strengthened morning newspapers, while at the same time bringing hard times to the traditionally strong afternoon and evening papers. Principally, the growth of television network news, the flight to the suburbs from the inner cities, and urban problems affecting late-day home deliveries all weakened afternoon dailies. Possibly most important of all was the economy. As prices rose, particularly for labor and newsprint, newspapers raised rates, forcing advertisers to choose between papers—not divide their advertising, as many had previously done. If a newspaper rose to a certain dominance, there was often a snowball effect: advertisers realized that more people could be reached through the larger newspaper, so in an effort to cut costs they eliminated the weaker one. Once the momentum got going, there was not much that could be done. In some ways, this is what happened to the *Star*, exacerbated by the lack of attention to the competition. For far too long, no one at the *Star* had taken the *Post* seriously. But our advantage was not yet overwhelming. And I had learned, as had my father and Phil before me, what it feels like to be fighting for your life. We knew how far we'd go for a line of advertising or a new subscriber. Don and I still bear the scars. Young as he was, Don, too, understood that nothing stands still, that success can bring with it the roots of its own downfall.

In March 1977, Allbritton reached an agreement to trade or sell his Washington, D.C., radio station, which, according to the *Star*'s monthly publication for its employees, would "provide Star Communications with a guaranteed cash flow over the next 20 years." Indeed, only a month later Allbritton announced the first profitable quarter at the *Star* since several years before he took over. I wrote congratulating him, and he responded that he knew one swallow didn't make a spring, but that at last he saw light at the end of the tunnel, which he also realized might be a mirage.

The *Star* was a much-improved product, and Allbritton's brilliant moves in selling his radio and smaller television stations put him in a far stronger financial position. I was worried, but not as much as when, in early February 1978, Time Inc. announced that it was buying the *Star*. (Allbritton was keeping the valuable television station.) Now we were faced with the powerful, rich, professional, savvy Time Inc., which we saw as an even greater threat than the Texas millionaire. Time's people tried new ideas, invested vast sums, and used *Time* magazine's foreign correspondents to run foreign news in the *Star*. And they spent even more money than Allbritton had on promotion. The theme "Today's News Today" began to appear on billboards everywhere. On radio and television the message about the new *Star* was delivered by "tough-talking 'private ears' " Sam and Janet Evening, radio characters who "snoop[ed] around Washington dredging up scoops" all to the tune of "Some Enchanted Evening." *The Christian Science Monitor* ran an article about the increased competition between the *Post* and the *Star* headed "Star Wars Come to Washington."

One of the first things the new editor of the *Star* did under the Time Inc. regime was to exhume a five-part profile of me by Lynn Rosellini that initially had been suggested by Joe Allbritton himself as a kind of hands-off look at me. In the end, he had ordered it killed because he thought it was so negative. Time Inc.'s people at the *Star* resurrected it, promoting it to the skies and even running the first two parts of the series on the front page. I'm not exactly objective about the series and have never reread it, but my memory is vivid that I was portrayed as a sort of Jekyll-Hyde. Not that some of what Rosellini said wasn't true, but I was pictured so negatively that I feared no one would ever work for us again.

I got a lot of sympathetic mail, and the *Star* ran a highly supportive letter from Barry Goldwater, which I found all the more moving for his not being close to me. Goldwater wrote:

> Now I don't happen to be one the Washington Post has been kind to during my political life. In fact, I imagine I have suffered as much from its editorial and reportorial whims as any person in politics, but that's beside the point. There comes a time, in my opinion, when decency in reporting must have some consideration, and neither your reporter nor your publication showed any inclination toward that. You can be critical in a decent way of the manner in which Mrs. Graham conducts her business, but I don't believe you have any right to be critical of the way she has conducted her life, nor have you the right to be dishonest about it.

WITH TIME INC.'s arrival in town, it's a wonder that I had the time or inclination for anything else in my life, but several activities that were a mix of public and private provided me with both a reprieve from business concerns and a measure of fun and personal satisfaction. Bob McNamara, then president of the World Bank, had committed that institution to trying to help the nations of the so-called Third World. Northern countries were distressed by the radical rhetoric of the countries of the South and their irrational demands for billions of dollars in aid, and the countries of the South were angered at what they viewed as the insensitivity and heartlessness of the North. Bob's idea was to ask a group to look at these problems as individuals rather than as representatives of their countries, and he had tapped Willy Brandt, former chancellor of West Germany, to lead it; the group came to be known as the Brandt Commission.

Bob argued that it would be good for me to join, because it would expose me to an aspect of the world about which I knew little; because I would bring a sense of what was politically viable within the United States; and because it would be good for the *Post* and *Newsweek* to become more aware of these issues. Although I was reluctant to break our rule about not getting involved in organizations that took stands on issues, I decided there were times for exceptions to rules, and this was one. I accepted.

Sixteen persons were appointed to the commission, four of whom were former or current heads of government: Ted Heath from Great Britain, Pierre Mendès-France from France, Olof Palme from Sweden, and Chile's Eduardo Frei. Nine of the sixteen representatives were from the developing countries. Two of us—Peter Peterson, my old friend from the Nixon administration, and I—were from the United States. It was perfectly clear that I was a token woman from the North, counterbalanced later by the addition of a Malaysian businesswoman, Khatijah Ahmad.

The first of our meetings took place in December of 1977 at Gymnich Castle near Bonn. For me, it was like plunging into another world, one where people spoke peculiar languages, in all of which they tossed around strange acronyms while bantering about meetings and reports from the past, United Nations subdivisions, and the functions of the Bank and the IMF. Since we sat alphabetically, it was only natural that several twosomes developed. My friendship with Ted Heath—my "G" to his "H"—grew over the two years of our seat assignments.

For most of that first meeting—indeed, for most of the first year—I said little or nothing, too intimidated by the unfamiliar issues and the experts around me. Gradually, through the meals, the walks, the informal gatherings over tea or drinks, the atmosphere began to change. And in certain areas, things were warming up a little faster than I realized. One of the most radical of the Third Worlders, a famous ladies' man, surprised me by inviting me to his room. I thanked him for the compliment but said I followed an old adage, "Never where you work." He replied that he heeded another one, "Never say never." The atmosphere had certainly grown more friendly.

As the time for the final meeting drew near, none of us could see how we were possibly going to produce a report; the commission seemed to consist of prima donnas who rarely agreed on anything. But our chairman was clearly determined to push through a report at the final meeting. During an exasperating afternoon session, Brandt, beet-red and breathing heavily, blew his top, made a final statement, and withdrew completely, depressed at our lack of progress. The remaining commissioners decided that Shridath (Sonny) Ramphal of Guyana from the South and Ted Heath from the North should work with Michael Hoffman, Brandt's aide, on the final draft. We met one more time and, led by Ted, worked our way through comments on all the sections. By great good luck, Ted later recalled, Brandt was delayed in arriving in England, and Ted seized the moment to force decisions and get the report accepted.

What effect did it have? Quite a lot in certain European countries; very little, if any, in the United States. We had arrived at a negotiated consensus. There were things in the report to which all of us took exception, but you had to sign it or not, and we all did. In the end, the report turned out to be exactly what it was designed not to be, with the various commissioners basically representing their states or constituencies.

I spoke to Ben about the report before it was released, saying that, though I knew this kind of thing didn't much interest him, I thought it mattered and hoped he would make sure it got the kind of news play it deserved. Ben's attention span was not always perfect, but I was positively disbelieving when I located the story of the commission's report on page 25 of the *Post*. Even *The New York Times* had put it on page 3. I was so angry I was absolutely unable to speak to Ben for twenty-four hours lest I explode. He had simply forgotten.

I suppose I did contribute something by imploring the editors of *Newsweek* to focus on the issues—in fact, urging them to do a cover story on the Third World. I knew it wouldn't be a thriller but thought it was something we owed our readers. After considerable foot-dragging, *Newsweek* finally did a cover story, some time shortly after the Brandt Report was issued. To the not-so-secret satisfaction of the editors, it was the worst-selling issue of the year.

DURING THIS PERIOD, while I was still publisher of the paper, more of my energy was going to The Washington Post Company than to *The Washington Post* itself. I had been thinking for quite a while about turning the paper over to Don, but was struggling with several questions: When was the transition best for Don? When was it best for me? When was it best for the *Post*?

Toward the end of 1978, when I had been publisher in title for nearly ten years and in essence for some years before that, I decided the time was ripe. I was enough detached as a parent to know that Don was ready; he has always been more mature than his years—always hardworking, conscientious, decent, bright, and able. And I needed to concentrate on the chairman and chief-executive-officer aspects of the company, which were growing more and more demanding. At the same time, I had come to the conclusion that there had to be a change in the editorial page. I couldn't solve Phil Geyelin's problems for him, and the situation had grown difficult for everyone. I thought that Phil should retire and that Meg should become editor, and I knew Don agreed, but for two reasons I didn't want to be the one to make the change. First, Meg was my friend, and I worried that such a move on my part—in essence, promoting my friend—might be perceived negatively. More important, I had learned when I began to work and made my own first major move—bringing Ben to the *Post*—that there was a completely different relationship with the people you put in place as contrasted with the people you inherited from your predecessor. I didn't want Don to inherit my editor, even if it was someone on whom we agreed; I felt strongly that he ought to have the opportunity to name his own editor.

So I decided to act at the beginning of the following year. On January 10, 1979, at a routine expanded staff meeting, I turned over the title of publisher of the *Post* to Don. Having made my announcement, I went on to answer publicly some of the questions I had been wrestling with privately: what would it mean and why now. "To the question of why now, the answer, in fact, is easy. It is because Don is ready and I am ready. Actually, I suspect Don was ready before I was," I told the staff. Don, with his usual grace, responded, "My mother has given me everything but an easy act to follow."

My father, Phil, my son, and I all had in common a love of the newspaper business. But Don is also very different from the other three of us. To begin with, he was far more qualified in experience and temperament than we were at the time each of us took over. He had edited both the *St. Albans News* and the *Harvard Crimson*. Newspapering clearly was where his interests lay. When he was in Vietnam, we had written each other about his future on the *Post*. By then he had decided to put off coming to the paper in order to learn more about the world. He strongly believed that you couldn't "be a good newspaperman if you've done nothing but work for newspapers all your life."

Besides Phil, others whom he respected had suggested to him that doing many different things and having many different experiences was the best possible preparation for any job. Don had particularly learned from John Gardner, and from Scotty Reston, who told him that he thought "the important thing was that no one should be able to say to someone 'You just don't understand my situation.' " He wrote me in December 1967, "Instinctively, I see that once I start working for *The Post*, I won't ever work for anyone else again. And there is a hell of a lot I want to do before then."

Don began, after Vietnam, by becoming a policeman in the District of Columbia. The *Post's* much-loved, longtime reporter on the police beat, Al Lewis, came to see me when he heard the news, saying, "I can stop this. It's way too dangerous. We don't want him running around doing that." In some ways, I didn't want it either—it *was* dangerous and it worried me—but I also knew that it was what Don wanted and that he had good reasons for choosing to do it. Oddly, he seemed to grow up noticeably more in the time he spent in the police department than in the previous two years in the army. I asked him why that was so and he responded, "Oh, that's easy. In the army you just do as you're told all day long, while on the police force you're constantly having to make your own decisions in difficult circumstances on the spot."

Don started at the *Post* as a metro reporter beginning in January 1971. He then moved through various jobs in a number of departments, from being a general clerk in accounting to assistant home-delivery manager in circulation, from promotion clerk to outside sales representative in classified and retail advertising, from assistant production manager to *Newsweek's* Los Angeles bureau.

In the fall of 1974, Ben Bradlee had a problem with the sports department: two managers were battling with each other and the section clearly was feeling the effects. Without telling me, Ben resolved the problem by offering the job of sports editor to Don. I had counted on furthering Don's training program by getting him more involved on the business side of the company and was somewhat irritated with Ben for resolving his problem at my expense, but I also saw it as a great mid-career management job for Don. Because it combined his passion for the editorial side of the business with his love of sports, I could hardly frustrate him by not agreeing. So I acceded to the move on condition that Don go in and out in a year and that he replace himself, which he did brilliantly with George Solomon.

In his year at the helm of sports, Don worked harder than anyone I'd ever seen. I once found him at his desk at three in the morning and asked him why he was there. His response was that, since he'd done a stint in production, he knew exactly how many late scores it was possible to send down to the composing room between 2:00 and 3:00 a.m., and still get the paper out on time.

When his year in Sports was up, Don became assistant general manager, and it was from that vantage point that he was so helpful to me and so instrumental to the paper during the pressmen's strike. I knew then that he was more than ready to take over as publisher. The relationship between him and me might have been immensely difficult, but we have both worked to make it smooth. It's difficult to have a parent for your boss; to have that parent be your mother is even harder. Don deserves the major share of the credit for making our professional relationship a happy one.

Once he was publisher, Don named Meg to succeed Phil Geyelin as the editorial-page editor, with all the expectable stresses and strains. She reinvigorated the page and ever since has edited it and the op-ed page, and written her column for the *Post* and *Newsweek*, with great distinction.

Though I had always known Don would one day become publisher, what I hadn't foreseen is that it would be so hard for me to give it up. But the move was an enormous emotional wrench, which I had to steel myself to endure because I knew it was right. "Publisher of the *Post*" is a title I would miss. I loved being directly involved with the paper and was intensely emotionally attached to it. The early years of participation with my father and Phil in the struggle to survive and my own dramatic years as publisher had left me with an immeasurable and immutable love for the *Post*, but I wasn't going to hang on too long just because I enjoyed it all so much.

So I had withdrawal pangs, but I left with a more-than-full-time and challenging job as head of the company—chairman and chief executive officer, responsible for the growth, soundness, and economic health of a half-billion-dollar company with five thousand employees and about two thousand shareholders.

BY THE FALL of 1979, the company was doing pretty well from a financial point of view—there had been a slight run-up in the stock—but as always there were problems, including the ongoing difficulties at the *Trenton Times* and *Inside Sports* and an earnings decline. I was feeling less than confident about my ability to turn any of this around. Warren and I were driving down to Glen Welby for the weekend when, as tactfully and gently as he could, he broke the news to me that Bill Ruane and Sandy Gottesman, close friends of his and investors who had bought a lot of *Post* stock for themselves and for their clients, were going to sell tens of millions of dollars' worth of it. Ruane managed the Sequoia Fund, and Gottesman was a managing partner at the First Manhattan Company, and these groups were about to sell all or half of their Post stock.

Warren had pondered how best to deliver this news, and he tried sugar-coating it in every way he could. I have to admit that my immediate response was to burst into tears. Here were these terribly clever investors, reputed to have such great judgment, who no longer believed in us; others surely would be leaving in droves. I considered their move a referendum on my management of the company, and it was clear I was found wanting.

Warren did his desperate best to console me, explaining that Bill considered he had done so well on Post stock that it added up to too much of some of his portfolios. He was keeping his own stock. "You don't know Wall Street," Warren tried to reassure me. "People don't think in a long-term way there. When your stock reaches $100, Wall Street will buy it." Naturally, I thought he was just trying to make me feel better; it was absurd to think that the stock would ever reach $100. I was not consoled.

Warren, of course, had a totally different perspective from mine on what Bill and Sandy were doing. He viewed it as an enormous plus in the lifetime of the company, almost like the *Times-Herald* merger. Though he knew I'd be profoundly distressed by the idea, he realized right away how much the company would benefit in future profits by their selling their stock. He tried to convince me that we should be holding a party, adding, "Don't worry. We'll just buy what they sell. It will be good for us and they'll regret it." Although I didn't stop worrying, we did buy in the stock at an average price of $21.91, which Sandy and Bill had bought before two splits at an equivalent price of $6.50.

Once, much later, Warren and I discussed women bursting into tears in business situations and I reminded him of our ride to Glen Welby. "Well," he said, smiling, "we made several hundred million dollars then. The next time you burst into tears, call me first." He added, "Look at it this way, Kay. If you hadn't bought it in, *I* would have burst into tears, so one of us had to cry."

From this point on, I really concentrated on trying to get the company straightened out. I resigned from most of the outside boards on which I had been serving—the University of Chicago and George Washington University among them, as well as Allied Chemical—and became much more actively involved with groups associated with the media and with newspapers: the Bureau of Advertising, the board of the Associated Press, and, most important, the board of the American Newspaper Publishers Association.

Given all the company's problems with which I was dealing at the time, it may have been crazy to have been involved so actively with all three of these industry organizations, but since none of them had any other women, it served a purpose for them and was helpful with the industry, as well as helping me become more familiar with some of the larger problems that media companies face.

The Bureau of Advertising, on which I served from 1971 through 1979, bumping up to its executive board from 1980 to 1982, had not been a favorite of Phil's, but I found it a congenial place. Its board had a decidedly lopsided composition at the time: not only was it all-male and all-white, but it was business- not editorial-oriented.

The eighteen directors on the AP board are elected by the membership, and anyone wishing to serve has to campaign for election, which I found difficult. Although I'd been warned that most people didn't get elected on their first try, I was still disappointed when I was defeated on mine. The following year, in April 1974, I was better organized and won, becoming the first woman member of the board, on which I served the allotted three terms until 1983.

I had been elected to ANPA's board in 1973, again the first woman, but this time not until a man who actively opposed women members had himself left the board. I wrote Lori Wilson, Al Neuharth's wife: "The view of 'The Good Ole Boys' will not die except generationally. Their view of the 'lovely ladies' and toasts to the wives will be with us for the rest of our ANPA lives!"

In those years, the chairmanship of the board alternated each two-year term between men associated with big and small papers, and under a very undemocratic procedure the incumbent chairman essentially chose or designated his successor. In 1979, Al Neuharth, who was the group's chairman at the time, approached me with the idea that I become chairman after the tenure of a nice, able man, Len Small, who ran a group of Illinois papers and was slated to succeed Al. The idea had never entered my head, but Al was firm in his conviction that I should be willing to take on the job, pointing out that if I didn't there was no other woman in the foreseeable future who would be there to do it. Little by little, I came to agree that I should be available—another barrier to crack—and that it might be interesting as well. I said if he could pull it off I'd like it, so Len invited me to succeed him when his term was up in 1981 and made it known that this was to happen.

But another tragedy hurled me into yet another job with little or no preparation. Len was killed in an automobile accident and, with almost no warm-up, I was handed a new time-consuming responsibility nearly two years before I expected it, becoming chairman of ANPA in April of 1980. Managing a big, all-male (except for me), diverse organization—small and big papers have very different points of view and interests—was one more stressful obligation. It was inconceivably intimidating for me, at first, to preside over the two-day committee meetings and the conventions, and in between to deal with the staff at the headquarters in Reston, Virginia. In addition, I had to wrestle with the dawning problems of electronic news and the challenge of the phone companies.

AROUND THE COMPANY, I was dealing with matters ranging from the circulation outlook at the *Post* and *Newsweek*, to newsprint costs, to continuing profit problems at PNS. I tried to concentrate on strategic planning for the company and hoped to make progress in the divisions and to improve the way in which each related to the others. We still needed a sounder growth policy in corporate. I had been thinking and working and picking the brains of various people for years about growth issues but had seen little or no progress. I was also thinking about the importance of performance appraisals and rewards, financial and otherwise. As always, there were people problems.

In the early summer of 1979, I went through another painful turnover at *Newsweek*. Ed Kosner had been a very successful number two under Oz Elliott, but without Oz he was having difficulty managing the large staff. Ed was a journalist of rare gifts but not yet a manager. Morale was at a low point. One person described to me what was happening as being "like the magazine having a nervous breakdown."

Peter Derow and I spent a lot of time discussing what to do, and again I'm afraid I listened to him and took his advice against my instincts. For one thing, I told Peter that, if Ed was in so much trouble, we had to warn him. Peter's answer was, "Absolutely not; if you do that, he's so unpredictable he might walk right out the door." Stupidly, I gave in to Peter's fears and didn't have the blunt talk with Ed that anyone under danger of dismissal has every right to expect and that can often be effective.

In the meantime, I'd been approached by an editor whom I knew at firsthand to be highly skilled in newspapers and whose skills I thought would be transferrable to a newsweekly. This was someone I had worked with and trusted, who wanted the job and who I thought would be perfect. But when I discussed it with Peter, he discouraged me from taking a risk by bringing in a non-news weekly editor. Again I acceded to what I believed was his better judgment. So we went back to Lester Bernstein, once *Newsweek*'s national and managing editor, who we thought would make a safe transition for a few years until we found another editor. I knew instantly that this was a wrong move when the first thing Lester did was take a month's vacation.

When Peter and I broke the news to Ed, he was naturally upset and bitter, and he had a valid cause for complaint, since neither of us had ever fully aired our differences with him. There was a meeting to let the editorial staff know about the changes. Ed walked in, said, "I am leaving the magazine," and then walked out of the room and out of the building. I stood up directly afterwards, said I was sorry for the abruptness of it, and praised Ed and Lester; then I, too, left. I wanted nothing more than to escape, and there was such a large crowd waiting for an elevator that I walked down the stairs from the fortieth floor to the twelfth, where the corporate offices were.

It was another change of editors at the top—and yet another chance for people to skewer me for being a difficult woman. I have noticed that, when an editor got changed, it was often the people under him who had complained the most vocally who then criticized me the loudest for the "way" it was done—so sudden, so unexpected, so cruel. Privately, however, people told me it was a move that had to be made at the time to help *Newsweek*. We went through two more unsuccessful tries at the editorship before we finally came up with Rick Smith.

There were more changes to come. My relationship with Mark Meagher was not an easy one and was growing more and more trying as I realized that here was yet another executive who had not worked out as I had hoped. Mark was a good person with great abilities in certain areas, but he was probably too young and inexperienced to have been rushed to the top of the company as president and chief operating officer. In July 1980, we announced that Mark would resign at the end of the year. The decision had been all the more difficult because I was fond of him personally. This may have been the low point of my business life; it was certainly one of the most painful and discouraging times I'd had. Mark's departure got writ large in my mind not just as my personal failing but, rather, as a sign that the whole company was in turmoil. Corporate was certainly not well run. We hadn't grown in any sensible or substantive way, and *Newsweek* was in managerial confusion. This time, the press really beat up on me, even exaggerating the number of changes among the top executives, in part because of a misreading of our organization chart and a mixing up of the company with the paper.

There was no one within the company to whom I could turn as a new president; I was going to have to look outside. Unfortunately, I was so shaken and discouraged by the personnel mistakes we'd made that I feared we wouldn't search for a replacement in the right way. My reputation as a difficult person to work with made a search hard under the best of circumstances, and stories were circulating that no one but Don could become president, because who would want to be sandwiched between a mother and a son. But Don was still very young and had just taken over the *Post* as publisher the year before.

Just as I began to look for help, Peter Derow, who by now had become a director of the company and chairman of *Newsweek* as well as president, after Bob Campbell's retirement, suggested that we bring in a consulting firm to study the company and be an administrative help while I was trying to run it alone. I thought there was merit to the idea, so we hired McKinsey and Company, and for the next year there were repeated meetings between people from McKinsey and from our company, going endlessly over what we'd done and what we hoped to do. I was increasingly baffled about the whole consultation process, which seemed to be little more than McKinsey's regurgitating what we had told them in a slightly different but not very helpful way.

The most imprudent suggestion made by McKinsey in its report was that we should stop buying in the stock: it had been all right to do at $20 and

$21, but now that the stock had reached $26 it was no longer a good idea. I actually took this advice for a while, although, as Warren has repeatedly said, anyone would have told me the company was probably worth more than $400 million on the market and that the stock-market value was about a quarter of that amount. Perhaps no one at McKinsey ever stopped to do that math. Afterwards, Don referred to the page in McKinsey's report on which the suggestion had been made as the "half-billion-dollar page," given that that's what it probably cost us in lost value to the company.

At the same time, I worked with a headhunter in my quest for a new company president. There were numerous meetings with the headhunter and with various candidates, none of whom seemed very plausible, and many of whom seemed remote from what I had in mind. They were either condescending to me or obsequious, and neither alternative appealed to me in any way. This activity went on for nearly a year, with me essentially running the company alone, with help from Marty Cohen, our financial vice-president and treasurer, and a management group that included the division heads and the few other corporate officers. It was a rough year, and I had no reason to think it was going to get any better until I resolved the management problems.

In November 1980, an additional worry came when Mobil Oil Company President William Tavoulareas sued the *Post* for libel for a story we'd run a year earlier by reporter Patrick Tyler detailing some of his business dealings. This lawsuit dragged on in various courts; one jury awarded the plaintiffs compensatory and punitive damages of $2.05 million in 1982, a decision overturned by a judge, then reinstated. Finally, the U.S. Court of Appeals ruled on March 13, 1987, that the 1979 story was "substantially" true and was not libelous, and after more than seven years, the case came to a close, with a decision in our favor.

By the time of the lawsuit, the cumulative effect of the pressures and anxiety and activities on so many levels at once took its toll. On a visit to New York in March of 1981 to make a speech to an advertising group, I contracted pneumonia, spent twelve days in the hospital there, and returned home extremely weak.

Immediately on my return, I got a call from Jim Shepley, president of Time Inc. and chairman of the *Star*, asking to meet me. This signaled yet another dramatic moment in our lives—mine and Don's, at least. Jim's call meant that Time Inc. was ready to do something about the *Star* and wanted to talk about the possibility of a joint operating agreement.

Our family had always wanted and welcomed the competition and felt that everyone was better off with it than without it, so Don and I and Warren had many meetings with our lawyers and the *Star*'s representatives trying to arrive at an agreement. We were still negotiating when, ten days after our last meeting, officials from Time Inc. held a press conference to announce the closing of the *Star* in two weeks. I actually heard the news on the radio while I was in my car on my way to work. The announcement left me with a range of emotions: first and foremost, I was deeply sad that it had come to this, that Washington was to lose a fine paper that had many loyal readers, not to mention employees, who would be devastated. I was also numbed by the reality of this final victory of sorts—bittersweet though it was—after all the years of struggle. This was not a competitor we hated but one we respected.

There was some talk of possible buyers for the *Star*, but that seemed unlikely. Rupert Murdoch, Walter Annenberg, Mortimer Zuckerman, and Armand Hammer were all mentioned as considering making proposals. To prevent anyone from merely buying the paper in order to profit from selling its assets, Time put some fairly rigorous requirements on any buyer. We at the *Post* continued to talk to people at the *Star*, and to others, Al Neuharth and Armand Hammer among them, about possible alternative joint operating agreements, but, in the end, there seemed no way to save the *Star*.

On August 7, 1981, the 128-year-old *Star* ceased publication. There was no gloating. As Don said, this was "a sad day for Washington and the newspaper business." The city and the country had lost a great American newspaper. A *Post* editorial a few days later stated, "Nobody wanted the *Star* to go out, but it is gone. Sadness, nostalgia, anger, sentimentality and apprehension have all been stirred by its loss, and these feelings have been shared by the people at the *Post*."

I knew the *Star*'s folding would present problems as well as opportunities for us, including resentment of our dominance and of the loss of the other much-beloved voice. There was predictable bitterness. Unless one understands newspaper economics and the inevitability of what happens when some degree of dominance is achieved, the tendency is to blame the remaining paper for being ruthless.

Almost a month later, when it was clear that no one would come forward to revive the fallen *Star*, we bought its land, building, and presses. We hired a number of its writers, most notably Mary McGrory. We picked up enough of its circulation so that, even with our new Springfield plant, we desperately needed the building and presses—and we're still printing there. Not a year passed before the opening of the *Washington Times* newspaper, founded and funded by the Unification Church. Its circulation and advertising are weak, but the paper does provide a lively, conservative editorial voice—at vast expense to the church. Presumably its backers feel that their presence in the nation's capital and access to the government are worth the price.

THE BEGINNING OF the end of the *Star* was not the only dramatic occurrence that spring of 1981. The previous fall, an article by one of our
new, young (twenty-six), bright reporters, Janet Cooke, had appeared on
the front page of the *Post*. "Jimmy's World," a piece about an eight-year-
old heroin addict, created a major impact on the community. The story
was sent out on the news-service wire and became a national and even an
international *cause célèbre*.

We felt the story was so good and so well written that we submitted it
for a Pulitzer Prize, which it won. The day after the prize was announced,
though, the whole story began to unravel, as it was revealed that there
were inconsistencies and exaggerations—if not untruths—in the way
Cooke had portrayed her own life. When the biographies of the Pulitzer
winners appeared in various newspapers, Vassar College called us to say
that Cooke had not only not graduated from there with honors, but had
not graduated at all; she had attended but left after a year for the University of Toledo, where she had received a bachelor's degree, not a master's,
as she'd claimed. People on the *Toledo Blade* called the Associated Press to
say that their records of Cooke's credentials didn't jibe with those that
were appearing in wire stories. When we checked what Cooke had listed
as her own credentials, we found that they didn't correspond to what she'd
written elsewhere—for instance, it turned out that she didn't speak several
languages.

On April 15, 1981, Janet Cooke finally confessed to *Post* editors that
she had fabricated the story. "Jimmy" turned out to be a composite, and
the quotes attributed to the child were, in fact, invented. Certain events
Cooke had described as having eyewitnessed never happened. Ben sent a
telegram to a long list of news organizations saying: "It is with great sadness and regret that I inform you that Janet Cooke, *The Washington Post*
reporter awarded the Pulitzer Prize for feature writing Monday, has determined that she cannot accept the award. . . . She regrets these events as
much as *The Washington Post* regrets them. She has offered her resignation, and it has been accepted."

We immediately assigned our ombudsman, Bill Green, to write about
what happened and why, believing that this was the most objective way to
hang out every detail of our embarrassment and to help us all understand
where we'd gone wrong. Many things had indeed gone wrong. At almost
no point was Cooke asked hard questions about what she was reporting.
She was trusted, and she wrote so well that no one thought to check the
facts of the story. The editors all relied on each other, so that the story had
gone from desk to desk until it eventually ended up on the front page.
Even her bio had not been sufficiently checked when she was hired.

I believe that we did all the right things after the fact. We revealed the
truth in excruciating and embarrassing detail. We apologized editorially.

We examined the system that had let it happen. Bill Green asked some tough questions—including whether race (she was black) helped Cooke advance faster than she should have—and drew a number of conclusions: the business of trusting reporters had gone too far; young reporters were looking for a Watergate under every rock; the scramble for journalistic prizes was poisonous; new reporters shouldn't be pushed so fast; the editors didn't listen enough to lurking doubts below them.

Janet Cooke blamed the paper for putting too much pressure on reporters to get what Woodward called the "Holy Shit" story instead of solid reporting. She accused us of creating competition among reporters to get on the front page. The journalism faculty at Howard University filed a complaint against the *Post* relating to the Cooke affair. *The New Republic* titled one of its articles on the matter "Deep Throat's Children."

I felt for Don Graham, who was then the publisher and who took on a very tough news conference and handled it well. I stuck out our collective neck even farther by calling Tom Winship, then chairman of the American Society of Newspaper Editors, a group that was meeting in Washington shortly after the prize was returned, to ask him if he was planning a session on the affair. He said he wasn't, and that at this late date there was no place for it. My response was: "You'll be the laughingstock of the industry if you don't do the program. I personally dread it, but it's the big ethical issue of the moment. You'd better find the time." Tom agreed and scheduled an early-bird meeting, heavily attended, in which our editors got pummeled. I was proud that Don Graham stood there by Ben, often with his arm around Ben's shoulder. Also right there was our incomparable former editor, Russ Wiggins, who, with his usual wry humor, said, "I feel great about the state of the American press. Every editor I saw assured me this couldn't have happened at his paper."

We took a terrible drubbing from all sides, and rightly so in some ways. Clearly, we had made mistakes and some of our procedures were not functioning properly. But I felt that the self-righteousness on the part of many in the industry, assuming it couldn't have happened in other places, was not only spiteful but shortsighted. I later told an ANPA gathering that there was a real danger that, in our efforts not to have such a thing happen again, "we will become so nervous we will go to the other extreme, and not do the job that a free press is supposed to do."

To ADD TO MY ANXIETIES during this difficult period, Peter Derow told me he'd found another job—ironically, back at CBS. He was quite willing to start in again on what was wrong with me and the company, but by this time I'd grown tougher and told him that once was enough. It seemed to irritate him not to be able to do a repeat monologue on my failings.

Only as the search for a new company president grew a little more or-ganized did I become more optimistic about the future. I held interview after interview with various candidates, at first not quite knowing what it was I was looking for, but somehow feeling I'd know it when I saw it. The search went on for so long that I began referring to it as "the search for Mr. Wonderful." But over the course of the process, I came to realize that I did have an idea of the goals of the company, and the search process helped me crystallize that idea while at the same time helping me define the qualities I was looking for in a president.

At last, in early July 1981, when I interviewed Dick Simmons—who had been president of Dun & Bradstreet—I instantly saw in him a number of the qualities I knew I needed and wanted, including a proven track record as a manager. A few days later, Warren, Don and Mary Graham, and I had dinner with Dick at my house. He and I then met together for several hours on a Saturday, talking comfortably. Two weeks later, I ex-tended an offer to Dick to become president and chief operating officer of The Washington Post Company. The search for "Mr. Wonderful," which had taken more than a year, had ended.

— *Chapter Twenty-eight* —

D ICK SIMMONS'S arrival helped make the decade of the 1980s the best years from a business point of view both for the company and for me. The Washington Post Company began achieving its goals of sustaining earnings growth, developing new businesses, and building for the future. And a great weight was lifted from my shoulders. I no longer dreaded the meetings to discuss plans, options, acquisitions. Without the tension that had existed for so long between me and whoever occupied that office across the conference room from mine, the future seemed more certain—and more positive. I realized only in retrospect how tough the previous years had been. Working became a pleasure again. Without recognizing it, I had gotten to the point where, the better things were going under my management, the more unhappy I became that the results weren't even better. Many of Dick's first moves helped make those results better yet, and, equally important, he helped me gain some perspective on how the company was doing, what we should be doing, and what we could expect to do.

In some ways, Dick and I were an unusual duo. We are very different from each other in style and temperament, yet were remarkably compatible. In time, we almost shared the company's top two jobs. He was much more than a chief operating officer; he was my partner and friend. His true and sure sense of himself helped keep him untroubled by my peculiar managerial background and my tendency to call Warren about any problem or opportunity. I tried always to give Dick the credit he deserved, as well as to give him a free rein in all operating aspects of the company. He in turn seemed very unbothered by my higher profile.

Dick moved fast and with assurance. In late October 1981, just a few weeks into his tenure, we announced that we were selling the *Trenton Times* to Allbritton Communications. And a few days later, we announced that we were engaged in discussions relating to the sale of *Inside Sports*, which had lost a lot of money and showed few signs of turnaround or possible improvement. I knew it had to be sold and was relieved when Dick moved quickly to do it. The sales of these two properties significantly reduced the company's earnings for that year but allowed us to focus our efforts on the development of our core businesses, which were all setting new records for revenue.

Dick also took the lead in looking for growth opportunities in line with the main mission of our company, related to the way people communicate. In 1982, we took our first step into the electronic age by getting into the cellular-telephone business. A few years later, after building some of the first cellular systems in the United States, we divested ourselves of what we had acquired in this area. It was a strategic exit based on our own recognition that those companies with market dominance had a significant advantage over the smaller players, of whom we were certainly one. Nevertheless, we did very well financially. (Alan Spoon, who later became president of the company, deserves much of the credit here.)

In 1983, we acquired a small electronic-information company called Legi-Slate, a database publisher that is now the nation's leading provider of online information on federal legislative and regulatory activity. We also got into cable programming, specifically related to sports, by acquiring about 50 percent of SportsChannel Associates, a network that telecast leading professional sports events to New York–area cable subscribers. These businesses, too, were later sold.

In November 1983, we successfully launched a national weekly edition of *The Washington Post*, an idea I had heard discussed since almost the first years of my father's ownership of the paper. This edition now has a circulation of well over 100,000. Because the *Post* is a local paper, geared to the Washington metropolitan-area market, it was never feasible for us to undertake a truly national daily edition, but this weekly tabloid of selected *Post* articles on politics and government satisfies many people's desire to follow the *Post*'s political reporting.

Late in 1984, we acquired a tutoring-and-test-preparation company, the Stanley H. Kaplan Company (now called the Kaplan Educational Centers), which interested Dick more than it did me. I confess that my lack of interest was reflected in my saying to Dick, "I don't give a shit about it, but if you think it will be profitable, let's do it." Not only has it worked out well for us, despite some ups and downs, but it has considerably more purpose and potential than I realized.

In 1985, we purchased 20 percent of the common stock of Cowles Media Company, owners of the *Minneapolis Star Tribune* and some other, smaller properties. That interest has grown over the years, and we now hold 28 percent.

We were less successful in several other areas. Early in 1982, we tried to buy the *Des Moines Register*, a paper and a company I respected greatly and would have loved to acquire, but we weren't the highest bidder. Just after we launched the weekly, we bought a 20-percent interest in the *National Journal*, a magazine about the federal government, but after being involved for three years we let Times Mirror acquire it. We looked hard at the number-two paper both in Chicago, the *Sun-Times*, and in Houston, the *Post*, but didn't go any further.

As a company, we have been conservative in our growth—perhaps too conservative—but as the eighties ended we were not left with a load of debt and the resulting need to sell the good properties, as were many other companies, who let their desire for growth overwhelm their judgment. We turned down the *Denver Post*, which was bought by the Times Mirror Company with disastrous results. Sometimes the things you don't do are as important as the things you do.

My major frustration in the first few years after Dick's arrival was that we were still not regarded by the financial world as a hot property, which kept our stock undervalued. This, however, worked to our advantage, since we continued our consistent pattern of buying in the stock, which helped us later.

Of all our attempts to grow, our most spectacular success and the best acquisition that Dick and I made together was cable, which began with our purchase of fifty-three cable systems from Capital Cities Communications Company, a purchase finalized in January 1986. Throughout 1985, Warren had helped his friend Tom Murphy, CEO of Cap Cities, acquire the ABC network. I was happy for both of them when the deal went through, at least until I realized the implications for me vis-à-vis Warren, who pointed out the obvious—that he would be going on the board of Cap Cities/ABC and would therefore have to get off ours. By then, Warren had been a board member for eleven years and never missed a meeting. Telling me this was hard for him; he knew I would feel bereft, to say the least, but he assured me he would still be at the other end of the telephone, that we would see each other as much as usual, that he would not vanish from my life. Even so, I was disturbed and saddened by the news.

In fact, it worked out well. Warren kept his shares in our company and remained involved with us. More important, as a sort of consolation prize, Murphy allowed us to bid on Cap Cities' cable systems, whereas that company divested everything else through investment bankers. Warren kept a correct distance from the negotiations, which were carried on between the Post Company and Cap Cities exclusively. We ran numbers, deliberated, discussed at length, argued among ourselves, and finally completed the acquisition for $350 million, much the biggest acquisition in the company's history—and the one that propelled us forward to our highest rank in the Fortune 500, that of 263 in both 1986 and 1987. By adding new customers and purchasing other small systems, Post-Newsweek Cable has now grown from 350,000 to 580,000 subscribers. And, happily, Warren is now back on our board, after serving Cap Cities/ABC for ten years, when it was sold to Disney.

At *Newsweek*, after years of tough going, we had begun to turn things around. One of the most painful failures on my part was that both the business and the editorial sides of the magazine kept undergoing managerial turmoil, each for different reasons. With editorial, I was directly responsible for the problem, and it took a long time to get it right. I still sensed great pools of ill-will and even disloyalty at *Newsweek*. Part of this may have been due to the excessive management turnover, but some of it certainly was the result of the natural competition between those working for the company in Washington and those working in New York. I finally offered Rick Smith the editorship, and knew he'd be just right for the job when he responded with, "Don't worry, I won't fuck it up."

Indeed he didn't. Under his strong leadership, first as editor and later as president, the whole mood improved—yet another example for me of how things get better when management acts together. Even with the problems newsmagazines have experienced in the new environment, *Newsweek* has had many fine successes and a great deal of solid growth. In the mid-1990s, *Newsweek* came to be considered the best of the newsmagazines, with its stellar writers like Jon Alter, Bob Samuelson, Jane Bryant Quinn, Allan Sloan, George Will, Meg, and many more. I felt a great deal of satisfaction.

Post-Newsweek Stations began to do better and better as well. Our stations cover all three major networks, so that, as Warren once pointed out, "anything achieved is independent of whether any one network happens to be hot at the moment." Joel Chaseman proved that he could operate the television stations so well under Dick's direction that their margins grew competitive with the best in the business. Our television news was as distinguished as that of the *Post* and *Newsweek*. All of the stations (including the two we have since acquired in Texas: KPRC in Houston and KSAT in San Antonio), now ably led by Bill Ryan, were and continue to be leaders in news. Following the demise of the *Star*, the *Post*'s penetration of its market was around 50 percent daily and 70 percent Sunday through most of the 1980s—by far the highest of any major U.S. metropolitan daily.

Out of everything we accomplished during the eighties, I was proudest of our improved management of the company, an area in which Dick was particularly strong. I once said I would like to win a Pulitzer Prize for management, and finally I was able to believe that we were becoming a truly well-run company. What's more, the effects of better management began to show. Our core businesses improved immeasurably in profitability, so that after a few years the company really took off: for several years,

The Washington Post Company led all companies in our field in a number of ways. Probably more important to me than any public acknowledgment of our gains, however, was what Warren thought about how we were doing. In mid-1984, he sent Don, Dick, and me a memo saying that he had just gone through a recent survey of publishing companies that charted their performance in various areas. He pointed out that, when Berkshire Hathaway bought its first shares in The Washington Post Company in the spring of 1973, the cost was $10.6 million, and the market value in 1984 for those shares was $140 million. He had gone down the list of publishing companies in the survey and run the numbers to calculate what would have happened if he had spent this same $10.6 million at the same moment in the shares of the other companies listed. In any other company, he would have fallen far short of what he had earned with Post Company stock, so he concluded: "Instead of thanks a million—make it thanks anywhere from $65 to $110 million." It got even better later.

AFTER ALL THE years of struggle, things had finally started to go smoothly for the company and for me. Though I never stopped worrying altogether—it's not in my nature—the business of the company was going well enough, and I had enough confidence in Dick, that I began to relax a little and to enjoy a larger life again.

As the editorial corporate head of the company, I had always felt strongly that part of my job was to follow important world issues that could affect the company and its holdings, but I hadn't always been in a position to give this responsibility the time and attention I felt it deserved. Starting in the late 1970s, I had taken some trips with a few editors and reporters—Meg and Jim Hoagland almost always going along—to one or several countries, to observe for ourselves what we had been reading about in the pages of our own publications. The number of these trips picked up in the early 1980s, largely because Dick's steady hand would be at the helm while I was gone.

On one of the first of these trips, at the request of the Romanians, we interviewed their communist dictator, Nicolae Ceausescu, in the very palace where he and his wife were later killed. He spent the entire interview complaining of his treatment by the West, while we tried to ask questions about his persecution of different religious and ethnic groups and his repression of dissent. The interview was stilted, to say the least: we took turns asking predetermined questions which he answered at length and mechanically. His long answers were shortened by our interpreter to, "He says, 'Welcome.' "

In 1978, the high point of a trip to West Africa was a visit to open a school in a small village a few hours outside of Abidjan, the relatively

affluent capital of the Ivory Coast. Accompanied by a young couple from
the U.S. Embassy, we were welcomed by most of the village, led by a chief
in robes and derby hat, despite the 105-degree heat and oppressive humidity. At an outdoor banquet, he made a speech in French declaring what
an honor it was to have me there as the seventeenth-most-important person in the world, a description he had obviously picked up from a poll that
had appeared in *U.S. News & World Report*. From then on, Jim Hoagland
enjoyed referring to me as *"numéro dix-sept."*

In 1980, I scheduled a trip to the Middle East with Meg and Jim, to
include, at Henry Kissinger's suggestion, Saudi Arabia as well as Egypt
and Israel. We were not sure the Saudis would receive two women, but
embassy officials—and, more important, Prince Bandar, an influential
member of the royal family then in this country training with the Army
Air Force—told us we would be welcome. Meg and I had been so thoroughly briefed about how to dress and how generally to comport ourselves while in Saudi Arabia that we were in a state of mild terror as we
landed, but we were told that our even being allowed to disembark from
the front of the plane represented real progress: only a few years previously, Pat Nixon and Nancy Kissinger had had to exit through a door at
the back of the plane.

Women were simply invisible in Saudi Arabia. We saw them only
once during our visit—at the house of Sheik Ahmed Zaki Yamani, then
minister of petroleum and mineral resources, where he had assembled a
small group of very Westernized technicians, middle managers in government, and their wives. By contrast, a dinner at the home of Prince Abdullah, then the third-most-powerful man in the country and the head of its
National Guard, turned out to be something out of the Thousand and
One Arabian Nights. We drove up to his palace, Meg and I dressed de-
murely in long skirts and long-sleeved blouses, covering everything we
possibly could, and stepped into a large oval room around the walls of
which members of the Guard sat cross-legged, with full military regalia
over their Arab robes, leather straps lined with bullets crossed over their
chests. They stared at us as we were led to seats elevated above theirs but
surrounding a kind of throne that was positioned even higher than ours,
in which sat Prince Abdullah. We learned later that Abdullah had had to
explain to his men for an hour beforehand why he had to have these two
American women to dinner.

In Egypt, we interviewed President Sadat at his country home. We
had several small tape recorders going as he talked, the Egyptians a single
large one; we were impressed to see a man emerge as if by magic from behind the bushes in the garden to change the tape. Sadat kept addressing
me personally with brutally offensive remarks about some of his neighbors. He would say, "Jimmy"—referring to Carter—"told me I can't say

this, Katharine, of King Hussein," and then he would go on to make some derisive and cutting remark. He also had some biting things to say about Henry Kissinger. But it was an interesting interview, and everyone went straight to work writing it up for the *Post* and *Newsweek*. We were amused when an Egyptian government man appeared, somewhat embarrassed, to ask us for a copy of our tapes from the interview, since their recorder hadn't worked. Later, we were dumbstruck to discover that, whereas we had observed their ground rules and had omitted all the startling remarks Sadat had made, the transcript of the interview ran in its entirety in an Egyptian paper, complete with the acerbic asides addressed to me. I hate to think of the repercussions these may have caused.

While we were in Egypt, I asked to see the shah of Iran, to whom the Egyptians had given refuge, and at the last minute they agreed to allow Jim and me in. The shah was perfectly willing, even eager, to talk at length and on the record, and indeed he spoke for two hours, flaying the British and the Americans for turning their backs on him. He regretted, as Jim noted in the lead to his story, "having followed 'a policy of surrender' to his opponents during his final days in power and said he wished he had used military force to put down the demonstrations that broke his rule." He told us that it was his own miscalculations, coupled with conflicting signals from the American and British governments, that had caused him to fail. Our interview with the shah turned out to be his final one, since he died shortly thereafter.

In Israel, nothing equaled our last dinner there, which was hosted by the director general of the Ministry of Foreign Affairs—a dinner that degenerated into a savage attack on the *Post* in general and its editorial policy in particular. At one point, Meg spoke up to rebut these attacks, saying that the Israelis needed to understand that one couldn't help being humbled by all that the Jews had experienced in Europe and by the danger they were in now—and that nobody she knew thought otherwise—but "what we were writing was our idea of what had to be done to avoid a terrible fate." With that, the questions began and grew increasingly hostile. The Israelis were especially vicious to Meg, who, being Jewish, was someone they thought ought to espouse their views uncritically.

One of the most bizarre of the interviews we held during these trips was with Muammar Qaddafi of Libya. Jim Hoagland, Chris Dickey of *Newsweek*, and I had gone to North Africa in 1988 to take a closer look at the growth of fundamentalism there. We succeeded in a last-minute request to interview Qaddafi, who was in Algeria at the time with the leaders of that country and Tunisia, and we were flown to where the leaders were meeting and where we were to see Qaddafi. We were all startled to be told that he wanted to see me alone first, but I walked into our agreed-upon meeting place and Qaddafi received me in a small room, rising from a leather chair to greet me politely. We exchanged small talk, and then he quickly led the discussion to Bob Woodward's book on the CIA, *Veil*, which had just come out, and in which Bob had reported on the CIA's having collected information about certain of Qaddafi's proclivities, alleging that he had been known to wear makeup and high-heeled shoes and that his aides had bought a toy teddy bear for him. Qaddafi, like everyone else, was concerned about what had been written about him. What I particularly noticed was his eyes; they never stopped rolling around, looking everywhere but straight at you. He used an interpreter, but seemed to know a lot of English, and occasionally even corrected the interpreter's attempt to soften his language.

My meeting with Qaddafi went on long enough so that Jim got edgy, and finally he and Chris decided to interrupt. When the interview was over, I asked if I could take Qaddafi's picture. When he agreed, my camera inconveniently jammed. I was so frustrated that I gave it a powerful hit, and it somehow worked. I got a sufficiently good photo so that *Newsweek* used it in a story and gave me a credit as a free-lancer, as well as a check for $87.50, which I framed.

Probably the most demanding interview on all our trips was the one we did with Soviet leader Mikhail Gorbachev later that year. Jim and I had been working on setting up an interview with the Soviet president for about five years and through three different presidents: Chernenko had agreed, but was taken ill and died; Andropov had then given us hope of an interview when he, too, got sick and died. When Gorbachev came along, I immediately started again, and was frustrated when both Tom Brokaw of NBC and *Time* magazine preceded us. Finally, just before a summit meeting with President Reagan, an interview in Moscow was granted, and we worked terribly hard preparing for it, right up to the last minute.

When we went into the meeting room, Gorbachev came on in his usual strong, charismatic way, but as soon as we sat down and began asking questions, there was a noticeable change in his manner. He was no less articulate than he had been when I'd met him at official functions in Washington, but he seemed strangely subdued in voice and demeanor, even "laid back" in the physical sense. However, he started sitting upright and tensing up as the questions grew distasteful to him, reacting almost physically to questions about possible dissension in the Politburo and the jailing of vocal dissidents. Nevertheless, he answered at length in a very controlled fashion until he cut off the interview abruptly after the fifth question, which was about human rights.

So nervous was Gorbachev about any hint of dissension in the Central Committee that he had Nikolai Shishlin, an important Central Committee official, call the *Post*'s Moscow bureau to pass on the message that he didn't want to be quoted as mentioning the names of anyone from the

Politburo. Bob Kaiser took the call from Shishlin, who also said that, since President Gorbachev didn't want any Politburo person named in the transcript of questions that had been asked, we would have to reformulate one of the questions that had specifically referred to Yegor Ligachev, a conservative antireformer and Gorbachev's reputed chief rival at the time. Shishlin told Kaiser, "Let's play this by Moscow rules." Kaiser's response was that, since he was asking us to use the Soviets' official transcript of the interview rather than our own, only I could make that decision.

After we insisted that it was impossible for us to delete Ligachev's name from the interview, Shishlin called the bureau again to say that Gorbachev himself wanted Georgi Arbatov—the Soviet Union's foremost "Americanologist"—to deliver a message to me. Arbatov found me in the apartment of Gary Lee, the *Post*'s Moscow correspondent, where several of us had gathered, and he and I went into a separate room so that he could talk with me alone. He argued hard that we owed this small favor to Gorbachev, who had granted me the big favor of the interview. I said I was sorry but this was not a favor within my power to grant; once we had asked a question, it was unthinkable to go back and edit the question. We wouldn't even do this for our own president, much less another country's. I held firm.

After a while, we joined the others, and when he rose to leave, Shishlin, who had accompanied Arbatov, looked at me and said, "Don't worry. You won't be arrested." We never learned why Gorbachev was so sensitive about having Ligachev's name mentioned, and soon thereafter, as Bob Kaiser pointed out, "Gorbachev willingly answered a question about his relations with Ligachev, with no sign of sensitivity."

The Gorbachev interview was in some ways the cap of all these trips with Meg and Jim and others, which were such an important part of my life for fifteen years or more—we logged tens of thousands of miles over the years in traveling to South Africa, the Philippines, China, Korea, Japan, India, and countries throughout the Middle East and South America. Although Don was the publisher of the *Post* and editorially responsible for the paper, with his encouragement I stayed involved in ways that never interfered with his authority. These trips were one way. Receiving certain foreign visitors was another. Often, people I had met abroad came to Washington, and I would invite them to the *Post* for editorial lunches. I also often entertained people at my house. For the most part I didn't give public dinners just for the sake of giving them; they almost always served some purpose. Frequently, the guests of honor were people we had met on our editorial trips. Both President Kaunda of Zambia and President Mugabe of Zimbabwe came when they were in Washington, as did Willy Brandt, Václav Havel, and Helen Suzman.

Occasionally, because I had the room and the facilities to accommodate sizable groups, and because I had the staff to bring an event together

without too much effort, I was asked by go-betweens to entertain prominent visitors. This was the case with President Febres Cordero of Ecuador
and with the king and queen of Jordan. I was happy to do it, though somewhat to my dismay I began to see myself mentioned in the press as a
"prominent Washington hostess"—a term I very much disliked. Again, it
seemed to me a sexist way of viewing what I was doing, which, to me, was
a natural part of my job.

I also felt strongly that it was part of my job to keep up with people in
and out of office. It was all in my day's work to get to know those in government and help them know journalists. Many of my dinners involved
members of various administrations over the years and could be described
as political, although they were always nonpartisan, or at least bipartisan.

I have been friends with presidents from both political parties, but any
relationship, even an old one, can grow strained when you become—as I
did—a symbol of a major newspaper and magazine and the target of presidential displeasure. This occurred with Johnson, Nixon, and Bush, but,
curiously, not much with Reagan. Ford was professionally friendly. Except
for entertaining the Clintons on Martha's Vineyard when they were there
on vacation, I have had little contact with them; they have been polite but
are of a younger generation, so it's perfectly natural.

Those who come to Washington as president and who haven't lived
here and known the city (as had, for example, Jack Kennedy, Lyndon
Johnson, and even Richard Nixon) seem to have a skewed idea of socializ-
ing between people from the press and people from the administration.
There are those in both groups who feel that we shouldn't see each other
except in working situations. Though I recognize that this issue of friendships or relationships is a touchy one, I take a different view. A hands-off
approach may be best for those who are covering people in the government, but for a publisher I feel sure openness is best. I consider it the role
of the head of a newspaper to be bipartisan and to bring journalists together with people from government. I think that an easy relationship is
constructive and useful for both sides: it helps the publication by opening
doors, and provides those who are covered in the news with the knowledge of whom they can suggest ideas to, complain to, or generally deal
with. When people don't feel easy enough to call, they just sit there grinding their teeth. I fear unspoken anger. Especially, people who may disagree on politics must still be able to communicate, and it's crucial for all
of us in the press to listen to all sides.

Jimmy Carter was one of those outsider presidents who found it difficult to find the right *modus operandi* for Washington. One spring night just
a year into Carter's presidency, Ben Bradlee and I gave a reception for the
American Society of Newspaper Editors, which was meeting in Washington. There must have been three dozen or so editors from all over the

country, so I tried very hard to round up members of the government and people from the White House to meet them. Hamilton Jordan, Carter's chief of staff, sent a polite but firm regret. Incredibly, I never even received an answer from the press secretary, Jody Powell. Thinking how stupid it was for the press secretary to ignore an event involving so many top editors, I called his office and asked to speak to him. I was told he was in a meeting. I explained about the party and that I felt it would be useful for him to attend. Still no answer, and he didn't come.

Some years later, after Carter had left office, another such party took place. Powell was present, and he and his wife, Nan, were charming—in fact, he brought a harmonica and danced and sang late into the evening. Later, too, I got to know Hamilton Jordan, and his ability and his charm were evident. I gave a dinner for him at which my toast began, "Hamilton, welcome to the establishment." He replied that if he had joined earlier Jimmy Carter might still be in the White House. I don't know that that's true, but I do believe that the Carter administration missed some good opportunities.

With all of Carter's troubles both inside and outside Washington during his presidency, it was no surprise when Ronald Reagan defeated him to become the fortieth president of the United States. I had met the Reagans several years before they came to Washington as president and first lady. Truman Capote told me he had gotten to know them in the course of some research he was doing on death sentences, in which he had become interested after writing *In Cold Blood*. "Honey, I know you won't believe me, but you'd really like them," Truman told me in his falsetto voice. Truman was right: we got along well and began a long friendship that puzzled many people in Washington.

When the Reagans first came to Washington after the election, they gave a dinner for Washingtonians who were active in one way or another. I was unable to accept because of an out-of-town speech, but decided to invite them in return and was delighted when they accepted. Shaping a dinner for a president is tricky; there is a delicate line to be drawn as one tries to center it on them—to give them a good time—and, in a sense, to ignore all else, including hurt feelings and pressure from people who would like to be there or think they should be there.

The night the Reagans arrived for the dinner, my two wonderful longtime maids, Lucy and Dora, were leaning out a second-floor window, watching the limousine pull up. They saw President-elect Reagan step out and embrace me, kissing me on both cheeks. Dora, a forceful and funny woman, turned to Lucy and said, "I hope she enjoyed that because that's the last time that will ever happen." Dora was wise in the ways of Washington and ordinarily right, but in this instance she was wrong.

In our toasts at that first dinner, we spoke about the advantages of knowing each other, which both the president-elect and I firmly believed in. For Reagan, however, there were repercussions from coming to dinner at my house. The political right was appalled. One newspaper featured a photograph of him embracing me, which *The Wall Street Journal* called "a photograph that may upset arch-conservatives almost as much as the famous one of Jimmy Carter bussing Leonid Brezhnev at the Vienna summit." Howard Phillips, head of the Conservative Caucus, lit into Reagan in remarks at the Religious Roundtable, saying, "You cannot always have Kay Graham going to your cocktail parties and smiling at you. If by June the Washington establishment is happy with Ronald Reagan, then you should be unhappy with Ronald Reagan."

With some ups and downs, we managed to remain friends throughout the eight years of Reagan's administration. At some point Nancy and I started lunching together regularly. At first, just the two of us would have long gossipy lunches; later, Meg joined us, either at my house or hers. Probably the most public time Nancy and I had was a weekend she spent with me on the Vineyard in August 1985. I couldn't imagine Nancy on the liberal and distinctly unchic Vineyard and thought Mike Deaver was mad to suggest such a thing, but when I invited her, she said yes right away, and she came, along with the Deavers and Meg and Warren. It was a typical Vineyard weekend, very informal, with walks on the beach and casual dinners. I think Nancy enjoyed it, and I know I did—despite the solid week of work and planning.

Our last dinner at my house was in November, after the election, in 1988, just as the Reagans were getting ready to leave Washington for California. Security surrounding the president had gotten much tighter. Although my door sits way back from the street, I was asked to put up a tent so that the president could get out of his car concealed from view. When I brought them in, I was told not to take them into the living room, because by then it was too crowded, but I simply ignored this and did so, and they were both quickly surrounded by well-wishing friends. The throng created one minor problem when someone knocked against a glass, which spilled a drink with ice onto the floor. I was dumbstruck at seeing the president of the United States down on his hands and knees in the middle of the crowd, picking up the ice. On the phone the next day, Nancy told me this reminded her of something that had happened in the hospital after the assassination attempt. The president, who was not supposed to get out of bed, went to the bathroom and spilled some water on the floor in the process. When attendants came in, he was on his hands and knees wiping it up. Asked why, he said he was afraid the nurse would get into trouble.

THE NATURAL ARM'S-LENGTH relationship between the government and the press always takes on an even more adversarial nature during any presidential campaign. The election year of 1988 was no exception. There were the usual stresses and strains with both Bush and Michael Dukakis, his Democratic opponent, and there were some unusual ones. Both candidates, of course, complained about our coverage of their campaigns. Both visited the paper for editorial lunches, but our troubles with each of them mounted sharply, as did our editorial dismay at their campaigns.

I had known George Bush for years, not intimately but pleasantly. My father had invested in the oil company Bush had started as a young man, and I liked both George and Barbara and thought of them as fine moderate Republicans in the tradition of his father, Senator Prescott Bush, whom I had also known. I hadn't seen much of them in the previous eight years, when he had served as vice-president, but was well aware that he had been loyal to Reagan, politically as well as personally.

Newsweek, however, had gotten on the wrong side of the candidate when it published—the very week Bush had announced his intention to run for president—a cover story on the vice-president titled "Fighting the Wimp Factor." The "wimp" label had been a thorn in the Bush campaign flesh since that time. The profile of Bush had been fair and complete, but the effect of the word "wimp" crying out from the cover on newsstands everywhere was hard to overcome.

What followed was not untypical: the Bush people distanced themselves from *Newsweek* reporters. Finally, in September 1988, a meeting was set up at the vice-president's residence, between Rick Smith, Evan Thomas, and me from *Newsweek*, and Bush, Jim Baker, and Craig Fuller, Bush's chief of staff. Bush claimed that the whole story had been wildly distorted by playing up the word on the cover, for which he accurately blamed the editors. His family, whom he'd asked to cooperate on the story, was naturally upset and angry and had advised him that further cooperation with the magazine, in any but a technically correct manner, would only prove the point: that he was indeed a wimp.

I earnestly tried to explain about the complicated newsweekly process, until Bush, without relenting, said that Rick Smith and Jim Baker should talk. As the vice-president and I walked toward the door, he whispered to me in the nicest possible way, "We'll work it out, but don't tell them." Rick did get together with Baker and managed to clear the air enough so that we could do the necessary background reporting, but the issue never really died and was compounded by others.

We—that is, reporters and editors from both the *Post* and *Newsweek*—had, of course, also met with Dukakis. Throughout the winter and spring, he had made a poor impression in several areas, but especially in national-security policy. His campaign manager called me late in the campaign and said the candidate would like to meet with several of us informally. I went with a group from the *Post* and *Newsweek*, hoping we would see a side of Dukakis we hadn't seen before and get to know him a little as an individual. We all sat around his hotel room and he talked, but nothing new was said and nothing personal about his views was revealed.

Despite his campaign, which I disliked, I voted for Bush; I thought Dukakis too inexperienced to govern. It was my only Republican vote for president. After Bush was elected, our relations were unexpectedly cool if not hostile throughout the four years of his administration. I rarely saw him and Barbara, except occasionally in long receiving lines. Perhaps my amicable relations with the Reagans, and with George Shultz, for whom the Bushes had no love, compounded our problems. These cool or antagonistic relationships are part of life in Washington and are accepted as such, but I often think how self-defeating they are and how much better polite professional relations would serve political figures *and* journalists in situations like this. I agreed with a charming message I got from George McGovern after he had been defeated for the presidency. He recalled making some bitter remarks about a couple of our columnists at a dinner party, but wrote me:

> I have regretted that outburst and I have also established that the maximum time I can carry a grudge is about three months. This note is simply to say that I have now forgotten all campaign grudges. It is just too difficult trying to remember which people I'm supposed to shun.

With rare exceptions, I feel strongly that McGovern's rule is an appropriate one for all of us. The longer I live, the more I observe that carrying around anger is most debilitating to the person who bears it.

IN THE IMMEDIATE years following Phil's death, it was terribly difficult for me to separate my work life from my private life; they were clearly so intermingled. For years, I had been on a kind of automatic pilot, trying to give attention to so many aspects of life at once—with two children still at home in the first years, friends, business acquaintances, always too much work, too many meetings, too many dinner parties. Fortunately, somewhere along the line, perhaps with the help of lessons learned from the women's movement, I began to have a happier time in my private life.

Family and friends have always been vital to me, but at some point I started to enjoy other people as well, to connect more, even to appreciate male friends more. There were always men in my life—romances and close friends—and I enjoyed them all. As long as Phil was alive, I so adored him that I never thought about another relationship. In truth, that "one-man woman" thinking stayed with me for years, and vestiges are there still. I have often been asked why I never remarried. In my early years at work, I resented the question, which I felt would not be asked of a male publisher. I usually answered that I really didn't know why. I still don't know all the reasons, but what I came to understand was that my job made it difficult, if not impossible.

Men who appeal to me are strong, bright, tough, and involved, but that kind of man would probably not accept my own active and absorbing life. Those men need more attention and emotional energy than I had left over at the end of any working day, and I wasn't looking for a prince consort. In fact, I wasn't looking at all. Because I was so engrossed in what I was doing, I rarely gave a thought to possible remarriage. When I did think of it, it occurred to me that, although the idea had some appeal, it would almost surely never happen. When you've lived alone for a number of years, I'm afraid that you begin to realize how hard it would be to accommodate to living with someone else, adjusting to or even indulging his desires and his life. It was clear to me that I was married to my job, and that I loved it.

When marriage works—and it does take a lot of work—it's the best way to live. I enjoy being around married people who really love each other, are constantly polite and caring about each other, and between whom you feel a real and supportive relationship. Henry and Nancy Kissinger are examples for me of two people who are very much in love with each other. Henry teases, complains, whines at this or that, but he once told me he couldn't exist without Nancy. Scotty and Sally Reston had a model marriage for nearly fifty years. I loved watching them together and understood how much they meant to each other. Scotty wrote me once, "I cannot imagine how I could have endured these years without Sally and do not know how you have borne them without your guy." What I believe to be true is that I couldn't have borne the dreariness of life without Phil had my life remained the one I had before he died. But mine was a changed life, and I couldn't imagine a new marriage working for me once I took over the Post Company.

Being single poses some difficulties, however, especially for weekends in the country, vacations, and summers—moments when two people together do much better. After a while, I knew I had to figure out some way to spend these times alone or with my family. Buying a house on Martha's Vineyard was a step that altered my life very much for the better and added greatly to my happiness. When I first found the house, it was completely tumble-down, having been rented by people who basically camped in it, but I loved its shape and the way it sat on the beautiful land. From my first look at it, I began to imagine that the house could become a fam-

ily center if the children liked it, or they could leave grandchildren with
me if they wanted to travel. Since I bought it in 1972 and renovated it the
following year, I have spent every August there, and my children and
grandchildren love it as much as I do. My stays there always restore me.

So the Vineyard helped my summers, and my friends helped throughout the year. The lives of those of us who stay on in Washington change
somewhat with a change of administrations, but our core friendships remain pretty much the same. There is a saying about relationships in
Washington: "If you want a friend in Washington, get a dog." Maybe because I've always lived here, because this is in a very real sense my hometown, I've found that not to be at all true. I'm sure it's different if you
arrive here as a member of a new administration: it always takes a while to
make new friends in a strange town, and undoubtedly there will be people
who try to wangle friendships with those in power in order to use them for
one reason or another.

Jim Jones, a congressman who had been defeated for election to the
Senate in 1986 and is now our ambassador to Mexico, was quoted as saying he had learned during his tenure here about "friends and friends of
convenience." But I see nothing wrong with the fact that people in power
often deal with others on more than one level. Sometimes you become
friends with people with whom you work because of some common interest or just because you have to work together. But there are also relationships that start out that way yet cross over to become real friendships that
last forever. Some of my deepest friendships began with an administration
person whom I got to know because of my association with the paper—
Bob McNamara and Henry Kissinger come immediately to mind—but
grew over time into relationships whose core had nothing to do with politics or work. This is true of others as well—Paul Nitze, Douglas Dillon,
Mac Bundy, Jack Valenti, Joe Califano, Larry Eagleburger. In business,
the same is true for my relationship with Ed Ney, whom I met because he
was head of Young and Rubicam, but with whom I have maintained a
friendship. What began as another business relationship with the head of
the Hecht Company, Allan Bloostein, also developed into something beyond that for me.

George Shultz and I had been friends when he was in Nixon's Cabinet, and he was one of the few administration officials who remained
friends with me through Watergate. I admired and liked him. We remet at
dinner at Meg's house when he returned as secretary of state under President Reagan. He asked if I was still playing tennis and said he'd love to
play, so I worked him into a game the following weekend, and we fell into
a routine of Sunday games with more or less the same foursome. We soon
added Saturday games and ended up playing every weekend for six years,
unless he was away on trips. He loved the game so much that he went to

great lengths to be there. Once he was engaged in some heavy negotiations having to do with the Middle East, and I assumed he would skip tennis, but he insisted on playing. Wondering how he had gotten out of his meetings, I asked him what he had told Yitzhak Shamir, with whom he had been talking. It didn't surprise me at all to learn that he had said, "I'm going to play tennis." Another time, during a particularly hard match, Bill Webster, then head of the FBI, and I both went for the same ball and collided. I went down so hard I was afraid I'd broken my hip, and a baseball-sized lump quickly formed on my rear end. In the car, George asked if I was all right or if he should take me to an emergency room. "I'm fine," I told him, "but I have this huge bump on my behind. If it weren't for your security men, I'd let you feel it."

From driving together to and from our games, our friendship deepened. I must have spent as much time with George as anyone in Washington except Obie, his devoted wife, who died recently. But I never learned anything professional from him in all those hours we spent in his car, though I must say it was apparent that something was wrong during Iran-Contra; he would make oblique remarks and was visibly disturbed and down. Always, George was the soul of discretion and integrity.

I don't believe that whom I was or wasn't friends with interfered with our reporting at any of our publications or at the stations. Most of the editors didn't know or care whom I knew. More important, I understood my priorities. In any altercation between the publications and people who were friends, I backed our reporters. Occasionally, if I thought we'd been unfair, I would ask about it, but only in an effort to try to ensure even-handed treatment. If there is a complete conflict of interest—that is, if a friendship develops and the paper has to report something negative that has to do with your friend—you either lose the friend or, if you're lucky, have one who is big enough to forgive, and eventually maybe forget.

I WAS MOVING inexorably toward the end of my seventh decade, and was enjoying myself increasingly with each passing year. Up to now, I had never minded getting older; in fact, I hadn't thought about it much. But 1987 was a landmark year—the year I turned seventy—and this was a birthday I really did mind. My friend Luvie Pearson had tried to soften the blow by assuring me, "Seventy is nothing. It's when you hit seventy-five that you really begin to feel it and then you feel it increasingly." From my experience, I think she had it just about right, but I didn't know that at the time and was bothered about being seventy. I certainly didn't want to broadcast my age to the world, especially not to the business world, so I was not interested in a party. Polly and Clayton Fritchey and Bob McNamara and I planned a motor trip in and around San Francisco and

Yosemite and the Napa Valley, timed deliberately so that I would be gone on my birthday.

What I hadn't reckoned on was Lally's persistence. A strong figure in my life from her very earliest childhood, Lally had combined forces with my three sons to override my real feelings and convince me to go along with the idea of a small party to be given by her and her brothers and their spouses. Reluctantly, I acceded to their wishes, insisting only that it had to be kept to really close friends and family. Lally agreed but applied her own definition of "close friends and family." To my horror (and delight, in the end), we wound up with over six hundred guests in a huge auditorium in Washington. The guests came from all periods of my life and from all over the world. Lally had gone to great trouble to have the huge room decorated with enormous bouquets of beautiful roses, coaxed out to full bloom, on each table. In an anteroom, there were blown-up pictures of me from every phase of my life, including one of a report card from the Madeira School. Many people had worked on a four-page mock edition of the *Post* with a banner headline that read "Katharine Graham Says 'No' to Birthday: Rejects Any Hoopla, Opts for a Quiet Evening at Home." Don was master of ceremonies, and Lally had arranged for eight toasts. Art Buchwald got off a great line: "The fantastic turnout tonight can only be attributed to one thing—fear." President Reagan wound up his words about friendship with, "Here's looking at you, kid," as he raised his champagne glass.

Although, for me, the party was a genuine reflection of how filled with friends was my life, as I got older I naturally began to lose some of these friends, who, as Joe Alsop used to say, had been "gathered." During the 1980s, there were many deaths with which I had to deal, beginning with that of my brother, Bill, a wonderful human being, sweet, generous, respected in his profession, and much of the time deeply unhappy.

Joe Alsop himself was another great loss, one that came toward the end of the decade. In the last several years of his life, he and I had become closer than ever. Perhaps the fact that we were both alone then—he and Susan Mary had separated—strengthened our connection. The traffic and phone calls between our Georgetown houses were almost constant. I not only enjoyed Joe's company but in some ways depended on it. We needed each other: he was important in my life, and I in his. More than almost anyone I knew, Joe gave pleasure and got pleasure. He once said, "Boredom, emptiness, complacency are the real enemies—and never experience!" And he was right.

I also lost my dear friend Luvie Pearson, on whom I had counted a great deal for so many years. She was wise, funny, brave, and tolerant. Her devoted friend Malcolm Forbes gave an eightieth birthday party for her on his yacht, which was then anchored in New York Harbor. Luvie looked as beautiful as ever, her sculptured, bony face, lanky frame, and long blond hair seemed never to have changed. But she confided to me that she was getting less able to take care of herself—she was bothered by arthritis in her hands—and feared having to leave her tiny house in Georgetown for a retirement home. Two years later, just as her health was getting precarious, Luvie died suddenly, on a bridge weekend, exactly the way she would have wanted. Her absence left me very sad, but I couldn't begrudge my friend her merciful death. She died the way anyone would hope to—with all her marbles, and not too painfully, too early, or too late.

Because I am at a point in my life where I am losing friends to death with increasing frequency, I have tried to follow Joe Alsop's advice and example to keep developing younger friends. I do that both because I enjoy people of all ages and also to guard against loneliness. Polly, my closest friend for nearly fifty years, remains dear to me, always thoughtful, kind, energetic, funny, and brave. My friendship with Meg has grown and deepened over the years to an extent for which I am infinitely grateful. Liz Hylton, my treasured assistant who began working with me even before Phil's death, remains my most consistent support. I am still close to my sisters Bis and Ruth, and we talk often and visit each other when we can.

BY THE LATE 1980s, the Washington Post Company was clearly a success. The stock had skyrocketed during Dick's fine operating years beyond my wildest dreams, reaching $300 per share, amazing to me. We were outperforming our competition in all our divisions. Our quality was higher than ever. We were, as Warren once said, "maximizing a tail wind."

Beyond Dick's obvious contributions to the success of the company, I think there were several things that helped us achieve what we did. Some of our success had to do with being a family company. At the *Star*, family involvement got out of hand—too many families, for one thing—but I think that family-owned companies bring special qualities to the table and that family members can bring singular attributes to a business enterprise. Possibly, quality may be nourished most easily by a family, whose perspective extends beyond the immediate horizon. There are exceptions, to be sure, but family members can provide stability and continuity, and family ownership can prevent takeovers, which is important to smooth operations in this period of disruptive and often ill-considered mergers and acquisitions.

Another factor that nudged us along the way was that we never took success for granted. In all our divisions, our businesses competed hard in every sense with our direct competition. We tried never to lose a subscription we had a chance of holding. We worked never to let an inch or a dollar of advertising slip away without a fight. We always anguished over being beaten on a story—and still do.

I believe that our concentration on journalistic excellence was a good business approach as well as a necessary editorial strategy. I think that this was yet another reason for our ultimate success: that we operated under the philosophy—which I have espoused and practiced from the time I took over the company, and which I believe my father and Phil did before me and Don is doing now—that journalistic excellence and profitability go hand in hand. The reason for putting it that way in the beginning was to try to reassure Wall Street that I cared about profitability. We had spent large sums on building up the editorial products at the *Post*, *Newsweek*, and the stations and had risked a lot on publishing the Pentagon Papers as we were going public and the Watergate stories later. I wanted badly to answer the question of why anyone would invest in this company. I had to try to assure Wall Street that I wasn't some madwoman, interested only in risks and editorial issues, but that I was also concerned with how we ran our business.

This twin concept had come to me not as a matter of profit margins and business goals but more as a problem of management. I thought if you did one thing well—focused on a quality product—the results would follow. It's clear that the mathematics of such thinking didn't seem to be with us; after all, in mathematical equations it is said that only one variable can be maximized at a time. But I think that we helped prove the compatibility of these two goals.

Ours was a good record and a good run, and it was finally beginning to be recognized as such by the industry. Warren was kind enough to talk about the company under my direction at a special awards lunch given in 1987 by the Center for Communications in New York, at which I was the guest of honor. He emphasized what he called the less-well-reported parts of the story of the company's success. At that time our record of earnings-per-share increases was better than that of any of the outstanding companies in our field. The average growth for the top six media companies was 1,550 percent since 1964; ours—at 3,150 percent—was just more than double that. (What Warren didn't say, of course, was how much his sage advice had had to do with this record.) Warren also joked to the group that he had once found a sheet of paper prominently displayed on my desk that said, "Assets on the left, liabilities on the right."

In December 1988, *Business Month* ran a cover story on the "Five Best Managed Companies," which put The Washington Post Company on this short list with Apple, Merck, Rubbermaid, and Wal-Mart. A few years later, I received *Fortune* magazine's Business Hall of Fame award, a consummate and, for me, truly gratifying honor.

So much of the success for which we were being recognized was directly attributable to Dick. During his tenure, earnings per share grew at an annual compounded rate of 22.5 percent, and return on equity averaged 26 percent. Beyond whatever tangible accomplishments could be pointed to or measured, Dick set a high standard of professional management for the company. That's why it was so difficult to think about his ever leaving. But almost from the beginning, he had warned me that he wanted to retire when he was still young enough to teach and to pursue some of his other interests.

As his ninth year at the company drew to a close, Dick began to talk about retiring, and at least a year before the company's annual-meeting date in May 1991, he set the date for his departure. I prevailed on him to stay on the board and to remain as president of the *International Herald Tribune* for five years, so that we would maintain our close ties.

As 1991 dawned, it was clear to me that Dick's impending departure meant that it was time for me to step down, too. I was always concerned lest inertia, or the lack of desire to give up, lead me to stay too long on the job. I had seen companies hurt or even ruined by an owner/CEO not stepping down at the right time, so I was glad when Dick's move, in a sense, made up my mind for me. I also felt it was fitting that the new team of Don Graham as president and Alan Spoon, then serving as president of *Newsweek* but in line to succeed Dick as the company's chief operating officer, move up together. So Dick and I stepped down at the same time from our positions as chief operating and chief executive officers.

In our 1991 annual report, Don wrote a lovely, personal, and highly unusual piece to find in an annual report. "If you're looking for objectivity," he began, "please turn the page." He retraced my arrival on the scene, and my lonely place as the only woman in the Fortune 500 for so many years. He noted financial results and highlighted editorial issues and events since 1963. He recalled my residual self-doubts. "At a Christmas lunch," Don wrote, "one of her guests asked everyone around the table what they wished they had done earlier in life. Most said they wished they'd been centerfielders or movie stars. Kay said she wished she'd gone to Harvard Business School"—which is still true of me today.

I was unsure how I would react at the inevitable moment of stepping down and worried that I would miss the authority and being the ultimate responsible person in the Post Company. Fortunately, it hasn't been as difficult as I'd imagined. Perhaps part of this is because I relate well to both Don and Alan, and they are careful to keep me informed. Perhaps, too, it's because it was a gradual departure for me. At the suggestion of several of the company's directors, I retained the title of chairman for two and a half more years, relinquishing it in September of 1993, when I became chairman of the three-person executive committee of the company, consisting of Don and Alan and me.

Ben's retirement, a few months after mine in 1991, when he reached the age of seventy, completed a smooth transition on the editorial side

from Ben and me to Len Downie and Don. The predictable negative stories appeared here and there to the effect that Don and Len were lower-
key, more interested in local news, and more—well, boring. This was the
same kind of story that had appeared about me when I was new: people are
judgmental about young managers and like to compare them unfavorably
with their predecessors. But Len had gradually taken over running the
news side of the paper from Ben in the preceding five years, as Don had
taken over the paper and some of what I did at the company—he'd already
been publisher for more than twelve years when he became president, and
later chairman.

Ben had indeed, as we said in our annual report that year, "redefined
The Post for a generation of Washingtonians." His retirement was a moving event—or series of events, I should say. It was all done as Ben did
everything, with great style. Just before he walked out of the newsroom on
August 31, there was to be a small farewell cake-and-champagne party for
him. It turned into a mass uprising, with many spontaneous speeches and
stories told about the legendary Ben—stories about people whose lives he
had touched, so many uniquely Ben incidents, not all of them printable.
No one wanted to leave. After three hours, Don remarked that one of the
reporters had brought her new baby with her that day and the baby was
about to celebrate her third birthday. On that note, Ben walked out of the
newsroom and out of the building, but certainly not out of the life of the
Post. He remains vice-president-at-large—a title at which he always
grins—with an office on the *Post*'s executive floor. His energy and charm
are undiminished. He is busy and happy and productive, and has written a
fascinating and well-received memoir, a book in which we hear his true
voice—the best kind of book.

Without the major responsibilities that went along with my title, I had
to try to reshape my life, to give it some new form that would serve not
merely to fill my days but to give some real meaning to what my friend
Luvie used to call the "last lap." It's hard for people who leave power to relinquish certain enjoyable things—the inside seat, the privileged conversations, the ultimate responsibility, and the many other perquisites that go
along with the kind of job I had had for so long. Admittedly, many of us
get spoiled by all of the benefits of our jobs. I certainly did. But I also believe it's healthy to have to return to a more normal life. There are advantages to private pleasures, probably more so if you have managed to
maintain some balance during your years at the top, which I tried to do.
But of course I am still spoiled in many ways—certainly by being able to
pursue the myriad interests in my life and by having a staff both in the office and at home to support me in all that I do.

In configuring a new way of life, I tried to understand what I needed
to retain from my old one. I knew it was important to keep active physi-

cally and mentally. I have returned to playing bridge, which I love, and hope to take up golf and maybe even continue tennis. Most important, though, is to keep working; I knew that I essentially never wanted *not* to work. To me, working is a form of sustenance, like food or water, and nearly as essential. Perhaps this was a direct genetic inheritance from my parents. I knew, too, that, though I would still be involved with the company on a part-time basis, I needed something else.

Reorganizing my working life meant finding a new kind of balance. I focused initially on continuing to do some things for the company, and becoming more involved in education and writing these memoirs.

Why dare to write a book? What makes any of us think that someone else would be interested in stories from our own past? For me, there was a mixture of motives. I had been thinking about my parents, who, with their drive, discipline, eccentricity, and wealth, might be of interest even to nonfamily people. Also, I felt that Phil's story had not been told. His brains, ability, and charm were legendary among his friends, but no one had written fully about him and his accomplishments, as well as about his devastation by his largely untreated manic-depression.

Partly, I wanted to look at my own life, because my personal history contains elements that were both unexpected and unrepeatable. I recognize the inherent danger of being self-serving and have tried to retain as much detachment as possible, but I wanted to tell what happened just as I saw it. And in the process, I hoped to arrive at some understanding of how people are formed by the way they grow up and further molded by the way they spend their days.

It is ironic that I became so intensely interested in education, which took up so much of my mother's later life; possibly, this was another of her legacies to me. I believe, as she did, that education is not only the most important societal problem but the most interesting. Of course, there are countless numbers of education projects being implemented and enormous sums being spent across the country, but I wanted to do something simple and direct—perhaps make life a little better for a few children, without trying to prove anything or getting encumbered in a large bureaucracy. Along with a very able, inspiring, and determined younger partner, Terry Golden, I have helped launch an early-childhood education project in the Anacostia section of Washington, D.C. Though the project as a whole has grown larger than I had envisioned, it concentrates on two housing projects, Frederick Douglass Community Homes and Stanton Dwellings, and aims at helping mostly single and unemployed parents be involved in the education of their children. We have raised enough money to help create a community service center for parents, with a small day-care unit for up to fifteen infants, and a new school for one hundred Head Start children from the ages of two to four. Our hope is that this is a public/private endeavor that can be replicated in other areas of the District, as well as elsewhere. I anticipate continuing to work on education issues when this project ends.

Fulfilling work, writing, keeping up with my old friends, adding new ones—these are the things I concentrate on now, as well as relating to my children and their families. My children remain remarkably close, even when they are having differences with each other or with me. I have not chronicled their adult lives so as not to intrude on their privacy, but I feel grateful to have been able to spend so much time with each of them.

Lally published two books and then became a newspaper-and-magazine journalist, writing a good deal for the *Los Angeles Times*, *New York* magazine, and *Parade*. The *Post* began regularly printing a column by her in 1991, and I take enormous pride in the quality of her writing and admire how hard she works at it. She has traveled the world and interviewed more leaders than I ever did. Her daughters, Katharine and Pamela, are well launched on their own professional careers.

My son Bill, after working as a lawyer at Williams and Connolly and at the Los Angeles public defender's office, and teaching law at UCLA, started an investment partnership. As tough a critic as Warren has admired his approach and work, at which Bill has demonstrably succeeded. At the same time, he is one of the most devoted parents I know. Of all my children, it is Bill who most loves the Vineyard; he has built a house next door to mine there, which means that I am able to see him and his teenage children, Edward and Alice, regularly.

Steve has lived in New York City all his adult life, and after working for Mike Nichols and Lewis Allen in the theater, he became a producer of plays, producing works by Sam Shepard, Athol Fugard, E. R. Gurney, and other contemporary playwrights. He also founded the New York Theatre Workshop, a nonprofit group devoted to producing plays by little-known American writers. The workshop produced early plays by John Guare, among others, and staged the original production of *Rent*, a current Broadway hit and Tony-winner. Steve then became a doctoral candidate in English at Columbia University and is now publisher of the Ecco Press, one of America's best literary presses. In 1996, *Rent* and a poet published by Ecco, Jorie Graham (formerly married to Billy), won Pulitzer Prizes, giving Steve two in a year when the *Post* had none. Steve's wife, Cathy, an illustrator, is also involved in community work in New York.

I am lucky to have Don and Mary in Washington. They have brought up four children—Liza, Laura, Will, and Molly—who now range in age from twenty-four to fourteen. Mary gave up being a lawyer after practicing for some years and devotes herself to writing, being involved with the children, and her own community interests.

It is my family and the engrossing pleasures I've mentioned that help me face the unavoidable problems of age and the inevitable loss of friends. I will be publishing this book when I am seventy-nine. I've been fortunate in life-style, in health, and in having so many interests, but old age is no barrel of laughs. Even if you are generally healthy, there are things—your heart (atrial fibrillation), your hips (arthritis), general slowing down mentally and physically—that make denial of aging an impossibility. People begin to take your arm, ask if you want an elevator, and generally treat you like a relic. Though they have nothing but the best and most solicitous of motives, it's hard not to feel condescended to.

At the same time, there are positive aspects to being old. Worry, if not gone altogether, no longer haunts you in the middle of the night. And you are free—or freer—to turn down the things that bore you and spend time on matters and with people you enjoy.

I am grateful to be able to go on working and to like my new life so well that I don't miss the old one. It's dangerous when you are older to start living in the past. Now that it's out of my system, I intend to live in the present, looking forward to the future.

— *Index* —

— *Photographic Credits* —

The photographs in this book are reproduced by permission and courtesy of the following (page numbers refer to photographic inserts):

Associated Press: page 22, bottom

AP/Wide World Photos: page 20, bottom; page 21, top

Photograph by Cecil Beaton. Courtesy *Vogue*. Copyright © 1967 The Condé-Nast Publications: page 25, bottom

Walter Bennett/*Time* Magazine (Reprinted by permission): page 14

Chase-Greenbrier: page 13, bottom

First Lieutenant Joseph E. Curz III: page 24, center

Ellsworth Davis/*The Washington Post:* page 28, center

Alfred Eisenstaedt, *Life* Magazine, © Time Inc.: page 69, bottom

Arthur Ellis/*The Washington Post:* page 17

Freudy Photo: page 16

© Mark Godfrey: page 21, bottom

Katharine Graham: page 26, top left

Harris & Ewing: page 8

Chris Johns: page 3, top

John McDonnell/*The Washington Post:* page 28, bottom

Harry Naltchayan/*The Washington Post:* page 23, bottom; page 25, top; page 29 (both)

Newsweek Staff Photo: page 27, top

Lona O'Connor/Detroit *Free Press:* page 49, top

Yoichi R. Okamoto: page 19, bottom

Lloyd Oleman: page 7, top right

Tony Rollo/*Newsweek:* page 26, bottom left

San Francisco *Call-Bulletin:* page 18, center

Edward Steichen (Reprinted by permission of Joanna T. Steichen): page 1, top left and right; page 5; page 7, bottom left; page 11

© 1956 Time Inc. (Reprinted by permission): page 13, top

Vytas Valaitas/*Newsweek:* page 15 (both)

Washington Post Staff Photo: page 6, top; page 18, bottom; page 19, top; page 23, top; page 24, bottom; page 27, bottom

Linda Wheeler/*The Washington Post:* page 22, top

Official White House Photo: page 30 (both)

All other photographs are from the collections of the Meyer and Graham families.

A NOTE ON THE TYPE

This book was set in Janson, a typeface long thought to have been made by the Dutchman Anton Janson, who was a practicing typefounder in Leipzig during the years 1668–1687. However, it has been conclusively demonstrated that these types are actually the work of Nicholas Kis (1650–1702), a Hungarian, who most probably learned his trade from the master Dutch typefounder Dirk Voskens. The type is an excellent example of the influential and sturdy Dutch types that prevailed in England up to the time William Caslon (1692–1766) developed his own incomparable designs from them.

Composed by American–Stratford Graphic Services,
Brattleboro, Vermont

Printed and bound by Quebecor Printing,
Martinsburg, West Virginia

Designed by Virginia Tan and Cassandra Pappas